TRADE ASSOCIATIONS
AND
PROFESSIONAL BODIES OF THE UNITED KINGDOM

RELATED TITLES OF INTEREST

The *Encyclopedia of Associations* Series
consists of the following volumes:

Volume 1: *National Organizations of the U.S.*
This primary volume furnishes details on more than 22,000 national and international nonprofit trade and professional associations, social welfare and public affairs organisations, religious, sports, and hobby groups, and other types of organisations that consist of voluntary members and that are headquartered in the U.S. Entries are arranged by subject and provide complete contact information and a description of activities, including publications, computerized services, and convention schedules. The 200,000-line alphabetical Name and Keyword Index lists all groups in both Volume 1 and *International Organizations*. It also cites thousands of entities that sound like (but aren't) national nonprofit membership organisations and gives a source of information for each. Index bound separately.

Volume 2: *Geographic and Executive Indexes*
Two sections. The Geographic Index lists alphabetically by state and city all the associations that are arranged by subject in Volume 1. Included are complete addresses, telephone numbers, names of executives, and Volume 1 entry numbers. The Executive Index lists alphabetically by surname all the executives mentioned in Volume 1, followed by their titles, names of their organisations, complete addresses, telephone numbers, and Volume 1 entry numbers.

Volume 3: *Supplement*
This supplement to Volume 1 provides full entries describing newly formed and newly found associations not listed in the main volume. Also included are approximately 10,000 major changes (association names, addresses, telephone numbers, executive officers, and mergers and other changes in status) between editions for some 4,000 associations listed in Volume 1.

International Organizations
This companion to Volume 1 provides detailed descriptions of more than 10,000 international nonprofit membership organisations (including multinational and binational groups and national organisations based outside of the U.S.). Uses the same subject arrangement and entry format as Volume 1. Includes Geographic, Executive, and Name and Keyword Indexes.

International Organizations Supplement
Provides full entries describing newly formed and newly found organisations not listed in International Organizations. Included with purchase of the main volume.

Regional, State, and Local Organizations
A five-volume guide to more than 47,000 regional, state, and local nonprofit membership organisations in all 50 states, the District of Columbia, and the U.S. territories of Guam, Puerto Rico, and Virgin Islands, with virtually no overlap of entries in Volume 1. Entries in each volume are listed alphabetically by state and city. Each volume includes an alphabetical Name and Keyword Index. The five volumes cover the following geographic areas: Great Lakes (IL, IN, MI, MN, OH, WI), Northeastern (CT, ME, MA, NH, NJ, NY, PA, RI, VT), Southern and Middle Altantic (AL, DE, DC, FL, GA, KY, MD, MS, NC, PR, SC, TN, VA, VI, WV), South Central and Great Plains (AR, IA, KS, LA, MO, NE, ND, OK, SD, TX), and Western (AK, AZ, CA, CO, GU, HI, ID, MT, NM, NV, OR, UT, WA, WY).

Encyclopedia of Associations Series on CD-ROM–Gale Global Access: Associations
This new CD-ROM database supplies access to more than 79,000 descriptive entries, the equivalent of 18 volumes on a single disc. Included are some 22,000 national associations of the U.S.; 47,000 regional, state, and local U.S. associations; 10,000 international associations (including multinational and binational groups and national organisations based outside the U.S.). The user is able to perform a wide range of searches through the entire file, with 15 searchable indexes. A 12-month subscription includes slipcase package containing the compact disc, retrieval software on diskette, and documentation. Replacement disc with new information is supplied after six months.

Encyclopedia of Associations Series Online
Available through DIALOG Information Services Inc. as File 114. Provides detailed descriptions of some 22,000 national associations of the U.S., 10,000 international, binational, and foreign national groups, and 47,000 regional, state, and local U.S. associations.

TRADE ASSOCIATIONS
AND
PROFESSIONAL BODIES OF THE UNITED KINGDOM

An Alphabetical and Subject-Classified Guide
to approximately 3500 organisations

10th EDITION

1991

edited by Patricia Millard

GALE RESEARCH INTERNATIONAL LTD.
LONDON

Published in the United Kingdom by Gale Research International Limited.
Published simultaneously in the United States by Gale Research Inc.
(An affiliated company of Gale Research International Limited)

A CIP catalogue record for this book is available from the British Library.

Printed in Great Britain by Bookcraft (Bath) Ltd.

ISBN 0-8103-8385-3

Copyright © 1991 by
Gale Research International

NOTICE

CONTENTS

Foreward vii

Preface to the Tenth Edition ix

PART ONE

Alphabetical List of Trade Associations and Professional Bodies 1

PART TWO

Chambers of Commerce, Trade, Industry and Shipping 311

United Kingdom Offices of Overseas Chambers of Commerce 321

INDEXES

Subject Index 323

Geographic Index by Town 387
(Excluding London Postal Districts)

FOREWORD

For almost thirty years, **TRADE ASSOCIATIONS AND PROFESSIONAL BODIES OF THE UNITED KINGDOM** has been the key resource for businesses and libraries providing reliable information on organisations throughout England, Scotland, Wales and Northern Ireland.

TRADE ASSOCIATIONS AND PROFESSIONAL BODIES OF THE UNITED KINGDOM is now published by Gale Research International Limited, publishers of the **ENCYCLOPEDIA OF ASSOCIATIONS.** The encyclopedia has served as the only comprehensive source of information on national nonprofit organisations headquartered in the Uniited States. Now in its 26th edition, the original title has been joined by a series of association titles.

In the current economic climate, keeping in touch with the relevant organisations is more important than ever. Since new organisations are continually being formed and dissolved, while others move their location, it is important to have a well researched, up-to-date resource which saves both time and frustration.

For this new edition of TAPBUK, all of the organisations included in the previous edition were contacted and invited to update their entries. In addition, over one thousand telephone calls were made to track down organisations which had moved, changed their names, or gone out of business. New entries have also been included, and a special effort has been made to add European/international organisations with headquarters or secretariats in the United Kingdom. We feel confident that the tenth edition of TAPBUK is both comprehensive and up-to-date.

In order to help up keep information as accurate and up-to-date as possible, we would appreciate hearing about any changes in the trade assocaitions or professional bodies included in this edition. We would also like to know about any associations not yet listed.

Please contact:

> The Editor
> *Trade Assns* and Professional Bodies of the UK
> **GALE RESEARCH INTERNATIONAL LTD.**
> 2-6 Boundary Row
> London SE1 8HN
> ENGLAND
>
> Telephone: 071-865-0190
> Fax: 071-865-0192

We also welcome your comments or suggestions.

PREFACE TO TENTH EDITION

In the United Kingdom, the trade and professional association is strong and varied. This edition contains close to 4,000 organisations, its largest coverage. It would be expected that the decline of traditional industries and corporate mergers might restrict the growth of new associations, but this is not the case. For every organisation that closes or merges, new technologies and products give rise to their own representative body. The United Kingdom has always had strong trade and professional associations, unlike, for example, other European countries where the chamber of commerce movement is strong at the expense of the trade association.

Trade and professional organisations are first and foremost representational, which is undoubtedly why new industries give rise to new associations. Each sector and sub-sector demands that its own interests are covered, exclusive to itself. The need for rationalisation may be great, but the need for a focal point of individual interests is greater, hence the increased size of this new edition.

This tenth edition follows a similar format to previous editions, but with expanded notes where appropriate. Trade and professional organisations are listed in strict alphabetical order in part one. Limited company status has been omitted as has any prefix (e.g. The) as in previous editions.

The section of chambers of commerce is in alphabetical order by town or area and the listing for overseas chambers with UK locations is also in order of country.

Where a telephone number is not given, it is at the wish of the officer in question. Fax numbers are provided and when no fax is used, a telex number is listed.

The abbreviations used are: St for Street and Rd for Road. Saint is only written in full where it could be mistaken for the street abbreviation.

The subject index has been streamlined for ease of use and fully cross-referenced. The geographical index does not include those organisations located within the central London postal districts and, where possible, outlying conurbations are indexed under the nearest major town. Postal codes now obviate the need for county names in most cases.

All entries have been verified by each organisation and we are very grateful to the large majority who so kindly and promptly returned their details. All the remainder have been checked by telephone.

Thanks are due to the editorial and production team at Gale and in particular to Catherine Shephard who has co-ordinated previous editions and who was invaluable in all stages of the compilation of this edition.

April 1991   Patricia Braun [Millard]

Alphabetical List of Trade Associations and Professional Bodies

★1★

Abrasive Industries Association
Fairgreen House
Sawbridgeworth
Stevenage   CM21 9AY
Phone: 0279 600602
Fax: 0279 726488

Concerned with grinding wheels and bonded abrasive products

★2★

Adhesive Tape Manufacturers Association
20-21 Tooks Court
London   EC4A 1LA
Phone: 071-831 7581
Fax: 071-405 1291

★3★

Adult Residential Colleges Association
Headlands
Church Lane
Washbrook
Ipswich   IP8 3HF
Phone: 0473 86737

Members are short-term residential colleges used primarily for adult education

★4★

Advanced Manufacturing Technology Research Institute
Hulley Rd
Hurdsfield

Macclesfield   SK10 2NE
Phone: 0625 425421
Fax: 0625 434964

Promotes research and development in the machine tools and related fields

★5★

Advertising Association
Abford House
15 Wilton Rd
London   SW1V 1NJ
Phone: 071-828 2771
Fax: 071-391 0376

A federation representing advertisers, agencies, the media and related support services

★6★

Advertising Film & Videotape Producers Association
26 Noel St
London   W1V 3RD
Phone: 071-434 2651
Telex: 071-434 9002

Represents the producers of television commercials

★7★

Advertising Film Rights Society
26 Noel St
London   W1V 3RD
Phone: 071-434 2651
Fax: 071-434 9002

★8★
Advertising Standards Authority
Brook House
2-16 Torrington Place
London   WC1E 7HN
Phone: 071-580 5555
Fax: 071-631 3051

★9★
Advisory Centre for Education
18 Victoria Park Square
London   E2 9PB
Phone: 081-980 4596

★10★
Advisory Committee on Pollution of the Sea
57 Duke St
London   W1M 5DH
Phone: 071-499 0704
Fax: 071-493 3092

For the preservation of protection of the world's seas from pollution by human activity

★11★
Advisory Council for the Education of Romany & other Travellers
Moot House
The Stow
Harlow   CM20 3AG
Phone: 0279 418666

Formed to advance the education of gypsies/travellers

★12★
Aerodrome Owners Association
c/o Bristol Airport
Bristol   BS19 3DW
Phone: 0275 874805

★13★
Affiliation of Honourable Photographers
68 Barcombe Rd
Brighton   BN1 9JR
Phone: 0273 606067

Members are professional photographers and managers

★14★
Aggregate Concrete Block Association
60 Charles St
Leicester   LE1 1FB
Phone: 0533 536161
Fax: 0533 514568

★15★
Agricultural & Food Research Council
Wiltshire Court
Farnsby St
Swindon   SN1 5AT
Phone: 0793 514242
Fax: 0793 514788

★16★
Agricultural Co-operative Training Council
23 Hanborough Business Park
Long Hanborough
Oxford   OX7 2LH
Phone: 0993 883577
Fax: 0993 883576

★17★
Agricultural Education Association
c/o J B Dakers
Scottish Agricultural College
Cleeve Gardens
Oakbank Rd
Perth   PH1 1HF
Phone: 0738 36611
Fax: 0738 27860

★18★
Agricultural Engineers' Association
Samuelson House
Paxton Rd
Peterborough   PE2 0LT
Phone: 0733 31381
Fax: 0733 370664

Membership includes manufacturers and importers of agricultural tractors and agricultural machinery

★19★
Agricultural Law Association
c/o R Mackay
Nunton Cottage
Nunton

Salisbury SP5 4HW
Phone: 0722 329276

Promotes the study, knowledge and understanding of the law relating to forestry and agriculture

★20★
Agricultural Lime Producers' Council
156 Buckingham Palace Rd
London SW1W 9TR
Phone: 071-730 8194
Fax: 071-730 4355

★21★
Agricultural Manpower Society
c/o Farm Management Unit
University of Reading
Earley Gate
Reading RG6 2AT
Phone: 0734 875123 ext. 8479
Telex: 847813

For practitioners, scientists, researchers and teachers active in agriculture, horticulture and forestry

★22★
Agricultural Show Exhibitors' Association
Station Office
The Old Railway Station
Little Bealings
Woodbridge IP13 6LT
Phone: 0473 611282
Fax: 0473 610116

Serving the interests of all categories of exhibitors at agricultural shows

★23★
Air League
c/o Royal Aeronautical Society
4 Hamilton Place
London W1V 0BQ
Phone: 071-491 0470
Fax: 071-499 6230

For individuals involved in the aerospace industry, civil and military aviation and government agencies

★24★
Aircraft Owners & Pilots Association
50a Cambridge St
London SW1V 4QQ
Phone: 071-834 5631
Fax: 071-834 8623

★25★
Aircraft Research Association
Manton Lane
Bedford MK41 7PF
Phone: 0234 50681
Fax: 0234 328584

Activities include the operating of transonic and other wind tunnels, together with the manufacture of aircraft models for testing

★26★
Airship Association
c/o 16 Temple Sheen
London SW14 7RP
Phone: 081-876 7046

Members are aeronautical engineers interested in the possibilities offered by airships

★27★
Alliance of British Clubs
PO Box 32
Stockport SK1 1ER
Phone: 061-485 8804
Fax: 061-486 1014

★28★
Alliance of Independent Retailers
Anbrian House
Saint Mary's St
Worcester WR1 1HA
Phone: 0905 612733
Fax: 0905 21501

★29★
Alliance of Independent Travel Agents
Independent House
65 Lincoln Rd
Peterborough PE1 25D
Phone: 0733 558588
Fax: 0733 558582

To provide independent ABTA travel agents with the same benefits and services that are available to multiple travel agents

★30★
Alliance of Literary Societies
c/o Birmingham Midland Institute
Margaret St
Birmingham   B3 3BS
Phone: 021-236 3591

★31★
**Alliance of Small Firms & Self-
   Employed People**
33 The Green
Calne   SN11 8DJ
Phone: 0249 817003
Fax: 0249 817003

★32★
Alliance of Video Retailers
Tobacco Wharf
50 Porters Walk
London   E1 9SF
Phone: 071-702 9681
Fax: 071-481 1102

Members operate video libraries

★33★
Allied Brewery Traders' Association
85 Tettenhall Rd
Wolverhampton   WV3 9NF
Phone: 0902 22303
Fax: 0902 333419

★34★
Almshouse Association
Billingbear Lodge
Wokingham
Reading   RG11 5RU
Phone: 0344 52922

Members are almshouse foundations which
provide accommodation for the elderly

★35★
Aluminium Can Recycling Association
Suite 308
1 Mex House
52 Blucher St
Birmingham   B1 1QU
Phone: 021-633 4656
Fax: 021 633 4698

★36★
Aluminium Extruders Association
Broadway House
Calthorpe Rd
Birmingham   B15 1TN
Phone: 021-456 1103
Fax: 021-456 2274

★37★
Aluminium Federation
Broadway House
Calthorpe Rd
Birmingham   B15 1TN
Phone: 021-456 1103
Fax: 021-456 2274

★38★
Aluminium Finishing Association
Broadway House
Calthorpe Rd
Birmingham   B15 1TN
Phone: 021-456 1103
Fax: 021-456 2274

Formerly: British Anodising Association

★39★
**Aluminium Foil Container
   Manufacturers Association**
38 & 42 High St
Bidford-on-Avon   B50 4AA
Phone: 0789 773347
Fax: 0789 490088

★40★
**Aluminium Powder & Paste
   Association**
Broadway House
Calthorpe Rd
Birmingham   B15 1TN
Phone: 021-456 1103
Fax: 021-456 2274

★41★
**Aluminium Primary Producers
   Association**
Broadway House
Calthorpe Rd
Birmingham   B15 1TN
Phone: 021-456 1103
Fax: 021-456 2274

★42★
Aluminium Rolled Products Manufacturers Association
Broadway House
Calthorpe Rd
Birmingham   B15 1TN
Phone: 021-456 1103
Fax: 021-456 2274

★43★
Aluminium Stockholders Association
Todd Rd
St Helens   WA9 1JD
Phone: 0744 23051
Fax: 0744 24757

★44★
Aluminium Window Association
Suites 323-324
Golden House
28-31 Great Pulteney St
London   W1R 3DD
Phone: 071-494 4651
Fax: 071-287 9010

★45★
Amalgamated Chimney Engineers
PO Box 35
Stoke-on-Trent   ST4 7NU
Phone: 0782 744311
Fax: 0782 747300

Members are companies which install chimneys

★46★
Ambulance Service Institute
c/o R Jones
Hampshire Ambulance HQ
10 City Rd
Winchester   SO23 8PD
Phone: 0962 860421

★47★
Anaesthetic Research Society
c/o Dr J W Sear
Nuffield Dept of Anaesthetics
John Radcliffe Hospital
Headington
Oxford   OX3 9DU
Phone: 0865 64711

★48★
Anatomical Society of GB & Ireland
c/o Professor D Brynmor Thomas
Dept of Biology & Preclinical Medicine
Bute Medical Buildings
St Andrews   KY16 9TS
Phone: 0334 76161   ext. 7106

★49★
Ancient Monuments Society
St Andrew-by-the-Wardrobe
Queen Victoria St
London   EC4V 5DE
Phone: 071-236 3934

★50★
Angling Foundation
23 Brighton Rd
Croydon   CR2 6EA
Phone: 0602 841703
Fax: 0602 841001

★51★
Angling Trade Association
10th Floor
Prudential House
Wellesley Rd
Croydon   CR0 9XY
Phone: 081-681 1242
Fax: 081-681 0012

Manufactures and suppliers of fishing tackle, clothing and accessories

★52★
Animal Diseases Research Association
Moredun Research Institute
408 Gilmerton Rd
Edinburgh   EH17 7JH
Phone: 031-664 3262
Fax: 031-664 8001

★53★
Animal Health Distributors Association
41 Barrack Square
Martlesham Heath
Ipswich   IP5 7RF
Phone: 0473 625891
Fax: 0473 610652

★54★
Antiquarian Booksellers Association
Suite 2, 26 Charing Cross Rd
London WC2H 0DG
Phone: 071-379 3041

Members are bookselling firms and dealers in rare books and manuscripts who have traded for more than five years

★55★
Antiquarian Horological Society
New House
High St
Ticehurst
Tunbridge Wells TN5 7AL
Phone: 0580 200125

The study of all mattters relating to the art and history of time measurement

★56★
Apparel Knitting & Textiles Alliance
c/o C M Purvis
British Apparel Textiles Centre
7 Swallow Place
London W1H 1LD
Phone: 071-491 9702
Fax: 071-491 9764

★57★
Arab Horse Society
Windsor House
The Square
Ramsbury
Salisbury SN8 2PE
Phone: 0672 20782
Fax: 0672 20880

Promotes the breeding of purebred Arabian horses

★58★
Arboricultural Association
Ampfield House
Ampfield
Romsey S051 9PA
Phone: 0794 68717

All aspects of arboriculture including the management, care, cultivation and improvement of trees and woodlands grown for amenity

★59★
Architects & Surveyors Institute
15 Saint Mary St
Chippenham SN15 3JN
Phone: 0249 444505
Fax: 0249 443602

Formed by the amalgamation of the faculty of Architects & Surveyors with the Construction Surveyors Institute

★60★
Architects Registration Council of the UK
73 Hallam St
London W1N 6EE
Phone: 071-580 5861

★61★
Architectural Aluminium Association
c/o B Edam
Willesborough Industrial Park
Ashford TN24 0TD
Phone: 0233 622008
Fax: 0233 646252

★62★
Architectural Association
34-36 Bedford Square
London WC1B 3ES
Phone: 071-636 0974
Fax: 071-436 8740

Covering educational aspects of architecture and design

★63★
Architectural Precast Cladding Association
75-79 High St
Aldershot GU11 1BY
Phone: 0252 312122
Fax: 0252 343081

★64★
Army Records Society
c/o Dept of War Studies
Royal Military Academy
Sandhurst

Camberley GU15 4PQ
Phone: 0276 63344 ext. 2440

All aspects of British military history including correspondence and eye witness accounts of battles and companys

★65★
Art Metalware Manufacturers' Association
10 Vyse St
Birmingham B18 6LT
Phone: 021-236 2657
Fax: 021-236 3921

★66★
Art Workers Guild
6 Queen Square
London WC1N 3AR
Phone: 071-837 3474

Membership is open to artists, craftsmen, architects and others engaged in design or the practice of the visual arts

★67★
Arthritis & Rheumatism Council
41 Eagle St
London EC1R 4AR
Phone: 071-405 8572

★68★
Article Number Association
6 Catherine St
London WC2B 5JJ
Phone: 071-836 3398
Fax: 071-240 8149

Standard bar code symbols for goods sold through automatic check-out in stores

★69★
Arts Development Association
The Arts Centre
Vane Terrace
Darlington DL3 7AX
Phone: 0325 465930

A national alliance for individuals and organisations promoting the arts at local and regional level

★70★
Asbestos Removal Contractors Association
Friars House
6 Parkway
Chelmsford CM2 0NF
Phone: 0245 259744
Fax: 0245 490722

Represents the interests of companies engaged in the removal or handling of asbestos - containing insulation from existing structures, plant and pipework

★71★
Aslib *see* Association for Information Management

★72★
Associated Scottish Life Offices
23 St Andrew Square
Edinburgh EH2 1AQ
Phone: 031-556 7171
Fax: 031-557 6702

Members are chief executives of Scottish life insurance companies

★73★
Association for all Speech Impaired Children
347 Central Markets
Smithfield
London EC1A 9NH
Phone: 071-236 3632
Fax: 071-236 8115

To promote the interests of young people with speech or language difficulties

★74★
Association for Astronomy Education
c/o R Kibble
34 Acland Crescent
London SE5 8EQ
Phone: 071-274 0530

★75★
Association for British Music
2 Union Place
Boston PE21 6PS
Phone: 0205 60541

★76★
Association for Business Sponsorship of the Arts
60 Gainsford St
London   SE1 2NY
Phone: 071-378 8143
Fax: 071-407 9527

★77★
Association for Child Psychology & Psychiatry
Argyle House
29-31 Euston Rd
London   NW1 2SD
Phone: 071-278 4861
Fax: 071-837 9143

Concerned with the mental health and development of children

★78★
Association for Clinical Research
11 Uxbridge St
London   W8 7TQ
Phone: 081-892 6033
Fax: 081-891 1735

★79★
Association for Dance Movement Therapy
c/o L G Higgens
Arts Therapies Dept
Springfield Hospital
Glenburnie Rd
London   SW17 7DJ
Phone: 081-769 0924

★80★
Association for Denture Prosthesis
Oak Wood, Brickhill Rd
Leighton Buzzard   LU7 OBA
Phone: 052523 7736

★81★
Association for Education & Training Technology
Blythe Centre
BMA House
Tavistock Square

London   WC1H 9JP
Phone: 071-388 7976
Fax: 071-388 2181

For individuals and organisations interested in institutional information technology

★82★
Association for Eye Research
c/o Professor G L Ruskell
Dept of Optometry & Visual Science
City University
311-321 Goswell Rd
London   EC1V 7DD
Phone: 071-253 4399   ext. 4305
Fax: 071-837 8068

★83★
Association for Family Therapy
c/o Pauline Jenkins
6 Heal Seddon
Danescourt
Cardiff   CF5 2QX
Phone: 0222 554594

To help families who suffer distress as a result of problems such as family break-down, bereavement, physical handicap, ill-health and other physical and emotional problems

★84★
Association for Industrial Archaeology
c/o Ironbridge Gorge Museum
The Wharfage
Ironbridge
Telford   TF8 7AW
Phone: 0952 452751
Fax: 0952 452204

★85★
Association for Information Management
Information House
20-24 Old St
London   EC1V 9AP
Phone: 071-253 4488
Fax: 071-430 0514

All aspects of information management handling

★86★
Association for Language Learning
c/o C Wilding
16 Regent Place
Rugby CV21 2PN
Phone: 0788 546443
Fax: 0778 544149

★87★
**Association for Literary & Linguistic
   Computing**
c/o Dept of English
University College of North Wales
Bangor LL57 2DG
Phone: 0248 351151 ext. 2213
Fax: 0248 370451

Promotes the development of computer sciences, computer services and computer applications in literary and linguist research

★88★
**Association for Management
   Education & Development**
c/o M Greatorex
21 Catherine St
Covent Garden
London WC2B 5JS
Phone: 071-439 1188
Fax: 071-734 8367

★89★
**Association for Neighbourhood
   Councils**
Council House
Victoria Square
Birmingham B1 1GB

★90★
**Association for Payment Clearing
   Services**
Mercury House
Triton Court
14 Finsbury Square
London EC2A 1BR
Phone: 071-628 7080
Fax: 071-206 5527

An aspect of banking practice

★91★
**Association for Petroleum &
   Explosives Administration**
Hinchingbrooke Cottage
Brampton Rd
Huntingdon PE18 8NA
Phone: 0480 457344
Fax: 0480 414958

★92★
Association for Residential Care
c/o Junes Churchill
The Old Rectory
Church North
Old Whittinghton
Chesterfield S41 9QY
Phone: 0246 455881

★93★
**Association for Sandwich Education &
   Training**
c/o R M Brewer
Sheffield City Polytechnic
Pond St
Sheffield S1 1WB
Phone: 0742 532135
Fax: 0742 725757

★94★
Association for Science Education
College Lane
Hatfield AL10 9AA
Phone: 07072 67411
Fax: 07072 66532

The teaching of science in schools and colleges at all levels

★95★
Association for Stammerers
Unit 309
156 Blackfriars Rd
London SE1 8EN
Phone: 071-721 7166
Fax: 071-721 7109

Self-help organisation aimed at assisting individuals with stammering speech patterns

★96★
Association for Student Counselling
c/o A Barty
Central St Martin College of Art & Design
Southampton Row
London   WC1B 4AP
Phone: 071-753 9090
Fax: 071-242 0240

★97★
Association for Studies in the Conservation of Historic Buildings
c/o Institute of Archaeology
31-34 Gordon Square
London   WC1H OPY
Phone: 071-387 7050

★98★
Association for Teaching Psychology
c/o British Psychological Society
48 Princess Rd East
Leicester   LE1 7DR
Phone: 0533 549568
Fax: 5533 470987

★99★
Association for Technological Education in Schools
78 Alderson Drive
Doncaster   DN2 6DB
Phone: 0302 61588

★100★
Association for the Conservation of Energy
9 Sherlock Mews
London   W1M 3RH
Phone: 071-935 1495

★101★
Association for the Education & Welfare of the Visually Handicapped
24 Vicarage Rd
Birmingham   B17 0SP
Phone: 021-426 6815

★102★
Association for the Instrumentation, Control & Automation Industry in the UK
Leicester House
8 Leicester St
London   WC2H 7BN
Phone: 071-437 0678
Fax: 071-437 4901

Formely Scientific Instrument Manufacturers' Association of GB

★103★
Association for the Prevention of Disabilities
9 High St
London   NW10
Phone: 081-965 5743

To prevent and alleviate mental handicap and developmental disabilities and to promote clinical research and advance education in the causes of mental handicap and developmental disabilites

★104★
Association for the Prevention of Theft in Shops
180 Wardour St
London   W1V 3AA
Phone: 071-505 1695
Fax: 071-741 4815

★105★
Association for the Reform of Latin Teaching
c/o R Davies
2 Eggar's Cottages
Long Sutton
Basingstoke   RG25 1SZ

★106★
Association for the Scientific Study of Anomalous Phenomena
c/o Dr Hugh Pincott
St Aldhelm
20 Paul St
Frome   BA11 1DX
Phone: 0373 51777

Research into all paranormal, anomalous and related phenomena

★107★
Association for the Study &
Preservation of Roman Mosaics
c/o P Johnson
Roman Research Trust
Littlecote Roman Villa
Hungerford   RG17 0SS
Phone: 06723-356

★108★
Association for the Study of Medical
Education
2 Roseangle
Dundee   DD1 4LR
Phone: 0382 26801

★109★
Association for the Study of Primary
Education (ASPE)
c/o J Morris
Education Office
Touthill Close
Peterborough   PE1 1JU
Phone: 0733 556214

A national body committed to the advancement of primary education by promoting collaborative study and action involving the
main professional groups

★110★
Association for the Teaching of the
Social Sciences
Pineleigh
Silverdale Rd
Arnside
Carnforth   LA5 0EH
Phone: 0244 683011

★111★
Association of Accommodation &
Welfare Officers
c/o M J Howells
Staffordshire Polytechnic
College Rd
Stoke-on-Trent   ST4 2DE
Phone: 0782 744531   ext. 3441
Fax: 0782 744035

For accommodation officers of colleges and
polytechnics

★112★
Association of Accounting Technicians
154 Clerkenwell Rd
London   EC1R 5AD
Phone: 071-837 6970
Telex: 269615

★113★
Association of Agricultural Education
Staffs
c/o Cumbria College
Newton Rigg
Penrith   CA11 0AH
Phone: 0768 63791

★114★
Association of Agriculture
Victoria Chambers
16-20 Strutton Ground
London   SW1P 2HP
Phone: 071-222 6115
Fax: 071-233 1517

Advances understanding of all aspects of
agriculture, food production and the countryside

★115★
Association of Anaesthetists of GB &
Ireland
9 Bedford Square
London   WC1B 3RA
Phone: 071-631 1650

★116★
Association of Applied Biologists
c/o Institute of Horticultural Research
Wellesbourne
Stratford upon Avon   CV35 9EF
Phone: 0789 470382
Fax: 0789 470234

★117★
Association of Art Historians
c/o Pamela Courtney
Albert House
Monnington-on-Wye

Hereford HR4 7NL
Phone: 09817 344
Fax: 09817 335

Members are individuals directly concerned with the advancement of the study of the history of art and design

★118★
Association of Assistant Librarians
c/o Library Association
7 Ridgmount St
London WC1E 7AE
Phone: 071-636 7543
Fax: 071-436 7218

Catering primarily for student librarians, paraprofessionals and professional library and information workers in the early stages of their careers

★119★
Association of Authorised Public Accountants
10 Cornfield Rd
Eastbourne BN21 4QE
Phone: 0323 410412
Fax: 0323 647204

Members are accredited statutory auditors

★120★
Association of Authors' Agents
20 John St
London WC1N 2DR
Phone: 071-405 6774
Telex: 297903

★121★
Association of Average Adjusters
Irongate House
22-30 Dukes Place
London EC3A 7LP
Phone: 071-283 9033

★122★
Association of Bankrupts
c/o John McQueen
4 Johnson Close
Abraham Heights

Lancaster LA1 5EU
Phone: 0524 64305
Fax: 0524 844001

Provides assistance and advice to bankrupts and debtors

★123★
Association of Bee-Keeping Appliance Manufacturers of GB
c/o P B Smith
Beehive Works
Wragby
Lincoln LN3 5LA
Phone: 0673 858555
Fax: 0673 857004

★124★
Association of Blind Chartered Physiotherapists
c/o V Jones
91 Nursery Rd
Birmingham B15 3JY
Phone: 021-454 4692

★125★
Association of Blind Piano Tuners
c/o A F Spencer
24 Fairlawn Grove
London W4 5EH
Phone: 081-995 0295

★126★
Association of Board Makers
Papermakers House
Rivenhall Rd
Westlea
Swindon SN5 7BE
Phone: 0793 886086
Fax: 0793 886182

★127★
Association of Boys' Clubs Organisers
c/o National Association of Boys' Clubs
369 Kennington Lane
London SE11 5QY
Phone: 071-793 0787
Fax: 071-820 9815

★128★
Association of British Aviation Consultants
c/o 19 Cliveden Place
London   SW1W 8HD
Phone: 071-259 9338
Fax: 071-730 1985

★129★
Association of British Chambers of Commerce
Sovereign House
212a Shaftesbury Avenue
London   WC2H 8EW
Phone: 071-240 5831
Fax: 071-379 6331

★130★
Association of British Climatologists
c/o L F Musk
Geography Dept
University of Manchester
Oxford Rd
Manchester   M13 9PL
Phone: 061-273 3333   ext. 3243
Fax: 061-273 4407

Areas covered include atmospheric pollution, climate change and climate variability

★131★
Association of British Consortium Banks
c/o Intermax Bank
29 Gresham St
London   EC2U 7LP
Phone: 071-606 7777

★132★
Association of British Container Lessors
c/o Acugreen Ltd
Bush House
Merewood Avenue
Headington
Oxford   OX3 8EH
Phone: 0865 64888
Telex: 837178

★133★
Association of British Correspondence Colleges
6 Francis Grove
London   SW19 4DT

★134★
Association of British Credit Unions
Unit 307
Westminster Business Square
339 Kennington Lane
London   SE11 5QY
Phone: 071-582 2626
Fax: 071-587 1774

Members of credit unions are co-operatively run, locally-based savings and loans institutions

★135★
Association of British Dental Surgery Assistants
DSA House
29 London St
Fleetwood   FY7 6JY
Phone: 03917 78631
Fax: 03917 73099

★136★
Association of British Directory Publishers
93a Blenheim Crescent
London   W11 2EQ
Phone: 071-221 9089

★137★
Association of British Dispensing Opticians
22 Nottingham Place
London   W1M 4AT
Phone: 071-935 7411

★138★
Association of British Editors
8-16 Great New St
London   EC4P 4ER
Phone: 0480 492133
Fax: 0480 492805

Provides a forum for the study and enhancement of press, television and radio journalism

★139★
Association of British Factors & Discounters
Hind Court, 147 Fleet St
London   EC4A 2BU
Phone: 071-353 1213
Telex: 298681

★140★
Association of British Fire Trades
48a Eden St
Kingston upon Thames   KT1 1EE
Phone: 081-549 5855
Fax: 081-547 1564

★141★
Association of British Generating Set Manufacturers
c/o D Hughes
Broadcrown
Mill St
Stone
Stafford   ST15 8BA
Phone: 0785 817513

★142★
Association of British Health Care Industries
Consort House
26-28 Queensway
London   W2 3RX
Phone: 071-221 4612
Fax: 071-229 4708

Members include medical equipment manufacturers, pharmaceutical companies, consultants, architects and health care planners

★143★
Association of British Independent Oil Exploration Companies
c/o D G M Boyd
New Bond Street House
1 New Bond St
London   W1Y 9PE
Phone: 071-499 0771
Fax: 071-491 3025

★144★
Association of British Insurers
Aldermary House
Queen St
London   EC4N 1TT
Phone: 071-248 4477
Fax: 071-489 1120

For insurance companies licensed to operate in the UK

★145★
Association of British Introduction Agencies
25 Abingdon Rd
London   W8 6AH
Phone: 071-938 1011

Members are marriage bureaux and introduction agencies

★146★
Association of British Investigators
10 Bonner Hill Rd
Kingston upon Thames   KT1 3EP
Phone: 081-546 3368
Fax: 081-546 7701

Members are individual private investigators with more than two years experience

★147★
Association of British Laundry Cleaning & Rental Services *now* Textile Services Association

★148★
Association of British Library & Information Studies Schools
c/o Helen Chandler
Dept of Library & Information Studies
Manchester Polytechnic
All Saints
Manchester   M15 6BH
Phone: 061-051 3581

★149★
Association of British Manufacturers of Photographic Cine & Audiovisual Equipment
1 West Ruislip Station

Ruislip   HA4 7DW
Phone: 0895 634515
Fax: 0895 631219

★150★
**Association of British Market
    Research Companies**
11 Great Marlborough St
London   W1V 1DE
Phone: 071-734 1171

★151★
Association of British Meat Processors
217 Central Markets
Smithfield
London   EC1A 9LH
Phone: 071-489 0005
Fax: 071-248 4733

★152★
**Association of British Mining
    Equipment Companies**
Royal Victoria Hotel
Station Rd
Sheffield   S4 7YE
Phone: 0742 737334
Fax: 0742 730194

Trade association covering all aspects of mining in the UK and abroad

★153★
Association of British Neurologists
c/o Professor D A S Compston
Dept of Neurology
Addenbrooke's Hospital
Hills Rd
Cambridge   CB2 2QQ
Phone: 0223 217091
Fax: 0223 242474

★154★
**Association of British Offshore
    Industries**
Great Guildford House
30 Great Guildford St
London   SE1 0HS
Phone: 071-928 9199
Fax: 071-928 6599

The exploitation of the sea and the sea-bed

★155★
Association of British Orchestras
Francis House
Francis St
London   SW1P 1DE
Phone: 071-828 6913
Fax: 071-828 5504

Represents the collective interests of professional orchestras including youth and college
orchestras

★156★
**Association of British Paediatric
    Nurses**
c/o Central Nursing Office
Hospital for Sick Children
Great Ormond St
London   WC1N 3JH
Phone: 071-405 9200   ext. 303

A professional forum that enables paediatric
nurses to maintain and/or improve the care of
sick children

★157★
**Association of British Pewter
    Craftsmen**
136 Hagley Rd
Birmingham   B16 9PN
Phone: 021-454 4141
Fax: 021-454 4949

★158★
**Association of British Picture
    Restorers**
Station Avenue
Kew   TW9 3QA
Phone: 081-948 5644

★159★
**Association of British Plywood &
    Veneer Manufacturers**
Russell Square House
10-12 Russell Square
London   WC1B 5AE
Phone: 081-804 2424
Fax: 081-804 1293

★160★
Association of British Preserved Milk
Manufacturers
19 Cornwall Terrace
London   NW1 4QP
Phone: 071-486 7244
Fax: 071-487 7434

★161★
Association of British Private
Detectives
PO Box 389
Moseley
Birmingham   B13 8QU
Phone: 021-449 7735

★162★
Association of British Professional
Conference Organisers
54 Church St
Tisbury
Salisbury   SP3 6NH
Phone: 0747 870490

★163★
Association of British Riding Schools
Old Brewery Yard
Penzance   TR18 2SL
Phone: 0736 69440
Fax: 0736 51390

★164★
Association of British Roofing Felt
Manufacturers
Central House
32-66 High St
London   E15 2PS
Phone: 081-519 4872
Fax: 081-519 5483

★165★
Association of British Sailmakers
2 Orchard Rd
Locks Heath
Southampton   SO3 6PR
Phone: 0489 584061
Fax: 0489 584061

Provides an arbitration service between cus-
tomers, suppliers and sailmakers

★166★
Association of British Salted Fish
Curers & Exporters
c/o Cawoods Fish Curers
Essex St
Hull   HU4 6PR
Phone: 0482 562128
Fax: 0482 507731

★167★
Association of British Science Writers
Fortress House
23 Savile Row
London   W1X 1AB
Phone: 071-494 3326

Members are medical and scientific journalists

★168★
Association of British Security
Officers
PO Box 389
Moseley
Birmingham   B13 8QU
Phone: 021-449 7735

★169★
Association of British Solid Fuel
Appliance Manufacturers
14 Pall Mall
London   SW1Y 5LZ
Phone: 071-930 7171

★170★
Association of British Spectroscopists
c/o Dr D Bowen
Discovery Spectrometry
Pfizer Central Research Laboratories
Sandwich   CTB 9NY
Phone: 0304 616161

★171★
Association of British Steriliser
Manufacturers
c/o M D H Ltd
Walworth Rd
Andover   SP10 5AA
Phone: 0264 62111
Fax: 0264 56452

★172★
Association of British Theatre Technicians
4 Great Pulteney St
London   W1R 3DF
Phone: 071-434 3901

Covering theatre planning and all technical aspects of theatrical presentation

★173★
Association of British Theological & Philosophical Libraries
c/o Alan Jesson
Bible Society's Library
University Library
West Rd
Cambridge   CB3 9DR
Phone: 0223 333000   ext. 3075
Fax: 0223 333160

★174★
Association of British Travel Agents
55-57 Newman St
London   W1P 4AH
Phone: 071-637 2444
Fax: 071-637 0713

★175★
Association of British Wild Animal Keepers
12 Tackley Rd
Bristol   BS5 6UG

An association for all those involved in the keeping and conservation of wildlife

★176★
Association of Brokers & Yacht Agents
c/o Mrs R Boxall
Petersfield Rd
Whitehill
Bordon
Alton   GU35 9BU
Phone: 04203 3862
Fax: 04203 88328

★177★
Association of Bronze & Brass Founders
136 Hagley Rd

Birmingham   B16 9PN
Phone: 021-454 4141
Fax: 021-454 4949

★178★
Association of Builders' Hardware Manufacturers
Heath St
Tamworth   B79 7JH
Phone: 0827 52337
Fax: 0827 310827

Trade association for manufacturers of architectural ironwork, sliding door components and other building supplies

★179★
Association of Building Component Manufacturers
Service House
61-63 Rochester Rd
Aylesford   ME20 7BS
Phone: 0622 715577
Fax: 0622 882215

Membership includes component manufacturers, contractors and suppliers

★180★
Association of Burglary Insurance Surveyors
Aldermary House
Queen St
London   EC4P 4JD
Phone: 071-248 4477
Fax: 071-489 1120

★181★
Association of Business Administration Studies
c/o C Oham
PO Box 70
London   E13 8BQ
Phone: 081-534 1511

★182★
Association of Business Advertising Agencies
c/o IPS Advertising
Crown House
Hartley Wintney

Basingstoke   RG27 8NW
Phone: 0251 264041
Fax: 0251 264223

Advertising agencies involved in business-to-business advertising

★183★
Association of Business Centres
29-30 Warwick St
London   W1R 5RD
Phone: 071-439 0623

★184★
Association of Business Executives
William House, 14 Worple Rd
London   SW19 4DD
Phone: 081-879 1973
Telex: 879 1983
Fax: 01-946 7153

★185★
Association of Button Merchants
78-80 Borough High St
London   SE1 1XG
Phone: 071-403 2300
Fax: 071-403 8140

★186★
Association of Calendered UPV Suppliers
Fountain Precinct
1 Balm Green
Sheffield   S1 3AF
Phone: 0742 766789
Fax: 0742 766213

★187★
Association of Career Teachers
c/o Miss R Yaffe
Hillsboro
Castledine St
Loughborough   LE11 2DX
Phone: 0509 214617

★188★
Association of Carton Board Makers
Papermaker House
Rivenhall Rd
Westlea

Swindon   SN5 7BE
Phone: 0793 886086
Fax: 0793 886182

★189★
Association of CCTV Surveyors
PO Box 13
Market Harborough   LE16 9SJ
Phone: 0858 432054
Fax: 0858 434743

Members are involved in the application of closed-circuit TV including the surveying of water sewage equipment

★190★
Association of Ceral Food Manufacturers *now* incorporated into Food & Drink Federation

★191★
Association of Certification Bodies
c/o British Standards Institution
2 Park St
London   W1A 2BS
Phone: 071-629 9000
Fax: 071-495 1612

★192★
Association of Charity Officers
c/o Valerie Barrow
RICS Benevolent Fund
2nd Floor
Tavistock House North
Tavistock Square
London   WC1H 9RJ
Phone: 071-387 0578

Members are officials of benevolent funds and registered charities giving non-contributing relief

★193★
Association of Charter Trustees & Urban Parish Councils
30 Church St
Kidderminster   DY10 2AX
Phone: 0562 66131

★194★
Association of Cheese Processors
19 Cornwall Terrace

London NW1 4QP
Phone: 071-486 7244
Fax: 071-487 4734

★195★
Association of Chief Architects of Scottish Local Authorities
c/o West Lothian District Council
Blackburn Rd
Bathgate EH4 2EF
Phone: 0506 53521
Fax: 041-227 2870

★196★
Association of Chief Education Social Workers
c/o B Thompson
54 Partridge Close
Ayton Village
Washington NE38 0ES
Phone: 091-477 1011 ext. 2740

★197★
Association of Chief Officers of Probation
c/o B Weston
20-30 Lawefield Lane
Wakefield WF2 8SP
Phone: 0924 361156
Fax: 0924 372837

The association promotes and co-ordinates the work of the probation services. Its members are chief, deputy chief and assistant chief probation offices throughout the UK.

★198★
Association of Chief Police Officers of England, Wales & Northern Ireland
New Scotland Yard, Broadway
London SW1H 0BG
Phone: 071-230 2456

★199★
Association of Chief Police Officers (Scotland)
Police Headquarters
Fettes Avenue
Edinburgh EH4 1RB
Phone: 031-311 3051
Fax: 031-311 3052

★200★
Association of Chief Technical Officers
c/o Keith Feltham
Horsham District Council
Horsham RH12 1RL
Phone: 0403 64191

★201★
Association of Child Psychotherapists
Burgh House
New End Square
London NW3 1LT
Phone: 071-794 8881

★202★
Association of Circulation Executives
c/o Mrs J Fellows
The Guardian
119 Farringdon Rd
London EC1R 3ER
Phone: 071-278 2332
Fax: 071-833 0873

Concerned with the distribution and marketing of national newspapers and magazines

★203★
Association of Circus Proprietors of GB
c/o M Clay
Mellor House
Primrose Lane
Mellor
Blackburn BB1 9DN
Phone: 0254 672222
Fax: 0254 631723

An employers association concerned with the continuous improvement of standards of animal welfare and the general control of the British circus industry

★204★
Association of Civil Defence & Emergency Planning Officers
c/o Emergency Planning Dept
Shire Hall
Mold
Chester CH7 6NR
Phone: 0352 2121 ext. 3019
Fax: 0352 58240

★205★
Association of Clinical Biochemists
Royal Society of Chemistry
Burlington House
Piccadilly
London   WV1 0BM
Phone: 071-437-8656
Fax: 071-437 8883

Includes chemical pathology mainly in district, general and teaching hospitals

★206★
Association of Clinical Pathologists
57 Lower Belgrave St
London   SW1W 0LR
Phone: 071-730 0078

★207★
Association of College Registrars & Administrators
c/o Kingston College of Further Education
Latchmere Rd
Kingston upon Thames   KT2 5XT
Phone: 081-541 4940

★208★
Association of Colleges for Further & Higher Education
c/o Swindon College
Regent Circus
Swindon   SN1 1PT
Phone: 0703 513193
Fax: 0703 641794

★209★
Association of Coloprociology of GB & Ireland
c/o Royal College of Surgeons
35-43 Lincoln's Inn Fields
London   WC2A 3PN
Phone: 071-405 3747

A multidisciplinary association to promote standards and training

★210★
Association of Commonwealth Universities
John Foster House
36 Gordon Square
London   WC1H OPF
Phone: 071-387 8572
Fax: 071-387 2655

★211★
Association of Community Health Councils for England & Wales
30 Drayton Park
London   N5 1PB
Phone: 081-690 8405

★212★
Association of Community Technical Aid Centres
c/o Royal Institution
Colquitt St
Liverpool   L1 4DE
Phone: 051-708 7607

To assist voluntary organisations and community groups in obtaining correct advice to undertake and run building or environmental improvement projects

★213★
Association of Community Workers in the UK
Grindon Lodge
Beech Grove Rd
Newcastle upon Tyne   NE4 6RS
Phone: 091-272 4341

★214★
Association of Company Registration Agents
20 Holywell Row
London   EC2A 4JB
Phone: 071-377 0381
Telex: 071-377 6648

★215★
Association of Conference Executives
Riverside House
High St
Huntingdon   PE18 6SG
Phone: 0480 457595
Fax: 0480 411341

For individuals who plan and organise meetings

★216★
Association of Conservation Officers
c/o E M Marten
25 Willington Rd
Cople
Bedford   MK44 3TH
Phone: 0234 686500

★217★
Association of Consultant Architects
Buchanans Wharf
Redcliff Backs
Bristol   BS1 6HT
Phone: 0272 293379
Fax: 0272 256008

Represents the interests of architects engaged in private practice

★218★
Association of Consulting Actuaries
c/o Waton & Sons
Waton House
London Rd
Reigate   RH2 9PQ
Phone: 081-688 8040
Fax: 0737 241496

★219★
Association of Consulting Engineers
c/o Brigadier H C Woodrow
Alliance House
12 Caxton St
London   SW1H 0QL
Phone: 071-222 6557
Fax: 071-222 0750

Members are individuals who are independent consulting engineers in private practice, either on their own account or as partners, principals or consultants in consulting engineering firms

★220★
Association of Consulting Scientists
11 Rosemont Rd
London   NW3 6NG
Phone: 071-794 2433

Membership is open to independent consultants practising in all branches of science and technology

★221★
Association of Contemporary Historians
c/o Dr A Polonski
Dept of International History
London School of Economics
Houghton St
London   WC2A 2AD
Phone: 071-405 7107

★222★
Association of Control Manufacturers
Leicester House
8 Leicester St
London   WC2H 7BN
Phone: 071-437 0678
Fax: 071-437 4901

Switches for appliances, thermal controls and time controls

★223★
Association of Corporate Trustees
2 Withdean Rise
Brighton   BN1 6YN
Phone: 0273 504276

Corporate trustees are involved in the fields of law, taxation, investment and related technical and practical matters

★224★
Association of Cost & Executive Accountants
Tower House
141-149 Fonthill Rd
London   N4 3HF
Phone: 071-272 3925
Fax: 071-281 5723

Professional society for accountants, financial directors, financial controllers and commercial consultants

★225★
Association of Cost Engineers
Lea House
5 Middlewhich Rd

Sandbach   CW11 9XL
Phone: 0270 764798
Fax: 0270 766180

Cost engineering embraces activities such as estimating, cost control, construction management, investment appraisal and risk analysis

★226★
Association of Councillors
c/o F Pickles
Town Hall
Ramsden St
Huddersfield   HD1 2TA
Phone: 0484 422122
Fax: 0484 435073

For elected members of local authorities

★227★
Association of County Archivists
c/o C North
Cornwall Record Office
County Hall
Truro   TR1 3AY
Phone: 0872 73698

★228★
Association of County Chief Executives
c/o I G Caulfield
Shire Hall
Warwick   CV34 4RR
Phone: 0926 410410
Fax: 0926 410302

★229★
Association of County Councils
66a Eaton Square
London   SW1W 9BH
Phone: 071-235 1200
Fax: 071-235 9549

Represents local government in England and Wales

★230★
Association of County Public Health Officers
c/o N J Durnford
Wiltshire County Council

Trowbridge   BA14 8JW
Phone: 0225 753641
Fax: 0225 752891

★231★
Association of County Supplies Officers
c/o A J Gaskell
Purchasing Dept
Buckinghamshire County Council
County Hill
Aylesbury   HP20 1YG
Phone: 0296 383651
Fax: 0296 383470

★232★
Association of Couriers in Tourism
c/o A Ormandy
80 Wickway Court
Cator St
London   SE15 6QD
Phone: 071-703 9708

★233★
Association of Cycle Traders
31a High St
Tunbridge Wells   TN1 1XN
Phone: 0892 526081
Fax: 0892 544278

★234★
Association of Dental Hospitals of the UK
c/o Birmingham Dental Hospital
St Chad's Queensway
Birmingham   B4 6NN
Phone: 021-236 8611
Fax: 021-625 8815

★235★
Association of Design & Arts Studies
84 Addison Rd
London   W14 8ED
Phone: 071-602 2072

Independent colleges and tutors specialising in the fine and decorative arts, applied arts and all aspects of design

★236★
**Association of Direct Labour
   Organisations**
6th Floor
Peter House
Oxford St
Manchester M1 5AZ
Phone: 061-236 8433
Fax: 061-236 6479

Members provide direct services and work
with local authorities using private sector
companies

★237★
**Association of Directors of Education
   in Scotland**
c/o W D C Semple
40 Torphichen St
Edinburgh EH3 8JJ
Phone: 031-229 9166
Fax: 031-229 0059

★238★
**Association of Directors of Public
   Health**
c/o Dr J M Richards
Dept of Public Health Medicine
Tower Hamlets Health Authority
48 Ashfield St
London E1 2AJ
Phone: 071-377 7129

★239★
**Association of Directors of Recreation,
   Leisure & Tourism**
c/o M P Graham
5 The Cross
Forfar DD8 1BX
Phone: 0307 65101
Fax: 0307 67158

★240★
**Association of Directors of Social
   Work**
c/o M Hartnoll
Department of Social Work
Grampian Regional Council
Woodmill House
Westburn Rd

Aberdeen AB9 2LU
Phone: 0224 664957
Fax: 0224 664992

The advancement of social work in Scotland

★241★
**Association of Directors of Social
   Services**
c/o R J Lewis
Town Hill
Stockport SK1 3XE
Phone: 061-474 7896
Fax: 0734 873521

★242★
Association of Disabled Professionals
170 Benton Hill
Horbury
Wakefield WF4 5HW
Phone: 0924 270335
Fax: 0924 270335

Seeks to improve the education, rehabilitation and employment opportunities for disabled people

★243★
**Association of Distributors of
   Advertising Material**
c/o R Radice
27 Brunswick Square
Gloucester GL1 1UN
Phone: 0452 308100
Fax: 0452 300912

Promotes the door-to-door distribution of
leaflets and samples through the network of
weekly free newspapers

★244★
**Association of District Council
   Treasurers**
c/o A Scholes
City Treasurer
City Hall
Norwich NR2 1NH
Phone: 0603 622233 ext. 2550
Fax: 0603 760006

★245★
Association of District Councils
26 Chapter St

London   SW1P 4ND
Phone: 071-233 6868
Fax: 071-233 6537

Representing the non-metropolitan district councils in England and Wales

★246★
Association of District Secretaries
c/o 9 Margaret Rd
Bishopsworth
Bristol   BS13 9DQ
Phone: 0272 647299
Fax: 0272 645700

★247★
Association of Domestic Management
3 Hagg Bank Cottages
Hagg Bank
Wylam   NE41 8JY
Phone: 0661 853845

The national body for dometic service managers, support and hotel service managers in the health service, local authority establishments and in the private sector

★248★
Association of Drainage Authorities
3 Royal Oak Passage
High St
Huntingdon   PE18 6EA
Phone: 0480 411123
Fax: 0480 431107

★249★
Association of Educational Advisers in Scotland
c/o G Cox
Darroch Annex
7 Gillespie St
Edinburgh   EH3 9NH
Phone: 031-229 6989

★250★
Association of Educational Psychologists
c/o Ms A Baumber
3 Sunderland Rd
Durham   DH1 2LH
Phone: 091-384 9512

★251★
Association of Electrical Machinery Trades
Phelps House
133a Saint Margaret's Rd
Twickenham   TW1 1RG
Phone: 081-744 2389
Fax: 081-744 2180

Representing the UK repairers and merchandisers of industrial electrical machinery, particularly electric motors

★252★
Association of Engineering Distributors
c/o G K Edwards
74 Chester Rd
Birmingham   B36 7BU
Phone: 021-776 7474
Fax: 021-776 7605

Covering all stockists of engineers manufacturers tools and equipment

★253★
Association of Entertainment & Arts Management
c/o J B A Sharples, Ashleigh Holly Rd
Windermere   CA23 2AG
Phone: 09662 2244

★254★
Association of Environment Conscious Builders
Windlake House
The Pump Field
Coaley
Gloucester   GL11 5DX
Phone: 0453 890757

To generate more environmental awareness with the building and construction industry

★255★
Association of European Machine Tool Merchants
117 High St
Berkhamsted   HP4 2DJ
Phone: 0442 876262
Fax: 0442 874996

★256★

Association of European Trade Mark Proprietors

852 Melton Rd

Thurmaston

Leicester LE4 8BN

Phone: 0533 640080

Fax: 0533 640141

Members are companies who own trade marks or provide services to trademark owners

★257★

Association of Exhibition Organisers

207 Market Towers

Nine Elms Lane

London SW8 5NQ

Phone: 071-627 3946

Fax: 071-488 0574

★258★

Association of Facilities Managers

26 Euston Centre

London NW1 3JL

Phone: 081-367 2481

Fax: 0440 703376

Facilities are properties where people are accommodated and work. Facilities management concerns all aspects of providing, maintaining, developing and improving those facilities

★259★

Association of Fish Canners *now* incorporated into Food & Drink Federation

★260★

Association of Flow Survey Contractors

c/o Morgan Moore Engineering Ltd

Pennine House

48 West St

Middlesbrough TS2 1LZ

Phone: 0642 218171

Fax: 0642 224215

★261★

Association of Franchised Distributors of Electronic Components

Owles Hall

Buntingford

Royston SG9 9PL

Phone: 0763 71209

Fax: 0763 73255

★262★

Association of Free Magazines & Periodicals

27 Brunswick Square

Gloucester GL1 1UN

Phone: 0452 308100

Fax: 0452 300912

Free newspaper publishers who also publish magazines and periodicals serving special interest groups

★263★

Association of Free Newspapers

c/o B Older

27 Brunswick Square

Gloucester GL1 1UF

Phone: 0452 308100

Fax: 0452 300912

★264★

Association of Futures Brokers & Dealers *now* incorporated into Securities and Futures Authority

★265★

Association of Genealogists & Record Agents

c/o Mrs P Berner

15 Dover Close

Hill Head

Fareham PO14 3SV

Phone: 0329 662512

Members are self-employed genealogists and record searchers

★266★

Association of General Practitioner Community Hospitals

Shepherds Spring Medical Centre

Cricketers Way

Andover   SP10 5DG
Phone: 0264 361126

★267★
Association of Golf Club Secretaries
c/o R Burniston
7a Beaconsfield Rd
Weston-super-Mare   BS23 1YE
Phone: 0934 641166

★268★
Association of Golf Writers
c/o R Laidlaw
Evening Standard
2 Derry St
London   W8 5EE
Phone: 071-938 7624

Members are journalists covering golf

★269★
Association of Graduate Careers Advisory Services
c/o C J Phillips
Manchester University Careers Service
Crawford House
Oxford Rd
Manchester   M14 9QS
Phone: 061-275 2828
Fax: 061-275 2850

★270★
Association of Graduate Recruiters
c/o R Cockman
Sheraton House
Castle Park
Cambridge   CB3 0AX
Phone: 0223 356720
Fax: 0223 356720

For organisations which recruit and employ graduates or which offer services in connection with graduate recruitment

★271★
Association of Greyboard Makers
Papermaker House
Rivenhall Rd
Westlea
Swindon   SN5 7BE
Phone: 0793 886086
Fax: 0793 886182

★272★
Association of Guide-Booking Agency Services
c/o A Ormandy
80 Wickway Court
Cator St
London   SE15 6QD
Phone: 071-703 9708

★273★
Association of Gypsy Organisations
c/o Dr D S Kenrick
61 Blenheim Crescent
London   W11 2EG
Phone: 071-727 2916

★274★
Association of Heads of Independent Schools
c/o Rougemont School
Stow Hill
Newport   NP4 4EB

★275★
Association of Heads of Outdoor Education Centres
Aberglasyn Hall
Beddgelert
Caernarfon   LL55 4YF
Phone: 0766 86233

★276★
Association of Health Care Information & Medical Records Officers
c/o Trevor Tyrrell Associates
Aumberry Gap
Loughborough   LE11 1AA
Phone: 0509 233141
Fax: 0509 610279

★277★
Association of High Pressure Water Jetting Contractors
c/o N G Allen
28 Eccleston St
London   SW1W 9PY
Phone: 071-730 7605
Fax: 071-730 7110

★278★
Association of Higher Academic Staff in Colleges of Education in Scotland
c/o Moray House College of Education
Holyrood Rd
Edinburgh EH8 8AQ
Phone: 031-556 8455

★279★
Association of Higher Education Institutions Concerned with Home Economics
c/o L Ecroyd
Bradford & Ilkley Community College
Wells Rd
Ilkley LS29 9RD
Phone: 0943 609010

★280★
Association of Hispanists of GB & Ireland
c/o Dr D Mackenzie
Dept of Hispanic Studies
University of Birmingham
PO Box 363
Birmingham B15 2TT
Phone: 021-414 6038

★281★
Association of Illustrators
1 Colville Place
London W1P 1HN
Phone: 071-636 4100

★282★
Association of Incorporated Managers & Administrators
25 Sunnybank Rd
Manchester M13 0XF
Phone: 061-248 6844

An educational body covering all aspects of the theory and practice of economic, commercial and industrial managements and adminstration

★283★
Association of Independant Crop Consultants
Church Farmhouse
Ingoldsby

Grantham NG33 4EJ
Phone: 0476 85790
Fax: 0476 85790

★284★
Association of Independent Businesses
133 Copeland Rd
London SE15 3SB
Phone: 071-277 5158

★285★
Association of Independent Cinemas
Theatre One Cinema, Ford St
Coventry CV1 5FN
Phone: 0203 20446

★286★
Association of Independent Computer Specialists
Leicester House
8 Leicester St
London WC2H 7BN
Phone: 071-437 0678

Members are consultants, programmers and software designers

★287★
Association of Independent Electricity Producers
c/o South West One Ltd
Herodsfoot
Liskeard PL14 4QX
Phone: 0579 21300
Fax: 0579 20586

A trade association representing the independent electricity industry; members are independent generators of electricity

★288★
Association of Independent Libraries
c/o J Allen
Portico Library
57 Moseley St
Manchester M2 3HY
Phone: 061-236 6785

★289★
Association of Independent Museums
Dundee Industrial Heritage
Maritime House

26 East Dock St
Dundee DD1 4HY
Phone: 0382 25282

★290★
Association of Independent Producers
now incorporated into Producers
Association

★291★
**Association of Independent Radio
Contractors**
46 Westbourne Rd
London W2 5SH
Phone: 071-727 2646
Fax: 0352

★292★
Association of Independent Railways
c/o M Burton
85 Balmoral Rd
Gillingham
Kent ME7 4QG
Phone: 0634 52672

★293★
**Association of Independent Tobacco
Specialists**
c/o D C Higgins
Re-Salis Drive
Hampton Lovett Industrial Estate
Droitwich DR9 0QF
Phone: 0905 794579
Fax: 0905 794502

★294★
**Association of Independent Tour
Operators**
PO Box 180
Isleworth TW7 7EA
Phone: 081-569 8092
Fax: 081-568 8330

★295★
**Association of Industrial Graphics &
Nameplate Manufacturers**
31 Keats Rd
Coventry CV2 5J2
Phone: 0203 448879
Fax: 0203 553949

★296★
**Association of Industrial Road Safety
Officers**
c/o Andrew Howard
Automobile Association
Fanum House
Basingstoke RG21 2EA
Phone: 0256 493038

★297★
**Association of Information Officers in
the Pharmaceutical Industry**
c/o Division of Gastroenterology
Glaxo Group Research
Greenford Rd
Greenford UB5 0HE
Phone: 081-422 3434

★298★
**Association of Installers & Unvented
Hot Water Systems (Scotland &
Ireland)**
2 Walker St
Edinburgh EH3 7LB
Phone: 031-225 2255
Fax: 031-226 7638

★299★
**Association of Insurance & Risk
Managers in Industry & Commerce**
6 Lloyds Ave
London EC3N 3AX
Phone: 071-480 7610

★300★
**Association of Interior Design Degree
Courses**
c/o Dept of 3D Design
Nottingham Polytechnic
Burton St
Nottingham NG1 4BU
Phone: 0602 418418 ext. 2414
Fax: 0602 486404

★301★
**Association of International
Accountants**
South Bank Building
Kingsway
Gateshead

Newcastle upon Tyne   NE11 0JS
Phone: 091-482 4409

★302★
**Association of International Bond
    Dealers**
7 Limeharbour
London   E14 9NQ
Phone: 071-538 5656
Fax: 071-538 4902

★303★
**Association of Investment Trust
    Companies**
c/o J W Rath
6th Floor
Park House
16 Finsbury Circus
London   EC2M 7JJ
Phone: 071-588 5347
Fax: 071-638 1803

★304★
Association of Invoice Factors
47 Brunswick Place
London   N1 6EE

★305★
**Association of Jute Spinners &
    Manufacturers**
148 Nethergate
Dundee   DD1 4EA
Phone: 0382 25881
Fax: 23584

★306★
Association of Law Costs Draftsmen
c/o D Boyd
66 Ravensbourne Park Crescent
London   SE6 4YP
Phone: 071-623 2011

★307★
Association of Law Teachers
c/o J Coles
Manchester College of Arts & Technology
Lower Hardman St
Manchester   M3 3FP
Phone: 061-831 7791

★308★
**Association of Learned & Professional
    Society Publishers**
c/o B T Donovan
48 Kelsey Lane
Beckenham   BR3 3NE
Phone: 081-658 0459

★309★
Association of Legal Personnel
Stone House
275 Greenwich High Rd
London   SE10 8NB
Phone: 081-853 3585
Fax: 081-853 3761

★310★
**Association of Licensed Aircraft
    Engineers**
The Old Court House
London Rd
Ascot   SL5 7EN
Phone: 0344 26138
Fax: 0344 21340

★311★
Association of Light Alloy Refiners
Broadway House
Calthorpe Rd
Birmingham   B15 1TN
Phone: 021-456 1103
Fax: 021-452 1897

★312★
Association of Lighting Designers
3 Apollo Studies
Charlton Kings Rd
London   NW5 2SW
Phone: 071-482 4224
Fax: 071-284 0636

Members are professional lighting designers

★313★
**Association of Lightweight Aggregate
    Manufacturers**
c/o Tarmac Pellite Ltd, John Hadfield
    House
Dale Rd

Matlock DE4 3PL
Phone: 0629 580300
Fax: 0629 580204

★314★
Association of Little Presses
89a Petherton Rd
London N5 2QT
Phone: 071-226 2657

Members are individuals operating as small presses/publishers

★315★
Association of Loading & Elevating Equipment Manufacturers
Carolyn House
22-26 Dingwall Rd
Croydon CR0 9XF
Phone: 081-681 1680
Fax: 081-681 2134

★316★
Association of London Authorities
36 Old Queen St
London SW1H 9JF
Phone: 071-222 7799
Fax: 071-799 2339

★317★
Association of London Borough Engineers & Surveyors
c/o C E Carter
London Borough of Merton
Crown House
London Rd
Morden SM4 5DX
Phone: 081-545 3050
Fax: 081-545 4105

★318★
Association of London Chief Librarians
c/o Central Library
Barking 1G11 7NB
Phone: 081-517 8666
Fax: 081-594 1156

★319★
Association of London Clubs
c/o Farmers Club
3 Whitehall Court

London SW1A 2EL
Phone: 071-930 3751

★320★
Association of Magisterial Officers
35 High St
Crawley RH10 1BQ
Phone: 0293 547515
Fax: 0293 616418

★321★
Association of Magistrates' Courts
c/o H Whittaker
C2 Division
Home Office
50 Queen Anne's Gate
London SW1H 9AT
Phone: 0533 527822

For people wishing to work professionally in magistrates' courts

★322★
Association of Mail Order Publishers
1 New Burlington St
London W1X 1FD
Phone: 071-437 0706

The trade association of companies selling books, periodicals and music direct to the public

★323★
Association of Makers of Newsprint
Papermaker House
Rivenhall Rd
Westlea
Swindon SN5 7BE
Phone: 0793 886086
Telex: 0793 886182

★324★
Association of Makers of Packaging Papers
Papermaker House
Rivenhall Rd
Westlea
Swindon SN5 7BE
Phone: 0793 886086
Fax: 0793 886182

★325★
Association of Makers of Printings & Writings
Papermaker House
Rivenhall Rd
Westlea
Swindon   SN5 7BE
Phone: 0793 886086
Fax: 0793 886182

★326★
Association of Makers of Soft Tissue Papers
Papermaker House
Rivenhall Rd
Westlea
Swindon   SN5 7BE
Phone: 0793 886086
Fax: 0793 886182

★327★
Association of Malt Products Manufacturers
60 Claremont Rd
Surbiton   KT6 4RH
Phone: 081-390 2022
Telex: 291561

★328★
Association of Manufacturers Allied to the Electrical & Electronic Industries
Leicester House
8 Leicester St
London   WC2H 7BN
Phone: 071-437 0678
Fax: 071-437 4901

Covers cable connectors and overhead line fittings, emergency lighting luminaires and industrial immersion heaters

★329★
Association of Manufacturers of Domestic Electrical Appliances
Leicester House
8 Leicester St
London   WC2H 7BN
Phone: 071-437 0678
Fax: 071-494 1094

★330★
Association of Manufacturing Chemists
Sidcup House
12-18 Station Rd
Sidcup   DA15 7EH
Phone: 081-302 2522
Fax: 081-302 1690

Covers international debt collection and credit enquiry

★331★
Association of Marine Catering Superintendents
30-32 Saint Mary Axe
London   EC3A 8ET
Phone: 071-227 2725

★332★
Association of Marine Engineering Schools
c/o E C Knowles
Dept of Mechanical, Marine & Production Engineering
Liverpool Polytechnic
Byrom St
Liverpool   L3 3AF
Phone: 051-207 3581   ext. 2024

★333★
Association of Market Survey Organisations
c/o Millward Brown
Olympus Avenue
Tachbrook Park
Warwick   CV34 6RJ
Phone: 0926 36425
Fax: 0926 833600

Members are marketing research companies

★334★
Association of Master Lightermen & Barge Owners
Central House
32-66 High St
London   E15 2PS
Phone: 081-519 4872
Fax: 081-519 5483

Covering the Port of London

★335★
Association of Master Upholsterers
564 North Circular Rd
London NW2 7QB
Phone: 081-205 0465

Upholstered furniture, car trimming, carpet
planning, bedding and the like

★336★
Association of Meat Inspectors in GB
44 Parkfield Rd
Taunton TA1 4SF
Phone: 0823 333201

★337★
Association of Media Independents
34 Grand Avenue
London N10 3BP
Phone: 081-883 9854
Fax: 081-444 6473

Members are companies engaged in planning
and buying advertising media

★338★
Association of Medical Research
Charities
Tavistock House South
Tavistock Square
London WC1H 9LG
Phone: 071-383 0490
Fax: 071-383 0507

★339★
Association of Medical Secretaries,
Practice Administrators &
Receptionists
Tavistock House North
Tavistock Square
London WC1H 9LN
Phone: 071-387 6005
Fax: 071-388 2648

An organisation formed to encourage high
standards among persons engaged in medical
secretarial employment

★340★
Association of Medical Technologists
c/o Medical Physics Dept
Freeman Hospital

Newcastle upon Tyne NE7 7DN
Phone: 091-284 3111 ext. 3485

★341★
Association of Metal Sprayers
5 Pinley Way
Solihull B91 3YG

★342★
Association of Metropolitan
Authorities
35 Great Smith St
London SW1P 3BJ
Phone: 071-222 8100
Fax: 071-222 0878

★343★
Association of Model Agents
The Clockhouse
Saint Catherine's Mews
London SW3 2PX
Phone: 071-584 6466

★344★
Association of Mortgage Lenders
c/o C Gordon Sheridan
Winslade Park
Exeter EX5 10S
Phone: 0392 282140
Fax: 0392 420830

★345★
Association of Motor Racing Circuit
Owners
Westway House
Castle Combe
Chippenham SN14 7EY
Phone: 0249 782417
Fax: 0249 782392

★346★
Association of Motor Vehicle Teachers
c/o T Mellard
23 Hilland Drive
Bishopston
Swansea SA3 3AJ
Phone: 0441 282843

★347★
Association of Municipal Engineers
1 Great George St
London   SW1P 3AA
Phone: 071-222 7722
Fax: 071-222 7500

Members are civil engineers working in the public service sector

★348★
Association of Music Advisers in Scotland
c/o E Luke
Borders Regional HQ
Newtown St Boswells
Roxburgh   TD6 0SA
Phone: 0835 23301   ext. 484

★349★
Association of National Health Service Supplies Officers *now* National Association of National Health Care Supplies Managers

★350★
Association of National Park Officers
c/o S Copeland
Old Vicarage
Bondgate
Helmsley   YO6 3BP
Phone: 0439 70657
Fax: 0439 70691

★351★
Association of National Tourist Office Representatives in the UK
42d Compayne Gardens
London   NW6 3RY
Phone: 071-624 5817

★352★
Association of Newspaper & Magazine Wholesalers
1 Whitehall St
Rochdale   OL16 1DU
Phone: 0706 354540
Fax: 0706 350448

Representing wholesale newspaper and regional distributors in England and Wales but excluding Greater London

★353★
Association of Newspaper & Magazine Wholesalers
Regent House
89 Kingsway
London   WC2B 6RH
Phone: 071-242 3458
Fax: 071-405 1128

★354★
Association of Noise Consultants
20-26 Cursitor St
London   EC4A 1HY
Phone: 071-405 2088

Members offer services relating to environmental noise and vibration, acoustic testing, architectural acoustics design and industrial noise reduction

★355★
Association of Nursery Training Colleges
c/o Princess Christian College
26 Wilbraham Rd
Manchester   M14 6JX
Phone: 061-224 4560

★356★
Association of Official Shorthandwriters
2 New Square
Lincoln's Inn
London   WC2A 3RU
Phone: 071-405 9884

★357★
Association of Optometrists
Bridge House
233-234 Blackfriars Rd
London   SE1 8NW
Phone: 071-261 9661
Fax: 071-261 0228

★358★
Association of Oriental Carpet Traders of London
c/o D V Robertson
8 Baker St

London W1M 1DA
Phone: 071-486 5888
Fax: 071-487 3686

★359★
Association of Paediatric Anaesthetists
of GB and Ireland
c/o Dr S E F Jones
Children's Hospital
Ladywood Middleway
Birmingham B16 8ET
Phone: 021-454 4851
Fax: 021-456 4697

★360★
Association of Painting Craft Teachers
c/o M Thomas
5 Raven Court
Churchwood Drive
St Leonards-on-Sea
Hastings TN38 9RL
Phone: 0424 853282

For all engaged in education and training
through-out the painting and decorating
industry including technology and related
skills associated with interior and exterior
decoration, vehicle painting, industrial finishing and signwork

★361★
Association of Pensioneer Trustees
c/o I D Hammond
James Hay Pension Trustees Ltd
Albany House
3-5 New St
Salisbury SP1 2PH
Phone: 0722 338333
Fax: 0722 411008

Membership is open to all individuals or
companies approved by the Superannuation
Funds Office of the Inland Revenue as pensioneer trustees

★362★
Association of Personal Assistants &
Secretaries
14 Victoria Terrace
Leamington Spa CV31 3AB
Phone: 0926 424844
Fax: 0926 451988

★363★
Association of Photographers
9-10 Domingo St
London EC1Y OTA
Phone: 071-608 1441
Fax: 071-253 3007

★364★
Association of Photographic
Laboratories
9 Warwick Court
London WC1R 5DJ
Phone: 071-405 2762
Fax: 071-831 2413

★365★
Association of Playing Field Officers &
Landscape Managers
c/o K Hill
1 Cowley Rd
Tuffley
Gloucester GL4 0HT
Phone: 0452 417693

Members are managers of sports grounds,
both local authority and privately owned

★366★
Association of Pleasurecraft Operators
on Inland Waterways
35a High St
Newport
Telford TF10 8JW
Phone: 0952 813572
Fax: 0952 820363

★367★
Association of Point-of-Sale
Advertising
c/o Batiste Group
Pembroke House
Campsbourne Rd
London N8 7PE
Phone: 081-340 3291
Fax: 081-341 4840

★368★
Association of Police & Court
Interpreters
c/o B El-Nour
PO Box 1977

London W11 3SE
Phone: 071-229 1167
Fax: 071-229 1203

★369★
Association of Police Surgeons
Creaton House
Creaton
Northampton NN6 8ND
Phone: 060124 722

Members are medical practitioners who regularly assist or advise the police in medical or forensic cases

★370★
Association of Polytechnic Teachers
Caxton Chambers
81 Albert Rd
Portsmouth PO5 2SQ
Phone: 0705 818625
Fax: 0705 838187

★371★
Association of Practising Accountants
c/o M J Snyder
Devonshire House
146 Bishopsgate
London EC2M 4JX
Phone: 071-377 8888
Fax: 071-247 7048

Members are medium-sized firms of chartered accountants

★372★
Association of Principals of Colleges
c/o Dr J R Gorrie
Chichester College of Technology
Westgate Fields
Chichester PO19 15B
Phone: 0243 786321
Fax: 0243 775783

★373★
Association of Principals of Sixth Form Colleges
c/o D Kelly
Palmer's College
Grays
Romford RM17 51D
Phone: 0325 370121

★374★
Association of Print & Packaging Buyers
Watford College
Hempsted Rd
Watford WD1 3EZ
Phone: 0923 57660
Fax: 0923 57556

★375★
Association of Printing Machinery Importers
c/o G D Thomas
16 Melville St
Ryde PO33 2AF
Phone: 0983 65135
Fax: 0983 616877

★376★
Association of Professional Composers
34 Hanway St
London W1P 9DE
Phone: 071-436 0919
Fax: 071-436 1913

Covering all forms of musical composition

★377★
Association of Professional Computer Consultants
Penn House
16 Peterborough Rd
Harrow HA1 2XN
Phone: 081-422 6460

Members are independent consultants who are free of ties with computer suppliers, software houses and bureaux

★378★
Association of Professional Foresters
Brokerwood House
Brokerwood
Westbury BA13 4EH
Phone: 0373 822238
Fax: 0373 858474

Represents all involved in forestry management, either as managers or suppliers of goods and services

★379★
Association of Professional Music Therapists
68 Pierce Lane
Fulbourn
Cambridge CB1 5DL
Phone: 0223 880377

★380★
Association of Professional Recording Studios
2 Windsor Square
Silver St
Reading RG1 2TH
Phone: 0734 756218
Fax: 0734 756216

★381★
Association of Professional Video Distributors
PO Box 25
Godalming GU7 1PL
Phone: 04868 23429

★382★
Association of Professions for the Mentally Handicapped People
Greytree Lodge
Second Avenue
Ross-on-Wye HR9 7HT
Phone: 0989 62630

★383★
Association of Project Managers
85 Oxford Rd
High Wycombe HP11 2DX
Phone: 0494 440090
Fax: 0494 28937

Primarily concerned with building and allied interests

★384★
Association of Property Unit Trusts
c/o A P W Jones
MIM Ltd
11 Devonshire Square
London EC2M 4YR
Phone: 071-214 1274
Fax: 071-214 1630

★385★
Association of Public Analysts
c/o M Barnett
Dr A Voelcher & Sons Ltd
380 Bollo Lane
London W3 8QU
Phone: 081-993 2421

★386★
Association of Public Analysts of Scotland
c/o Strathclyde Regional Chemist Dept
8 Elliot Place
Glasgow G3 8EJ
Phone: 041-227 2367
Fax: 041-227 2224

Public analysts serve local authorities by providing their expertise in food law enforcement

★387★
Association of Publishers' Educational Representatives
c/o S W Hall
88 Haven Close
Cookridge
Leeds LS16 6SG
Phone: 0532 673956

★388★
Association of Qualitative Research Practitioners
c/o Hudson, Payne & Iddiols
8 Buckingham St
London WC2N 6BY
Phone: 071-930 8111

★389★
Association of Quality Management Consultants
4 Beyne Rd
Olivers Battery
Winchester SO22 4JW
Phone: 0962 866969
Fax: 0962 866969

★390★
Association of Radical Midwives
62 Greetby Hill

Ormskirk   L39 2DT
Phone: 0695 572776

Members are midwives, students midwives and others interested in improving maternity care

★391★
Association of Railway Preservation Societies
3 Orchard Close
Watford   WD1 3DU
Phone: 0923 221280
Fax: 0923 241023

★392★
Association of Recognised English Language Schools
2 Pontypool Place
London   SE1 8QF
Phone: 071-242 3136
Fax: 071-928 9378

Member organisations operate schools for the teaching of English as a foreign language

★393★
Association of Recreation Managers
Lower Basildon
Reading   RG8 9NE
Phone: 0491 874222
Fax: 0491 874059

★394★
Association of Registered Care Homes
852 Melton Rd
Thurmaston
Leicester   LE4 8BN
Phone: 0533 692467
Fax: 0533 640141

Membes are owners of private residential and nursing homes

★395★
Association of Registered Chauffeurs
Unit 8
Metropolitan Wharf
Wapping Wall
London   E1 9SS
Phone: 071-481 1223
Fax: 071-480 6287

★396★
Association of Registrars of Scotland
7 East Fergus Place
Kirkcaldy   KY1 1XT
Phone: 0592 262023

★397★
Association of Religious in Education
53 Cromwell Rd
London   SW7 2EH
Phone: 071-584 6617

★398★
Association of Relocation Agents
105 Hanover St
Edinburgh   EH2 1DJ
Phone: 031-220 2505

Relocation agents work in the private and corporate sectors helping people who have to move because of job relocation

★399★
Association of Residential Letting Agents
18-21 Jermyn St
London   SW1Y 6HP
Phone: 071-734 0655

The regulatory body for companies dealing in the field of letting and for individual managers of residential property

★400★
Association of Retired Persons
Parnell House
19 Wilton Rd
London   SW1V 1LW
Phone: 071-895 8880
Fax: 071-834 3829

Retirement planning for people over 50

★401★
Association of Road Traffic Sign Makers
72 Victoria Rd
Trowbridge   BA14 7LD
Phone: 0225 753501
Fax: 0225 777702

★402★
Association of Scottish Local Health Councils
21 Torphichen St
Edinburgh   EH3 8HX
Phone: 031-229 2344

★403★
Association of Sea Fisheries Committees of England & Wales
11 Clive Avenue
Lytham St Annes   FY8 2RU
Phone: 0253 721848

For the enforcement of fisheries regulations, byelaws and fisheries management

★404★
Association of Sexual & Marital Therapists
PO Box 62
Sheffield   S10 3TS

★405★
Association of Shell Boilermakers
The Meadows
Ryleys Lane
Alderley Edge   SK9 7UU
Phone: 0625 582346
Fax: 0625 586351

★406★
Association of Shopfront Section Manufacturers
411 Limpsfield Rd
The Green
Warlingham   CR3 9HA
Phone: 0883 624691

★407★
Association of Show & Agricultural Organisations
The Showground
Winthorpe
Newark   NG24 2NY
Phone: 0636 702627

★408★
Association of Ski Schools in GB
c/o Cairdsport Ski Schools
Aviemore Centre

Aviemore   PH22 1PL
Phone: 0479 810310
Fax: 0479 810689

To promote skiing as an enjoyable, safe sport by ensuring that qualified instruction is given

★409★
Association of Social Research Organisations
Regent's College
Inner Circle
London   NW1 4NS
Phone: 071-487 7413
Fax: 071-487 7590

★410★
Association of Speakers Clubs
c/o P Dawkins
3 Leawood Croft
Holloway
Matlock   DE4 5BN
Phone: 0629 534619

Covers training in public speaking

★411★
Association of Stainless Fastener Distributors
c/o G K Edwards
74 Chester Rd
Birmingham   B36 7BU
Phone: 021-776 7474
Fax: 021-776 7605

★412★
Association of Street Lighting Contractors
34 Pishiobury Drive
Sawbridgeworth
Stevenage   CM21 0AE
Phone: 0279 722390
Fax: 0279 726583

Members undertake highway and street lighting schemes for local authorites, civic contractors and estate developers

★413★
Association of Structural Fire Protection Contractors & Manufacturers
c/o J G Fairley
PO Box 111
Aldershot GU11 1YW
Phone: 0252 21322
Fax: 0252 333901

★414★
Association of Subscription Agents
Periodicals Division
Beaver House
Hythe Bridge St
Oxford OX1 2SN
Phone: 0865 792792 ext. 212
Fax: 0865 791438

★415★
Association of Sun Tanning Organisations
32 Grayshott Rd
London SW11 5TT
Phone: 071-228 6077

Members manufacture, sell or operate sun tanning salons and leisure centres and promote their safety

★416★
Association of Supervisors of Midwives
c/o Maternity Unit
James Paget Hospital
Lowestoft Rd
Gorleston
Great Yarmouth NR31 6LA
Phone: 0493 600611 ext. 269

★417★
Association of Suppliers to the Furniture Industry
PO Box 10
Epping CM16 7RR
Phone: 0378 78873
Fax: 0378 72217

★418★
Association of Surgeons of GB & Ireland
c/o Royal College of Surgeons
35-43 Lincoln's Inn Fields
London WC2A 3PN
Phone: 071-405 6753
Fax: 071-430 9235

For consultant general surgeons

★419★
Association of Teachers in Geology
now Earth Science Teachers' Association

★420★
Association of Teachers of Mathematics
7 Shaftesbury St
Derby DE3 8YB
Phone: 0332 46599

★421★
Association of Teachers of Printing & Allied Subjects
c/o R F Underwood
12 Station Rd
Kirby Muxloe
Leicester LE9 9EJ
Phone: 0533 541818 ext. 260

★422★
Association of Teachers of Singing
c/o C J Schooling
Sideways House
146 Greenstead Rd
Colchester CO1 2SN
Phone: 0206 867462

★423★
Association of Teaching Hospital Pharmacists
c/o P Sharott
District Pharmacist
Charing Cross Hospital
Fulham Palace Rd
London W6 8RF
Phone: 081-846 1141
Fax: 081-846 7493

★424★
Association of Telephone Information & Entertainment Providers
48 Grafton Way
London   W1P 5LB
Phone: 071-387 2838
Fax: 071-388 4932

★425★
Association of Temporary & Interim Executive Services
36-38 Mortimer St
London   W1N 7RB
Phone: 071-323 4300
Fax: 071-255 2878

★426★
Association of the British Pharmaceutical Industry
12 Whitehall
London   SW1A 2DY
Phone: 071-930 3477
Fax: 071-930 3290

Representing manufacturers of medicines not advertised to the public

★427★
Association of Timber Agents & Brokers
Russell Square House
10-12 Russell Square
London   WC1B 5AE
Phone: 071-436 3636
Fax: 071-436 6603

★428★
Association of Trading Standards Officers
c/o P B Nelson
Dept of Consumer Services
Bexley Civic Offices
Broadway
Bexleyheath   DA6 7LB
Phone: 081-303 7777   ext. 2778
Fax: 081-301 4937

★429★
Association of Tutors Incorporated
27 Radburn Court

Dunstable   LU6 1HW

Members are principals of tutorial colleges, agencies and private tutors

★430★
Association of UK Media Librarians
c/o S Adair
London Weekend Television
South Bank
London   SE1 9LT
Phone: 071-261 3734
Fax: 071-928 6948

★431★
Association of University Professors of French & Heads of French Departments
c/o Professor J Birkett
Dept of French
University of Birmingham
PO Box 363
Birmingham   B15 2TT
Phone: 021-414 5963
Fax: 021-414 5966

★432★
Association of University Teachers
1 Pembridge Rd
London   W11 3HJ
Phone: 071-221 4370
Fax: 071-727 6547

★433★
Association of University Teachers (Scotland)
6 Castle St
Edinburgh   EH2 3AT
Phone: 031-226 6694
Fax: 031-226 2066

★434★
Association of Users of Research Agencies
c/o Incorporated Society of British Advertisers
44 Hertford St
London   W1Y 8AE
Phone: 071-499 7502

For organisations using companies providing market research services

★435★
Association of Valuers of Licensed Property
c/o A G Cooper
310 Ewell Rd
Surbiton   KT6 7AL
Phone: 081-390 7833
Fax: 081-390 6709

★436★
Association of Vehicle Recovery Operators *now* incorporated with Retail Motor Industry Federation

★437★
Association of Veterinary Anaesthetists of GB & Ireland
c/o Dr A M Nolan
Dept of Veterinary Pharmacology
University of Glasgow
Bearsden Rd
Glasgow   G1 1QH
Phone: 041-334 8855

★438★
Association of Veterinary Teachers & Research Workers
c/o Dr D J Taylor
Dept of Veterinary Pathology
University of Glasgow
Bearsden Rd
Glasgow   G61 1QH
Phone: 041-339 8855

★439★
Association of Vice-Principals of Colleges
c/o Dr J D Ledger
Reading College of Technology
Crescent Rd
Reading   RG1 5RQ
Phone: 0734 583501
Fax: 0734-352271

Members are second-tier managers in colleges

★440★
Association of Wagon Builders & Repairers
c/o K G Rose
26 Mayfield
Rowledge
Farnham   GU10 4DZ
Phone: 025125 4358
Fax: 025125 4358

Members design, build and repair rail freight wagons

★441★
Association of Webbing Load Restraint Equipment Manufacturers
22 Cauldon Close
Leek   ST13 5SH
Phone: 0538 386826

★442★
Association of Welding Distributors
1 Hull Rd
York   YO1 3JF
Phone: 0904 415720
Fax: 0904 425158

★443★
Association of Wholesale Woollen Merchants
The Old Post Office
Dunchideock
Exeter   EX2 9TU
Phone: 0392 832559

★444★
Association of Workers for Maladjusted Children
c/o Allan Rimmer
Redhill School
East Sutton
Maidstone   ME17 3DQ
Phone: 0622 843104

For those working with children and adolescents who are emotionally disturbed or who have behavioural and/or learning problems

★445★
Association of X-ray Equipment Manufacturers
Leicester House
8 Leicester St
London   WC2H 7BN
Phone: 071-437 0678
Fax: 071-437 0391

All types of medical X-ray and associated equipment

★446★
Athletic Clothing Manufacturers Association
c/o R Archbell
Star Sports Wear Ltd
Denby Dale Rd
Thornes
Wakefield   WF2 7AY
Phone: 0924 291441
Fax: 0924 291441

★447★
Audio Engineering Society
Lent Rise Rd, Burnham
Slough   SL1 7NY
Phone: 0628 663725
Fax: 0628 667002

★448★
Audio Visual Association
46 Manor View
London   N3 2SR
Phone: 081-349 2429

★449★
Auger Boring Association
56 Britton St
London   EC1M 5NA
Phone: 071-253 8955
Fax: 071-251 1939

★450★
Authors' Licensing & Collecting Society
7 Ridgmount St
London   WC1E 7AE
Phone: 071-255 2034
Fax: 071-323 0486

Collecting society for writers

★451★
Automated Material Handling Systems Association
Scammell House
High St
Ascot   SL5 7JF
Phone: 0344 23800
Fax: 0344 291197

★452★
Automatic Door Suppliers Association
411 Limpsfield Rd
The Green
Warlingham   CR3 9HA
Phone: 0883 624961
Fax: 0883 626841

To promote standards of safety in the installation and use of automatic doors

★453★
Automatic Indentification Manufacturers
c/o I G Smith
The Old Vicarage
Haley Hill
Halifax   HX3 6DR
Phone: 0422 359161
Fax: 0422 355604

Automatic identification systems are used primarily in manufacturing and retailing

★454★
Automatic Vending Association of Britain
Bassett House
High St
Banstead   SM7 2LZ
Phone: 0737 357211
Fax: 0737 370501

★455★
Automotive Distributors Federation
68-70 Coles Hill Rd
Birmingham   B36 8AB
Phone: 021-784 3535
Fax: 021 784 4411

Members are wholesale distributors and manufacturers of motor components and accessories

★456★
Aviation Insurance Offices' Association
c/o London Aviation Insurance Group
110-112 Fenchurch St
London   EC3M 5LH
Phone: 071-623 3175
Telex: 888748

★457★
Baby Equipment Hirers Association
4 Santon Close
Kirkham
Blackpool   PR4 3HF
Phone: 0772 685513

Members operate home-based baby equipment hiring services

★458★
Baby Products Association
60 Claremont Rd
Surbiton   KT6 4RH
Phone: 081-390 2022
Fax: 081-390 2027

★459★
Bacon & Meat Manufacturers' Association *now* British Meat Manufacturers' Association

★460★
Badminton Association of England
c/o National Badminton Centre
Bradwell Rd
Loughton Lodge
Milton Keynes   MK8 9LA
Phone: 0908 568822
Fax: 0908 566922

★461★
Bakery Allied Traders' Association
now incorporated into Food & Drink Federation

★462★
Ball & Roller Bearing Manufacturers Association
136 Hagley Rd
Birmingham   B16 9PN
Phone: 021-454 4141
Fax: 021-454 4141

★463★
Ballroom Dancers Federation
c/o W Laird
151 Brudenell Rd
London   SW17 8DF
Phone: 081-672 8176

Members are professional ballroom dancers concerned with competition, demonstration, and cabaret, coaching and adjudicating

★464★
Baltic Air Charter Association
6 The Office Village
Romford Rd
London   E15 4EA
Phone: 081-519 3909
Telex: 28768
Fax: 081-519 6967

★465★
Bar Association for Commerce, Finance & Industry
2 Plowden Buildings
Middle Temple Lane
London   EC4Y 9AT
Phone: 071-583 4937

Members are barristers practising in commerce, finance and industry

★466★
Bar Association for Local Government
c/o Milton Keynes Borough Council
1 Saxon Gate East
Milton Keynes   MK9 3HG
Phone: 0908 682205
Fax: 0908 682456

Incorporating Society of Local Government Barristers

★467★
Barge & Canal Development Association
c/o Peter L Smith
33 Walnut Crescent
Peacock Estate
Wakefield   WF2 0EU
Phone: 0924 366677

★468★
Barristers' Clerks' Association
24 Chancery Lane
London WC2A 1LS
Phone: 071-583 5141

★469★
Basketware Importers Association
85-87 Westbourne Park Rd
London W2 5QJ
Phone: 071-229 9766
Fax: 071-243 0077

Members are importers of basketware and wicker furniture

★470★
Bathroom & Kitchen Distributors Association
c/o T Parker
58 Beaumont Rd
Cambridge CB1 4PX
Phone: 0223 466640
Fax: 0223 412323

The supply of building materials and accessories to builders merchants and ironmongers

★471★
BCIRA Cast Metals Technology
Alvechurch
Birmingham B48 7QB
Phone: 0527 66414
Fax: 0527 585070

All aspects of foundry technology

★472★
BEAMA
Leicester House
8 Leicester St
London WC2H 7BN
Phone: 071-437 0678
Fax: 071-437 4901

A federation of trade associations serving the industrial electrical, electronic and allied manufacturing industries

★473★
BEAMA Ancillery Metering Equipment Manufacturers' Association
Leicester House
8 Leicester St
London WC2H 7BN
Phone: 071-437 0678
Fax: 071-437 4901

★474★
BEAMA Capacitor Manufacturers' Association
Leicester House
8 Leicester St
London WC2H 7BN
Phone: 071-437 0678
Fax: 071-437-4901

★475★
BEAMA Interactive & Mains Systems Association
Leicester House
8 Leicester St
London WC2H 7BN
Phone: 071-437 0678
Fax: 071-437 4901

★476★
BEAMA Metering Association
Leicester House
8 Leicester St
London WC2H 7BN
Phone: 071-437 0678
Fax: 071-437 4901

★477★
BEAMA Transmission & Distribution Association
Leicester House
8 Leicester St
London WC2H 7BN
Phone: 071-437 0678
Fax: 071-437 4901

★478★
Bedding Plant Growers Association
c/o Jane Connor
Agriculture House
25 Knightsbridge
London SW1X 7NJ
Phone: 071-235 5077
Fax: 071-235 3526

★479★
Betting Office Licensees Association
Francis House
Francis St
London SW1P 1DE
Phone: 071-630 0667

★480★
Bibliographical Society
c/o British Library
Dept of Humanities & Social Sciences
Great Russell St
London WC1B 3DG
Phone: 071-323 7567
Fax: 071-323 7736

★481★
Bicycle Association of GB
Starley House
Eaton Rd
Coventry CV1 2FH
Phone: 0203 553838
Fax: 0203 228366

★482★
Billiards & Snooker Control Council
92 Kirkstall Rd
Leeds LS3 1LT
Phone: 0532 440586
Fax: 0532 468418

★483★
Biochemical Society
59 Portland Place
London W1N 3AJ
Phone: 071-580 5530
Fax: 071-323 1136

★484★
Bioindustry Association
1 Queen Anne's Gate
London SW1H 9BT
Phone: 071-222 2809
Fax: 071-222 8876

★485★
Biological Engineering Society
c/o Royal College of Surgeons
35-43 Lincoln's Inn Fields

London WC2A 3PN
Phone: 071-242 7750

The application of technology to all aspects of medicine and biology

★486★
Biscuit Cake Chocolate &
   Confectionery Alliance
11 Green St
London W1Y 3RF
Phone: 071-629 8971
Fax: 071-493 4885

Representing the interests of bakers and confectioners in the UK

★487★
Bitumen Roof Coating Manufacturers
   Association *now* European Liquid
   Roofing Association

★488★
Black Bolt & Nut Association of GB
Blundell House
Torrington Avenue
Coventry CV4 9GU
Phone: 0203 446496
Fax: 0203 466074

★489★
Blanket Manufacturers Association
60 Toller Lane
Bradford BD8 9BZ
Phone: 0274 491241
Fax: 0274 547320

★490★
Board of Airline Representatives in the
   UK
c/o British Airways
200 Buckingham Palace Rd
London SW1W 9TA
Phone: 071-821 4124
Fax: 071-821 4090

Members are scheduled British and foreign airlines operating to or from and within the UK or with offices in the UK

★491★
Boarding Schools Association
Watendlath
Bug Hill
Warlingham   CR6 9LT
Phone: 0883 624717

Covers schools, both maintained and independent, with boarding facilities

★492★
Boiler & Radiator Manufacturers Association
11th Floor
Savoy Tower
77 Renfrew St
Glasgow   G2 3BZ
Phone: 041-332 0826
Fax: 041-332 5788

★493★
Book Development Council
19 Bedford Square
London   WC1B 3HJ
Phone: 071-580 6321
Fax: 071-636 5375

★494★
Book Packagers Assocation
93a Blenheim Crescent
London   W11 2EQ
Phone: 071-221 9089

★495★
Book Publishers' Representatives' Association
3 Carolina Way
Tiptree   CO5 0DW
Phone: 0621 816710

★496★
Bookmakers' Association
22 Malthouse Lane
Birmingham   B8 1SP
Phone: 021-327 3031

★497★
Booksellers Association of GB & Ireland
Minster House
272-274 Vauxhall Bridge Rd
London   SW1V 1BA
Phone: 071-834 5477
Fax: 071-834 8812

★498★
Boot & Shoe Manufacturers' Association
Unit 10d
Printing House Yard
15a Hackney Rd
London   E2 7PR
Phone: 071-739 1678
Fax: 071-739 8724

★499★
Borough Engineers' Society
c/o Dept of Operations
Blackburn Council
Davyfield Rd
Blackburn   BB1 2LX
Phone: 0254 583555
Fax: 0254 662916

★500★
Brewers Association of Scotland
6 Saint Colme St
Edinburgh   EH3 6AD
Phone: 031-225 4681
Fax: 031-220 1132

★501★
Brewers' Society
42 Portman Square
London   W1H OBB
Phone: 071-486 4831
Fax: 071-935 3991

Members are brewery companies and licensed retailers

★502★
Brewing Research Foundation
Lyttel Hall
Nutfield
Redhill   RH1 4HY
Phone: 0737 82272

★503★
Brick Development Association
Woodside House
Winkfield

Windsor   SL4 2DX
Phone: 0344 885651
Fax: 0344 890129

Representing clay and calcium silicate brick manufacturers

★504★
British & International Golf Greenkeepers' Association
Aldwark
Alne
York   YO6 2NS
Phone: 034 73581
Fax: 034 738864

★505★
British & Irish Association of Law Librarians
c/o H C Boucher
Pinsent & Co
Post & Mail House
26 Colmore Circus
Birmingham   B4 6BH
Phone: 021-200 1050
Fax: 021-200 1040

To promote the better administration and exploitation of law libraries and legal information units by further education and training

★506★
British Abrasives Federation
Fairgreen House
Sawbridgeworth
Stevenage   CM21 9AY
Phone: 0279 600602
Fax: 0279 726488

★507★
British Academy of Experts
c/o M Cohen
90 Bedford Court Mansions
Bedford Avenue
London   WC1B 3AE
Phone: 071-637 0333
Fax: 071-637 1893

A professional society and qualifying body for independent experts experienced in a wide range of professional, commercial and industrial disciplines

★508★
British Academy of Film & Television Arts
195 Piccadilly
London   W1V 9LG
Phone: 071-465 0277
Fax: 071-734 1792

★509★
British Accounting Association
c/o Professor K Maunders
Dept of Accounting
Hull University
Hull   HU6 7RX
Phone: 0482 466391

★510★
British Activity Holiday Association
Norton Terrace
Llandrindod Wells   LD1 6AE
Phone: 0597 823902
Fax: 0597 824085

★511★
British Acupuncture Association
34 Alderney St
London   SW1Y 4EU
Phone: 071-834 1012

★512★
British Adhesives & Sealants Association
33 Fellowes Way
Stevenage   SG2 8BW
Phone: 0438 358514

★513★
British Advertising Gift Distributors Association
1 West Ruislip Station
Ruislip   HA4 7DW
Phone: 0895 622154
Fax: 0895 631219

★514★
British Aerobatic Association
c/o D Britten
Gracious Pond Farm
Gracious Pond Rd
Chobham

Woking GU24 8HL
Phone: 093287 3332
Fax: 093287 3333

For aerobatic flying enthusiasts

★515★
British Aerosol Manufacturers' Association
Kings Buildings
Smith Square
London SW1P 3JJ
Phone: 071-828 5111
Fax: 071-834 8436

★516★
British Agencies for Adoption & Fostering
11 Southwark St
London SE1 1RQ
Phone: 071-407 8800
Fax: 071-403 6970

Members include local authority and voluntary adoption agencies and professionals
working in adoption, fostering and social
work with children

★517★
British Aggregate Construction Materials Industries
156 Buckingham Palace Rd
London SW1W 9TR
Phone: 071-730 8194
Fax: 071-730 4355

The trade association representing the aggre-
gates, bituminous coated materials, surfaces
and ready-mixed concrete industries

★518★
British Agricultural & Garden Machinery Association
14 Church St
Rickmansworth WD3 1RQ
Phone: 0923 720241
Fax: 0923 896063

★519★
British Agricultural & Horticultural Plastics Association
5 Belgrave Square

London SW1X 8PH
Phone: 071-235 9483
Fax: 071-235 8045

★520★
British Agricultural Export Council
c/o London Chamber of Commerce
69 Cannon St
London EC4N 5AB
Phone: 071-248 4444
Fax: 071-489 0391

★521★
British Agricultural History Society
c/o Institute of Agricultural History &
   Museum of
English Rural Life
University of Reading
Whiteknights Park
Reading RG6 2AG
Phone: 0734 318660
Fax: 0734 314404

Covers world agricultural history including
the social, economic and technical aspects of
rural studies

★522★
British Agrochemicals Association
4 Lincoln Court
Lincoln Rd
Peterborough PE1 2RP
Phone: 0735 49225

★523★
British Air Survey Association
c/o BKS Surveys Ltd
47 Ballycairn Rd
Coleraine BT51 3HZ
Phone: 0265 52311
Fax: 0265 57637

★524★
British Aluminium Foil Rollers Association
c/o British Alcan Foil Ltd
North Woolwich Rd
London E16 2BQ
Phone: 071-476 6111
Fax: 071-511 7903

★525★
**British Amusement Catering Trades
  Association**
Bacta House
122 Clapham Common North Side
London   SW4 9SP
Phone: 071-228 4107
Fax: 071-223 0257

★526★
**British Anaesthetic & Respiratory
  Equipment Manufacturers
  Association;**
The Stables
Sugworth Lane
Radley
Oxford   OX14 2HX
Phone: 0865 736393
Fax: 0865 736393

★527★
British Angora Goat Society
c/o National Agricultural Centre
Stoneleigh
Kenilworth   CV8 2LG
Phone: 0203 696722
Fax: 0203 696729

★528★
British Anodising Association *now*
  Aluminium Finishing Association

★529★
British Antique Dealers' Association
20 Rutland Gate
London   SW7 1BD
Phone: 071-589 4128
Fax: 071-581 9083

★530★
**British Approvals Board for
  Telecommunications**
Claremont House
34 Molesey Rd
Hersham
Walton-on-Thames   KT12 4RQ
Phone: 0932 222289
Fax: 0932 229756

Assessment evaluation and approval for tele-communications apparatus intended for connection to the UK public networks

★531★
British Approvals for Fire Equipment
48a Eden St
Kingston upon Thames   IT1 1EE
Phone: 081-541 1950
Fax: 081-547 1564

★532★
British Archaeological Association
24 Lower St
Hernham
Salisbury   SP2 8EY

To promote the study of archaeology and preservation of national antiquities

★533★
British Art Medal Society
c/o M Jones
Dept of Coins & Medals
British Museum
Great Russell St
London   WC1B 3DG
Phone: 071-636 1555   ext. 658
Fax: 071-323 8480

★534★
British Arts Festivals Association
PO Box 925
London   N6 5XX
Phone: 081-348 4117

★535★
**British Association for Accident &
  Emergency Medicine**
c/o Royal College of Surgeons
Lincoln's Inn Fields
London   WC2A 3PN
Phone: 071-831 9405
Fax: 071-405 0318

Membership is available to doctors whose professional commitment is to accident and emergency medicine

★536★
British Association for Behavioural Psychotherapy
59 Revelstoke Rd
London   SW18 5NG
Phone: 081-944 1133
Fax: 081-879 3326

★537★
British Association for Brazing & Soldering
Abington Hall
Abington
Cambridge   CB1 6AL
Phone: 0223 891162
Fax: 0223 892588

★538★
British Association for Chemical Specialities
John Marshall House
246-254 High St
Sutton
Surrey   SM1 1PA
Phone: 081-643 0689
Fax: 081-770 7103

Trade association of companies manufacturing speciality chemicals, maintenance products and disinfectants

★539★
British Association for Commercial & Industrial Education
16 Park Crescent
London   W1N 4AP
Phone: 071-636 5351

★540★
British Association for Counselling
37a Sheep St
Rugby   CV21 3BX
Phone: 0788 578328
Fax: 0788 562189

★541★
British Association for Dramatherapists
The Old Mill
Tolpuddle
Dorchester   DT2 7EX

The application of dramatic programmes in remedial education and therapeutic practice

★542★
British Association for Early Childhood Education
111 City View House
463 Bethnal Green Rd
London   E2 9QY
Phone: 071-739 7594

The education and welfare of children from birth through the early stages of primary education

★543★
British Association for Immediate Care
31c Lower Brook St
Ipswich   IP4 1AQ
Phone: 0473 218407

★544★
British Association for Jazz Education
c/o R Paton
Dept of Music
Bishop Otter College
College Lane
Chichester   PO17 4PE
Phone: 0243 787911

★545★
British Association for Language Teaching now Association for Language Learning

★546★
British Association for Local History
Shopwyke Hall
Chichester   PO20 6BQ
Phone: 0243 787639
Fax: 0243 787639

★547★
British Association for Service to the Elderly
119 Hassell St

Newcastle under Lyme ST5 1AX

Phone: 0782 661033

Fax: 0782 712725

Concerned with the health and welfare of elderly people

★548★
British Association for Shooting & Conservation

Marford Mill

Rossett

Wrexham LL12 0HL

Phone: 0244 570881

Fax: 0244 571678

★549★
British Association for Soviet Slavonic & East European Studies

c/o Dr J Shapero

Social Science & Administration Dept

Goldsmith College

Lewisham Way

London SE14 6NW

Phone: 081-692 7171

Professional association of university teachers/researchers in the areas of Russian and east European languages, literatures and history

★550★
British Association for the Advancement of Science

23 Savile Row

London W1X 1AB

Phone: 071-494 3326

Fax: 071-734 1658

Seeks to enhance public understanding and awareness of science and technology and its impact on society

★551★
British Association of Advisers & Lecturers in Physical Education

Nelson House

3-6 The Beacon

Exmouth EX8 3AG

Phone: 0395 263247

★552★
British Association of Aesthetic Plastic Surgeons

c/o Royal College of Surgeons

35-43 Lincoln's Inn Fields

London WC2A 3PN

Phone: 071-405 2234

Fax: 071-831 4041

★553★
British Association of Art Therapists

11a Richmond Rd

Brighton BN2 3RL

★554★
British Association of Barbershop Singers

c/o P Jones

6 Boundary Rd

Ashford TW15 3LU

Phone: 0784 241868

Fax: 0455 202198

Promotes barbershop harmony singing and co-ordinates the activities of registered barbershop harmony clubs

★555★
British Association of Beauty Therapy & Cosmetology

2nd Floor

34 Imperial Square

Cheltenham GL50 1QZ

Phone: 0242 570284

Fax: 0242 222177

★556★
British Association of British Mountain Guides

c/o J Nicholson

Crawford House

Precont Centre

Booth St East

Manchester M13 9RZ

Phone: 061-273 5835

Fax: 061-274 3233

★557★
British Association of Canned Food Importers & Distributors

152-160 City Rd

London   EC1V 2NP
Phone: 071-253 9421

★558★
British Association of Canoe Trades
c/o D F Patrick
P & H Fibreglass Ltd
Station Rd
West Hallam
Derby   DE7 6HB
Phone: 0602 320155
Fax: 0602 327177

★559★
**British Association of Clothing
   Machinery Manufacturers**
1st Floor
159-163 Great Portland St
London   W1N 5FD
Phone: 071-636 7564

Members are engaged in the manufacture of
clothing machinery or specialised machinery
for the clothing and allied trades

★560★
**British Association of Colliery
   Management**
3i7 Nottingham Rd
Old Basford
Nottingham
Phone: 0602 785819
Fax: 0602 422279

★561★
British Association of Concert Agents
26 Wadham Rd
London   SW15 2LR
Phone: 081-874 5742
Fax: 081-877 0434

Umbrella organisation for classical concert
agents, artist managers and other professionals in the classical music business

★562★
**British Association of Conference
   Towns**
International House
43 Dudley Rd

Tunbridge Wells   TN1 1LB
Phone: 0892 33442

The professional association representing all
the major and many of the smaller conference
destinations in the UK

★563★
**British Association of Cosmetic
   Surgeons**
c/o J Schetrumpf
17 Harley St
London   W1N 1DA
Phone: 071-323 5728
Fax: 071-323 5314

★564★
**British Association of Cultured Pearl
   Importers**
c/o Ms L B Snead
10 Vyse St
Birmingham   B18 6LT
Phone: 021-236 2657

★565★
British Association of Dermatologists
3 St Andrew's Place
Regent's Park
London   NW1 4LB
Phone: 071-935 8576
Fax: 071-224 0321

★566★
**British Association of Domiciliary Care
   Officers**
c/o J Hamilton-Hall
72 Woodsend Rd
Manchester   M31 2GX
Phone: 061-748 4438

Membership is open to managers of home
help, home care, day care, domiciliary care,
community meals services and any other service encompassing care in the community

★567★
British Association of Electrolysists
c/o M Anderson
18 Stokes End
Haddenham
Thame   HP17 8DX
Phone: 0844 290721

★568★
**British Association of Feed
  Supplement Manufacturers**
Mill House
The Hill
Cranbrook TN17 3AH
Phone: 0580 714204
Fax: 0580 714337

★569★
**British Association of Friends of
  Museums**
c/o E Cass
548 Wilbraham Rd
Manchester M21 1LB
Phone: 061-236 8585

★570★
**British Association of Golf Course
  Architects**
5 Oxford St
Woodstock
Oxford OX7 1TQ
Phone: 0993 811976
Fax: 0993 812448

★571★
**British Association of Golf Course
  Constructors**
2 Angel Court
High St
Market Harborough LE16 7HN
Phone: 0858 464346
Fax: 0858 434734

★572★
**British Association of Green Crop
  Driers**
25 Frant Rd
Tunbridge Wells TN2 5JT
Phone: 0892 37777
Fax: 0892 24593

The dehydration and processing of forage
crops

★573★
**British Association of Hotel
  Accountants**
c/o R Kett
PO Box 128

Edgware HA8 6TR
Phone: 081-952 0673
Fax: 081-831 8626

★574★
**British Association of Hotel
  Reservations Representatives**
35-37 Grosvenor Gardens
London SW1W 0BS
Phone: 071-630 9954
Telex: 8950918

★575★
**British Association of Industrial
  Editors**
3 Locks Yard
High St
Sevenoaks TN13 1LT
Phone: 0732 459331
Fax: 0732 461757

A professional association primarily for editors of house journals

★576★
**British Association of Landscape
  Industries**
Landscape House
9 Henry St
Keighley BD21 3DR
Phone: 0535 606139
Fax: 0535 610269

★577★
**British Association of Leisure Parks,
  Piers & Attractions**
25 Kings Terrace
London NW1 0JP
Phone: 071-383 7942
Fax: 071-383 7925

★578★
**British Association of Manipulative
  Medicine**
c/o Dr D Goldman
46 Scots Lane
Bromley BR2 0LL
Phone: 081-650 3906

★579★
British Association of Nature Conservationists
c/o C Hatton
2 Ravensfield Rd
London   SW17 8SE

★580★
British Association of Numismatic Societies
c/o K F Sugden
Dept of Numismatics
The University
Oxford Rd
Manchester   M13 9PL
Phone: 061-275 2661

★581★
British Association of Occupational Therapists
6-8 Marshalsea Rd
London   SE1 1HL
Phone: 071-357 6480

★582★
British Association of Operating Department Assistants
c/o S E Garner
Guardian House
92-94 Foxberry Rd
London   SE4 2SH
Phone: 081-692 8943
Fax: 081-691 8415

The main aim of members is to ensure that the needs of the health service can be met by a staff group responsible for patient care in an increasingly technological environment

★583★
British Association of Oral & Maxillofacial Surgeons
Royal College of Surgeons
35-43 Lincoln's Inn Fields
London   WC2A 3PN
Phone: 071-405 8074
Fax: 071-405 0318

★584★
British Association of Orthodontists
c/o C Kettler
15 Foster Hill Rd
Bedford   MK40 2ES
Phone: 0234 357570

★585★
British Association of Otolaryngologists
c/o Royal College of Surgeons
35-43 Lincoln's Inn Fields
London   WC2A 3PN
Phone: 071-405 8373
Fax: 071-405 0318

Covering the interests of ear, nose and throat specialists

★586★
British Association of Paper Exporters
c/o G W Flutter
George Stanley Paper Ltd
137-139 Euston Rd
London   NW1 2AT
Phone: 071-388 1506
Fax: 071-338 0007

★587★
British Association of Paragliding Clubs
c/o J Burdett
18 Talbot Lane
Leicester   LE1 4LR
Phone: 0533 51300
Fax: 0533 530318

Represents the interests of parascenders and parascending clubs

★588★
British Association of Pharmaceutical Physicians
1 Wimpole St
London   W1M 8AE
Phone: 071-491 8610
Fax: 071-499 2405

★589★
British Association of Picture Libraries & Agencies
13 Woodberry Crescent

London N10 1PJ
Phone: 081-883 2531
Fax: 081-883 9215

★**590**★
British Association of Plastic Surgeons
c/o Royal College of Surgeons
35-43 Lincoln's Inn Fields
London WC2A 3PN
Phone: 071-831 5161
Fax: 071-831 4041

★**591**★
**British Association of Pool Table
    Operators**
c/o M Ferris
Bulkeley House
Stockport Rd
Cheadle SK8 2AA
Phone: 061-491 1068
Fax: 061-428 5595

★**592**★
**British Association of Professional
    Hairdressing Employers**
1a Barbon Close
London WC1N 3JX
Phone: 071-405 7184

The employers' association for hair salon
groups

★**593**★
**British Association of
    Psychotherapists**
c/o J Lawrence
121 Hendon Lane
London N3 3PR
Phone: 081-346 1747
Fax: 081-785 4622

Offers training in adult or child psychotherapy to persons working in allied professions

★**594**★
British Association of Removers
3 Churchill Court
58 Station Rd
Harrow HA2 7SA
Phone: 081-861 3331
Fax: 081-861 3332

★**595**★
British Association of Seed Analysts
c/o Mrs J Moore
3 Whitehall Court
London SW1A 2EQ
Phone: 071-930 3611
Fax: 071-930 3952

★**596**★
**British Association of Settlements &
    Social Action Centres**
13 Stockwell Rd
London SW9 9AU
Phone: 071-733 7428

A national network of multi-purpose
organisations seeking to tackle the causes
and effects of poverty and discrimination, primarily in inner city and urban areas

★**597**★
British Association of Ski Instructors
Grampian Rd
Aviemore PH22 1RL
Phone: 0479 810407
Fax: 0479 811222

★**598**★
British Association of Social Workers
16 Kent St
Birmingham B5 6RD
Phone: 021-622 3911

★**599**★
**British Association of State Colleges
    in English Language Teaching**
c/o T Cole
Hull College of Further Education
Queens Gardens
Hull HU1 3DG
Phone: 0482 29943
Fax: 0482 219079

An association of educational institutions
offering English courses for overseas students

★**600**★
**British Association of Surgical
    Oncology**
c/o Royal College of Surgeons
35-43 Lincoln's Inn Fields

London   WC2A 3PN
Phone: 071-405 5612
Fax: 0318

★601★
**British Association of Symphonic
  Bands & Wind Ensembles**
c/o A R Veal
3 Northbrook Rd
Solihull   B90 3NT
Phone: 021-744 1529

★602★
**British Association of Teachers of the
  Deaf**
c/o Icknield High School
Riddy Lane
Luton   LU3 2AH
Phone: 0582 596599

For qualified teachers of the deaf and those
working in educating deaf people

★603★
**British Association of the Hard of
  Hearing**
7-11 Armstrong Rd
London   W3 7JL
Phone: 081-743 1110

★604★
British Association of Tourist Officers
c/o Marketing Bureau
Saint Andrews Court
Saint Andrews St
Plymouth   PL1 2AH
Phone: 0752 261125
Telex: 45121

★605★
British Association of Toy Retailers
24 Baldwyn Gardens
London   W3 6HL
Phone: 081-993 2894
Fax: 081-992 0408

★606★
**British Association of Trade Computer
  Label Manufacturers**
Papermakers House
Rivenhall Rd

Westlea
Swindon   SN5 7BE
Phone: 0793 886086
Fax: 0793 886182

★607★
**British Association of Urological
  Surgeons**
c/o Royal College of Surgeons
35-43 Lincoln's Inn Fields
London   WC2A 3PN
Phone: 071-405 1390
Fax: 071-404 5048

★608★
British Astronomical Association
Burlington House
Piccadilly
London   W1V 9AG
Phone: 071-734 4145

For astronomical societies and amateur
astronomers

★609★
British Audio Dealers Association
PO Box 229
London   N1 7UU
Phone: 071-226 5500
Fax: 071-359 7620

★610★
**British Automatic Sprinkler
  Association**
10 Chellaston Rd
Wigston
Leicester   LE8 1FR
Phone: 0533 884420

★611★
**British Aviation Archaeological
  Council**
8 Holly Rd
Oulton Broad
Lowestoft   NR32 3NH
Phone: 0502 585421

For individuals interested in aviation history
particularly military aircraft

★612★
British Ball Clay Producers' Federation
Park House
Courtenay Park
Newton Abbot TQ12 4PS
Phone: 0626 332345
Fax: 0626 332344

★613★
British Ballet Organization
39 Lonsdale Rd
London SW13 9JP
Phone: 081-748 1241
Fax: 081-748 1301

★614★
British Balloon & Airship Club
Box 1006
Birmingham B5 5RT
Phone: 021-643 3224

★615★
British Bankers' Association
10 Lombard St
London EC3V 9EL
Phone: 071-623 4001
Fax: 071-283 7037

Trade association for banks authorised by the Bank of England to trade in the UK

★616★
British Bathroom Council
Federation House
Station Rd
Stoke-on-Trent ST4 2RT
Phone: 0782 747074
Fax: 0782 744102

★617★
British Battery Makers' Society *see*
    Society of Battery Manufacturers

★618★
British Battery Manufacturers Association
7 Buckingham Gate

London SW1E 6JS
Phone: 071-630 5454
Fax: 071-630 5767

Representing the primary dry-cell, non-chargeable battery manufacturers, including environmental and safety aspects

★619★
British Bee-Keepers' Association
National Agricultural Centre
Stoneleigh
Kenilworth CV8 2LZ
Phone: 0203 696679

★620★
British Beer-Mat Collectors Society
10 Coombe Hill Crescent
Thame OX9 2EH
Phone: 084421 5792

★621★
British Biophysical Society
c/o Dr K R Fox
Dept of Physiology & Pharmacology
University of Southampton
Southampton SO9 3TU
Phone: 0703 594374
Fax: 0703 514319

★622★
British Blind & Shutter Association
Heath St
Tamworth B79 7JH
Phone: 0827 52337
Fax: 0827 310827

★623★
British Boatbuilders Association
20 Queens Rd
Aberdeen AB1 6YT
Phone: 0224 645454
Fax: 0224 644701

★624★
British Bobsleigh Association
Springfield House
Woodstock Rd
Coulsdon CR5 3HJ
Phone: 0737 555152
Fax: 0737 556832

★625★
British Bottlers' Institute
PO Box 16
Alton GU34 4NZ
Phone: 0420 23632

A forum for those concerned with the bottling, canning and packaging of beverages and supporting industries

★626★
British Box & Packaging Association
Papermakers House
Rivenhall Rd
Westlea
Swindon SN5 7BE
Phone: 0793 886086
Fax: 0793 886182

★627★
British Branded Hosiery Group
c/o D M Batt
Couture Marketing Ltd
Station Rd
Stoney Stanton
Leicester LE9 6LU
Phone: 045527 2322
Telex: 045527 4395

★628★
British Bronze & Brass Ingot Manufacturers Association
136 Hagley Rd
Birmingham B16 9PN
Phone: 021-454 4141
Fax: 021-454 4949

★629★
British Brush Manufacturers' Association
35 Bill Rd
Northampton NN1 5DD
Phone: 0604 22023
Fax: 0604 31252

Covering brushes, brooms, paint rollers & paint pads

★630★
British Burn Association
c/o Dr J Kearney
Regional Tissue Bank

Pinderfields General Hospital
Aberford Rd
Wakefield WF1 4DG

★631★
British Business Graduates Society
c/o City of London Polytechnic
84 Moorgate
London EC2M 6SQ
Phone: 0277 73385

Representing the interests of business graduates and furthering business education

★632★
British Butterfly Conservation Society
Tudor House
Quorn
Loughborough LE12 8AD
Phone: 0509 412870

★633★
British Button Manufacturers Society
63 Stanley Hill Avenue
Amersham HP7 9BA
Phone: 0494 722458

★634★
British Cable Makers' Confederation
Cable House, 56 Palace Rd
East Molesey KT8 9DW
Phone: 081-941 4079
Fax: 081-783 0104

A trade association which represents British manufacturers of insulated metallic and optical fibre cables and wires for the transmission and distribution of electrical power and communications

★635★
British Calcium Carbonates Federation
24 Fearnley Rd
Welwyn Garden City AL8 6HW
Phone: 0707 324538

★636★
British Canoe Union
Mapperley Hall
Lucknow Avenue
Nottingham NG3 5FA
Phone: 0602 691944

★637★
British Car Wash Association
c/o K Pond
Oakstead Holdings
The Pinnacles
Elizabeth Way
Harlow   CM19 1AR
Phone: 0279 443221
Fax: 0279 439800

★638★
**British Caramel Manufacturers'
  Association** *now* incorporated into
  Food & Drink Federation

★639★
**British Carpet Manufacturers'
  Association**
72 Dean St
London   W1V 5HB
Phone: 071-734 9853
Fax: 071-734 9856

★640★
British Carpets Export Council
72 Dean St
London   W1V 5HB
Phone: 071-734 9853
Fax: 071-734 9856

★641★
British Cartographic Society
c/o C Beattie
13 Sheldrake Gardens
Hordle
Lymington   SO41 0FJ
Phone: 0425 618679

★642★
British Carton Association
11 Bedford Row
London   WC1R 4DX
Phone: 071-242 6904
Fax: 071-405 7784

Covering the folding carton and paperboard packaging industry

★643★
British Casino Association
Leicester House
8 Leicester St
London   WC2H 7BN
Phone: 071-437 0678
Fax: 071-437 4901

★644★
British Cast Iron Research Association
  see BCIRA Cast Metals Technology

★645★
British Cattle Veterinary Association
Green Farm
Fretherne
Saul
Gloucester   GL2 7J6
Phone: 0452 740816

★646★
British Cave Research Association
c/o BCM BCRA
London   WC1N 3XX

★647★
British Cement Association
Wexham Springs
Slough   SL3 6PL
Phone: 0753 662727
Fax: 0753 660499

Members are producers of cement and concrete.

★648★
British Ceramic Confederation
Federation House
Station Rd
Stoke-on-Trent   ST4 2SA
Phone: 0782 744631
Fax: 0782 744102

Represents and services the British Ceramic Gift & Tableware Manufacturers' Association, British Clayware Land Drain Industry, British Electro-Ceramic Manufacturers' Association, British Industrial Ceramic Manufacturers' Association, Clay Roofing Tile Council, Institute of Clayworkers, National Federation of Clay Industries and Refractories Association of GB

★649★
British Ceramic Plant & Machinery Manufacturers' Association
PO Box 107
Broadstone
Bournemouth   BH18 8LQ
Phone: 0202 695566
Fax: 0202 605295

★650★
British Ceramic Research
Queens Rd
Penkhull
Stoke-on-Trent   ST4 7LQ
Phone: 0782 45431
Fax: 0782 412331

Covering ceramic whitewares, heavy clays, refractories, industrial ceramics and testing services

★651★
British Ceramic Tile Council
Federation House
Station Rd
Stoke-on-Trent   ST4 2RU
Phone: 0782 747147
Fax: 0782 744102

The trade association for UK manufacturers of ceramic wall, floor and fireplace tiles

★652★
British Chain Manufacturers Association
c/o D Williams-Allden
Midland House
New Rd
Halesowen
Birmingham   B63 3HY
Phone: 021-550 9390

Formerly: Machine Made Chain Manufacturers Association

★653★
British Chemical Distributors & Traders Association
Suffolk House
George St
Croydon   CR0 0YN
Phone: 081-686 4545
Fax: 081-688 7768

★654★
British Chemical Engineering Contractors Association
1 Regent St
London   SW1Y 4NR
Phone: 071-839 6514
Fax: 071-930 3466

★655★
British Chess Federation
9a Grand Parade
St Leonards-on-Sea
Hastings   TN38 0DD
Phone: 0424 442500
Telex: 338625

★656★
British Chicken Association
High Holborn House
52-54 High Holborn
London   WC1V 6SX
Phone: 071-242 4683
Fax: 071-831 0624

★657★
British Chiropractic Association
Premier House
10 Greycoat Place
London   SW1P 1SB
Phone: 071-222 8866

Concerned with treatment of spinal disorders by specialised manipulative techniques

★658★
British Christmas Tree Growers Association
12 Lauriston Rd
London   SW19 4TQ
Phone: 081-946 2695
Fax: 081-947 0211

★659★
British Classification Society
c/o C Orton
Institute of Archaeology
31-34 Gordon Square
London   WC1H 0PY
Phone: 071-387 7050   ext. 4749

★660★
British Clayware Land Drain Industry
  see British Ceramic Confederation

★661★
British Clock & Watch Manufacturers'
  Association
Upton Hall
Upton
Newark NG23 5TE
Phone: 0636 813795
Fax: 0636 812258

★662★
British Clothing Industry Association
7 Swallow Place
London W1R 7AA
Phone: 071-408 0020
Fax: 071-493 6276

★663★
British Coal Exporters' Federation
Victoria House
Southampton Row
London WC1B 4DH
Phone: 071-405 0034
Fax: 071-831 5181

★664★
British College of Naturopathy &
  Osteopathy
6 Netherhall Gardens
London NW3 5RR
Phone: 071-435 6464
Fax: 3630

★665★
British College of Optometrists
10 Knaresborough Place
London SW5 0TG
Phone: 071-373 7765
Fax: 071-373 1143

★666★
British Colostomy Association
15 Station Rd
Reading RG1 1LG
Phone: 0734 391537
Fax: 0734 569095

★667★
British Colour Makers' Association
PO Box 58
Tadworth KT20 5SH
Phone: 0737 353253

★668★
British Combustion Equipment
  Manufacturers Association
The Fernery
Market Place
Midhurst GU29 9DP
Phone: 0730 812782
Fax: 0730 813366

★669★
British Commercial Rabbit Association
c/o Mrs S McGeoch
Fairfield House
Sound
Nantwich CW5 8BG
Phone: 0270-780248

For rabbit farmers, breeders and ancillary products

★670★
British Compressed Air Society
Leicester House
8 Leicester St
London WC2H 7BN
Phone: 071-437 0678
Fax: 071-734 0462

★671★
British Compressed Gases Association
26 Brighton Rd
Crawley RH10 6AA
Phone: 0293 35915
Fax: 0293 37965

★672★
British Computer Society
13 Mansfield St
London W1M 0BP
Phone: 071-637 0471
Fax: 071-631 1049

The professional body for information technology

★673★
British Confectioners Association
8 Wilbury Avenue
Cheam SM2 7DU
Phone: 081-642 5166

Including bread and cake but not sugar confectionery

★674★
British Constructional Steelwork Association
c/o G K Edwards
74 Chester Rd
Birmingham B36 7BU
Phone: 021-776 7474
Fax: 021-776 7605

★675★
British Consultants Bureau
Suite 1
Westminster Palace Gardens
1-7 Artillery Row
London SW1P 1RJ
Phone: 071-222 3651
Fax: 071-222 3664

Members are multi-disciplined and concerned with promoting skills and interests overseas

★676★
British Contract Furnishing Association
PO Box 384
London N12 8HF
Phone: 081-445 8694
Fax: 081-445 8620

Members are manufacturers and contract furnishers

★677★
British Copyright Council
c/o G Adams
29-39 Berners St
London W1P 4AA
Phone: 071-359 1895
Fax: 071-359 1895

A forum for the bodies speaking for those who create or hold interests or copyright in literary, dramatic, musical or artistic works and those who perform them

★678★
British Cotton Growing Association
3 Shortlands
London W6 8RT
Phone: 081-741 9090
Fax: 081-846 0950

★679★
British Council of Ballroom Dancing
87 Parkhurst Rd
London N7 0LP
Phone: 071-609 1386

★680★
British Council of Maintenance Associations
c/o D Baird
The Old Barn
Barber Booth
Edale
Sheffield S30 2ZL
Phone: 0433 670391

Represents the interest of maintenance engineers nationally and internationally

★681★
British Council of Organisations of Disabled People
St Mary's Church
Greenlaw St
London SE18 5AR
Phone: 081-316 4184

★682★
British Council of Physical Education
c/o Chelsea School of Human Movement
Brighton Polytechnic
Trevin Towers
Gaudick Rd
Eastbourne BN20 7SP
Phone: 0323 21400

★683★
British Council of Shopping Centres
c/o College of Estate Management
Whiteknights Park
University of Reading

Reading   RG6 2AW
Phone: 0734 861101
Fax: 0734 755344

For the development and improvement of shopping facilities

★684★
British Crop Protection Council
49 Downing St
Farnham   GU9 7PH
Phone: 0252 733072
Fax: 0252 727194

★685★
British Cryogenics Council
c/o N Heiberg
Cryophysics Ltd
Unit 4
Avenue Two
Station Lane Industrial Estate
Witney
Oxford   OX8 6YD
Phone: 0993 773681
Fax: 0993 705826

★686★
British Crystallographic Association
c/o Dr A J Smith
Dept of Chemistry
University of Sheffield
Sheffield   S5 7HS
Phone: 0742 768555   ext. 4476
Fax: 0742 738673

★687★
British Cutlery & Silverware Association
Light Trades House
3 Melbourne Avenue
Sheffield   S10 2QJ
Phone: 0742 663084
Fax: 0742 670910

★688★
British Cycling Federation
36 Rockingham Rd
Kettering   NN16 8HG
Phone: 0536 412211
Fax: 0536 412142

★689★
British Deaf Association
38 Victoria Place
Carlisle   CA1 1HU
Phone: 0228 48844
Fax: 0228 41420

★690★
British Decorators Association
6 Haywra St
Harrogate   HG1 5BL
Phone: 0423 567292

★691★
British Deer Farmers' Association
Holly Lodge
Spencers Lane
Berkswell
Coventry   CV7 7BZ
Phone: 0203 465957
Fax: 0203 469063

★692★
British Deer Producers' Society
Beale Centre
Lower Basildon
Reading   RG8 9NH
Phone: 0734 844094

★693★
British Deer Society
Beale Centre
Lower Basildon
Reading   RG8 9NH
Phone: 0734 844094

★694★
British Dental Association
64 Wimpole St
London   W1M 8AL
Phone: 071-935 0875

★695★
British Dental Hygienists' Association
c/o A Craddock
13 The Ridge
Yatton
Bristol   BS19 4DQ
Phone: 0934 833932

★696★
British Dental Trade Association
Merritt House
Hill Avenue
Amersham HP6 5BQ
Phone: 0494 431010
Fax: 0494 431360

★697★
British Diabetic Association
10 Queen Anne St
London W1M 0BD
Phone: 071-323 1531
Fax: 071-637 3644

Provides information and advice on living
with diabetes and supports research into the
disease and its complications

★698★
British Dietetic Association
7th Floor
Elizabeth House
22 Suffolk St
Queensway
Birmingham B1 1LS
Phone: 021-643 5483

★699★
British Digestive Foundation
3 St Andrew's Place
London NW1 4LB
Phone: 071-580 1155

★700★
British Direct Marketing Association
Grosvenor Gardens House
33-35 Grosvenor Gardens
London SW1W 0BS
Phone: 071-630 7322
Fax: 071-828 7125

★701★
British Display Society
70a Crayford High St
Dartford DA1 4FF
Phone: 0322 555755

★702★
British Disposable Products
Association
Papermakers House
Rivenhall Rd
Westlea
Swindon SN5 7BE
Phone: 0793 886086
Fax: 0793 886182

Manufacturers of catering disposables

★703★
British Doll Artists Association
c/o 67 Victoria Drive
Bognor Regis PO21 2TD
Phone: 0243 823538

★704★
British Dragonfly Society
c/o R I Silsby
1 Haydn Ave
Purley
Croydon CR8 4AG
Phone: 081-668 5859

To promote and encourage the study and
conservation of dragonflies and their natural
habitats, especially in the UK

★705★
British Drilling Association
PO Box 113
Brentwood CM15 9DS
Phone: 0277 73456
Fax: 0277 374405

★706★
British Dyslexia Association
c/o G Yelland
98 London Rd
Reading RG1 5AU
Phone: 0734 351927
Fax: 0734 668271

★707★
British Ecological Society
Burlington House
Piccadilly
London W1V 0LQ
Phone: 071-434 2641

★708★
British Edible Pulse Association
c/o Mrs C Craig
54 Cambridge St
Grantham   NG31 6EX
Phone: 0476 70001
Fax: 0476 70001

★709★
**British Educational Equipment
   Association**
20 Beaufort Court
Admirals Way
London   E14 9XL
Phone: 071-537 4997
Fax: 071-537 4846

Members are manufacturers and distributors
of products and services for education

★710★
**British Educational Management &
   Administration Society**
c/o L Martin
110a Blackheath Hill
London   SE10 8AG
Phone: 071-798 3394

★711★
**British Educational Research
   Association**
c/o Dr G Wallace
Derbyshire College of Higher Education
Western Rd
Mickleover
Derby   DE3 5GX
Phone: 0332 47181

★712★
British Effluent & Water Association
5 Castle St
High Wycombe   HP13 6RZ
Phone: 0494 444544
Fax: 0494 446185

Members are companies supplying effluent
and water treatment plant and equipment

★713★
British Egg Association
High Holborn House, 52-54 High Holborn

London   WC1V 6SX
Phone: 071-242 4683
Fax: 071-831 0624

For commercial egg producers

★714★
British Egg Products Association
61 Prestbury Crescent
Woodmansterne
Croydon   SM7 3PJ
Phone: 0737 357048

★715★
**British Electrical & Allied
   Manufacturers Association** *see*
   BEAMA

★716★
British Electrical Systems Association
Granville Chambers
2 Radford St
Stone   ST15 8DA
Phone: 0785 812426
Telex: 0785 818157

Members are manufacturers of cable management, protection and support products

★717★
**British Electro-Ceramic Manufacturers
   Association** *see* British Ceramic
   Confederation

★718★
**British Electro-Static Manufacturers
   Association**
Croxteth Hall
Ripley
Guildford   GU23 6EX
Phone: 0483 225435
Fax: 0784 461393

To promote the specification and use of Brit-
ish-made static elimination equipment, anti-
static materials and associated products

★719★
British Electroless Nickel Society
1 Bryn Trystion
Cynwyd

Denbigh LL21 0LP
Phone: 0490 2833
Telex: 0490 3288

Electroless nickel technology has wide applications in the aerospace, electronics, mining,
oil engineering and automotive industries

★720★
British Electrotechnical Approvals
Board
Mark House
9-11 Queens Rd
Hersham
Walton-on-Thames KT12 5NA
Phone: 0932 244401
Fax: 0932 226603

★721★
British Entertainment & Dancing
Association
14 Oxford St
London W1N 0HL
Phone: 071-636 0851

★722★
British Epilepsy Association
Anstey House
40 Hanover Square
Leeds LS3 1BE
Phone: 0532 439393
Fax: 0532 428804

★723★
British Equestrian Federation
c/o British Equestrian Centre
Stoneleigh
Kenilworth CV8 2LR
Phone: 0203 696697
Fax: 0203 696484

★724★
British Equestrian Trade Association
Wothersome Grange
Bramham
Wetherby LS23 6LY
Phone: 0532 892267
Fax: 0532 893352

Members are equestrians, retailers and manufacturers

★725★
British Equine Veterinary Association
c/o Mrs A E Ewen
Hartham Park
Corsham SN13 0QB
Phone: 0249 715723
Fax: 0249 715920

Members are practising veterinary surgeons
and professionals interested in equine practice, teaching and research

★726★
British Esperanto Association
140 Holland Park Avenue
London W11 4UF
Phone: 071-727 7821

Members are booksellers offering books on
esperanto

★727★
British Essence Manufactuers'
Association *now* incorporated into
Food & Drink Federation

★728★
British Essential Oils Association
152-160 City Rd
London EC1V 2NP
Phone: 071-253 9421
Fax: 071-250 0965

★729★
British Exhibition Contractors
Association
Kingsmere House
Graham Rd
London SW19 3SR
Phone: 081-543 3888
Fax: 081-543 4036

The trade association representing contractors and suppliers who build and equip British and overseas exhibition stands

★730★
British Exhibition Venues Association
International House
43 Dudley Rd
Tunbridge Wells TN1 1LB
Phone: 0892 33442

★731★
British Exporters Association
16 Dartmouth St
London   SW1H 9BL
Phone: 071-222 5419
Fax: 071-222 2782

The organisation representing export houses

★732★
British Fabric Association
12 Elm Park Rd
Pinner   HA5 3LA
Phone: 081-866 3798

★733★
**British Facsimile Industry Consultative
  Committee**
9-19 London Rd
Newbury   RG13 1JL
Phone: 0635 523344
Fax: 0635 550678

The trade association for manufacturers of fax
machines

★734★
British Fantasy Society
15 Stanley Rd
Morden   SM4 5DE
Phone: 081-540 9443

For devotees of fantasy, horror and related
fields in literature, art and the cinema

★735★
British Fashion Council
7 Swallow Place
London   W1R 7HA
Phone: 071-408 0020
Fax: 071-493 6276

★736★
**British Federation of Care Home
  Proprietors**
852 Melton Rd
Thurmaston

Leicester   LE4 8BN
Phone: 0533 640095
Fax: 0533 640141

Members are owners of private residential
and nursing homes, catering for all categories, elderly, young, physically and mentally
handicapped and disabled

★737★
British Federation of Film Societies
21 Stephen St
London   W1V 1PL
Phone: 071-255 1444
Fax: 071-436 7950

★738★
**British Federation of Hotel, Guest
  House & Self-Catering Associations**
5 Sandicroft Rd
Blackpool   FY1 2RY
Phone: 0253 52683

Representing the small family-run hotels,
guest houses and self-caterers

★739★
British Federation of Music Festivals
198 Park Lane
Macclesfield   SK11 6UD
Phone: 0625 28297

★740★
**British Federation of Printing
  Machinery & Supplies**
55-56 Lincoln's Inn Fields
London   WC2A 3LJ
Phone: 071-831 3303

★741★
British Federation of Young Choirs
2 Heathcoat St
Loughborough   LE11 3BW
Phone: 0509 211664
Fax: 0509 233749

To encourage and stimulate choral singing
amongst young people

★742★
**British Fibreboard Packaging
  Association**
2 Saxon Court
Freeschool St
Northampton NN1 1ST
Phone: 0604 21002
Fax: 0604 20636

★743★
British Field Sports Society
59 Kennington Rd
London SE1 7PZ
Phone: 071-928 4742

★744★
**British Film & Television Producers'
Association** *see* Producers'
Association

★745★
British Film Designers Guild
52 Holland Park Mews
London W11 3SP
Phone: 071-221 3828
Fax: 071-211 1978

To advance the interests of the art department
in feature films

★746★
British Film Institute
21 Stephen St
London W1P 1PL
Phone: 071-255 1444
Telex: 27624

★747★
**British Fire Protection Systems
  Association**
48a Eden St
Kingston upon Thames KT1 1EE
Phone: 081-549 5855
Fax: 081-547 1564

★748★
British Fire Services Association
86 London Rd
Leicester LE2 0QR
Phone: 0533 542879

Covers both fire brigades and salvage corps

★749★
British Flat Roofing Council
38 Bridlesmith Gate
Nottingham NG1 2GQ
Phone: 0602 507733
Fax: 0602 504122

★750★
**British Floorcovering Manufacturers
  Association**
c/o R J M Crawt
125 Queens Rd
Brighton BN1 3YW
Phone: 0273 29271
Fax: 0273 28114

Concerned only with vinyl and linoleum
floorcoverings

★751★
**British Flue & Chimney Manufacturers
  Association**
Sterling House
6 Furlong Rd
Bourne End
Maidenhead SL8 5DG
Phone: 06285 31186
Fax: 06285 810423

Members are manufacturers and sole distributors of factory-made chimneys and flue
products

★752★
British Fluid Power Association
235-237 Vauxhall Bridge Rd
London SW1V 1EJ
Phone: 071-233 7044
Fax: 071-828 1917

For the hydraulic and pneumatic fluid power
industry

★753★
**British Fluid Power Distributors
  Association**
235-237 Vauxhall Bridge Rd
London SW1V 1EJ
Phone: 071-233 7044
Fax: 071-828 1917

Represents the interests of British distributors
of hydraulic and pneumatic components

★754★
British Fluoridation Society
64 Wimpole St
London   W1M 8AL
Phone: 071-486 7007

★755★
British Flute Society
c/o J Keeling
88 Lexden Rd
West Bergholt
Colchester   CO6 3BW

★756★
British Food Export Council
301-344 Market Towers
1 Nine Elms Lane
London   SW8 5NQ
Phone: 071-622 0188
Fax: 071-627 5972

★757★
**British Footwear Manufacturers
   Federation**
Royalty House
72 Dean St
London   W1V 5HB
Phone: 071-437 5573
Fax: 071-494 1300

★758★
British Forging Industry Association
245 Grove Lane
Birmingham   B20 2HB
Phone: 021-554 3311
Fax: 021-523 0761

★759★
British Foundry Association
Bridge House
121 Smallbrook Queensway
Birmingham   B5 4JP
Phone: 021-643 3377
Fax: 021-643 5064

★760★
British Fragrance Association
6 Catherine St

London   WC2B 5JJ
Phone: 071-836 2460
Fax: 071-836 0580

★761★
British Franchise Association
Thames View
Newton Rd
Henley-on-Thames   RG9 1HG
Phone: 0491 578050
Fax: 0491 573517

Members are engaged in the distribution of
goods and services through independent outlets under franchise agreements

★762★
British Friction Materials Council
2 Newman Rd
Bromley   BR1 1RJ
Phone: 081-290 5522
Fax: 081-460 9156

Covering brake linings and clutch facing
manufacture

★763★
British Frozen Food Federation
2nd Floor
Barclays Bank Chambers
55 High St
Grantham   NG31 6NE
Phone: 0476 590194
Fax: 0476 590152

★764★
**British Fruit & Vegetable Canners'
   Association** *now* incorporated into
   Food & Drink Federation

★765★
**British Fruit Juice Importers
   Association**
c/o F A Haynes
63 Wray Park Rd
Reigate   RH2 0EQ
Phone: 0737 242832
Fax: 0737 223486

★766★
British Fur Trade Association
25 Little Trinity Lane

London   EC4V 2AA
Phone: 071-248 5947
Fax: 071-236 3420

★767★
**British Furniture Manufacturers'
  Federation Associations**
30 Harcourt St
London   W1H 2AA
Phone: 071-724 0854
Fax: 071-723 0622

★768★
British Gear Association
St James's House
Frederick Rd
Birmingham   B15 1JJ
Phone: 021-456 3445
Telex: 917944

★769★
British Geological Survey
Keyworth
Nottingham   NG12 5GG
Phone: 06077 6111
Fax: 06077 6391

Formerly: Institute of Geological Sciences

★770★
British Geotechnical Society
c/o Institution of Civil Engineers
1-7 Great George St
London   SW1P 3AA
Phone: 071-630 0726

★771★
British Geriatrics Society
1 St Andrew's Place
London   NW1 4LB
Phone: 071-935 4004
Fax: 071-224 0454

To promote scientific developments of geriat-
ric medicine, improve medical and social services for elderly people and promote
measures which will improve health throughout adult life to ensure better fitness on
achieving old age

★772★
British Glass Confederation
Northumberland Rd
Sheffield   S10 2UA
Phone: 0742 686201
Fax: 0742 681073

A merger of Glass Manufacturers Association
with the British Glass Industry Research
Association

★773★
British Gliding Association
3rd Floor
Kimberley House
Vaughan Way
Leicester   LE1 4SE
Phone: 0533 531051

★774★
British Goat Society
34-36 Fore St
Bovey Tracey
Newton Abbot   TQ13 9AD
Phone: 0626 833168

★775★
British Goose Producers Association
High Holborn House
52-54 High Holborn
London   WC1V 6SX
Phone: 071-242 4683
Fax: 071-831 0624

★776★
British Grassland Society
c/o Institute for Grassland & Animal
  Production
Hurley
Maidenhead   SL6 5LR
Phone: 0628 823626

Seeks to increase the production and use of
grass and forage crops in agriculture

★777★
British Grit Association
c/o N Kirkham
69 Woodthorne Rd South
Wolverhampton   WV6 8SN
Phone: 0902 752631

★778★
British Growers Association
86 Colston St
Bristol   BS1 5BB
Phone: 0272 299800
Telex: 0272 252504

★779★
British Guild of Travel Writers
c/o Formula Communications
Parnell House
19-28 Wilton Rd
London   SW1V 1LW
Phone: 071-834 6996
Fax: 071-834 5660

★780★
**British Hacksaw & Bandsaw Makers'
   Association**
Light Trades House
3 Melbourne Avenue
Sheffield   S10 2QJ
Phone: 0742 663084
Fax: 0742 670910

★781★
British Hallmarking Council
St Philips House
St Philips Place
Birmingham   B3 2PP
Phone: 021-200 3300
Fax: 021-200 3330

Members are individuals appointed by the
Government and assay officers of Great Britain

★782★
British Hand Knitting Confederation
c/o F Shackleton
Nappa House
Scott Lane
Riddlesden
Keighley   BD20 5BU
Phone: 0535 603450

Representing the interests of hand knitting
yarn spinners

★783★
**British Hang Gliding & Paragliding
   Association**
Cranfield Airfield
Cranfield   MK43 0YR
Phone: 0234 751688

★784★
British Hardmetal Association
Light Trades House
3 Melbourne Avenue
Sheffield   S10 2QJ
Phone: 0742 663084
Fax: 0742 670910

★785★
**British Hardware & Housewares
   Manufacturers' Association**
35 Billing Rd
Northampton   NN1 5DD
Phone: 0604 22023
Fax: 0604 31252

★786★
British Hardware Federation
20 Harborne Rd
Birmingham   B15 3AB
Phone: 021-454 4385
Fax: 021-452 1812

★787★
British Hat Guild
Commerce House
Stuart St
Luton   LU1 5AU
Phone: 0582 23456
Fax: 0582 419422

Members are manufacturers, wholesalers and
retailers

★788★
**British Hay & Straw Merchants
   Association**
52 Park Meadow
Hatfield   AL9 5HP
Phone: 0707 268807

★789★
British Health Care Association
The Courtyard
Allerton Park
Knaresborough HG5 0SE
Phone: 0423 331295
Fax: 0423 331296

Represents private health care schemes

★790★
British Health Care Export Council
now Association of British Health
Care Industries

★791★
British Health Food Trade Association
Angel Court
High St
Godalming GU7 1DT
Phone: 0483 426450
Fax: 0483 426921

★792★
**British Health-Care Trade & Industry
Council** *now* merged into
Association of British Health Care
Industries

★793★
British Hedgehog Preservation Society
Knowbury House
Knowbury
Ludlow SY8 3LQ

★794★
British Helicopter Advisory Board
Building C2
Fairoaks Airport
Chobham
Woking GU24 8HX
Phone: 0276 856100
Fax: 0276 856126

All aspects of helicopter operation

★795★
British Herbal Medicine Association
c/o R A Hill
Field House
Lye Hole Lane
Redhill

Bristol BS18 7TB
Phone: 0934 862994

Members are importers, manufacturers, herbal
practitioners, herbal retailers, wholesalers and
health food shops

★796★
British Herpetological Society
c/o Zoological Society
Regent's Park
London NW1 4RY
Phone: 081-452 9578

The study of reptiles and amphibians

★797★
British Hire Cruiser Federation
19 Acre End St
Eynsham
Oxford OX8 1PE
Phone: 0865 880107

★798★
**British Holiday & Home Parks
Association**
Chichester House
31 Park Rd
Gloucester GL1 1LH
Phone: 0452 26911
Fax: 0452 307226

The representative body for own-
ers/managers of park homes, caravans, cha-
lets, tents and all types of self-catering
accommodation

★799★
British Holistic Medical Association
179 Gloucester Place
London NW1 2XA
Phone: 071-262 5299

★800★
British Home Furnishing Bureau
126-128 Cromwell Rd
London SW7 4ET
Phone: 071-373 7744

★801★
British Homoeopathic Association
27a Devonshire St

London W1N 1RJ
Phone: 071-935 2163

★802★
British Honey Importers & Packers Association
152-160 City Rd
London EC1Y 8PD
Phone: 071-253 9421
Fax: 071-250 0965

★803★
British Horn Society
c/o J Wates
Paxman Ltd
116 Long Acre
London WC2E 9PA
Phone: 071-240 3642

★804★
British Horological Institute
Upton Hall
Upton
Newark NG23 5TE
Phone: 0636 813795
Fax: 0636 812258

The professional body for individuals

★805★
British Horse Society
British Equestrian Centre, Stoneleigh
Kenilworth CV8 2LR
Phone: 0203 696697
Fax: 0203 692357

★806★
British Hotels, Restaurants & Caterers Association
40 Duke St
London W1M 6HR
Phone: 071-499 6641
Telex: 296619

★807★
British Humanist Association
13 Prince of Wales Terrace
London W8 5PG
Phone: 071-937 2341

★808★
British Hypnotherapy Association
1 Wythburn Place
London W1H 5WL
Phone: 071-723 4443

Concerned with professional standards in the treatment of nervous disorders

★809★
British Ice Hockey Association
517 Christchurch Rd
Bournemouth BH1 4AG
Phone: 0202 303946
Fax: 0202 398005

★810★
British Importers Confederation
3rd Floor
Kemp House
152-160 City Rd
London EC1V 2NP
Phone: 071-253 9421
Fax: 071-250 0965

★811★
British Incoming Tour Operators' Association
18a Coulson St
London SW3 3NB
Phone: 071-581 4101
Fax: 071-225 3834

Representing the interests of companies deriving a substantial part of their income from the provision of tours and tourism services within the UK for visitors from overseas

★812★
British Independent Grocers Association
17 Farnborough St
Farnborough GU14 8AG
Phone: 0252 515001

Membership is comprised of independent grocers, off-licences, convenience stores, operators and other categories of grocery-related retailers

★813★
British Independent Plastic Extruders' Association
c/o J K Foster
89 Cornwall St
Birmingham   B3 3BY
Phone: 021-236 1866
Fax: 021-200 1389

Members manufacture extrusions in nearly all plastic materials and carry out a wide range of finishing and fabrication operations

★814★
British Independent Steel Producers Association
5 Cromwell Rd
London   SW7 2HX
Phone: 071-581 0231
Fax: 071-589 4009

Trade association for the independent sector of the UK steel industry

★815★
British Industrial Biological Research Association
Woodmansterne Rd
Carshalton   SM5 4DS
Phone: 081-643 4411
Fax: 081-661 7029

Research into toxicology and promotes health and safety with chemicals

★816★
British Industrial Ceramic Manufacturers' Association see
British Ceramic Confederation

★817★
British Industrial Fasteners Federation
Blundell House
Torrington Avenue
Coventry   CV4 9GU
Phone: 0203 466496
Fax: 0203 466074

★818★
British Industrial Furnace Constructors Association
8th Floor
Bridge House
Smallbrook Queensway
Birmingham   B5 4JP
Phone: 021-643 3377
Fax: 021-643 5064

★819★
British Industrial Truck Association
c/o G Coates
Scammell House
High St
Ascot   SL5 7JF
Phone: 0344 23800
Fax: 0344 291197

★820★
British Institute of Agricultural Consultants
c/o 3 Elm Close
Campton
Shefford
Stevenage   SG17 5PE
Phone: 0525 60000
Fax: 0525 60156

★821★
British Institute of Architectural Technicians
397 City Rd
London   EC1V 1NE
Phone: 071-278 2206
Fax: 071-837 3194

For individuals who have completed qualifying architectural technician examinations

★822★
British Institute of Cleaning Science
Whitworth Chambers
George Row
Northampton   NN1 1DF
Phone: 0604 230075

Professional body promoting training and education in the cleaning industry

★823★
British Institute of Embalmers
21c Station Rd
Knowle
Solihull   B93 0HL
Phone: 0564 778991
Fax: 0564 770812

★824★
British Institute of Industrial Therapy
Methuen St
Southampton S02 0FL
Phone: 0703 642988

★825★
British Institute of Innkeeping
51-53 High St
Camberley GU15 3RG
Phone: 0276 684449
Fax: 0276 23045

★826★
British Institute of Interior Design
   now incorporated into the Chartered
Society of Designers

★827★
**British Institute of International &
   Comparative Law**
17 Russell Square
London WC1B 5DR
Phone: 071-636 5802
Fax: 071-323 2016

★828★
**British Institute of Kitchen
   Architecture**
2 High St
Crowborough TN6 2QA
Phone: 08926 64636

★829★
British Institute of Management
Management House
Cottingham Rd
Corby NN17 1TT
Phone: 0536 204222
Fax: 0536 201651

★830★
British Institute of Mental Handicap
c/o Dr J Harris
Wolverhampton Rd
Kidderminster DY10 3PP
Phone: 0562 850251

★831★
**British Institute of Non-Destructive
   Testing**
1 Spencer Parade
Northampton NN1 5AA
Phone: 0604 30124
Fax: 0604 231489

★832★
British Institute of Organ Studies
c/o Dr C Kent
Dept of Music
University of Reading
35 Upper Redlands Rd
Reading RG1 5JE
Phone: 0734 318416

★833★
**British Institute of Practical
   Psychology**
67 Highbury New Park
London N5 2EZ
Phone: 071-226 3569

★834★
**British Institute of Professional
   Photography**
2 Amwell End
Ware SG12 9HN
Phone: 0920 464011
Fax: 0920 487056

Covers all branches of professional photography

★835★
British Institute of Radiology
36 Portland Place
London W1N 4AT
Phone: 071-580 4085
Telex: 071-255 3209

A multi-disciplinary society furthering all aspects of radiology and the radiological sciences

★836★
British Institute of Sports Coaches
2 College Close
Beckett Park
Leeds LS6 3QH
Phone: 0532 753365

★837★
British Institute of Surgical Technologists
1 Webbs Court
Buckhurst Avenue
Sevenoaks TN13 1LZ
Phone: 0732 458868
Fax: 0732 459225

★838★
British Institute of Traffic Education Research
Kent House
Kent St
Birmingham B5 6QF
Phone: 021-622 2402
Fax: 021-622 3450

★839★
British Insurance & Investment Brokers' Association
14 Bevis Marks
London EC3A 7NT
Phone: 071-623 9043
Fax: 071-626 9676

Representing insurance brokers and independent financial advisers

★840★
British Insurance Law Association
Bedford Court Mansions
90 Bedford Avenue
London WC1B 3AE
Phone: 071-637 0333
Fax: 071-637 1893

★841★
British Interactive Video Association
24 Stephenson Way
London NW1 2HD
Phone: 071-387 2233
Fax: 071-387 5373

★842★
British Interlingua Society
c/o Flat 14
Ventnor Court
Wostenholm Rd
Sheffield S7 1LB
Phone: 0742 582931

★843★
British Interlining Manufacturers Association
32 Skircoat Green
Halifax HX3 0RX
Phone: 0422 824236
Fax: 0422 824436

★844★
British Internal Combustion Engine Research Institute
111-112 Buckingham Avenue
Slough Trading Estate
Slough SL1 4PH
Phone: 0753 811899
Fax: 0753 811898

★845★
British International Freight Association
Redfern House
Browells Lane
Feltham TW13 7EP
Phone: 081-844 2266
Fax: 081-890 5546

For companies and staff engaged in freight forwarding

★846★
British Interplanetary Society
27-29 South Lambeth Rd
London SW8 1SZ
Phone: 071-735 3160
Fax: 071-820 1504

All aspects of space research and technology

★847★
British Investment Casting Trade Association
Bordesley Hall
The Holloway
Alvechurch
Birmingham B48 1QA
Phone: 0527 584770
Fax: 0527 584771

★848★
British Iron & Steel Consumers' Council
16 Berwyn Rd

Richmond-on-Thames   TW10 5BS
Phone: 081-878 4898

Represents interests of British steel users on all issues of policy affecting their steel supplies, both in the UK and internationally

★849★
British Isles Bee Breeders' Association
c/o A Knight
11 Thomson Drive
Codnor
Derby   DE5 9RU
Phone: 0773 745287

Concerned with the conservation, restoration, study, selection and improvement of the native and near native honeybees of Britain and Ireland

★850★
British Jazz Society
10 Southfield Gardens
Twickenham   TW1 4SZ
Phone: 081-892 0133

★851★
British Jewellers' Association
10 Vyse St
Birmingham   B18 6LT
Phone: 021-236 2657
Fax: 021-236 3921

★852★
British Jewellery & Giftware Federation
10 Vyse St
Birmingham   B1 6LT
Phone: 021-236 2657
Fax: 021-236 3921

★853★
British Judo Association
c/o G Kenneally
9 Islington High St
London   N1 9LQ
Phone: 071-833 4424
Telex: 27830

★854★
British Judo Council
1a Horn Lane

London   W3 9NJ
Phone: 081-992 9454

★855★
British Junior Chamber
12 Regent Place
Rugby   CV21 2PN
Phone: 0788 572795
Fax: 0788 542091

A voluntary training body

★856★
British Kinematograph Sound & Television Society
547-549 Victoria House
Vernon Place
London   WC1B 4DJ
Phone: 071-242 8400
Fax: 071-405 3567

All aspects of film and television production and distribution

★857★
British Kitchen Furniture Manufacturers
82 New Cavendish St
London   W1M 8AD
Phone: 071-580 5588
Fax: 071-631 3872

★858★
British Laboratory Ware Association
Guild House
30-32 Worple Rd
London   SW19 4EF
Phone: 081-946 2548
Fax: 081-879 1219

All types of laboratory equipment

★859★
British Lace Federation
c/o R G Walton
The Hermitage
Gonalston
Nottingham   NG14 7JA
Phone: 0602 663541
Fax: 0602 605981

★860★
British Ladder Manufacturers Association
c/o E J Abbey
38 Empress Avenue
West Mersea
Colchester CO5 8EX
Phone: 0206 382666

★861★
British Laminated Plastic Fabricators Association
c/o British Plastics Federation
5 Belgrave Square
London SW1X 8PH
Phone: 071-235 9483
Fax: 071-235 8045

★862★
British Lawnmower Manufacturers Federation
2 Newman Rd
Bromley BR1 1RJ
Phone: 081-290 5522
Fax: 081-460 9156

★863★
British Lead Manufacturers Association *now* Lead Sheet Association

★864★
British Leather Confederation
Leather Trade House
Kings Park Rd
Northampton NN3 1JD
Phone: 0604 494131
Fax: 0604 648220

★865★
British Leathergoods Manufacturers Association
10 Vyse St
Birmingham B1 3HJ
Phone: 021-236 2657
Fax: 021-236 3921

★866★
British Lichen Society
c/o Dr O W Purvis
Dept of Botany
Natural History Museum
Cromwell Rd
London SW7 5BD
Phone: 071-938 9351
Fax: 071-938 9260

★867★
British List Brokers Association
16 The Pines
Broad St
Guildford GU3 3BH
Phone: 0483 301311
Fax: 0483 506331

Covering the provision of specialist mailing lists

★868★
British Lock Manufacturers Association
Heath St
Tamworth B79 7JH
Phone: 0827 52337
Fax: 0827 310827

★869★
British Lubricants Federation
16 Hyde Lane
Danbury
Chelmsford CM3 4QS
Phone: 0245 412104
Fax: 0245 416742

★870★
British Management Data Foundation
Highfield
Longridge
Sheepscombe
Stroud GL6 7QU
Phone: 0452 813211
Fax: 0452 812527

★871★
British Marine Equipment Association
4th Floor
30 Great Guildford St

London   SE1 0HS
Phone: 071-928 9199
Fax: 071-928 6599

★872★
British Marine Equipment Council
4th Floor
30 Great Guildford St
London   SE1 0HS
Phone: 071-928 9199
Fax: 071-928 6599

Member companies supply equipment for all
types of ships, for the offshore oil and gas
industry and for pollution control

★873★
British Marine Industries Federation
Boating Industry House
Vale Rd
Oatlands
Weybridge   KT13 9NS
Phone: 0932 854511
Fax: 0932 852874

The trade association for companies operating within the leisure and pleasure side of the
market as well as some commercial vessels
such as small fishing vessels, tugs and
barges.

★874★
British Masonry Drill Bit Association
Light Trades House
3 Melbourne Avenue
Sheffield   S10 2QJ
Phone: 0742 663084
Fax: 0742 670910

★875★
British Materials Handling Federation
8th Floor
Bridge House
Smallbrook Queensway
Birmingham   B5 4JP
Phone: 021-643 3377
Fax: 021-643 5064

★876★
British Measurement & Testing
  Association
c/o Dr J Wilson
National Physical Laboratory
Building 31, North Lodge
Queens Rd
Teddington   TW11 0LW
Phone: 081-943 5524

Concerned with the application of measurement at all levels of accuracy

★877★
British Meat Manufacturers'
  Association
19 Cornwall Terrace
London   NW1 4QP
Phone: 071-935 7980
Fax: 071-487 4734

★878★
British Medical Acupuncture Society
Newton House
Newton Lane
Lower Whitley
Warrington   WA4 4JA
Phone: 092 573727

Members are family doctors and hospital specialists who practice acupuncture alongside
more conventional techniques

★879★
British Medical Association
BMA House
Tavistock Square
London   WC1H 9JP
Phone: 071-387 4499
Fax: 071-383 6400

★880★
British Medical Ultrasound Society
36 Portland Place
London   W1N 3DG
Phone: 071-636 3714
Fax: 071-323 2175

The advancement of the science and technology of ultrasonics as applied in medicine

★881★
British Menswear Guild
Wool House
Carlton Gardens
London   SW1Y 5AE
Phone: 071-839 2620
Fax: 071-976 1924

★882★
British Merchant Banking & Securities Houses Association
6 Frederick's Place
London   EC2R 8BT
Phone: 071-796 3606
Fax: 071-796 4345

Representing merchant banking interests

★883★
British Metal Castings Council
Bridge House
Smallbrook Queensway
Birmingham   B5 4JP
Phone: 021-643 3377
Fax: 021-643 5064

★884★
British Metal Finishing Suppliers Association *now* British Surface Treatment Suppliers Association

★885★
British Metallurgical Plant Constructors' Association
Room 629
162-168 Regent St
London   W1R 5TB
Phone: 071-734 3031
Telex: 28905

★886★
British Microcomputers Manufacturers Group *see* British Office Technology Manufacturers Alliance

★887★
British Microlight Aircraft Association
Bullring
Deddington

Oxford   OX5 4TT
Phone: 0869 38888
Fax: 37116

★888★
British Migraine Association
178a High Rd
Byfleet
Weybridge   KT14 7ED
Phone: 0932 352468
Fax: 0202 393776

★889★
British Milksheep Association
5g St Andrew's Square
Droitwich   WR9 8HE
Phone: 0905 776257
Fax: 0905 775635

★890★
British Model Soldier Society
c/o D Pearce
22 Lynwood Rd
London   W5 1JJ
Phone: 081-998 5230

To promote the hobby of military modelling and collecting

★891★
British Motor Ship Owners Association
Central House
32-66 High St
London   E15 2PS
Phone: 081-519 4872
Fax: 081-519 5483

The body concerned with coastal and short-sea shipping

★892★
British Motorcyclists Federation
129 Seaforth Avenue
New Malden   KT3 6JU
Phone: 081-942 7914
Fax: 081-949 6215

★893★
British Mountaineering Council
Crawford House
Precinct Centre

Booth St East
Manchester   M13 9RZ
Phone: 061-273 5835

★894★
British Music Hall Society
c/o Daphne Masterton
Brodie & Middleston Ltd
68 Drury Lane
London   WC2B 5SP
Phone: 071-836 3289

★895★
British Music Information Centre
10 Stratford Place
London   W1N 9AE
Phone: 071-499 8567

★896★
British Music Society
30 High Beeches
Gerrards Cross   SL9 7HX
Phone: 0753 884970

Promotes the work of lesser-known British composers, primarily from the years 1850-1950

★897★
British Mycological Society
c/o Dr G Beakes
Dept of Biology
Ridley Building
University of Newcastle upon Tyne
Newcastle upon Tyne   NE1 7RU
Phone: 091-222 6000
Fax: 091-261 1182

★898★
British Narrow Fabrics Association
c/o A H Green
4th Floor
York House
91 Granby St
Leicester   LE1 6EA
Phone: 0533 545490
Fax: 0533 550548

Covers elastic, trimmings, braids, ribbons, tapes, labels and webbing

★899★
British National Committee for Non-Destructive Testing *now* British Measurement & Testing Association

★900★
British National Committee for Electroheat
c/o M J Thelwell
30 Millbank
London   SW1P 4RD
Phone: 071-834 2333   ext. 6339
Fax: 071-931 0356

★901★
British National Committee on Space Research *see* Interdisciplinary Scientific Committee on Space Research

★902★
British National Committee on Large Dams
c/o N Tyler
1-7 Great George St
London   SW1P 3AA
Phone: 071-222 7722
Fax: 071-222 7500

★903★
British Naturalists' Association
c/o J F Pearton
48 Russell Way
Higham Ferrers
Wellingborough   NN9 8EJ
Phone: 0933 314672
Fax: 0933 410449

To encourage education, study and research in all branches of natural history and wildlife conservation

★904★
British Nautical Instrument Trade Association
105 West George St
Glasgow   G2 1QP
Phone: 041-221 7020
Fax: 041-248 7409

★905★
British Naval Equipment Association
4th Floor
30 Great Guildford St
London SE1 0HS
Phone: 071-928 9199
Fax: 071-928 6599

Members are companies supplying ships' equipment and services for the naval sector

★906★
British Needlecrafts Council
143 Queens Rd
Halifax HX1 4LN
Phone: 0422 351215
Fax: 0422 320642

★907★
British Non-Ferrous Metals Federation
10 Greenfield Crescent
Birmingham B15 3AU
Phone: 021-456 3322
Telex: 021-456 1394

Members are fabricators of copper and copper-based alloys

★908★
British Nonwovens Manufacturers' Association
c/o P A Truelove
26 The Butts
Brentford TW8 8BL
Phone: 081-560 6576

★909★
British Nuclear Energy Society
c/o P Bacos
Institution of Civil Engineers
1-7 Great George St
London SW1P 3AA
Phone: 071-222 7722
Fax: 071-222 7500

★910★
British Nuclear Forum
22 Buckingham Gate

London SW1E 6LB
Phone: 071-828 0116
Fax: 071-828 0110

Member companies are engaged in funding, building, operating and supplying services to Britain's nuclear power stations

★911★
British Numismatic Society
c/o W Slayter
63 West Way
Edgware HA8 9LA
Phone: 081-958 8753

★912★
British Numismatic Trade Association
P O Box 82
Coventry CV5 6SW
Phone: 0203 677976
Fax: 0203 677985

★913★
British Nutrition Foundation
15 Belgrave Square
London SW1X 8PS
Phone: 071-235 4904
Fax: 071-235 5336

★914★
British Oat & Barley Millers Association *now* incorporated into Food & Drink Federation

★915★
British Occupational Hygiene Society
1 St Andrew's Place
London NW1 4LB
Phone: 071-486 4860
Fax: 071-224 2376

★916★
British Office Systems & Stationery Federation
6 Wimpole St
London W1M 8AS
Phone: 071-637 7692
Fax: 071-436 3137

Concerned with all aspects of office machinery including computer hardware and software

★917★
British Office Technology Manufacturers Alliance
Owles Hall
Buntingford
Royston SG9 9PL
Phone: 0763 71209
Fax: 0763 73225

Covering the interests of UK manufacturers of information technology products

★918★
British Offshore Support Vessels Association
30-32 St Mary Axe
London EC3A 8ET
Phone: 071-283 2922
Fax: 071-626 8135

★919★
British Oil Spill Control Association
4th Floor
Great Guildford House
30 Great Guildford St
London SE1 0HS
Phone: 071-928 9199
Fax: 071-928 6599

Covering all aspects of marine and industrial pollution control

★920★
British Ophthalmic Lens Manufacturers & Distributors' Association
37-41 Bedford Row
London WC1R 4JH
Phone: 071-405 8101
Fax: 071-831 2707

Covering the interests of companies in the manufacture and distribution of lenses

★921★
British Orchid Growers Association
c/o Mrs A Rittershausen
2 Golvers Hill Rd
Kingsteignton
Newton Abbot TQ12 3BP
Phone: 0626 52065

★922★
British Organic Farmers Association
86 Colston St
Bristol BS1 5BB
Phone: 0272 299666
Fax: 0272 252504

★923★
British Orienteering Federation
Riversdale
Dale Rd North
Darley Dale
Matlock DE4 2HX
Phone: 0629 734042
Fax: 0629 733769

Competitive navigation on foot, with the aid of map and compass

★924★
British Ornithologists' Union
c/o Dept of Ornithology
British Museum
Tring HP23 6AP
Phone: 0442 890080

★925★
British Orthopaedic Association
c/o Royal College of Surgeons
35-43 Lincoln's Inn Fields
London WC2A 3PN
Phone: 071-405 6507
Fax: 071-831 2676

★926★
British Orthoptic Society
Tavistock House North
Tavistock Square
London WC1H 9HX
Phone: 071-387 7992

★927★
British Osteopathic Association
c/o Dr R S MacDonald
8-10 Boston Place
London NW1 6QH
Phone: 071-262 5250

★928★
British Overseas & Commonwealth Banks Association
c/o Hong Kong & Shanghai Bank
99 Bishopsgate
London   EC2P 2LA
Phone: 071-638 2366
Fax: 071-638 2125

★929★
British Paediatric Association
5 St Andrew's Place
London   NW1 4LB
Phone: 071-486 6151
Fax: 071-486 6004

★930★
British Paper & Board Industry Federation
Papermaker House
Rivenhall Rd
Westlea
Swindon   SN5 7BE
Phone: 0793 886086
Fax: 0793 886182

★931★
British Paper Machinery Makers Association
127 Stockport Rd
Marple
Stockport   SK6 6AF
Phone: 061-427 7111
Fax: 061-449 0526

★932★
British Parachute Association
c/o D Oddy
Wharf Way
Glen Parva
Leicester   LE2 9TF
Phone: 0533 785271
Fax: 0533 477662

★933★
British Parking Association
17 The Croft
Chiswell Green
St Albans   AL2 3AR
Phone: 0727 57206

Members represent central and local government, consultants, contractors, engineers, planners, architects, car park operators and equipment manufacturers

★934★
British Pasta Products Association
now incorporated into Food & Drink Federation

★935★
British Peanut Council
c/o Overseas Farmers Group Ltd
71-73 Carter Lane
London   EC4V 5EQ
Phone: 071-236 6135
Fax: 071-248 1081

★936★
British Pest Control Association
c/o R J Straud
3 St James' Court
Friar Gate
Derby   DE1 1ZU
Phone: 0332 294288
Fax: 0332 295904

★937★
British Pharmacological Society
c/o Dr T Maclagan
Dept of Pharmacology
Royal Free Hospital
School of Medicine
Rowland Hill St
London   NW3 2PF
Phone: 071-794 0500

★938★
British Philatelic Federation
107 Charterhouse St
London   EC1M 6PT
Phone: 071-251 5040

For private collectors, clubs and dealers

★939★
British Phonographic Industry
Roxburghe House
273-287 Regent St

London   W1R 7PB
Phone: 071-629 8642
Fax: 071-493 3667

★940★
British Photobiology Society
c/o Dr R H Douglas
Dept of Optometry & Visual Science
City University
311-321 Goswell Rd
London   EC1V 7DD
Phone: 071-253 4399
Fax: 071-250 0837

The scientific study of photobiology and its application to maintenance of health in animal, plant and human life

★941★
British Photographers' Liaison Committee
9-10 Domingo St
London   EC1Y OTA
Phone: 071-608 1441
Fax: 071-253 3007

★942★
British Photographic Association
Carolyn House
22-26 Dingwall Rd
Croydon   CRO 9XF
Phone: 081-681 1680
Fax: 081-681 2134

★943★
British Photographic Export Group
1 West Ruislip Station
Ruislip   HA4 7DW
Phone: 0895 634515
Fax: 0895 631219

★944★
British Photographic Importers' Association
Carolyn House
22-26 Dingwall Rd
Croydon   CRO 9XF
Phone: 081-688 4422
Fax: 081-681 2134

★945★
British Plastics Federation
5 Belgrave Square
London   SW1X 8PH
Phone: 071-235 9483
Fax: 071-235 8045

★946★
British Plastics Stockholders' Association
21c Station Rd
Knowle
Solihull   B93 0HL
Phone: 0564 778990
Fax: 0564 770812

Members are multi-product distributors of plastics products

★947★
British Plumbing Fittings Manufacturers Association
10 Greenfield Crescent
Birmingham   B15 3AU
Phone: 021-456 3322
Fax: 021-456 1394

Represents UK manufacturers of tube fittings made of copper or copper alloy materials for connecting pipes to convey water or gas

★948★
British Polarological Research Society
Operational-Polarology Research Laboratory
UK Polarosciences RE2
Teakwood
Spring Gardens
Ventnor   PO38 1QX

Fundamental research into biopolarological communication-sensing, transmission, and control phenomena

★949★
British Polyolefin Textiles Association
148 Nethergate
Dundee   DD1 4EA
Phone: 0382 25881
Fax: 0382 23584

To promote and protect the interests of the UK polypropylene extrusion and weaving industries

★950★
British Ports Federation
7th Floor
Victoria House
Vernon Place
London   WC1B 4LL
Phone: 071-242 1200
Fax: 071-405 1069

★951★
British Pot Plant Growers Association
see Bedding Plant Growers
Association

★952★
British Pottery Managers' Association
c/o Dept of Ceramics
Staffordshire Polytechnic
College Rd
Stoke-on-Trent   ST4 2DE
Phone: 0782 744531
Fax: 0782 744035

★953★
**British Poultry Breeders & Hatcheries
   Association**
High Holborn House
52-54 High Holborn
London   WC1V 6SX
Phone: 071-242 4683
Fax: 071-831 0624

★954★
British Poultry Federation
High Holborn House
52-54 High Holborn
London   WC1V 6SX
Phone: 071-242 4683
Fax: 071-831 0624

★955★
British Powder Metal Federation
c/o G K Edwards
74 Chester Rd
Castle Bromwich
Birmingham   B36 7BU
Phone: 021-776 7474
Fax: 021-776 7605

Formerly: British Metal Sinterings Association

★956★
British Precast Concrete Federation
60 Charles St
Leicester   LE1 1FB
Phone: 0533 536161
Fax: 0533 514568

★957★
**British Pressure Gauge Manufacturers
   Association**
136 Hagley Rd
Birmingham   B16 9PN
Phone: 021-454 4141
Fax: 021-454 4949

★958★
British Printing Industries Federation
11 Bedford Row
London   WC1R 4DX
Phone: 01-242 6904
Fax: 01-405 7784

★959★
**British Production & Inventory Control
   Society**
c/o R G Turner
University of Warwick Science Park
Sir William Lyons Rd
Coventry   CV4 7EZ
Phone: 0203 692266

★960★
**British Promotional Merchandise
   Association**
Osborn House
21-25 Lower Stone St
Maidstone   ME15 6YT
Phone: 0622 671081

★961★
British Property Federation
35 Catherine Place
London   SW1E 6DY
Phone: 071-828 0111
Fax: 071-834 3442

The trade association of the property industry; membership includes property development companies, property investment
companies, banks, insurance companies,
pension funds, residential landlords, multiple
retailers and professional firms

★962★
British Psycho-Analytical Society
63 New Cavendish St
London W1M 7RD
Phone: 071-580 4952
Fax: 071-327 5312

★963★
British Psychological Society
St Andrews House
48 Princess Rd East
Leicester LE1 7DR
Phone: 0533 549568
Fax: 0533 470787

Members are graduate physiologists

★964★
British Public Works Association
c/o J Marsh
Millis House
The Causeway
Staines TW18 3BX
Phone: 0748 452748

★965★
British Pump Manufacturers Association
Carlyle House
235-237 Vauxhall Bridge Rd
London SW1V 1EJ
Phone: 071-931 0476
Fax: 071-828 0667

The liquid pump manufacturers trade association

★966★
British Pyrotechnists Association
Peat House
1 Watereloo Way
Leicester LE1 6LP
Phone: 0533 471122
Fax: 0533 547626

★967★
British Quality Association
10 Grosvenor Gardens
London SW1W 0DQ
Phone: 071-823 5608
Fax: 071-824 8030

All aspects of product quality advancement

★968★
British Rabbit Council
Purefoy House
7 Kirk Gate
Newark NG24 1AD
Phone: 0636 76042

★969★
British Racketball Association
c/o R Bishop
22 Crookham Close
Birmingham B17 8RR
Phone: 021-429 3380

★970★
British Radio & Electronic Equipment Manufacturers' Association
Landseer House
19 Charing Cross Rd
London WC2H 0ES
Phone: 071-930 3206
Fax: 071-839 4613

Covers manufacturers of radio and television receivers, video recorders, teletext receivers, viewdata terminals and all consumer electronic products

★971★
British Ready Mixed Concrete Association
1 Bramber Court
2 Bramber Rd
London W14 9PBN
Phone: 071-381 6582
Fax: 071-381 8770

★972★
British Record Society
c/o P L Dickinson
College of Arms
Queen Victoria St
London EC4V 4BT
Phone: 071-236 9612

★973★
British Records Association
18 Padbury Court

London   E2 7EH
Phone: 071-729 1415

Concerned with the preservation and use of historical records

★974★
British Refrigeration Association
Sterling House
6 Furlong Rd
Bourne End
Maidenhead   SL8 5DG
Phone: 0628 531186
Fax: 0628 810423

Trade association representing manufacturers, contractors, wholesalers and distributors of refrigeration plant, equipment and components

★975★
British Reinforcement Manufacturers Association
20-21 Tooks Court
London   EC4A 1LB
Phone: 071-831 7581
Fax: 071-405 1291

★976★
British Resin Manufacturers' Association
Queensway House
2 Queensway
Redhill   RH1 1QS
Phone: 0737 768611
Fax: 0737 761685

★977★
British Resorts Association
c/o I Gill
PO Box 9
Margate
Southend-on-Sea   CT9 1XZ
Phone: 0843 225511   ext. 2164
Fax: 0843 290906

Members are local authorities and tourist boards

★978★
British Retail Florists Association
c/o W Hart
49 Meadway

Enfield   EN3 6NX
Phone: 0992 767645

★979★
British Retailers Association *see* Retail Consortium

★980★
British Retinitis Pigmentosa Society
c/o Mrs L Cantor
Greens Norton Court
Greens Norton
Towcester   NN12 8BS

Retinitis pigmentosa is a group of hereditary disease affecting the eyes and leading to sight deterioration

★981★
British Rig Owners' Association
30-32 St Mary Axe
London   EC3A 8ET
Phone: 071-283 2922
Fax: 071-626 8135

All aspects of design, construction, equipment and operation of mobile offshore units

★982★
British Road Federation
Pillar House
194-202 Old Kent Rd
London   SE1 5TG
Phone: 071-703 9769
Fax: 071-701 0029

★983★
British Robot Association
Aston Science Park
Love Lane
Birmingham   B7 4BJ
Phone: 021-359 0981
Fax: 021-359 7520

Members are suppliers of robotics and automation equipment

★984★
British Rubber Industry Training Organisation
Scala House
Holloway Circus

Birmingham B1 1EQ
Phone: 021-643 9599
Fax: 021-631 3297

Members are companies associated with the rubber industry

★985★
British Rubber Manufacturers Association
90 Tottenham Court Rd
London W1P 0BR
Phone: 071-580 2794
Fax: 071-631 5471

Membership covers manufacturers of rubber and polyurethane products

★986★
British Safety Council
National Safety Centre
62 Chancellor's Rd
London W6 9RS
Phone: 081-741 1231
Fax: 081-741 4551

★987★
British Schools Gymnastics Association
c/o Mrs H M Macleod
Talbot Cottage
Forest Rd
Wokingham
Reading RG11 5SG
Phone: 0344 420215

★988★
British Schools' Canoeing Association
Fairplay House
Wickham Bishops
Chelmsford CM8 3JL
Phone: 0621 891213

★989★
British Science Fiction Association
29 Thornville Rd
Hartlepool TS26 8EW

★990★
British Scrap Federation
16 High St
Brampton

Huntingdon PE18 8TU
Phone: 0480 455249
Fax: 0480 453680

★991★
British Screen Advisory Council
13 Bateman St
London W1V 6EB
Phone: 071-437 9617
Fax: 071-734 7143

Representing organisations and individuals within the film, television and video industries in the UK

★992★
British Secondary Metals Association
25 Park Rd
Runcorn WA7 4SS
Phone: 0928 572400
Fax: 0928 580493

★993★
British Security Industry Association
Security House
Barbourne Rd
Worcester WR1 1RS
Phone: 0905 21464
Fax: 0905 613625

Covers guard and patrol, transport and distribution, security systems, CCTV, safe and lock and security equipment

★994★
British Seeds Council
Agriculture House
25 Knightsbridge
London SW1X 7NJ
Phone: 071-235 5077
Fax: 071-235 3526

★995★
British Shippers' Council
Hermes House
Saint John's Rd
Tunbridge Wells TN4 9UZ
Phone: 0892 26171
Fax: 0892 34989

Represents the interests of British importers and exporters in relation to the movement of their goods to and from overseas

★996★
British Shops & Stores Association
Middleton House
Main Rd
Middleton Cheney
Banbury OX17 2TN
Phone: 0295 712277
Fax: 0295 711665

Formerly: Drapers Chambers of Trade

★997★
British Show Jumping Association
c/o British Equestrian Centre
Stoneleigh
Kenilworth CV8 2LR
Phone: 0203 696516
Fax: 0203 696685

★998★
British Sign Association
Swan House
207 Balham High Rd
London SW17 7BQ
Phone: 081-675 7241
Fax: 081-675 1636

★999★
British Ski Federation
258 Main St
East Calder
Edinburgh EH53 0EE
Phone: 0506 884343
Fax: 0506 882952

The governing body for the sport of skiing

★1000★
British Slot Car Racing Association
c/o C M Frost
48 Wiltshire Gardens
Bransgore
Christchurch
Bournemouth BH23 8BJ
Phone: 0425 72060

The controlling body for slot racing model cars in the UK

★1001★
British Small Animal Veterinary Association
5 St George's Terrace

Cheltenham GL50 3PT
Phone: 0242 584354

★1002★
British Social Biology Council
69 Eccleston Square
London SW1V 1PJ
Phone: 071-834 2091

★1003★
British Society for Clinical Neurophysiology
c/o Dr H Morgan
Dept of Clinical Neurophysiology
Burden Neurological Hospital
Stoke Lane
Bristol BS16 1QT
Phone: 0272 701212   ext. 2929

Medical and scientific study of the nervous system

★1004★
British Society for Music Therapy
69 Avondale Avenue
Barnet EN4 8NB
Phone: 081-368 8879

Promotes the use and development of music therapy in treatment, education, rehabilitation and training of children and adults suffering from emotional, physical or mental handicap

★1005★
British Society for Nutritional Medicine
PO Box 3AP
London W1N 3AP
Phone: 071-436 8532
Fax: 071-580 3910

★1006★
British Society for Parasitology
c/o Professor C Arme
Dept of Biological Science
University of Keele
Keele ST5 5BG
Phone: 0782 621111
Fax: 0782 630007

★1007★
British Society for Rheumatology

3 St Andrew's Place
London NW1 4LB
Phone: 071-224 3739
Fax: 071-224 0156

For the treatment and prevention of rheumatic diseases

★1008★
British Society for Strain Measurement

39 Heaton Rd
Newcastle upon Tyne NE6 1SB
Phone: 091-265 9188
Fax: 091-276 2090

Covers the engineering aspects of strain measurement, stress analysis, and associated technologies

★1009★
British Society for Surgery of the Hand

c/o Royal College of Surgeons
35-43 Lincoln's Inn Fields
London WC2A 3PN
Phone: 071-831 5161
Fax: 071-831 4041

★1010★
British Society for the History of Science

31 High St
Stanford in the Vale
Faringdon
Swindon SNL 8LH
Phone: 0367 710223

To promote and further the study of the history and philosophy of science

★1011★
British Society for the History of Medicine

c/o Dr J M T Ford
Warders
East St
Tonbridge TN9 1LA

★1012★
British Society for the Study of Infection

c/o Dr J A N Emslie
Ruchill Hospital
Glasgow G20 9NB
Phone: 041-946 7120
Fax: 041-946 4359

★1013★
British Society for the Study of Prosthetic Dentistry

c/o R D Welfare
Eastman Dental Hospital
256 Gray's Inn Rd
London WC1X 8LD
Phone: 071-837 3646 ext. 2115

★1014★
British Society of Animal Production

PO Box 3
Penicuik
Edinburgh EH26 0RZ
Phone: 031-445 4508

★1015★
British Society of Audiology

80 Brighton Rd
Reading RG6 1PS
Phone: 0734 660622
Fax: 0734 351915

★1016★
British Society of Baking

Maclaren House
Scarbrook Rd
Croydon CR9 1QH
Phone: 081-688 7788
Fax: 081-688 8375

★1017★
British Society of Cinematographers

11 Croft Rd
Chalfont St Peters
Gerrards Cross SL9 9AE
Phone: 0753 888052

Members are directors of photography working in motion pictures

★1018★
British Society of Commerce
c/o 25 Bridgeman Terrace
Wigan   WN1 1TD
Phone: 0942 43572

★1019★
British Society of Dowsers
Sycamore Cottage
Tamley Lane
Hastingleigh
Ashford   TN25 5HW
Phone: 0233 75253

The scientific principles of dowsing including the knowledge of its application to the search for subterranean watercourses, cavities, tunnels, ores and other entities

★1020★
British Society of Experimental & Clinical Hypnosis
c/o Dept of Psychology
Middlewood Hospital
Sheffield   S6 1TP
Phone: 0742 852222

★1021★
British Society of Gastroenterology
3 St Andrew's Place
London   NW1 4LB
Phone: 071-387 3534
Fax: 071-487 3734

★1022★
British Society of Hypnotherapists
c/o S Young
37 Orbain Rd
London   SW6 7JZ
Phone: 071-385 1166

Specialising in the treatment of nervous disorders and addictions

★1023★
British Society of Medical & Dental Hypnosis
151 Otley Old Rd
Leeds   LS16 6HN
Phone: 0532 613077

To promote the use of hypnotic techniques in medicine and dentistry

★1024★
British Society of Painters in Oils
c/o L Simpson
41 Lister St
Ilkley   LS29 9ET
Phone: 0943 609075

★1025★
British Society of Painters in Oils, Pastels & Acrylics
c/o L Simpson
41 Lister St
Ilkley   LS29 9ET
Phone: 0943 609075

★1026★
British Society of Perfumers
c/o K B Shipp, Glebe Farmhouse, Mears Ashby Rd, Wilby
Wellingborough   NN8 2UQ
Phone: 0933 76546

Members are individual creative perfumers

★1027★
British Society of Periodontology
c/o Dr T F Walsh
Charles Clifford Dental Hospital
Wellesley Rd
Sheffield   S10 2SZ
Phone: 0742 670444
Fax: 0742 665326

Members are dental surgeons

★1028★
British Society of Plant Breeders
Woolpack Chambers
Market St
Ely   CB7 4ND
Phone: 0353 664211
Fax: 0353 661156

★1029★
British Society of Rheology
c/o C Moules
Kruss UK Ltd
5-6 Carrington House
37 Upper King St
Royston   SG8 9AZ
Phone: 0763 244280
Fax: 0763 244298

★1030★
British Society of Scientific Glassblowers
21 Grebe Avenue
Eccleston Park
St Helens WA10 3QL
Phone: 051-709 1438

★1031★
British Sociological Association
Room 701
Columbia House
69 Aldwych
London WC2B 4DX
Phone: 071-955 7303

★1032★
British Soft Drinks Association
6 Catherine St
London WC2B 5JJ
Phone: 071-836 2460
Fax: 071-836 5559

Members are manufacturers, factors and franchisors of still and carbonated soft drinks, concentrates, freeze drinks, fruit juices and packaged waters

★1033★
British Soluble Coffee Manufacturers Association *now* incorporated into Food & Drink Federation

★1034★
British Spectacle Frame Makers' Association
37-41 Bedford Row
London WC1R 4JH
Phone: 071-405 8101
Fax: 071-831 2797

★1035★
British Sports & Allied Industries Federation
10th Floor
Prudential House
Wellesley Rd
Croydon CRO 9XY
Phone: 081-681 1242
Fax: 081-681 0012

★1036★
British Sports Association for the Disabled
34 Osnaburgh St
London NW1 3ND
Phone: 071-383 7277
Fax: 071-383 7332

★1037★
British Starch Industry Association
now incorporated into Food & Drink Federation

★1038★
British Stationery & Office Products Federation *now* British Office Systems & Stationery Federation

★1039★
British Structural Bearings Manufacturers Association
20-21 Tooks Court
Cursitor St
London EC4A 1LA
Phone: 071-464 0131
Fax: 071-464 6018

★1040★
British Sugar Beet Seed Producers Association
c/o A R Withyman
23 New Rd
Spalding PE11 1DH
Phone: 0775 2261
Fax: 0775 67525

★1041★
British Sugarcraft Guild
Wellington House
Messeter Place
London SE9 5DP
Phone: 081-859 6943

★1042★
British Sunbed Hire Federation
32 North Bridge Rd
Doncaster DN5 9AN
Phone: 0302 364067
Fax: 0302 730453

★1043★
British Surface Treatment Suppliers
   Association
136 Hagley Rd
Birmingham B16 9PN
Phone: 021-454 4141
Fax: 021-454 4949

Formerly: British Metal Finishing Suppliers
Association

★1044★
British Surfing Association
Champions Yard
Penzance TR18 2SS
Phone: 0736 60250
Fax: 0736 60250

The official body for the sport of surfing

★1045★
British Surgical Export Group
1 Webbs Court
Buckhurst Avenue
Sevenoaks TN13 1LZ
Phone: 0732 558868
Fax: 0732 459225

Covering surgical equipment manufacturers
interests

★1046★
British Surgical Trades Association
1 Webbs Court
Buckhurst Avenue
Sevenoaks TN13 1LZ
Phone: 0732 458868
Fax: 0732 459225

★1047★
British Tape Industry Association
Carolyn House
22-26 Dingwall Rd
Croydon CR0 9XF
Phone: 081-681 1680
Fax: 081-681 2134

Trade association for the manufacture of
audio and videotape

★1048★
British Tattoo Artists Federation
389 Cowley Rd

Oxford OX4 2BS
Phone: 0865 716877

★1049★
British Tenpin Bowling Association
114 Balfour Rd
Ilford IG1 4JD
Phone: 081-478 1745
Fax: 081-514 3665

★1050★
British Tensional Strapping
   Association
c/o J L T Smith
133 Lichfield St
Walsall WS1 1SL
Phone: 0922 23513
Fax: 0922 724331

★1051★
British Textile By-Products
   Association
115 Windsor Rd
Oldham
Manchester OL8 1RQ
Phone: 061-624 3611
Fax: 061-627 0058

★1052★
British Textile Confederation
7 Swallow Place
London W1H 1LD
Phone: 071-491 9702
Fax: 071-491 9764

★1053★
British Textile Employers' Association
Reedham House
31 King St West
Manchester M3 2PF
Phone: 061-834 7871
Telex: 666737

Members are spinners, weavers and finishers
of cotton and other textiles

★1054★
British Textile Machinery Association
20 Ralli Courts, West Riverside

Manchester   M3 5FL
Phone: 061-834 2991
Fax: 061-834 7380

★1055★
British Thematic Association
107 Charterhouse St
London   EC1M 6PT
Phone: 071-251 5040
Fax: 071-490 4253

For philatelists who collect stamps by theme rather than by country

★1056★
British Thoracic Society
1 St Andrew's Place
London   NW1 4LB
Phone: 071-486 7766

★1057★
British Timber Merchants' Association
Stocking Lane
Hughenden Valley
High Wycombe   HP14 4JZ
Phone: 024-024 3602
Fax: 024-024 5487

Represents all sides of the industry: sawmillers, timber merchants, specialist fencing producers, paper, board and chipboard mills and agents

★1058★
British Tinnitus Association
105 Gower St
London   WC1E 6AH
Phone: 071-387 8033

Tinnitus affects hearing adversely

★1059★
British Toy & Hobby Manufacurers Association
80 Camberwell Rd
London   SE5 0EG
Phone: 071-701 7271
Fax: 071-708 2437

★1060★
British Toymakers Guild
124 Walcot St

Bath   BA1 5BG
Phone: 0225 442440

Members are craftsmen toymakers, shops, galleries and collectors

★1061★
British Trampoline Federation
152a College Rd
Harrow   HA1 1BH
Phone: 081-863 7278

★1062★
British Trout Association
104 Parkway
London   NW1 7AN
Phone: 071-911 0313
Fax: 071-911 0315

Covering the interests of trout and other fish farmers

★1063★
British Trust for Conservation Volunteers
36 Saint Mary's St
Wallingford   OX10 0EU
Phone: 0491 39766
Fax: 0491 39646

★1064★
British Trust for Ornithology
National Centre for Ornithology
The Nunnery
Nunnery Place
Thetford   IP24 2PU
Phone: 044282 3461
Fax: 044282 8455

Members are ornithological conservation and research volunteers and the trust collects information on the distribution, numbers, movements and habits of birds in Britain, particularly problems relating to conservation and land use

★1065★
British Tugowners' Association
6th Floor
Central House
32-66 High St

London E15 2PS
Phone: 081-519 4872
Fax: 081-519 5483

★1066★
British Tunnelling Society
1-7 Great George St
London SW1P 3AA
Phone: 071-222 7722
Fax: 071-222 7500

★1067★
British Turf & Landscape Irrigation Association
c/o P Shildrick
3 Ferrands Park Way
Harden
Bingley BD16 1HZ
Phone: 0535 273188

★1068★
British Turkey Federation
High Holborn House
52-54 High Holborn
London WC1V 6SX
Phone: 071-242 4683
Fax: 071-831 0624

★1069★
British Turned-Parts Manufacturers Association
136 Hagley Rd
Birmingham B16 9PN
Phone: 021-454 4141
Fax: 021-454 4949

★1070★
British Unidentified Flying Object Research Association
16 Southway
Burgess Hill
Haywards Heath RH15 9ST
Phone: 0444 236738

★1071★
British Universities Film & Video Council
55 Greek St

London W1V 5LR
Phone: 071-734 3687
Fax: 071-287 3914

Encourages the use, production and study of audio-visual media, materials and techniques for teaching and research in higher education

★1072★
British Urban & Regional Information Systems Association
c/o D Ward
Social Services Dept
Hampshire County Council
The Castle
Winchester SO23 8UG
Phone: 0962 841841 ext. 7257

To improve communications between people concerned with information systems in local and central government, the health service and the academic world

★1073★
British Urban Regeneration Association
19-21 High St
Sutton
Surrey SM1 1NF
Phone: 081-643 4877
Fax: 081-642 1313

★1074★
British Urethane Foam Contractors Association
26 Warwick Row
Coventry CV1 1EY
Phone: 0203 25018

★1075★
British Vacuum Council
47 Belgrave Square
London SW1X 8QX
Phone: 071-235 6111
Fax: 071-259 6002

★1076★
British Valve & Actuator Manufacturers Association
8th Floor
Bridge House
Smallbrook Queensway

Birmingham   B5 4JP

Covers industrial valves and actuators for the control of fluids and gases

★1077★
British Vehicle Rental & Leasing Association
13 Saint Johns St
Chichester   PO19 1UU
Phone: 0243 786782
Fax: 0243 533851

★1078★
British Venture Capital Association
c/o Victoria Mudford
3 Catherine Place
London   SW1E 6DX
Phone: 071-233 5212
Fax: 071-931 0563

Members provide venture capital funds

★1079★
British Veterinary Association
7 Mansfield St
London   W1M 0AT
Phone: 071-636 6541
Fax: 071-436 2970

★1080★
British Videogram Association
22 Poland St
London   W1V 3DD
Phone: 071-437 5722
Fax: 071-437 0477

Representing the interests of copyright-owning publishers of pre-recorded video cassettes and video discs in the UK

★1081★
British Vintage Wireless Society
c/o P Leggatt
Garretts Farm
Pankridge St
Crondall
Farnham   GU10 5RU
Phone: 0252 850948

Provides a forum for people with an interest in wireless history and old wireless equipment

★1082★
British Waste Paper Association
Alexander House Business Centre
Station Rd
Aldershot   GU11 1BQ
Phone: 0252 344454
Fax: 0252 23417

★1083★
British Watch & Clock Makers' Guild
West Wick
Marsh Rd
Burnham-on-Crouch   CM0 8NE
Phone: 0621 783104

★1084★
British Water Industries Group
9 Harley St
London   W1N 2AL
Phone: 071-436 7541
Fax: 071-436 7393

Members provide services and products covering water resource management, water treatment and supply, waste water and industrial effluent treatment

★1085★
British Water Ski Federation
390 City Rd
London   EC1V 2QA
Phone: 071-833 2855
Fax: 071-837 5879

★1086★
British Watercolour Society
c/o L Simpson
41 Lister St
Ilkley   LS29 9ET
Phone: 0943 609075

★1087★
British Waterfowl Association
c/o Mrs C J Winskill
6 Caldicott Close
Over Winsford
Crewe   CW7 1LW
Phone: 0606 594150

★1088★
British Wholesale Traders Association
74 Waterloo St
Glasgow   G2 7LY
Phone: 041-248 4797

★1089★
British Wind Energy Association
4 Hamilton Place
London   W1V 0BQ
Phone: 071-499 3515
Fax: 071-499 6230

★1090★
British Wood Preserving & Damp-
   Proofing Association
6 The Office Village
4 Romford Rd
London   E15 4ED
Phone: 081-519 2588
Fax: 081-519 3444

★1091★
British Wood Pulp Association
73 Billington Rd
Leighton Buzzard   LU7 8TG
Phone: 0525 379038

★1092★
British Wood Turners Association
78 St Marks Avenue
Salisbury   SP1 3DW
Phone: 0722 328032
Fax: 0722 333558

★1093★
British Woodworking Federation
82 New Cavendish St
London   W1M 8AD
Phone: 071-580 5588
Fax: 071-631 3872

Members manufacture builders woodwork

★1094★
British Woven Wire Export Association
c/o Mrs R Barclay
Locker Wire Weavers Ltd
Church St

Warrington   WA1 2SU
Phone: 0925 51212
Fax: 0925 444386

★1095★
Broadcasting Press Guild
25 Court House Gardens
London   N3 1PU
Phone: 081-346 0643

An association of journalists who cover
broadcasting in the national, regional and
trade press

★1096★
Builders Merchants Federation
15 Soho Square
London   W1V 5FB
Phone: 071-439 1753
Fax: 071-734 2766

Members are concerned with the distribution
of all building timber, plumbing, heating and
decorating materials to the trade and to the
public

★1097★
Building Conservation Trust
Apartment 39
Hampton Court Palace
East Molesey
Kingston upon Thames   KT8 9BS
Phone: 081-943 2277

Promotes the proper maintenance, repair and
improvement of houses and flats of all types

★1098★
Building Contractors Federation
82 New Cavendish St
London   W1M 8AD
Phone: 071-580 5588
Fax: 071-631 3872

★1099★
Building Employers Confederation
82 New Cavendish St
London   W1M 8AD
Phone: 071-580 5588
Fax: 071-631 3872

★1100★
Building Equipment & Materials Metal Trades Organisations
11th Floor, Savoy Tower
77 Renfrew St
Glasgow G2 3BZ
Phone: 041-332 0826
Fax: 041-332 5788

Represents the interests of manufacturers of builders castings, metal baths, boilers, sinks and solid fuel appliances

★1101★
Building Materials Export Group
26 Store St
London WC1E 7BT
Phone: 071-323 3770
Fax: 071-323 0307

★1102★
Building Research Establishment
Garston
Watford WD2 7JR
Phone: 0923 894040
Fax: 0923 664010

★1103★
Building Services Research & Information Association
Old Bracknell Lane West
Bracknell RG12 4AH
Phone: 0344 426511
Fax: 0344 487575

Covers mechanical and electrical services associated with buildings

★1104★
Building Societies Association
3 Savile Row
London W1X 1AF
Phone: 071-437 0655
Fax: 071-734 6416

★1105★
Bulb Distributors Association
Springfields Gardens, Camelgate
Spalding PE12 6ET
Phone: 0775 724843
Fax: 0775 711209

★1106★
Bureau of Freelance Photographers
Focus House
497 Green Lanes
London N13 4BP
Phone: 081-882 3315

★1107★
Bus & Coach Council
52 Lincoln's Inn Fields
London WC2A 3LZ
Phone: 071-831 7546
Fax: 071-242 0053

★1108★
Bus Advertising Council
10 Jamestown Rd
London NW1 7BY
Phone: 071-482 3000

★1109★
Business & Technician Education Council
Central House
Upper Woburn Place
London WC1H 0HH
Phone: 071-388 3288
Fax: 071-387 6068

Approves vocational courses in a wide range of subjects throughout the UK and, in some overseas countries, awards qualifications

★1110★
Business Aircraft Users' Association
PO Box 29
Wallingford OX10 0AG
Phone: 0491 37903

Representing the aviation interests of companies owning or using aircraft for business purposes

★1111★
Business Archives Council
185 Tower Bridge Rd
London SE1 2UF
Phone: 071-407 6110

To encourage the preservation of the archives of the British business community and to promote the study of business history

★1112★
Business Equipment & Information Technology Association
Leicester House
8 Leicester St
London WC2H 7BN
Phone: 071-437 0678
Fax: 071-437 4901

Members interests cover communications and data processing, dictation, filing and storage equipment, mailing systems, microfilm, office machines and systems and reprographic equipment

★1113★
Butter Information Council
Tubs Hill House
London Rd
Sevenoaks TN13 1BL
Phone: 0732 460060
Fax: 0732 459403

★1114★
Buttonhook Society
2 Romney Place
Maidstone ME15 6LE

★1115★
Cable Programme Providers Group
34 Grand Avenue
London N10 3BP
Phone: 081-883 9854
Fax: 081-444 6473

★1116★
Cable Television Association
50 Frith St
London W1V 5TE
Phone: 071-437 0549
Fax: 071-734 2546

★1117★
Cadmium Association
c/o M Cook
42-46 Weymouth St
London W1N 3LQ
Phone: 071-499 8425
Fax: 071-493 1555

Membership covers mining companies and users of cadmium

★1118★
Calcium Silicate Brick Association
24 Fearnley Rd
Welwyn Garden City AL8 6HW
Phone: 0707 324538

Members are manufacturers of bricks and brick-making machinery

★1119★
Campden Food & Drink Research Association
Chipping Campden GL55 6LD
Phone: 0386 840319
Fax: 0386 841306

Members are companies involved in food, drink and allied industries including packaging and process innovation

★1120★
Camping & Outdoor Leisure Association
58 Station Approach
Ruislip HA4 6SA
Phone: 081-842 1111
Fax: 081-842 0090

★1121★
Can Makers Information Service
36 Grosvenor Gardens
London SW1W OEB
Phone: 071-629 9621
Fax: 071-730 9364

Represents the interests of the manufacturers of drinks cans

★1122★
Canine Studies Institute
London Rd
Lily Hill
Bracknell RG12 6QN
Phone: 0344 420898

To improve the quality of training in animal care

★1123★
Car Radio Industry Specialists Association
1 Crosmont Drive
Toothill

Swindon SN5 8LR
Phone: 0793 873221
Fax: 0793 881700

Members are specialist retailers and manufacturers covering all auto electrical systems

★1124★
Careers Research & Advisory Centre
Sheraton House, Castle Park
Cambridge CB3 0AX
Phone: 0223 460277
Telex: 94011229
Fax: 0223 460178

★1125★
Carers National Association
29 Chilworth Mews
London W2 3RG
Phone: 071-724 7776
Fax: 071-723 8130

To cover the interests of people caring for elderly or infirm relatives

★1126★
Case Makers' Association
37-41 Bedford Row
London WC1R 4JH
Phone: 071-405 8101
Telex: 071-831 2797

Dealing with the ophthalmic optical industry

★1127★
Castor Manufacturers (UK) Association
12 The Spinney
Handsworth Wood
Birmingham B20 1NR
Phone: 021-554 7340
Fax: 0384 892422

Domestic, hospital and industrial furniture castors

★1128★
Catering Equipment Distributors Association of GB
c/o J N Humphry-Baker
16 Merrilyn Close

Claygate
Esher KT10 0EQ
Phone: 0372 66354
Fax: 0372 68023

★1129★
Catering Equipment Manufacturers Association
Carlyle House
235-237 Vauxhall Bridge Rd
London SW1V 1EJ
Phone: 071-233 7011
Fax: 071-828 0667

★1130★
Catering Managers Association of GB
c/o P Godbold
Mount Pleasant
Egton
Whitby Y021 1UE
Phone: 0947 85514

★1131★
Catering Teachers' Association
c/o I Littlewood
Runshaw Tertiary College
Langdale Rd
Leyland
Preston PR5 2DQ
Phone: 0772 432511
Fax: 0772 622295

Professional association for those concerned with all aspects of education and training in the food and accommodation service industry

★1132★
Cathedral Architects Association
32-34 Mosley Rd
Newcastle upon Tyne NE1 1DF
Phone: 091-232 3884

★1133★
Cathedral Organists' Association
c/o Royal School of Church Music
Addington Palace
Croydon CR9 5AD
Phone: 081-654 7676

★1134★
Catholic Teachers' Federation
c/o M H Emm
24 Knowlands Rd
Monkspath
Solihull   B90 4UG
Phone: 021-745 4265

★1135★
Cement Admixtures Association
Harcourt
The Common
Kings Langley
Watford   WD4 8BL
Phone: 0923 264314

To encourage the safe and effective use of admixtures in concrete and sand mixes

★1136★
Central Association of Agricultural Valuers
c/o C Harwood
Estate Office
New College
Oxford   OX1 3BN
Phone: 0865 724015

Members are land agents, valuers and auctioneers

★1137★
Central Association of Bee-Keepers
c/o M R English
6 Oxford Rd
Teddington   TW11 OPZ
Phone: 081-977 5867

★1138★
Central Council for Education & Training in Social Work
Derbyshire House
Saint Chad's St
London   WC1H 8AD
Phone: 071-278 2455

★1139★
Central Council of Physical Recreation
Francis House
Francis St

London   SW1P 1DE
Phone: 071-828 3163
Fax: 071-630 8820

★1140★
Central Council of Probation Committees
38 Belgrave Square
London   SW1X 8NT
Phone: 071-245 9364

★1141★
Central Council of the Irish Linen Industry
Lambeg Rd
Lisburn   BT27 4RL
Phone: 0846 677377
Fax: 0846 670470

★1142★
Central Criminal Court Journalists' Association
Press Room
Central Criminal Court
Old Bailey
London   EC4M 7EH
Phone: 071-248 3277

★1143★
Central Entertainment Agents Council
PO Box 112
Eastbourne   BN22 8RQ
Phone: 0323 38965
Fax: 0323 38946

Members are licensed entertainment agents

★1144★
Centre for Agricultural Strategy
University of Reading
1 Earley Gate
Reading   RG6 2AT
Phone: 0734 318150
Fax: 0734 352421

To provide independent and continuing assessments of agricultural and countryside development and their implications for the balanced use of land

★1145★
Centre for Information Media &
   Technology
c/o Hatfield Polytechnic
College Lane
Hatfield   AL10 9AB
Phone: 0707 279691
Fax: 0707 279115

★1146★
Centre for Information on Language
   Teaching & Research
Regent's College
Inner Circle
London   NW1 4NS
Phone: 071-486 8221

★1147★
Centre for Interfirm Comparison
Capital House
48 Andover Rd
Winchester   SO23 7BH
Phone: 0962 844144
Fax: 0962 843180

★1148★
Centre for Policy on Ageing
25-31 Ironmonger Row
London   EC1V 3QP
Phone: 071-253 1787
Fax: 071-490 4206

To promote policies which will result in
higher standards of care and a better lifestyle
for the elderly

★1149★
Centre for Urban Educational Studies
Lawn Lane
London   SW8 1TU
Phone: 071-735 0656
Fax: 071-582 3750

★1150★
Centre of Management in Agriculture
c/o P James
Farm Management Unit
University of Reading
PO Box 236

Reading   RG6 2AT
Phone: 0734 351458

To promote training in all aspects of agricultural management

★1151★
Certificated Bailiffs' Association of
   England & Wales
c/o S Smith
Bibby & Co
Graphic House
152-154 High St
Rayleigh   SS6 7BF
Phone: 0268 773629

★1152★
Chain Testers' Association of GB *now*
   Lifting Equipment Engineers
   Association

★1153★
Chamber of Coal Traders
Victoria House
Southampton Row
London   WC1B 4DH
Phone: 071-405 0034
Fax: 071-831 5181

Distribution of solid fuel by wholesale, retail,
railborne and seaborne means

★1154★
Champagne Agents Association
71 Lincoln's Inn Fields
London   WC2A 3JF
Phone: 071-404 3131
Fax: 071-405 1453

★1155★
Channel Tunnel Association
2 Tyrell Gardens
Windsor   SL4 4DH
Phone: 0753 859161

All aspects of a fixed Channel link between
the UK and France

★1156★
Chartered Association of Certified
   Accountants
29 Lincoln's Inn Fields

London WC2A 3EE
Phone: 071-242 6855
Telex: 24381

Professional and examining body

★1157★
Chartered Building Societies Institute
c/o P Harrington
19 Baldock St
Ware SG12 9DH
Phone: 0920 465051
Fax: 0920 460016

★1158★
Chartered Institute of Arbitrators
24 Angel Gate
City Rd
London EC1V 2RS
Phone: 071-837 4483
Fax: 071-837 4185

★1159★
Chartered Institute of Bankers
10 Lombard St
London EC3V 9AS
Phone: 071-623 3531
Fax: 071-283 1510

An educational body

★1160★
Chartered Institute of Building
Englemere
Kings Ride
Ascot SL5 8BJ
Phone: 0344 23355
Fax: 0344 23467

★1161★
Chartered Institute of Loss Adjusters
Manfield House
376 Strand
London WC2R 0LR
Phone: 071-240 1496
Fax: 071-836 0340

★1162★
**Chartered Institute of Management
  Accountants**
63 Portland Place

London W1N 4AB
Phone: 071-637 2311
Fax: 071-631 5309

The professional body for cost and management accountants, financial directors and controllers

★1163★
Chartered Institute of Marketing
Moor Hall
Cookham
Maidenhead SL6 9QH
Phone: 06285 24922
Fax: 06285 31382

★1164★
Chartered Institute of Patent Agents
Staple Inn Buildings
High Holborn
London WC1V 7PZ
Phone: 071-405 9450
Fax: 071-430 0471

The professional body for patent agents and others in the intellectual property field

★1165★
**Chartered Institute of Public Finance
  & Accountancy**
3 Robert St
London WC2N 6BH
Phone: 071-895 8823
Fax: 071-895 8825

Professional accountancy body for the public sector

★1166★
Chartered Institute of Transport
80 Portland Place
London W1N 4DP
Phone: 071-636 9952
Fax: 071-637 0511

A professional body whose members are engaged in all branches of transport or physical distribution

★1167★
**Chartered Institution of Building
  Services Engineers**
222 Balham High Rd

London SW12 9BS
Phone: 081-675 5211
Fax: 081-675 5449

A learned society dedicated to the promotion of the art, science and practice of building services including heating, ventilating, air conditioning, electrical services and illumination engineering

★1168★
Chartered Insurance Institute
20 Aldermanbury
London EC2V 7HY
Phone: 071-606 3835
Fax: 071-726 0131

★1169★
Chartered Society of Designers
29 Bedford Square
London WC1B 3EG
Phone: 071-631 1510
Fax: 071-580 2338

Representing designers practising in fashion and textiles, interior design, product design and graphics

★1170★
Chartered Society of Physiotherapy
14 Bedford Row
London WC1R 4ED
Phone: 01-242 1941

★1171★
Chemical Industries Association
Kings Building
Smith Square
London SW1P 3JJ
Phone: 071-834 3399
Fax: 071-834 4469

Members are manufacturers, processors, providers of services and employers in the chemical and allied industries

★1172★
Chemical Recovery Association
c/o J Looker
9 Larch Grove
Paddock Wood
Tonbridge TN12 6LA
Phone: 089283 3587

★1173★
Chest Heart & Stroke Association
Tavistock House North
Tavistock Square
London WC1H 9JE
Phone: 071-387 3012

★1174★
Chief & Assistant Chief Fire Officers Association
10-11 Pebble Close
Amington
Tamworth B77 4RD
Phone: 0827 61516

★1175★
Chief Building Surveyors' Society
c/o C S Birks
Property Dept
Hereford & Worcs County Council
Bath St
Hereford HR1 2HQ
Phone: 0432 352211
Fax: 0432 352627

Members are senior officers within counties or boroughs responsible for the maintenance of their authority's properties

★1176★
Chief Leisure Officers Association
20 Essex Rd
Stevenage SG1 3EX
Phone: 0438 353073

All aspects of local government leisure services

★1177★
Chilled Food Association *now* incorporated into Food & Drink Federation

★1178★
China & Glass Retailers' Association
M16 Victoria House
Vernon Place
London WC1B 4DA
Phone: 071-404 0520
Fax: 071-242 4996

★1179★
China Clay Association
John Keay House
St Austell   PL25 4DJ
Phone: 0726 74482
Fax: 0726 623019

★1180★
Choir Schools Association
c/o King's School
College Green
Worcester   WR1 2LH
Phone: 0905 23016

★1181★
Chromatographic Society
c/o J A Challis
Nottingham Polytechnic
Burton St
Nottingham   NG1 4BU
Phone: 0602 500596
Fax: 0602 500614

★1182★
Church Monuments Society
c/o C Easter
18 Cotmore Way
Chillington
Kingsbridge   TQ7 2HU
Phone: 0548 580001

Promotes the care and conservation of funer-
ary monuments, sculpture and other memori-
als associated with burial

★1183★
Cinema Advertising Association
127 Wardour St
London   W1V 4AD
Phone: 071-439 9531
Fax: 071-439 2395

To promote, monitor and maintain standards
of cinema advertising

★1184★
Cinema Theatre Association
40 Winchester St
London   SW1V 4NF
Phone: 071-834 0549

★1185★
Cinematograph Exhibitors' Association
   of GB & Ireland
1st Floor
Royalty House
72-73 Dean St
London   W1V 5HB
Phone: 071-734 9551

★1186★
Circle of Wine Writers
c/o B Cooper
North Lodge
Redleaf
Tunbridge Wells   TN11 8HY
Phone: 0892 870555

★1187★
Civic Catering Association
c/o Leisure Department
Trencherfield Mill
Wallgate
Wigan   WN3 4EF
Phone: 0942 828500

★1188★
Clarinet & Saxaphone Society of GB
167 Ellerton Rd
Tolworth
Surbiton   KT6 7UB
Phone: 081-390 8307

★1189★
Classical Association
c/o R Wallace
Dept of Classics
University of Keele
Keele   ST5 5BG
Phone: 0782 621111
Fax: 0782 613847

Promotes the teaching of classical subjects

★1190★
Clay Pigeon Shooting Association
107 Epping New Rd
Buckhurst Hill   IG9 5TQ
Phone: 081-505 6221
Fax: 081-506 0739

★1191★
Clay Pipe Development Association
Drayton House
30 Gordon St
London WC1H 0AN
Phone: 071-388 0025
Fax: 071-387 1324

The trade association for manufacturers of vitrified clay drain and sewer pipes and fittings

★1192★
Clay Roofing Tile Council *see* British Ceramic Confederation

★1193★
Cleaning & Hygiene Suppliers' Association
John Marshall House
246-254 High St
Sutton
Surrey SM1 1PA
Phone: 081-643 0689
Fax: 081-770 7103

Trade association of companies engaged in the supply of cleaning and hygiene products, equipment and systems to industry, commerce, institutions and catering establishments

★1194★
Cleaning & Support Services Association
Suite 73-74
Hop Exchange
London SE1 1FY
Phone: 071-403 2747
Fax: 071-403 1984

★1195★
Clothing & Footwear Institute
71 Brushfield St
London E1 6AA
Phone: 071-247 1696

Covers design, production and educational aspects

★1196★
Coal Merchants' Federation
21 Baldock St

Ware SG12 9DH
Phone: 0920461 628

Retail distribution of solid fuel

★1197★
Coal Preparation Plant Association
The Fountain Precinct
1 Balm Green
Sheffield S1 3AF
Phone: 0742 766789
Fax: 0742 766213

★1198★
Coated Abrasives Manufacturers' Association
Fairgreen House
Sawbridgeworth
Stevenage CM21 9AY
Phone: 0279 600602
Fax: 0279 726488

Concerns the roll stock surface coated abrasives industry

★1199★
Cocoa Association of London
1 St Katherine's Docks
London E1 9AX
Phone: 071-481 2080
Fax: 071-702 9924

★1200★
Coffee Trade Federation
c/o R E Shimell
146a High St
Tonbridge TN9 1BB
Phone: 0732 770332
Fax: 0732 770362

★1201★
Coir Association
62 Wilson St
London EC2A 2BU
Phone: 071-782 0007
Fax: 071-782 0939

Represents UK and overseas importers and exporters of coir products

★1202★
Coke Oven Managers' Association
Waveney House
Adwick Rd
Mexborough S64 0BS
Phone: 0709 582991

★1203★
Cold Rolled Sections Association
Centre City Tower
7 Hill St
Birmingham B5 4UU
Phone: 021-643 5494
Fax: 021-643 7738

★1204★
Cold Storage & Distribution Federation
Tavistock House North
Tavistock Square
London WC1H 9HZ
Phone: 071-388 7766
Fax: 071-388 1533

★1205★
Collaborative International Pesticides Analytical Council
c/o 5 Pondwick Rd
Harpenden AL5 2HG
Phone: 0582 715887

★1206★
College of Ophthalmologists
3 Bramber Court
2 Bramber Rd
London W14 9PQ
Phone: 071-385 6281
Fax: 071-381 1799

Formely Ophthalmological Society of the UK

★1207★
College of Osteopaths & Practitioners
110 Thorkhill Rd
Thames Ditton KT7 0UW
Phone: 081-905 1395

★1208★
College of Preceptors
Coppice Row
Theydon Bois
Epping CM16 7DN
Phone: 0992 812727
Fax: 0992 814690

Professional membership/examinations body for teachers and educationalists

★1209★
College of Radiographers
14 Upper Wimpole St
London W1M 8BN
Phone: 071-935 5726
Fax: 071-487 3483

★1210★
College of Speech & Language Therapists
6 Lechmere Rd
London NW2 5BU
Phone: 081-459 8521
Fax: 081-459 8913

Qualified speech therapists working for the relief of disorders of communication among both adults and children

★1211★
Combined Edible Nut Trade Association
62 Wilson St
London EC2A 2BU
Phone: 071-782 0007
Fax: 071-782 0939

★1212★
Combined Heat & Power Association
Grosvenor Gardens House
35-37 Grosvenor Gardens
London SW1W 0BS
Phone: 071-828 4077
Fax: 071-828 0310

★1213★
Combustion Engineering Association
PO Box 15
Farm Rd
Aberaman
Aberdare CF44 6YZ
Phone: 0685 879119
Fax: 0685 878104

Promotes efficiency in the utilisation of all types of fuel

★1214★
Commercial Art Directors Association
Shepperton Studios
Studios Rd
Shepperton TW17 0QD
Phone: 0932 562611
Fax: 0932 568989

★1215★
Commercial Horticulture Association
96 Church St
Great Bedwyn
Marlborough SN8 3PF
Phone: 0672 870392

For manufacturers and suppliers to the commercial horticultural trade, particularly for those participating in exhibitions

★1216★
Commercial Rabbit Association *now*
British Commercial Rabbit Association

★1217★
Commercial Trailer Association
c/o A Smith
Forbes House
Halkin St
London SW1X 7DS
Phone: 071-235 7000
Fax: 071-235 7112

★1218★
Committee of Advertising Practice
Brook House
2-16 Torrington Place
London WC1E 7HN
Phone: 071-580 5555
Fax: 071-631 3051

The industry body to ensure that press advertising obeys the code of Advertising Practice

★1219★
Committee of Directors of Polytechnics
c/o Dr M S Lewis
Kirkman House
12-14 Whitfield St
London W1P 6AX
Phone: 071-637 9939
Fax: 071-436 4966

To further the development of the polytechnic approach to higher education

★1220★
Committee of London & Scottish Bankers
10 Lombard St
London EC3V 9AP
Phone: 071-283 8866
Fax: 071-283 7037

★1221★
Committee of Marketing Organisations
c/o Incorporated Society of British Advertisers
44 Hertford St
London W1Y 8AE
Phone: 071-499 7502
Fax: 071-629 5355

★1222★
Committee of Scottish Clearing Bankers
19 Rutland Square
Edinburgh EH1 2DD
Phone: 031-229 1326
Fax: 031-229 1852

★1223★
Committee of Vice-Chancellors & Principals
c/o T U Burgner
29 Tavistock Square
London WC1H 9EZ
Phone: 071-387 9231
Fax: 071-388 8649

Members are executive heads of all the universities in the UK

★1224★
Commonwealth & Overseas Fire Services Association
Queensway House
2 Queensway
Redhill RH1 1QS
Phone: 0737 768611
Telex: 948669

★1225★
Commonwealth Association of Architects
66 Portland Place
London W1N 4AD
Phone: 071-636 8276
Fax: 071-255 1541

★1226★
Commonwealth Association of Surveying & Land Economy
16 St Mary-at-Hill
London EC3R 8EE
Phone: 071-283 8961
Fax: 071-283 8966

National professional societies concerned with land surveying, quantity surveying and land economy

★1227★
Commonwealth Engineers Council
c/o Institution of Civil Engineers
1-7 Great George St
London SW1P 3AA
Phone: 071-222 7722
Fax: 071-222 7500

★1228★
Commonwealth Journalists Association
Castle House
27 Castlereagh St
London W1H 5YR
Phone: 071-262-1054
Fax: 071-724 6925

★1229★
Commonwealth Lawyers Association
c/o Law Society
50 Chancery Lane
London WC2A 1SX
Phone: 071-242 1222
Fax: 071-831 0057

Membership consits of bars, law societies and lawyers throughout the Commonwealth

★1230★
Commonwealth Magistrates' & Judges' Association
28 Fitzroy Square

London W1P 6DD
Phone: 071-387 4889
Fax: 071-383 0757

To advance the law by promoting the independence of the judiciary

★1231★
Communication, Advertising & Marketing Education Foundation
Abford House
15 Wilton Rd
London SW1V 1NJ
Phone: 071-828 7506
Fax: 071-391 0356

An examinations board serving the communications industry.

★1232★
Community Radio Association
119 Southbank House
Black Prince Rd
London SE1 7SJ
Phone: 071-582 8732

Community radio stations are non profit making, locally owned and controlled, volunteer based and provide training and access to the communities they serve

★1233★
Community Transport Association
Highbank
Halton St
Hyde
Manchester SK14 2NY
Phone: 061-366 6685
Fax: 061-367 8396

★1234★
Company Chemists Association
1 Thane Rd West
Nottingham NG2 3AA
Phone: 0602 592831
Fax: 0602 595097

Covers the interests of multiple retail chemists

★1235★
Composers' Guild of GB
34 Hanway St

London W1P 7DE
Phone: 071-436 0007
Fax: 071-436 1913

Members are composers of classical music

★1236★
Comprehensive Prescription House
Association
37-41 Bedford Row
London WC1R 4JH
Phone: 071-405 8101
Fax: 071-831 2797

Members are companies who transfer opticians prescriptions into spectacles

★1237★
Compressed Air Equipment
Distributors Association
c/o G K Edwards
74 Chester Rd
Birmingham B36 7BU
Phone: 021-776 7474
Fax: 021-776 7605

Members are stockists or distributors of compressed air/pneumatic equipment

★1238★
Computer & Peripheral Equipment
Trade Association
1 High St
Maidenhead SL6 1JN
Phone: 0628 782728

★1239★
Computing Services Association
Hanover House
73-74 High Holborn
London WC1V 6LE
Phone: 071-405 2171
Fax: 071-404 4119

The trade association for the computing software and services industry

★1240★
Concrete Block Paving Association
60 Charles St
Leicester LE1 1FB
Phone: 0533 536161
Fax: 0533 514568

★1241★
Concrete Brick Manufacturers
Association
60 Charles St
Leicester LE1 1FB
Phone: 0533 536161
Fax: 0533 514568

★1242★
Concrete Pipe Association
60 Charles St
Leicester LE1 1FB
Phone: 0533 536161
Fax: 0533 514568

Member companies manufacture precast drainage products

★1243★
Concrete Society
Devon House
12-15 Dartmouth St
London SW1H 9BL
Phone: 071-222 1822
Fax: 071-222 5099

★1244★
Confederation of Aerial Industries
Suite 106
Grosvenor Gardens House
33-37 Grosvenor Gardens
London SW1W OBS
Phone: 071-828 0625
Fax: 071-828 0507

Members are contractors, manufacturers, retailers or wholesalers of domestic aerial installations including entryphones, warden call or other communication systems

★1245★
Confederation of Associations of
Specialist Engineering Contractors
ESCA House
34 Palace Court
London W2 4JG
Phone: 071-229 2488
Fax: 071-727 9268

★1246★
Confederation of British Associations
852 Melton Rd
Thurmaston
Leicester LE4 8BN
Phone: 0533 640083
Fax: 0533 640141

All aspects of trade and professional association management and practice

★1247★
Confederation of British Industry
Centre Point
103 New Oxford St
London WC1A 1DU
Phone: 071-379 7400
Fax: 071-240 1578

The employers' organistion covering large and small firms and trade associations

★1248★
Confederation of British Wool Textiles
60 Toller Lane
Bradford BD8 9BZ
Phone: 0274 491241
Fax: 0274 547320

Representing wool importers, merchants, combers, spinners, cloth manufacturers, dyers and finishers

★1249★
Confederation of Information Communication Industries
19 Bedford Square
London WC1B 3HJ
Phone: 071-580 6321
Fax: 071-636 5375

★1250★
Conference & Lecturers in Craft & Design Education
c/o G Harrison
Brunel University
Runnymede Campus
Egham
Staines TW20 0JZ
Phone: 0784 431341

★1251★
Conference for Independent Further Education
Lovehayne Farm
Southleigh
Colyton
Exeter EX13 6JE
Phone: 0404 87241

★1252★
Conference of Catholic Secondary Schools & Colleges
c/o P F Fursey
St Thomas Becket School
Huyton-with-Roby
Liverpool L36 6EG
Phone: 051-489 2489

For head teachers of Roman Catholic maintained and independent secondary schools and colleges

★1253★
Conference of Drama Schools
c/o Central School of Speech & Drama
Eton Avenue
London NW3 3HY
Phone: 071-722 8183

★1254★
Conference of Heavy Engineering Industries Abnormal Loads Committee
Leicester House
8 Leicester St
London WC2H 7BN
Phone: 071-437 0678
Fax: 071-437 4901

★1255★
Conference of University Administrators
c/o R Ives
University of Manchester
Oxford Rd
Manchester M13 9PL
Phone: 061-275 2063

★1256★
Conference of University Teachers of German in GB & Ireland
c/o Dr J L Flood
Institute of Germanic Studies
29 Russell Square
London WC1B 5DP
Phone: 071-580 2711
Fax: 071-436 3497

★1257★
Conservation Foundation
1 Kensington Gore
London SW7 2AR
Phone: 071-823 8842
Fax: 071-823 8791

★1258★
Conservation Trust
National Environmental Education Centre
George Palmer Site
Northumberland Ave
Reading RG2 7PW
Phone: 0734 868442
Fax: 0734 314051

For teachers, companies, voluntary organisations and individuals interested in increasing environmental understanding and awareness

★1259★
Conservatory Association
2nd Floor
Goodwin House
George St
Huntingdon PE18 6BU
Phone: 0480 458271

★1260★
Construction Fixings Association
Light Trades House
3 Melbourne Avenue
Sheffield S10 2QJ
Phone: 0742 663084
Fax: 0742 670910

★1261★
Construction Industry Computing Association
Guildhall Place

Cambridge CB2 3QQ
Phone: 0223 311246

Promotes the appropriate use of computers and information technology in the construction industry

★1262★
Construction Industry Research & Information Association
6 Storey's Gate
London SW1P 3AU
Phone: 071-222 8891
Fax: 071-222 1708

Identifies the research needs of the construction industry

★1263★
Construction Plant-Hire Association
c/o N G Allen
28 Eccleston St
London SW1W 9PY
Phone: 071-730 7117
Fax: 071-730 7110

★1264★
Construction Surveyors Institute *now*
Architects & Surveyors Institute

★1265★
Consultant Quantity Surveyors Association
5-15 Cromer St
London WC1H 8LS
Phone: 071-837 0940
Fax: 071-278 2192

★1266★
Consultative Council of Professional Management Organisations
c/o Institute of Chartered Secretaries & Administrators
16 Park Crescent
London W1M 4HA
Phone: 071-580 4741
Fax: 071-323 1132

★1267★
Consumer Credit Association of the UK
Queens House
Queens Rd
Chester CH1 3BQ
Phone: 0244 312044
Fax: 0244 318035

★1268★
Consumer Credit Trade Association
1st Floor
159-163 Great Portland St
London W1N 5FD
Phone: 071-636 7564

Represents the interests of companies providing and operating credit, leasing and rental facilities

★1269★
Contract Cleaning & Maintenance Association
Suite 73-74 Hop Exchange
24 Southwark St
London SE1 1TY
Phone: 071-403 2747
Fax: 071-403 1984

★1270★
Contract Flooring Association
4c St Mary's Market
Nottingham NG1 4PH
Phone: 0602 411126
Fax: 0602 412238

★1271★
Contractors Mechanical Plant Engineers
20 Knave Wood Rd
Kemsing
Sevenoaks TN15 6RH
Phone: 09592 2628

★1272★
Convention of Scottish Local Authorities
Rosebery House
9 Haymarket Terrace
Edinburgh EH12 5XZ
Phone: 031-346 1222
Fax: 031-346 0055

Covers regional and district councils in Scotland

★1273★
Cooperative Employers Association
Holyoake House
Hanover St
Manchester M60 0AS
Phone: 061-832 4300
Fax: 061-831 7684

Members are employed by retail cooperative societies

★1274★
Cooperative Union
Holyoake House
Hanover St
Manchester M60 0AS
Phone: 061-832 4300
Fax: 061-831 7684

The national federation of UK retail cooperative societies

★1275★
Copper Development Association
Orchard House
Mutton Lane
Potters Bar EN6 3AP
Phone: 0707 50711
Fax: 0707 42769

★1276★
Copper Smelters & Refiners Association
10 Greenfield Crescent
Birmingham B15 3AU
Phone: 021-456 3322
Fax: 021-456 1394

★1277★
Cork Industry Federation
62 Leavesden Rd
Weybridge KT13 9BX
Phone: 0932 848416

★1278★
Cornish Mining Development Association
Roundway
Sennen
Penzance   TR19 7AW
Phone: 0736 871320

To foster, encourage, develop and protect the metalliferous mining industry of Britain in general and Devon and Cornwall in particular

★1279★
Coroners' Society of England & Wales
c/o Dr John Burton
HM Coroners Court
7 Orchard Rise
Richmond-on-Thames   TW10 5BX
Phone: 081-876 5386

★1280★
Corporate Hospitality Association
PO Box 67
Kingswood
Tadworth   KT20 6LG
Phone: 0737 833963
Fax: 0737 833507

★1281★
Corporation of Estate Agents
Castle Hedingham,
Halstead   CO9 3EN
Phone: 0787 60600

★1282★
Corporation of Insurance & Financial Advisors
6-7 Leapale Rd
Guildford   GU1 4JX
Phone: 0483 39121
Fax: 0483 301847

Members are independent financial advisers

★1283★
Corrugated Case Materials Association
Papermakers House
Rivenhall Rd
Westlea
Swindon   SN5 7BE
Phone: 0793 886086
Fax: 0793 886182

★1284★
Cosmetic, Toiletry & Perfumery Association
35 Dover St
London   W1X 3RA
Phone: 071-491 8891
Fax: 071-493 8061

Covers manufacturers and suppliers

★1285★
Cottage Garden Society
c/o Mrs C Tordoff
5 Nixon Close
Thornhill
Dewsbury   WF12 0JA
Phone: 0924 468469

★1286★
Council for Acupuncture
Panther House
38 Mount Pleasant
London   WC1X 0AP
Phone: 071-837 8026
Fax: 071-278 3608

An umbrella organisation for the five main professional associations of acupuncturists

★1287★
Council for British Archaeology
112 Kennington Rd
London   SE11 6RE
Phone: 071-582 0494
Fax: 071-587 5152

★1288★
Council for Complementary & Alternative Medicine
38 Mount Pleasant
London   WC1X 0AP
Phone: 071-409 1440

Ensures cooperation between professional bodies representing acupuncture, chiropractice, homoeopathy, medical herbalism, naturopathy, and osteopathy

★1289★
Council for Dance Education & Training
5 Tavistock Place

London WC1H 9SN
Phone: 071-388 5770

★1290★
Council for Educational Advance
c/o Temple House
9 Upper Berkeley St
London W1H 8BY
Phone: 071-402 5608
Fax: 071-402 5600

★1291★
Council for Environmental Conservation *now* Environment Council

★1292★
Council for Environmental Education
University of Reading
London Rd
Reading RG1 5AQ
Phone: 0734 756061
Fax: 0734 756264

The national body for the co-ordination and promotion of environmental education in England, Wales and Northern Ireland

★1293★
Council for Licensed Conveyancers
3c Cairngorm House
203 Marsh Wall
London E14 9YT
Phone: 071-537 2953
Fax: 071-537 3827

★1294★
Council for Music in Hospitals
c/o Sylvia Lindsay
340 Lower Rd
Little Bookham
Leatherhead KT23 4EF
Phone: 0372 458264

★1295★
Council for Name Studies in GB & Ireland
c/o I A Fraser
School of Scottish Studies

University of Edinburgh
27 George Square
Edinburgh EH9 9LD
Phone: 031-667 6504162

Research into placenames and personal names

★1296★
Council for National Academic Awards
344-354 Grays Inn Rd
London WC1X 8BP
Phone: 071-278 4411

★1297★
Council for National Parks
London Ecology Centre
45 Shelton St
London WC2H 9HJ
Phone: 071-240 3603

★1298★
Council for Professions Supplementary to Medicine
Park House
184 Kennington Park Rd
London SE11 4BU
Phone: 071-582 0866
Fax: 071-820 9684

Professions covered include chiropody, dietetics, medical laboratory sciences, occupational therapy, orthoptics, physiotherapy, and radiography

★1299★
Council for the Accreditation of Correspondence Colleges
27 Marylebone Rd
London NW1 5JS
Phone: 071-935 5391

★1300★
Council for the Advancement of Communication with Deaf People
School of Education
University of Durham
Pelaw House
Durham DH1 1TA
Phone: 091-374 3607

★**1301**★
Council for the Protection of Rural England
25 Buckingham Palace Rd
London SW1W OPP
Phone: 071-976 6433
Fax: 071-702 9769

Members are individuals interested in the preservation of rural areas of the UK

★**1302**★
Council for the Registration of Gas Installers
140 Tottenham Court Rd
London W1P 9LN
Phone: 071-387 9185
Fax: 071-388 0317

★**1303**★
Council of British Fire Protection Equipment *now* Fire Industry Council

★**1304**★
Council of European & Japanese National Shipowners' Associations
30-32 St Mary Axe
London EC3A 8ET
Phone: 071-623 3281
Fax: 071-621 9986

★**1305**★
Council of Forest Industries of British Columbia
Tileman House
131-133 Upper Richmond Rd
London SW15 2TR
Phone: 081-788 4446
Fax: 081-789 0148

Members produce a range of forest products including lumber, pulp, newsprint, paper, plywood and the like, which are marketed worldwide

★**1306**★
Council of Local Education Authorities
66a Eaton Square
London SW1W 9BH
Phone: 071-235 1200
Fax: 071-235 8458

★**1307**★
Council of Mechanical & Metal Trades Associations
Artillery House, Artillery Row
London SW1P 1RT
Phone: 01-799 1579
Telex: 8812939
Fax: 01-799 1852

★**1308**★
Council of Mechanical & Metal Trades Associations *now* Mechanical & Metal Trades Confederation

★**1309**★
Council of Mining & Metallurgical Institutions
44 Portland Place
London W1N 4BR
Phone: 071-580 3802
Fax: 071-436 5388

To promote development of the world's mineral resources

★**1310**★
Council of Mortgage Lenders
c/o C Trench
3 Savile Row
London W1X 1AF
Phone: 071-437 0655
Fax: 071-734 6416

★**1311**★
Council of Outdoor Specialists
c/o N Reed
Poster Media Ltd
Victory House
14 Leicester Square
London WC2H 7NB
Phone: 071-629 6652
Fax: 071-408 0600

Covering poster and outdoor advertising

★**1312**★
Council of Photographic News Agencies
30 New Bridge St

London EC4V 6BN
Phone: 071-248 6730
Fax: 071-489 8982

Members are photographic news picture companies supplying the media with news, sport and stock pictures

★1313★
Council of Regional Arts Associations
Litton Lodge
13a Clifton Rd
Winchester SO22 5BP
Phone: 0962 851063
Fax: 0962 842033

★1314★
Council of Science & Technology Institutes
20 Queensberry Place
London SW7 2DZ
Phone: 071-581 8333
Fax: 071-823 9409

★1315★
Council of Subject Teaching Associations
c/o A R Hall
15 Courthill Terrace
Rochester ME1 3NX
Phone: 0634 826357

★1316★
Council of Voluntary Welfare Work
Duke of York's HQ
Kings Rd
London SW3 4RY
Phone: 071-730 3161

★1317★
Council on International Educational Exchange
c/o D Spuck
33 Seymour Place
London W1H 6AT
Phone: 071-706 3008
Fax: 071-724 8468

Membership includes colleges, universities, secondary schools and youth-serving agencies

★1318★
Country Houses Association
41 Kingsway
London WC2B 6UB
Phone: 071-836 1624

★1319★
Country Landowners' Association
16 Belgrave Square
London SW1X 8PQ
Phone: 071-235 0511
Fax: 071-235 4696

Members are owners of rural land

★1320★
Country Music Association
Suite 3
52 Haymarket
London SW1Y 4RP
Phone: 071-930 2445
Fax: 071-930 2446

Members are individuals and companies engaged in the country music industry world-wide

★1321★
County Education Officers' Society
c/o S Sharpe
County Education Dept
Buckingham County Council
County Hall
Aylesbury HP20 1UZ
Phone: 0296 395000 ext. 2602

★1322★
County Emergency Planning Officers' Society
Emergency Planning Dept
Wiltshire County Council
County Hall
Trowbridge BA14 8JE
Phone: 0225 753641 ext. 3510
Fax: 0225 777424

★1323★
County Planning Officers' Society
Gloucestershire County Council
Shire Hall

Gloucester GL1 2TN
Phone: 0452 425650
Fax: 0452 425034

★1324★
**County Road Safety Offices'
Association**
Castle Court
Shire Hall
Cambridge CB3 0AP
Phone: 0223 317781
Fax: 0223 317735

★1325★
County Surveyors' Society
c/o J J Stansfield
Suffolk County Council
St Edmund House
Rope Walk
Ipswich IP4 1LZ
Phone: 0473 83000

★1326★
Covered Conductors Association
Cable House
56 Palace Rd
East Molesey KT8 9DW
Phone: 081-941 4079
Fax: 081-783 0104

★1327★
Crafts Council
44a Pentonville Rd
London N1 9BY
Phone: 071-278 7700
Fax: 071-837 6891

★1328★
Craftsmen Potters Association
William Blake House
7 Marshall St
London W1V 1FD
Phone: 071-437 7605
Fax: 071-287 9954

★1329★
Creamery Proprietors' Association
19 Cornwall Terrace

London NW1 4QP
Phone: 071-486 7244
Fax: 071-487 4734

Covering manufacture and distribution of milk products.

★1330★
Creative Services Association
c/o F Fearne
FCA Mavity Ltd
2 Brick St
London W1Y 7DF
Phone: 071-409 0440
Fax: 071-499 0698

★1331★
Cremation Society of GB
2nd Floor
Brecon House
16-16a Albion Place
Maidstone ME14 5DZ
Phone: 0622 688292
Fax: 0622 686698

★1332★
Cricket Council
Lord's Cricket Ground
St John's Wood Rd
London NW8 8QZ
Phone: 071-286 4405
Fax: 071-289 5619

★1333★
Crime Reporters' Association
c/o Press Room
New Scotland Yard
London SW1H 0BG
Phone: 071-222 1157

★1334★
Crime Writer's Association
c/o Anthea Fraser
PO Box 172
Tring HP23 5LP
Phone: 044 282 8496

Membership is primarily for published writers of crime fiction or non-fiction who are residing in the UK

★1335★
Criminal Bar Association
c/o A Rafferty
4 Brick Court
London EC4N 2AY
Phone: 071-413 0353

★1336★
Critics' Circle
c/o Peter Hepple
47 Bermondsey St
London SE1 3XT
Phone: 071-403 1818
Fax: 071-403 1418

Professional association of critics of drama, music, films, ballet, radio and television

★1337★
Critics' Guild
9 Compayne Gardens
London NW6 3DG
Phone: 071-624 7579

Members are press critics covering all the arts

★1338★
Croquet Association
c/o B C Macmillan, Hurlingham Club,
  Ranelagh Gardens
London SW6 3PR
Phone: 071-736 3148

★1339★
Cruising Association
Ivory House
St Katharine's Docks
London E1 9AT
Phone: 071-481 0881

Members are cruising yachtsmen

★1340★
Curriculum Association
c/o Professor R Moon
School of Education
Open University
Walton Hall
Milton Keynes MK7 6AA
Phone: 0908 652374
Fax: 0908 653744

★1341★
Cutlery & Allied Trades Research Association
Light Trades House
3 Melbourne Avenue
Sheffield S10 2QJ
Phone: 0742 769736
Fax: 0742 670910

★1342★
Cystic Fibrosis (Mucoviscidosis) Association
c/o Linda Johnson
3 Lecky St
London SW7 3QP
Phone: 071-373 8300

★1343★
Dairy Trade Federation
19 Cornwall Terrace
London NW1 4QP
Phone: 071-486 7244
Fax: 071-487 4734

Representing processors and distributors of milk and milk products

★1344★
Dealer Advertising Information Service
Ladybellegate House
Longsmith St
Gloucester GL1 2HT
Phone: 0452 308200
Fax: 0452 300698

★1345★
Decorative Gas Fire Manufacturers Association
Bridge House
10 Freemantle Business Centre
Millbrook Rd East
Southampton SO1 0JR
Phone: 0703 631593
Fax: 0703 634497

To promote the credibility and safety of decorative gas fires to ensure acceptable standards

★1346★
Decorative Lighting Association
Bryn House
Bryn

Bishop's Castle SY9 5LE
Phone: 05884 658
Fax: 05884 669

★1347★
Defence Manufacturers Association
Park House
Broadford
Shalford
Guildford GU4 8DW
Phone: 0483 579333
Fax: 0483 36717

★1348★
Dehydrated Potato Association *now*
incorporated into Food & Drink
Federation

★1349★
Delicatessen & Fine Food Association
6 The Broadway
Thatcham
Newbury RG13 4JA
Phone: 0635 69033
Fax: 0635 69058

★1350★
Design & Industries Association
19 Lawn Crescent
Kew TW9 3NR
Phone: 081-940 4925

★1351★
Design & Technology Association
Smallpiece House
27 Newbold Terrace East
Leamington Spa CV32 4ES
Phone: 0926 315984
Fax: 0926 337881

For teachers in state and independent schools

★1352★
Design Business Association
29 Bedford Square
London WC1B 3EG
Phone: 071-631 1510
Fax: 071-580 2338

Members are consultancies who promote the
use of design by business and other organisations

★1353★
Design Council
28 Haymarket
London SW1Y 4SU
Phone: 071-839 8000
Fax: 071-935 2130

★1354★
**Designers & Art Directors Association
of London**
12 Carlton House Terrace
London SW1Y 5AH
Phone: 071-839 2964
Fax: 071-925 2645

★1355★
Despatch Association
55 Blockley Rd
Wembley HA0 3LN
Phone: 081-904 7868
Fax: 081-904 2021

Members provide courier service

★1356★
Dessert & Cake Mixes Association
now incorporated into Food & Drink
Federation

★1357★
Diabetes Foundation
177a Tennison Rd
London SE25 5NF
Phone: 081-656 5467

Research into the cure for diabetes and education to enable diabetics to avoid the long-
term complications of the disease

★1358★
**Diamond Industrial Products
Association**
Fair Green House
Sawbridgeworth
Stevenage CM21 9AJ
Phone: 0279 600602

★1359★
Diecasting Society
Queensway House
2 Queensway

Redhill   RH1 1QS
Phone: 0737 768611
Fax: 0737 760467

★1360★
Direct Mail Producers Association
34 Grand Avenue
London   N10 3BP
Phone: 081-883 9854
Fax: 081-444 6473

★1361★
Direct Selling Association
29 Floral St
London   WC2E 9DP
Phone: 071-497 1234
Fax: 071-497 3144

The marketing of goods direct to the consumer, omitting wholesale and retail outlets

★1362★
Directors Guild of GB
Suffolk House
1-8 Whitfield Place
London   W1P 5SF
Phone: 071-383 3858
Fax: 071-383 5173

Members are directors in theatre, film, television, radio, opera and dance

★1363★
Directory Publishers Association
93a Blenheim Crescent
London   W11 2EQ
Phone: 071-221 9089

★1364★
Disability Alliance Education & Research Association
1st Floor
East Universal House
88-94 Wentworth St
London   E1 7SN
Phone: 071-240 0806

Concerning the rights, benefits and services for all people with disabilities and their families

★1365★
Disabled Drivers' Association
The Hall
Ashwellthorpe
Norwich   NR16 1EX
Phone: 0508 41449

★1366★
Display Producers & Screen Printers Association *now* Screen Printing Association

★1367★
Disposable Hypodermic & Allied Equipment Manufacturers' Association of Europe
551 Finchley Rd
London   NW3 7BJ
Phone: 071-431 2187
Fax: 071-794 5271

Members are manufacturers of single-use hypodermic syringes, needles and related products

★1368★
Disposable Nappy Association
c/o A Monroe
Monroe & Forser
37 Soho Square
London   W1V 5DG
Phone: 071-439 7177
Fax: 071-437 0553

★1369★
District Auditors' Society
c/o J McWhirr
District Audit Office
1st Floor
Sheffield House
Lytton Way
Stevenage   SE1 3HB
Phone: 0438 351570
Fax: 0438 362367

★1370★
District Council Technical Association
c/o A M Travis
Town Hall

Weston-Super-Mare   BS23 1UJ
Phone: 0934 631701
Fax: 0934 418194

★1371★
District Planning Officers' Society
c/o J Colby
Dept of Planning
Royal Borough of Windsor & Maidenhead
Aston House
York Rd
Maidenhead   SL6 1PS
Phone: 0628 33155   ext. 2042
Fax: 0628 770098

★1372★
Diving Medical Advisory Committee
28-30 Little Russell St
London   WC1A 2HN
Phone: 071-405 7045
Fax: 071-831 2581

For medical doctors specialising in hyperbaric (diving) medicine

★1373★
Domestic Appliance Service Association
Hazeldene
Wengeo Lane
Ware   SG12 0EG
Phone: 0920 465928
Fax: 0992 581443

Members are private firms servicing and repairing all gas or electric domestic appliances

★1374★
Domestic Coal Consumers' Council
Gavrelle House
2 Bunhill Row
London   EC1Y 8LL
Phone: 071-638 8929

Dealing with the supply, quality and price of housecoal and smokeless fuel

★1375★
Domestic Heating Council
2 Walker St

Edinburgh   EH7 3LB
Phone: 031-225 2255
Fax: 031-226 7638

★1376★
Domestic Heating Society
King's Shade Walk
122 High St
Epsom   KT19 8AU
Phone: 0372 376312

Members are manufacturers, contractors and consultants covering domestic and commercial heating

★1377★
Domestic Manufacturing Stationers' Association
6 Wimpole St
London   W1M 8AS
Phone: 071-637 7692
Telex: 21201

★1378★
Door & Shutter Manufacturers Association
Heath St
Tamworth   B79 7JH
Phone: 0827 52337
Fax: 0827 310827

★1379★
Drapers Chamber of Trade *now* British Shops & Stores Association

★1380★
Draught Proofing Advisory Association
PO Box 12
Haslemere   GU27 3AH
Phone: 0428 54011
Fax: 0428 51401

★1381★
Drawing Office Material Manufacturers & Dealers Association
25-27 Oxford St

London W1R 1RF
Phone: 071-734 2971
Fax: 071-494 1764

Graphic and reprographic suppliers association

★1382★
Drilling & Sawing Association
Kensington House
Suffolk St
Queensway
Birmingham B1 1LN
Phone: 021-643 4577

Members are contractors and suppliers in the concrete cutting industry

★1383★
Drinking Fountain Association
105 Wansunt Rd
Bexley DA5 2DN
Phone: 0322 528062

★1384★
Driving Instructors Association
Safety House
Beddington Farm Rd
Croydon CR0 4XZ
Phone: 081-660 3333
Fax: 081-665 5565

★1385★
Dry Stone Walling Association of GB
c/o YFC Centre
National Agricultural Centre
Stoneleigh
Kenilworth CV8 2LG
Phone: 021-378 0493

★1386★
Dry-Lining & Partition Association
82 New Cavendish St
London W1M 8AD
Phone: 071-580 5588
Fax: 071-436 5398

Concerned with dry linings, ceilings and dry permanent or demountable partitions

★1387★
Duck Producers Association
High Holborn House
52-54 High Holborn
London WC1V 6SX
Phone: 071-242 4683
Fax: 071-831 0624

★1388★
Ductile Iron Producers Asssociation
8th Floor, Bridge House
Smallbrook Queensway
Birmingham B5 4JP
Phone: 021-643 3377
Fax: 021-643 5064

★1389★
Dyslexia Institute
133 Gresham Rd
Staines TW18 2AJ
Phone: 0784 463851
Fax: 0784 460747

Concerned with teaching and teacher training

★1390★
Earth Science Teachers Association
c/o G Sparks
36 High View Rd
Guildford GU2 5RT
Phone: 0483 572399

For teachers of geology and earth sciences at all levels

★1391★
Ecclesiastical History Society
c/o Dr V G Davis
Queen Mary & Westfield College
Kidderpore Avenue
London NW3 7ST
Phone: 071-435 7141
Fax: 071-794 2173

★1392★
Ecological Design Association
20 High St
Stroud GL5 1AS
Phone: 0453 752985

Focuses on the environmental dimension in design

★1393★
Economic History Society
c/o E G Ray
1 Greville Rd
Cambridge   CB1 3QG

★1394★
Economics Association
Maxwelton House
41-43 Boltro Rd
Haywards Heath   RH16 1BJ
Phone: 0444 455084

Represents teachers of economics and related subjects in schools and colleges and pro- motes the teaching of these subjects within a broadly-based curriculum

★1395★
Educational Centres Association
c/o Dominic Delahunt
Chequer Centre
Chequer St
London   EC1Y 8PL
Phone: 071-251 4158

Seeks to secure access to resources and activity bases for learning, specially designed or converted for adult use

★1396★
Educational Development Association
c/o B Pinfield
34 Newhouse Crescent
Norden
Rochdale   OL11 5RR
Phone: 0706 42829

Teachers' association for in-service training

★1397★
Educational Institute of Design, Craft & Technology now Design & Technology Association

★1398★
Educational Institute of Scotland
46 Moray Place
Edinburgh   EH3 6BH
Phone: 031-225 6244
Fax: 031-220 3151

★1399★
Educational Publishers Council
19 Bedford Square
London   WC1B 3HJ
Phone: 071-580 6321
Fax: 071-636 5375

Members publish educational and academic books and journals

★1400★
Educational Television Association
King's Manor
Exhibition Square
York   YO1 2EP
Phone: 0904 433929

Promotes the use of television and video for educational purposes

★1401★
Electric Battery Manufacturers Association now Society of British Battery Manufacturers

★1402★
Electric Steel Makers' Guild
c/o J W Piper
56 Shakespeare Crescent
Dronfield
Sheffield   S18 6ND
Phone: 0246 417601

Concerning the manufacture of steel in elec- tric furnaces

★1403★
Electric Vehicle Association of GB
Leicester House
8 Leicester St
London   WC2H 7BN
Phone: 071-872 6205
Fax: 071-437 4901

A forum for the UK interests of those whose business is derived from battery-powered equipment and electric vehicles

★1404★
Electrical & Electronic Insulation Association
Leicester House
8 Leicester St

London WC2H 7BN
Phone: 071-437 0678
Fax: 071-437 4901

★1405★
Electrical Contractors Association
34 Palace Court
London W2 4HY
Phone: 071-229 1266
Fax: 071-221 7344

★1406★
Electrical Contractors Association of Scotland
Bush House
Bush Estate
Edinburgh EH26 05B
Phone: 031-445 5577
Fax: 031-445 5548

★1407★
Electrical Installation Equipment Manufacturers Association
Leicester House
8 Leicester St
London WC2H 7BN
Phone: 071-437 0678
Fax: 071-734 2354

★1408★
Electrical Wholesalers Federation
Panton House
25-27 Haymarket
London SW1Y 4EN
Phone: 071-930 2002
Fax: 071-930 4102

★1409★
Electricity Association
c/o R Farrance
30 Millbank
London SW1P 4RD
Phone: 071-834 2333

★1410★
Electricity Consumers' Council
Brook House
2-16 Torrington Place
London WC1E 7LL
Phone: 071-724 3431

★1411★
Electro-Acoustic Music Association
now Sonic Arts Network

★1412★
Electro-Medical Trade Association
Consort House
26-28 Queensway
London W2 3RX
Phone: 071-221 4612

★1413★
Electro-Physiological Technologists' Association
c/o E Smith
Neurophysiology Dept
Selly Oak Hospital
Raddlebarn Rd
Birmingham B29 6JD
Phone: 021-472 5313

Members are medical technicians, doctors and scientists involved in neurophysiology

★1414★
Electronic Components Industry Federation
Romano House
399-401 Strand
London WC2R 0LT
Phone: 071-497 2311
Fax: 071-497 2335

Covering components, accessories and materials

★1415★
Electronic Engineering Association
Leicester House
8 Leicester St
London WC2H 7BN
Phone: 071-872 6216
Fax: 071-434 3477

★1416★
Embroiderers' Guild
Apartment 41
Hampton Court Palace
East Molesey KT8 9AU
Phone: 081-943 1229

★1417★
Employers' Association of the Linen & Cotton Handkerchief & Household Goods Wages Council
Reedham House
31 King St West
Manchester M3 2PF
Phone: 061-832 9291
Fax: 061-833 1740

★1418★
Energy Industries Council
Newcombe House
45 Notting Hill Gate
London W11 3LQ
Phone: 071-221 2043
Fax: 071-221 8813

Trade association of companies providing capital equipment and services for the energy industries including petrochemicals

★1419★
Energy Systems Trade Association
PO Box 16
Stroud GL5 5EB
Phone: 0453 873568

★1420★
Engineering Council
10 Maltravers St
London WC2R 3ER
Phone: 071-240 7891
Fax: 071-240 7517

★1421★
Engineering Employers' Federation
Broadway House
Tothill St
London SW1H 9NQ
Phone: 071-222 7777
Fax: 071-222 2782

★1422★
Engineering Equipment & Materials Users Association
14-15 Belgrave Square

London SW1X 8PS
Phone: 071-235 5316
Fax: 071-245 6937

Members are industrial users of engineering equipment, material and stores

★1423★
Engineering Industries Association
16 Dartmouth St
London SW1H 9BL
Phone: 071-222 2367
Fax: 071-222 2782

Trade association for technical and electrical engineering companies

★1424★
Engineering Teaching Equipment Manufacturers Association
PO Box 8
Brockenhurst
Lymington SO42 7ZZ
Phone: 0590 22854
Fax: 071-537 4846

Members design and manufacture equipment to meet the need for technology teaching and training

★1425★
Engineers' Hand Tools Association
Light Trades House
3 Melbourne Avenue
Sheffield S10 2QJ
Phone: 0742 663084
Fax: 0742 670910

★1426★
English Association
The Vicarage
1 Priory Gardens
London W4 1TT
Phone: 081-995 4236

For the understanding and appreciation of English language and literature

★1427★
English Basketball Association
48 Bradford Rd
Leeds LS28 6DF
Phone: 0532 361166

★1428★
English Bowling Association
Lyndhurst Rd
Worthing   BN11 2AZ
Phone: 0903 820222
Fax: 0903 820444

★1429★
English Bowling Federation
62 Frampton Place
Boston   PE21 8EL
Phone: 0205 366201

★1430★
English Country Cheese Council
5-7 John Princes St
London   W1M 0AP
Phone: 071-499 7822
Telex: 298632

★1431★
English Curling Association
66 Preston Old Rd
Freckleton
Preston   PR4 1PD
Phone: 0772 634154

To promote curling and provide facilities at ice rinks

★1432★
English Indoor Bowling Association
290a Barking Rd
London   E6 3BA
Phone: 081-470 1237

★1433★
English National Board for Nursing, Midwifery & Health Visiting
Victory House
170 Tottenham Court Rd
London   W1P 0HA
Phone: 071-388 3131
Fax: 071-383 4031

★1434★
English Place-Name Society
c/o School of English Studies
University of Nottingham
University Park

Nottingham   NG7 2RD
Phone: 0602 484848

★1435★
English Schools Cricket Association
c/o C J Cooper
68 Hatherley Rd
Winchester   SO22 6RR
Phone: 0962 65773

★1436★
English Schools Football Association
c/o C S Allatt
4a Eastgate St
Stafford   ST16 2NQ
Phone: 0785 51142
Fax: 0785 55485

★1437★
English Schools Swimming Association
c/o D Redman
3 Maybank Grove
Liverpool   L17 6DW
Phone: 051-427 3707

★1438★
English Schools Table Tennis Association
c/o L C H Engelberg
Badger Lane
Derby   DE5 6FG
Phone: 0246 590164

To promote the sport of table tennis among school boys and girls between the ages of 8 and 19

★1439★
English Ski Council
c/o D King
Area Library Building
Queensway Mall
The Cornbrow
Halesowen
Birmingham   B63 4AJ
Phone: 021-501 2341

The governing body of the sport for English skiers, membership is open to clubs, educational establishments, youth organisations and the like

★1440★
English Table Tennis Association
Queensbury House
Havelock Rd
Hastings   TN34 1HF
Phone: 0424 722525
Fax: 0424 422103

The governing body

★1441★
English Vineyard Association
c/o Commander G L Bond
38 West Park
London   SE9 4RH
Phone: 081-857 0452

Members own vineyards over half an acre; associates own vineyards less than half an acre. Membership also include companies dealing with vineyards and their requirements

★1442★
Entertainment Agents Association
4 Keyes House
Dolphin Square
London   SW1V 3NA
Phone: 071-834 0515
Fax: 0261

The trade association for theatrical employment agents

★1443★
Entertainment Industry Suppliers Association
42 Cranbown St
London   WC2H 7AN
Phone: 071-437 4761
Fax: 071-287 0315

★1444★
Envelope Makers' & Manufacturing Stationers' Association
44 St Martin's Approach
Ruislip   HA4 7QQ
Phone: 0895 632867

★1445★
Environment Council
80 York Way

London   N1 9AG
Phone: 071-278 4736
Fax: 071-837 9688

The umbrella body for non-governmental UK organisations concerned with environmental conservation

★1446★
Environmental Communicators Organisation
c/o A Massam
8 Hooks Cross
Watton-at-Stone
Hertford   SG14 3RY
Phone: 0920 830527

Members are environmental journalists

★1447★
Environmental Education Advisors Association
c/o Mr Moseley
Environmental Education Advisor
Education Dept
Old County Hall
Truro   TR1 3BA
Phone: 0872 74282   ext. 3401
Fax: 0872 222490

★1448★
Ephemera Society
12 Fitzroy Square
London   W1P 5HQ
Phone: 071-387 7723

Conservation and study of printed and hand-written ephemera

★1449★
Equipment Leasing Association
18 Upper Grosvenor St
London   W1X 9PB
Phone: 071-491 2783
Fax: 071-629 0396

★1450★
Ergonomics Society
c/o Dept of Human Sciences
University of Technology

Loughborough   LE1 3TU
Phone: 0509 234904

The study of man in the working environment
and the application of physiological, psychological and anatomical knowledge to improve
the design of work

★1451★
Esperanto Teachers Association
140 Holland Park Avenue
London   W11 4UF
Phone: 071-727 7821

★1452★
Estate Agents Services Association
29 Alexander St
London   W2 5NU
Phone: 071-229 4837
Fax: 071-229 4837

★1453★
European Asbestos & Recycling
  Association
Friars House
6 Parkway
Chelmsford   CM2 0NF
Phone: 0245 259744

★1454★
European Association of Science
  Editors
13 Wimpole St
London   W1M 7AB
Phone: 071-636 3175
Fax: 071-636 3175

★1455★
European Association of Teachers
20 Brookfield
Highgate West Hill
London   N6 6AS
Phone: 081-340 9136

★1456★
European Caravan Federation
c/o W R Innes
PO Box 1
Langport

Taunton   TA10 9HP
Phone: 0458 251821
Fax: 0458 74367

★1457★
European Catering Association
1 Victoria Parade
Richmond-on-Thames   TW9 3NB
Phone: 081-940 4464

Members are catering managers, directors,
contract caterers and suppliers previously the
Industrial Catering Association

★1458★
European Committee of
  Manufacturers, Compressors,
  Vacuum Pumps & Pneumatic Tools
Leicester House
8 Leicester St
London   WC2H 7BN
Phone: 071-437 0678
Fax: 071-734 0462

★1459★
European Committee of
  Manufacturers of Electrical
  Installation Equipment
Leicester House
8 Leicester St
London   WC2H 7BN
Phone: 071-437 0678
Fax: 071-734 2354

★1460★
European Confederation of Medical
  Suppliers Associations
551 Finchley Rd
London   NW3 5BJ
Phone: 071-431 2187
Fax: 071-794 5271

Representing companies in the non-pharma-
ceutical healthcare field

★1461★
European Council of International
  Schools
c/o T M Maybury
21b Lavant St

Petersfield   GU32 3EL
Phone: 0730 68244
Fax: 0730 67914

A professional association of international schools in over 100 countries. Members are mainly English language primary and secondary schools offering an American, British and/or international curriculum

★1462★
European Desalination Association
c/o Dr W T Hanbury
Dept of Mechanical Engineering
University of Glasgow
Glasgow   G12 8QQ
Phone: 041-776 5221
Fax: 041-776 1772

For individuals interested in the process of desalination and other methods of water treatment

★1463★
European Federation of Conference Towns
c/o G V Smith
137 Sheen Rd
Richmond-on-Thames   TW9 1YJ
Phone: 081-940 3431
Fax: 081-322 1920

Advice and assistance on planning meetings, exhibitions and events in European cities

★1464★
European Federation of Corrosion
c/o Institute of Metals
1 Carlton House Terrace
London   SW1Y 5DB
Phone: 071-839 4071
Fax: 071-839 2289

★1465★
European Federation of Dairy Retailers
c/o Dairy Trade Federation
19 Cornwall Terrace
London   NW1 4QP
Phone: 071-486 7244
Fax: 071-487 4734

★1466★
European Federation of Honey Packers & Distributors
152-160 City Rd
London   EC1V 2NP
Phone: 071-253 9421
Fax: 071-250 0965

★1467★
European Federation of Societies for Ultrasound in Medicine & Biology
c/o L Surry
The Studio
45 Bond St
London   W5 5AS
Phone: 081-567 9307
Fax: 081-991 0559

All aspects of medical ultrasound

★1468★
European Fishing Tackle Trade Association
102 Old St
London   EC1V 9AY
Phone: 071-251 3438
Fax: 071-250 4164

For manufacturers, wholesalers and distributors of fishing tackle and accessories

★1469★
European Flexible Intermediate Bulk Container Association
140 Camphill Rd
Broughty Ferry
Dundee   DD5 2NF
Phone: 0382 480049
Fax: 0382 480130

★1470★
European Flexographic Technical Association
6 The Tynings
Cleveland
Bristol   BS21 7YP
Phone: 0272 878090
Fax: 0272 878090

★1471★
European Food Brokers Association
10 Wellbank
Hook Norton
Banbury   OX15 5LN
Phone: 0608 737176
Fax: 0608 730256

★1472★
European Food Law Association
Chadwick House
48 Rushworth St
London   SE1 0QT
Phone: 071-928 6006
Fax: 071-261 1960

★1473★
**European General Galvanizers
   Association**
London House
68 Upper Richmond Rd
London   SW15 2RP
Phone: 081-874 2122
Fax: 081-874 3251

★1474★
**European Glass Container
   Manufacturers' Committee**
Northumberland Rd
Sheffield   S10 2UA
Phone: 0742 686201
Fax: 0742 681073

★1475★
European Information Association
c/o I Thomson
European Documentation Centre
University College
Cardiff   CF1 3XT
Phone: 0222 874262
Fax: 0222 229740

Membership is open to individuals and
organisations providing or interested in information services relating to the European
Community and related organisations

★1476★
European Institute for the Media
c/o Professor George Wedell
The University

Oxford St
Manchester   M13 9PL
Phone: 061-273 2754
Fax: 061-273 8788

Policy-oriented research and development in
the fields of radio, television, the press and
related issues in mass communications

★1477★
**European Investment Casters'
   Federation**
The Holloway
Alvechurch
Birmingham   B18 7QB
Phone: 0527 584770
Fax: 0527 584771

★1478★
**European Lead Development
   Committee**
c/o Lead Development Association
42-46 Weymouth St
London   W1N 3LQ
Phone: 071-499 8422
Fax: 071-493 1555

★1479★
European Liquid Roofing Association
Maxwelton House
Boltro Rd
Haywards Heath   RG16 1BJ
Phone: 0444 417458
Fax: 0444 415616

★1480★
**European Malt Extract Manufacturers
   Association**
60 Claremont Rd
Surbiton   KT6 4RH
Phone: 081-390 2022
Fax: 081-390 2027

★1481★
**European Marketing & Promotion
   Association**
322 Kennington Park Rd
London   SE11 4PP
Phone: 071-582 9922
Fax: 071-582 1604

★1482★
European Marketing Association
18 St Peters Steps
Brixham

★1483★
European Motel Federation
c/o D B Westrup
36 Repton Drive
Newcastle under Lyme   ST5 3JF
Phone: 0782 617482

★1484★
**European Organisation of Caries
   Research**
c/o Professor C Robinson
Dept of Oral Biology
School of Dentistry
Clarendon Way
Leeds   LS2 9LU
Phone: 0532 336159
Telex: 0532 336158

Promotes research into dental caries and
related matter

★1485★
European Piano Teachers Association
c/o Carole Grindea
28 Emperor's Gate
London   SW7 4HS
Phone: 071-373 7307

Members are piano teachers and pianists
aiming to raise the standard of both teaching
and performance

★1486★
**European Plasticised PVC Film
   Manufacturers' Association**
The Fountain Precinct, 1 Balm Green
Sheffield   S1 3AF
Phone: 0742 766789
Fax: 0742 766213

★1487★
**European Plastics Distributors
   Association**
21c Station Rd
Knowle

Solihull   B93 0HL
Phone: 0564 778991
Fax: 0564 770812

Representing distributors of semi-finished
products

★1488★
**European Pressure Die Casting
   Committee**
c/o Zinc Development Association
42-44 Weymouth St
London   W1N 3LQ
Phone: 071-499 6636
Fax: 071-493 1555

★1489★
European Regional Airlines Association
Baker Site
Fairoaks Airport
Chobham
Woking   GU24 8HX
Phone: 0276 856495
Fax: 0276 857038

Members represent regional airlines, associ-
ate members are corporations and others
engaged in commercial aviation

★1490★
**European Society of Ophthalmic
   Plastic & Reconstructive Surgery**
c/o J R O Collin
Moorfields Eye Hospital
City Rd
London   EC1V 2PD
Phone: 071-253 3411

Members are surgeons interested in plastic
surgery around the eyes

★1491★
**European Sponsorship Consultants
   Association**
Copsham House
50 Broad St
London   EC1R 0HH
Phone: 071-251 2505

★1492★
European Tugowners Association
Central House
32-66 High St

London E15 2PS
Phone: 081-519 4872
Fax: 081-519 5483

★1493★
**European Wire Rope Information
   Service**
The Fountain Precinct
1 Balm Green
Sheffield S1 3AF
Phone: 0742 766789
Fax: 0742 766213

★1494★
Exhibition Industry Federation
Sheen Lane House
254 Upper Richmond Rd West
London SW14 8AG
Phone: 081-878 9130
Fax: 081-878 4712

The federation's aim is to increase exhibition
business throughout the UK and to extend
the range of exhibitors and exhibition visitors

★1495★
Export Buying Offices Association
74 Great Titchfield St
London W1P 7AF
Phone: 071-493 8141
Fax: 071-636 7225

★1496★
**Export Group for the Constructional
   Industries**
Kingsbury House
15-17 King St
London SW1Y 6QU
Phone: 071-930 5377

★1497★
External Wall Insulation Association
PO Box 12
Haslemere GU27 3AH
Phone: 0428 54011
Fax: 0428 51401

★1498★
Fabric Care Research Association
Forest House Laboratories
Knaresborough Rd

Harrogate HG2 7LZ
Phone: 0423 885977
Fax: 0423 880045

Membership covers organisations in textile
aftercare, dry cleaners, launderers, workwear
and textile rental

★1499★
Faculty of Actuaries
23 St Andrew Square
Edinburgh EH2 1AQ
Phone: 031-557 1575

★1500★
Faculty of Advocates
Advocates Library
Parliament House
Edinburgh EH1 1RF
Phone: 031-226 5071
Fax: 031-225 3642

★1501★
Faculty of Architects & Surveyors
   now Architects & Surveyors Institute

★1502★
Faculty of Astrological Studies
BM 7470
London WC1N 3XX
Phone: 071-700 3556

★1503★
Faculty of Building
12 High St
Elstree WD6 3EP
Phone: 081-207 0366
Fax: 081-950 1025

Covers construction, civil engineering and
allied interests

★1504★
Faculty of Business Education
c/o L V J Garner
The Old School
Pant Glas
Oswestry SY10 7HS
Phone: 0691 654019
Fax: 0691 670235

For teachers of commercial subjects in
schools and colleges

★1505★
Faculty of Church Music
27 Sutton Park
Blunsdon
Swindon SN2 4BB
Phone: 081-675 0180

★1506★
Faculty of Community Medicine
4 St Andrew's Place
London NW1 4LB
Phone: 071-935 0243

★1507★
Faculty of Dental Surgery
Royal College of Surgeons
35-43 Lincoln's Inn Fields
London WC2A 3PN
Phone: 071-405 3474
Fax: 071-831 9438

★1508★
Faculty of Homoeopathy
c/o Royal London Homoeopathic Hospital
Great Ormond St
London WC1N 3HR
Phone: 071-837 9469
Fax: 071-278 7900

★1509★
**Faculty of Royal Designers for
  Industry**
6-8 John Adam St
London WC2N 6EZ
Phone: 071-930 5115
Fax: 071-839 5805

★1510★
**Faculty of Secretaries &
  Administrators**
15 Church St
Godalming GU7 1EL
Phone: 0483 425144

For those engaged in secretarial, administrative or management work

★1511★
Fairground Society
c/o Rutland Cottage Museum
Hillgate

Whaplode St Catherines
Spalding PE12 6SF
Phone: 040634 379

★1512★
Farm & Rural Buildings Centre
c/o National Agricultural Centre
Stoneleigh
Kenilworth CV8 2LG
Phone: 0203 696503
Fax: 0203 696900

A reference source on farm buildings and fixed equipment

★1513★
Farriers Registration Council
PO Box 49
East of England Showground
Peterborough PE2 0GU
Phone: 0733 234451
Fax: 0733 370038

★1514★
Fauna & Flora Preservation Society
79-83 North St
Brighton BN1 1ZA
Phone: 0273 820445

Concern for the environment and its wildlife

★1515★
Federation against Copyright Theft
7 Victory Business Centre
Worton Rd
Isleworth TW7 6ER
Phone: 081-568 6646
Fax: 081-560 6364

Members are film and video companies taking action against piracy of copyright in films, television programmes and audio visual recordings

★1516★
**Federation of Agricultural Co-
  operatives**
17 Waterloo Place
Leamington Spa CV32 5LA
Phone: 0926 450445
Fax: 0926 883699

★1517★
Federation of Associations of
Specialists & Sub-Contractors
Hodwell House
Norton Rd
Stevenage SG1 2BB
Phone: 0438 743159
Fax: 0438 743165

★1518★
Federation of Automatic Transmission
Engineers
PO Box 25
Marple
Stockport SK6 5AD
Phone: 061-427 3050
Fax: 061-477 4303

★1519★
Federation of Bakers
20 Bedford Square
London WC1B 3HF
Phone: 071-580 4252
Fax: 071-255 1389

★1520★
Federation of British Artists
17 Carlton House Terrace
London SW1Y 5BD
Phone: 071-930 6844
Fax: 071-839 7830

★1521★
Federation of British Audio
Landseer House
19 Charing Cross Rd
London WC2H 0ES
Phone: 071-930 3206
Fax: 071-839 4613

Manufacturers of hi-fi equipment and accessories

★1522★
Federation of British Cremation
Authorities
4 Salisbury Rd
Carshalton SM5 3HA
Phone: 081-669 4521

★1523★
Federation of British Engineers' Tool
Manufacturers
Light Trades House
3 Melbourne Avenue
Sheffield S10 2QJ
Phone: 0742 663084
Fax: 0742 670910

★1524★
Federation of British Fire
Organisations *now* Fire Protection
Association

★1525★
Federation of British Hand Tool
Manufacturers
Light Trades House
3 Melbourne Avenue
Sheffield S10 2QJ
Phone: 0742 663084
Fax: 0742 670910

★1526★
Federation of British Kipperers,
Herring Merchants & Herring Trade
Quick Freezers Associations
1 East Craibstone St
Aberdeen AB9 1YH
Phone: 0224 581581
Fax: 0224 580119

★1527★
Federation of British Port Wholesale
Fish Merchants Association
Fish Dock Rd
Grimsby DN31 3NG
Phone: 0472 350022
Fax: 0472 240838

★1528★
Federation of Building Specialist
Contractors
82 New Cavendish St
London W1M 8AD
Phone: 071-580 5588
Fax: 071-681 3872

★1529★
Federation of Children's Book Groups
c/o M Adey
The Old Malthouse
Aldbourne
Marlborough   SN8 2DW

★1530★
Federation of Civil Engineering Contractors
Cowdray House
6 Portugal St
London   WC2A 2HH
Phone: 071-404 4020
Fax: 071-242 0256

★1531★
Federation of Clothing Designers & Executives
11 Prior Avenue
Sutton
Surrey   SM2 5HX
Phone: 081-642 1667

★1532★
Federation of Commodity Associations
c/o A Rucker
1 Commodity Quay
St Katharine's Dock
London   E1 9AX
Phone: 071-481 2080
Fax: 071-702 9924

★1533★
Federation of Communication Services
c/o J Malcolm
Keswick House
20 Anerley Rd
London   SE20 8ER
Phone: 081-778 5656
Fax: 8402

Represents the mobile communications industry including network operators, service providers, equipment manufacturers and suppliers, dealers in cellular PMR, Band III, paging, PCN, CT2 and all supporting businesses

★1534★
Federation of Crafts & Commerce
Federation House
Rodney Rd

Southsea
Portsmouth   PO4 8SY
Phone: 0705 817224
Fax: 0705 818592

★1535★
Federation of Dredging Contractors
5th Floor
Ingersoll House
9 Kingsway
London   WC2B 6XF
Phone: 071-240 9971
Fax: 071-240 9692

Primarily marine dredging

★1536★
Federation of Drum Reconditioners
20-21 Tooks Court
London   EC4A 1LB
Phone: 071-831 7581
Fax: 071-405 1291

★1537★
Federation of Engine Remanufacturers
Jefferson House
18 Orchard Lane
Guiseley
Leeds   LS20 9HZ
Phone: 0943 870825
Fax: 0943 870858

Promotes the reconstruction of gasoline and diesel engines

★1538★
Federation of Engineering Design Companies
Suite 106
Grosvenor Gardens House
35-37 Grosvenor Gardens
London   SW1W 0BS
Phone: 071-828 0625
Fax: 071-828 0507

★1539★
Federation of English Language Course Organisations
2 Pontypool Place
London   SE1 8QF
Phone: 071-242 3136
Telex: 28905

★1540★
Federation of Environmental Trade Associations
Sterling House
6 Furlong Rd
Bourne End
Maidenhead SL8 5DG
Phone: 06285 31186
Fax: 0628 810423

Encompasses trade associations in building services and environmental control industries

★1541★
Federation of Epoxy Resin Formulators & Applicators
c/o Charles Allen Associates
241 High St
Aldershot GU11 1TJ
Phone: 0252 336318

★1542★
Federation of Ethical Stage Hypnotists
c/o P Casson
Winston
Church Hill
Royston
Barnsley S71 4NH
Phone: 0226 722555

★1543★
Federation of European Marketing Research Associations
Studio 38
Wimbledon Business Centre
Riverside Rd
London SW17 0BA
Phone: 081-879 0709
Fax: 081-947 2637

Primarily industrial and technical interests

★1544★
Federation of Family History Societies
Benson Room
Birmingham & Midland Institute
Margaret St
Birmingham B3 3BS
Phone: 0743 65505

Information available on genealogical, heraldry and family history organisations worldwide having British ancestral connections.

★1545★
Federation of Fresh Meat Wholesalers
227 Central Markets
Smithfield
London EC1A 9LH
Phone: 071-329 0776
Fax: 071-329 0653

All aspects of wholesale fresh meat trades including slaughtering

★1546★
Federation of Garden & Leisure Manufacturers
96 Church St
Great Bedwyn
Marlborough SN8 3PF
Phone: 0672 7870392
Fax: 0672 870788

Covering the leisure gardening trade with an emphasis on exports

★1547★
Federation of Independent Advice Centres
London Regional Office
13 Stockwell Rd
London SW9 9AU
Phone: 051-709 6952
Fax: 7444

Trade association for independent and charitable advice centres

★1548★
Federation of London Wholesale Newspaper Distributers *now* incorporated with Association of Newspaper & Magazine Wholesalers

★1549★
Federation of Manufacturers of Construction Equipment & Cranes
Carolyn House
22-26 Dingwall Rd
Croydon CR0 9XF
Phone: 081-688 2727
Fax: 081-681 2134

Represents the interests of manufacturers of contractors plant

★1550★
Federation of Manufacturing Opticians
37-41 Bedford Row
London WC1R 4JH
Phone: 071-405 8101
Fax: 2797

★1551★
Federation of Master Builders
Gordon Fisher House
14-15 Great James St
London WC1N 3DP
Phone: 071-242 7583
Fax: 071-404 0296

Primarily for the small and medium-sized building firms

★1552★
Federation of Master Organ Builders
c/o D M Van Heck
Petersfield GU32 3AT
Phone: 0730 62151

★1553★
Federation of Merchant Tailors
32 Savile Row
London W1X 1AG
Phone: 071-734 0173

Concerned with the interests of retail bespoke tailors

★1554★
Federation of Music Industries
c/o Arthur Spencer-Bolland
24 Fairlawn Grove
London W4 5EH
Phone: 081-995 0295
Fax: 081-742 2396

★1555★
Federation of Oils, Seeds & Fats Associations
24 St Mary Axe
London EC3A 8ER
Phone: 071-283 2707
Fax: 071-623 1310

★1556★
Federation of Ophthalmic & Dispensing Opticians
113 Eastbourne Mews
London W2 6LQ
Phone: 071-258 0240
Fax: 071-724 1175

★1557★
Federation of Overseas Property Developers Agents & Consultants
PO Box 981
Brighton BN2 2FT
Phone: 0273 777647
Fax: 0273 779122

★1558★
Federation of Petroleum Suppliers
Suite 24
500 Manchester Rd East
Manchester M28 6NS
Phone: 061-779 5181
Fax: 061-790 2624

Representing distributors of petroleum products but excluding major oil companies

★1559★
Federation of Piling Specialists
20-21 Tooks Court
London EC4A 1LB
Phone: 071-831 7581
Telex: FAS: 071-405 1291

★1560★
Federation of Private Residents' Associations
11 Dartmouth St
London SW1H 9BL
Phone: 071-222 0037

For those holding long leases on their properties

★1561★
Federation of Recorded Music Societies
Withyfeld
192c Woodrow Forest
Melksham SN12 7RF
Phone: 0225 707710

★1562★
Federation of Recruitment &
  Employment Services
36-38 Mortimer St
London W1N 7RB
Phone: 071-323 4300
Fax: 071-255 2878

★1563★
Federation of Resource Centres
c/o Gloucestershire Play Resource Centre
Unit 2
1 Badminton Close
Naunton Lane
Cheltenham GL53 7BX
Phone: 0242 221700

★1564★
Federation of Sailing & Motor Cruising
  Schools
c/o Kay Compton
Staddlestones
Fletchworth Lane
Totton
Southampton SO4 2DZ
Phone: 0703 869956

★1565★
Federation of Small Mines of GB
29 King St
Newcastle under Lyme ST5 1ER
Phone: 0782 614618
Fax: 0782 717287

★1566★
Federation of Sports Goods
  Distributors
20 Costells Edge
Scaynes Hill
Haywards Heath RH17 7PY
Phone: 0444 86410

For retail sports shops

★1567★
Federation of Wholesale & Industrial
  Distributors Co-ordinating
  Committee
c/o J Hussey
The Old Post Office
Dunchideock

Exeter EX2 9TU
Phone: 0392 832559

Membership is open to all organisations representing distributors of consumer goods (non-food)

★1568★
Federation of Wholesale Distributors
36 The Goffs
Eastbourne BN21 1HD
Phone: 0323 24952
Fax: 0323 32820

★1569★
Federation of Wire Rope
  Manufacturers of GB
c/o C M Rainer
John Shaw Ltd
Sandy Lane
Worksop S80 3ES
Phone: 0909 473321
Fax: 0909 500199

★1570★
Fellowship of Engineering
2 Little Smith St
London SW1P 3DL
Phone: 071-222 2688
Fax: 071-233 0054

Members are chartered engineers in all the various branches

★1571★
Fellowship of Makers & Researchers
  of Historical Instruments
c/o Oxford University
Faculty of Music
St Aldate's
Oxford OX1 1DB
Fax: 0865 276128

Promotes the preservation, reconstruction and use of historical musical instruments

★1572★
Fellowship of Skilled Secretaries
20 Sylvan Way
West Wickham
Croydon BR4 9HB
Phone: 081-462 5030

★1573★
Fellowship of Sports Masseurs & Therapists
36 Lodge Drive
London N13 5JZ
Phone: 081-886 3120

★1574★
Fencing Contractors Association
23 St Johns Rd
Watford WD1 1PY
Phone: 0923 248895
Fax: 0923 31134

★1575★
Ferro Alloys & Metals Producers Association
The Fountain Precinct
1 Balm Green
Sheffield S1 3AF
Phone: 0742 766789
Fax: 0742 766213

★1576★
Fertiliser Manufacturers' Association
Greenhill House
Thorpe Wood
Peterborough PE3 6GF
Phone: 0733 331303
Fax: 0733 333617

★1577★
Fibre Building Board Organisation
1 Hanworth Rd
Feltham TW13 5AF
Phone: 081-751 6107

Represents manufacturers, agents, distributors and importers of fibre boards

★1578★
Fibre Cement Manufacturers' Association
PO Box 92
Elmswell
Bury St Edmunds IP30 9HS
Phone: 0359 259379
Fax: 0359 259385

★1579★
Field Studies Council
Preston Montford
Montford Bridge
Shrewsbury SY4 1HW
Phone: 0743 850674

★1580★
File Association
Light Trades House
3 Melbourne Avenue
Sheffield S10 2QJ
Phone: 0742 663084
Fax: 0742 670910

★1581★
Film & Television Lighting Contractors Association
20 Darwin Close
London N11 1TA
Phone: 081-361 2122

★1582★
Film & TV Press Guild
9 Compayne Gardens
London NW6 3DG

★1583★
Filtration Society
7 Manor Close
Oadby
Leicester LE2 4FE
Phone: 0533 720536

Covers filtration and separation in all industries

★1584★
Finance Houses Association
18 Upper Grosvenor St
London W1X 9PB
Phone: 071-491 2783
Fax: 071-629 0396

Represents companies providing instalment finance to industry and the consumer

★1585★
Financial Intermediaries, Managers & Brokers Regulatory Authority
Hertsmere House
Marsh Wall

London E14 9RW
Phone: 071-538 8860
Fax: 071-895 8579

★1586★
Fine Art Trade Guild
16-18 Frances Place
London SW6 1TT
Phone: 071-381 6616
Fax: 071-381 2596

Members are predominantly gallery owners and picture framers

★1587★
Fingerprint Society
c/o M Leadbetter
2 Priory Lane
Little Wymondley
Stevenage SG4 7HE
Phone: 0438 359292

Members are fingerprint and scene-of-the-crime officers and the Society's aim is to further the study of fingerprinting as a forensic science

★1588★
Fire Extinguishing Trades Association
48a Eden St
Kingston upon Thames KT1 1EE
Phone: 081-549 8839
Fax: 081-547 1564

★1589★
Fire Fighting Vehicle Manufacturers' Association
c/o A Smith
Forbes House
Halkin St
London SW1X 7DS
Phone: 071-235 7000
Fax: 071-235 7112

★1590★
Fire Industry Council
48a Eden St
Kingston upon Thames KT1 1EE
Phone: 081-549 8839
Fax: 081-547 1564

★1591★
Fire Protection Association
140 Aldersgate St
London EC1A 4HX
Phone: 071-606 3757
Fax: 071-600 1487

★1592★
Fish & Meat Spreadable Products Association *now* incorporated into Food & Drink Federation

★1593★
Fisheries Society of the British Isles
c/o Dr A P Scott
Fisheries Laboratory
Ministry of Agriculture, Fisheries & Food
Pakefield Rd
Lowestoft NR33 0HT

All aspects of fish biology and fishing science

★1594★
Fishing Boat Builders' Association
20 Queens Rd
Aberdeen AB1 6YT
Phone: 0224 645454
Fax: 0224 644701

★1595★
Fitness Industry Association
10 Barley Mow Passage
London W4 4PH
Phone: 081-994 6477
Fax: 081-994 1533

Members are commercial health clubs, local authority leisure centres, user groups, suppliers to the industry, consultants and individuals

★1596★
Flag Institute
10 Vicarage Rd
Chester CH2 3HZ
Phone: 0244 351335
Fax: 0244 341894

All aspects of flags and related subjects, members include manufacturers, museums, government departments and individuals

★1597★
Flat Glass Council
44-48 Borough High St
London SE1 1XB
Phone: 071-403 7177
Fax: 071-357 7458

★1598★
Flat Glass Manufacturers Association
Prescot Rd
St Helens WA10 3TT
Phone: 0744 28882
Fax: 0744 35525

★1599★
Flat Roofing Contractors Advisory Board
Maxwelton House
Boltro Rd
Haywards Heath RH16 1BJ
Phone: 0444 440027
Fax: 0444 415616

Covering built-up flat roofing and ancillary materials

★1600★
Flax & Linen Association
1 Bank St
Dundee DD1 1RN
Phone: 0382 25691

★1601★
Flax Merchants Association
c/o Malcom MacLaine Ltd
18-25 Eldon St
London EC2M 7LA
Phone: 071-638 8144
Telex: 8814395

★1602★
Flexible Intermediate Bulk Container Association
140 Camphill Rd
Broughty Ferry
Dundee DD5 2NF
Phone: 0382 480049
Fax: 0382 480130

★1603★
Flour Advisory Bureau
21 Arlington St
London SW1A 1RN
Phone: 071-493 2521
Fax: 071-493 6785

★1604★
Flour Milling & Baking Research Association
Chorleywood
Rickmansworth WD3 5SH
Phone: 09278 4111
Fax: 09278 4539

Fundamental chemical research, nutrition and toxicological work, development of new processes and instrumentation

★1605★
Flowers & Plants Association
Covent House
New Covent Garden Market
London SW8 5NX
Phone: 071-738 8044
Fax: 071-622 5307

To advertise and promote the sales of cut flowers and pot plants to the public in the UK

★1606★
Folklore Society
c/o University College
Gower St
London WC1E 6BT
Phone: 071-387 5894

★1607★
Folly Fellowship
Woodstock House
Winterhill Way
Burpham
Guildford GU4 7JX
Phone: 0483 65634

Concerned with the care and preservation of follies, grottoes and garden buildings

★1608★
Food & Drink Federation
6 Catherine St

London WC2B 5JJ
Phone: 071-836 2460
Fax: 071-836 0580

Represents the UK food manufacturing industry

★1609★
Food Additives Industry Association
Kings Building
Smith Square
London SW1P 3JJ
Phone: 071-834 3399
Fax: 071-834 4469

★1610★
Football Association
16 Lancaster Gate
London W2 3LW
Phone: 071-262 4542
Fax: 071-402 0486

★1611★
Football Writers' Association
c/o D Signy
223 Great North Way
London NW4 1PN
Phone: 081-203 0962

★1612★
Footwear Components Federation
c/o Chamberlain Phipps Ltd
Heathfield Way
Northampton NNS 7QV
Phone: 0604 750878
Fax: 0604 750878

★1613★
Footwear Distributors Federation
69-79 Fullham High St
London SW6 3JW
Phone: 071-371 5177
Fax: 071-371 0529

★1614★
Foreign Banks & Securities Houses Association
c/o I G Mackay
68 Lombard St
London EC3V 9LJ
Phone: 071-955 5495

★1615★
Foreign Exchange & Currency Deposit Brokers' Association
c/o D Rickson
Euro Brokers Ltd
Adelaide House
London Bridge
London EC4R 9EQ
Phone: 071-626 2691
Fax: 071-626 3820

Advisory body liaising between London brokers, banks and the Bank of England in all aspects of the foreign exchange market

★1616★
Foreign Press Association in London
11 Carlton House Terrace
London SW1Y 5AJ
Phone: 071-930 0445
Fax: 071-925 0469

Members are London-based foreign journalists, freelance foreign and British journalists, press and PR officers and embassy press attaches

★1617★
Forensic Science Society
Clarke House
18a Mount Parade
Harrogate HG1 1BX
Phone: 0423 506068
Fax: 0423 539048

Members are scientists, lawyers, pathologists, police officers, surgeons and odontologists

★1618★
Forestry Industry Committee of GB
Admel House
24 High St
London SW19 5DX
Phone: 081-944 6340
Fax: 081-944 6308

Membership consists of enterprises, organisations and professional associations within the private sector of the forestry industry, and encompasses activities from silvicultural research to the commercial processing of timber

★1619★
Fork Truck Hire Association
c/o H C Hinder
150 Poplar Rd South
London   SW19 3JY
Phone: 081-542 5396
Fax: 081-543 9234

★1620★
Formula Air Racing Association
c/o The Tiger Club
Redhill Aerodrome
Redhill
Phone: 0737 822212

★1621★
Fortress Study Group
c/o D W Quarmby
Blackwater Forge Home
Blackwater
Newport
Isle of Wight   PO30 3BJ
Phone: 0983 526207

All aspects of fortifications and their arma-
ments, especially works constructed to mount
or resist artillery

★1622★
**Foundation for Management
   Education**
Sun Alliance House
New Inn Hall St
Oxford   OX1 2QE
Phone: 0865 251486
Fax: 0865 723488

★1623★
**Foundry Equipment & Supplies
   Association**
Queensway House
2 Queensway
Redhill   RH1 1QS
Phone: 0737 768611
Fax: 0737 760467

★1624★
Fountain Society
16 Gayfere St

London   SW1P 3HP
Phone: 071-222 6037

Covering fountains, cascades and waterfalls

★1625★
Freight Transport Association
Hermes House
St Johns Rd
Tunbridge Wells   TN4 9UZ
Phone: 0892 26171
Fax: 0892 34989

Serving the interests of businesses concerned
with the movements of goods or freight by
road, rail, sea or air

★1626★
Freshwater Biological Association
The Ferry House
Ambleside   LA22 0LP
Phone: 09662 2468
Fax: 09662 6914

Includes biological, chemical and ecological
aspects of freshwater study

★1627★
Frozen Food Producers Association
now United Kingdom Association of
   Frozen Food Producers

★1628★
Fruit Importers Association
408-409 Market Towers
1 Nine Elms Lane
London   SW8 5NQ
Phone: 071-720 1387
Fax: 071-498 0058

Covers the fresh fruit and vegetable industries

★1629★
**Funeral Furnishing Manufacturers
   Association**
66-69 Devon St
Saltley
Birmingham   B7 4SL
Phone: 021-359 6868
Fax: 021-359 5438

★1630★
Fur Education Council
PO Box 1EW

London W1A 1EW
Phone: 071-935 4328

★1631★
Furniture History Society
c/o Furniture & Woodwork Collection
Victoria & Albert Museum
Cromwell Rd
London SW7 2RL
Phone: 071-373 7250

★1632★
**Furniture Industry Research
  Association**
Maxwell Rd
Stevenage SG1 2EW
Phone: 0438 313433
Fax: 0438 727607

All aspects of furniture performance and
associated materials

★1633★
Galvanizers Association
Wrens Court
56 Victoria Rd
Sutton Coldfield
Birmingham B72 1SY
Phone: 021-355 8838
Fax: 021-355 8727

★1634★
Gambica *see* Association for the
  Instrumentation Control &
  Automation Industry in the UK

★1635★
Game Conservancy Trust
Burgate Manor
Fordingbridge SP6 1EF
Phone: 0425 652381
Fax: 0425 655848

Scientific research in the conservation of
game as a supplementary crop

★1636★
Game Farmers Association
Oddington Lodge
Moreton-in-Marsh GL56 0UR
Phone: 0233 85610

★1637★
Gamekeepers' Association *now*
incorporated into the British
Association for Shooting &
Conservation

★1638★
Garage Equipment Association
c/o A Smith
Forbes House
Halkin St
London SW1X 7DS
Phone: 071-235 7000
Fax: 071-235 7112

★1639★
Garden Centre Association
38 Carey St
Reading RG1 7JS
Phone: 0734 393900

★1640★
Garden History Society
c/o 5 The Knoll
Hereford HR1 1RU
Phone: 0432 354479

★1641★
**Garden Industry Manufacturers
  Association**
20 Harborne Rd
Birmingham B15 3AB
Phone: 021-454 4385
Fax: 021-452 1812

★1642★
Garden Machinery Association
Church St
Rickmansworth WD3 1RQ
Phone: 0923 778255
Fax: 0923 896063

★1643★
Gas Consumers Council
Abford House
15 Wilton Rd
London SW1V 1LT
Phone: 071-931 0977
Fax: 071-630 9934

★1644★
Gauge & Tool Makers' Association
3 Forge House
Summerleys Rd
Princes Risborough   HP17 2HL
Phone: 0844 274222
Fax: 0844 274227

Concerned with jigs, fixtures, press tools, moulds and dies, measuring equipment and special tooling

★1645★
Gemmological Association of GB
27 Greville St
London   EC1N 8SU
Phone: 071-404 3334
Fax: 071-404 8843

★1646★
General Aviation Manufacturers & Traders Association
26 High St
Brill
Aylesbury   HP18 9ST
Phone: 0844 238389
Telex: 838807

Members are aircraft operators concerned with air taxi, charter and commuter light transportation

★1647★
General Aviation Safety Committee
Holly Tree Cottage
Park Corner
Nettlebed
Henley-on-Thames   RG9 6DP
Phone: 0491 641735

★1648★
General Council & Register of Naturopaths
6 Netherhall Gardens
London   NW3 5RR
Phone: 071-435 8728

★1649★
General Council & Register of Osteopaths
54 London St

Reading   RG1 4SQ
Phone: 0734 576585

★1650★
General Council of British Shipping
30-32 St Mary Axe
London   EC3A 8ET
Phone: 071-283 2922
Fax: 071-626 8135

Covering the interests of British ship owners, ship managers and associated companies

★1651★
General Council of the Bar
11 South Square
Gray's Inn
London   WC1R 5EL
Phone: 071-242 0082
Fax: 071-831 9217

The professional and governing body for barristers

★1652★
General Dental Council
37 Wimpole St
London   W1M 8DQ
Phone: 071-486 2171
Fax: 071-224 3294

Concerned with dental education at all levels and maintains the dentistry register and the rolls of dental auxiliaries

★1653★
General Dental Practitioners Association
GDPD House
High St
Thorpe-le-Soton
Clacton-on-Sea   CO16 0DY
Phone: 0255 861829
Fax: 0255 862346

★1654★
General Medical Council
44 Hallam St
London   W1N 6AE
Phone: 071-580 7642
Fax: 071-436 1384

★1655★
General Optical Council
41 Harley St
London W1N 2DJ
Phone: 071-580 3898
Fax: 071-436 3525

★1656★
General Products Association *now*
incorporated into Food & Drink
Federation

★1657★
General Studies Association
c/o Ampleforth College
York YO6 4ER
Phone: 0439 3361
Fax: 0439 3206

★1658★
General Teaching Council for Scotland
5 Royal Terrace
Edinburgh EH7 5AF
Phone: 031-557 6773

★1659★
Geographical Association
343 Fulwood Rd
Sheffield S10 3BP
Phone: 0742 670666

★1660★
Geological Society
Burlington House
Piccadilly
London W1V 0JU
Phone: 071-434 9944

★1661★
Geologists Association
Burlington House
Piccadilly
London W1V 9AG
Phone: 071-434 9298
Fax: 071-287 0280

Serving the interests of the amateur geologist

★1662★
Giftware Association
10 Vyse St

Birmingham B18 6LT
Phone: 021-236 2657
Fax: 021-236 3921

★1663★
**Gilt Edged Market Makers Association
  Committee**
7th Floor
The Stock Exchange
Old Broad St
London EC2N 1HP
Phone: 071-588 2355

★1664★
Gin & Vodka Assocation of GB
Strangford
Amport
Andover SP11 8AX
Phone: 0264 773089
Fax: 0264 773085

★1665★
Girls' Schools Association
130 Regent Rd
Leicester LE1 7PG
Phone: 0533 541619
Fax: 0533 471152

★1666★
Glass & Allied Trades Association
c/o E Ormond
Flat 7
3 Pond Rd
London SE3 9JL
Phone: 071-248 4444
Telex: 888941

Members are importers of glass and crystal
table ware

★1667★
Glass & Glazing Federation
44-48 Borough High St
London SE1 1XB
Phone: 071-403 7177
Fax: 071-357 7458

Members are manufacturers, processors and
installers of architectural glass and frames

★1668★
Glass Manufacturers Federation *see*
British Glass Confederation

★1669★
**Glassfibre Reinforced Cement
Association**
5 Upper Bar
Newport
Telford TF10 7EH
Phone: 0952 820397

★1670★
Glasshouse Crop Research Institute
see Institute of Horticulture

★1671★
Golf Ball Manufacturers Conference
23 Brighton Rd
Croydon CR2 6EA
Phone: 081-681 1242
Fax: 081-681 0012

★1672★
Good Gardeners Association
Two Mile Lane
Highnam
Gloucester GL2 8DW
Phone: 0452 305814

★1673★
Governing Bodies Association
The Flat
Lambdens
Beenham
Reading RG7 5JY
Phone: 0734 302677

Concerning independent boys public schools

★1674★
**Governing Bodies of Girls Schools
Association**
Windleshaw Lodge
Withyham
Tunbridge Wells TN7 4BD

★1675★
Grain & Feed Trade Association
28 St Mary Axe

London EC3A 8ED
Phone: 071-283 5146
Fax: 071-626 4449

★1676★
Grand National Archery Society
7th St
National Agricultural Centre
Stoneleigh
Kenilworth CV8 2LG
Phone: 0203 696631
Fax: 0203 696900

The governing body for the sport of archery

★1677★
Graphic Reproduction Federation
c/o Chantrey Vellacott
Russell Square House
10-12 Russell Square
London WC1B 5LF
Phone: 071-436 3666

★1678★
Great Britain Pistol Council
4 Queens Gardens
Ossett
Wakefield WF5 8BD

★1679★
**Great Britain Target Shooting
Federation**
Lord Roberts House
Bisley Camp
Brookwood
Woking GU24 0NP
Phone: 0934 712145
Fax: 04867 6392

★1680★
Greeting Card & Calendar Association
6 Wimpole St
London W1M 8AS
Phone: 071-637 7692
Fax: 071-436 3137

★1681★
Guernsey Growers Association
Grange House
The Grange
St Peter Port

Channel Island
Phone: 0481 24227

★1682★
Guild of Agricultural Journalists
c/o D Gomery
47 Court Meadow
Rotherfield TN6 3LP
Phone: 089-285 3187

★1683★
Guild of Air Pilots & Air Navigators
Cobham House
291 Gray's Inn Rd
London WC1X 8QF
Phone: 071-837 3323
Fax: 071-833 3190

★1684★
Guild of Architectural Ironmongers
8 Stepney Green
London E1 3JU
Phone: 071-790 3431
Fax: 071-790 8517

★1685★
Guild of Aviation Artists
71 Bondway
London SW8 1SQ
Phone: 071-735 0634

★1686★
Guild of British Animation
25 Noel St
London W1V 3RD
Phone: 071-434 2651
Fax: 071-434 9002

★1687★
Guild of British Film Editors
c/o A E Cox
Travair
Spurlands End Rd
Great Kingshill
High Wycombe HP1 2QX
Phone: 0494 712313

★1688★
Guild of British Newspaper Editors
Bloomsbury House
Bloomsbury Square
74-77 Great Russell St
London WC1B 3DA
Phone: 071-636 7014
Fax: 071-631 5119

★1689★
Guild of Business Travel Agents
Premier House
10 Greycoat Place
London SW1P 1SB
Phone: 071-222 2744

★1690★
Guild of Church Musicians
c/o J Ewington
Hillbrow
Godstone Rd
Bletchingley
Reigate RH1 4PJ
Phone: 0883 743168

The examining body for church musicians including singers in choirs

★1691★
Guild of Conservation Food Producers
c/o B D Lloyd-James
PO Box 157
Bradwell Common
Milton Keynes MK13
Phone: 0908 641042
Fax: 0908 691043

Members have wide experience in the production of foods using traditional farming practices and limit the number of pesticides and other chemicals on crops, restricting these to low-toxicity, biodegradable forms

★1692★
Guild of Experienced Motorists
East Grinstead House
East Grinstead RH9 1UF
Phone: 0342 324444

★1693★
Guild of Film Production Accountants & Financial Administrators
c/o Twickenham Film Studios
St Margarets
Twickenham TW1 2AW
Phone: 081-892 4477
Fax: 081-891 5574

★1694★
Guild of Guide Lecturers
2 Bridge St
London SW1A 2JR
Phone: 071-839 7438

The professional association of registered tourist board guides in Great Britain

★1695★
Guild of Hairdressers
5 Sealand Rd
Chester CH1 4LE
Phone: 0244 382213

★1696★
Guild of Hospital Pharmacists
79 Camden Rd
London NW1 9ES
Phone: 071-267 4422
Fax: 071-284 1679

The representative organisation of hospital pharmacists employed in the National Health Service

★1697★
Guild of International Songwriters & Composers
Sovereign House
12 Trewartha Rd
Penzance TR20 9ST
Phone: 0736 762826
Fax: 0736 763328

★1698★
Guild of Jewish Journalists
c/o The Jewish Chronicle
25 Furnival St
London EC4A 1JT
Phone: 071-405 9252
Fax: 071-405 9040

★1699★
Guild of Master Craftsmen
166 High St
Lewes BN7 1XU
Phone: 0273 478449
Fax: 0273 478606

★1700★
Guild of Metal Perforators
Carolyn House
22-26 Dingwall Rd
Croydon CR0 9XF
Phone: 081-688 6101
Fax: 081-681 2134

★1701★
Guild of Motoring Writers
c/o S Scott-Fairweather
30 The Cravens
Smallfield
Crawley RH6 9QS
Phone: 034284 3294

★1702★
Guild of Newspaper Editors
c/o S Boyd
The Scotsman
North Bridge
Edinburgh EH1 1YT
Phone: 031-225 2468

★1703★
Guild of Professional After Dinner Speakers
12 Little Bornes
Alleyn Park
London SE21 8SE
Phone: 081-670 5585
Fax: 081-670 0055

★1704★
Guild of Railway Artists
c/o F P Hodges
45 Dickens Rd
Warwick CV34 5NS
Phone: 0926 499246

★1705★
Guild of Taxidermists
c/o D Ferguson
Glasgow Museum & Art Gallery
Kelvingrove
Glasgow C3 2LA
Phone: 041-357 3929

★1706★
Guild of Television Cameramen
1 Churchill Rd
Whitchurch
Tavistock PL19 9BU
Phone: 0822 614405

★1707★
Guild Of Travel Writers
c/o G Thomas
90 Corringway
London W5 3HA
Phone: 081-998 2223

Members are professional travel journalists

★1708★
Gun Trade Association
c/o N S Brown
Fairbourne Cottage
Bunny Lane
Timsbury
Romsey SO51 OPG
Phone: 0794 68443

Concerned with all aspects of the sporting firearm industry in the UK

★1709★
Gypsum Products Development Association
c/o Peat Marwick McLintock
1 Puddle Dock
London EC4V 3PD
Phone: 071-583 2104
Fax: 071-583 1886

★1710★
Hairdressing Council
12 David House
45 High St
London SE25 6HJ
Phone: 081-771 6205

The statutory authority for hairdressing

★1711★
Hairdressing Manufacturers' & Wholesalers' Association
Clare Cottage
Oakbank
Haywards Heath RH16 1RR
Phone: 0444 452580

★1712★
Hand Knitting Association
c/o F Shackleton
Nappa House
Scott Lane
Riddlesden
Keighley BD20 5BU
Phone: 0535 603450

Members are companies or individuals engaged in any process connected with the production or distribution of hand knitting yarns

★1713★
Handkerchief & Household Linens Association
C Blane and Son
85 Plantation Rd
Ballydougan
Portadown BT63 5MJ
Phone: 0762 341317
Fax: 0762 341318

★1714★
Handsaw Association
Light Trades House
Melbourne Avenue
Sheffield S10 2QJ
Phone: 0742 663084
Fax: 0742 670910

★1715★
Harris Tweed Association
Ballantyne House
84 Academy St
Inverness IV1 1LU
Phone: 0463 231270
Fax: 0463 221596

★1716★
HATRA *see* Hosiery & Allied Trade Research Association

★1717★
**Hawick Knitwear Manufacturers
  Association**
32 Commercial Rd
Hawick   TD9 7AD
Phone: 0450 72983
Fax: 0450 77909

★1718★
Headmasters' Conference
130 Regent Rd
Leicester   LE1 7PG
Phone: 0533 854810
Fax: 0533 471152

Professional association of headmasters of
independent schools

★1719★
Headteachers' Association of Scotland
c/o Jordanhill College of Education
Southbrae Drive
Glasgow   G13 1PP
Phone: 041-950 3248

★1720★
**Health Food Manufacturers'
  Association**
Angel Court
High St
Godalming   GU7 1DT
Phone: 0483 426450
Fax: 0483 426921

The association for manufacturers, distributors and suppliers to the health food trade

★1721★
Health Visitors' Association
50 Southwark St
London   SE1 1UN
Phone: 071-378 7255
Fax: 071-407 3521

Professional association of health visitors and
school nurses

★1722★
**Healthcare Financial Management
  Association**
3 Robert St

London   WC2N 6BH
Phone: 071-895 8823
Fax: 071-895 8825

Promotes professional standards of financial
practice in the management and audit of
health services

★1723★
Hearing Aid Council
Moorgate House
201 Silbury Boulevard
Milton Keynes   MK9 1LZ
Phone: 0908 585442

Members are employers and dispensers of
hearing aids in the private sector

★1724★
Hearing Aid Industry Association
c/o A & M Hearing Ltd
Faraday Rd
Crawley   RH10 2LS
Phone: 0279 722023
Telex: 8954575

Covering manufacturers, importers, wholesalers and retailers

★1725★
**Heating & Ventilating Contractors'
  Association**
ESCA House
34 Place Court
London   W2 4JG
Phone: 071-229 2488
Fax: 071-727 9268

Covering heating, ventilating, air conditioning, refrigeration, energy conservation, heat
recovery, heat pumps, piping, and domestic
engineering installation work

★1726★
**Heating, Ventilating & Air
  Conditioning Manufacturers'
  Association**
Sterling House
6 Furlong Rd
Bourne End
Maidenhead   SL8 5DG
Phone: 0628 531186
Fax: 0628 810423

★1727★
Heavy Transport Association
c/o J Dyne
Aaron & Partners
Grosvenor Court
Foregate St
Chester CH1 1HG
Phone: 0244 315366
Fax: 0244 350660

Members are professional operators of special type vehicles and equipment pertaining to the heavy haulage industry

★1728★
Hen Packers Association
High Holborn House
52-54 High Holborn
London WC1V 6SX
Phone: 071-242 4683
Fax: 071-831 0624

★1729★
Heraldry Society
44-45 Museum St
London WC1A 1LY
Phone: 071-430 2172

Including armoury, genealogy and kindred subjects

★1730★
Herb Society
PO Box 415
London SW1P 2HE

★1731★
Herring Buyers Association
46 Moray Place
Edinburgh EH3 6BQ
Phone: 031-225 4548
Telex: 727868

★1732★
High Performance Pipe Association
Service House
61-63 Rochester Rd
Aylesford

Maidstone ME20 7BS
Phone: 0622 882093
Fax: 0622 882215

Members are manufacturers of ultra-rib uPVC gravity sewer system and associated products

★1733★
Highway & Traffic Technicians Association *now* Institute of Highway Incorporated Engineers

★1734★
Historic Houses Association
2 Chester St
London SW1X 7BB
Phone: 071-259 5688
Fax: 071-259 5590

Members are owners of historic houses, castles and gardens

★1735★
Historical Association
59a Kennington Park Rd
London SE11 4LH
Phone: 071-735 3901

Promotes the study and teaching of history at all educational levels

★1736★
Historical Breechloading Smallarms Association
c/o Imperial War Museum
Lambeth Rd
London SE1 6HZ
Phone: 071-416 5270

★1737★
Historical Commercial Vehicle Society
Iden Grange
Cranbrook Rd
Staplehurst TN12 0ET
Fax: 893227

For people interested in historic commercial vehicles over twenty years old

★1738★
Historical Metallurgy Society
c/o R Ward
1 Carlton House Terrace

London SW1Y 5DB
Phone: 071-839 4071
Fax: 071-839 4813

All aspects of metallurgical history including preservation of early iron blast furnaces and archaeometallurgy

★1739★
Hockey Association
16 Northdown St
London N1 9BG
Phone: 071-837 8878
Fax: 071-837 8163

★1740★
Home & Contract Furnishing Textiles Association
Reedham House
31 King St West
Manchester M3 2PF
Phone: 061-832 8684
Fax: 061-833 1740

★1741★
Home & School Council
81 Rustlings Rd
Sheffield S11 7AB
Phone: 0742 662467

Concerned with home-school relationships

★1742★
Home Brewing & Winemaking Manufacturers Association
Beechtree House
60 Saint Mary's Rd
Weybridge KT13 9PZ
Phone: 0932 848724
Fax: 0932 844613

★1743★
Home Brewing & Winemaking Trade Association
21 Cole Park Rd
Twickenham TW1 1HP
Phone: 081-891 1253

★1744★
Home Laundering Consultative Council
7 Swallow Place

London W1K 7AA
Phone: 071-408 0020
Fax: 071-493 6276

★1745★
Honey Importers & Packers Association
152-160 City Rd
London EC1V 2NP
Phone: 071-253 9421
Fax: 071-250 0065

★1746★
Hop Merchants' Association
Nettlestead Oast
Paddock Wood
Tonbridge TN12 6DA
Phone: 081-947 8551
Fax: 081-879 0589

Members trade in hops grown in England

★1747★
Horticultural & Contractors' Tools Association
Light Trades House
3 Melbourne Avenue
Sheffield S10 2QJ
Phone: 0742 663084
Fax: 0742 670910

★1748★
Horticultural Trades Association
19 High St
Theale
Reading RG7 5AH
Phone: 0734 303132
Fax: 0734 323453

Members are growers, seedsmen and retailers in the amenity andleisure horticultural industry

★1749★
Hosiery & Allied Trades Research Association
7 Gregory Boulevard
Nottingham NG7 6LD
Phone: 0602 623311
Fax: 0602 625450

★1750★
Hospital Disposable Fabric Convertors' Association
c/o Surgikos Ltd
Kirkton Campus
Livingston EH54 7AT
Phone: 0506 413441
Fax: 0506 414116

★1751★
Hospital Doctors' Association
The Old Court House
London Rd
Ascot SL5 7EN
Phone: 0344 26613

Concerned with the interests of junior hospital doctors

★1752★
Hospital Physicists' Association *see*
Institute of Physical Sciences in Medicine

★1753★
Hotel, Catering & Institutional Management Association
191 Trinity Rd
London SW17 7HN
Phone: 081-672 4251

★1754★
House Builders Federation
82 New Cavendish St
London W1M 8AD
Phone: 071-580 5588
Fax: 071-631 3872

Members are private housing developments companies

★1755★
Hydrographic Society
c/o M Boreham
Polytechnic of East London
Longbridge Rd
Dagenham RM8 2AS
Phone: 081-597 1946
Fax: 081-590 9730

The science of surveying at sea

★1756★
Hydrological Society
c/o Institution of Civil Engineers
1 Great George St
London SW1P 3AA
Phone: 071-630 0726
Fax: 071-222 7500

★1757★
Ice Cream Alliance
90-94 Gray's Inn Rd
London WC1X 8AH
Phone: 071-405 0712

★1758★
Ice Cream Federation
1 Green St
London W1Y 3RG
Phone: 071-629 0655
Fax: 071-499 9095

★1759★
Ileostomy Association of GB & Ireland
Amblehurst House
Black Scoth Lane
Mansfield NG18 4PF
Phone: 0623 28099

★1760★
Immigration Law Practitioners' Association
115 Old St
London EC1V 9JR
Phone: 071-250 1671

★1761★
Imperial Society of Teachers of Dancing
Euston Hall
Birkenhead St
London WC1H 8BE
Phone: 071-837 9967
Fax: 071-833 5981

A qualifying body for all forms of dance

★1762★
Importers of Madeira Wine
c/o Mathew Clark & Sons Ltd
183-185 Central St

London EC1V 8DR
Phone: 071-253 7646
Fax: 071-251 0263

★1763★
Incorporated Association of Architects & Surveyors
Jubilee House
Billing Brook Rd
Weston Favell
Northampton NN3 4NW
Phone: 0604 404121
Fax: 0604 784220

★1764★
Incorporated Association of Organists
24 Hither Green Lane
Abbey Park
Redditch B98 9BW
Phone: 0527 65555

An educational body whose objective is to advance the art of organ playing at all levels

★1765★
Incorporated Association of Preparatory Schools
138 Kensington Church St
London W8 4BN
Phone: 071-727 2316

Heads of independent preparatory schools

★1766★
Incorporated Brewers' Guild
8 Ely Place
London EC1N 6SD
Phone: 071-405 4565
Telex: 912881

For individuals

★1767★
Incorporated Phonographic Society
c/o Bishopsgate Institute
230 Bishopsgate
London EC2M 4QH
Phone: 071-247 6844

★1768★
Incorporated Society for Psychical Research
1 Adam & Eve Mews

London W8 6UG
Phone: 071-937 8984

★1769★
Incorporated Society of British Advertisers
44 Hertford St
London W1Y 8AE
Phone: 071-499 7502
Fax: 071-629 5355

★1770★
Incorporated Society of Licensed Trade Stocktakers
15 Deanburn Walk
Bo'ness EH51 ONB
Phone: 0506 825227

A certifying body for professional stocktakers

★1771★
Incorporated Society of Managers & Administators
25 Sunnybank Rd
Longsight
Manchester M13 OXF
Phone: 061-248 6844
Telex: 66637

★1772★
Incorporated Society of Musicians
10 Stratford Place
London W1N 9AE
Phone: 071-629 4413

For professional musicians (performers, teachers and composers)

★1773★
Incorporated Society of Organ Builders
c/o D M Van Heck
Petersfield GU32 3AT
Phone: 0730 62151

★1774★
Incorporated Society of Valuers & Auctioneers
3 Cadogan Gate

London SW1X OAS
Phone: 071-235 2282
Fax: 071-235 4390

Members are professionally qualified valuers,
auctioneers, estate agents and surveyors

★1775★
Independent Cellular Retailers
Federation
c/o Cole Communications
1 Central St
Manchester M2 5WR
Phone: 061-832 1638
Fax: 061-832 1641

Members are retailers of cellular telephones

★1776★
Independent Contractors Association
852 Melton Rd
Thurmaston
Leicester LE4 8BN
Phone: 0533 640083
Fax: 0533 640161

Members are independent computer contractors

★1777★
Independent Film Distributors'
Association
c/o S Brooks
Glenbuck Films
Glenbuck Rd
Surbiton KT6 6BT
Phone: 081-399 0022
Fax: 081-399 6651

★1778★
Independent Film, Video &
Photography Association
79 Wardour St
London W1V 3PH
Phone: 071-439 0460

★1779★
Independent Footwear Retailers'
Association
24 Fairlawn Grove
London W4 5EH
Phone: 081-994 6259

★1780★
Independent Healthcare Association
22 Little Russell St
London WC1A 2HT
Phone: 071-430 0537
Fax: 071-242 2681

★1781★
Independent National Computing
Association
852 Melton Rd
Thurmaston
Leicester LE4 8BN
Phone: 0533 640579
Fax: 0533 640141

For independent contractors

★1782★
Independent Programme Producers
Association
50-51 Berwick St
London W1A 4RD
Phone: 071-439 7034
Fax: 071-494 2700

The trade association for British independent
television producers

★1783★
Independent Publishers Guild
25 Cambridge Rd
Hampton
East Moseley TW12 2JL
Phone: 081-979 0250

Membership is open to publishing companies
which publish and produce books under their
own imprint, also to packagers and suppliers.
All are independent of any owning group or
consortia

★1784★
Independent Schools Association
c/o Boys British School
East St
Saffron Walden CB10 1LS
Phone: 0799 23619

★1785★
Independent Schools Bursars'
  Association
Woodlands
Closewood Rd
Denmead
Portsmouth PO7 6JD
Phone: 0705 264506

★1786★
Independent Schools Careers
  Organisation
12-18 Princess Way
Camberley GU15 3SP
Phone: 0276 21188

★1787★
Independent Schools Information
  Service
56 Buckingham Gate
London SW1E 6AG
Phone: 071-630 8793
Fax: 071-630 5013

★1788★
Independent Schools Joint Council
25 Victoria St
London SW1H 0EX
Phone: 071-222 4957

★1789★
Independent Secretarial Training
  Association
16 Marlborough Crescent
London W4 1HF

★1790★
Independent Television Association
Knighton House
56 Mortimer St
London W1N 8AN
Phone: 071-636 6866
Fax: 071-580 7892

Represents the interests of the ITV programme companies appointed by the Independent Broadcasting Authority

★1791★
Independent Theatre Council
Unit 129 West
Westminster Business Square
Durham St
London SE11 5JH
Phone: 071-820 1712

★1792★
Independent Waste Paper Processors
  Association
25 High St
Daventry NN11 4BG
Phone: 0327 703223
Fax: 0327 300612

★1793★
Industrial Agents Society
c/o N Higson
Herring Son & Dawe
26-28 Sackville St
London W1X 2QL
Phone: 071-734 8155
Fax: 071-437 1742

Representing surveyors and agents specialising in industrial property

★1794★
Industrial Catering Association *see*
  European Catering Association

★1795★
Industrial Cleaning Machine
  Manufacturers' Association
Leicester House
8 Leicester St
London WC2H 7BN
Phone: 071-437 0678
Fax: 071-437 4901

★1796★
Industrial Fire Protection Association
  of GB *see* Fire Protection
  Association

★1797★
Industrial Marketing Research
  Association
11 Bird St

Lichfield WS13 6PW
Phone: 0543 263448
Fax: 0543 250929

★1798★
Industrial Participation Association
87-95 Tooley St
London SE1 2RA
Phone: 071-403 6018
Fax: 071-407 9083

★1799★
Industrial Safety (Protective Equipment) Manufacturers Association
Central House
32-66 High St
London E15 2PS
Phone: 081-519 4872
Fax: 081-519 5483

★1800★
Industrial Society
3 Carlton House Terrace
London SW1Y 5DG
Phone: 071-839 4300

Concerned with practical problems which arise from all aspects of employment and industrial relations

★1801★
Industrial Tyre Association
Gothic Cottage
Tintern Parva
Chepstow NP6 6SQ
Phone: 0291 689534

★1802★
Industrial Water Society
1 Tolson's Mill
Lichfield St
Fazeley
Tamworth B78 3QB
Phone: 0827 289558
Fax: 0827 250408

Individuals who help industry and commerce to use water wisely and economically and protect the environment against effluent discharge

★1803★
Industry & Environment Association
77 Temple Sheen Rd
London SW14 7RS
Phone: 081-876 3367

★1804★
Industry Council for Packaging & the Environment
Premier House
10 Greycoat Place
London SW1P 1SB
Phone: 071-222 8866
Fax: 071-222 5358

A trade organisation which brings together all sectors of industry involved in the manufacture of packaging and the manufacture and retailing of packaged goods

★1805★
Infant & Dietetic Food Association
now incorporated into Food & Drink Federation

★1806★
Infection Control Nurses' Association
c/o Mrs J M Lawrence
Dept of Microbiology
Edgware General Hospital
Edgware HA8 0AD
Phone: 081-952 2381

★1807★
Inland Waterways Amenity Advisory Council
1 Queen Anne's Gate
London SW1H 9BT
Phone: 071-222 4939
Fax: 071-222 1811

The organisation advises on the use and development of cruising waterways for amenity and recreation

★1808★
Inland Waterways Association
114 Regent's Park Rd

London NW1 8UQ
Phone: 071-586 2556

Covers the restoration, retention and development of inland waterways for commercial and recreational use

★1809★
Insolvency Practitioners Association
18-19 Long Lane
London EC1A 9HE
Phone: 071-600 3601
Fax: 071-600 3602

★1810★
Institute for Animal Health
Compton Laboratory
Newbury RG16 ONN
Phone: 0635 578411

Concerned with research into animal diseases

★1811★
Institute for Complementary Medicine
21 Portland Place
London WIN 3AF
Phone: 071-636 9543

For practitioners in all branches of alternative medicine

★1812★
Institute for Consumer Ergonomics
73 Swingbridge Rd
Loughborough LE11 OJB
Phone: 0509 236161
Fax: 0509 610725

★1813★
Institute for Fiscal Studies
180-182 Tottenham Court Rd
London W1P 9LE
Phone: 071-636 3784

★1814★
Institute for International Communication
21 Meadowcourt Rd
London SE3 9EU
Phone: 081-318 9555
Fax: 081-318 9057

Members teach English to managers from abroad

★1815★
Institute for International Research
44 Conduit St
London W1R 9FD
Phone: 071-434 0301
Fax: 071-437 2336

★1816★
Institute for Scientific Information
132 High St
Uxbridge UB8 1DP
Phone: 0895 30085
Fax: 0895 56710

★1817★
Institute for Social Inventions
24 Abercorn Place
London NW8 9XP
Phone: 071-229 7253

★1818★
Institute for Social Studies in Medical Care
14 South Hill Park
London NW3 2SB
Phone: 071-794 7793

★1819★
Institute for the Study of Drug Dependence
1-11 Hatton Place
London EC1N 8ND
Phone: 071-430 1991
Fax: 071-404 4415

★1820★
Institute of Acoustics
c/o C M MacKenzie
PO Box 320
St Albans AL1 1PZ
Phone: 0727 48195
Fax: 0727 50553

★1821★
Institute of Actuaries
Staple Inn Hall
High Holborn
London WC1V 7QJ
Phone: 071-242 0106
Fax: 071-405 2482

★1822★
Institute of Administrative Management
40 Chatsworth Parade
Petts Wood
Orpington BR5 1RW
Phone: 0689 75555
Fax: 0689 70891

Members are individuals from industry and commerce involved in personnel managers and office administration

★1823★
Institute of Advanced Motorists
IAM House
359-365 Chiswick High Rd
London W4 4HS
Phone: 081-994 4403
Fax: 081-994 9249

★1824★
Institute of Agricultural Secretaries
c/o National Agricultural Centre
Stoneleigh
Kenilworth CV8 2LZ
Phone: 0203 696592
Fax: 0203 696900

★1825★
Institute of Animal Health
Ash Rd
Pirbright
Woking GU24 0NF
Phone: 0483 232441
Telex: 859137

★1826★
Institute of Animal Physiology & Genetics Research
Roslin
Edinburgh EH25 9PS
Phone: 031-440 2726
Fax: 031-440 0434

★1827★
Institute of Animal Physiology
Babraham
Cambridge CB2 4AT
Phone: 0223 832312
Fax: 0223 836122

★1828★
Institute of Architectural Ironmongers
8 Stepney Green
London E1 3JU
Phone: 071-790 3431
Fax: 071-790 8517

★1829★
Institute of Asphalt Technology
Unit 18
Central Trading Estate
Staines TW18 4XE
Phone: 0784 465387
Fax: 0784 463700

★1830★
Institute of Auctioneers & Appraisers in Scotland
10 Glenfinlas St
Edinburgh EH3 6YY
Phone: 031-226 5541
Fax: 031-226 2278

★1831★
Institute of Automotive Engineer Assessors
1 Love Lane
London EC2V 7JJ
Phone: 071-606 8744
Fax: 071-606 4057

Members are concerned to develop the science of design, manufacture and related technology of motor vehicles together with the science of repair and the insurance risks arising from the use of road vehicles

★1832★
Institute of Bankers in Scotland
20 Rutland Square
Edinburgh EH1 2DE
Phone: 031-229 9869
Fax: 031-229 1852

★1833★
Institute of Baths & Recreation Management
Gifford House
36-38 Sherrard St

Melton Mowbray   LE13 1XJ
Phone: 0664 65531
Fax: 0664 501155

Fosters the study of the technique and operation of swimming pools and indoor recreation centres

★1834★
Institute of Biology
20 Queensberry Place
London   SW7 2DZ
Phone: 071-581 8333
Fax: 071-823 9409

★1835★
Institute of Brewing
33 Clarges St
London   W1Y 8EE
Phone: 071-499 8144
Fax: 071-499 1156

For the advancement of education especially in the sciences of brewing, fermentation and distillation

★1836★
Institute of British Bakers
50 Sandygate Rd
Sheffield   S10 5RY
Phone: 0742 663383

★1837★
Institute of British Carriage & Automobile Manufacturers
31 Redstone Farm Rd
Hall Green
Birmingham   B28 9N4
Phone: 021-778 4354
Fax: 021-702 2615

★1838★
Institute of British Detective Investigative Security & Forensic Specialists
PO Box 389
Moseley
Birmingham   B13 8QU
Phone: 021-449 7735

★1839★
Institute of British Foundrymen
3rd Floor
Bridge House
121 Smallbrook Queensway
Birmingham   B5 4JP
Phone: 021-643 4523
Fax: 021-631 2872

★1840★
Institute of British Geographers
1 Kensington Gore
London   SW7 2AR
Phone: 071-584 6371

★1841★
Institute of Builders' Merchants
Parnall House
5 Parnall Rd
Staple Tye
Harlow   CM18 7PP
Phone: 0279 419650

★1842★
Institute of Building Control
21 High St
Ewell
Epsom   KT17 1SB
Phone: 081-393 6860
Fax: 081-393 1083

★1843★
Institute of Burial & Cremation Administration
c/o Robert Coates, The Gatehouse
Kew Meadow Path
Richmond-on-Thames   TW9 4EN
Phone: 081-876 8056

★1844★
Institute of Careers Officers
27a Lower High St
Stourbridge   DY8 1TA
Phone: 0384 376464

Professional body for those engaged in careers advisory work

★1845★
Institute of Carpenters
c/o J G Fairley
P O Box 111
Aldershot GU11 1YW
Phone: 0252 21302
Fax: 0252 333901

★1846★
Institute of Ceramics
Shelton House
Stoke Rd
Shelton
Stoke-on-Trent ST4 2DR
Phone: 0782 202116
Fax: 0782 202421

★1847★
**Institute of Charity Fund Raising
  Managers**
208 Market Towers
1 Nine Elms Lane
London SW8 5NQ
Phone: 071-627 3436
Fax: 3508

★1848★
**Institute of Chartered Accountants of
  Scotland**
27 Queen St
Edinburgh EH2 1LA
Phone: 031-225 5673
Telex: 727530
Fax: 031-225 3813

★1849★
**Institute of Chartered Accountants in
  England & Wales**
Chartered Accountants' Hall
Moorgate Place
London EC2P 2BJ
Phone: 071-628 7060
Fax: 071-920 0547

★1850★
Institute of Chartered Foresters
22 Walker St
Edinburgh EH3 7HR
Phone: 031-225 2705

★1851★
**Institute of Chartered Secretaries &
  Administrators**
16 Park Crescent
London W1N 4AH
Phone: 071-580 4741
Fax: 071-323 1132

★1852★
Institute of Chartered Shipbrokers
24 St Mary Axe
London EC3A 8DE
Phone: 071-283 1361
Fax: 071-283 1245

★1853★
Institute of Chiropodists
91 Lord St
Southport PR8 1SA
Phone: 0704 546141
Fax: 0704 500477

Members are qualified chiropodists both in
private practice and working for the National
Health Service

★1854★
**Institute of Civil Defence & Disaster
  Studies**
Bell Court House
11 Blomfield St
London EC2M 7AY
Phone: 071-588 3700

The professional body for emergency planning and civil defence officers and members
of civil defence units

★1855★
Institute of Classical Studies
c/o University of London
31-34 Gordon Square
London WC1H OPY
Phone: 071-387 7050 ext. 4726

★1856★
Institute of Clay Technology
High Trees
Brunswood Rd

Matlock   DE4 3PA
Phone: 0629 55302

All matters affecting the working of clay for use in production of bricks, tiles, pipes and similar products

★1857★
Institute of Clayworkers *see* British Ceramic Confederation

★1858★
Institute of Clerks of Works of GB
41 The Mall
London   W5 3TJ
Phone: 081-579 2917
Fax: 081-579 0554

★1859★
Institute of Clinical Aromatherapy
22 Bromley Rd
London   SE6 2TP
Phone: 081-690 6681

★1860★
Institute of Commerce
Marlowe House
Station Rd
Sidcup   DA5 7BJ
Phone: 081-302 0261
Fax: 081-302 4169

To promote and develop business education

★1861★
Institute of Commercial Management
ICM House
17 Hinton Rd
Bournemouth   BH1 2EE
Phone: 0202 290999
Fax: 0202 293497

An international examining body for business and management students

★1862★
Institute of Community Development
c/o Incorporated Society of Managers & Administrators
25 Sunnybank Rd
Longsight

Manchester   M13 0XF
Phone: 061-248 6844
Telex: 66637

★1863★
Institute of Company Accountants
40 Tyndalls Park Rd
Bristol   BS8 1PL
Phone: 0272 738261
Fax: 0272 238292

All aspects of accountancy and financial management

★1864★
Institute of Concrete Technology
PO Box 255
Beaconsfield
High Wycombe   HP9 1JE
Phone: 0494 674572

★1865★
Institute of Consumer Advisers
5 Cemetery Rd
Stapleford
Nottingham   NG9 8AP

★1866★
Institute of Contemporary History
4 Devonshire St
London   W1N 2BH
Phone: 071-636 7247

Research institute and library for European contemporary history

★1867★
Institute of Cooperative Directors
Holyoake House
Hanover St
Manchester   M60 0AS
Phone: 061-832 4300
Fax: 061-831 7684

Representing the retail cooperative trades

★1868★
Institute of Credit Management
Easton House
Easton-on-the-Hill

Stamford   PE9 3NH
Phone: 0780 56777
Fax: 0780 51610

The professional body for those involved in the credit management for both the public and private sectors

★1869★
Institute of Data Processing Management
IDPM House
Edgington Way
Ruxley Corner
Sidcup   DA14 5HR
Phone: 081-308 0747
Fax: 081-308 0604

A qualifying body particularly concerned with data processing in business administration

★1870★
Institute of Directors
116 Pall Mall
London   SW1Y 5ED
Phone: 071-839 1233
Fax: 071-930 1949

Represents the interests of individual business leaders

★1871★
Institute of Domestic Heating & Environmental Engineers
37a High Rd
Benfleet
Phone: 0268 754266

★1872★
Institute of Economics & Statistics
St Cross Building
Manor Rd
Oxford   OX1 3UL
Phone: 0865 271073
Fax: 0865 271094

★1873★
Institute of Ecotechnics
24 Old Gloucester St
London   WC1N 3AL
Phone: 071-242 7367

★1874★
Institute of Employment Consultants
6 Guildford Rd
Woking   GU22 7PX
Phone: 0483 766442
Fax: 714979

Educational and training body for individual recruitment professionals

★1875★
Institute of Employment Rights
98 St Pancras Way
London   NW1 9NZ
Phone: 071-482 3892
Fax: 071-482 3906

An independent organisation acting as a focal point for the spread of new ideas in the field of labour law. Members include trade union secretaries and labour law academics and practitioners

★1876★
Institute of Energy
18 Devonshire St
London   W1N 2AU
Phone: 071-580 7124
Fax: 071-580 4420

A professional body concerned with the effective provision, conversion transmission and use of energy in all its forms

★1877★
Institute of Engineers & Technicians
100 Grove Vale
London   SE22 8DR
Phone: 081-693 1255
Fax: 081-299 0862

The professional body for engineers, technicians and students

★1878★
Institute of Entertainment & Arts Management
3 Trinity Rd
Scarborough   YO11 2TD
Phone: 0723 367449

Members are individuals working in the management of theatres, entertainment centres, arts and allied industries

★1879★
Institute of Environmental Assessment
c/o Dr T Coles
Unit 6
The Old Malt House
Spring Gardens
Grantham NG31 6JP
Phone: 0476 68100
Fax: 0476 76476

Members are employed in environmental consultancies, local authorities, industry or educational establishments

★1880★
**Institute of European Trade &
   Technology**
64 West Smithfield
London EC1A 9DY
Phone: 071-606 2930
Fax: 071-606 2935

★1881★
**Institute of Executive Engineers &
   Officers** *now* Institution of
   Incorporated Executive Engineers

★1882★
Institute of Explosives Engineers
6th Floor
Epic House
Charles St
Leicester LE1 3SH
Phone: 0533 538915
Fax: 0533 511754

★1883★
Institute of Export
Export House
64 Clifton St
London EC2A 4HB
Phone: 071-247 9812

★1884★
Institute of Facilities Management
40 Chatsworth Parade
Petts Wood
Orpington BR5 1RW
Phone: 0689 75555

★1885★
Institute of Family Therapy
43 New Cavendish St
London W1M 7RG
Phone: 071-935 1651

Members teach and practice family therapy and develop standards in the assessment and treatment of families

★1886★
Institute of Field Archaeologists
Metallurgy & Materials Building
University of Birmingham
PO Box 363
Birmingham B15 2TT
Phone: 021-471 2788
Fax: 021-414 3952

★1887★
**Institute of Financial & Management
   Studies**
25 Stratfield Rd
Kidlington
Oxford OX5 1DH
Phone: 08675 77858

★1888★
Institute of Financial Accountants
   now International Asssociation of
   Book-keepers

★1889★
Institute of Financial Planning
Hereford House
East St
Hereford HR1 2LU
Phone: 0432 274891
Fax: 0432 353375

A professional body for people providing financial advice and services either as independents or as company representatives

★1890★
Institute of Fisheries Management
c/o Balmaha
Coldwells Rd
Holmer
Hereford
Phone: 0432 276225

★1891★
Institute of Food Science & Technology of the UK

5 Cambridge Court
210 Shepherds Bush Rd
London W6 7NL
Phone: 071-603 6316
Fax: 071-602 9936

★1892★
Institute of Freight Forwarders *now*
British International Freight
Association

★1893★
Institute of Freshwater Ecology

Windermere Laboratory
Far Sawrey
Ambleside LA22 0LP
Phone: 09662 2468/9
Fax: 09662 6914

★1894★
Institute of Grocery Distribution

Grange Lane
Letchmore Heath
Watford WD2 8DQ
Phone: 0923 857141
Fax: 0923 852531

Covers manufacturing, wholesaling distribution and retailing in the grocery trades

★1895★
Institute of Groundsmanship

19-23 Church St
Wolverton
Milton Keynes MK12 5LG
Phone: 0908 312511
Fax: 0908 311140

★1896★
Institute of Group Analysis

1 Daleham Gardens
London NW3 5BY
Phone: 071-431 2693

The professional association for group-analytic psychotherapists

★1897★
Institute of Health Education

14 High Elm Rd
Hale Barns
Altrincham WA15 0HS
Phone: 061-980 8276
Fax: 061-980 7446

Members are individuals concerned with the promotion of health and the prevention of illness in all sections of the community at home, school, work and leisure

★1898★
Institute of Health Services Management

75 Portland Place
London W1N 4AN
Phone: 071-580 5041

★1899★
Institute of Heraldic & Genealogical Studies

79-82 Northgate
Canterbury CT1 1BA
Phone: 0227 768664
Fax: 0227 765617

Offers a series of assessment tests and examinations leading to a range of qualifications in genealogical method and practice

★1900★
Institute of Highway Incorporated Engineers

20 Queensberry Place
London SW7 2DR
Phone: 071-823 9093
Fax: 071-823 9409

Dealing with all aspects of construction, highway and traffic engineering and transportation

★1901★
Institute of Holistic Therapies

c/o M Tradewell
PO Box 37
Scarborough YO11 1AR

★1902★
Institute of Home Economics
Aldwych House
71-91 Aldwych
London   WC2B 4HN
Phone: 071-404 5532
Fax: 071-242 1117

★1903★
Institute of Home Safety
c/o C A Rand
132 North Rd
Dartford   DA1 3NB
Phone: 081-854 8888   ext. 8076

Members are professionals working in the field of home accident prevention

★1904★
Institute of Horticulture
80 Vincent Square
London   SW1P 2PE
Phone: 071-976 5951
Fax: 071-630 6060

Members are professionally engaged in all aspects of horticulture industry management, and the growing and marketing of all edible and decorative crops

★1905★
Institute of Hospital Engineering
Cumberland Business Centre
Northumberland Rd
Portsmouth   PO5 1DS
Phone: 0705 823186
Fax: 0705 815927

The professional body for all concerned with health estate management and engineering in both the private and public sectors

★1906★
Institute of Housing
Octavia House
Westwood Way
Coventry   CV4 8JP
Phone: 0203 694433
Fax: 0203 695110

★1907★
Institute of Hydrology
Maclean Building
Crowmarsh Gifford
Wallingford   OX10 8BB
Phone: 0491 38800
Fax: 0491 32256

★1908★
Institute of Information Scientists
44 Museum St
London   WCIA ILY
Phone: 071-831 8003
Fax: 071-430 1270

★1909★
Institute of Insurance Brokers
Higham Business Centre
Midland Rd
Higham Ferrers
Northampton   NN9 8DW
Phone: 0933 410003
Fax: 0933 410020

For registered insurance brokers

★1910★
Institute of Internal Auditors
13 Abbeville Mews
88 Clapham Park Rd
London   SW4 7BX
Phone: 071-498 0101
Fax: 071-978 2492

★1911★
Institute of International Licensing Practitioners
c/o J Bingham-Dore
105 Onslow Square
London   SW7 3LU
Phone: 071-584 5749

For independent licensing consultants and agents

★1912★
Institute of Inventors
19 Fosse Way
London   W13 0BZ
Phone: 081-998 3540
Fax: 081-991 1309

★1913★
Institute of Legal Cashiers
1st Floor
136 Well Hall Rd
London   SE9 6SN
Phone: 081-294 2021
Fax: 081-294 2001

Members are book-keepers, accountants and administrators working in legal practices

★1914★
Institute of Legal Executives
Kempston Manor
Kempston
Bedford   MK42 7AB
Phone: 0234 841000
Fax: 0234 840373

The professional body for persons employed by or working for solicitors

★1915★
Institute of Leisure & Amenity Management
ILAM House
Lower Basildon
Reading   RG8 9NE
Phone: 0491 874222
Fax: 0491 874059

The professional body for managers working in art and entertainment complexes, health and fitness clubs, museums, parks, playgrounds and sports centres

★1916★
Institute of Linguists
Mangold House
24a Highbury Grove
London   N5 2EA
Phone: 071-359 7445
Fax: 071-354 0202

★1917★
Institute of Logistics & Distribution Management
Douglas House
Queens Square
Corby   NN17 1PL
Phone: 0536 205500
Fax: 0536 400979

★1918★
Institute of London Underwriters
49 Leadenhall St
London   EC3A 2BE
Phone: 071-488 2424
Fax: 071-702 3010

The trade association for insurance companies transacting marine, aviation and transport business on the London insurance market

★1919★
Institute of Machine Woodworking Technology
c/o E H Williams
Lawley
Great Ryton
Dorrington
Shrewsbury   SY5 7LN
Phone: 074373 8124

Covering the field of woodworking from the conversion of log and round timber, sawmilling, building, joinery etc to the numerous branches concerned with woodwork manufacturing and various forms of composition timber and plastics

★1920★
Institute of Maintenance & Building Management
Keats House
30 East St
Farnham   GU9 7SW
Phone: 0252 710994

Membership consists of public service employees engaged in building and maintenance work

★1921★
Institute of Management Consultants
5th Floor
32-33 Hatton Garden
London   EC1N 8DL
Phone: 071-242 2140
Fax: 071-831 4597

★1922★
Institute of Management Services
1 Cecil Court
London Rd

Enfield EN2 6DD
Phone: 081-363 7452
Fax: 081-367 8149

Members are primarily concerned with work study, organisation and methods and related techniques

★1923★
Institute of Management Specialists
58 Clarendon Ave
Leamington Spa CV32 4SA
Phone: 0924 55498

Management specialists assist in the formulation of policy, implementing departmental decisions and monitoring results

★1924★
Institute of Manpower Studies
Mantell Building
University of Sussex
Falmer
Brighton BN1 9RF
Phone: 0273 686751
Fax: 0273 690430

A focus of knowledge and practical experience in manpower management, the operation of labour markets and employment and training policy

★1925★
Institute of Marine Engineers
76 Mark Lane
London EC3R 7JN
Phone: 071-481 8493
Fax: 071-488 1854

Members are involved in marine engineering, naval architecture and offshore and sub-sea engineering

★1926★
Institute of Market Officers
c/o A Fretwell
7 Locke Avenue
Barnsley S70 1QH
Phone: 0226 203314

For the administration of markets, fairs, abattoirs and cold storage

★1927★
Institute of Masters of Wine
Five Kings House
1 Queen St Place
London EC4R 1QS
Phone: 071-236 4427
Fax: 071-329 0298

★1928★
Institute of Materials Management
Cranfield Institute of Technology
Cranfield MK43 0AL
Phone: 0234 750323
Fax: 0234 750875

Covering management techniques, control systems and technology related to the movement of materials and goods in manufacturing, warehousing and distribution

★1929★
Institute of Mathematics & its Applications
Maitland House
Warrior Square
Southend-on-Sea SS1 2JY
Phone: 0702 354020
Fax: 0702 354111

★1930★
Institute of Measurement & Control
87 Gower St
London WC1E 6AA
Phone: 071-387 4949
Fax: 071-388 8431

The science and practice of measurement and control technology and its application

★1931★
Institute of Medical Ethics
Tavistock House North
Tavistock Square
London WC1H 9LG
Phone: 071-387 8132

★1932★
Institute of Medical Laboratory Sciences
12 Queen Anne St

London W1M 0AU
Phone: 071-636 8192
Fax: 071-436 4946

★1933★
Institute of Metal Finishing
Exeter House
48 Holloway Head Rd
Birmingham B1 1NQ
Phone: 021-622 7387
Fax: 021-666 6316

Metal finishing processes include electro-plating, organic (paint) finishing, anodising, printed circuitry and ancillary methods of surface treatment

★1934★
Institute of Metals
1 Carlton House Terrace
London SW1Y 5DB
Phone: 071-839 4071
Fax: 071-839 2289

★1935★
Institute of Motorcycling
c/o Murray Evans Associates
7 Buckingham Gate
London SW1E 6JS
Phone: 071-630 5454
Fax: 071-630 5767

★1936★
Institute of Musical Instrument Technology
c/o Frank Fowler
134 Crouch Hill
London N8 9DX
Phone: 081-340 2271

★1937★
Institute of Ophthalmology
Judd St
London WC1H 9QS
Phone: 071-387 9621

Teaching and research into eye diseases and other causes of blindness

★1938★
Institute of Packaging
Sysonby Lodge
Nottingham Rd
Melton Mowbray LE13 0NU
Phone: 0664 500055
Fax: 0664 64164

A professional organisation concerned with education, training and qualifying standards in packaging technology

★1939★
Institute of Paper Conservation
c/o C Hampson
Leigh Lodge
Leigh
Worcester WR6 5LB
Phone: 0886 32323

Membership is open to all having an interest in paper and its conservation including librarians, archivists, bookbinders, paper scientists, artists, historians and other specialists

★1940★
Institute of Patentees & Inventors
Suite 505a
Triumph House
189 Regent St
London W1R 7WF
Phone: 071-242 7812

★1941★
Institute of Personnel Management
IPM House
35 Camp Rd
London SW19 4UW
Phone: 081-946 9100
Telex: 947203

★1942★
Institute of Petroleum
61 New Cavendish St
London W1M 8AR
Phone: 071-636 1004
Fax: 701-255 1472

★1943★
Institute of Pharmacy Management
 International
c/o G Knowles
Seaways Cottage
Marine Rd
Hoylake
Liverpool   L47 2AS
Phone: 051-632 3760
Fax: 051-632 6400

Members are pharmaceutical chemists

★1944★
Institute of Physical Sciences in
 Medicine
4 Campleshon Rd
York   YO2 1PE
Phone: 0904 610821
Fax: 0904 612279

Professional organisation for medical physicists and bioengineers working in or supporting the health service

★1945★
Institute of Physics
47 Belgrave Square
London   SW1X 8QX
Phone: 071-235 6111
Fax: 071-259 6002

Professional body whose members represent
all aspects of pure and applied physics

★1946★
Institute of Plumbing
64 Station Lane
Hornchurch   RM12 6NB
Phone: 04024 72791
Fax: 04024 48987

Professional association for independent registered plumbers and students

★1947★
Institute of Practitioners in Beauty
c/o Mrs H Shaw
3rd Floor
42 Albemarle St
London   W1X 3FE
Phone: 071-629 3884

Open to individual qualified beauticians

★1948★
Institute of Practitioners in
 Advertising
44 Belgrave Square
London   SW1X 8QS
Phone: 071-235 7020
Fax: 071-245 9904

Representing advertising agencies and the
people who work in them

★1949★
Institute of Printing
8 Lonsdale Gardens
Tunbridge Wells   TN1 1NU
Phone: 0892 38118

★1950★
Institute of Professional Investigators
31a Wellington St
Blackburn   BB1 8AF
Phone: 0254 680072

Members are criminal, police or civil investigators, handwriting experts, pathologists and
similar

★1951★
Institute of Psycho-Analysis
63 New Cavendish St
London   W1M 7RD
Phone: 071-580 4952

★1952★
Institute of Psychosexual Medicine
11 Chandos St
London   W1M 9DE
Phone: 071-580 0631

★1953★
Institute of Public Loss Assessors
14 Red Lion St
Chesham
Amersham   HP5 1HB
Phone: 0494 782342

★1954★
Institute of Public Relations
15 Northburgh St

London EC1V 0PR
Phone: 071-253 5151
Fax: 071-490 0588

The professional body for individuals

★1955★
Institute of Purchasing & Supply
Easton House
Easton-on-the-Hill
Stamford PE9 3NZ
Phone: 0780 56777
Fax: 0780 51610

The professional body for purchasing, supply and materials management staff in the public and private sectors of industry, local and central government

★1956★
Institute of Purchasing Management
Purchasing House
1 Fox Lane
Little Bookham
Leatherhead KT23 3AT
Phone: 0372 54131
Fax: 0372 52572

★1957★
Institute of Qualified Private Secretaries
126 Farnham Rd
Slough SL1 4XA
Phone: 0753 22395
Fax: 0403 864094

★1958★
Institute of Quality Assurance
8-10 Grosvenor Gardens
London SW1W 0DQ
Phone: 071-730 7154
Fax: 071-824 8030

Covering education and training in quality assurance

★1959★
Institute of Quarrying
7 Regent St

Nottingham NG1 5BY
Phone: 0602 411315
Fax: 0602 484035

A professional body for managers, technologists and specialist personnel in the quarrying industry

★1960★
Institute of Refractories Engineers
15 St Benedicts Rd
Wombourne
Wolverhampton WV5 9HP
Phone: 0902 894799

★1961★
Institute of Refrigeration
Kelvin House
76 Mill Lane
Carshalton SM5 2JR
Phone: 081-647 7033
Fax: 081-773 0165

A professional body to promote the advancement of refigeration in all its applications

★1962★
Institute of Rent Officers
c/o M R Webber
Musgrave House
Musgrave Row
Exeter EX4 3TW
Phone: 0392 72321
Fax: 0392 210069

★1963★
Institute of Risk Management
140 Aldersgate St
London EC1A 4HY
Phone: 071-796 2119
Fax: 071-796 2120

Risk management requires familiarity with areas such as fire engineering, security, occupational safety, insurance and legal liability and all aspects covering the financial loss which follows accidents

★1964★
Institute of Road Safety Officers
c/o E M Marsh
31 Dyers Close
West Buckland

Taunton   TA21 9JU
Phone: 0823 255670

★1965★
Institute of Road Transport Engineers
1 Cromwell Place
London   SW7 2JF
Phone: 071-589 3744
Fax: 071-225 0494

Members are transport engineers and others responsible for the care of road freight and passenger vehicles

★1966★
Institute of Roofing
24 Weymouth St
London   W1A 3FA
Phone: 071-436 0387
Fax: 071-637 5215

★1967★
Institute of Safety & Public Protection
c/o R M Chapman
Rotherham Metropolitan Borough Council
38 Moorgate Rd
Rotherham   S60 2BU
Phone: 0709 373731   ext. 3104

★1968★
Institute of Sales & Marketing Management
31 Upper George St
Luton   LU1 2RD
Phone: 0582 411130
Fax: 0582 453640

★1969★
Institute of Sales Promotion
Arena House
66-68 Pentonville Rd
London   N1 9HS
Phone: 071-837 5340
Fax: 071-837 5326

Trade association representing sales promotion agencies, promoters and suppliers

★1970★
Institute of Science Technology
Mansell House
22 Bore St

Lichfield   WS13 6LP
Phone: 0543 251346
Fax: 0543 415804

Professional organisation for laboratory technicians

★1971★
Institute of Scientific & Technical Communicators
PO Box 479
Luton   LU1 4QR
Phone: 0582 400316

Covers communication techniques, engineering, science and the dissemination of information

★1972★
Institute of Sheet Metal Engineering
Exeter House
48 Holloway Head Rd
Birmingham   B1 1NQ
Phone: 021-622 2860
Fax: 021-666 6316

★1973★
Institute of Shorthand Writers
2 New Square
Lincoln's Inn
London   WC2A 3RU
Phone: 071-405 9884

The promotion of the more efficient practice of shorthand writing in connection with legal proceedings

★1974★
Institute of Social Psychiatry
c/o Sutton Manor Clinic
Stapleford Tawney
Romford   RM4 1SR
Phone: 0992 814661

★1975★
Institute of Sound & Communications Engineers
4b High St
Burnham

Slough SL1 7JH
Phone: 0628 667633
Fax: 0628 665882

Provides an interface between individuals in
the various sound and communication industries employed by companies or practising as
independent engineers or consultants

★1976★
Institute of Sports Sponsorship
Francis House
Francis St
London SW1P 1DE
Phone: 071-828 8771
Fax: 071-630 8820

Members are agencies involved in business
sponsorship of sporting events

★1977★
Institute of Statisticians
43 St Peters Square
Preston PR1 7BX
Phone: 0772 204237
Fax: 0772 204476

★1978★
Institute of Sterile Services
  Management
c/o D Keeton
Grantham & Kesteven General Hospital
Manthorpe Rd
Grantham NG31 8DG
Phone: 0476 65232 ext. 4477

★1979★
Institute of Supervisory Management
22 Bore St
Lichfield WS13 6LP
Phone: 0543 251346
Fax: 0543 250929

★1980★
Institute of Swimming Pool Engineers
c/o M W Alcock
94 Morley Grove
Harlow CM20 1ED
Phone: 0279 626364
Fax: 0279 626300

★1981★
Institute of Swimming Teachers &
  Coaches
Lantern House
38 Lester Rd
Loughborough LE11 2AG
Phone: 0509 264357

★1982★
Institute of Tape Learning
c/o Educational Tapes Ltd
PO Box 4
Hemel Hempstead HP3 8BT
Phone: 0442 251346

★1983★
Institute of Taxation
12 Upper Belgrave St
London SW1X 8BB
Phone: 071-235 9381
Fax: 071-235 2562

★1984★
Institute of the Furniture Warehousing
  & Removing Industry
3 Churchill Court
58 Station Rd
Harrow HA2 7SA
Phone: 081-861 3331
Fax: 081-861 3332

★1985★
Institute of the Motor Industry
Fanshaws
Brickendon
Hertford SG13 8PQ
Phone: 0992 86521
Fax: 0992 86548

Professional body for individuals working
throughout the industry

★1986★
Institute of Trade Mark Agents
4th Floor
Canterbury House
2-6 Sydenham Rd
Croydon CR0 9EX
Phone: 081-686 2052
Fax: 081-680 5723

★1987★
Institute of Trading Standards Administration
4-5 Hadleigh Business Centre
351 London Rd
Hadleigh SS7 2BT
Phone: 0702 559922
Fax: 0702 559902

The professional body for those engaged in the administration and enforcement of trading standards and consumer protection legislation

★1988★
Institute of Training & Development
Marlow House
Institute Rd
Marlow SL7 1BD
Phone: 0628 890123
Fax: 0628 890208

For those involved in human resource development

★1989★
Institute of Transactional Analysis
BM Box 4104
Old Gloucester St
London WC1N 3XX
Phone: 071-405 0463

Transactional analysis is an aspect of psychotherapy used in a variety of ways including management training, school teaching and counselling

★1990★
Institute of Translation & Interpreting
318a Finchley Rd
London NW3 5HT
Phone: 071-794 9931
Fax: 071-435 2105

Members are freelance and staff translators and interpretors

★1991★
Institute of Transport Administration
32 Palmerston Rd

Southampton SO1 1LL
Phone: 0703 631380
Fax: 0703 634165

Members are professional transport managers primarily from the road haulage sector

★1992★
Institute of Travel & Tourism
113 Victoria St
St Albans AL1 3TJ
Phone: 0727 54395
Fax: 0727 47415

★1993★
Institute of Travel Management
1 Richmond Mews
London W1V 5AG
Phone: 071-437 9556
Fax: 071-434 0200

★1994★
Institute of Trichologists
228 Stockwell Rd
London SW9 9SU
Phone: 071-733 2056

Provides scientific training of individuals qualified to advise and treat hair and scalp disorders

★1995★
Institute of Vehicle Recovery
201 Great Portland St
London W1N 6AB
Phone: 071-580 9122
Fax: 071-580 6376

★1996★
Institute of Vitreous Enamellers
c/o J D Gardom
PO Box 1
Ripley DE5 3EB
Phone: 0773 743136

★1997★
Institute of Wastes Management
9 Saxon Court
St Peters Gardens
Northampton NN1 1SX
Phone: 0604 20426
Fax: 0604 21339

★1998★
Institute of Welfare Officers
254 Hanging Ditch
Corn Exchange
Manchester M4 3BQ
Phone: 061-832 6541
Telex: 669362

★1999★
Institute of Wood Science
Stocking Lane
Hughenden Valley
High Wycombe HP14 4NU
Phone: 0240 245374

Concerned with the scientific, technical, practical and general knowledge of timber and wood-based materials

★2000★
Institute of Word Processing
18 Upper Shirley Rd
Croydon CR0 5EA

★2001★
Institution of Agricultural Engineers
West End Rd
Silsoe
Bedford MK45 4DU
Phone: 0525 61096

The professional body for engineers, scientists, technologists and managers in the agricultural and allied industries, including forestry, food processing and agrochemicals

★2002★
Institution of Analysts & Programmers
Charles House
36 Culmington Rd
London W13 9NH
Phone: 081-567 2118
Fax: 081-567 4379

Members consist of those professionally engaged in computer programming or systems analysis for commerce, industry or the public service

★2003★
Institution of British Engineers
Royal Liver Building
6 Hampton Place

Brighton BN1 3DD
Phone: 0273 734274

★2004★
Institution of British Telecommunications Engineers
2-12 Gresham St
London EC2V 7AG
Phone: 071-356 8050
Fax: 071-356 7942

★2005★
Institution of Chemical Engineers
165-171 Railway Terrace
Rugby CV21 3HQ
Phone: 0788 78214
Fax: 0788 60833

The qualifying body for chemical engineers

★2006★
Institution of Civil Engineering Surveyors
26 Market St
Altrincham WA14 1PF
Phone: 061-928 8074

★2007★
Institution of Civil Engineers
1-7 Great George St
London SW1P 3AA
Phone: 071-222 7722
Fax: 071-222 7500

Incorporating engineers and technicians

★2008★
Institution of Corrosion Science & Technology
PO Box 253
Leighton Buzzard LU7 7WB
Phone: 0525 851771
Fax: 0525 376690

★2009★
Institution of Diagnostic Engineers
3 Wycliffe St

Leicester   LE1 5LR
Phone: 0537 592552
Fax: 0537 592444

Concerned with the diagnosis of deterioration of plant and machinery and the development of faults

★2010★
Institution of Diesel & Gas Turbine Engineers
c/o K S Edmanson
PO Box 43
Bedford   MK40 7JB
Phone: 0234 214340
Telex: 886841

Covers diesel, gas and duel-fuel engines, gas turbines, their applications and related technologies

★2011★
Institution of Electrical Engineers
Savoy Place
London   WC2R 0BL
Phone: 071-240 1871
Fax: 071-240 7735

All branches of electrical and electronic engineering, including control engineering, radio and automation

★2012★
Institution of Electronics & Electrical Incorporated Engineers
Savoy Hill House
Savoy Hill
London   WC2R 0BS
Phone: 071-836 3357
Fax: 071-497 9006

The professional body for individuals in every sphere of activity where electronic or electrical technology has a role to play

★2013★
Institution of Engineering Designers
Courtleigh
Westbury Leigh
Westbury   BA13 3TA
Phone: 0373 822801
Fax: 0373 858085

★2014★
Institution of Engineers & Shipbuilders in Scotland
Charing Cross Tower
10 Elmbank Gardens
Glasgow   G2 4HT
Phone: 041-248 3721

★2015★
Institution of Environmental Health Officers
Chadwick House
48 Rushworth St
London   SE1 0QT
Phone: 071-928 6006
Fax: 071-261 1960

★2016★
Institution of Environmental Sciences
c/o A D Baillie
14 Princes Gate
London   SW7 1PU
Phone: 081-766 6755

★2017★
Institution of Fire Engineers
148 New Walk
Leicester   LE1 7QB
Phone: 0533 553654
Fax: 0533 471231

A professional organisation to promote and improve the science and practice of fire extinction, fire prevention and fire engineering

★2018★
Institution of Gas Engineers
17 Grosvenor Crescent
London   SW1X 7ES
Phone: 071-245 9811
Fax: 071-245 1229

★2019★
Institution of Geologists
Burlington House, Piccadilly
London   W1V 9AG
Phone: 071-734 0751

★2020★
Institution of Highways &
**   Transportation**
3 Lygon Place
London   SW1W 0JS
Phone: 071-730 5245
Fax: 071-730 1628

★2021★
Institution of Incorporated Executive
**   Engineers**
Wix Hill House
West Horsley
Godalming   KT24 6DZ
Phone: 0483 222383
Fax: 0483 224321

For engineers specialising in engineering
management

★2022★
Institution of Industrial Managers
Rochester House
66 Little Ealing Lane
London   W5 4XX
Phone: 081-579 9411
Fax: 081-579 2244

The professional body for industrial managers
who are concerned with developing and raising the standards of industrial works and factory management

★2023★
Institution of Lighting Engineers
Lennox House
9 Lawford Rd
Rugby   CV21 2DZ
Phone: 0788 576492
Fax: 0788 540145

Promotes advancements in the science and
art of efficient lighting

★2024★
Institution of Mechanical Engineers
1 Birdcage Walk
London   SW1H 9JJ
Phone: 071-222 7899
Fax: 071-222 4557

Members are chartered mechanical engineers
together with engineers aspiring to that level

of competence and others from associated
professions

★2025★
Institution of Mechanical Incorporated
**   Engineers**
3 Birdcage Walk
London   SW1H 9JN
Phone: 071-222 7899
Fax: 071-222 4557

★2026★
Institution of Mining & Metallurgy
44 Portland Place
London   W1N 4BR
Phone: 071-580 3802
Fax: 071-430 5388

Members are metallurgists, geologists, mining and petroleum engineers

★2027★
Institution of Mining Electrical &
**   Mining Mechanical Engineers**
60 Silver St
Doncaster   DN1 1HT
Phone: 0302 360104
Telex: 0302 730399

A professional body for engineers interested
in promoting safety in electrical and mechanical engineering

★2028★
Institution of Mining Engineers
Danum House
South Parade
Doncaster   DN1 2DY
Phone: 0302 360104
Fax: 0302 340554

★2029★
Institution of Nuclear Engineers
1 Penerley Rd
London   SE6 2LQ
Phone: 081-698 1500
Telex: 8812093

★2030★
Institution of Occupational Safety &
**   Health**
222 Uppingham Rd

Leicester   LE5 0QG
Phone: 0533 768424
Fax: 0533 460423

The professional body for individual safety and health practitioners in the UK

★2031★
Institution of Plant Engineers
77 Great Peter St
London   SW1P 2EZ
Phone: 071-233 2855
Fax: 071-233 2604

The design, selection, installation, maintenance and control of fixed or mobile plant, equipment and services

★2032★
Institution of Population Registration
c/o N D Stephens
96 Herongate Rd
London   E12 5EQ
Phone: 071-351 3941

★2033★
Institution of Production Engineers
66 Little Ealing Lane
London   W5 4XX
Phone: 081-579 9411

★2034★
Institution of Public Health Engineers
now incorporated with Institution of Water & Environmental Management

★2035★
Institution of Railway Signal Engineers
1 Bedlake Close
Bedlake Hall
Dawlish   EX7 9SA
Phone: 0626 888096

★2036★
Institution of Structural Engineers
11 Upper Belgrave St
London   SW1X 8BH
Phone: 071-235 4535
Fax: 071-235 4294

Professional body for qualified structural engineers

★2037★
Institution of Water & Environmental Management
15 John St
London   WC1N 2EB
Phone: 071-831 3110
Fax: 071-405 4967

A multi-disciplinary body for engineers and scientists

★2038★
Institution of Water Officers
Heriot House
12 Summerhill Terrace
Newcastle upon Tyne   NE4 6EP
Phone: 091-230 5150
Fax: 091-230 2880

Concerned with education, training and registration

★2039★
Institution of Works & Highways Management
Dalkeith House
Dalkeith Place
Kettering   NN16 0BS
Phone: 0536 411077

Members are civil engineers with particular emphasis on the municipal, public and private sectors of the construction industry

★2040★
Institutional Fund Managers' Association
6th Floor
Park House
16 Finsbury Circus
London   EC2M 7JP
Phone: 071-638 1639
Fax: 071-920 9186

★2041★
Instock Footwear Suppliers Association
c/o S Clare-Hay
Castlefields
Newport Rd
Stafford   ST16 1BQ
Phone: 0785 211311
Fax: 0785 211680

★2042★
Insurance Adjusters Association
152 Commercial St
London   E1 6NU
Phone: 071-377 0282

★2043★
Insurance Brokers Registration Council
15 St Helen's Place
London   EC3A 6DS
Phone: 071-588 4387

★2044★
Insurance Institute of London
Aldermary House
10-15 Queen St
London   EC4N 1ST
Phone: 071-248 3892

★2045★
Interational Council of Museums
c/o C R Hill
Dept of Public Services
Natural History Museum
Cromwell Rd
London   SW7 5BD
Phone: 071-589 6323

★2046★
**Interdisciplinary Scientific Committee
on Space Research**
c/o C R Argent
Royal Society
6 Carlton House Terrace
London   SW1Y 5AG
Phone: 071-839 5561
Fax: 071-930 2170

★2047★
**Interior Decorators & Designers
Association**
Crest House
102-104 Church Rd
Teddington   TW11 8PY
Phone: 081-977 1105
Fax: 081-943 3151

Members are individual interior decorators, designers and trade suppliers

★2048★
**International Accounting Standards
Committee**
41 Kingsway
London   WC2B 6YU
Phone: 071-240 8781
Fax: 071-379 0048

Consists of professional accountancy bodies with members in over 70 countries

★2049★
International Advertising Association
39a London Rd
Kingston upon Thames   KT2 6ND
Phone: 081-546 4809
Fax: 081-549 3476

★2050★
**International Airline Passengers
Assocation**
Carolyn House
Dingwall Rd
Croydon   CR9 2ZQ
Phone: 081-681 6555
Fax: 081-681 0234

Members are frequent, primarily business travellers

★2051★
**International Anatomical
Nomenclature Committee**
c/o Professor R Warwick
Dept of Anatomy
Guy's Hospital Medical School
London Bridge
London   SE1 9RT
Phone: 071-955 5000   ext. 5646

★2052★
**International Association Against
Painful Experiments on Animals**
c/o C Smith
PO Box 215
St Albans   AL3 4RD
Phone: 0727 835386

Animal welfare organisations united to abolish the use of animals for research purposes

★2053★
International Association for the Protection of Industrial Property
c/o M Ellis
2-3 Cursitor St
London   EC4A 1BQ
Phone: 071-405 4405   ext. 228
Fax: 071-405 9339

Concerned with protecting patents, trade marks and designs

★2054★
International Association for Vehicle System Dynamics
c/o Professor R Sharp
School of Mechanical Engineering
Cranfield Institute of Technology
Wharley End
Cranfield   MK43 0AL
Phone: 0234 750111
Fax: 0234 750875

Vehicle dynamics is a science based on the theory of motion of ground-based vehicle systems

★2055★
International Association for Educational & Vocational Guidance
c/o K Hall
Dept of Economic Development
Gloucester House
Chichester St
Belfast   BT11 1GP
Phone: 0232 235211
Fax: 0232 248761

★2056★
International Association for Teachers of English as a Foreign Language
c/o J Norcott
3 Kingsdown Chambers
Kingsdown Park
Tankerton
Whitstable   CT5 2DJ
Phone: 0227 276528
Fax: 0227 274415

★2057★
International Association of Agricultural Economics
Queen Elizabeth House
21 St Giles
Oxford   OX1 3LA
Phone: 0865 273609
Fax: 0865 73607

★2058★
International Association of Book-keepers
Burford House
44 London Rd
Sevenoaks   TN13 1AS
Phone: 0732 458080
Fax: 0732 455848

A professional body serving employees at the first level of work in financial accounting

★2059★
International Association of Dry Cargo Shipowners
5th Floor
39 Dover St
London   W1X 3RB
Phone: 071-629 7079
Fax: 071-493 7865

Concerned solely with the welfare of the dry bulk sector of shipping

★2060★
International Association of Fish Meal Manufacturers
Hoval House
Orchard Parade
Mutton Lane
Potters Bar   EN6 3AR
Phone: 0707 42343
Fax: 0707 45489

National fish meal and oil producing organisations and companies

★2061★
International Association of Group Psychotherapy
c/o Dr S Whiteley
Wheelwrights Cottage
Wheelers Lane
Brockham

Reigate   RH3 7LA
Phone: 0737 7843446
Fax: 0737 221711

★2062★
**International Association of Music
   Libraries**
c/o Helen Mason
Music & Drama Library
Brayford House
Lucy Tower St
Lincoln   LN1 1XN
Phone: 0522 552855
Fax: 0522 552858

★2063★
**International Association of
   Navigation Schools**
c/o Capt M M Cornish
Glasgow College of Maritime Studies
21 Thistle St
Glasgow   G5 9XB
Phone: 041-429 3201   ext. 31
Fax: 041-420 1690

★2064★
**International Association of Packaging
   Research Institutes**
Eyot Lodge
Petworth Rd
Chiddingfold
Guildford   GU8 4UA
Phone: 0428 682098
Fax: 0428 682098

★2065★
**International Association of Research
   Institutes for the Graphic Arts
   Industry**
18 The Ridgeway
Fetcham Park
Leatherhead   KT22 9AZ
Phone: 0372 376161

Conducts multilateral research projects and
exchanges information on research and
development in printing and allied industries

★2066★
**International Association of Seed
   Crushers**
8 Salisbury Square
London   EC4P 4AN
Phone: 071-822 5296
Telex: 28395

Covering oils, seeds and vegetable fats

★2067★
**International Association of Textile
   Dyers & Printers**
Reedham House
31 King St West
Manchester   M3 2PF
Phone: 061-832 9279

Members are European trade associations
operating in the textile finishing industry

★2068★
**International Association of Tour
   Managers**
397 Walworth Rd
London   SE17 2AW
Phone: 071-703 9154
Fax: 071-703 0358

★2069★
**International Association of University
   Professors of English**
c/o John Lawlor
Merevale
Crewe Rd
Madeley Heath
Crewe   CW3 9LQ

To promote the study of English language
and literature at university level

★2070★
**International Association on Water
   Pollution Research & Control**
1 Queen Anne's Gate
London   SW1H 9BT
Phone: 071-222 3848
Fax: 071-233 1197

★2071★
**International Audiology Society to
   Help the Deaf**
16 Nithsdale Rd

Weston-super-Mare   BS23 4JR
Phone: 0934 415207

Members are deaf people eager to learn lip reading, discriminate speech and have clear speech

★2072★
International Bar Association
2 Harewood Place
London   W1R 9HB
Phone: 071-629 1206
Fax: 071-409 0456

★2073★
International Bee Research Association
18 North Rd
Cardiff   CF1 3DY
Phone: 0222 372409
Telex: 262433

Co-ordinates bee research work and research on pollination

★2074★
International Cargo Handling Co-ordination Association
71 Bondway
London   SW8 1SH
Phone: 071-793 1022
Fax: 071-820 1703

★2075★
International Cement Bonded Particleboard Federation
Maxwell Rd
Stevenage   SG1 2EP
Phone: 0438 741299
Fax: 0438 741301

★2076★
International Centre for Conservation Education
Greenfield House
Guiting Power
Cheltenham   GL54 5TZ
Phone: 0451 850777
Fax: 0451 850705

★2077★
International Chamber of Commerce
14-15 Belgrave Square

London   SW1X 8PS
Phone: 071-823 2811
Fax: 071-235 5447

★2078★
International Chamber of Shipping
30-32 St Mary Axe
London   EC3A 8ET
Phone: 071-283 2922
Fax: 6268135

For national associations of ship owners and individual shipping companies

★2079★
International Cocoa Organization
22 Berners St
London   W1P 3DB
Phone: 071-637 3211
Fax: 071-631 0114

For cocoa exporting and importing countries

★2080★
International Cocoa Trades Federation
now Cocoa Association of London

★2081★
International Coffee Organization
22 Berners St
London   W1P 4DD
Phone: 071-580 8591
Fax: 071-580 6129

Covering co-operation between coffee exporting and coffee importing countries

★2082★
International Coil Winding Association
69 Queensway
Barwell
Leicester   LE9 8GD
Phone: 0455 841351
Fax: 0455 841309

Members manufacture machinery, coil wound products, goods or allied interests

★2083★
International Commercial Property Association
c/o Hillier Parker May & Rowden
77 Grosvenor St

London W1A 2BT
Phone: 071-629 7666
Fax: 071-491 9146

★2084★
International Commission on Irrigation & Drainage
1-7 Great George St
London SW1P 3AA
Phone: 071-222 7722
Fax: 071-222 7500

★2085★
International Commission on Radiological Protection
c/o Dr H Smith
PO Box 35
Didcot OX11 0RJ
Phone: 0235 833929
Fax: 0235 832832

★2086★
International Commission on Zoological Nomenclature
c/o Natural History Museum
Cromwell Rd
London SW7 5BD
Phone: 071-938 9387

★2087★
International Committee of Toy Industries
80 Camberwell Rd
London SE5 0EG
Phone: 071-701 7271
Fax: 071-708 2437

★2088★
International Confederation of Midwives
10 Barley Mow Passage
London W4 4PH
Phone: 081-994 6477
Fax: 081-994 1533

★2089★
International Conference in Composite Structures
c/o Professor I H Marshall
Paisley College of Technology

High St
Paisley PA1 2BE
Phone: 041-848 3562
Fax: 041-887 0812

A forum for contact between specialists in the structural application of composite materials

★2090★
International Consumer Electronics Association
Landseer House, 19 Charing Cross Rd
London WC2H 0ES
Phone: 071-930 3206
Fax: 071-839 4613

★2091★
International Copper Association
Brosnan House
Darkes Lane
Potters Bar EN6 1BW
Phone: 0707 44577
Fax: 0707 44904

★2092★
International Council for Bird Preservation
32 Cambridge Rd
Girton
Cambridge CB3 0PJ
Phone: 0223 277318
Telex: 0223 277200

A federation of organisations interested in preserving bird species

★2093★
International Council for Technical Communication
Strathmore
Hitchin Rd
Letchworth SG6 3LL
Phone: 0462 685854

An association of societies whose objectives are to improve the standards of writing, speaking and graphic communication in all applications of science and technology

★2094★
International Council of Ballroom Dancing
87 Parkhurst Rd

London N7 0LP
Phone: 071-609 1386

★2095★
International Council of Graphic Design Associations
c/o V Mullin
PO Box 398
London W11 4UG
Phone: 071-603 8494
Fax: 071-371 6040

Members are national professional graphic design associations seeking to raise the standard of graphic design and professional practice

★2096★
International Council of Hides & Skins Traders Association
20-21 Tooks Court
London EC4A 1LB
Phone: 071-831 7581
Fax: 071-405 1291

★2097★
International Council of Marine Industry Associations
Boating Industry House
Vale Rd
Weybridge KT13 9NS
Phone: 0932 854511
Fax: 0932 852874

Promotes boating as an international recreational activity

★2098★
International Council on Monuments & Sites
10 Barley Mow Passage
London W4 4PH
Phone: 081-994 6477

★2099★
International Dance Teachers' Association
76 Bennett Rd
Brighton BN2 5JL
Phone: 0273 685652

The association for qualified dance teachers

★2100★
International Deep Drawing Research Group
c/o Roger Pearce
School of Industrial Science
Cranfield Institute of Technology
Cranfield MK43 0AL
Phone: 0234 750111
Telex: 825072

A forum for international collaboration on matters relevant to the forming of sheet metal

★2101★
International Dental Federation
64 Wimpole St
London W1M 8AL
Phone: 071-935 7852
Fax: 071-486 0183

★2102★
International Farm Management Association
c/o Farm Management Unit
University of Reading
Earley Gate
Reading RG6 2AR
Phone: 0734 351458
Fax: 0734 352421

For individuals concerned with the planning, production and marketing of agricultural commodities

★2103★
International Federation for Modern Languages & Literatures
c/o Professor David Wells
Dept of German
Birkbeck College
Malet St
London WC1E 7HX
Phone: 071-631 6103
Fax: 071-631 6270

★2104★
International Federation for Theatre Research
c/o Professor Michael Anderson, Darwin College, University of Kent
Canterbury CT2 7NY
Phone: 0227 764000

★2105★
International Federation of Airworthiness
58 Whiteheath Avenue
Ruislip HA4 7PW
Phone: 0895 672504
Fax: 0895 676656

All aspects of airworthiness, maintenance, design and operation

★2106★
International Federation of Aromatherapists
4 East Mearn Rd
London SE21 8HA

★2107★
International Federation of Business & Professional Women
16 Cloisters House
8 Battersea Park Rd
London SW8 4BG
Phone: 071-738 8323
Fax: 071-622 8528

★2108★
International Federation of Dental Anaesthesiology Societies
c/o P Sykes
Wilmington Lodge
19 Dunstable St
Ampthill MK45 2NJ
Phone: 0525 403205

Promote study and practice of improved methods of anaesthesia, analgesia and sedation in dentistry

★2109★
International Federation of Essential Oils & Aroma Trades
152-160 City Rd
London EC1V 2NP
Phone: 071-253 9421
Fax: 071-250 0965

For producers, compounders and traders of fragrance and flavour materials

★2110★
International Federation of Multiple Sclerosis Societies
3-9 Heddon St
London W1R 7LE
Phone: 071-734 9120
Fax: 071-287 2587

★2111★
International Federation of Park & Recreation Administration
The Grotto
Lower Basildon
Reading RG8 9NE
Phone: 0491 874222
Fax: 0491 874059

★2112★
International Federation of Prestressing
c/o Institution of Structural Engineers
11 Upper Belgrave St
London SW1X 8BH
Phone: 071-235 4535
Fax: 071-235 4294

★2113★
International Federation of Settlements
c/o Dr C Kunz
Birmingham Settlement
318 Summer Lane
Birmingham B19 3RL
Phone: 021-359 3562
Fax: 021-359 6357

Covers settlements, community centres and neighbourhood houses to help people in need

★2114★
International Federation of Shipmasters Associations
202 Lambeth Rd
London SE1 7JY
Phone: 071-261 0450

★2115★
International Federation of Societies of Cosmetic Chemists
Delaport House
57 Guildford St
Luton LU1 2NL
Phone: 0582 26661
Fax: 0582 405217

★2116★
International Federation of Stamp Dealers Associations
27 John Adam St
London WC2N 6HZ
Phone: 071-930 8333
Fax: 071-930 1163

★2117★
International Federation of the Periodical Press
5 Saint Matthew St
London SW1P 2JT
Phone: 071-873 8158
Fax: 071-873 8167

★2118★
International Federation of the Phonographic Industry
54 Regent St
London W1R 5PJ
Phone: 071-434 3521
Fax: 071-439 9166

Represents the producers and distributors of sound and audio visual recording on copyright and other legal matters

★2119★
International Federation of Tour Operators
66 High St
Lewes BN7 1XG
Phone: 0273 475332
Fax: 0273 483746

★2120★
International Federation of Training & Development Organisations
c/o K Gardner
22 Sapperton

Cirencester GL7 6LQ
Phone: 0285 76305
Fax: 0285 76579

★2121★
International Food Information Service
Lane End House
Shinfield
Reading RG2 9BB
Phone: 0734 883895
Fax: 0734 885065

★2122★
International Fur Trade Federation
20-21 Queenhithe
London EC4V 3AA
Phone: 071-489 8159
Telex: 917513

Members trade, manufacture or process fur skins

★2123★
International General Produce Association
24 St Mary Axe
London EC3A 8ER
Phone: 071-283 5511
Fax: 071-623 1310

★2124★
International Glaciological Society
Lensfield Rd
Cambridge CB2 1ER
Phone: 0223 355974
Fax: 0223 336543

All aspects of snow and ice studies

★2125★
International Glaucoma Association
c/o Kings College Hospital
Denmark Hill
London SE5 9RS
Phone: 071-274 6222 ext. 2934

★2126★
International Guild of Opticians
113 Eastbourne Mews

London W2 6LQ
Phone: 071-258 0240
Fax: 071-724 1175

Members are opticians, optical companies and optical employers engaged in optical dispensing

★2127★
International Health & Beauty Council
109 Felpham Rd
Felpham PO22 7PW
Phone: 0243 860320

★2128★
International Hospital Federation
2 St Andrew's Place
London NW1 4LB
Phone: 071-935 9487

★2129★
International Institute for Conservation of Historic & Artistic Works
6 Buckingham St
London WC2N 6BA
Phone: 071-839 5975
Fax: 071-976 1564

★2130★
International Institute for Environment & Development
3 Endsleigh St
London WC1H 0DD
Phone: 071-388 2117
Fax: 071-388 2826

★2131★
International Institute for Strategic Studies
23 Tavistock St
London WC2E 7NQ
Phone: 071-379 7676
Fax: 071-836 3100

Concerned with all international security problems including arms control and disarmament

★2132★
International Institute of Communications
Tavistock House South
Tavistock Square
London WC1H 9LF
Phone: 071-388 0671
Fax: 071-380 0623

Relating to media and electronic communication

★2133★
International Institute of Risk & Safety Management
National Safety Centre
Chancellor's Rd
London W6 9RS
Phone: 081-741 1231
Fax: 081-741 4555

The study and research into accident prevention and occupational health in industry

★2134★
International Institute of Security
292a Torquay Rd
Paignton TQ3 2ET
Phone: 0803 554849
Fax: 0803 529203

The professional body specialising in the provision of security measures against loss through theft, fire, fraud, other damage and waste

★2135★
International Institute of Social Economics
Enholmes Hall
Patrington
Hull HU12 0PR
Phone: 0964 630033
Telex: 51317

★2136★
International Institute of Sports Therapy
109 Felpham Rd
Felpham PO22 7PW
Phone: 0243 860320

★2137★
International Institute of Synthetic Rubber Producers
Britannia House
Glenthorne Rd
London W6 0LF
Phone: 081-748 3955
Fax: 081-748 3898

★2138★
International Law Association
Charles Clore House
17 Russell Square
London WC1B 5DR
Phone: 071-323 2978
Fax: 071-323 3580

The study and advancement of international law both private and public, comparative law, the unification of law and making proposals for solving conflicts in law

★2139★
International Lead & Zinc Study Group
Metro House
58 St Jame's St
London SW1A 1LD
Phone: 071-499 9373
Fax: 071-493 3725

Representative of producing and consuming countries

★2140★
International Map Collectors Society
c/o W H S Pearce
29 Mount Ephraim Rd
London SW16 1NQ
Phone: 081-769 5041

★2141★
International Maritime Industries Forum
15a Hanover St
London W1R 9HG
Phone: 071-493 4559
Fax: 071-491 0736

Membership embraces shipowners, shipbuilders, oil companies, bankers, insurance companies and similar

★2142★
International Maritime Pilots Association
c/o HQS Wellington
Temple Stairs
Victoria Embankment
London WC2R 2PN
Phone: 071-240 3973

★2143★
International Maritime Satellite Organisation
40 Melton St
London NW1 2EQ
Phone: 071-387 9089
Fax: 071-387 2115

Satellite telecommunications

★2144★
International Meat Trade Association
217 Central Markets
Smithfield
London EC1A 9LH
Phone: 071-489 0005
Fax: 071-248 4733

★2145★
International Medical Society of Paraplegia
c/o National Spinal Injuries Centre
Stoke Mandeville Hospital
Aylesbury HP21 8AL
Phone: 0296 84111

★2146★
International Mohair Association
Mohair House
68 The Grove
Ilkley LS29 9PA
Phone: 0943 817149
Fax: 0943 817150

★2147★
International Optometric & Optical League
10 Knaresborough Place

London   SW5 0TG
Phone: 071-370 4765
Fax: 071-373 1143

Concerned with optometric education world-wide

★2148★
**International Petroleum Industry
   Environmental Conservation
   Association**
1st Floor
1 College Hill
London   EC4R 2RA
Phone: 071-248 3447

★2149★
International Phonetic Association
c/o Dr P J Roach
Dept of Linguistics & Phonetics
University of Leeds
Leeds   LS2 9JT
Phone: 0532 333562
Fax: 0532 333566

To promote the scientific study of phonetics
and its various practical appplications

★2150★
**International Planned Parenthood
   Federation**
Regent's College
Inner Circle
London   NW1 4NS
Phone: 071-486 0741
Fax: 071-487 7450

★2151★
International Police Association
1 Fox Rd
West Bridgford
Nottingham   NG2 6AJ
Phone: 0602 813638

Members are police officers either on active
service or retired

★2152★
**International Powered Access
   Federation**
P O Box 16

Billingshurst   RH14 9YU
Phone: 040-372 2015
Fax: 040-372 2014

★2153★
International Press Institute
Dilke House
Malet St
London   WC1E 7JA
Phone: 071-636 0703
Fax: 071-580 8349

★2154★
**International Press
   Telecommunications Council**
Ascent Four Building
Great South West Rd
Heathrow
Hounslow   TW14 8LX
Phone: 081-751 3336
Fax: 081-751 3473

To safeguard and promote the telecommun-
cations interest of the world's press

★2155★
**International Primary Aluminium
   Institute**
New Zealand House
Haymarket
London   SW1Y 4TE
Phone: 071-930 0528
Fax: 071-321 0183

For producers of primary aluminium world-
wide

★2156★
**International Primary Market
   Association**
c/o D Hazell
1-3 College Hill
London   EC4R 2RA
Phone: 071-248 0933
Fax: 071-489 9316

Represents the interests of managers of new
issues of debt for the public and corporate
sectors

★2157★
International Professional Security Association
292a Torquay Rd
Paignton TQ3 2ET
Phone: 0803 554849
Fax: 0803 529203

A professional body to promote the science and professional practices of all applications of industrial and commercial security

★2158★
International Property Lawyers Association
18 Manor Park
Tunbridge Wells TN1 1JJ
Phone: 0892 510222
Fax: 0892 510333

An international network of English-speaking property lawyers for purchase of foreign real estate

★2159★
International Publishers' Advertising Representatives Association
525-527 Fulham Rd
London SW6 1HF
Phone: 071-385 7723
Fax: 071-381 8884

★2160★
International Register of Oriental Medicine
Green Hedges House
Green Hedges Avenue
East Grinstead RH19 1DZ
Phone: 0342 313106

★2161★
International Rubber Research & Development Board
Chapel Building
Brickendonbury
Hertford SG13 8NP
Phone: 0992 584966
Telex: 817449

Co-operation on rubber research among producing countries

★2162★
International Rubber Study Group
8th Floor
York House
Empire Way
Wembley HA9 0PA
Phone: 081-903.7727
Fax: 081-903 2848

Members are producers and consumers of natural and synthetic rubber products

★2163★
International Salvage Union
Central House
32-66 High St
London E15 2PS
Phone: 081-519 4872
Fax: 081-519 5483

★2164★
International Sheepdog Society
c/o A Hendry
Chesham House
47 Brownham Rd
Bedford MK40 2AA
Phone: 0234 52672

★2165★
International Ship Electric Service Association
4th Floor
Diamond House
37-38 Hatton Garden
London EC1N 8TB
Phone: 071-405 6506
Fax: 071-836 6819

Members are marine and industrial electro-technical service companies

★2166★
International Ship Suppliers Association
235 The Broadway
London SW19 1SD
Phone: 081-543 9161
Fax: 081-543 9162

Members are concerned with supplying merchant shipping with ships stores

★2167★
International Shipping Federation
30-32 St Mary Axe
London EC3A 8ET
Phone: 071-283 2922
Fax: 071-283 9138

A world-wide organisation concerned with all matters relating to the employment and safety of merchant seamen

★2168★
International Society for Boundary Elements
c/o Dr C A Brebbia
Ashurst Lodge
Ashurst
Southampton S04 2AA
Phone: 0703 293223
Fax: 0703 292853

Boundary elements technology is a computerised system of engineering research, development and design

★2169★
International Society for Evolutionary Protistology
c/o Dr S Moss
School of Biological Sciences
Portsmouth Polytechnic
Portsmouth P01 2DY
Phone: 0705 842024
Fax: 0705 842070

Protists are unicellular or acellular organisms comprising protozoa, algae, fungi and some viruses

★2170★
International Society for Music Education
Music Education, Information & Research Centre
University of Reading
London Rd
Reading RG6 1NY
Phone: 0734 318846
Fax: 0734 352080

★2171★
International Society for Soil Mechanics & Foundation Engineering
c/o Dept of Engineering
University of Cambridge
Trumpington St
Cambridge CB2 1PZ
Phone: 0223 355020
Fax: 0223 332662

Members are involved in geotechnology and its engineering applications

★2172★
International Society for the Prevention of Water Pollution
c/o R Earl
Little Orchard
Bentworth
Alton GU34 5RB
Phone: 0420 62225

Aims to prevent and cure pollution of seas, lakes, rivers and streams worldwide

★2173★
International Society of Interior Designers
1st Floor
6 Chelsea Garden Market
Chelsea Harbour
London SW10 0XE
Phone: 071-352 5513
Fax: 071-376 4685

★2174★
International Society of Paediatric Oncology
c/o Yorkshire Regional Cancer Organisation
Cookridge Hospital
Leeds LS16 6QB
Phone: 0532 673411 ext. 403
Fax: 0532 611427

Research and treatment of malignant diseases in children

★2175★
International Sugar Organization
28 Haymarket

London   SW1Y 4SP
Phone: 071-930 3666
Fax: 071-930 0401

Covering the export and import of sugar

★2176★
International Tanker Owners Pollution
Federation
Staple Hall
Stonehouse Court
87-90 Houndsditch
London   EC3A 7AX
Phone: 071-621 1255
Telex: 887514

Members are independent and oil company
tanker owners

★2177★
International Tea Committee
Sir John Lyon House
5 High Timber St
London   EC4V 3NH
Phone: 071-248 4672
Fax: 071-248 3011

Tea producers and consumers

★2178★
International Tin Research Institute
Kingston Lane
Uxbridge   UB8 3PJ
Phone: 0895 72406
Fax: 0895 51841

Research into tin, its alloys and compounds

★2179★
International Truss Plate Association
c/o Twinaplate Ltd
Threemilestones
Truro   TR4 9LD
Phone: 0872 79525
Fax: 0872 222150

★2180★
International Trust for Zoological
Nomenclature
c/o Natural History Musum
Cromwell Rd
London   SW7 5BD
Phone: 071-938 9387

★2181★
International Tube Association
46 Holly Walk
Leamington Spa   CV32 4HY
Phone: 0926 334137
Fax: 0926 314755

Members are involved in the international
unification of tube production and processing

★2182★
International Tungsten Industry
Association
280 Earls Court Rd
London   SW5 9AS
Phone: 071-373 7413
Fax: 071-835 1486

Concerned with the production and consumption of tungsten

★2183★
International Tyre, Rubber & Plastics
Federation
7 Tilney Way
Reading   RG6 4AD
Phone: 0734 869031

Members are primarily concerned with waste
tyres, their disposal and recycling

★2184★
International Underwater Engineering
Contractors
28-30 Little Russell St
London   WC1A 2HN
Phone: 071-405 7045
Fax: 071-831 2581

★2185★
International Union for Surface
Finishing
c/o Dr T R Gabe
17 Alexandra Grove
London   N12 2HE
Phone: 081-445 6881

★2186★
International Union of Anthropological
& Ethnological Sciences
University College of North Wales

Bangor   LL57 2DG
Phone: 0248 351151

A world organisation of social and biological
anthropological scientists and institutions
whose work is also of interest to archaeologists and linguistics specialists

★2187★
**International Union of Aviation
    Insurers**
6 Lovat Lane
London   EC3R 8DT
Phone: 071-626 5314
Telex: 8952022

★2188★
**International Union of Credit &
    Investment Insurers**
17-18 Dover St
London   W1X 3PB
Phone: 071-409 2008
Fax: 071-495 6082

Covering export credit insurance transactions

★2189★
International Union of Crystallography
5 Abbey Square
Chester   CH1 2HU
Phone: 0244 342878
Fax: 0244 314888

★2190★
**International Union of Microbiological
    Societies**
c/o Professor S W Glover
Dept of Genetics
Ridley Building
University of Newcastle upon Tyne
Newcastle upon Tyne   NE1 7RU
Phone: 091-222 7695
Fax: 091-261 1182

★2191★
International Vegetarian Union
Kings Drive
Marple

Stockport   SK6 6NQ
Phone: 061-427 5850
Fax: 061-926 9182

Promotes vegetarianism and the development
of vegetarian societies

★2192★
**International Visual Communications
    Association**
5-6 Clipstone St
London   WC1P 7EB
Phone: 071-580 0962
Fax: 071-436 2606

The promotion and use of screen communications

★2193★
**International Water Supply
    Association**
1 Queen Anne's Gate
London   SW1H 9BT
Phone: 071-222 8111
Fax: 071-222 7243

Concerned with the public supply of water
through pipes for domestic, agricultural and
industrial purposes and the control, provision
and protection of the necessary water
resources

★2194★
**International Waterfowl & Wetlands
    Research Bureau**
Slimbridge
Gloucester   GL2 7BX
Phone: 0453 890624
Fax: 0453 890827

Promotes research and conservation of
waterfowl and their wetland habitat

★2195★
**International Wire & Machinery
    Association**
44 Holly Walk
Leamington Spa   CV32 4HY
Phone: 0926 334137
Fax: 0926 334137

For manufacturers of wire, cable and fibre
optic components and suppliers of related
production and process machinery

★2196★
International Wool Secretariat
Wool House
6 Carlton Gardens
London SW1Y 5AE
Phone: 071-930 7300
Fax: 071-930 8884

Representing the wool producing countries

★2197★
Intumescent Fire Seals Association
Stocking Lane, Hughenden Valley
High Wycombe HP14 4ND
Phone: 024024 3091
Fax: 024024 5487

★2198★
Investment Managers Regulatory Organisation
Broadwalk House
5 Appold St
London EC2A 2LL
Phone: 071-628 6022
Fax: 071-920 9285

★2199★
Investor Relations Society
1st Floor
St Alphage House
2 Fore St
London EC2Y 5DA
Phone: 071-588 2966
Fax: 071-256 6930

Members comprise senior executives with management responsibilities for investor relations, including specialists in public affairs, finance directors and company secretaries

★2200★
Irish Linen Guild
Lambeg Rd
Lisburn BT27 4RL
Phone: 0846 677377
Fax: 0846 670470

★2201★
Issuing Houses Association *now*
British Merchant Banking & Securities Houses Association

★2202★
Jewellery Distributors' Association of GB
10 Vyse St
Birmingham B18 6LT
Phone: 021-236 2657
Fax: 021-236 3921

★2203★
Jockeys' Association of GB
39 Kingfisher Court
Hambridge Rd
Newbury RG14 5SJ
Phone: 0635 44102
Fax: 0635 37932

★2204★
Joint Association of Classical Teachers
31-34 Gordon Square
London WC1H 0PY
Phone: 071-387 0348

For teachers and lecturers in the field of classics, classical civilisation, ancient history and archaeology

★2205★
Joint British Committee for Stress Analysis
c/o Professor J Croll
Dept of Civil Engineering
University of London
Gower St
London WC1E 6BT
Phone: 071-387 7050 ext. 2721
Telex: 296273

★2206★
Joint Care Committee
c/o Patricia Braun
2/41 Myddelton Square
London EC1R 1YB
Phone: 071-837 6874
Fax: 071-837 5264

Representative of the private healthcare sector

★2207★
Joint Committee of National Amenity Societies
c/o Ancient Monuments Society
St Andrew-by-the-Wardrobe
Queen Victoria St
London   EC4V 5DE
Phone: 071-236 3934

★2208★
Joint Council for Welfare of Immigrants
115 Old St
London   EC1V 9JR
Phone: 071-251 8706
Fax: 071-253 3832

★2209★
Joint Industrial Council for the Wholesale Grocery & Provision Trade
18 Fleet St
London   EC4Y 1AS
Phone: 071-353 8894

Covers England and Wales only

★2210★
Joint Industry Board for the Electrical Contracting Industry
Kingswood House
47-51 Sidcup Hill
Sidcup   DA14 6HP
Phone: 081-302 0031
Fax: 081-309 1103

★2211★
Joint University Council
c/o Royal Institute of Public Administration
Regents's College
Inner Circle
London   NW1 4NS
Phone: 071-935 0496
Fax: 071-486 7746

Co-ordinates and develops the work of universities, university colleges, polytechnics and other relevant centres

★2212★
Justices' Clerks' Society
c/o A R Heath
Court House
Homer Rd
Solihull   B91 3RD
Phone: 021-705 8101

★2213★
Jute Importers' Association
c/o Barrie & Nairn
49 Meadowside
Dundee   DD1 1EH
Phone: 0382 23044
Fax: 0382 201383

Covering the importation of raw jute

★2214★
Jute Spinners & Manufacturers Association
148 Nethergate
Dundee   DD1 4EA
Phone: 0382 25881
Fax: 0382 23584

★2215★
Kitchen Specialists Association
PO Box 311
Worcester   WR1 1DN
Phone: 0905 726066
Fax: 0905 726469

Members design, supply or install fitted kitchens

★2216★
Knitting Industries' Federation
7 Gregory Boulevard
Nottingham   NG7 6NB
Phone: 0602 621081
Fax: 0602 625450

★2217★
Lambeg Industrial Research Association
Glenmore House
Lambeg Rd

Lisburn   BT27 4RJ
Phone: 0846 662255
Fax: 0846 661691

Covering textiles and plastics with particular emphasis on linen, other long-staple natural fibres and polyolefins

★2218★
Land Drainage Contractors Association
c/o National Agricultural Centre
Stoneleigh
Kenilworth   CV8 2LG
Phone: 0203 696683
Fax: 0203 696900

FAX: 0203 696900

★2219★
Land Institute
16 Third Avenue
Worthing   BN14 9NZ
Phone: 0903 37292

★2220★
Landscape Institute
12 Carlton House Terrace
London   SW1Y 5AH
Phone: 071-738 9166
Fax: 071-738 9134

The professional association for landscape architects, landscape managers and landscape scientists

★2221★
Landscape Research Group
Leuric
North Rd
South Kilworth
Lutterworth   LE17 6DU
Phone: 0858 575530
Fax: 0858 575002

A multi-disciplinary body to encourage education, interest and research in the field of landscape

★2222★
Lard Association
c/o N Jackson
CWS Ltd
Edible Oils & Fats Factory

Liverpool Rd
Manchester   M30 6BB
Phone: 061-775 3061
Fax: 061-777 9108

★2223★
Law Centres Federation
18-19 Warren St
London   W1P 5DP
Phone: 071-387 8570
Fax: 071-387 8368

★2224★
Law Society
113 Chancery Lane
London   WC2A 1PL
Phone: 071-242 1222
Fax: 071-405 9522

The professional body for solicitors in England & Wales

★2225★
Law Society of Scotland
26 Drumsheugh Gardens
Edinburgh   EH3 7YR
Phone: 031-226 7411
Fax: 031-225 2934

★2226★
Lawn Tennis Association
Queen's Club
Barons Court
London   W14 9EG
Phone: 071-385 2366
Telex: 8956036

★2227★
Lead Contractors Association
31 Marsh Rd
Pinner   HA5 5NL
Phone: 081-4291 0628
Fax: 081-868 0110

Promotes the use of specialist lead work contractors and the use of lead sheet in building

★2228★
Lead Development Association
42-46 Weymouth St

London W1N 3LO
Phone: 071-499 8422
Fax: 071-493 1555

Covers mining companies, metal producers, traders, semi-fabricators and users

★2229★
Lead Sheet Association
42-46 Weymouth St
London W1N 3LQ
Phone: 071-224 0055
Fax: 071-493 1555

Covering the manufacture of lead sheet and pipe

★2230★
Lead Smelters & Refiners Association
42-46 Weymouth St
London W1N 3LQ
Phone: 071-224 0055
Fax: 071-493 1555

★2231★
Leather Institute *now* British Leather Confederation

★2232★
Leather Producers' Association
Leather Trade House
Kings Park Rd
Northampton NN3 1JD
Phone: 0604 494131
Fax: 0604 648220

★2233★
Leicester & District Knitting Industry Association
53 Oxford St
Leicester LE1 5XY
Phone: 0533 541608
Fax: 0533 542273

★2234★
Leisure & Outdoor Furniture Association
60 Claremont Rd
Surbiton KT6 4RH
Phone: 081-390 2022
Fax: 081-390 2027

★2235★
Leisure Studies Association
Chelsea School of Human Movement
Brighton Polytechnic
Gandick Rd
Eastbourne BN20 7SP

An independent body of researchers, planners, policy-makers, administrators and practitioners involved in leisure issues

★2236★
Letter File Manufacturers Association
6 Wimpole St
London W1M 8AS
Phone: 071-637 7692
Fax: 071-436 3137

★2237★
Librarians of Institutes & Schools of Education
c/o R W Kirk
School of Education
21 University Rd
Leicester LE1 7RF
Phone: 0533 523735
Fax: 0533 523653

Members are university education librarians serving teacher training

★2238★
Library Association
7 Ridgmount St
London WC1E 7AE
Phone: 071-636 7543
Fax: 071-436 7218

The central body for library and information professionals, concerned with education, training and practice

★2239★
Licensed Taxi Drivers Association
9-11 Woodfield Rd
London W9 2BA
Phone: 071-286 1046
Fax: 071-286 2494

★2240★
Licensing Executives Society
c/o Dr R C Cass
266 Malden Rd

New Malden KT3 6AR
Phone: 081-949 2509
Fax: 081-942 5245

Members are lawyers, patent agents, consultants and others who deal with product
licensing and technology transfer

★2241★
Life Assurance & Unit Trust Regulatory Authority
Centre Point
103 New Oxford St
London WC1A 1QH
Phone: 071-379 0444
Fax: 071-379 4121

★2242★
Life Insurance Association
Citadel Houe
Station Approach
Chorleywood
Rickmansworth WD3 5PF
Phone: 0923 285333
Fax: 0923 285333

For financial advisers, both independent and
tied, and managers in financial services

★2243★
Lifting Equipment Engineers Association
Waggoners Court
The Street
Manuden
Bishop's Stortford CM23 1DW
Phone: 0279 816504
Fax: 0279 816524

Members interests include all aspects of lifting equipment

★2244★
Light Metal Founders Association
136 Hagley Rd
Birmingham B16 9PN
Phone: 021-454 4141
Fax: 021-454 4949

★2245★
Light Music Society
Lancaster Farm
Chipping Lane

Langridge
Preston PR3 2NB
Phone: 0772 783646

★2246★
Light Rail Transit Association
35 Wimbledon Place
Bradwell Common
Milton Keynes MK13 8DR

Formed to advocate the retention and development of light rail systems and tramways

★2247★
Lighting Industry Federation
Swan House
207 Balham High Rd
London SW17 7BQ
Phone: 081-675 5432
Fax: 081-673 5880

★2248★
Lightweight Cycle Association of GB
c/o Witcomb Cycles Ltd
21-25 Tanners Hill
London SE8 4PJ
Phone: 081-692 1734

Promotes the use of craftsmen-built cycle
framesets

★2249★
Lightweight Cycle Manufacturers' Association
c/o Witcomb Cycles Ltd
21-25 Tanners Hill
London SE8 4PJ
Phone: 081-692 1734

Members are craftsmen in cycle frameset
building

★2250★
Linen Sewing Thread Manufacturers' Association of GB & N Ireland
Hilden
Lisburn BT27 4RR
Phone: 0846 672231
Fax: 0846 607121

★2251★
Linguistics Association of GB
c/o Dr N Fabb
Dept of English
University of Strathclyde
Glasgow   G1 1XH
Phone: 041-553 4150
Fax: 041-552 3493

★2252★
Liquefied Petroleum Gas Industry Technical Association
Alma House
Alma Rd
Reigate   RH2 0AZ
Phone: 0737 224700
Fax: 0737 241116

★2253★
Liquid Food Carton Manufacturers Association
c/o T E Grimes
Smallfield Fitzhugh Tillet & Co
30b Wimpole St
London   W1M 8AA
Phone: 071-486 3337

★2254★
Livestock Auctioneers' Market Committee for England & Wales
Surveyor Court
Westwood Way
Coventry   CV4 8JE
Phone: 071-334 3832
Telex: 071-334 3800

All matters effecting the marketing of cattle, sheep and pigs

★2255★
Livestock Traders Association of GB
Regent House
Clinton Avenue
Nottingham   NG5 1AZ
Phone: 0602 608171
Fax: 0602 603665

★2256★
Lloyd's Aviation Underwriters' Association
Lloyds Building
Lime St
London   EC3M 7DQ
Phone: 071-327 4045
Fax: 071-626 2389

★2257★
Lloyd's Motor Underwriters' Association
Irongate House
Dukes Place
London   EC3A 7LP
Phone: 071-626 7006
Fax: 071-929 1224

★2258★
Lloyd's Underwriters Association
Lloyds Building
1 Lime St
London   EC3M 7DQ
Phone: 071-626 9420
Fax: 071-626 2389

★2259★
Lloyd's Underwriters' Non-Marine Association
6th Floor
Chesterfield House
26-28 Fenchurch St
London   EC37 2DU
Phone: 071-623 9191
Fax: 071-626 2389

★2260★
Local Authority Caterers Association
33 Grangefield Rd
Guildford   GU4 7NR
Phone: 0483 35523

★2261★
Local Authority Valuers Association
c/o E Turner
Estate Officer
Trafford Borough Council
Manchester   M32 0TH
Phone: 061-872 2101   ext. 4204
Fax: 061-234 1299

★2262★
Local Government Management Board
41 Belgrave Square
London   SW1X 8NZ
Phone: 071-235 6081
Fax: 071-235 1257

The local authorities employers association

★2263★
Locomotive & Carriage Institution
c/o J E Lunn
69 Avondale Close
Horley
Crawley   RH6 8BN
Phone: 0293 773239

To advance knowledge on all aspects of railway operation and maintenance

★2264★
London & Provincial Antique Dealers'
  Association
535 Kings Rd
London   SW10 0SZ
Phone: 071-823 3511
Fax: 071-823 3522

Members are antique and fine art dealers throughout the UK

★2265★
London Adventure Playground
  Association
279 Whitechapel Rd
London   E1 1BY
Phone: 071-377 0314
Fax: 071-247 4490

★2266★
London Association of Master
  Decorators
2 Upper Melton Terrace
Melton
Woodbridge   IP12 1QJ
Phone: 0394 380787

Members are decorating and painting companies in the London area

★2267★
London Association of Master
  Stonemasons
82 New Cavendish St

London   W1M 8AD
Phone: 071-580 5588
Fax: 071-631 3872

★2268★
London Boroughs Association
23 Buckingham Gate
London   SW1E 6LB
Phone: 071-834 6788
Fax: 071-834 6940

★2269★
London Discount Market Association
39 Cornhill
London   EC3V 3NU
Phone: 071-623 1020   ext. 2356
Fax: 071-623 0404

★2270★
London District Surveyors Association
c/o P S Johnson
Perceval House
14-16 Uxbridge Rd
London   W5 2HL
Phone: 081-758 5623
Fax: 081-579 6872

Members are district surveyors working in the inner and outer boroughs of London

★2271★
London Fish & Poultry Retailers'
  Association
c/o R H Cayless
66 Aberdour Rd
Goodmayes
Ilford   IG3 9PG
Phone: 081-590 4200

★2272★
London Fish Merchants Association
36 Billingsgate Market
87 West India Dock Rd
London   E14 8ST
Phone: 071-515 2655
Fax: 071-538 2618

★2273★
London Footwear Manufacturers Association
Unit 10d
Printing House Yard
15a Hackney Rd
London E2 7PR
Phone: 071-739 1678
Fax: 071-739 5124

★2274★
London Insurance & Reinsurance Market Association
41-43 Mincing Lane
London EC3R 7AE
Phone: 071-480 5999
Fax: 071-283 6726

★2275★
London International Financial Futures Exchange
Royal Exchange
London EC3V 3PJ
Phone: 071-623 0444

★2276★
London Jute Association
c/o R E Shimell
146a High St
Tonbridge TN9 1BB
Phone: 0732 770332
Fax: 0732 770362

★2277★
London Regional Passengers Committee
Golden Cross House
8 Duncannon St
London WC2N 4JF
Phone: 071-839 1898
Telex: 071-839 8971

Represents the interests of users of bus, underground and rail passengers in and around London

★2278★
London Sisal Association
146a High St

Tonbridge TW9 1DB
Phone: 0732 770332
Fax: 0732 770362

★2279★
London Sugar Brokers' Association
66 Mark Lane
London EC3R 7HS
Phone: 071-480 9339
Fax: 071-480 9500

★2280★
London Tugowners Association
Alexandra House
Royal Pier Rd
Gravesend DA12 2DJ
Phone: 0474 359361
Fax: 0474 321380

★2281★
London Wharfingers Association
Central House
32-66 High St
London E15 2PS
Phone: 081-519 4872
Fax: 081-519 5483

★2282★
Loss Prevention Council
140 Aldersgate St
London EC1A 4HY
Phone: 071-606 3757
Fax: 071-600 1487

★2283★
Low Temperature Coal Distillers Association of GB
c/o Coalite Group Plc
PO Box 21
Chesterfield S44 6AB
Phone: 0246 822281
Telex: 54250

★2284★
Lute Society
103 London Rd
Oldham

Manchester OL1 4BW
Phone: 061-624 4369

Membership covers musicians, instrument makers and universities

★2285★
Machine Tool Technologies
Association
62 Bayswater Rd
London W2 3PS
Phone: 071-402 6671
Fax: 071 724 7250

For all concerned with the machine tool and equipment trades, whether as manufacturers or importers

★2286★
Machinery Users' Association
Saville House
2 Lindsey St
London EC1A 9HP
Phone: 071-796 3481
Telex: 071-796 4891

Represents industry and commerce on all aspects of rating law and practice

★2287★
Made-up Textile Association
148 Nethergate
Dundee DD1 4EA
Phone: 0382 25881
Fax: 0382 23584

Members are companies engaged in the manufacture and processing of heavy industrial textiles

★2288★
Magistrates' Association
28 Fitzroy Square
London W1P 6DD
Phone: 071-387 2353
Fax: 071-383 4020

★2289★
Magnesite & Chrome Brickmakers
Association
The Fountain Precinct
1 Balm Green

Sheffield S1 3AF
Phone: 0742 766789
Fax: 0742 766213

★2290★
Mail Order Traders' Association
25 Castle St
Liverpool L2 4TD
Phone: 051-236 7581
Fax: 051-227 2548

★2291★
Mail Users' Association
3 Pavement House
The Pavement
Hay-on-Wye HR3 5BU
Phone: 0497 821357
Fax: 0497 821360

★2292★
Malaysian Rubber Producers' Research
Association
Tun Abdul Razak Laboratory
Brickendonbury
Hertford SG13 8NL
Phone: 0992 584966
Fax: 0992 554837

Research into natural rubber and innovation in processing and use of natural rubber and natural rubber latex

★2293★
Malt Distillers Association of Scotland
1 North St
Elgin IV30 1UA
Phone: 0343 544077
Fax: 0343 548523

★2294★
Mammal Society
Dexter House
2 Royal Mint Court
London EC3N 4XX
Phone: 071-265 0808

★2295★
Management Consultancies
Association
11 West Halkin St

London SW1X 8JL
Phone: 071-235 3897

★2296★
Manila Hemp Association
c/o Mrs P J Shadbolt
25 Beaufort Court
Admiral's Way
London E14 9XL
Phone: 071-538 5383
Fax: 071-538 2007

★2297★
Manorial Society of GB
104 Kennington Rd
London SE11 6RE
Phone: 071-735 6633
Fax: 071-582 7022

Promotes the history of the British Isles through the better understanding of local traditions

★2298★
Manpower Society
c/o M P Bradney
Old Rickyard
School Lane
Newton Burgoland
Leicester LE6 1SL
Phone: 0530 70965

Promotes the study of manpower policy, management and planning utilisation

★2299★
Manufacturers' Agents' Association of GB & Ireland
Somers House
1 Somers Rd
Reigate RH2 9DU
Phone: 0737 241025
Telex: 00737 224537

★2300★
Margarine & Shortening Manufacturers' Association *now* incorporated into Food & Drink Federation

★2301★
Marine Engine & Equipment Manufacturers' Association
56 Braycourt Avenue
Walton-on-Thames KT12 2BA
Phone: 0932 224910
Fax: 0932 852874

★2302★
Marine Librarians' Association
c/o Marine Society
202 Lambeth Rd
London SE1 7JW
Phone: 071-261 9535
Fax: 071-401 2537

★2303★
Marine Society
202 Lambeth Rd
London SE1 7JW
Phone: 071-261 9535
Fax: 071-401 2537

★2304★
Marine Trades Association *now* British Marine Industries Federation

★2305★
Marine Training Association
Rycote Place
30-38 Cambridge St
Aylesbury HP20 1RS
Phone: 0296 434943
Fax: 0296 437124

★2306★
Market Research Society
15 Northburgh St
London EC1V 0AH
Phone: 071-490 4911
Fax: 071-490 0608

The professional association for those using survey techniques for marketing, social and economic research

★2307★
Marketing Society
Stanton House
206 Worple Rd

London SW20 8PN
Phone: 081-879 3464
Fax: 081-879 0362

The professional body for senior practising
marketing people

★2308★
Marquee Contractors Association
47 Osborne Rd
Croydon CR7 8PD
Phone: 081-653 1988
Fax: 081-653 2932

Marquee hire

★2309★
Martial Arts Commission
15-16 Deptford Broadway
London SE8 4PE
Phone: 081-691 3433
Fax: 081-692 8900

Governing body for all martial arts except
judo

★2310★
Master Carvers Association
c/o D Reid
23 Fishergate
York YO1 4AE
Phone: 0904 659121
Fax: 0904 640018

★2311★
Master Craftsmen's Association &
Retail Export Group
47 Maddox St
London W1R 0EQ
Phone: 071-629 5047

★2312★
Master Locksmiths Association
Units 4 & 5
Woodford Halse Business Park
Great Central Way
Woodford Halse
Daventry NN11 6SU
Phone: 0327 62255
Fax: 0327 62539

★2313★
Master Music Printers & Engravers
Association
2-10 Plantation Rd
Amersham HP6 6HJ
Phone: 0494 725525

Membership consists of employers in the lith-
ographic printing and music engraving industries

★2314★
Master Photographers Association
Hallmark House
97 East St
Epsom KT17 1EA
Phone: 0372 726123
Fax: 0372 728214

★2315★
Master Tanners Association
80-86 Lord St
Liverpool L2 1TW
Phone: 051-708 9023
Fax: 051-709 4635

★2316★
Masters of Basset Hounds Association
Yew Tree Cottage
Haselton
Cheltenham GL54 4DX
Phone: 0451 60500

★2317★
Masters of Deerhounds Association
c/o Dr J W Peek
Bilboa House
Dulverton
Tiverton
Phone: 0398 23475

★2318★
Masters of Draghounds Association
Wisper Wood
School Lane
Nutley
Uckfield TN22 3PG
Phone: 082-571 3180

★2319★
Masters of Foxhounds Association
Parsloes Cottage
Bagendon
Cirencester
Phone: 028583 470
Fax: 028583 737

★2320★
Mastic Asphalt Council & Employer's Federation
Lesley House
6-8 Broadway
Bexleyheath DA6 7LE
Phone: 081-298 0411
Fax: 081-298 0381

★2321★
Mathematical Association
259 London Rd
Leicester LE2 3BE
Phone: 0533 703877

For teachers and students of mathematics and mathematical education at all levels

★2322★
Mechanical & Metal Trades Confederation
235-237 Vauxhall Bridge Rd
London SW1V 1EJ
Phone: 071-233 7011
Fax: 071-828 0667

★2323★
Mechanical Handling Engineers Association
8th Floor
Bridge House
Smallbrook Queensway
Birmingham B5 4JP
Phone: 021-643 3377
Fax: 021-643 5064

The association of designers and manufacturers of conveyors and related systems and equipment engineering

★2324★
Mechanical-Copyright Protection Society
Elgar House
41 Streatham High Rd
London SW16 1ER
Phone: 081-769 4400
Fax: 081-769 8792

Concerned with music recording copyright

★2325★
Media Circle
c/o Rosemary Michael
Advertising Association
Abford House
15 Wilton Rd
London SW1V 1NJ
Phone: 071-828 2771
Fax: 071-931 0376

Representing advertisers, agencies, the media and related services

★2326★
Media Society
Church Cottage
East Rudham
Fakenham PE31 8QZ
Phone: 048-522 664
Fax: 048-522 8155

★2327★
Media Studies Association
c/o Brennan Publications
148 Birchover Way
Allestree
Derby DE3 2RW
Phone: 0332 551884

Promotes exchange of ideas between teachers and practitioners of broadcasting and journalism

★2328★
Medical Journalists' Association
14 Hovendens
Sissinghurst TN17 2LA
Phone: 0580 713920

★2329★
Medical Officers of Schools Association

c/o Dr Elizabeth Pryce-Jones
Community House, 124 Middleton Rd
Morden   SM4 6RW
Phone: 081-685 9922

★2330★
Medical Women's Federation

Tavistock House North
Tavistock Square
London   WC1H 9HX
Phone: 071-387 7765

The professional association of women doctors in Great Britain and Northern Ireland

★2331★
Membrane Switch Manufacturers' Association

Leicester House
7 Leicester St
London   WC2H 7BN
Phone: 071-437 0678
Fax: 071-437 4901

★2332★
Menswear Association of Britain

37-39 Cheval Place
London   SW7 1EU
Phone: 071-225 3635
Fax: 071-589 3787

Represents retailers of mens and boys wear

★2333★
Mental After Care Association

Bainbridge House
Bainbridge St
London   WC1A 1HP
Phone: 071-436 6194

To provide residential care and other sevices within the community for adults recovering from mental health problems

★2334★
Mental Health Film Council

380 Harrow Rd

London   W9 9HU
Phone: 071-286 2346

To promote the effective use of the media in promotion of mental health

★2335★
Metal Finishing Association

27 Fredericks St
Birmingham   B1 3HJ
Phone: 021-236 2657
Telex: 334003

★2336★
Metal Packaging Manufacturers Association

Elm House
19 Elmshott Lane
Cippenham
Slough   SL1 5QS
Phone: 0628 605203
Fax: 0628 665597

Trade association of companies involved in the manufacture of light metal containers, closures and fitments

★2337★
Metal Roofing Contractors Association

c/o J Wilson
31 Great Newton St
Liverpool   L3 5RN
Phone: 051-709 5951
Fax: 051-709 2872

★2338★
Metalforming Machinery Makers' Association

Queensway House
2 Queensway
Redhill   RH1 1QS
Phone: 0737 768611
Fax: 0737 760467

★2339★
Metamorphic Association

c/o G Saint-Pierre
67 Ritherden Rd
London   SW17 8QE
Phone: 081-672 5951

A technique used in holistic therapy

★2340★
Metropolitan Public Gardens Association
3 Mayfield Rd
Croydon CR4 6DN
Phone: 081-689 4197

★2341★
Microwave Association
8 High St
Hurstpierpoint
Brighton BN6 9TZ
Phone: 0273 834716
Fax: 0273 834306

Covers microwave ovens, cookware and accessories

★2342★
Midland General Galvanizers Association
93 Tettenhall Rd
Wolverhampton WV3 9PE
Phone: 0902 26726
Fax: 0902 26028

★2343★
Military Historical Society
c/o J Gaylor
30 Edgeborough Way
Bromley BR1 2UA
Phone: 081-460 7341

Covers research into the dress, arms, history and tradition of Britain's armed forces and those of the Commonwealth

★2344★
Milking Machine Manufacturers' Association
Yorkings
Grange Park
Ross-on-Wye HR9 6EA
Phone: 0600 890597

★2345★
Milling Cutter & Toolbit Association
Light Trades House
3 Melbourne Avenue
Sheffield S10 2QJ
Phone: 0742 663084
Fax: 0742 670910

★2346★
Mineral Industry Research Organisation
6 St James's Square
London SW1Y 4LD
Phone: 071-930 2399
Fax: 071-930 3249

Promotes science and technology relating to the finding, mining and processing of minerals and to their refining and recovery from any source

★2347★
Mineralogical Society of GB & Ireland
41 Queen's Gate
London SW7 5HR
Phone: 071-584 7916

To further the knowledge of mineralogy, crystallography, geochemistry and petrology

★2348★
Minerals Engineering Society
32 Field Rise, Littleover
Derby DE3 7DE
Phone: 0332 766812

★2349★
Miners' Lamp Manufacturers' Association
Queensway House
2 Queensway
Redhill RH1 1QS
Phone: 0737 768611
Fax: 0737 761685

★2350★
Mining Association of the UK
6 St James's Square
London SW1Y 4LD
Phone: 071-930 2399
Fax: 071-930 3249

Covering the interests of the mining of metals and minerals in any part of the world

★2351★
Mining Institute of Scotland
14 Pendreich Grove
Bonnyrigg
Edinburgh EH19 2EH
Phone: 031-663 5264

★2352★
Minor Metals Trades Association
6th Floor
Central House
32-66 High St
London   E15 2PS
Phone: 081-519 4872
Fax: 081-519 5483

★2353★
Mobile & Outside Caterers Association of GB
7 Hamilton Way
Wallington   SM6 9NJ
Phone: 081-669 8121
Fax: 081-647 1128

★2354★
Modern Humanities Research Association
c/o Professor David Wells
Dept of German
Birkbeck College,Malet St
London   WC1E 7HX
Phone: 071-631 6103
Fax: 071-631 6270

For scholars working in the fields of modern European languages and literature

★2355★
Modern Language Association *now* incorporated with Association for Language Learning

★2356★
Modern Pentathlon Association of GB
Wessex House
Silchester Rd
Tadley
Reading   RG26 6PX
Phone: 0734 810111
Fax: 0734 819817

★2357★
Money Advice Association
Aizlewood's Mill
Nursery St

Sheffield   S3 8GG
Phone: 0742 823165
Fax: 0742 823150

Assistance to debtors

★2358★
Monumental Brass Society
c/o 57 Leeside Crescent
London   NW11 0HA

Promotes the preservation and study of monumental brasses and incised slabs together with the study of lost brasses

★2359★
Mortar Producers' Association
74 Holly Walk
Leamington Spa   CV32 4JD
Phone: 0926 38611

★2360★
Motor Agents Association *now* Retail Motor Industry Federation

★2361★
Motor Barge Owners Association *now* incorporated with Association of Master Lightermen & Barge Owners

★2362★
Motor Industry Research Association
Watling St
Nuneaton   CV10 0TU
Phone: 0203 348541
Fax: 0203 343772

★2363★
Motor Schools Association of GB
182a Henthon Moor Rd
Stockport   SK4 4DY
Phone: 061-443 1611
Fax: 061-443 1699

Trade and professional association for driving instructors

★2364★
Motor Vehicle Dismantlers' Association of GB
15-17 Green Lane
Castle Bromwich

Birmingham B36 0WY
Phone: 021-776 7311
Fax: 021-776 7795

★2365★
Motorcycle Industry Association
Starley House
Eaton Rd
Coventry CV1 2FH
Phone: 0203 227427
Fax: 0203 229175

For manufacturers and importers of motorcyles, components and accessories

★2366★
Motorcycle Retailers Association *now* incorporated with Retail Motor Industry Federation

★2367★
Multiple Sclerosis Society of GB & Ireland
25 Effie Rd
London SW6 1EE
Phone: 071-736 6267

★2368★
Multiple Shoe Retailers' Association
Bedford House
69-79 Fulham Rd
London SW6 3JW
Phone: 071-391 5177
Fax: 0529

★2369★
Museum Training Institute
Kershaw House
55 Well St
Bradford BD1 5PS
Phone: 0274 391056
Fax: 0274 394890

Sets occupational standards for the museum, art gallery and heritage profession

★2370★
Museums Association
34 Bloomsbury Way

London WC1A 2SF
Phone: 071-404 4767
Fax: 071-430 0167

Representing museums and art galleries and their employees

★2371★
Mushroom Growers' Association
2 Saint Pauls St
Stamford PE9 2BE
Phone: 0780 66688
Fax: 0780 66558

★2372★
Music Advisers' National Association
c/o B Ley
Education Office
Shire Hall
Gloucester GL1 2TP
Phone: 0452 425300

★2373★
Music Film & Video Producers' Association
26 Noel St
London W1V 3RD
Phone: 071-434 2651
Fax: 071-434 9002

★2374★
Music Industries Association
7 The Avenue
Datchet
Slough SL3 9DH
Phone: 0753 41963
Fax: 0753 47190

Wholesalers and distributors of musical instruments

★2375★
Music Masters' & Mistresses' Association
c/o A Morris
Bedford School
Bedford MK40 2TU
Phone: 0234 59419

Members are musicians teaching in independent schools

★2376★
Music Publishers' Association
7th Floor
Kingsway House
103 Kingsway
London   WC2B 6QX
Phone: 071-831 7591
Fax: 071-242 0612

★2377★
Music Retailers Association
PO Box 249
London   W4 5EX
Phone: 081-994 7592

★2378★
Muzzle Loaders Association of GB
PO Box 493
Rhyl   LL18 5XG
Phone: 0745 584981

Concerned with the use and study of antique firearms, particularly the safe and effective use of muzzle loading rifles, pistols and shot-guns

★2379★
Names Society
32 Speer Rd
Thames Ditton   KT7 0PW
Phone: 081-398 0761

Dealing with the popularity of first names, the meaning of surnames and related aspects

★2380★
National & International Society for Education through Art
7a High St
Corsham   SN13 0ES
Phone: 0249 714825
Fax: 0249 716138

★2381★
National Adult School Organisation
Masu Centre
Gaywood Croft
Cregoe St
Birmingham   B15 2ED
Phone: 021-622 3400

★2382★
National Anglers' Council
11 Cowgate
Peterborough   PE1 1LZ
Phone: 0733 54084

★2383★
National Artists Association
79 Royal College St
London   NW1 2EW

★2384★
National Association for Curriculum Enrichment & Extension
Ohmagen
Nettleton Rd
Burton
Chippenham   SN14 7LR
Phone: 045421 395

★2385★
National Association for Design Education
c/o F Zanker
26 Dorchester Close
Mansfield   NG18 4QW
Phone: 0623 631551

★2386★
National Association for Education in the Arts
13 Back Lane
South Luffenham
Oakham   LE15 8NQ
Phone: 0780 721115
Fax: 0780 721401

★2387★
National Association for Environmental Education
Wolverhampton Polytechnic
Walsall Campus
Gorway
Walsall   WS1 3BD
Phone: 0922 31200

★2388★
**National Association for Gifted
  Children**
Park Campus
Boughton Green Rd
Northampton NN2 7AL
Phone: 0604 792300

To assist children with outstanding talents to
fulfil their potential, and to give support to
parents, teachers and others professionally
concerned with their development

★2389★
**National Association for Higher
  Education in Film & Video**
c/o West Surrey College of Art & Design
Falkner Rd
Farnham GU9 7DS
Phone: 0252 722441
Fax: 0252 733869

★2390★
**National Association for Maternal &
  Child Welfare**
1 South Audley St
London W1Y 6JS
Phone: 071-493 2601
Fax: 071-491 2772

Concerned with all aspects of education

★2391★
**National Association for Mental After-
  care in Registered Care Homes**
c/o P A Burns
The Mews Studio
102e Longstone Rd
Eastbourne BN21 3SJ
Phone: 0323 35662
Fax: 0323 32072

Members run residential and nursing homes
for people who are, or who have been, suffering from a mental disorder

★2392★
**National Association for Mental
  Health**
22 Harley St
London W1N 2ED
Phone: 071-637 0741
Fax: 071-323 0061

★2393★
**National Association for Organic
  Gardening**
Ryton-on-Dunsmore
Coventry CV8 3LG
Phone: 0203 303517

★2394★
**National Association for Outdoor
  Education**
c/o C Care
50 Highview Avenue
Grays
Romford RM17 6RU
Phone: 0708 855228

To further the recognition of outdoor education as an accepted approach to learning

★2395★
**National Association for Pastoral Care
  in Education**
c/o D Lambourn
Education Dept
University of Warwick
Coventry CV4 7AL
Phone: 0203 523810

★2396★
**National Association for Primary
  Education**
c/o T Scholey
University Centre
University of Leicester
Barrack Rd
Northampton NN2 6AF
Phone: 0604 30180

Membership includes teachers, school communities, parents and all interested in the primary phase of schooling and child
development

★2397★
**National Association for Remedial
  Education**
2 Lichfield Rd
Stafford ST17 4JX
Phone: 0785 46872
Fax: 0785 41187

Concerned with the prevention, investigation
and treatment of learning difficulties, from

whatever source, which hinder educational development

★2398★
National Association for Staff Development in Further & Higher Education
30 St Helena Rd
Colchester   CO3 3BA
Phone: 0206 571258

★2399★
National Association for Teaching English & other Community Languages to Adults
Hall Green College
Floodgate St
Birmingham   B5 5SU
Phone: 021-778 2311   ext. 290
Fax: 021-616 1303

Aims to advance the education of adults resident in the UK whose first language is not English

★2400★
National Association for the Care & Resettlement of Offenders
169 Clapham Rd
London   SW9 0PU
Phone: 071-582 6500
Fax: 071-735 1673

★2401★
National Association for the Support of Small Schools
c/o Molly Stiles
91 King St
Norwich   NR1 1PH
Phone: 0603 613088

★2402★
National Association for the Teaching of English
c/o Birley School Annexe
Fox Lane
Sheffield   S12 4SW
Phone: 0742 390081

The teaching of English at all levels

★2403★
National Association for the Teaching of Drama
30 Heathdene Rd
London   SW16 3PD
Phone: 081-679 3661

★2404★
National Association for the Welfare of Children in Hospital
29-31 Euston Rd
London   NW1 2SD
Phone: 071-833 2041

A partnership of parents and professionals working to promote the best health care for children at home or in hospital

★2405★
National Association for Voluntary Hostels
Fulham Palace
Bishops Avenue
London   SW6 6EA
Phone: 071-731 4205

All aspects of hostel management and the care of single, homeless people

★2406★
National Association of Advisers in Craft Design & Technology
124 Kidmore Rd
Reading   RG4 7NB
Phone: 0734 470615

Members are local authority education advisers and inspectors

★2407★
National Association of Advisory Officers for Special Education
c/o C Dyer
32a Pleasant Valley
Saffron Walden   CB11 4AP

★2408★
National Association of Agricultural Contractors
Huts Corner
Tilford Rd
Hindhead   GU26 6SF
Phone: 042873 5360

★2409★
National Association of Almshouses
see Almshouse Association ·

★2410★
National Association of Approved Driving Instructors
90 Ash Lane
Halebarns
Altrincham WA15 8PB
Phone: 061-980 5907

Members are individual Department of Transport approved driving instructors

★2411★
National Association of Arc Welding Equipment Repairers
c/o G K Edwards
74 Chester Rd
Birmingham B36 7BU
Phone: 021-776 7474
Fax: 021-776 7605

★2412★
National Association of Archery Coaches
c/o J Adams
132 Hamstead Hall Rd
Birmingham B20 1JB
Phone: 021-554 8840

★2413★
National Association of Bereavement Services
c/o J Webster
68 Charlton St
London NW1 1JR
Phone: 071-388 2153

★2414★
National Association of Bookmakers
Tolworth Tower
Ewell Rd
Surbiton KT6 7EL
Phone: 081-390 8222
Fax: 081-390 8222

★2415★
National Association of Boys' Clubs
369 Kennington Lane
London SE11 5QY
Phone: 071-793 0787

★2416★
National Association of Breeders' Services
c/o Herdwise (UK) Ltd
Barclays Bank Chambers
North End
Bedale
Ripon DL8 1AB
Phone: 0677 24216
Fax: 0677 24778

For private companies supplying bovine semen

★2417★
National Association of British & Irish Millers
21 Arlington St
London SW1A 1RN
Phone: 071-493 2521
Fax: 071-493 6785

★2418★
National Association of British Market Authorities
c/o Brian Ormshaw
19 Derwent Avenue
Milnrow
Rochdale OL16 3UD
Phone: 0706 57740

An association of local authorities owning and/or operating livestock markets

★2419★
National Association of Careers & Guidance Teachers
c/o I H Lee
34 Station Rd
Hesketh Bank
Preston PR4 6SP
Phone: 0772 814258

★2420★
National Association of Catering Butchers
217 Central Markets
Smithfield

London   EC1A 9LH
Phone: 071-489 0005
Fax: 071-248 4733

★2421★
National Association of Chimney Sweeps

PO Box 35
Stoke-on-Trent   ST4 7NU
Phone: 0782 744311
Fax: 0782 747300

Formed to improve the standards of the chimney sweeping profession and to create appropriate qualifications

★2422★
National Association of Chimney Lining Engineers

PO Box 35
Stoke-on-Trent   ST4 7NU
Phone: 0782 744311
Fax: 0782 747300

Members are companies using a system of pumped in situ chimney lining

★2423★
National Association of Cider Makers

now incorporated into Food & Drink Federation

★2424★
National Association of Cigarette Machine Operators

Unit 2
Waymills Industrial Estate
Whitchurch
Shrewsbury   SY13 1TT
Phone: 0948 4850

★2425★
National Association of Citizens Advice Bureaux

Myddelton House
115-123 Pentonville Rd
London   N1 9LZ
Phone: 071-833 2181
Fax: 071-833 4371

★2426★
National Association of Colleges in Distributive Education & Training

c/o J Turner
39 The Birches
London   N21 4NJ
Phone: 081-360 4409

Furtherance and development of education and training for those employed in the distributive trades

★2427★
National Association of Colliery Managers

137 Station Rd
Lingfield   RH7 6DZ
Phone: 0342 833716
Fax: 0737 60425

★2428★
National Association of Counsellors in Education

c/o B W Vaughan
10 Durham St
Swindon   SN1 3HS
Phone: 0793 35378

To promote the acceptance of counselling as a profession within the educational system

★2429★
National Association of Deafened People

c/o Royal National Institute for the Deaf
105 Gower St
London   WC1E 6AH
Phone: 071-387 8033
Fax: 071-388 2346

★2430★
National Association of Decorative & Fine Arts Societies

8a Grosvenor Place
London   SW1W 0EN
Phone: 071-233 5433

★2431★
National Association of Development Education Centres

6 Endsleigh St

London WC1H 0DX
Phone: 071-388 2670

★2432★
National Association of Estate Agents
Arbon House
21 Jury St
Warwick CV34 4EH
Phone: 0926 496800
Fax: 0926 400953

A professional body for individuals in practice
as estate agents

★2433★
**National Association of Family
  Planning Doctors**
27 Sussex Place
London NW1 4RG
Phone: 071-724 2441
Fax: 071-723 0575

★2434★
**National Association of Farriers,
  Blacksmiths & Agricultural
  Engineers**
Avenue R
7th St
National Agricultural Centre
Stoneleigh
Kenilworth CV8 2LG
Phone: 0203 696595
Fax: 0203 696708

★2435★
**National Association of Fastener
  Stockholders**
c/o G K Edwards
74 Chester Rd
Birmingham B36 7BU
Phone: 021-776 7474
Fax: 021-776 7605

Members are stockists/distributors of industrial fasteners

★2436★
**National Association of Field Studies
  Officers**
Arnfield Tower Field Study Centre
Manchester Rd
Tintwhistle

Manchester SK14 7NE
Phone: 04574 2420

★2437★
National Association of Fire Officers
10 Cuthbert Rd
Croydon CRO 3RB
Phone: 081-686 8863
Fax: 081-681 8875

★2438★
**National Association of Flower
  Arrangement Societies of GB**
21 Denbigh St
London SW1V 2HF
Phone: 071-828 5145

★2439★
**National Association of Funeral
  Directors**
618 Warwick Rd
Solihull B91 1AA
Phone: 021-711 1343

★2440★
National Association of Goldsmiths
St Dunstan's House
Carey Lane
London EC2V 8AB
Phone: 071-726 4374
Fax: 071-726 4873

Members include retail jewellers, silversmiths
and horologists

★2441★
**National Association of Governors &
  Managers**
81 Rustlings Rd
Sheffield S11 7AB
Phone: 0742 662467

Information, training and advice for school
governors

★2442★
**National Association of Head Teachers
  & Deputies**
1 Heath Square
Boltro Rd

Haywards Heath   RH16 1BL
Phone: 0444 458133
Fax: 0444 416326

For heads and deputies of all types of schools in the UK

★2443★
National Association of Health Estate Managers
c/o H Potts
St Mary's Hospital
14 Pope's Lane
Colchester   CO3 3JL
Phone: 0206 769244 ext. 260

★2444★
National Association of Health Service Personnel Officers
c/o Ms N Bartley
Merseyside Regional Health Authority
Hamilton House
24 Pall Mall
Liverpool   L36 1AL
Phone: 051-236 4620

★2445★
National Association of Health Authorities
Birmingham Research Park
Vincent Drive
Birmingham   B15 2SQ
Phone: 021-471 4444
Fax: 021-414 1120

★2446★
National Association of Health Stores
c/o J Scorrot
Chamber of Commerce Building
Unit D2
Boston Industrial Estate
Norfolk St
Boston   PE21 9HG
Phone: 0205 362626

★2447★
National Association of Health Service Security Officers
c/o W G Collins
District Security Officer

West Glamorgan Health Authority
36 Orchard St
Swansea   SA1 5AQ
Phone: 0792 458066
Fax: 0792 655364

★2448★
National Association of Health & Exercise Teachers
112a Great Russell St
London   WC1B 3NQ
Phone: 071-580 4451
Fax: 071-637 0753

★2449★
National Association of Holiday Centres
10 Bolton St
London   W1Y 8AU
Phone: 071-499 8000
Fax: 071-629 4460

★2450★
National Association of Hospital Broadcasting Organisations
PO Box 2481
London   W2 1JR
Phone: 071-402 8815

★2451★
National Association of Hospital Fire Officers
c/o B Clarke
District Risk Manager
St Bartholomew's Hospital
West Smithfield
London   EC1 7BE
Phone: 071-601 8054
Fax: 071-601 8057

★2452★
National Association of Industrial Distributors
74 Chester Rd
Birmingham   B4 7SY
Phone: 021-776 7474
Fax: 021-776 7655

★2453★
National Association of Industries for the Blind & Disabled
43a High St South
Dunstable LU6 3RA
Phone: 0582 606796

★2454★
National Association of Inland Waterway Carriers
9-11 Jameson St
Hull HU1 3HR
Phone: 0482 27281

★2455★
National Association of Inspectors & Educational Advisers
1 Heath Square
Boltro Rd
Haywards Heath RH16 1BL
Phone: 0444 441279
Fax: 0444 416326

★2456★
National Association of Investment Clubs
Tower Buildings
Water St
Liverpool L3 1PQ
Phone: 051-236 6262
Fax: 051-236 6004

★2457★
National Association of Language Advisers
c/o J Lee
Westbury Centre
Ripple Rd
Barking IG11 7PT
Phone: 0483 572881   ext. 29

★2458★
National Association of Leagues of Hospital Friends
2nd Floor
Fairfax House
Causton Rd
Colchester CO1 1RJ
Phone: 0206 761227

★2459★
National Association of Licensed House Managers
9 Coombe Lane
London SW20 8NE
Phone: 081-947 3080

★2460★
National Association of Lift Makers
Leicester House
8 Leicester St
London WC2H 7BN
Phone: 071-437 0678
Fax: 071-437 4901

An association covering lifts, escalators, passenger conveyors and paternosters

★2461★
National Association of Local Councils
108 Great Russell St
London WC1B 3LD
Phone: 071-637 1865

Covers English parish and town councils and Welsh community councils

★2462★
National Association of Loft Insulation Contractors
PO Box 12
Haslemere GU27 3AH
Phone: 0428 54011
Fax: 0428 51401

★2463★
National Association of Master Bakers
21 Baldock St
Ware SG12 9DH
Phone: 0920 468061
Fax: 0920 461632

★2464★
National Association of Mathematics Advisors
c/o A Hibbert
Taberner House
Park Lane
Croydon CR9 1TP
Phone: 081-686 4433   ext. 2147

Members are mathematics inspectors and advisers to local educational authorities and provide information on mathematics education

★2465★
National Association of Memorial Masons
Crown Buildings
High St
Aylesbury HP20 1SL
Phone: 0296 434750
Fax: 0296 431332

Employers' organisation for the memorial masonry trade

★2466★
National Association of National Health Care Supplies Managers
c/o Mrs C B Jones
Hillingdon Health Authority
Royal Lane
Hillingdon
Uxbridge UB8 3QW
Phone: 0895 72181
Fax: 0895 811031

Members are engaged in the management of supplies used in direct health care provision

★2467★
National Association of Orientation & Mobility Instructors
c/o Miss J M Hollis
107 Cowper St
Brighton BN3 5BL
Phone: 0273 735609

★2468★
National Association of Paper Merchants
Papermaker House
Rivenhall Rd
Westlea
Swindon SN5 7BE
Phone: 0793 886086
Fax: 0793 886182

★2469★
National Association of Pension Funds
12-18 Grosvenor Gardens

London SW1W ODH
Phone: 071-730 0585
Fax: 071-730 2595

All matters relating to the provision of retirement and allied benefits

★2470★
National Association of Perry Makers
c/o J D Brown
Allied Vintners Ltd
Kilver St
Shepton Mallet BA4 5ND
Phone: 0749 343333
Fax: 0749 345673

★2471★
National Association of Plumbing, Heating & Mechanical Services Contractors
Ensign House
Westwood Way
Coventry CV4 8BA
Phone: 0203 470626
Fax: 0203 470942

★2472★
National Association of Postgraduate Medical Education Centre Administrators
c/o J Woodings
Burton District Hospital
Belvedere Rd
Burton upon Trent DE13 0RB
Phone: 0283 66333

★2473★
National Association of Principal Agricultural Education Officers
c/o R A Holtom
Staffordshire College of Agriculture
Robaston
Penkridge
Stafford ST19 5PH
Phone: 0785 712209
Fax: 0785 715701

★2474★
National Association of Prison Visitors
c/o Mrs A G McKenna
46b Hartington St

Bedford   MK41 7RL
Phone: 0234 359763

★2475★
**National Association of Probation
   Officers**
3-4 Chivalry Rd
London   SW11 1HT
Phone: 071-223 4887

★2476★
**National Association of Public Golf
   Courses**
35 Sinclair Grove
London   NW11 9JH
Phone: 071-734 2421

★2477★
National Association of Racial Equality
1st Floor
8-16 Coronet St
London   N1 6HD
Phone: 071-739 6658

★2478★
**National Association of Radiator
   Specialists**
c/o R Paterson
Heath Cottage
25 Long St
Wheaton Aston
Stafford   ST19 9NF
Phone: 0785 840086

Concerning the manufacture and repair of
radiators fixed to internal combustion engines
and industrial heat exchange equipment

★2479★
**National Association of Range
   Manufacturers**
34 St Margarets Rd
Ruislip   HA4 7NY
Phone: 0895 638114

★2480★
**National Association of Retail
   Furnishers**
17-21 George St
Croydon   CR9 1TQ
Phone: 081-680 8444

★2481★
**National Association of Scaffolding
   Contractors**
82 New Cavendish St
London   W1M 8AD
Phone: 071-580 5588
Fax: 071-436 5398

★2482★
**National Association of School Meals
   Organisers** *now* Local Authority
Caterers Association

★2483★
**National Association of Schoolmaster
   & Union of Women Teachers**
Hillscourt Education Centre
Rednal
Birmingham   B45 8RS
Phone: 021-453 6150
Fax: 021-453 7224

★2484★
**National Association of Seed Potato
   Merchants**
Suite A
Palmer House
Palmer Lane
Coventry   CV1 1FN
Phone: 0203 553949
Fax: 0203 553949

★2485★
National Association of Shopfitters
411 Limpsfield Rd
Warlingham   CR6 9HA
Phone: 0883 624961
Fax: 0883 626841

★2486★
National Association of Shopkeepers
Lynch House
91 Mansfield Rd
Nottingham   NG1 3FN
Phone: 0602 475046

Primarily for small retailers and traders

★2487★
National Association of Social Workers in Education
116 Greenhill Rd
Winchester SO22 5DG
Phone: 0962 62876

★2488★
National Association of Sole Practitioners
8 South Parade
Summertown
Oxford OX2 7JZ
Phone: 0865 310991
Fax: 0865 56181

Members are solicitors who are the sole partner in a practice

★2489★
National Association of Solid Fuel Wholesalers
Victoria House
Southampton Row
London WC1B 4DH
Phone: 071-405 0034
Fax: 071-831 5181

★2490★
National Association of Sound & Lighting Companies
Park House
East Dulwich
London SE22 8RY
Phone: 081-693 1734

★2491★
National Association of Specialist Anglers *see* Angling Foundation

★2492★
National Association of Steel Stockholders
Gateway House
High St
Birmingham B4 7SY
Phone: 021-632 5821
Fax: 021-643 6645

★2493★
National Association of Teachers of Dancing
56 The Broadway
Thatcham
Newbury RG13 4HP
Phone: 0635 68888

★2494★
National Association of Teachers of Home Economics
Hamilton House
Mabledon Place
London WC1H 9BJ
Phone: 071-387 1441

★2495★
National Association of the Launderette Industry
79 Glen Eyre Rd
Southampton SO2 3NN
Phone: 0703 766328
Fax: 0703 766328

★2496★
National Association of Theatre Nurses
22 Mount Parade
Harrogate HG1 1BV
Phone: 0423 508079
Fax: 0423 531613

Members are trained nurses working in theatre, anaesthetics, recovery and sterile supply units

★2497★
National Association of Toastmasters
c/o M Nicholls
Albany House
Albany Crescent
Claygate
Esher KT10 0PF
Phone: 0372 68022

★2498★
National Association of Toy Distributors
3 Dean Farrar St
London SW1H 9LG
Phone: 071-222 0441
Fax: 071-222 1064

★2499★
National Association of Toy Retailers
24 Baldwyn Gardens
London   W3 6HL
Phone: 081-993 2894
Fax: 081-992 0408

★2500★
National Association of Trade
** Protection Societies**
4-6 New St
Leicester   LE1 5NB
Phone: 0533 531951

★2501★
National Association of Tripedressers
60 Claremont Rd
Surbiton   KT6 4RH
Phone: 081-390 2027
Fax: 081-390 2027

★2502★
National Association of Victims
** Support Schemes**
Cranmer House
39 Brixton Rd
London   SW9 6DZ
Phone: 071-735 9166
Fax: 071-582 5712

Victim support offers information, practical
help and emotional support to victims of
crime

★2503★
National Association of Voluntary Help
** Organisers**
c/o Mrs J Hawthore
Winwick Hospital
Winwick
Warrington   WA2 8RR
Phone: 0722 336262

★2504★
National Association of Warehouse
** Keepers**
Walter House
418-422 Strand

London   WC2R 0PT
Phone: 071-836 5522
Fax: 071-379 6904

Representing the interests of public warehouse keepers

★2505★
National Association of Waste
** Disposal Contractors**
Mountbarrow House
6-20 Elizabeth St
London   SW1W 9RB
Phone: 071-824 8882
Fax: 071-824 8753

★2506★
National Association of Water Power
** Users**
c/o Cdr G C Chapman
The Rock
South Brent
Torquay   TQ10 9JL
Phone: 0364 72185

★2507★
National Association of Women's
** Clubs**
5 Vernon Rise,
London   WC1X 9EP
Phone: 071-837 1434

★2508★
National Association of Youth Hostel
** Wardens**
c/o N K Jordon
Youth Hostel
Mounton Rd
Chepstow   NP6 6AA
Phone: 0727 55215

★2509★
National Association of Youth
** Orchestras**
c/o Carol Main
Ainslie House
11 Saint Colme St
Edinburgh   EH3 6AG
Phone: 031-225 4606

★2510★
National Association of Youth &
Community Education Officers
c/o J Tate
Cross Park
Ringmore
Kingsbridge   TQ7 4HW
Phone: 0548 810238

The professional body for officers and advisers employed by local authorities in the field of social education

★2511★
National Audio Visual Aids Library
George Building
Normal College
Bangor   LL57 2PZ
Phone: 0248 370144
Fax: 0248 351415

★2512★
National Autistic Society
276 Willesden Lane
London   NW2 5RB
Phone: 081-451 1114
Fax: 081-451 5865

★2513★
National Automobile Safety Belt
Association
60 Claremont Rd
Surbiton   KT6 4RH
Phone: 081-390 2027
Fax: 081-390 2022

★2514★
National Bed Federation
251 Brompton Rd
London   SW3 2EZ
Phone: 071-589 4888
Fax: 071-823 7009

Represents manufacturers of beds, mattresses and pillows

★2515★
National Board for Nursing, Midwifery
& Health Visiting for Northern
Ireland
RAC House
79 Chichester St

Belfast   BT1 4JE
Phone: 0232 238152

★2516★
National Board for Nursing, Midwifery
& Health Visiting for Scotland
22 Queen St
Edinburgh   EH2 1JX
Phone: 031-226 7371
Fax: 031-225 9970

★2517★
National Caravan Council
Catherine House
Victoria Rd
Aldershot   GU11 1SS
Phone: 0252 318251
Fax: 0252 22596

Members include manufacturers, distributors, park operators and suppliers of components, accessories and services

★2518★
National Care Homes Association
5 Bloomsbury Place
London   WC1A 2QA
Phone: 071-436 1871
Fax: 071-436 1193

Members run residential care homes for the infirm

★2519★
National Carpet Cleaners Association
45 Seymour Rd
St Albans   AL3 5HN
Phone: 0727 862101

★2520★
National Cattle Breeders' Association
c/o R W Kershaw-Dalby
Lawford Grange
Lawford Heath
Rugby   CV23 9HG
Phone: 0788 565264
Fax: 0788 567142

★2521★
National Caving Association
c/o 3 Valletort Rd
Stoke

Plymouth PL1 5PH
Phone: 0752 563588

★2522★
National Cavity Insulation Association
PO Box 12
Haslemere GU27 3AH
Phone: 0428 654011
Fax: 0428 651401

★2523★
National Centre of Tribology
c/o United Kingdom Atomic Energy
   Authority
Risley
Warrington WA3 6AT
Phone: 0925 252640
Fax: 0925 252579

All aspects of lubrication, friction and wear

★2524★
National Chamber of Trade
Enterprise House
59 Castle St
Reading RG1 7SN
Phone: 0734 566744
Fax: 0734 567963

★2525★
National Children's Bureau
8 Wakley St
London EC1V 7QE
Phone: 071-278 9441
Fax: 071-278 9512

To improve communication and co-ordination between those connected with the care
and well-being of children and their families -
normal, deprived and handicapped

★2526★
**National Childrens' Wear Association
   of GB & NI**
40-42 Oxford St
London W1N 9FJ
Phone: 071-636 1833
Fax: 071-631 3748

★2527★
National Church Crafts Association
c/o A C Rose
Henwood Decorative Metal Studios
The Bayle
Folkestone CT20 1SQ
Phone: 0303 50911
Fax: 0303 850224

★2528★
National Clayware Federation
7 Castle St
Bridgwater TA6 3DT
Phone: 0278 458251
Fax: 0278 428358

Scope covered includes chimney pots, flue
liners, airbricks and ridge tiles

★2529★
National Cold Storage Federation *see*
   Cold Storage & Distribution
   Federation

★2530★
**National College of Hypnosis &
   Psychotherapy**
12 Cross St
Nelson BB9 7EN
Phone: 0282 699378

★2531★
**National Committee of Skal Clubs of
   the UK**
21 Churchfield Rd
Poole
Bournemouth BH15 2QL
Phone: 0202 749311
Fax: 0202 391744

Members are executives working the travel
and tourism industry

★2532★
**National Confederation of Parent-
   Teacher Associations**
2 Ebbsfleet Industrial Estate
Stonebridge Rd
Northfleet
Gravesend DA11 9DS
Phone: 0474 560618
Fax: 0474 564418

★2533★
National Conference of Friendly Societies
Room 313
Victoria House
Vernon Place
London WC1B 4DP
Phone: 071-242 1923

★2534★
National Consumer Credit Federation
98-100 Holme Lane
Sheffield S6 4JW
Phone: 0742 348101

★2535★
National Contractors Group
82 New Cavendish St
London W1M 8AD
Phone: 071-580 5588
Fax: 071-631 3872

Building contractors

★2536★
National Council for Advisers for Educational Technology
c/o P Baker
Centre for Educational Technology
Herrick Rd
Leicester LE2 6DJ
Phone: 0533 709759

The professional body for local education authority officers concerned with the development of educational and information technology in England and Wales

★2537★
National Council for Baking Education
20 Bedford Square
London WC1B 3HF
Phone: 071-580 4252
Fax: 071-580 4252

★2538★
National Council for Drama Training
5 Tavistock Place
London WC1H 9FF
Phone: 071-387 3650

★2539★
National Council for Educational Standards
c/o Mrs M Smith
1 Hinckley Way
Esher KT10 0BD
Phone: 081-398 1253

★2540★
National Council for Educational Technology
3 Devonshire St
London W1N 2BA
Phone: 071-636 4186
Fax: 071-636 2163

★2541★
National Council for Mother Tongue Teaching
5 Musgrave Crescent
London SW6 4PT
Phone: 071-736 2134

★2542★
National Council for Schools Sports
c/o D Lomas
21 Northampton Rd
Croydon CR0 7HB
Phone: 081-656 8857

★2543★
National Council for Special Education
Exhall Grange
Wheelwright Lane
Coventry CV7 9HP
Phone: 0203 362414

To further the education and welfare of all who are in any way handicapped

★2544★
National Council for Teacher-centred Professional Development
c/o K Martin
Somerset Education Centre
Park Rd
Bridgwater TA6 7HS
Phone: 0278 423721
Fax: 0278 428181

★2545★
National Council for the Conservation of Plants & Gardens
c/o The Pines
Wisley Gardens
Woking GU23 6QB
Phone: 0483 211465
Fax: 0483 211003

Aims to conserve garden plants for future generations

★2546★
National Council for Vocational Qualifications
222 Euston Rd
London NW1 2BZ
Phone: 071-387 9898
Fax: 071-387 0978

★2547★
National Council for Voluntary Organisations
26 Bedford Square
London WC1B 3HU
Phone: 071-636 4066
Fax: 071-436 3188

★2548★
National Council for Voluntary Youth Services
Wellington House
29 Albion St
Leicester LE1 6GD
Phone: 0533 471400
Fax: 0533 548573

★2549★
National Council of Building Material Producers
26 Store St
London WC1E 6BD
Phone: 071-323 3770
Fax: 071-323 0307

★2550★
National Council of Psychotherapists & Hypnotherapy Register
1 Clovelly Rd
London W5 5HF
Phone: 081-567 0262

★2551★
National Council of Voluntary Child Care Organisations
8 Wakley St
London EC1V 7QE
Phone: 071-833 3319
Fax: 071-833 8637

Co-ordinates child care agencies in the voluntary sector

★2552★
National Council of Women of GB
36 Danbury St
London N1 8JU
Phone: 071-354 2395

★2553★
National Council on Inland Transport
5 Pembridge Crescent
London W11 3DT
Phone: 071-727 4689

Concerned with public transport for passengers and goods

★2554★
National Cricket Association
c/o Lord's Cricket Ground
St John's Wood Rd
London NW8 8QZ
Phone: 071-289 6098

★2555★
National Dairy Council
5-7 John Princes St
London W1M 0AP
Phone: 071-499 7822
Fax: 071-408 1353

★2556★
National Dairy Producers Association
c/o G T Davies
Perthi Mwyar
Hayscastle
Haverfordwest SA62 5PR
Phone: 0348 840789

★2557★
National Dairymen's Association
19 Cornwall Terrace

London NW1 4QP
Phone: 071-935 4562
Fax: 071-487 4734

★2558★
National Deaf Childrens' Society
45 Hereford Rd
London W2 5AH
Phone: 071-229 9272
Fax: 071-243 0195

★2559★
National Diabetes Foundation *now*
Diabetes Foundation

★2560★
National Dried Fruit Trade Association
152-160 City Rd
London EC1V 2NP
Phone: 071-253 9421
Fax: 071-250 0965

★2561★
National Early Music Association
8 Covent Garden
Cambridge CB1 2HR
Phone: 0223 315681

★2562★
**National Edible Oil Distributors'
Association** *now* incorporated into
Food & Drink Federation

★2563★
National Education Association
c/o Mrs M Smith
1 Hinckley Way
Esher KT10 0BD
Phone: 081-398 1253

★2564★
National Egg Marketing Association
High Holborn House
52-54 High Holborn
London WC1V 6SX
Phone: 071-242 4683
Fax: 071-831 0624

★2565★
National Electronics Council
Room 211
Savoy Hill House
Savoy Hill
London WC2R 0BU
Phone: 071-836 4264

Concerned with the social impact of the introduction of electronic equipment

★2566★
National Energy Efficiency Association
18 Devonshire St
London W1N 2AV

The professional association for managers of energy

★2567★
**National Engineering Construction
Employers' Association**
Broadway House
Tothill St
London SW1H 9NQ
Phone: 071-222 7777
Fax: 071-233 1930

★2568★
National Exhibitors Association
29a Market Square
Biggleswade SG18 8AQ
Phone: 0767-316255
Fax: 0767-316430

Members are organisations and companies attending exhibitions

★2569★
National Farmers' Union
Agriculture House
25-31 Knightsbridge
London SW1X 7NJ
Phone: 071-235 5077
Fax: 071-235 3526

Membership is restricted to working farmers

★2570★
National Farmers' Union of Scotland
17 Grosvenor Crescent
Edinburgh EH12 5EN
Phone: 031-337 4333
Fax: 031-337 4127

★2571★
National Federation of Anglers
Halliday House
2 Wilson St
Derby   DE1 1PG
Phone: 0322 362000

★2572★
National Federation of Bus Users
6 Holmhurst Lane
St Leonards-on-Sea
Hastings   TN37 7LW
Phone: 0424 752424

Seeks to improve bus services, bus design and passenger facilities

★2573★
National Federation of City Farms
c/o Avon Environmental Centre
Junction Rd
Brislington
Bristol   BS4 3JP
Phone: 0272 719109

For community-run city farm and garden projects

★2574★
National Federation of Clay Industries
see British Ceramic Confederation

★2575★
National Federation of Community Organisations
8-9 Upper St
London   N1 OPQ
Phone: 071-226 0189

Helping to promote and develop facilities for recreation and leisure-time occupation to improve the conditions of life of local residents

★2576★
National Federation of Consumer Groups
12 Mosley St
Newcastle upon Tyne   NE1 1DE
Phone: 091-261 8259

★2577★
National Federation of Demolition Contractors
Cowdray House
6 Portugal St
London   WC2A 2HH
Phone: 071-404 4020
Fax: 071-430 2680

★2578★
National Federation of Fish Friers
Federation House
289 Dewsbury Rd
Leeds   LS11 5HW
Phone: 0532 713291
Fax: 0532 717571

Representing bona fide fish and chip shop proprietors

★2579★
National Federation of Fishermen's Organisations
Marsden Rd
Fish Docks
Grimsby   DN31 3SG
Phone: 0472 352141
Fax: 0472 242486

Representative body for full-time commercial fishermen

★2580★
National Federation of Fishmongers
34 St Margarets Rd
Ruislip   HA4 7NY
Phone: 0895 638114

Incorporating poultry, game and rabbit traders

★2581★
National Federation of Fruit & Potato Trades
103-107 Market Towers
Nine Elms Lane
London   SW8 5NQ
Phone: 071-627 3391
Fax: 071-498 1191

Representing wholesaleing and importing of fresh fruit, vegetables, potatoes and flowers

★2582★
National Federation of Hide & Skin Markets
51 Hill Ave
Amersham   HP6 5BX
Phone: 0494 728428

★2583★
National Federation of Housing Co-operatives
88 Old St
London   EC1V 9AX
Phone: 071-608 2494
Fax: 071-490 5280

★2584★
National Federation of Housing Associations
175 Gray's Inn Rd
London   WC1X 8UP
Phone: 071-278 6571
Fax: 071-955 8696

★2585★
National Federation of Inland Wholesale Fish Merchants
West India Dock Rd
London   E14 5ST
Phone: 071-515 2655

★2586★
National Federation of Master Steeplejacks Lightning Conductor Engineers
6th Floor
Epic House
Charles St
Leicester   LE1 3SH
Phone: 0533 538915
Fax: 0533 511754

★2587★
National Federation of Master Window Cleaners
Summerfield House
Harrogate Rd
Stockport   SK5 6HQ
Phone: 061-432 8754

★2588★
National Federation of Meat Traders
1 Belgrove
Tunbridge Wells   TN1 1YW
Phone: 0892 541412
Fax: 0892 35462

Members include independent retail butchers, slaughterhouse operators, bacon curers and small goods manufacturers

★2589★
National Federation of Music Societies
Francis House
Francis St
London   SW1P 1DE
Phone: 071-828 7320
Fax: 071-828 5504

Members belong to amateur music clubs, choral and orchestral societies

★2590★
National Federation of Painting & Decorating Contractors
82 New Cavendish St
London   W1M 8AD
Phone: 071-580 5588
Fax: 071-631 3872

★2591★
National Federation of Plastering & Dry Lining Partition Contractors
82 New Cavendish St
London   W1M 8AD
Phone: 071-580 5588
Fax: 071-631 3872

★2592★
National Federation of Playgoers' Societies
c/o Mrs E Bunclark
18 Seymour Rd
Westcliffe-on-Sea
Southend-on-Sea   SS0 8NJ
Phone: 0702 74391

★2593★
National Federation of Retail Newsagents
Yeoman House
11 Sekforde St

London   EC1R 0HD
Phone: 071-253 4225
Fax: 071-250 0927

Members are mainly independent retail newsagents and some managers of multiple newsagents

★2594★
National Federation of Roofing Contractors
24 Weymouth St
London   W1N 3FA
Phone: 071-436 0387
Fax: 071-637 5215

★2595★
National Federation of Scale & Weighing Machine Manufacturers
1 Totteridge Avenue
High Wycombe   HP13 6XG
Phone: 0494 30430
Fax: 0494 446788

★2596★
National Federation of Sea Anglers
14 Bank St
Newton Abbot   TQ12 2JW
Phone: 0626 331330

★2597★
National Federation of Self-Employed
140 Lower Marsh
London   SE1 7AE
Phone: 071-928 9272
Fax: 071-401 2544

Members are self-employed workers and small businesses

★2598★
National Federation of Self-Help Organisations
150 Townmead Rd
London   SW6 2RA
Phone: 071-731 8440

For ethnic minority groups

★2599★
National Federation of Spiritual Healers
Old Manor Farm Studio
Church St
Sunbury-on-Thames   TW16 6RG
Phone: 0932 783164

★2600★
National Federation of Taxicab Associations
c/o S Thresh
41 Maple Drive
Huntingdon   PE18 7JE
Phone: 0480 432223

★2601★
National Federation of Terrazzo-Mosaic Specialists
PO Box 50
Banstead   SM7 2RD
Phone: 0737 360673

★2602★
National Federation of Voluntary Literacy Schemes
Cambridge House
131 Camberwell Rd
London   SE5 0HF
Phone: 071-703 8083

To promote and develop the work of voluntary adult basic education schemes

★2603★
National Federation of Wholesale Poultry Merchants
1 Belgrove
Tunbridge Wells   TN1 1YW
Phone: 0892 541412
Fax: 0892 35462

★2604★
National Federation of Women's Institutes
39 Eccleston St
London   SW1W 9NT
Phone: 071-730 7212

★2605★

**National Federation of Young Farmers
  Clubs**

c/o National Agricultural Centre
Stoneleigh
Kenilworth CV8 2LG
Phone: 0203 696544
Fax: 0203 696900

★2606★

**National Federation of Zoological
  Gardens of GB & Ireland**

c/o Zoological Society
Regent's Park
London NW1 4RY
Phone: 071-586 0230
Fax: 071-483 4436

★2607★

National Fillings Trades Association

263 Monton Rd
Manchester M30 9LF
Phone: 061-788 9018
Fax: 061-787 7741

For manufacturers of synthetic and natural
filling materials

★2608★

**National Fireplace Council
  Manufacturers' Association**

PO Box 35
Stoke-on-Trent ST4 7NU
Phone: 0782 44311
Fax: 0782 747300

★2609★

**National Foundation for Educational
  Research in England & Wales**

The Mere
Upton Park
Slough SL1 2DQ
Phone: 0753 74123

★2610★

National Game Dealers Association

1 Belgrove

Tunbridge Wells TN1 1YW
Phone: 0892 541412
Fax: 0892 35462

Trade organisation whose members cover
wholesale and export game

★2611★

**National Glass Reinforced Plastics
  Construction Federation**

82 New Cavendish St
London W1M 8AD
Phone: 071-580 5588
Fax: 071-436 5398

★2612★

**National Golf Clubs Advisory
  Association**

Victoria Mill
Buxton Rd
Bakewell DE4 1DA
Phone: 0629 813844

★2613★

National Hairdressers' Federation

11 Goldington Rd
Bedford MK40 3JY
Phone: 0234 60332
Fax: 0234 269337

Members own hairdressing salons

★2614★

National Hedgelaying Society

c/o Miss M A Ellis
YFC Centre
National Agricultural Centre
Stoneleigh
Kenilworth CV8 2LG
Phone: 0203 696544
Fax: 0203 696900

To encourage the craft of hedgelaying and to
maintain local styles

★2615★

National Home Improvement Council

26 Store St
London WC1E 7BT
Phone: 071-636 2562

★2616★
National House-Building Council
58 Portland Place
London W1N 4BU
Phone: 071-580 9381
Fax: 071-580 4255

★2617★
**National Housing & Town Planning
  Council**
14-18 Old St
London EC1V 9AB
Phone: 071-251 2363
Telex: 071-608 2830

Membership includes individuals and
organisations concerned with housing, planning or environmental issues

★2618★
**National Illumination Committee of
  GB**
c/o Chartered Institution of Building
  Services Engineers
Delta House
222 Balham High Rd
London SW12 9BS
Phone: 081-675 5211
Fax: 081-675 5449

★2619★
**National Inspection Council for
  Electrical Installation Contracting**
Vintage House
37 Albert Embankment
London SE1 7UJ
Phone: 071-582 7746
Fax: 071-820 0831

To protect users of electricity against unsafe
or unsound electrical installations

★2620★
**National Institute for Biological
  Standards of Control**
Blanche Lane
South Mimms
Potters Bar EN6 3QG
Phone: 0707 54753
Fax: 0707 46730

★2621★
National Institute for Social Work
5-7 Tavistock Place
London WC1H 9SS
Phone: 071-387 9681

★2622★
**National Institute of Adult Continuing
  Education**
19b De Montfort St
Leicester LE1 7GE
Phone: 0533 551451
Fax: 0533 854514

★2623★
**National Institute of Agricultural
  Botany**
Huntingdon Rd
Cambridge CB3 0LE
Phone: 0223 276381
Fax: 0223 277602

Crop variety and seed testing

★2624★
National Institute of Carpet Fitters
Wira House
West Park
Ring Rd
Leeds LS16 6QL
Phone: 0532 743721
Telex: 557189

★2625★
**National Institute of Economic &
  Social Research**
2 Dean Trench St
London SW1P 3HE
Phone: 071-222 7665
Fax: 071-222 1435

★2626★
National Institute of Fresh Produce
440 Market Towers
Nine Elms Lane
London SW8 5NN
Phone: 071-720 4465
Fax: 071-720 2047

★2627★
National Institute of Hardware
3 Morton St
Leamington Spa CV32 5SY
Phone: 0926 421284
Fax: 0926 833478

★2628★
National Institute of Medical Herbalists
c/o Mrs Chacksfield
9 Palace Gate
Exeter EX1 1JA
Phone: 0392 426022

★2629★
National Joint Consultative Committee for Building
18 Mansfield St
London W1M 9FG
Phone: 071-580 5588
Fax: 071-631 3872

★2630★
National Joint Council for Civil Air Transport
121 Clare Rd
Stanwell
Staines TW19 7QP
Phone: 0784 254034
Fax: 0784 250314

★2631★
National Joint Council for the Flat Glass Industry
44-48 Borough High St
London SE1 1XB
Phone: 071-403 7177
Fax: 071-357 7458

See also Flat Glass Council

★2632★
National Joint Council for the Building Industry
18 Mansfield St
London W1M 9FG
Phone: 071-580 1740

★2633★
National Joint Council for the Motor Vehicle Retail & Repair Industry
201 Great Portland St
London W1N 6AB
Phone: 071-580 9122
Fax: 071-580 6376

★2634★
National Joint Industrial Council for the Gas Industry
Rivermill House
152 Grosvenor Rd
London SW1V 3JL
Phone: 071-821 1444
Telex: 938529

★2635★
National League for the Blind & Disabled
2 Tenterden Rd
London N17 8BE
Phone: 081-808 6030

★2636★
National Licensed Victuallers' Association
2 Downing St
Farnham GU9 7NX
Phone: 0252 714448
Telex: 0252 723742

Members are free traders and tenants of public houses

★2637★
National Market Traders Federation
c/o R J Toller
Hampton House
Hawshaw Lane
Hoyland
Barnsley S74 0HA
Phone: 0226 749021

★2638★
National Master Tile Fixers Association
20-21 Tooks Court
Cursitor St

London EC4A 1LA
Phone: 071-831 7581
Fax: 071-405 1291

★2639★
National Materials Handling Centre
c/o Cranfield Institute of Technology
Cranfield MK43 0AL
Phone: 0234 750323
Fax: 0234 750875

★2640★
National Metal Trades Federation
Savoy Tower
77 Renfrew St
Glasgow G2 3BZ
Phone: 041-332 0826
Fax: 041-332 5788

★2641★
National Music Council of GB
10 Stratford Place
London W1N 9AE
Phone: 071-436 0007

Membership is open to music societies and related organisations

★2642★
National Osteoporosis Society
c/o L Edwards
Barton Meade House
PO Box 10
Radstock
Bath BA3 3YB
Phone: 0761 32472
Fax: 0761 37903

Provides help and support for sufferers from this bone disease

★2643★
National Panel Products Association
Clareville House
26-27 Oxendon St
London SW1Y 4EL
Phone: 071-839 1891
Fax: 071-930 0094

★2644★
National Pawnbrokers' Association
1 Bell Yard

London WC2A 2JP
Phone: 071-242 1114
Fax: 071-405 4266

★2645★
National Pharmaceutical Association
40-42 Saint Peter's St
St Albans AL1 3NP
Phone: 0727 832161
Fax: 0727 40858

The association for proprietors of retail pharmacies

★2646★
National Philatelic Society
107 Charterhouse St
London EC1M 6PT
Phone: 071-251 5040
Fax: 071-490 4253

Membership is open to both dealers and collectors

★2647★
National Pig Breeders' Association
7 Rickmansworth Rd
Watford WD1 7HE
Phone: 0923 34377
Fax: 0923 246491

Members are pig farmers, pedigree pig breeders and pig breeding companies

★2648★
National Pistol Association
21 Letchworth Gate Centre
Protea Way
Letchworth SG6 1JT
Phone: 0462 679887
Fax: 0462 481183

Promotes the sport of target shooting

★2649★
National Playing Fields Association
25 Ovington Square
London SW3 1LQ
Phone: 071-584 6445
Fax: 071-581 2402

★2650★
National Pony Society
Brook House
25 High St
Alton GU34 1AW
Phone: 0420 88333

★2651★
National Portraiture Association
60 Fitzjames Avenue
London W14 2JG
Phone: 071-602 0892
Fax: 071-602 0892

★2652★
**National Prefabricated Building
   Association**
PO Box 3
Kenilworth CV8 1SD
Phone: 0926 851165

★2653★
National Pure Water Association
Meridan
Cae Goody Lane
Ellesmere
Oswestry SY12 9DW
Phone: 0691 623015

To protect public water supplies from all
forms of contamination including fluoridation

★2654★
**National Register of Hypnotherapists
   & Psychotherapists**
12 Cross St
Nelson BB9 7EN
Phone: 0282 699378

★2655★
**National Register of Warranted
   Builders**
14 Great James St
London WC1N 3DP
Phone: 071-242 7583
Fax: 071-404 0296

★2656★
National Renderers Association
101 Wigmore St

London W1H 9AB
Phone: 071-493 1546
Fax: 071-493 5526

Concerned with the recycling of animal by-
products

★2657★
National Retail Training Council
Bedford House
69-79 Fulham High St
London SW6 3JW
Phone: 071-371 5021
Fax: 071-371 9160

★2658★
National Retreat Centre
24 South Audley St
London W1Y 5DL
Phone: 071-493 3534

★2659★
National Rifle Association
c/o Brigadier P G A Prescott
Bisley Camp
Brookwood
Woking GU24 0PB
Phone: 0483 797777

★2660★
National Sawmilling Association
Clareville House
26-27 Oxendon St
London SW1Y 4EL
Phone: 071-839 1891
Fax: 071-930 0094

★2661★
National School Band Association
Cottage 1
Arden Hall
Bredbury
Stockport SK6 2RY
Phone: 061-494 7569

To foster an interest in music through the
playing of brass and woodwind instruments
and the formation of brass and wind bands in
schools

★2662★
National School Sailing Association
c/o South Kent Professional Development
  Centre
Chart Rd
Folkestone   CT19 4EW
Phone: 0303 278621
Fax: 0303 270330

★2663★
National Sheep Association
The Sheep Centre
Malvern   WR13 6PH
Phone: 0684 892661
Fax: 0684 892663

★2664★
National Skating Association of GB
15-27 Gee St
London   EC1V 3RE
Phone: 071-253 3824

★2665★
National Small Woods Association
Red House
Hill Lane
Birmingham   B43 6LZ
Phone: 021-358 0461

★2666★
National Small-Bore Rifle Association
Lord Roberts House
Bisley Camp
Brookwood
Woking   GU24 0NP
Phone: 04867 6969
Fax: 04867 6392

Governing body for small-bore, air rifle and
pistol target shooting

★2667★
**National Society for Clean Air &
  Environmental Protection,**
136 North St
Brighton   BN1 1RG
Phone: 0273 26313
Fax: 0273 735802

★2668★
**National Society for Education in Art
  & Design**
7a High St
Corsham   SN13 0ES
Phone: 0249 714825
Fax: 716138

Members are interested in all aspects of art,
craft and design education

★2669★
National Society for Epilepsy
c/o Chalfont Centre for Epilepsy
Chalfont St Peter
Gerrards Cross   SL9 0RJ
Phone: 02407 3991
Fax: 02407 71927

★2670★
**National Society of Allotment &
  Leisure Gardeners**
O'Dell House
Hunters Rd
Corby   NN17 1JE
Phone: 0536 66576

The central body of organised gardeners
encouraging the formation of gardening
associations and giving help to amateur gardeners

★2671★
**National Society of Master Pattern
  Makers**
Queensway House
2 Queensway
Redhill   RH1 1QS
Phone: 0737 768611
Fax: 0737 760467

★2672★
National Society of Master Thatchers
c/o J A Dunkley
Hi-View
Little St
Yardley Hastings
Northampton   NN7 1EZ
Phone: 060129 293

★2673★
National Sulphuric Acid Association
140 Park Lane
London W17 4DT
Phone: 071-495 0414
Telex: 21724

★2674★
National Supervisory Council for Intruder Alarms *see* Loss Prevention Council

★2675★
National Tenants Organization
182 Sparrow Farm Drive
Feltham TW14 ODD
Phone: 081-890 8928

★2676★
National Therapeutic & Osteopathic Society
c/o F Bailey
14 Marford Rd
Wheathampstead AL4 8AS
Phone: 0582 833950

★2677★
National Toy Libraries Association
68 Churchway
London NW1 1LT
Phone: 071-387 9592

★2678★
National Trainers Federation
42 Portman Square
London W1H OAP
Phone: 071-935 2055

Members are racehorse trainers

★2679★
National Turf Grass Council
3 Ferrands Park Way
Harden
Bingley BD16 1HZ
Phone: 0535 273188

Concerned with all matters relevant to amenity or non-agricultural grassland, particularly its use for sport and recreation

★2680★
National Tyre Distributors' Association
Elsinore House
Buckingham St
Aylesbury HP20 2NQ
Phone: 0296 395933
Fax: 0296 88675

★2681★
National Union of Residents' Association
6 Dalmeny Rd
Carshalton SM5 4PP
Phone: 081-647 3683
Fax: 081-773 4003

★2682★
National Union of Townswomen's Guilds
Chamber of Commerce House
75 Harborne Rd
Birmingham B15 3DA
Phone: 021-456 3435
Telex: 338224

★2683★
National Vegetable Research Station Association *now* Wellesbourne Vegetable Research Association

★2684★
National Waterways Transport Association
Central House
32-66 High St
London E15 2PS
Phone: 081-519 4872
Fax: 081-519 5483

★2685★
National Wool Textile Export Corporation
c/o G Richardson
Lloyds Banks Chambers
43 Hustlegate
Bradford BD1 1PE
Phone: 0274 724235
Fax: 0274 723124

★2686★
Natural Environment Research Council
Polaris House
North Star Avenue
Swindon SN2 1EU
Phone: 0793 41500
Fax: 0793 411501

Government establishment which co-ordinates research into geology, geophysics, oceanography, hydrology, marine and fresh-water biology and atmosphere

★2687★
Natural Sausage Casing Association
70 Sandy Lane
Cheam SM2 7EP
Phone: 081-642 7907

★2688★
Natural Slate Quarries Association
c/o H A Pritchard Bryn
Llanllechid
Bangor LL57 3LG
Phone: 0248 600476

Concerned with roofing slates, architectural products and dampcourse slates, slate powder and granules

★2689★
Nautical Institute
202 Lambeth Rd
London SE1 7LQ
Phone: 071-928 1351
Fax: 071-401 2537

Members are qualified mariners in navies and the merchant marine

★2690★
Naval Historical Collectors & Research Association
17 Woodhill Avenue
Portishead
Bristol BS20 9EX
Phone: 0272-848318

All aspects of naval history and interests including battles, naval medals, social history, ships and maritime postal history

★2691★
Needleloom Felt Manufacturers' Association
3 Manchester Rd
Bury BL9 0DR
Phone: 061-764 5401
Fax: 061-764 1114

★2692★
Needlemakers Association
c/o Needles Industry Ltd
Studley
Redditch B80 7AS
Phone: 0527 852301
Fax: 0527 852604

★2693★
Network for Alternative Technology & Technology Assessment
c/o Energy & Environment Research Unit
Faculty of Technology
Open University
Walton Hall
Milton Keynes MK7 6AA
Phone: 0908 653197
Fax: 0908 653744

Promotes the development of alternative technology for retrievable energy sources, alternative food production, transport, building construction, design and work organisation

★2694★
Newspaper Conference
Bloomsbury House, Bloomsbury Square,
  74-77 Great Russell St
London WC1B 3DA
Phone: 071-636 7014
Fax: 071-631 5119

For the London editors of regional newspapers in membership of the Newspaper Society

★2695★
Newspaper Publishers Association
34 Southwark Bridge Rd

London   SE1 9EU
Phone: 071-928 6928
Fax: 071-928 2067

The trade association for national daily and Sunday newspapers

★2696★
Newspaper Society
Bloomsbury House,Bloomsbury Square,74-77 Great Russell St
London   WC1B 3DA
Phone: 071-636 7014
Fax: 071-631 5119

Memberhsip is confined to the publishers of regional and local daily and weekly newspapers

★2697★
Nickel Development Institute
c/o European Technical Information Centre
Alvechurch
Birmingham   B48 7QB
Phone: 0527 584777
Fax: 0527 585562

★2698★
Noise Abatement Society
PO Box 8
Bromley   BR2 0UH
Phone: 081-460 3146
Telex: 8953679

★2699★
North East Coast Institution of Engineers & Shipbuilders
Great North House
Sandyford Rd
Newcastle upon Tyne   NE1 8ND
Phone: 091-230 1515

★2700★
Northern Furniture Manufacturers Association
c/o J G Mellors & Co
Salisbury House
Salisbury Grove

Leeds   LS12 2AS
Phone: 0532 794676
Fax: 0532 794607

Members are companies engaged in furniture manufacture, upholstery and french polishing

★2701★
Northern Ireland Association for Mental Health
80 University St
Belfast   BT7 1HE
Phone: 0232 228474
Fax: 0232 234940

★2702★
Northern Ireland Association of Youth Clubs
Hampton
Glenmachan Park
Belfast   BT4 2PJ
Phone: 0232 760067
Fax: 0232 768799

★2703★
Northern Ireland Bankers' Association
Stokes House
17-25 College Square East
Belfast   BT1 6DE
Phone: 0232 327551

★2704★
Northern Ireland Builders Merchants' Association
6 Grey Point, Helen's Bay
Bangor
Co Down   BT19 1LE
Phone: 0247 853233

★2705★
Northern Ireland Dairy Trade Federation
c/o M B McCartney
123-137 York St
Belfast   BT15 1AB
Phone: 0232 248358
Fax: 0232 233210

★2706★
Northern Ireland Grain Trade Association
10 Arthur St
Belfast BT1 4GD
Phone: 0232 323274
Fax: 0232 439364

★2707★
Northern Ireland Hotels & Caterers Association
108-110 Midland Building
Whitla St
Belfast BT15 1JP
Phone: 0232 351110
Fax: 0232 351504

★2708★
Northern Ireland Master Painters' Association
16 The Square, Ballygowan
Newtownards BT23 6HU
Phone: 0238 528384

★2709★
Northern Ireland Retail Fish Trade Association
393 Ormeau Rd
Belfast BT7 3GP
Phone: 0376 571391

★2710★
Northern Ireland Timber Importers Association
6 Grey Point, Helen's Bay
Bangor
Co Down BT19 1LE
Phone: 0247 853233

★2711★
Northern Ireland Wholesale Merchants' & Manufacturers' Association
10 Arthur St
Belfast BT1 4GD
Phone: 0232 323274
Fax: 0232 439364

★2712★
Northern Ireland Wool Users' Association
c/o Ulster Carpet Mills
Portadown BT62 1EE
Phone: 0762 334433

★2713★
Nuclear Stock Association
21 London Rd
Great Shelford
Cambridge CB2 5DB
Phone: 0223 845834
Fax: 0223 845835

Members are plant propagators and fruit growers dedicated to ensuring the supply of healthy planting stock to the fruit growing industry

★2714★
Numerical Engineering Society
Rochester House
66 Little Ealing Lane
London W5 4XX
Phone: 081-579 9411
Fax: 081-579 2244

Concerned with the control of machines by numerical methods

★2715★
Occupational Hygiene Products Distributors Association
c/o G K Edwards
74 Chester Rd
Birmingham B36 9BU
Phone: 021-776 7474
Fax: 021-776 7605

★2716★
Office of Health Economics
12 Whitehall
London SW1A 2DY
Phone: 071-930 9203

★2717★
Offshore Contractors Council
Suites 41-48
Kent House
87 Regent St

London W1R 7HF
Phone: 071-437 1935
Fax: 071-287 8635

★2718★
Oil & Chemical Plant Constructors' Association
Suites 41-48
87 Regent St
London W1R 7HF
Phone: 071-734 5246
Fax: 071-287 8635

★2719★
Oil & Colour Chemists' Association
967 Harrow Rd
Wembley HA0 2SF
Phone: 081-908 1086
Fax: 081-908 1219

Members are involved in the paint, printing ink and allied industries

★2720★
Omnibus Society
c/o E B H Chapwell
The Spinney
Meadow Rd
Ashtead KT21 1QR
Phone: 0372 272631

For individuals interested in road passenger transport including vehicles, routes, ticket systems, history and future development

★2721★
Open Spaces Society
25a Bell St
Henley-on-Thames RG9 2BA
Phone: 0491 573535

Concerning the protection of common land, town and village greens, open spaces and rights of way

★2722★
Operational Research Society
Neville House
14 Waterloo St
Birmingham B2 5TX
Phone: 021-643 0236

★2723★
Ophthalmic Exhibitors' Association
37-41 Bedford Row
London WC1R 4JH
Phone: 071-405 8101
Fax: 071-831 2797

★2724★
Ophthalmic Prescription Manufacturers' Association
37-41 Bedford Row
London WC1R 4JH
Phone: 071-405 8101
Fax: 071-831 2797

Members are companies looking after the interests of ophthalmic prescription houses who transform opticians prescriptions into complete spectacles

★2725★
Optical Frame Importers' Association
37-41 Bedford Row
London WC1R 4JH
Phone: 071-405 8101
Fax: 071-831 2797

★2726★
Optical Information Council
57a Old Woking Rd
Byfleet
Woking KT14 6LF
Phone: 09323 53283

★2727★
Orders & Medals Research Society
c/o N G Gooding
123 Turnpike Link
Croydon CR0 5NU
Phone: 081-680 2701

Members are individuals, companies and military museum representatives

★2728★
Organic Food Manufacturers Federation
The Tithe House
Peaseland Green
East Dereham NR20 3DY
Phone: 0362 83314
Fax: 0362 83398

★2729★
Organisation of European Aluminium Smelters
Broadway House
Calthorpe Rd
Birmingham B15 1TN
Phone: 021-456 1103
Fax: 021-452 1897

★2730★
Organisation of Professional Users of Statistics
Lancaster House
More Lane
Esher KT10 8AP
Phone: 0372 63121

★2731★
Organisation of Teachers of Transport Studies
c/o S Goss
PO Box 4UZ
London W1A 4UZ
Phone: 071-631 3833

★2732★
Oriental Ceramic Society
31b Torrington Square
London WC1E 7JL
Phone: 071-636 7985

★2733★
Osteopathic Association Of GB
62 Messina Avenue
London NW6 4LE
Phone: 071-372 3206
Fax: 071-372 3206

The professional body for osteopathic practitioners

★2734★
Outdoor Advertising Association of GB
Centric House
390-391 Strand
London WC2R OLT
Phone: 071-240 2181
Fax: 071-497 8977

Members are poster advertising contractors

★2735★
Outdoor Advertising Council
Central House
390-391 The Strand
London WC2 R04
Phone: 071-240 2181
Fax: 071-222 1064

★2736★
Outdoor Writer's Guild
c/o K Spencer
1 Warwick Avenue
Newcastle upon Tyne NE16 5QR
Phone: 091-488 1947
Fax: 091-488 6718

★2737★
Overhead Transmission Line Contractors
c/o Eve Group plc
Minster House
Plough Lane
London SW17 0AZ
Phone: 081-946 3085
Fax: 081-946 2156

★2738★
Overseas Press & Media Association
c/o Sinclairs
32 Queen Anne St
London W1M 9LB
Phone: 071-323 0886
Fax: 071-734 4033

For advertising representatives of overseas media

★2739★
Packaging & Industrial Films Association
The Fountain Precint, 1 Balm Green
Sheffield S1 3AF
Phone: 0742 766789
Fax: 0742 766213

★2740★
Packaging Distributors Association
Papermakers House
Rivenhall Rd
Westlea

Swindon   SN5 7BEL
Phone: 0793 886086
Fax: 0793 886182

★2741★
Paddle Steamer Preservation Society
17 Stockfield Close
Hazlemere
High Wycombe   HP15 7LA
Phone: 049-481 2979

★2742★
Paint Research Association
Waldegrave Rd
Teddington   TW11 8LD
Phone: 081-977 4427
Fax: 081-943 4705

★2743★
Paintmakers Association of GB
6th Floor
Alembic House
93 Albert Embankment
London   SE1 7TY
Phone: 071-582 1185

The trade association for the manufacturers of painted and of surface coatings in the UK

★2744★
Palaeontographical Society
c/o British Geological Survey
Keyworth
Nottingham   NG12 5GG
Phone: 06077 6111
Fax: 06077 6602

For figuring and describing British fossils

★2745★
Palaeontological Association
c/o Dr A Crame
British Antarctic Survey
High Cross
Madingley
Cambridge   CB3 OET
Phone: 0223 61188
Fax: 0223 62616

★2746★
Paper Agents' Association
86 Gaia Lane

Lichfield   WS13 7LS
Phone: 0543 251270

Representing overseas paper and board manufacturers

★2747★
Paper Makers' Allied Trades Association
c/o D G McNay
Hercules Ltd
Langley Rd
Manchester   M6 6JU
Phone: 061-736 4461
Fax: 061-745 7009

Membership covers suppliers of plant and raw materials to paper mills

★2748★
Parrot Society
c/o D Coombes
108b Fenlake Rd
Bedford   MK42 0EU
Phone: 0234 58922

Co-ordinates the study and conservation of all parrots and parrotlike birds other than budgerigars

★2749★
Partially Sighted Society
Queen's Rd
Doncaster   DN1 2NX
Phone: 0302 323132

★2750★
Partitioning Industry Association
692 Warwick Rd
Solihull   B91 3DX
Phone: 021-705 9270
Fax: 021-711 2892

★2751★
Passenger Shipping Association
93 Newman St
London   W1P 3LE
Phone: 071-491 7693
Fax: 071-636 9206

For passenger ship owners and operators

★2752★
Pastel Society
17 Carlton House Terrace
London SW1Y 5BD
Phone: 071-930 6844
Fax: 071-839 7830

★2753★
**Patent Glazing Contractors
  Association**
13 Upper High St
Epsom KT17 4QY
Phone: 03727 29191
Fax: 0372 729190

★2754★
Pathological Society of GB & Ireland
c/o 2 Carlton House Terrace
London SW1Y 5AF
Phone: 071-976 1260
Fax: 071-976 1267

★2755★
Patients Association
18 Victoria Park Square
London E2 9PF
Phone: 081-981 5676

★2756★
**Pedestrians Association for Road
  Safety**
1 Wandsworth Rd
London SW8 2XX
Phone: 071-735 3270

★2757★
Pensions Management Institute
124 Middlesex St
London E1 7HY
Phone: 071-247 1452
Fax: 071-375 0603

Professional body for all those employed in
the field of occupational pensions schemes

★2758★
PERA *see* Production Engineering
  Research Association of GB

★2759★
Performing Right Society
29-33 Berners St
London W1P 4AA
Phone: 071-580 5544
Fax: 071-631 4138

To license the public performing and broadcasting rights in non-dramatic copyright
music on behalf of composers and publishers

★2760★
Periodical Publishers Association
Imperial House
15-19 Kingsway
London WC2B 6UN
Phone: 071-379 6268
Fax: 071-379 5661

★2761★
Permaculture Association
c/o G Sobal
Old Cuming Farm
Buckfastleigh TQ11 0LT
Phone: 0364 43988

Advanced design principles for food production and sustainable lifestyles, especially per-
ennial crops and mixed plantings, water and
energy conservation

★2762★
**Permanent International Association
  of Navigation Congresses**
1-7 Great George St
London SW1P 3AA
Phone: 071-222 7722
Fax: 071-222 7500

★2763★
**Permanent International Association
  of Road Congresses**
Room 414
St Christopher House
Southwark St
London SE1 0TE
Phone: 071-921 4349
Fax: 071-921 4349

Aims to bring together people throughout the
world who are interested in the planning,
design, construction, maintenance and operation of road and associated topics including

road safety and the impact of roads on the environment

★2764★
Permanent Service for Mean Sea Level
Bidston Observatory
Birkenhead
Liverpool L43 7RA
Phone: 051-653 8633
Telex: 628591

Collects, analyses and publishes data on changes in global sea levels

★2765★
Permanent Way Institution
23 Reginald Rd
Wombwell
Barnsley S73 0HP
Phone: 0226 752605

Members are railway civil engineers, trackworkers and railway contractors

★2766★
Personal Managers' Association
1 Summer Rd
East Molesey KT8 9LX
Phone: 081-398 9796

For artists, technicians and writers in the entertainment industry

★2767★
Pet Food Manufacturers' Association *now* incorporated into Food & Drink Federation

★2768★
Pet Health Council
4 Bedford Square
London WC1B 3RA
Phone: 071-631 3795
Fax: 071-631 0602

Promotes the health and welfare of the companion animal in the interest of pet and human health

★2769★
Pet Trade & Industry Association
103 HighSt

Bedford MK40 1NE
Phone: 0234 273933
Fax: 0234 273550

Covering professional dog groomers, retail pet stores, manufacturers and distributors of livestock, pet food and accessories

★2770★
Petrol Pump Manufacturers Association
c/o Peat Marwick McLintock
1 Puddle Dock
London EC4V 3PD
Phone: 071-583 2104
Fax: 071-583 1886

★2771★
Petrol Retailers Association *now* incorporated with Retail Motor Industry Federation

★2772★
Petroleum Exploration Society of GB
Burlington House
Piccadilly
London W1V 9AG
Phone: 071-437 2258

★2773★
Pharmaceutical General Council (Scotland)
34 York Place
Edinburgh EH1 3HU
Phone: 031-556 2076

★2774★
Pharmaceutical Society of GB *now* Royal Pharmaceutical Society of GB

★2775★
Pharmaceutical Society of Northern Ireland
73 University St
Belfast BT7 1HL
Phone: 0232 326927
Fax: 0232 439919

★2776★
**Phenolic Foam Manufacturers
   Association**
c/o J G Fairley
P O Box 111
Aldershot GU11 1YW
Phone: 0252 21302
Fax: 0252 333901

★2777★
Philatelic Traders' Society
27 John Adam St
London WC2N 6HZ
Phone: 071-930 6465
Fax: 071-930 1163

Members are dealers, auctioneers, publishers
and manufacturers

★2778★
Philological Society
c/o Professor Theodora Bynon
School of Oriental & African Studies
Thornhaugh St
London WC1H 0XG
Phone: 071-637 2388
Fax: 071-436 3844

Formed to promote the study and knowledge
of the structure, affinities and history of languages

★2779★
**Photographic Instrument Repairing
   Authority**
c/o L H Frankham
166 Westcotes Drive
Leicester LE3 0SP
Phone: 0533 550825

★2780★
**Physical Education Association of GB
   & N Ireland**
Ling House
162 Kings Cross Rd
London WC1X 9DH
Phone: 071-278 9311

★2781★
Physiological Society
c/o Dr D Cotterall
School of Medicine

University of Leeds
Leeds LS2 9JT
Phone: 0532 445906
Fax: 0532 334381

★2782★
Phytochemical Society of Europe
c/o Professor P J Lea
Dept of Biological Sciences
University of Lancaster
Lancaster LA1 4YQ
Phone: 0524 65201
Fax: 0524 382212

Members are research scientists working in
the field of plant chemistry

★2783★
Piano Trade Suppliers Association
c/o D Hart
78-80 Borough High St
London SE1 1XG
Phone: 071-403 2300
Fax: 071-403 8140

Members are manufacturers of component
parts used in piano making

★2784★
**Pianoforte Manufacturers &
   Distributors' Association**
2nd Floor
20 Beach Rd
Lowestoft NR32 1EA
Phone: 0502 569931
Fax: 0502 569931

★2785★
Pianoforte Tuners' Association
c/o Mrs V M Addis
10 Reculver Rd
Herne Bay CT6 6LD
Phone: 0227 368808

★2786★
Pickles & Sauces Association *now*
   incorporated into Food & Drink
   Federation

★2787★
Pipe Jacking Association
c/o A Marshall
56 Britton St
London   EC1M 5NA
Phone: 071-353 8805
Fax: 071-251 1939

Representing contractors, suppliers and manufacturers in the pipe jacking and micro-tun-
nelling industries

★2788★
Pipeline Industries Guild
17 Grosvenor Crescent
London   SW1X 7ES
Phone: 071-235 7938
Fax: 071-235 0074

★2789★
Pipesmokers' Council
c/o M Butler
19 Elmington Rd
London   E8 3BY
Phone: 071-241 6950

★2790★
PIRA
Randalls Rd
Leatherhead   KT22 7RU
Phone: 0372 376161
Fax: 0372 377526

The UK technical centre for the paper and
board, printing and packaging industries

★2791★
Pizza & Pasta Association
29 Market Place
Wantage   OX12 8BG
Phone: 02357 72207
Fax: 02357 69044

★2792★
**Plastic Industrial Containers
   Association**
St Nicholas House
15-17 George St
Luton   LU1 5DJ

★2793★
Plastic Pipe Manufacturers Society
c/o Wenham Major
89 Cornwall St
Birmingham   B3 3BY
Phone: 021-236 1866
Fax: 021-200 1389

Members are UK manufacturers of plastic
pipes and/or fittings

★2794★
**Plastic Tanks & Cisterns
   Manufacturers' Association**
Birchfield Mill
Llangynwyd
Maesteg
Bridgend   CF34 9RY
Phone: 0656 733722

★2795★
Plastics & Rubber Institute
11 Hobart Place
London   SW1W 0HL
Phone: 071-245 9555
Telex: 071-823 1379

★2796★
**Plastics Crate Manufacturers'
   Association**
73 Horncastle Rd
Boston   PE21 9HY
Phone: 0205 369640

★2797★
**Plastics Land Drainage Manufacturers'
   Association**
Centre City Tower
7 Hill St
Birmingham   B5 4UU
Phone: 021-643 5494
Fax: 021-643 7738

★2798★
**Plastics Machinery Distributors
   Association**
208 Down House
Broomhill Rd
London   SW18 4JQ

★2799★
Plastics Stockholders' Association
now British Plastics Stockholders'
Association

★2800★
Plastics Window Federation
Federation House
87 Wellington St
Luton   LU1 5AF
Phone: 0582 456147
Fax: 0582 412215

★2801★
Poetry Society
21 Earls Court Square
London   SW5 9DE
Phone: 071-373 7861
Fax: 071-244 7388

★2802★
Point-to-Point Secretaries Association
c/o Lord Wolverton
97 Hurlingham Rd
London   SW6 3NL
Phone: 071-499 8562

★2803★
Police Federation (England & Wales)
15-17 Langley Rd
Surbiton   KT6 6LP
Phone: 081-390 2224
Fax: 081-390 2249

For police officers below the rank of superin-
tendent

★2804★
Police History Society
c/o P Shattle
Cambridgeshire Constabulary
Thorpewood Police Station
Thorpewood
Peterborough   PE3 6SD
Phone: 0733 63232
Telex: 32246

★2805★
**Police Superintendents' Association of
England & Wales**
67a Reading Rd
Pangbourne
Reading   RG8 7JD
Phone: 07357 4005

★2806★
Pool Promoters Association
25 Castle St
Liverpool   L2 4TD
Phone: 051-227 4181
Fax: 051-227 5958

Trade association of football pool promoters

★2807★
**Portable Electric Tool Manufacturers'
Association**
c/o Peat Marwick McLintock
1 Puddle Dock
London   EC4V 3PD
Phone: 071-583 2104
Fax: 071-583 1886

★2808★
Post Office Users National Council
Waterloo Bridge House
Waterloo Rd
London   SE1 8UA
Phone: 071-928 9458

★2809★
Postal History Society
c/o J Scott
Lower St Farmhouse
Hildenborough
Tonbridge   TN11 8PT
Phone: 0480 456254

★2810★
Postcard Association
6 Wimpole St
London   W1M 8AS
Phone: 071-637 7692
Fax: 071-436 3137

★2811★
Potato Processors Association *now*
incorporated into Food & Drink
Federation

★2812★
Poultry Industry Conference
High Holborn House
52-54 High Holborn
London WC1V 6SX
Phone: 071-242 4683
Fax: 071-831 0624

★2813★
Power Actuated Systems Association
Light Trades House
3 Melbourne Avenue
Sheffield S10 2QJ
Phone: 0742 663084
Fax: 0742 670910

★2814★
Power Fastenings Association
Heath St
Tamworth B79 7JH
Phone: 0827 52337
Fax: 0827 310827

To promote the safe use of pneumatic nailing
and staplingequipment

★2815★
Power Generation Contractors
  Association
Leicester House
8 Leicester St
London WC2H 7BN
Phone: 071-437 0678
Fax: 071-437 4901

★2816★
Pre-Packed Flour Association *now*
incorporated into Food & Drink
Federation

★2817★
Pre-Retirement Association of GB &
  Northern Ireland
The Nodus Centre
University Campus

Guildford GU2 5RX
Phone: 0483 39323

★2818★
Pre-School Playgroups Association
61-63 Kings Cross Rd
London WC1X 9LL
Phone: 071-833 0991
Fax: 071-837 4442

★2819★
Precast Flooring Federation
60 Charles St
Leicester LE1 1FB
Phone: 0533 536161
Fax: 0533 514568

★2820★
Prefabricated Aluminium Scaffold
  Manufacturers Association
c/o Building Centre
26 Store St
London WC1E 7BS
Phone: 071-323 3770
Fax: 071-323 0307

Promotes the safe use of aluminium access
equipment to users

★2821★
Prehistoric Society
c/o Museum Bookshop
36 Great Russell St
London WC1B 3PP
Phone: 071-580 4086

For the encouragement of prehistoric study
and excavation

★2822★
Pressed Felt Manufacturers
  Association
Hudcar Mills
Hudcar Lane
Bury BL9 6HD
Phone: 061-764 2262
Telex: 669000

★2823★
Primary History Association
St John's Wood County Primary School

Knutsford   WA16 8PA
Phone: 0565 4578

For primary teachers

★2824★
Printing Historical Society
St Bride Institute
Bride Lane
London   EC4Y 8EE
Phone: 071-353 3331

★2825★
Prison Officers' Association
Cronin House
245 Church St
London   N9 9HW
Phone: 081-803 0255
Fax: 081-803 1761

★2826★
Private Libraries Association
Ravelston
South View Rd
Pinner   HA5 3YD

An international society of private book collectors

★2827★
Process Plant Association
11 Brook St
Leighton Buzzard   LU7 8LQ
Phone: 0525 374386

The trade association for British manufacturers and fabricators of plant used by the chemical, petrochemical, oil gas, pharmacutical, mineral processing and solid wastes treatment industries

★2828★
Processed Vegetable Growers Association
133 Eastgate
Louth   LN11 9QG
Phone: 0507 602427

★2829★
Processed Woodchip, Sawdust & Woodflour Association
46 Chandos Avenue

London   N20 9DX
Phone: 081-446 2311

★2830★
Processors' & Growers' Research Organisation
Great North Rd
Thornhaugh
Peterborough   PE8 6HJ
Phone: 0780 782585
Fax: 0780 783993

Research for the agricultural and processing industries into peas, beans and other vegetable crops

★2831★
Procurators Fiscal Society
3 Queens Ferry St
Edinburgh   EHR 4RD
Phone: 031-226 4962
Fax: 031-220 4669

★2832★
Produce Packaging & Marketing Association
15 Hawley Square
Margate
Southend-on-Sea   CT9 1PF
Phone: 0843 225371
Fax: 0843 299662

Covering the fresh fruit and vegetable trades

★2833★
Producers' Association
Paramount House
162-170 Wardour St
London   W1V 4LA
Phone: 071-437 7700
Fax: 071-734 4564

The association for film and television producers

★2834★
Production Engineering Research Association of GB
Nottingham Rd
Melton Mowbray   LE13 0PB
Phone: 0664 501501
Fax: 0664 501264

★2835★
Professional Business & Technical Management

58 Clarendon Avenue
Leamington Spa CV32 4SA
Phone: 0926 55498

For professional staff involved in industry, computing, technology and associated management

★2836★
Professional Flight Instructors' Association

c/o Post Office
CSE Aviation
Oxford Airport
Kidlington
Oxford OX5 1RA
Phone: 0865 841234

★2837★
Professional Gardeners Guild

c/o Sophie Plebenga
Estate Office
Knebworth House
Knebworth
Stevenage SG3 6PY
Phone: 0438 812661
Fax: 0438 811908

★2838★
Professional Golfers' Association

Apollo House
The Belfry
Sutton Coldfield
Birmingham B76 9PT
Phone: 0675 470333
Fax: 0675 470674

★2839★
Professional Institutions Council for Conservation

61 Brown St
Manchester M62 2JX
Phone: 061-832 8888

★2840★
Professional Lighting & Sound Association

7 Highlight House
St Leonards Rd
Eastbourne BN21 3UH
Phone: 0323 40335
Fax: 0323 646905

Members are manufacturers and suppliers of discotheque and other sound and lighting entertainment equipment

★2841★
Professional Plant Users Group

c/o Landscape Institute
12 Carlton House Terrace
London SW1Y 5AH
Phone: 071-738 9166
Fax: 071-738 9134

For organisations who use plants in public and private landscaping

★2842★
Property Consultants Society

107a Tarrant St
Arundel BN18 7DP
Phone: 0903 883787

Members are estate agents, surveyors and consultants

★2843★
Proprietary Articles Trade Association

5 Caxton Way
Watford Business Park
Watford WD1 8UA
Phone: 0923 211647
Fax: 0923 211648

For retailers, wholesalers and manufacturers of proprietary pharmaceuticals

★2844★
Proprietary Association of GB

Vernon House
Sicilian Avenue
London WC1A 2QH
Phone: 071-242 8331

Represents manufacturers of non-prescription products sold directly to the public

★2845★
Proprietary Crematoria Association
The Lodge
Hartington Rd
Brighton   BN2 3PL
Phone: 0273 601601
Fax: 0273 655318

The administration of privately owned crematoria and cemeteries

★2846★
Provincial Booksellers' Fairs Association
PO Box 66
Cambridge   CB1 3PD
Phone: 0223 240921

Promotes the secondhand and antiquarian book trade

★2847★
Provincial Theatre Council
Bedford Chambers
The Piazza
London   WC2E 8HQ
Phone: 071-836 0971
Fax: 071-497 2543

★2848★
Public Relations Consultants Association
Willow House
Willow Place
London   SW1P 1JH
Phone: 071-233 6026
Fax: 071-828 4797

The trade association for consultancies offering public relations and corporate communication services

★2849★
Publishers Association
19 Bedford Square
London   WC1B 3HJ
Phone: 071-580 6321
Fax: 071-636 5375

★2850★
Pump Distributors Association of GB
PO Box 993
Pewsey

Marlborough   SN9 5ZA
Phone: 0672 851688
Fax: 0672 851688

★2851★
Quilters' Guild
Op 66
Dean Clough
Halifax   HX3 5AX
Phone: 0422 345631

To promote the art, understanding, appreciation, technique and heritage of patchwork, quilting and appliqué

★2852★
Racecourse Association
Winkfield Rd
Ascot   SL5 7HX
Phone: 0344 25912
Fax: 0344 27233

The trade association for licensed racecourses

★2853★
Racehorse Owners Association
42 Portman Square
London   W1H 9FF
Phone: 071-486 6977

★2854★
Radio Industry Council
Landseer House
19 Charing Cross Rd
London   WC2H 0ES
Phone: 071-930 3206
Fax: 071-839 4613

★2855★
Radio Society of GB
Lambda House
Cranborne Rd
Potters Bar   EN6 3JE
Phone: 0707 59015
Fax: 0707 45105

National hobby society for radio amateurs

★2856★
Radio, Electrical & Television Retailers' Association
RETRA House
1 Ampthill St

Bedford   MK42 9EY
Phone: 0234 269110
Fax: 0234 269609

Represents retailers of radio, television, audio and domestic electrical appliances

★2857★
Radionics Association
Baerlein House
Goose Green
Deddington
Banbury   OX5 4NZ
Phone: 0869 38852

Radionics is a method of healing at a distance through the medium of a specially designed instrument using the faculty of extra-sensory perception

★2858★
Railway Development Society
c/o Reg Snow
48 The Park
Great Bookham
Leatherhead   KT23 3LS
Phone: 0372 52863

★2859★
Railway Industry Association
6 Buckingham Gate
London   SW1E 6JP
Phone: 071-834 1426
Fax: 071-821 1640

★2860★
Ramblers Association
1-5 Wandsworth Rd
London   SW8 2XX
Phone: 071-582 6878

★2861★
Rating & Valuation Association
41 Doughty St
London   WC1N 2LF
Phone: 071-831 3505

★2862★
Rating Surveyors Association
Regal House
Mengham Rd

Hayling Island
Portsmouth   PO11 9BL
Phone: 0705 467415

★2863★
Reclamation Association
16 High St
Brampton
Huntingdon   PE18 8TU
Phone: 0480 455249
Fax: 0480 453680

★2864★
Recreation Managers Association of GB
5 Balfour Rd
Weybridge   KT13 8HE
Phone: 0932 841583

★2865★
Referees' Association
1 Westhill Rd
Coundon
Coventry   CV6 2AD
Phone: 0203 601701

The body for association football referees

★2866★
Refined Sugar Association
c/o D G Moon
Plantation House
Mincing Lane
London   EC3M 3HT
Phone: 071-626 1745
Fax: 071-283 3831

Members are active traders in white sugar

★2867★
Refractories Association of GB   see
British Ceramic Federation

★2868★
Refractory Contractors Association
Central House
32-66 High St
London   E15 2PS
Phone: 081-519 4872
Fax: 081-519 5483

★2869★
Refractory Users Federation
Suites 41-48
Kent House
87 Regent St
London W1R 7HF
Phone: 071-734 5247
Fax: 071-287 8635

★2870★
Refugee Council
3 Bondway
London SW8 1SJ
Phone: 071-582 6922

★2871★
Regional Studies Association
c/o Wharfdale Projects
15 Micawber St
London N1 7TB
Phone: 071-490 1128
Fax: 071-253 0095

For individuals and corporate groups
involved in urban and regional planning

★2872★
**Register of Traditional Chinese
   Medicine**
19 Trinity Rd
London N2 8JJ
Phone: 081-947 1879

★2873★
Registered Nursing Home Association
Calthorpe House
Hagley Rd
Birmingham B16 8QY
Phone: 021-454 2511
Fax: 021-454 0932

★2874★
**Release Paper Manufacturers
   Association**
Leicester House
8 Leicester St
London WC2H 7BN
Phone: 071-437 0678
Fax: 071-437 4901

★2875★
Remote Sensing Society
c/o Dept of Geography
University of Nottingham
University Park
Nottingham NG7 2RD
Phone: 0602 587611
Fax: 0602 420825

Remote sensing is the term given to the
acquisition and use of data about the earth
from sources such as aircraft, balloons, rock-
ets and satellites

★2876★
Research & Development Society
47 Belgrave Square
London SW1X 8QX
Phone: 071-235 6111
Fax: 071-259 6002

★2877★
Restaurateurs Association of GB
c/o I Fyfe
190 Queen's Gate
London SW7 5EU
Phone: 071-581 2444
Fax: 071-581 8261

★2878★
**Retail Confectioners & Tobacconists
   Association**
53 Christchurch Avenue
London N12 0DH
Phone: 081-445 6344
Fax: 081-446 1633

★2879★
Retail Consortium
Bedford House
69-79 Fulham High St
London SW6 3JW
Phone: 071-371 5185
Fax: 071-371 0529

Representing the majority of British retailers

★2880★
Retail Fruit Trade Federation
Office 3 Market Centre
Western International Market
Hayes Rd

Southall   UB2 5XT
Phone: 081-569 3090

Independent specialist fruiterers and green-grocery

★2881★
Retail Motor Industry Federation
201 Great Portland St
London   W1N 6AB
Phone: 071-580 9122
Fax: 071-580 6376

Representing the motor trade whose members sell, service, repair and recover all types of motor vehicles and sell petrol/diesel fuel

★2882★
Retread Manufacturers' Association
Brampton House
10 Queen St
Newcastle under Lyme   ST5 1ED
Phone: 0782 661944
Fax: 0782 712635

★2883★
Rice Association *now* incorporated into Food & Drink Federation

★2884★
Road Haulage Association
Roadway House
35 Monument Hill
Weybridge   KT13 8RN
Phone: 0932 841515
Fax: 0932 852516

Trade association for the hire-or-reward section of the industry

★2885★
Road Operators' Safety Council
52 Lincoln's Inn Fields
London   WC2A 3LZ
Phone: 071-242 8909

★2886★
Road Surface Dressing Association
c/o Ernst & Young
Cloth Hall Court
14 King St

Leeds   LS1 2JN
Phone: 0532 431221
Fax: 0532 434195

★2887★
Roast & Ground Coffee Association
now incorporated into Food & Drink Federation

★2888★
Romani Institute
c/o Dr D S Kenrick
61 Blenheim Crescent
London   W11 2EG
Phone: 071-727 2916

★2889★
Romantic Novelists' Association
9 Hillside Rd
Southport   PR8 4QB
Phone: 0704 60945

★2890★
Rose Trade Association
Chiswell Green Lane
St Albans   AL2 3NR
Phone: 0727 50461

★2891★
Rotating Electrical Machines Association
Leicester House
8 Leicester St
London   WC2H 7BN
Phone: 071-437 0678
Fax: 071-437 4901

All rotating electrical machines other than turbines, traction motors or machines for use in aircraft

★2892★
Royal Aeronautical Society
4 Hamilton Place
London   W1V 0BQ
Phone: 071-499 3515
Fax: 071-499 6230

The body for aerospace professionals

★2893★
Royal Agricultural Society of England
National Agricultural Centre
Stoneleigh
Kenilworth   CV8 2LZ
Phone: 0203 696969
Fax: 0203 696900

★2894★
Royal Anthropological Institute of GB & Ireland
50 Fitzroy St
London   W1P 5HS
Phone: 071-387 0455

★2895★
Royal Archaeological Institute
c/o Winifred Phillips
Society of Antiquaries
Burlington House
Piccadilly
London   W1V 0HS

★2896★
Royal Association for Disability & Rehabilitation
25 Mortimer St
London   W1N 8AB
Phone: 071-637 5400
Fax: 071-637 1827

★2897★
Royal Association in Aid of Deaf People
27 Old Oak Rd
London   W3 7HN
Phone: 081-743 6187
Fax: 081-740 6551

★2898★
Royal Association of British Dairy Farmers
55 Sleaford St
London   SW8 5AB
Phone: 071-627 2111
Fax: 071-978 1824

★2899★
Royal Astronomical Society
Burlington House
Piccadilly
London   W1V 0NL
Phone: 071-734 4582
Fax: 071-494-0166

A learned society to encourage and promote astronomy and geophysics

★2900★
Royal College of General Practitioners
14 Princes Gate
London   SW7 1PU
Phone: 071-581 3232
Fax: 071-225 3047

★2901★
Royal College of Midwives
15 Mansfield St
London   W1M 0BE
Phone: 071-580 6523
Fax: 071-436 3951

★2902★
Royal College of Nursing of the UK
20 Cavendish Square
London   W1M 0AB
Phone: 071-409 3333
Fax: 071-491 3859

★2903★
Royal College of Obstetricians & Gynaecologists
27 Sussex Place
London   NW1 4RG
Phone: 071-262 5425
Fax: 071-723 0575

★2904★
Royal College of Pathologists
2 Carlton House Terrace
London   SW1Y 5AF
Phone: 071-930 5861
Fax: 071-321 0523

★2905★
Royal College of Physicians
11 St Andrew's Place

London   NW1 4LE
Phone: 071-935 1174
Fax: 071-487 5218

★2906★
Royal College of Psychiatrists
17 Belgrave Square
London   SW1X 8PG
Phone: 071-235 2351
Fax: 071-245 1231

★2907★
Royal College of Radiologists
38 Portland Place
London   W1N 3DG
Phone: 071-636 4432
Fax: 071-323 3100

★2908★
Royal College of Surgeons of England
35-43 Lincoln's Inn Fields
London   WC2A 3PN
Phone: 071-405 3474
Telex: 071-831 9438

★2909★
Royal College of Veterinary Surgeons
32 Belgrave Square
London   SW1X 8QP
Phone: 071-235 4971
Fax: 071-245 6100

★2910★
Royal Economic Society
c/o Professor Z A Silberston
Imperial College of Science & Technology
Exhibition Rd
London   SW7 2AZ
Phone: 071-589 5111
Fax: 071-584 7596

Members are mainly professional economists in business, government service or higher education

★2911★
Royal Entomological Society
41 Queens Gate
London   SW7 5HU
Phone: 071-584 8361

★2912★
Royal Environmental Health Institute
   of Scotland
62 Virginia St
Glasgow   G1 1TX
Phone: 041-552 1533

★2913★
Royal Forestry Society of England,
   Wales & N Ireland
102 High St
Tring   HP23 4AF
Phone: 044-282 2028

To encourage the positive management of Britain's woodlands so that they may be conserved, improved and expanded

★2914★
Royal Geographical Society
1 Kensington Gore
London   SW7 2AR
Phone: 071-589 5466
Fax: 071-581 9918

★2915★
Royal Highland & Agricultural Society
   of Scotland
c/o Edinburgh Exhibition & Trade Centre,
   Ingliston
Edinburgh   EH28 8NF
Phone: 031-333 2444

★2916★
Royal Historical Society
c/o University College
Gower St
London   WC1E 6BT
Phone: 071-387 7532

★2917★
Royal Horticultural Society
80 Vincent Square
London   SW1P 2PE
Phone: 071-834 4333

★2918★
Royal Incorporation of Architects in
   Scotland
15 Rutland Square

Edinburgh EH1 2BE
Phone: 031-229 7545
Fax: 031-228 2188

★2919★
Royal Institute of British Architects
66 Portland Place
London W1N 4AD
Phone: 071-580 5533
Fax: 071-255 1541

The professional body for chartered architects

★2920★
Royal Institute of International Affairs
Chatham House
10 St James's Square
London SW1Y 4LE
Phone: 071-930 2233
Fax: 071-839 3593

★2921★
Royal Institute of Navigation
1 Kensington Gore
London SW7 2AT
Phone: 071-589 5021
Fax: 8671

★2922★
Royal Institute of Oil Painters
17 Carlton House Terrace
London SW1Y 5BD
Phone: 071-930 6844
Fax: 071-839 7830

★2923★
Royal Institute of Painters in Water Colours
17 Carlton House Terrace
London SW1Y 5BD
Phone: 071-930 6844
Fax: 071-839 7830

★2924★
Royal Institute of Philosophy
14 Gordon Square
London WC1H 0AG
Phone: 071-387 4130

★2925★
Royal Institute of Public Administration
Regent's College
Inner Circle
London NW1 4NS
Phone: 071-935 0496
Fax: 071-486 7746

★2926★
Royal Institute of Public Health & Hygiene
28 Portland Place
London W1N 4DE
Phone: 071-580 2731

Promotes the advancement of all aspects of public health, hygiene and preventative medicine

★2927★
Royal Institution of Chartered Surveyors
12 Great George St
London SW1P 3AD
Phone: 071-222 7000
Fax: 071-222 9430

★2928★
Royal Institution of Naval Architects
10 Upper Belgrave St
London SW1X 8BQ
Phone: 071-235 4622
Fax: 071-245 6959

★2929★
Royal Meteorological Society
104 Oxford Rd
Reading RG1 7LJ
Phone: 0734 568500
Fax: 0734 568571

★2930★
Royal Microscopical Society
37-38 St Clements
Oxford OX4 1AJ
Phone: 0865 248768
Fax: 0865 791237

Concerned with electron & optical micros-copy, histochemistry, cytochemistry and the examination of materials by microscopy and associated techniques

★2931★
Royal Musical Association
c/o Peter Owens
135 Purves Rd
London   NW10 5TH
Phone: 081-960 5239

★2932★
Royal National Institute for the Blind
224 Great Portland St
London   W1N 6AA
Phone: 071-388 1266

★2933★
Royal National Institute for the Deaf
105 Gower St
London   WC1E 6AH
Phone: 071-387 8033
Fax: 071-388 2346

★2934★
Royal National Rose Society
Chiswell Green Lane
St Albans   AL2 3NR
Phone: 0727 50461

★2935★
Royal Numismatic Society
c/o Dept of Coins & Medals
British Museum
Great Russell St
London   WC1B 3DG
Phone: 071-323 8585

★2936★
Royal Pharmaceutical Society of GB
1 Lambeth High St
London   SE1 7JN
Phone: 071-735 9141

The professional body for hospital, industrial, academic and retail pharmacists

★2937★
Royal Philatelic Society
41 Devonshire Place

London   W1N 1PE
Phone: 071-486 1044
Fax: 071-486 0803

★2938★
Royal Photographic Society
Milsom St
Bath   BA1 1DN
Phone: 0225 462841
Fax: 0225 448688

For individuals interested in the science and technology of photography, processing, radiography and holography

★2939★
Royal Scottish Forestry Society
11 Atholl Crescent
Edinburgh   EH3 8HE
Phone: 031-229 8180
Fax: 031-229 5611

★2940★
Royal Scottish Geographical Society
10 Randolph Crescent
Edinburgh   EH3 7TU
Phone: 031-225 3330

★2941★
Royal Scottish Society of Painters in Water-Colours
29 Waterloo St
Glasgow   G2 6BZ
Phone: 041-226 3838

★2942★
Royal Society
6 Carlton House Terrace
London   SW1Y 5AG
Phone: 071-839 5561
Fax: 071-930 9433

Promotes the natural sciences and their application to daily life

★2943★
Royal Society for Mentally Handicapped Children & Adults
123 Golden Lane

London EC1Y 0RT
Phone: 071-454 0454
Fax: 071-608 3254

Concerned with the well-being of people of all ages with a mental handicap/learning disability

★2944★
Royal Society for Nature Conservation
The Green
Witham Park
Waterside South
Lincoln LN2 7RJ
Phone: 0522 544400
Fax: 0522 511616

For all concerned with conserving wildlife in the UK

★2945★
Royal Society for the Encouragement of Arts, Manufactures & Commerce
8 John Adam St
London WC2N 6EZ
Phone: 071-930 5115
Fax: 071-839 5805

Addresses social and economic concerns, including industry, the environment and education together with the applied and fine arts

★2946★
Royal Society for the Prevention of Accidents
Cannon House
Priory Queensway
Birmingham B4 6BS
Phone: 021-233 2461
Fax: 021-236 2850

★2947★
Royal Society of British Artists
17 Carlton House Terrace
London SW1Y 5BD
Phone: 071-930 6844
Fax: 071-839 7830

★2948★
Royal Society of British Sculptors
108 Old Brompton Rd
London SW7 3RA
Phone: 071-373 5554

★2949★
Royal Society of Chemistry
Burlington House
Piccadilly
London W1V 0BN
Phone: 071-437 8656
Fax: 071-437 8883

The professional body for individual chemists

★2950★
Royal Society of Health
38a St George's Drive
London SW1V 4BH
Phone: 071-630 0121
Fax: 071-976 6847

Covers health and social care, nutrition, hygiene and the environment

★2951★
Royal Society of Literature
1 Hyde Park Gardens
London W2 2LT
Phone: 071-723 5104

★2952★
Royal Society of Marine Artists
17 Carlton House Terrace
London SW1Y 5BD
Phone: 071-930 6844
Fax: 071-834 7830

★2953★
Royal Society of Medicine
1 Wimpole St
London W1M 8AE
Phone: 071-408 2119
Fax: 071-355 3196

★2954★
Royal Society of Miniature Painters, Sculptors & Gravers
Westminster Gallery
Central Hall
Storey's Gate
London SW1H 9NH
Phone: 071-222 8010

★2955★
Royal Society of Musicians of GB
10 Stratford Place

London W1N 9AE
Phone: 071-629 6137

★2956★
Royal Society of Painter-Etchers & Engravers
Bankside Gallery
48 Hopton St
London SE1 9JH
Phone: 071-928 7521
Fax: 071-928 2820

Covering printmaking

★2957★
Royal Society of Painters in Water-Colours
Bankside Gallery
48 Hopton St
London SE1 9JH
Phone: 071-928 7521
Fax: 071-928 2820

★2958★
Royal Society of Portrait Painters
17 Carlton House Terrace
London SW1Y 5BD
Phone: 071-930 6844
Fax: 071-839 7830

★2959★
Royal Society of Tropical Medicine & Hygiene
26 Portland Place
London W1N 4EY
Phone: 071-580 2127

Promotes health and seeks to advance the study, control and prevention of tropical diseases

★2960★
Royal Statistical Society
25 Enford St
London W1H 2BH
Phone: 071-723 5882
Fax: 071-706 1710

★2961★
Royal Television Society
Tavistock House East
Tavistock Square

London WC1H 9HR
Phone: 071-387 1970
Fax: 071-387 0358

A forum for all who work in the television industry

★2962★
Royal Town Planning Institute
26 Portland Place
London W1N 4BE
Phone: 071-636 9107
Fax: 071-323 1582

★2963★
Royal Yachting Association
RYA House
Romsey Rd
Eastleigh
Southampton SO5 4YA
Phone: 0703 629962
Fax: 0703 629924

Governing body for the sport of yachting

★2964★
Rubber Stamp Manufacturers' Guild
6 Wimpole St
London W1M 8AS
Phone: 071-637 7692
Fax: 071-436 3137

★2965★
Rubber Trade Association of London
1st Floor
Wigham House
16-30 Wakering Rd
Barking IG11 8PG
Phone: 081-594 5346
Fax: 081-507 8017

★2966★
Rugby Football Union
Rugby Rd
Twickenham TW1 1DZ
Phone: 081-892 8161
Fax: 081-892 9816

★2967★
Rural Crafts Association
c/o Trevor Sears
Heights Cottage

Brook Rd
Wormley
Godalming   GU8 5UA
Phone: 0428 682292

★2968★
Rusk Manufacturers Association *now*
  incorporated into Food & Drink
  Federation

★2969★
**Safety Equipment Distributors
  Association**
c/o G K Edwards
74 Chester Rd
Birmingham   B36 7BU
Phone: 021-776 7474
Fax: 021-776 7605

★2970★
Sail Training Association
2a The Hard
Portsmouth   PO1 3PT
Phone: 0705 832055
Fax: 0705 815769

★2971★
Sailing Barge Association
Central House
32-66 High St
London   E15 2PS
Phone: 081-519 4872
Fax: 081-519 5483

★2972★
Salmon & Trout Association
Fishmongers' Hall
London Bridge
London   EC4R 9EL
Phone: 071-283 5838
Fax: 071-929 1389

Representing game anglers

★2973★
Salt Manufacturers Association
The Cottage
Oldfield Bank
Highgate Rd

Altrincham   WA14 4QZ
Phone: 061-941 2595

Salt for human consumption

★2974★
Salvage Association
Bankside House
107-112 Leadenhall St
London   EC3A 4AP
Phone: 071-623 1299
Fax: 071-626 4963

For the protection of commercial interests in
respect of wrecked and damaged property

★2975★
**Sand & Ballast Hauliers & Allied
  Trades Alliance**
c/o Mrs L A Bennett
16 Walter Rd
Wokingham
Reading   RG11 2UY
Phone: 0734 784324

★2976★
Sand & Gravel Association
Bramber Court
2 Bramber Rd
London   W14 9PB
Phone: 071-381 8778
Fax: 8770

Represents sand and gravel interests excluding sand for refractory or moulding purposes

★2977★
Saw Association
Light Trades House
3 Melbourne Avenue
Sheffield   S10 2QJ
Phone: 0742 663084
Fax: 0742 670910

★2978★
School & Group Travel Association
Honeycroft House
Pangbourne Rd
Upper Basildon
Pangbourne

Reading RG8 8LR
Phone: 0491 671631

Members are primarily travel companies organising tours foreducational and youth groups

★2979★
School Bookshop Association
6 Brightfield Rd
London SE12 8QF
Phone: 081-852 4953

Membership covers schools, libraries, bookshops, publishers, authors and parents concerned with the importance of book use and availability

★2980★
School Examination & Assessment Council
Newcombe House
45 Notting Hill Gate
London W11 3JB
Phone: 071-229 1234
Fax: 071-243 0542

★2981★
School Journey Association
48 Cavendish Rd
London SW12 0DG
Phone: 081-675 6636

Members are full-time teachers and the association promotes educational travel

★2982★
School Library Association
Liden Library
Barrington Close
Liden
Swindon SN3 6HF
Phone: 0793 617838

Membership embraces all concerned with the development of primary and secondary school libraries

★2983★
School of Herbal Medicine Phytotherapy
Bucksteep Manor
Bodle St Green

Hailsham BN27 4RJ
Phone: 0323 833812
Fax: 0323 833869

★2984★
School Secretaries' Association
c/o Miss D Hancox
King Edward VI Camp Hill School for Girls
Vicarage Rd
Birmingham B14 7QJ
Phone: 021-441 2150

★2985★
Schools Poetry Association
27 Pennington Close
Golden Common
Winchester SO21 1UR
Phone: 0962 712062

★2986★
Science Fiction Foundation
c/o J Day
Polytechnic of East London
Longbridge Rd
Dagenham RM8 2AS
Phone: 081-590 7722
Fax: 081-590 7799

Promotes the study of science fiction in education

★2987★
Scientific Instrument Manufacturers Association of GB *now* Association for the Instrumentation, Control & Automation Industry in the UK

★2988★
Scientific Instruments Research Association *see* Sira

★2989★
Scotch Quality Beef & Lamb Association
13th Avenue
Edinburgh Exhibition & Trade Centre
Ingliston
Edinburgh EH28 8NB
Phone: 031-333 5335
Fax: 031-333 2935

★2990★
Scotch Whisky Association
17 Half Moon St
London W1Y 7RB
Phone: 071-629 4384
Fax: 071-493 1398

★2991★
Scottish & N Ireland Plumbing Employers' Federation
2 Walker St
Edinburgh EH3 7LB
Phone: 031-225 2255
Fax: 031-226 7638

★2992★
Scottish Agricultural Arbiters' Association
10 Dublin St
Edinburgh EH1 3PR
Phone: 031-556 2993
Fax: 031-557 5542

★2993★
Scottish Agricultural Organisation Society
Claremont House
19 Claremont Crescent
Edinburgh EH7 4JW
Phone: 031-556 6574
Fax: 031-557 3060

★2994★
Scottish Assessors' Association
c/o Ian Rogers
30-31 Queen St
Edinburgh EH2 1LZ
Phone: 031-225 1339

★2995★
Scottish Association for Mental Health
Atlantic House
38 Gardner's Crescent
Edinburgh EH3 8DQ
Phone: 031-229 9687
Fax: 031-229 3558

★2996★
Scottish Association for Metals
c/o Dr J R Wilcox
Bell College of Technology
Hamilton
Glasgow ML3 OJB
Phone: 0698 283100
Fax: 0698 282131

★2997★
Scottish Association of Advisers in Physical Education
c/o Malcolm Renny, Newton Advisers Centre, Green Street Lane
Ayr KA8 8BH
Phone: 0292 260325

★2998★
Scottish Association of Directors of Water & Sewerage Services
c/o J M T Cockburn
Director of Water Services
Grampian Regional Council
Woodhill House
Westburn Rd
Aberdeen AB9 2LU
Phone: 0224 664900
Fax: 0224 697445

★2999★
Scottish Association of Geography Teachers
c/o J L Bairner
Bannockburn Secondary School
Bannockburn
Stirling
Phone: 0786 70229

★3000★
Scottish Association of Master Bakers
Atholl House
4 Torphichen St
Edinburgh EH3 8JQ
Phone: 031-229 1401
Fax: 031-229 8239

★3001★
Scottish Association of Milk Product Manufacturers
Phoenix House
South Avenue
Clydebank
Glasgow G81 2LG
Phone: 041-951 1170
Fax: 041-951 1129

★3002★
Scottish Association of Youth Clubs
Balfour House
17 Bonnington Grove
Edinburgh EH6 4DP
Phone: 031-554 2561

★3003★
Scottish Boat Builders Association
36 Renfield St
Glasgow G2 1BD
Phone: 041-248 6161
Fax: 041-204 1537

★3004★
Scottish Building Contractors Association
13 Woodside Crescent
Glasgow G3 7UP
Phone: 041-332 7144
Fax: 041-331 1684

★3005★
Scottish Building Employers Federation
13 Woodside Crescent
Glasgow G3 7UP
Phone: 041-332 7144
Fax: 041-331 1684

★3006★
Scottish Cement Merchants Association
79 West Regent St
Glasgow G2 2AW
Phone: 041-332 0922

★3007★
Scottish Commercial Travellers Association
c/o R M Wood
20 Anderson St
Airdrie ML6 0AA
Phone: 0236 56161
Fax: 0236 66149

★3008★
Scottish Committee of Optometrists
3 Castleton Crescent
Newton Mearns
Glasgow G71 5JX
Phone: 041-639 6483

★3009★
Scottish Community Education Council
West Coates House
90 Haymarket Terrace
Edinburgh EH12 5LQ
Phone: 031-313 2488
Fax: 031-313 2477

★3010★
Scottish Consumer Credit Association
22 Hamilton Rd
Glasgow G73 3DG
Phone: 041-647 2363
Fax: 041-643 1151

★3011★
Scottish Corn Trade Association
8 Melville Crescent
Edinburgh EH3 7PQ
Phone: 031-225 6834
Fax: 031-225 4049

★3012★
Scottish Council for Arbitration
55 Queen St
Edinburgh EH2 3PA
Phone: 031-220 4776

To administor arbitration in Scotland, both domestic and international

★3013★
Scottish Council for Educational Technology
74 Victoria Crescent Rd
Glasgow   G12 9JN
Phone: 041-334 9314
Fax: 041-334 6519

★3014★
Scottish Council for Research in Education
15 Saint John St
Edinburgh   EH8 8JR
Phone: 031-557 2944
Fax: 031-556 9454

★3015★
Scottish Council for Voluntary Organisations
18-19 Claremont Crescent
Edinburgh   EH7 4QD
Phone: 031-556 3882
Fax: 031-556 0279

★3016★
Scottish Daily Newspaper Society
Merchants House Buildings
30 George Square
Glasgow   G2 1EG
Phone: 041-248 2375
Fax: 041-248 2362

★3017★
Scottish Dairy Trade Federation
Phoenix House
South Avenue
Clydebank
Glasgow   G81 2LG
Phone: 041-951-1170
Fax: 041-951 1129

★3018★
Scottish Dance Teachers' Alliance
339 North Woodside Rd
Glasgow   G20 6ND
Phone: 041-339 8944

To promote and encourage Scottish dancing in all forms

★3019★
Scottish Decorators Federation
249 West George St
Glasgow   G2 4RB
Phone: 041-221 7090
Fax: 041-204 1902

★3020★
Scottish Employers' Council for the Clay Industries
c/o Wemyss Brick Co Ltd
Methil
Kirkcaldy   KY8 3QQ
Phone: 0592 712313
Fax: 0592 716349

★3021★
Scottish Engineering Employers' Association
105 West George St
Glasgow   G2 1QL
Phone: 041-221 3181
Fax: 041-204 1202

★3022★
Scottish Federation of Grocers' & Wine Merchants Associations
3 Loaning Rd
Edinburgh   EH7 6JE
Phone: 031-652 2482
Fax: 031-652 2896

★3023★
Scottish Federation of Meat Traders' Associations
3 Kinnoull St
Perth   PH1 5EN
Phone: 0738 37785

★3024★
Scottish Federation of Merchant Tailors
3 Randolph Crescent
Edinburgh   EH3 7UD
Phone: 031-225 5851
Telex: 72465

★3025★
Scottish Field Studies Association
c/o A Lavery
Kindrogan Field Centre
Enochdhu
Blairgowrie   PH10 7PG
Phone: 0250 81286

★3026★
Scottish Film Council
Dowanhill
74 Victoria Crescent Rd
Glasgow   G12 9JN
Phone: 041-334 4445
Fax: 041-334 8132

★3027★
Scottish Fishermen's Federation
18 Bon Accord Crescent
Aberdeen   AB1 2DE
Phone: 0224 582583
Fax: 0224 574958

★3028★
Scottish Flour Millers' Association
c/o Maurice Crichton, Hall of Caldwell,
   Uplawmoor
Glasgow   G78 4BW
Phone: 050585 248

★3029★
Scottish Glass Association
13 Woodside Crescent
Glasgow   G3 7UP
Phone: 041-332 7144
Fax: 041-331 1684

★3030★
Scottish Grocers Federation
3 Loaning Rd
Edinburgh   EH7 6JE
Phone: 031-652 2482
Fax: 031-652 2896

★3031★
Scottish Homing Union
231 Low Water Rd
Hamilton

Glasgow   ML3 7QN
Phone: 0698 286983

For keepers and trainers of homing pigeons

★3032★
Scottish House Builders Association
13 Woodside Crescent
Glasgow   G3 7UP
Phone: 031-332 7144
Fax: 031-331 1684

★3033★
Scottish Institute of Adult &
   Continuing Education
30 Rutland Square
Edinburgh   EH1 2BW
Phone: 031-229 6775
Fax: 031-229 6775

★3034★
Scottish Joint Industry Board for the
   Electrical Contracting Industry
c/o D D W Montgomery
Bush House
Bush Estate
Edinburgh   EH26 0SB
Phone: 031-445 5577
Fax: 031-445 5548

★3035★
Scottish Lace & Window Furnishing
   Association
1 Craigview Rd
Newmilns   KA16 9DQ
Phone: 0560 20041

★3036★
Scottish Landowners' Federation
39 Palmerston Place
Edinburgh   EH12 5AU
Phone: 031-220 4055
Fax: 031-220 4056

Representing owners of rural land in Scotland

★3037★
Scottish Law Agents Society
3 Albyn Place

Edinburgh EH2 4NQ
Phone: 031-225 7515
Fax: 031-220 1083

★3038★
Scottish Library Association
Motherwell Business Centre, Coursington Rd
Motherwell ML1 1PW
Phone: 0698 52526
Fax: 0698 52057

★3039★
Scottish Licensed Trade Association
10 Walker St
Edinburgh EH3 7LA
Phone: 031-225 5169
Fax: 031-220 4057

★3040★
Scottish Marine Biological Association
Dunstaffnage Marine Research Laboratory
PO Box 3
Oban PA34 4AD
Phone: 0631 62244
Fax: 0631 65518

★3041★
Scottish Master Plasterers' Association
12 Hill St
Edinburgh EH2 3LB
Phone: 031-225 5214
Fax: 031-226 2069

★3042★
Scottish Master Wrights & Builders Association
26 West Nile St
Glasgow G1 2PQ
Phone: 041-221 0011
Fax: 041-248 5117

★3043★
Scottish Milk Records Association
c/o Milk Marketing Board
Underwood Rd
Paisley PA3 1TJ
Phone: 041-887 1234
Fax: 041-889 1225

★3044★
Scottish Motor Trade Association
3 Palmerston Place
Edinburgh EH12 5AF
Phone: 031-225 3643
Fax: 031-220 0446

★3045★
Scottish Museums Council
County House
20-22 Torphichen St
Edinburgh EH3 8JB
Phone: 031-229 7465

★3046★
Scottish National Housing & Town Planning Council
c/o J M Brown
62 Hawkhead Rd
Paisley PA1 3NB
Phone: 041-889 7056

★3047★
Scottish Net Manufacturers Association
c/o J & W Stuart Ltd
Inveresk Industrial Estate
Musselburgh EH21 7PA
Phone: 031-665 2552
Fax: 031-653 6191

★3048★
Scottish Newspaper Proprietors' Association
48 Palmerston Place
Edinburgh EH12 5DE
Phone: 031-220 4353
Fax: 031-220 4344

The representative body for publishers of Scottish weekly newspapers

★3049★
Scottish Newspaper Publishers Association
48 Palmerston Place
Edinburgh EH12 5DE
Phone: 031-220 4353
Fax: 031-220 4344

★3050★
**Scottish Pelagic Fishermens
   Association**
21 Albert St
Aberdeen   AB9 8DA
Phone: 0224 632464
Fax: 0224 632184

★3051★
Scottish Pharmaceutical Federation
135 Buchanan St
Glasgow   G1 2JG
Phone: 041-221 1235
Fax: 041-221 5781

★3052★
Scottish Pipers' Association
c/o B MacDougall
5 Barrington Drive
Glasgow   G4 9DS
Phone: 041-334 6398

★3053★
Scottish Plant Owners Association
12 St Vincent Place
Glasgow   G1 2EQ
Phone: 041-248 3434
Fax: 041-221 1226

★3054★
Scottish Poetry Library Association
Tweeddale Court
14 High St
Edinburgh   EH1 1TE
Phone: 031-557 2876

★3055★
Scottish Police Federation
5 Woodside Place
Glasgow   G3 7PD
Phone: 041-332 5234
Fax: 041-331 2436

★3056★
Scottish Pre-School Play Association
14 Elliot Place
Glasgow   G3 8EP
Phone: 041-221 4148

★3057★
Scottish Provision Trade Association
George House
36 North Hanover St
Glasgow   G1 2AD
Phone: 041-552 3422
Fax: 041-552 2935

★3058★
Scottish Publishers Association
25a South West Thistle Street Lane
Edinburgh   EH2 1EW
Phone: 031-225 5795
Fax: 031-220 0377

Members are book publishers

★3059★
Scottish Salmon Smokers Association
163c Cargo Terminal
Turnhouse Rd
Edinburgh   EH12 OAL
Phone: 031-339 2468

★3060★
Scottish Scrap Association
112 West George St
Glasgow   G2 1QF
Phone: 041-332 7484
Fax: 041-333 0581

★3061★
**Scottish Secondary Teachers'
   Association**
15 Dundas St
Edinburgh   EH3 6QG
Phone: 031-556 5919
Fax: 031-556 1419

★3062★
**Scottish Seed & Nursery Trade
   Association**
12 Bruntsfield Crescent
Edinburgh   EH10 4HA
Phone: 031-447 1035
Fax: 031-447 0970

★3063★
Scottish Shooting Council
39 Pelstream Avenue

Stirling   FK7 0BG
Phone: 0786 75769

★3064★
Scottish Society for Conservation & Restoration
100 Holeburn Rd
Glasgow   G43 2XN
Phone: 041-637 4149

★3065★
Scottish Standing Conference of Voluntary Youth Organisations
Central Hall
West Tollcross
Edinburgh   EH3 8BP
Phone: 031-229 0339

★3066★
Scottish Steel Founders' Association
c/o P T Hughes
Glencast Ltd
Kirkland Works
Leven   KY8 2LE
Phone: 0333 23641
Fax: 0333 25734

★3067★
Scottish Timber Trade Association
John Player Building
Players Rd
Stirling Enterprise Park
Stirling   FK7 7RS
Phone: 0786 51623
Fax: 0786 74412

★3068★
Scottish Tourist Guides Association
c/o Miss C Ward
45 Learmouth Grove
Edinburgh   EH4 1BZ
Phone: 031-332 0490

★3069★
Scottish Vocational Education Council
Hanover House
24 Douglas St
Glasgow   G2 7NQ
Phone: 031-248 7900
Fax: 031-244 4996

★3070★
Scottish Wholesale Druggists Association
17 Smith's Place
Edinburgh   EH6 8NU
Phone: 031-554 1551

★3071★
Scottish Wirework Manufacturers' Association
c/o I W Reid
William Reed & Sons Ltd
162 Glenpark St
Glasgow   G31 1PG
Phone: 041-554 7081
Fax: 041-554 7162

★3072★
Scottish Woollen Industry Association
45 Moray Place
Edinburgh   EH3 6EQ
Phone: 031-225 3149
Fax: 031-220 4942

★3073★
Scottish Woollen Publicity Council
45 Moray Place
Edinburgh   EH3 6EQ
Phone: 031-225 3149
Fax: 031-220 4929

★3074★
Scottish Woollen Trade Mark Association
45 Moray Place
Edinburgh   EH3 6EQ
Phone: 031-225 3149
Fax: 031-220 4942

★3075★
Screen Printing Association
Association House
7a West St
Reigate   RH2 9BL
Phone: 0737 240792
Fax: 0737 240770

Formerly: Display Producers & Screen Printers Association

★3076★
Screw Thread Tool Manufacturers' Association
Light Trades House
3 Melbourne Avenue
Sheffield S10 2QJ
Phone: 0742 663084
Fax: 0742 670910

★3077★
Seasoning Manufacturers Association
now incorporated into Food & Drink Federation

★3078★
Secondary Heads Association
130 Regent Rd
Leicester LE1 7PG
Phone: 0533 471797
Fax: 0533 471152

For heads and deputies of secondary schools

★3079★
Securities & Futures Authority
Stock Exchange Tower
Old Broad St
London EC2N 1EQ
Phone: 071-256 9000
Fax: 071-334 8943

The regulatory body for dealers and advisers in securities, bonds, financial futures and options and corporate finance

★3080★
Securities & Investments Board
3 Royal Exchange Buildings
London EC3V 3NL
Phone: 071-929 0433
Fax: 071-929 0433

★3081★
Seed Crushers' & Oil Processors' Association *now* incorporated into Food & Drink Federation

★3082★
Sewing Machine Trade Association
c/o A Spencer-Bolland
24 Fairlawn Grove

London W4 5EH
Phone: 081-995 0411

★3083★
Shellfish Association of GB
Fishmongers' Hall
London Bridge
London EC4R 9EL
Phone: 071-283 8305
Fax: 071-929 1389

The trade association for shellfish cultivators, processors and distributors

★3084★
Sherry Producers Committee
71 Lincoln's Inn Fields
London WC2A 3JF
Phone: 071-405 6195
Fax: 071-405 1453

★3085★
Shetland Salmon Farmers' Association
80 Commercial St
Lerwick ZE1 ODL
Phone: 0595 5579
Fax: 0595 4494

★3086★
Shipowners Refrigerated Cargo Research Association
140 Newmarket Rd
Cambridge CB5 8HE
Phone: 0223 65101
Fax: 461522

All aspects relating to transportation of perishables by land, sea and air

★3087★
Shiprepairers & Shipbuilders Independent Association
33 Catherine Place
London SW1E 6DY
Phone: 071-828 0933

Represents firms in the private sector of the shiprepairing and shipbuilding industries

★3088★
Shop & Display Equipment Association
24 Croydon Rd

Caterham   CR3 6YR
Phone: 0883 348911
Fax: 343435

★3089★
Showmen's Guild of GB
Guild House
41 Clarence St
Staines   TW18 4SY
Phone: 0784 61805
Fax: 0784 461732

★3090★
Silk Association of GB
c/o L Rheinberg
Morley Rd
Tonbridge   TN9 1RN
Phone: 0732 351357
Telex: 95311
Fax: 0732 770217

★3091★
Silsoe Research Institute
Wrest Park
Silsoe
Bedford   MK45 5HS
Phone: 0525 60000
Fax: 0525 60156

Covering agricultural research

★3092★
Simplified Spelling Society
51 Purser's Cross Rd
London   SW6 4QY
Phone: 071-736 6821

To encourage the serious study of spelling

★3093★
**Simultaneous Interpretation
   Equipment Suppliers Association**
9 Hesper Mews
London   SW5 0HH
Phone: 071-373 9474

★3094★
Single Ply Association
125 Queen's Rd

Brighton   BN1 3YW
Phone: 0273 29271
Fax: 0273 28114

Formerly: The Flexible Roofing Association

★3095★
Single Ply Roofing Association
1f Upton Rd
Norwich   NR4 7PA
Phone: 0603 507835
Fax: 0603 503317

Concerned with the wider use of polymeric membranes capable of application as a single ply

★3096★
Sira
South Hill
Chislehurst
Orpington   BR7 5EH
Phone: 081-467 2636
Fax: 081-467 6515

Members are manufacturers and users of measurement instrumentation

★3097★
Skibob Association of GB
c/o K Rochfort
150 Canterbury Way
Stevenage   SG1 4BL
Phone: 0438 745201

★3098★
**Skin Hide & Leather Traders
   Association**
20-21 Tooks Court
Cursiton St
London   EC4A 1LB
Phone: 071-831 7581
Fax: 071-405 1291

★3099★
**Small Electrical Appliance Marketing
   Association**
Carolyn House
22-26 Dingwall Rd
Croydon   CR0 9XF
Phone: 081-681 1687
Fax: 081-681 2134

★3100★
**Small Independent Brewers'
Association**
2 Balfour Rd
London   N5 2HB
Phone: 071-359 8323
Fax: 071-354 3962

★3101★
Small Landlords Association
c/o Lilian Cline
28 Rosedene Avenue
London   SW16 2LT
Phone: 081-769 5060

Members are resident and non-resident landlords

★3102★
**Snack, Nut & Crisp Manufacturers
Association**
10 Wardour St
London   W1V 3HG
Phone: 071-439 2567
Telex: 071-439 2673

Members are engaged in the production of
potato crisps, savoury snacks and processed
nuts

★3103★
Snail Centre
Plas Newydd
90-92 Dinerth Rd
Colwyn Bay   LL28 4YH
Phone: 0492 48253
Fax: 0492 43124

Research into the production and farming of
edible snails

★3104★
Soap & Detergent Industry Association
PO Box 9
Hayes Gate House
Hayes   UB4 0JD
Phone: 081-573 7992
Fax: 081-848 9671

★3105★
Social Care Association
23a Victoria Rd

Surbiton   KT6 4JZ
Phone: 081-390 6831
Fax: 081-399 6183

Professional association for those involved in
social care, especially in residential and day
care

★3106★
Social History Society of the UK
c/o Centre for Social History
Furness College
Lancaster University
Lancaster   LA1 4YG
Phone: 0524 65201   ext. 2812

★3107★
Social Policy Association
c/o Dr A Erskine
Dept of Social Administration & Social
   Work
University of Glasgow
Lilybane House
Bue Gardens
Glasgow   G12 8RT
Phone: 041-339 8855   ext. 4520

★3108★
Social Research Association
9 Windsor Rd
London   N13 5PP
Phone: 081-886 2052

An aspect of market research

★3109★
Society for Applied Bacteriology
c/o Dr A Campbell
Seale-Hayne Faculty
Polytechnic South West
Newton Abbot   TP12 6NQ
Phone: 0626 52323

Membership is open to all concerned with
and engaged in the study of any aspect of
microbiology

★3110★
Society for Computers & Law
10 Hurle Crescent
Bristol   BS8 2TA
Phone: 0272 237393

Promotes the use of high technology in law

★3111★
Society for Drug Research
c/o B Cavilla
20 Queensberry Place
London   SW7 2DZ
Phone: 081-501 8333
Fax: 071-823 9409

Furthering research and education in the field
of relief of sickness

★3112★
**Society for Earthquake & Civil
    Engineering Dynamics**
1-7 Great George St
London   SW1P 3AA
Phone: 071-222 7722
Fax: 071-222 7500

★3113★
**Society for Education in Film &
    Television**
29 Old Compton St
London   W1V 5PL
Phone: 071-734 5455

★3114★
Society for Endocrinology
23 Richmond Hill
Bristol   BS8 1EN
Phone: 0272 734662
Fax: 0272 237489

★3115★
Society for Environmental Therapy
c/o H Davidson
521 Foxhall Rd
Ipswich   IP3 8LW
Phone: 0473 723552

The environmental causes of disease and
low-technology medicine. Membership is
open to both lay and professional people

★3116★
Society for Experimental Biology
Burlington House
Piccadilly
London   W1V 0LQ
Phone: 071-439 8732
Fax: 071-287 4786

Members are postgraduates and scientists

★3117★
Society for General Microbiology
Harvest House
62 London Rd
Reading   RG1 5AS
Phone: 0734 861345
Fax: 0734 314112

★3118★
Society for Italic Handwriting
c/o J Fricker
Highfields
Nightingale Rd
Guildford   GU1 1ER
Phone: 0483 68443

★3119★
Society for Low Temperature Biology
c/o Institute of Biology
20 Queensberry Place
London   SU7 2D2
Phone: 071-581 8333
Fax: 071-823 9409

Studying the effect of low temperatures on
living organisms

★3120★
Society for Nautical Research
c/o National Maritime Museum
Romney Rd
London   SE10 9NF
Phone: 081-858 4422

The study of ships and seafaring internationally

★3121★
**Society for Post-Medieval
    Archaeology**
c/o Museum of London
London Wall
London   EC2Y 5HN
Phone: 071-600 3699
Fax: 071-600 1058

Members include professional archaeologists,
historians, university libraries, institutions and
other interested individuals

★3122★
Society for Radiological Protection
c/o National Radiological Protection Board
Chilton
Didcot   OX11 0RQ
Phone: 0235 831600
Fax: 0235 833891

★3123★
**Society for Research into Higher
   Education**
c/o Cynthia Iliffe
University of Surrey
Guildford   GU2 5XH
Phone: 0483 39003
Fax: 0483 300803

★3124★
**Society for Research into
   Hydrocephalus & Spina Bifida**
c/o Dr R Bayston
Institute for Child Health
30 Guilford St
London   WC1N 1EH
Phone: 071-242 9789
Fax: 071-831 0488

For medical professionals to advance education and research

★3125★
**Society for the Advancement of
   Games & Simulation in Education**
c/o Mrs M Mamolias
48 Pemberton Rd
East Molesey   KT8 9LG
Phone: 0504 223054

★3126★
**Society for the Advancement of
   Anaesthesia in Dentistry**
59 Summerlands Avenue
London   W3 6EW
Phone: 081-993 6844

Promotes the teaching and progress of pain
control in dentistry

★3127★
**Society for the Prevention of
   Asbestosis & Industrial Diseases**
c/o N Tait
38 Drapers Rd
Enfield   EN2 8LU
Phone: 081-366 1640

Provides information on prevention and
advice to anyone affected by an industrial
disease

★3128★
**Society for the Promotion of Hellenic
   Studies**
31-34 Gordon Square
London   WC1H 0PP
Phone: 071-387 7495

Promotes the study of Greek language, literature, history and art in the ancient, Byzantine
and modern periods

★3129★
**Society for the Promotion of New
   Music**
10 Stratford Place
London   W1N 9AE
Phone: 071-491 8111

★3130★
**Society for the Promotion of Roman
   Studies**
31-34 Gordon Square
London   WC1H 0PP
Phone: 071-387 8157

For academics and classicists involved in
archaeology, art, literature and history of Italy
and the Roman Empire back to 700AD

★3131★
**Society for the Protection of Ancient
   Buildings**
37 Spital Square
London   E1 6DY
Phone: 071-377 1644
Fax: 5296

★3132★
Society for the Social History of Medicine
c/o Mary Fissell
Maths Tower
University of Manchester
Manchester   M13 9PL
Phone: 061-275 5910
Fax: 061-273 1123

★3133★
Society for Theatre Research
c/o Theatre Museum
1e Tavistock St
London   WC2E 7PA

★3134★
Society for Underwater Technology
c/o Cdr D R Wardle
76 Mark Lane
London   EC3R 7JN
Phone: 071-481 0750
Fax: 071-481 4001

For individuals interested in underwater technology, ocean science and offshore engineering

★3135★
Society of Analytical Psychology
1 Daleham Gardens
London   NW3 5BY
Phone: 071-435 7696
Fax: 071-431 1495

★3136★
Society of Antiquaries
Burlington House
Piccadilly
London   W1V 0HS
Phone: 071-734 0193
Fax: 071-287 6967

Concerning archaeology, art and architectural history, genealogy and heraldry

★3137★
Society of Antiquaries of Scotland
Royal Museum of Scotland, Queen St
Edinburgh   EH2 1JD
Phone: 031-225 7534   ext. 327

★3138★
Society of Apothecaries of London
Apothecaries Hall
Blackfriars Lane
London   EC4V 6EJ
Phone: 071-236 1189

Members are individual medical practitioners

★3139★
Society of Archer-Antiquaries
c/o D Elmy
61 Lambert Rd
Bridlington   YO16 5RD
Phone: 0262 601604

Research into all aspects of archery history

★3140★
Society of Architectural & Industrial Illustrators
PO Box 22
Stroud   GL5 3DH
Phone: 0453 882563

Members are illustrators, model makers and photographers working in architecture and industry

★3141★
Society of Archivists
Information House
20-24 Old St
London   EC1V 9AP
Phone: 071-253 4488

Members include archivists, records managers and conservators in central and local government, universities, charities and the business sector

★3142★
Society of Artists in Architecture
31 Park Hill Rd
Bromley   BR2 0JX
Phone: 071-930 6844

★3143★
Society of Arts Publicists
59 Knightsbridge
London   SW1X 7RA
Phone: 071-240 2430
Fax: 071-235 3671

★3144★
Society of Association Executives
Unit 6a
L/A Works
Alfred St
Westbury   BA13 3DY

★3145★
Society of Authors
84 Drayton Gardens
London   SW10 9SB
Phone: 071-373 6642

Members are authors or illustrators having full-length works published in the UK

★3146★
Society of Automotive-Electrical Technicians
c/o T R A Creedy
PO Box 62
Selsey
Chichester   PO20 OHJ
Phone: 0243 603736

Concerned with the development and application of electrical/electronic subjects for all forms of transport

★3147★
Society of Battery Manufacturers
Duddings
Timberscombe
Minehead
Phone: 0643 841252

★3148★
Society of Bookbinders
c/o J A Isaac
Lower Hammonds Farm
Ripley Lane
West Horsley
Godalming   KT24 6JP
Phone: 04865 3175

★3149★
Society of British Aerospace Companies
29 King St
London   SW1Y 6RD
Phone: 071-839 3231
Fax: 071-930 3577

★3150★
Society of British Battery Manufacturers
Duddings
Timberscombe
Dunster   TA24 7TB
Phone: 0643 841252

★3151★
Society of British Fight Directors
56 Goldhurst Terrace
London
Phone: 071-624 1837

Professional body of fight directors for film, theatre and television

★3152★
Society of British Gas Industries
36 Holly Walk
Leamington Spa   CV32 4LY
Phone: 0926 334357
Fax: 0926 450459

Representing the interests of contractors and suppliers of gas plant, gas appliances and equipment

★3153★
Society of British Match Manufacturers
Sword House
Totteridge Rd
High Wycombe   HP13 6EJ
Phone: 0494 33300
Fax: 0494 437459

★3154★
Society of British Neurological Surgeons
c/o T A H Hyde
Institute of Neurological Sciences
Southern General Hospital
1345 Govan Rd
Glasgow   GS1 4TF
Phone: 041-445 2466
Fax: 041-425 1915

★3155★
**Society of British Printing Ink
   Manufacturers**
Pira House
Randalls Rd
Leatherhead KT22 7RU
Phone: 0372 378628
Fax: 0372 377526

All matters connected with the manufacture
of printing inks, printers varnishes and printers rollers

★3156★
Society of British Snuff Blenders
20 Carclaze Rd
St Austell PL25 3AQ
Phone: 0726 66857

★3157★
Society of British Theatre Designers
4 Great Pulteney St
London W1R 3DF
Phone: 071-434 3901
Fax: 071-434 3903

★3158★
Society of British Water Industries
38 Holly Walk
Leamington Spa CV32 4LY
Phone: 0926 831530
Fax: 0926 450459

Members are engaged in producing products
for or offering services to both water and gas
industries

★3159★
Society of Business Economists
11 Bay Tree Walk
Watford WD1 3RX
Phone: 0923 37287

★3160★
Society of Cable Television Engineers
10 Avenue Rd
Dorridge
Solihull B93 8LD
Phone: 0564 774058
Fax: 0564 779032

★3161★
Society of Cardiological Technicians
c/o Dept of Medical Cardiology
Plymouth General Hospital
Greenbank Section
Plymouth
Phone: 0752 766843

★3162★
**Society of Catering & Hotel
   Management Consultants**
c/o Humble Arnold Associates
The Midden
Node Court
Drivers End
Codicote
Stevenage SG4 8TR
Phone: 0438 821444
Fax: 0438 821432

★3163★
Society of Chemical Industry
14-15 Belgrave Square
London SW1X 8PS
Phone: 071-235 3681
Fax: 071-823 1698

A multi-disciplinary body

★3164★
**Society of Chief Architects of Local
   Authorities**
c/o D Johnson
Teeside House
108a Borough Rd
Middlesbrough TS1 2HG
Phone: 0642 248155 ext. 3101
Fax: 0642 241288

★3165★
**Society of Chief Building Regulation
   Officers**
c/o W L Stemp
Greenholt
Springfield Rd
Verwood
Bournemouth BH21 6HN
Phone: 0202 675151 ext. 3212

★3166★
Society of Chief Electrical & Mechanical Engineers in Local Government
c/o P K Knight
County Architects Dept
Herts County Council
County Hall
Hertford
Phone: 0992 555070
Fax: 0992 555009

★3167★
Society of Chief Personnel Officers
c/o N J Sutcliffe, Charnwood Borough
  Council, Southfields
Loughborough   LE11 2TX
Phone: 0509 263151   ext. 2033
Fax: 0509 610626

For personnel officers working in local goverment

★3168★
Society of Chief Quantity Surveyors in Local Government
c/o D W Croser
46 The Drive
Amersham   HP7 9AD
Phone: 0494 727449

★3169★
Society of Chiropodists
53 Welbeck St
London   W1M 7HE
Phone: 071-486 3381
Fax: 071-935 6859

The professional body for state-registered chiropodists

★3170★
Society of Community Health Council Staff
c/o T Hicks
1st Floor
12 New North Parade
Huddersfield   HD1 5JP
Phone: 0484 435154

★3171★
Society of Community Medicine *now* Society of Public Health

★3172★
Society of Company & Commercial Accountants *now* Institute of Company Accountants

★3173★
Society of Construction Law
c/o Philip Ranner
6 Upper Stone St
Maidstone   ME15 6EX
Phone: 0622 687437

★3174★
Society of Consulting Marine Engineers & Ship Surveyors
6 Lloyds Avenue
London   EC3N 3AX
Phone: 071-488 3010

★3175★
Society of Cosmetic Scientists
Delaport House
57 Guildford St
Luton   LU1 2JN
Phone: 0582 26661
Fax: 0582 405217

★3176★
Society of County & Regional Public Relations Officers
c/o Graham Terry
Avon County Council
Avon House
The Haymarket
Bristol   BS99 7NF
Phone: 0272 290777
Telex: 44756

★3177★
Society of County Children's & Education Librarians
c/o R Boyd
Schools Library Service
Resource Centre
Parkway

Bridgwater   TA6 4RL
Phone: 0278 421015
Fax: 0278 444284

★3178★
Society of County Librarians
c/o M Messenger
County Library HQ
County Hall
Spetchley Rd
Worcester   WR5 2NP
Phone: 0905 763763
Fax: 0905 763000

★3179★
Society of County Secretaries
c/o A Fraser
Cumbria County Council
The Courts
Carlisle   CA3 8IZ
Phone: 0228 812204
Fax: 0228 26247

★3180★
**Society of County Trading Standards
   Officers**
c/o N I Cull
Trading Standards Dept
County Hall
Hertford   CG13 8DE
Phone: 0992 555651
Fax: 0992 555652

★3181★
Society of County Treasurers
c/o B Smith
Treasurers Dept
Staffordshire County Council
Eastgate St
Stafford   ST16 2NF
Phone: 0785 223121
Fax: 0785 54392

★3182★
Society of Dairy Technology
Crossley House
72 Ermine St
Huntingdon   PE18 6EZ
Phone: 0480 450741
Fax: 0480 431800

★3183★
Society of Designer-Craftsmen
c/o R O'Donoghue
24 Rivington St
London   EC2A 3DU
Phone: 071-739 3663

★3184★
**Society of Directors of Trading
   Standards in Scotland**
c/o H T Miller
Consumer Protection Dept
Sandwick Rd
Stornoway   PA87 2BW
Phone: 0851 3733   ext. 313
Fax: 0851 5349

★3185★
**Society of District Councils Public
   Relations Officers**
c/o Brian Portway
Public Relations Unit
Gravesham Borough Council
Civic Centre
Windmill St
Gravesend   DA12 1AU
Phone: 0474 337304
Fax: 0474 337453

★3186★
Society of Dyers & Colourists
82 Grattan Rd
Bradford   BD1 2JB
Phone: 0274 725138
Fax: 0274 392888

Concerned with developments in the science
and technology of colouration

★3187★
Society of Education Officers
21-27 Lambs Conduit St
London   WC1N 3NJ
Phone: 071-831 1973

The professional association representing
education officers who work in the management of local education authorities in
England, Wales and Northern Ireland

★3188★
Society of Electronic & Radio Technicians *now* incorporated in Institution of Electronics & Electrical Incorporated Engineers

★3189★
Society of Engineers
Parsifal College
527 Finchley Rd
London   NW3 7BG
Phone: 071-435 5600
Fax: 071-435 5600

A multi-disciplinary body of professional engineers

★3190★
Society of Environmental Engineers
Owles Hall
Buntingford
Royston   SG9 9PL
Phone: 0763 71209
Fax: 0763 73255

★3191★
Society of Equestrian Artists
c/o Julie Foyle
4 Woolgarth Farm
Blakes Lane
West Horsley
Godalming   KT24 6DX
Phone: 0483 222992

★3192★
Society of Film Distributors
Royalty House
72-73 Dean St
London   W1V 5HB
Phone: 071-437 4383
Fax: 071-734 0912

★3193★
Society of Fine Art Auctioneers
7 Blenheim St
London   W1Y 0AS
Phone: 071-629 2933

★3194★
Society of Fire Protection Engineers
c/o P M Hamblin
Sedgwick James Risk Services
4th Floor
Sedgwick House
Sedgwick Centre
London   E1 8DX
Phone: 071-481 5357
Fax: 071-377 3199

★3195★
Society of Floristry
c/o Stanley Coleman
The Old Schoolhouse
Payford
Gloucester   GL19 3HY
Phone: 0531 820809

Members are professional florists

★3196★
Society of Garden Designers
c/o R Williams
Rowan House
2 Winterton Drive
Speen
Newbury   RG13 1ND

★3197★
Society of Genealogists
14 Charterhouse Buildings
Goswell Rd
London   EC1M 7BA
Phone: 071-251 8799

For individuals interested in the study of genealogy and heraldry

★3198★
Society of Glass Technology
20 Hallam Gate Rd
Sheffield   S10 5BT
Phone: 0742 663168
Fax: 0742 665252

★3199★
Society of Graphic Fine Art
9 Newburgh St
London   W1V 1LH

★3200★
**Society of Headmasters of
   Independent Schools**
c/o A E R Dodds
Green Garth
Horsell Rise
Woking   GU21 4AY
Phone: 0486 262573

★3201★
Society of Hearing Aid Audiologists
c/o A Crego-Bourne
Bridle Croft
22a Bury Heath Rd
Epsom   KT17 4LS
Phone: 03727 25348

★3202★
Society of Homoeopaths
2 Artizan Rd
Northampton   NN1 4HU
Phone: 0604 21400
Fax: 0604 233900

★3203★
**Society of Hospital Linen Service &
   Laundry Managers**
c/o G Nixon
Bellsdyke Hospital
Bellsdyke Rd
Larbert
Falkirk   FK5 4SF
Phone: 0324 556131

Members are professional launderers
employed within the health service

★3204★
Society of Incentive Travel Executives
42 Clifden Rd
Twickenham   TW1 4LX
Phone: 081-744 2312

★3205★
Society of Indexers
16 Green Rd
Birchington
Herne Bay   CT7 6JZ

All types of indexing and particularly books
and perodicals

★3206★
**Society of Industrial Emergency
   Services Officers**
234-244 Stockwell Rd
London   SW9 9SP
Phone: 071-733 3388
Fax: 071-326 4240

The Society is concerned with emergencies
of all types affecting industry, including network disasters, accidents, vandalism and the
like

★3207★
Society of Industrial Tutors
c/o Jean Cooke
Middlesex Polytechnic
Queensway
Enfield   EN3 4SF
Phone: 081-804 8131   ext. 2229

The teaching of industrial studies to mature
students

★3208★
**Society of Information Technology
   Managers**
c/o R P Griffith
Northamptonshire County Council
Information Technology Services
Angel St
Northampton   NN1 1ED
Phone: 0604 236540

The professional organisation for local government officers responsible for recom-
mending corporate information technology
policy

★3209★
**Society of International Gas Tankers &
   Terminal Operators**
Staple Hall
87-90 Houndsditch
London   EC3A 7AX
Phone: 071-621 1422
Fax: 071-626 5913

Membership is open to owners and operators
of tankers carrying liquefied natural or petroleum gas and to the owners of marine terminals loading or receiving these cargoes

★3210★
Society of Investment Analysts
211-213 High St
Bromley   BR1 1NY
Phone: 081-464 0811
Fax: 081-313 0587

The professional body for members of the investment community applying formal analytical skills to research, portfolio management and related activites

★3211★
Society of Jewellery Historians
c/o Miss J Rudoe
Dept of Medieval & Later Acquisitions
British Museum
Great Russell St
London   WC1B 3DG
Phone: 071-636 1555
Fax: 071-323 8480

★3212★
Society of Laundry Engineers & Allied Trades
78-80 Borough High St
London   SE1 1XG
Phone: 071-403 2300
Fax: 071-403 8140

★3213★
Society of Leather Technologists & Chemists
1 Edges Court
Northampton   NN3 1UJ
Phone: 0604 647318

★3214★
Society of Licensed Victuallers
Heatherley
London Rd
Ascot   SL5 8DR
Phone: 0344 884440
Fax: 0344 884703

★3215★
Society of Local Authority Chief Executives
County Hall
Glenfield
Leicester   LE3 8RA
Phone: 0533 656220
Fax: 0533 656255

★3216★
Society of Local Council Clerks
c/o B D Farquhar
Council Offices
School Aycliffe Lane
Newton Aycliffe
Darlington   DL5 4ER
Phone: 0325 300700

★3217★
Society of London Art Dealers
c/o Lawrence Slingsby
91a Jermyn St
London   SW1Y 6JB
Phone: 071-930 6137
Fax: 071-321 0685

★3218★
Society of Master Printers of Scotland
48 Palmerston Place
Edinburgh   EH12 5DE
Phone: 031-220 4353
Fax: 031-220 4344

★3219★
Society of Master Shoe Repairers
St Crispin's House
21 Station Rd
Desborough
Kettering   NN14 2SA
Phone: 0536 760374

Trade association for independent shoe repairers throughout the UK

★3220★
Society of Metaphysicians
c/o J Williamson
Archers' Court
Stonestile Lane
Hastings   TN35 4PG
Phone: 0424 751577
Fax: 0424 751577

Covering parapsychological, paraphysical and intuitive sciences

★3221★
Society of Metropolitan Chief Trading Standards Officers
c/o P A Rose
Dept of Environmental Services
159-167 Upper St
London   N1 1RE
Phone: 071-354 7361

★3222★
Society of Metropolitan Treasurers
Civic Centre
Regent St
Gateshead
Newcastle upon Tyne   NE8 1HH
Phone: 091-477 1011
Fax: 091-478 3495

★3223★
Society of Miniaturists
c/o L Simpson
41 Lister St
Ilkley   LS29 9ET
Phone: 0943 609075

★3224★
Society of Motor Manufacturers & Traders
Forbes House
Halkin St
London   SW1X 7DS
Phone: 071-235 7000
Fax: 071-235 7112

Members include manufacturers and importers of cars, garage equipment, public service and commercial vehicles and related equipment

★3225★
Society of Museum Archaeologists
c/o Dr Stephen Greep
Tyne & Wear Museums Services
Blandford House
Blandford Square
Newcastle upon Tyne   NE1 4JA
Phone: 091-232 6789

For museum-based archaeologists

★3226★
Society of Occupational Medicine
6 St Andrew's Place
London   NW1 4LB
Phone: 071-486 2641

★3227★
Society of Parliamentary Agents
c/o I McCulloch
1 Dean Farrar St
London   SW1H ODY
Phone: 071-222 9458
Fax: 071-222 0650

★3228★
Society of Pension Consultants
Ludgate House
Ludgate Circus
London   EC4A 2AB
Phone: 071-353 1688
Fax: 071-353 9296

Members include organisations providing advice and/or services in connection with the setting up or running of a pension scheme

★3229★
Society of Pharmaceutical Medicine
1 Wimpole St
London   W1M 4AP
Phone: 071-493 7825

★3230★
Society of Picture Researchers & Editors
B M Box 259
London   WC1N 3XX
Phone: 081-404 5011

★3231★
Society of Ploughmen
Quarry Farm
Loversall
Doncaster   DN11 9DH
Phone: 0302 852469

★3232★
Society of Private Printers
c/o D Chambers
Ravelston
South View Rd

Pinner HA5 3YD

For owners of private printing presses

★3233★
Society of Producers of Advertising Music
c/o Nicki Sayes
Ashton House
Blackheath
Guildford GU4 8RD
Phone: 0438 898097

★3234★
Society of Professional Engineers
c/o P A Lancaster
Parsifal College
527 Finchley Rd
London NW3 7BG
Phone: 071-435 5600

Members are qualified engineers from all disciplines

★3235★
Society of Public Accountants
25 Bridgeman Terrace
Wigan WN1 1TD
Phone: 0942 821085

For non chartered non certified accountants engaged in public practice within the UK

★3236★
Society of Public Health
28 Portland Place
London W1N 4DE

The professional association of doctors and dentists working in the field of public health medicine, community health and community dentistry

★3237★
Society of Public Notaries of London
Baltic Exchange Building
24 St Mary Axe
London EC3A 8HD
Phone: 071-623 1357
Fax: 071-623 5428

★3238★
Society of Public Teachers of Law
c/o Professor David Casson
University of Buckingham
Buckingham MK18 1EG
Phone: 0280 814080

Members are individuals involved in teaching law at public universities

★3239★
Society of Radiographers
14 Upper Wimpole St
London W1M 8BN
Phone: 071-935 5726
Fax: 071-487 3483

★3240★
Society of Recorder Players
95 Salisbury Avenue
St Albans AL1 4TY
Phone: 0727 860740

★3241★
Society of Registration Officers
c/o P J Butt
Register Office
6a Bugle St
Southampton SO9 4XQ
Phone: 0703 631422

Members are officers who register births, marriages and deaths

★3242★
Society of Sales Management Administrators
40 Archdale Rd
London SE22 9HJ
Phone: 071-274 9533

The professional and examining body for people engaged in selling and marketing

★3243★
Society of Scottish Artists
3 Howe St
Edinburgh EH3 6TE
Phone: 031-557 2342

★3244★
Society of Scribes & Illuminators
c/o S Cavendish
54 Boileau Rd
London SW13 9BL
Phone: 081-748 9951

Members practice the crafts of writing, illuminating and lettering

★3245★
Society of Solicitors in the Supreme Courts of Scotland
c/o Alistair Brownlie
2 Abercromby Place
Edinburgh EH3 6JZ
Phone: 031-556 4070
Fax: 031-556 1624

★3246★
Society of Strip Illustration
7 Dilke St
London SW3 4JE
Phone: 081-677 6737

To promote the interests of professionals working in the field of comic strip

★3247★
Society of Surveying Technicians
Drayton House
30 Gordon St
London WC1H 0BH
Phone: 071-388 8008
Fax: 071-383 8008

Members are students and surveying technicians whose specialities include agriculture, building, hydrographics and quantity surveying

★3248★
Society of Teachers in Business Education
Sherwood House
High St
Crowthorne RG11 7AX
Phone: 0344 761612

★3249★
Society of Teachers of Speech & Drama
73 Berry Hill Rd

Mansfield NG18 4RU
Phone: 0623 27636

★3250★
Society of Television Lighting Directors
46 Batchworth Lane
Northwood HA6 3HG

Members are engaged in the direction and design of the creative aspect of television lighting

★3251★
Society of Theatre Consultants
4 Great Pulteney St
London W1R 3DF
Phone: 071-434 3904

For those practising as consultants on the technical problems involved in the design of theatres and other entertainment buildings

★3252★
Society of Town Planning Technicians
c/o Royal Town Planning Institute
26 Portland Place
London W1N 4BE
Phone: 071-636 9107
Fax: 1582

★3253★
Society of Typographical Designers
21-27 Seagrave Rd
London SW6 1RP
Phone: 071-381 8726
Fax: 8726

★3254★
Society of West End Theatre
Bedford Chambers
The Piazza
London WC2E 8HQ
Phone: 071-836 0971
Fax: 071-497 2543

Comprising managers and proprietors of theatres and producers of shows in London's west end, both in the commercial and subsidised sectors

★3255★
Society of Wildlife Artists
17 Carlton House Terrace
London   SW1Y 5BD
Phone: 071-930 6844
Fax: 071-839 7830

★3256★
Society of Women Writers &
**   Journalists**
c/o Mary Rensten
13 Warwick Avenue
Cuffley
Barnet   EN6 4RU
Phone: 0707 872311

★3257★
Society of Wood Engravers
c/o H Paynter
P O Box 355
Richmond-on-Thames   TW10 6LE
Phone: 081-940 3553

★3258★
Society of Young Publishers
c/o J Whitaker & Sons Ltd
12 Dyott St
London   WC1A 1DF
Phone: 071-836 8911

★3259★
Soil Association
86-88 Colston St
Bristol   BS1 5BB
Phone: 0272 290661
Fax: 0272 252404

Concerned with organic farming and gardening

★3260★
Solar Energy Society
c/o S Winkworth
King's College
Atkins Building, South Campden Hill Rd
London   W8 7AH
Phone: 071-333 4314
Fax: 071-937 7783

All aspects of renewable energy sources

★3261★
Solar Trade Association
Brackenhurst
Greenham Common South
Newbury   RG15 8HH
Phone: 0635 46561

Members are organisations with business interests in solar energy systems

★3262★
Solder Makers Association
c/o J Saw
Multicore Solders Ltd
Kelsey House
Wood Lane End
Hemel Hempstead   HP2 4RQ
Phone: 0442 233233
Fax: 0442 69554

★3263★
Solid Smokeless Fuels Federation
Devonshire House
Church St
Sutton-in-Ashfield
Mansfield   NG17 1AE
Phone: 0623 550411
Fax: 0623 441249

Provides advice on the efficient use of solid smokeless fuels and appliances

★3264★
Solids Handling & Processing
**   Association**
60 Claremont Rd
Surbiton   KT6 4RH
Phone: 081-390 2022
Telex: 291561

Members are manufacturers of equipment used in the handling and processing of particulate solids

★3265★
Solvents Industry Association
c/o Dr T H Farmer
57 Mymms Drive
Brookmans Park
Hatfield   AL9 7AE
Phone: 0707 55461

★3266★
Sonic Arts Network
1-4 West Heath Yard
174 Mill Lane
London NW6 1TB
Phone: 071-794 5638

For companies and individuals interested in electro-acoustic music

★3267★
Sound & Communications Contractors Association
4-b High St
Burnham
Slough SL1 7JH
Phone: 0628 667633
Fax: 0628 665882

Members install, permanently or temporarily, a wide range of audio systems

★3268★
Sound & Communications Industries Federation
4-b High St
Burnham
Slough SL1 7JH
Phone: 0628 667683
Fax: 0628 665882

★3269★
Sound & Communications Suppliers Association
4-b High St
Burnham
Slough SL1 7JH
Phone: 0628 67633
Fax: 0628 665882

Members supply a wide range of audio equipment

★3270★
Soup & Gravy Manufacturers Association *now* incorporated into Food & Drink Federation

★3271★
Soya Bean Meal Futures Association
24-28 St Mary Axe

London EC3A 8EP
Phone: 071-626 7985
Fax: 071-623 2917

★3272★
Spice Trade Association *now* incorporated into Food & Drink Federation

★3273★
Spiritualist Association of GB
33 Belgrave Square
London SW1X 8QB
Phone: 071-235 3351

★3274★
Sports Council
16 Upper Woburn Place
London WC1H 0QP
Phone: 071-388 1277
Fax: 071-383 5740

★3275★
Sports Council for Northern Ireland
House of Sport
Upper Malone Rd
Belfast BT9 52A
Phone: 0232 381222
Fax: 0232 682757

★3276★
Sports Turf Research Institute
St Ives Research Station
Bingley BD16 1AU
Phone: 0274 565131
Fax: 0274 561891

Covers the construction and maintenance of sport grounds, including non-grass surfaces

★3277★
Sports Writers' Association of GB
c/o Sports Council
16 Upper Woburn Place
London WC1H 0QP
Phone: 071-388 1277
Fax: 071-383 5740

★3278★
Sprayed Concrete Association
c/o J G Fairley
P O Box 111
Aldershot   GU11 1YW
Phone: 0252 21302
Fax: 0252 333901

★3279★
**Spring Research & Manufacturers'
  Association**
Henry St
Sheffield   S3 7EQ
Phone: 0742 760771
Fax: 0742 726344

★3280★
Squash Rackets Association
33-34 Warple Way
London   W3 0RQ
Phone: 081-746 1616
Fax: 081-746 0580

★3281★
Stage Management Association
Southbank House
Black Prince Rd
London   SE1 7SJ
Phone: 071-587 1514

For those working in professional stage management in the UK

★3282★
**Stainless Steel Fabricators'
  Association**
Savoy Tower
77 Renfrew St
Glasgow   G2 3BY
Phone: 041-332 0826
Fax: 041-332 5788

★3283★
Stainless Steel Industry Association
The Fountain Precinct
1 Balm Green
Sheffield   S1 3AF
Phone: 0742 766789
Fax: 0742 766213

★3284★
Standby Ship Operators Association
28-30 Little Russell St
London   WC1A 2HN
Phone: 071-405 0002
Fax: 071-831 2581

★3285★
**Standing Conference of Heads of
  Modern Languages in Polytechnics &
  other Colleges**
c/o R French
Wiltshire Building
Portsmouth Polytechnic
Hampshire Terrace
Portsmouth   PO1 2BJ
Phone: 0705 827681

★3286★
Standing Conference of Principals
PO Box 190
Cheltenham   GL50 3SJ
Phone: 0242 225925
Fax: 0242 221502

Members are heads of colleges and institutes in higher education

★3287★
**Standing Conference of Regional
  Advisory Councils for Further
  Education**
232 Vauxhall Bridge Rd
London   SW1V 1AU
Phone: 071-233 6199
Fax: 071-233 6191

★3288★
**Standing Conference on Physical
  Education in Teacher Education**
c/o Carnegie Dept
Leeds Polytechnic
Beckett Park
Leeds   LS6 3QS
Phone: 0532 832600

★3289★
**Standing Conference on Principals of
  Sixth Form & Tertiary Colleges**
c/o Chris Chapman
North Area College

Buckingham Rd
Stockport   SK4 3XE
Phone: 061-442 7494
Fax: 061-442 2166

★3290★
Statute Law Society
c/o Clifford Shanbury
186 City Rd
London   EC1V 2NU
Phone: 071-251 1644

For improving the form and manner in which statutes and delegated legislation are expressed, produced and published

★3291★
Steel Castings Research & Trade Association
7 East Bank Rd
Sheffield   S2 3PT
Phone: 0742 728647
Fax: 0742 730852

Membership comprises steel foundries, iron foundries, steel and roll producers, investment casting producers, ingot producers and suppliers of aluminium castings to the automotive and aerospace sectors

★3292★
Steel Construction Institute
Silwood Park
Ascot   SL5 7QN
Phone: 0344 23345
Fax: 0344 22944

Members are involved in all aspects of steel construction

★3293★
Steel Lintel Manufacturers Association
PO Box 10
Newport   NP9 0XN
Phone: 0633 290022
Fax: 0633 270280

★3294★
Steel Window Association
PO Box 43
Tring House

Tring   HP23 5PS
Phone: 0442 890768
Fax: 0442 890765

Includes curtain walling

★3295★
Stereoscopic Society
195 Gilders Rd
Chessington   KT9 2EB

Stereoscopy is the study of three-dimensional imagery created by photographic or other means

★3296★
Sterilised Suture Manufacturers' Association
c/o David Geck
154 Fareham Rd
Gosport
Portsmouth   PO13 0AS
Phone: 0329 224120
Fax: 0329 220213

Sterile absorbable and non-absorbable material

★3297★
Sterilization Packaging Materials Association
c/o John Emm
Norad Travel Ltd
2 Market Place
Radstock
Bath   BA3 2AE
Phone: 0761 33949

★3298★
Sterling Brokers Association
c/o Euro Brokers Sterling Ltd
Adelaide House
London Bridge Rd
London   EC4R 9EQ
Phone: 071-626 2691
Fax: 071-626 3815

★3299★
Stilton Cheese Makers Association
PO Box 11
Buxton   SK17 6PR
Phone: 0298 26224
Fax: 0298 24870

★3300★
Stone Federation
82 New Cavendish St
London   W1M 8AD
Phone: 071-580 5588
Fax: 071-631 3872

★3301★
Storage & Handling Equipment
   Distributors' Association
c/o G K Edwards
74 Chester Rd
Birmingham   B36 7BU
Phone: 021-776 7474
Fax: 021-776 7605

Members include stockists, designers and installers

★3302★
Storage Equipment Manufacturers
   Association
8th Floor
Bridge House
Smallbrook Queensway
Birmingham   B5 4JP
Phone: 021-643 3377
Fax: 021-643 5064

★3303★
Strategic Planning Society
17 Portland Place
London   W1N 3AF
Phone: 071-636 7737
Fax: 071-323 1692

Promotes strategic and long range planning in private, public and governmental organisations

★3304★
Strip Curtain Suppliers Association
235-241 Regent St
London   W1R 8JU
Telex: 547320

★3305★
Sugar Association of London
c/o D G Moon
Plantation House
Mincing Lane

London   EC3M 3HT
Phone: 071-626 1745
Fax: 071-283 3831

Concerned with the raw sugar trades

★3306★
Sugar Bureau
Duncan House
Dolphin Square
London   SW1V 3PW
Phone: 071-828 9465
Fax: 071-821 5393

All aspects of refined sugar

★3307★
Sugar Traders Association of the UK
66 Mark Lane
London   EC3R 7HS
Phone: 071-480 9339
Fax: 071-480 9500

★3308★
Super Tension Cables Group
56 Palace Rd
East Molesey   KT8 9DW
Phone: 081-941 4079
Fax: 081-783 0104

★3309★
Surf Life Saving Association of GB
14 Cathedral Yard
Exeter   EX1 1HJ
Phone: 0392 54364

★3310★
Surgical Dressing Manufacturers'
   Association
c/o D Holland
Robert Bailey & Son Plc
Dysart St
Stockport   SK2 7PF
Phone: 061-483 1133
Fax: 061-483 5587

★3311★
Surgical Textiles Conference
c/o D Crubtree
Vevnon Carus Ltd
Penworthan Mills

Preston PR1 9SN
Phone: 0772 744493 ext. 220
Fax: 0772 748754

Employers' association within the surgical dressings industry

★3312★
Suspended Access Equipment Manufacturers' Association
82 New Cavendish St
London W1M 8AD
Phone: 071-580 5588
Fax: 071-631 3872

★3313★
Suspended Ceilings Association
29 High St
Hemel Hempstead HP1 3AA
Phone: 0442 40313
Fax: 0442 42600

★3314★
Swimming Pool & Allied Trades Association
Spata House
1a Junction Rd
Andover SP10 3QT
Phone: 0264 356210
Fax: 0264 332628

★3315★
Swimming Teachers' Association
Anchor House
Birch St
Walsall WS2 8HZ
Phone: 0922 645097
Fax: 0922 720628

Caters for the interests of those qualified to teach aquatic subjects

★3316★
Table Jellies Association *now* incorporated into Food & Drink Federation

★3317★
Tableware Distributors Association
c/o D H Field
Commerce House
Festival Park

Stoke-on-Trent ST1 5BE
Phone: 0782 202222
Fax: 0782 202448

★3318★
Tachograph Analysis Association
c/o Dr N E Kirkwood
Merseyside Innovation Centre
131 Mount Pleasant
Liverpool L3 5TF
Phone: 051-708 0123

★3319★
Talking Newpaper Association of the UK
90 High St
Heathfield TN21 8JD
Phone: 04352 6102
Fax: 04352 5422

Providing local news on tape for visually impaired people

★3320★
Tavistock Institute of Human Relations
120 Belsize Lane
London NW3 5BA
Phone: 071-435 7111
Fax: 071-794 4661

Aims encompass the study of human relations in conditions of wellbeing, conflict and change in the community, the work group and the larger organisations, together with the promotion of the effectiveness of individuals and organisations

★3321★
Tea Brokers Association of London
Sir John Lyon House
Upper Thames St
London EC4V 3LA
Phone: 071-236 3368

★3322★
Tea Buyers' Association
Central House
32-66 High St
London E15 2PS
Phone: 081-579 4872
Fax: 081-519 5483

★3323★
Tea Council
Sir John Lyon House
5 High Timber St
London   EC4V 3NJ
Phone: 071-248 1024
Fax: 071-329 4568

★3324★
Tea Producers Association
Central House
32-66 High St
London   E15 2PS
Phone: 081-519 4872
Fax: 081-519 5483

★3325★
**Telecommunication Engineering &
  Manufacturing Association**
Leicester House
8 Leicester St
London   WC2H 7BN
Phone: 071-437 0678
Fax: 071-437 6047

★3326★
**Telecommunications Industry
  Association**
364-366 Fulham Rd
London   SW10 9UH
Phone: 071-351 7115
Fax: 071-352 6888

The trade association for manufacturers, distributors, dealers, maintainers, installers, service providers and consultants

★3327★
**Telecommunications Users'
  Association**
48 Percy Rd
London   N12 8BU
Phone: 081-445 0996
Fax: 081-455 1107

★3328★
Tenant Farmers' Association
Hadwyn House
Field Rd
Reading   RG1 6BJ
Phone: 0734 391121
Fax: 0734 502697

★3329★
Tertiary College Association
c/o S McLoughlin
Oswestry College
College Rd
Oswestry   SY11 2SA
Phone: 0691 653067
Fax: 0691 670243

★3330★
Textile Converters Association
c/o N Tetley
111 Philips Park Rd
Manchester   M11 3EY
Phone: 061-223 9456
Fax: 061-231 5516

Representing interests of converters of cotton, man-made and allied fibres

★3331★
Textile Distributors Association
The Old Post Office Dunchideock
Exeter   EX2 9TU
Phone: 0392 832559

★3332★
Textile Finishers' Association
Reedham House
31 King St West
Manchester   M3 2PF
Phone: 061-832 9279
Fax: 061-833 1740

★3333★
Textile Institute
10 Blackfriars St
Manchester   M3 5DR
Phone: 061-834 8457
Fax: 061-835 3087

All aspects of the textile industry

★3334★
Textile Research Council
Forest House Laboratories
Knaresborough Rd

Harrogate   HG2 7LZ
Phone: 0423 880349
Fax: 0423 880045

★3335★
Textile Services Association
7 Churchill Court
58 Station Rd
Harrow   HA2 7SA
Phone: 081-863 7755
Fax: 081-861 2115

Members are companies involved in laundry,
dry cleaning and textile rental

★3336★
Thames Passenger Services Federation
Central House
32-66 High St
London   E15 2PS
Phone: 081-519 4872
Fax: 081-519 5483

★3337★
Theatres Advisory Council
4 Great Pulteney St
London   W1R 3DF
Phone: 071-434 3901
Fax: 071-434 3903

Concerned with theatre preservation and new
theatre building

★3338★
Theatres National Committee
Bedford Chambers
The Piazza
London   WC2E 8HQ
Phone: 071-836 0971
Fax: 071-497 2543

Representative of all aspects of theatrical
management

★3339★
Theatrical Management Association
Bedford Chambers
The Piazza

London   WC2E 8HQ
Phone: 071-836 0971
Fax: 071-497 2543

Represents those concerned with theatrical
production, both commercial and subsidised,
outside London

★3340★
Thermal Insulation Contractors
Association
Kensway House
388 High Rd
Ilford   IG1 1TL
Phone: 081-514 2120
Fax: 081-478 1256

★3341★
Thermal Insulation Manufacturers &
Suppliers Association
c/o J G Fairley
P O Box 111
Aldershot   GU11 1YW
Phone: 0252 336318
Fax: 0252 333901

★3342★
Thoroughbred Breeders' Association
Stanstead House
The Avenue
Newmarket   CB8 9AA
Phone: 0638 661321
Fax: 0638 665621

★3343★
Timber & Brick Homes Consortium
Gable House
40 High St
Rickmansworth   WD3 1ES
Phone: 0923 778136
Fax: 0923 720724

Members specialise in the design, manufacture and construction of timber and brick
housing

★3344★
Timber Arbitrators Associations of the
UK
Clareville House
26-27 Oxendon St

London   SW1Y 4EL
Phone: 071-839 1891
Fax: 071-930 0094

★3345★
Timber Drying Association
Chiltern House
Stocking Lane
Hughenden Valley
High Wycombe   HP14 4ND
Phone: 0240 243091
Fax: 0240 245487

★3346★
**Timber Packaging & Pallet
  Confederation**
Heath St
Tamworth   B79 7JH
Phone: 0827 52337
Fax: 0827 310827

Members are manufacturers of pallets and
cases and also export packers

★3347★
**Timber Research & Development
  Association**
Chiltern House
Stocking Lane
Hughenden Valley
High Wycombe   HP14 4ND
Phone: 0240 243091
Fax: 0240 245487

Acts as the interface between timber as a natural resource and its commercial use as a
material

★3348★
Timber Trade Federation
Clareville House
26-27 Oxendon St
London   SW1Y 4EZ
Phone: 071-839 1891
Fax: 071-839 1891

For timber agents, importers and merchants

★3349★
Timber Trade Training Association
Stocking Lane
Hughenden Valley

High Wycombe   HP14 4NB
Phone: 0240 2442011
Fax: 0240 245051

Training association for the imported timber
trade

★3350★
Timeshare Council
23 Buckingham Gate
London   SW1E 6LB
Phone: 071-821 8845
Fax: 071-828 0739

★3351★
Tobacco Advisory Council
Glen House
Stag Place
London   SW1E 5AG
Phone: 071-828 2041
Fax: 071-630 9638

The trade association of companies manufacturing tobacco products in the UK

★3352★
Tool & Trades History Society
60 Swanley Lane
Swanley
Dartford   BR8 7JG
Phone: 0322 62271

For all interested in hand-tools and in the
skills and techniques of working wood,
metal, leather, stone and other materials, from
antiquity to the recent past

★3353★
Torry Research Station
135 Abbey Rd
Aberdeen   AB9 8DG
Phone: 0224 877071
Fax: 0224 874246

A research establishment concerned with fish
and shellfish science and technology

★3354★
Tour Operators Study Group
66 High St
Lewes   BN7 1XG
Phone: 0273 475332
Fax: 0273 483746

★3355★
Tourism Society
26 Grosvenor Gardens
London   SW1W 0DU
Phone: 071-730 4380
Fax: 071-730 9367

Membership includes professionals working in all sectors of the tourism and travel industry

★3356★
Town & Country Planning Association
17 Carlton House Terrace
London   SW1Y 5AS
Phone: 071-930 8903
Fax: 071-930 3280

★3357★
Toy & Giftware Importers Association
c/o R E Shimell
146a High St
Tonbridge   TN9 1BB
Phone: 0732 770332
Fax: 0732 770362

★3358★
Trade Mark Owners Association
30-35 Pall Mall
London   SW17 5LY
Phone: 071-925 2515
Fax: 071-925 2436

★3359★
Trade Marks Patents & Designs Federation
5th Floor
Henrietta House
9 Henrietta Place
London   W1M 9AG
Phone: 071-499 9320

★3360★
Trades Union Congress
Congress House
23-28 Great Russell St

London   WC1B 3LS
Phone: 071-636 4030
Fax: 071-636 0632

The body representing British trades unions working for improved economic and social conditions for members

★3361★
Traditional Acupuncture Society
1 The Ridgeway
Stratford upon Avon   CV37 9JL
Phone: 0789 298798

★3362★
Tramway & Light Railway Society
6 The Woodlands
Brightlingsea   CO7 0RY
Phone: 0206 304411

★3363★
Translators Association
84 Drayton Gardens
London   SW10 9SB
Phone: 071-373 6642

★3364★
Transport & Road Research Laboratory
Old Wokingham Rd
Crowthorne   RG11 6AU
Phone: 0344 773131
Fax: 0344 770356

Covering all aspects of traffic, safety features of roads, behaviour of road users, highway design and engineering, bridge design and vehicle safety

★3365★
Transport Association
9th Floor
Centre City Tower
7 Hill St
Birmingham   B5 4UU
Phone: 021-643 5494
Fax: 021-643 7738

★3366★
Transport Ticket Society
8 Eastfield Crescent
Yardley Gobion

Towcester NN12 7TT

Phone: 0908 542309

All aspects of fare collection systems

★3367★
Transport Users Consultative Committee

Golden Cross House
Strand
London WC2N 4JF
Phone: 071-839 1898

★3368★
Tree Council

35 Belgrave Square
London SW1X 8QN
Phone: 071-235 8854

★3369★
Tropical Growers' Association

9 Artillery Passage
London E1 7LJ
Phone: 071-375 0085
Fax: 071-247 9467

For individuals and companies interested in the cultivation of all tropical trees and plants including rubber, oil, palm, cocoa, bananas etc as crops

★3370★
Trussed Rafter Fabricators Association

24 Bishops Walk
Gunton St Peter
Lowestoft NR32 4JN
Phone: 0502 61515

★3371★
Twist Drill & Reamer Association

Light Trades House
3 Melbourne Avenue
Sheffield S10 2QJ
Phone: 0742 663084
Fax: 0742 670910

★3372★
Ulster Curers' Association

10 Arthur St
Belfast BT1 4GD
Phone: 0232 323274
Fax: 0232 439364

★3373★
Ulster Farmers' Union

475-477 Antrim Rd
Belfast BT15 3DA
Phone: 0232 370222
Telex: 0232 370739

★3374★
Underfeed Stoker Makers' Association

Lansbury Estates
Lower Guildford Rd
Knaphill
Woking GU21 2EP
Phone: 04867 86503

★3375★
Underwater Association for Scientific Research

c/o Dr M Pagett
Huntersbrook House
Hoggs Lane
Purton
Swindon SN5 9HQ
Phone: 0793 771557

Members are professional scientists or divers with an interest in underwater aspects of the sciences

★3376★
Union of Independent Companies

13 Knightsbridge Green
London SW1X 7QL
Phone: 071-581 4393
Fax: 071-581 3529

Membership open to all independent companies engaged in productive industry or in a directly supportive role

★3377★
Unit Trust Association

65 Kingsway
London WC2B 6TD
Phone: 071-831 0898
Telex: 071-831 9975

The trade association for unit trust management companies

★3378★
**United Kingdom & Ireland
  Particleboard Association**
Maxwell Rd
Stevenage SG1 2EP
Phone: 0438 741299
Fax: 0438 741301

★3379★
**United Kingdom Agricultural Supply
  Trade Association**
3 Whitehall Court
Whitehall Place
London SW1A 2EQ
Phone: 071-930 3611
Fax: 071-930 3952

★3380★
**United Kingdom Alliance of
  Professional Teachers of Dancing**
23 Alfred St
Blackpool FY1 4LH
Phone: 0253 752172
Fax: 0253 27178

To provide examination service and support
for the dance profession in all its forms

★3381★
**United Kingdom Association of
  Manufacturers of Bakers' Yeast**
now incorporated into Food & Drink
Federation

★3382★
**United Kingdom Association of Frozen
  Food Producers**
1 Green St
London W1Y 3RG
Phone: 071-629 0655
Fax: 071-499 7095

★3383★
United Kingdom Automation Council
87 Gower St
London WC1E 6AA
Phone: 071-387 4949
Fax: 071-388 8431

★3384★
United Kingdom Bartenders Guild
91-93 Gordon Rd
Birmingham B17 9HA
Phone: 021-427 8099

★3385★
**United Kingdom Council for
  Computing Development**
Glenthorne House
Hammersmith Grove
London W6 0LG
Phone: 081-741 7305
Fax: 081-741 5993

★3386★
**United Kingdom Credit Insurance
  Brokers' Committee**
Biiba House
14 Bevis Marks
London EC3A 7LH
Phone: 071-623 9043
Fax: 071-626 9676

★3387★
**United Kingdom Egg Producers
  Association**
East Dundry
Bristol BS18 8NJ
Phone: 0272 643498
Fax: 0272 643298

★3388★
**United Kingdom Environmental Law
  Association**
c/o Linklater & Paine
160 Aldersgate St
London EC1A 4LP
Phone: 071-606 7080
Fax: 071-600 2885

★3389★
**United Kingdom Federation of
  Business & Professional Women**
23 Ansdell St
London W8 5BN
Phone: 071-938 1729

★3390★
**United Kingdom Federation of Jazz
Bands**
c/o Mr Rogers
14 Dilyun Avenue
Hengoed
Cardiff CF8 7AG

★3391★
**United Kingdom Fellmongers
Association**
c/o 431 Wilmslow Rd
Manchester M20 9AD
Phone: 061-445 4235
Telex: 94013192

★3392★
United Kingdom Harp Association
c/o Charlotte Seale
33 Sandbrook Rd
London N16 0SH
Phone: 071-254 0419

★3393★
**United Kingdom Home Care
Association**
Premier House
Watson Mill Lane
Sowerby Bridge
Halifax HX6 3BW
Phone: 0422 835057
Fax: 0422 835058

Members are proprietors or managers providing care and/or nursing services to people in their own homes

★3394★
**United Kingdom Home Economics
Federation**
c/o Mrs P Marshall
8 Alms Hill Crescent
Sheffield S11 9QZ
Phone: 0742 362654

★3395★
**United Kingdom Industrial Space
Committee**
c/o Society of British Aerospace Companies
29 King St

London SW1Y 6RD
Phone: 071-839 3231
Fax: 071-930 3577

★3396★
**United Kingdom Institute for
Conservation**
37 Upper Addison Gardens
London W14 8AJ
Phone: 071-603 5643
Fax: 071-603 5643

For historic and artistic works

★3397★
United Kingdom Irrigation Association
c/o Professor M K V Carr
Silsoe College
Silsoe
Ampthill MK45 4DT
Phone: 0525 60428
Fax: 0525 61527

Members are primarily farmers and growers who irrigate, together with their suppliers and advisers

★3398★
**United Kingdom Jute Goods
Association**
c/o Chancery Vellacott
Russell Square House
10-12 Russell Square
London WC1B 5LF
Phone: 071-436 3666
Fax: 071-436 8884

★3399★
**United Kingdom Land & Hydrographic
Survey Association**
c/o N W Granger
33 Catherine Place
London SW1E 6DY
Phone: 071-828 0933
Fax: 071-834 5747

Represents UK companies engaged in all aspects of surveying

★3400★
United Kingdom Medical Equipment Industries Group
Leicester House
8 Leicester St
London WC2H 7BN
Phone: 071-437 0678
Fax: 071-437 4901

★3401★
United Kingdom Mineral Wool Association
c/o Eurisol (UK) Ltd
39 High St
Redbourn AL3 7LW
Phone: 0582 794624
Fax: 0582 794300

The trade association for manufacturers of glass wool and rock wool products which are used to give protection against fire, water penetration and noise

★3402★
United Kingdom Module Constructors Association
16 Rothesay Place
Edinburgh EH3 7SQ
Phone: 031-225 3688
Telex: 727901

Member companies are engaged in design, engineering and fabrication of modules and associated structures for oil and gas industries

★3403★
United Kingdom Offshore Operators Association
3 Hans Crescent
London SW1X OLN
Phone: 071-589 5255
Fax: 071-589 8961

Members work in the oil and gas companies which are designated operators of licences on the UK continental shelf

★3404★
United Kingdom Onshore Operators Group
Top Floor
Hedges House

153-155 Regent St
London W1R 7FD
Phone: 071-287 0327
Fax: 071-734 4967

A forum in which representatives of the oil industry may discuss matters relating to the exploration and drilling of oil and natural gas

★3405★
United Kingdom Petroleum Industry Association
9 Kingsway
London WC2B 6XH
Phone: 071-240 0289
Fax: 071-379 3102

Members are companies involved in the supply, refining and distribution of petroleum products

★3406★
United Kingdom Picture Editors Guild
c/o B Bodman
Press Association
85 Fleet St
London EC4P 3BE
Phone: 071-353 7440
Telex: 22330

★3407★
United Kingdom Preserves Manufacturers' Association *now* incorporated into Food & Drink Federation

★3408★
United Kingdom Provision Trade Federation
17 Clerkenwell Green
London EC1R 0DP
Phone: 071-253 2114
Fax: 071-608 1645

Primarily concerned with dairy products

★3409★
United Kingdom Reading Association
c/o M Cooper
Edge Hill College of Higher Education
St Helens Rd

Ormskirk L39 4QP
Phone: 0695 577505

Covering the teaching of language and reading skills

★3410★
United Kingdom Reclamation Council
16 High St
Brampton
Huntingdon PE18 8TU
Phone: 0480 455249
Fax: 0480 453680

★3411★
United Kingdom Renderers' Association
60 Claremont Rd
Surbiton KT6 4RH
Phone: 081-390 2022
Fax: 081-390 2027

★3412★
United Kingdom Rice Standards Association
152-160 City Rd
London EC1V 2NP
Phone: 071-253 9421
Fax: 071-250 0965

★3413★
United Kingdom Softwood Sawmillers' Association
16 Gordon St
Glasgow G1 3QE
Phone: 041-221 6551
Fax: 041-204 0507

★3414★
United Kingdom Standing Conference for Psychotherapy
c/o D Hamilton
167 Sumatra Rd
London NW6 1PN
Phone: 071-431 4379
Fax: 071-435 1945

To promote public health by encouraging high standards of training and practice and the wider provision of psychotherapy

★3415★
United Kingdom Standing Conference on Hospitality Management Education
c/o W Nevett
Hollings Faculty
Manchester Polytechnic
Old Hall Lane
Manchester M14 6HR
Phone: 061-247 2717
Fax: 061-257 3024

★3416★
United Kingdom Sugar Industry Association
Duncan House
Dolphin Square
London SW1V 3PW
Phone: 071-828 9465

★3417★
United Kingdom Tea Association
Central House
32-66 High St
London E15 2PS
Phone: 081-519 4872
Fax: 081-519 5483

★3418★
United Kingdom Technology Organisation
Rivendell
Upper Farringdon
Alton GU34 3EJ
Phone: 0420 58534
Telex: 858393

★3419★
United Kingdom Wool Growers Federation
17 Waterloo Place
Leamington Spa CV32 5LA
Phone: 0926 450445
Fax: 0926 881960

★3420★
United Society of Artists
207 Sunny Bank Rd

Potters Bar   EN6 2NH
Phone: 0707 57531

Members are painters in oils, water colours and pastels

★3421★
Universities Council for Adult & Continuing Education
c/o Professor C Duke
Dept of Continuing Education
University of Warwick
Coventry   CV4 7AL
Phone: 0203 523827
Fax: 0203 524223

★3422★
Universities Council for the Education of Teachers
c/o Mary Russell
58 Gordon Square
London   WC1H 0NT
Phone: 071-580 8000
Fax: 071-323 0577

★3423★
University, College & Professional Publishers Council
19 Bedford Square
London   WC1B 3HJ
Phone: 071-580 6321
Fax: 071-636 5375

★3424★
Uranium Institute
12th Floor
Bowater House
68 Knightsbridge
London   SW1X 7LT
Phone: 071-225 0303
Fax: 071-225 0308

Members are producers, handlers and organisations whose work is related to uranium and the nuclear fuel cycle

★3425★
Variety & Allied Entertainments Council of GB
8 Harley St

London   W1N 2AB
Phone: 071-636 6367
Fax: 071-935 0269

Covering managers and agents in the light, live entertainments business

★3426★
Vegan Society
7 Battle Rd
St Leonards-on-Sea
Hastings   OX1 2AY
Phone: 0424 427393
Fax: 0424 427393

Veganism is a way of living which seeks to exclude, as far as possible, all forms of exploitation of and cruelty to animals for food, clothing or other purposes

★3427★
Vegetable Protein Association *now* incorporated into Food & Drink Federation

★3428★
Vegetarian Society
53 Marloes Rd
London   W8 4QG
Phone: 071-937 7739

★3429★
Vehicle Builders' & Repairers' Association
102 Finkle Lane
Leeds   LS27 7TW
Phone: 0532 538333
Fax: 0532 380496

★3430★
Video Trade Association
54d High St
Northwood   HA6 1BL
Phone: 09274 29122
Fax: 0923 835980

Represents the interests of video retailers

★3431★
Videotex Industry Association
Preview House
Boundary Rd
Loudwater

High Wycombe   HP10 9QT
Phone: 06285 2913

★3432★
Vinegar Brewers' Federation
152-160 City Rd
London   EC1V 2NP
Phone: 071-253 9421
Fax: 071-250 0965

★3433★
Vintage Arms Association
17 The Fairway
Caister-on-Sea
Great Yarmouth
Phone: 0493 721613

Members are interested in antique and vintage weapons

★3434★
Vitreous Enamel Development Council
New House
High St
Ticehurst
Tunbridge Wells   TN5 7AL
Phone: 0580 200152

★3435★
Vodka Trade Association *now* Gin &
   Vodka Association of GB

★3436★
Voluntary Group Association
32-40 Headstone Drive
Harrow   HA3 5QT
Phone: 081-863 5511
Telex: 923215

Trade association for the independent grocery groups

★3437★
Wall Covering Distributors Association
c/o R Veal
137 Dale St
Liverpool   L2 2JL
Phone: 051-236 2144
Fax: 051-236 2140

★3438★
Wallcovering Manufacturers
   Association of GB
Alembic House
93 Albert Embankment
London   SE1 7TY
Phone: 071-582 1185
Fax: 071-735 0616

★3439★
Wallpaper, Paint & Wallcovering
   Retailers Association
PO Box 44
Walsall   WS3 1TD
Phone: 0922 31134
Fax: 0922 723703

★3440★
Waste Disposal Engineers Association
c/o M Terry
South East Wales Waste Management
11 Hill St
Pontypridd   CF37 2TU
Phone: 0443 406441
Fax: 0443 493920

★3441★
Watch & Clock Importers Association
   of GB
278 Lymington Avenue
London   N22 6JN
Phone: 081-888 7617

★3442★
Water Companies' Association
14 Great College St
London   SW1P 3RX
Phone: 071-222 0644
Fax: 071-222 3366

★3443★
Water Research Centre
Henley Rd
Medmenham
Marlow   SL7 2HD
Phone: 0491 571531
Fax: 0491 579094

Research on all aspects of water technology
and water pollution

★3444★
Water Services Association of England & Wales
1 Queen Anne's Gate
London   SW1H 9BT
Phone: 071-222 8111
Fax: 071-222 1811

★3445★
Web Offset Newspaper Association
74-77 Great Russell St
London   WC1B 3DA
Phone: 071-636 7014
Fax: 071-631 5119

★3446★
Welding Institute
Abington Hall
Abington
Cambridge   CB1 6AL
Phone: 0223 891162
Fax: 0223 892588

Activities cover all aspects of welding technology

★3447★
Welding Manufacturers' Association
Leicester House
8 Leicester St
London   WC2H 7BN
Phone: 071-437 0678
Fax: 071-437 4901

★3448★
Well Drillers Association
PO Box 13
Market Harborough   LE16 9SJ
Phone: 0858 432054
Fax: 0858 434743

★3449★
Wellesbourne Vegetable Research Association
Wellesbourne
Warwick   CV35 9EF
Phone: 0789 470382
Fax: 0789 470552

Provides a channel of communication through which the vegetable industry can keep in touch with current developments in horticultural research

★3450★
White Metal Casting Association
25 Long St
Wheaton Aston
Stafford   ST19 9NF
Phone: 0785 840086

★3451★
Wholesale Cash & Carry Association
36 The Goffs
Eastbourne   BN21 1HD
Phone: 0323 24952

★3452★
Wholesale Confectionery & Tobacco Alliance
11 The Green
Keswick Gardens
Fetcham
Leatherhead   KT22 9XE
Phone: 0372 52235
Fax: 0372 52015

★3453★
Wholesale Delivered Catering Association *now* Federation of Wholesale Distributors

★3454★
Wholesale Delivered Group Trade Association
36 The Goffs
Eastbourne   BN21 1HD
Phone: 0323 24952

★3455★
Wholesale Floorcovering Distributors' Association
The Old Post Office Dunchideock
Exeter   EX2 9TU
Phone: 0392 832559

★3456★
Wholesale Grocers' Association of Scotland
12 Broughton Place

Edinburgh EH1 3RX
Phone: 031-556 8753

★3457★
Wider Share Ownership Council
Juxon House
94 St Pauls Churchyard
London EC4M 8EH
Phone: 071-248 9155 ext. 3323
Fax: 071-248 9155 EXT 3031

★3458★
Wildfowl & Wetlands Trust
Slimbridge
Gloucester GL2 7BT
Phone: 0453 890333
Fax: 0453 890527

★3459★
Wine & Spirit Association of GB & N Ireland
Five Kings House
1 Queen St Place
London EC4R 1XX
Phone: 071-248 5377
Fax: 071-489 0322

★3460★
Wiping Cloth Manufacturers' Association
c/o D Foulkes
39 Greenway
Braunston
Daventry NN1 7JT
Phone: 0788 890965

★3461★
Wire & Wire Rope Employers' Association
4th Floor
Alpha House
Rowlandsway
Manchester M22 5RG
Phone: 061-436 3200
Fax: 061-436 3994

★3462★
Wire Products Association
c/o D J Thrower
Mail Pak Ltd

23 St Aubuns Rd
London SE19 3AA
Phone: 081-771 6444
Fax: 081-771 5614

★3463★
Wire Rope Export Conference
c/o C M Rainer
John Shaw Ltd
Sandy Lane
Worksop S80 3ES
Phone: 0909 473321
Fax: 0909 500199

★3464★
Women's Engineering Society
Dept of Civil Engineering
Imperial College of Science & Technology
Exhibition Rd
London SW7 2BU
Phone: 071-589 5111 ext. 4731

★3465★
Wood Wool Slab Manufacturers Association
26 Store St
London WC1E 7BT
Phone: 071-323 3770
Fax: 071-323 0307

★3466★
Woodworkers', Builder's & Miscellaneous Tools Association
Light Trades House
3 Melbourne Avenue
Sheffield S10 2QJ
Phone: 0742 663084
Fax: 0742 670910

★3467★
Woodworking Machinery Suppliers Association
PO Box 10
Epping CM16 7RR
Phone: 0378 78873
Fax: 0378 72217

★3468★
World Arabian Horse Organisation
Capital House
11 Waterfront Quay
Manchester M5 2XW
Phone: 061-872 3952
Telex: 9312100251

Concerned with the welfare and survival of the arabian horse

★3469★
World Association of Sarcoidosis
149 Harley St
London W1N 1HG
Phone: 071-935 4444

Sarcoidosis is characterised by inflammation of the lungs, eyes, skin and other tissue

★3470★
World Bureau of Metal Statistics
27a High St
Ware SG12 9BA
Phone: 0920 461274
Fax: 0920 464258

Concerning non-ferrous metals statistics worldwide

★3471★
World Jersey Cattle Bureau
Wuthering Heights
St Lawrence
Jersey
Phone: 0534 61572
Fax: 0534 65569

★3472★
World Petroleum Congresses
61 New Cavendish St
London W1M 8AR
Phone: 071-636 1004
Fax: 071-255 1472

Provides a forum for discussing the problems of the oil industry on a worldwide basis

★3473★
World Pheasant Association
PO Box 5
Child Beale Wildlife Trust

Basildon
Reading RG8 9PF
Phone: 0735 5140

The conservation of all game birds

★3474★
World Ploughing Organisation
Whiteclose
Longtown
Carlisle CA6 5TY
Phone: 0228 791153

Members are ploughing competition organisers

★3475★
World Professional Billiards & Snooker Association
27 Oakfield Rd
Bristol BS8 2AT
Phone: 0272 744491
Fax: 0272 744931

★3476★
World Ship Society
35 Wickham Way
Haywards Heath RH16 1UJ
Phone: 0444 413066

Caring for the needs of ship enthusiasts

★3477★
World Small Animal Veterinary Association
c/o Dr P G C Bedford
Royal Veterinary College
Hawkshead Lane
Hatfield AL9 7TA
Phone: 0707 55486
Fax: 0707 52090

Members are involved in teaching and research related to cats, dogs, caged birds and other small animals

★3478★
World Society for the Protection of Animals
1a Park Place
Lawn Lane

London SW8 1UA
Phone: 071-793 0540
Fax: 071-793 0208

Members are national animal welfare societies who promote efforts for the protection of
animals and the conservation of their environment

★3479★
World's Poultry Science Association
c/o T E Whittle
19 Kildoon Drive
Maybole KA19 8AZ
Phone: 0655 83074

★3480★
Woven Wire Association
c/o Locker Wire Weavers Ltd
Church St
Warrington WA1 2SU
Phone: 0925 51212
Fax: 0925 444386

Provides technical information and standards
for the woven wire cloth industry

★3481★
Writing Equipment Society
4 Greystones Grange Crescent
Sheffield S11 7JL
Phone: 0742 667140

The conservation and study of writing instruments and accessories

★3482★
Writing Instruments Association
6 Wimpole St
London W1M 8AS
Phone: 071-637 7692
Fax: 071-436 3137

★3483★
**Yacht Brokers Designers & Surveyors
  Association**
Wheel House
Petersfield Rd
Whitehill
Bordon

Alton GU35 9BU
Phone: 04203 3862
Fax: 04203 88328

Members are yacht and small craft brokers,
designers, agents or surveyors

★3484★
Yacht Charter Association
60 Silverdale
New Milton BH25 7DE
Phone: 0425 619004

★3485★
Yacht Harbour Association
Hardy House
Somerset Rd
Ashford TN24 8EW
Phone: 0233 643837
Fax: 0233 642490

★3486★
Yachting Journalists Association
c/o S Ansell
The Glider Centre
Bishop's Waltham
Southampton SO3 1DH
Phone: 0489 89631
Fax: 0489 892416

★3487★
Zinc Alloy Die Casters Association
42-46 Weymouth St
London W1N 3LQ
Phone: 071-499 6636
Fax: 071-493 1555

★3488★
Zinc Development Association
42-46 Weymouth St
London W1N 3LQ
Phone: 071-499 8422
Fax: 071-493 1555

Covers mine and metal producers, users,
merchants and traders

★3489★
**Zinc Pigment Development
  Association**
42-44 Weymouth St

London   W1N 3LQ
Phone: 071-499 6636
Fax: 071-493 1555

★3490★
Zip Fastener Manufacturers'
Association
Centre City Tower
7 Hill St
Birmingham   B5 4UU
Phone: 021-643 5494
Fax: 021-643 7738

★3491★
Zoological Society of London
Regent's Park
London   NW1 4RY
Phone: 071-722 3333
Fax: 071-483 4436

Chambers of Commerce, Trade, Industry, and Shipping

Aberdeen Chamber of Commerce
15 Union Terrace   Phone: 0224 641222
Aberdeen AB9 1HF   Fax: 0224 644326

Aldershot & District Chamber of Commerce
4-6 Gordon Rd
Aldershot GU11 1HE   Phone: 0252 310113

Altrincham & District Chamber of Commerce & Trade
272 Brooklands Rd
Manchester M23 9HD   Phone: 061-973 7925

Andover & District Chamber of Commerce
PO Box 47
Andover SP10 1RH   Phone: 0264 65275

Ashford Chamber of Trade, Commerce & Industry
Ashford House
County Square   Phone: 0233 620960
Ashford TN23 1YB

Ayr Chamber of Commerce
12 Alloway Place   Phone: 0292 264696
Ayr KA7 2AG   Fax: 0292 610647

Ballymena & District Chamber of Commerce & Industry
c/o S Kyle
44 Broadway Avenue   Phone: 0266 652424
Ballymena BT43 7AA   Fax: 0266 47610

Barking & Dagenham Chamber of Commerce
16-18 Cambridge Rd
Barking IG11 8NW   Phone: 081-591 6966

Barnsley Chamber of Commerce & Industry
Commerce House   Phone: 0226 201166
Westgate   Fax: 0226 298606
Barnsley S70 2DX

Barnstaple & Braunton District Chamber of Commerce & Trade
c/o B V Jackson
Bridge Buildings
The Strand   Phone: 0271 72812
Barnstaple EX32 8LZ

Basingstoke District Chamber of Commerce
51-57 New Market
Square   Phone: 0265 52275
Basingstoke RG21 1HT

Bath Chamber of Commerce
16 Abbey Churchyard   Phone: 0225 460655
Bath BA1 1PB   Telex: 449212

Birmingham Chamber of Industry & Commerce
Chamber of Commerce
House   Phone: 021-454 6171
75 Harborne Rd   Fax: 021-455 8670
Birmingham B15 3DH

Birmingham Chamber of Trade
136 Hagley Rd   Phone: 021-454 4141
Birmingham B16 9PN   Fax: 021-454 4949

Blackburn & District Incorporated Chamber of Industry & Commerce
4a Strawberry Bank   Phone: 0254 55493
Blackburn BB2 6AA   Telex: 635165

Bolton Chamber of Commerce & Industry
Silverwell House   Phone: 0204 33896
Silverwell St   Fax: 0204 361780
Bolton BL1 1PX

Boston & District Chamber of Commerce
Unit 2D
Boston Industrial
  Centre   Phone: 0205 351144
Norfolk St
Boston PE21 2HG

Bournemouth Chamber of Trade &
  Commerce
Carrington House
1 Wootton Gardens
Bournemouth   Phone: 0202 553257
  BH1 1PB

Bradford Chamber of Commerce
Commerce House   Phone: 0274 728166
Cheapside   Fax: 0274 370860
Bradford BD1 4JZ

Brent Chamber of Commerce
44 Craven Park Rd
London NW10 4AE   Phone: 081-965 7272

Brentford Chamber of Commerce
c/o J Tibbles
31 Braemar Rd   Phone: 081-568 8925
Brentford TW8 0NR

Bristol Chamber of Commerce &
  Industry   Phone: 0272 737373
16 Clifton Park   Telex: 449752
Bristol BS8 3BY   Fax: 0272 745365

Bromley Borough Chamber of Commerce
7 Palace Grove
Shortlands   Phone: 081-460 8974
Bromley BH1 3HA

Burnley & District Chamber of Commerce
16 Kerby Walk   Phone: 0282 36555
Burnley BB11 2DE   Fax: 0282 35620

Burton upon Trent & District Chamber of
  Commerce & Industry
158 Derby St
Burton upon Trent   Phone: 0283 63761
  DE14 2NZ   Fax: 0283 510753

Burton upon Trent Chamber of Commerce
240 Branston Rd
Burton upon Trent   Phone: 0283 31711
  DE14 3BT

Bury & District Chamber of Commerce
Lloyds Bank Chambers   Phone: 061-764 8640
4 Bolton St   Fax: 061-761 1108
Bury BL9 0LQ

Cambridge & District Chamber of
  Commerce & Industry
c/o P W Homer
The Business Centre   Phone: 0223 237414
Station Rd   Fax: 0223 237405
Cambridge CB4 4LF

Camden Chambers of Commerce
51 Lambs Conduit St   Phone: 071-405 2515
London WC1N 3NB

Cardiff Chamber of Commerce & Industry
91-92 Saint Mary St   Phone: 0222 481648
Cardiff CF1 1DW   Fax: 0222 489785

Cardiff Chamber of Trade
c/o E L Dutton
PO Box 735   Phone: 0222 889010
Cardiff CF4 5ZU   Fax: 0222 383988

Carlisle Chamber of Commerce
4 Brunswick St   Phone: 0228 26288
Carlisle CA1 1PP

Central & West Lancashire Chamber of
  Commerce & Industry
9-10 Eastway Business
  Village   Phone: 0772 653000
Oliver's Place   Fax: 0772 655544
Fulwood
Preston PR2 4WT

Central Scotland Chamber of Commerce
Suite A
Haypark
Marchmont Ave   Phone: 0324 716868
Polmont   Telex: 778583
Falkirk FK2 0NZ

Cheltenham Chamber of Commerce
4 Royal Crescent   Phone: 0242 515051
Cheltenham GL50 3DA

Chester & North Wales Chamber of
  Commerce
1st Floor
Reliance House   Phone: 0244 378776
Waterloo Rd   Fax: 0244 378701
Chester CH2 2AL

Chesterfield & North Derbyshire Chamber
  of Commerce
Canal Wharf   Phone: 0246 203456
Chesterfield S41 7NA   Fax: 0246 203173

Colchester & District Chamber of Trade &
  Commerce
1 High St   Phone: 0206 765277
Colchester CO1 1DA   Fax: 0206 578073

Coventry Chamber of Commerce & Industry
123 Saint Nicolas St   Phone: 0203 633000
Coventry CV1 4FD   Fax: 0203 552908

Croydon Chamber of Commerce & Industry
Commerce House   Phone: 081-680 2165
21 Scarbrook Rd   Fax: 081-688 4587
Croydon CR9 6HY

Derby & Derbyshire Chamber of Commerce & Industry
New Enterprise House
Saint Helens St   Phone: 0332 47031
Derby DE1 3GY   Fax: 0332 382028

Doncaster Chamber of Commerce & Industry
c/o G J Mangan
50 Christchurch Rd   Phone: 0302 341000
Doncaster DN1 2QN   Fax: 0302 328382

Dorking & District Chamber of Commerce
Regency House
South St   Phone: 0306 881204
Dorking RH4 2EL

Dorset Chamber of Commerce & Industry
Upton House
Upton Country Park   Phone: 0202 682000
Poole BH17 7BJ   Fax: 0202 680315

Dover Chamber of Commerce
3 Waterloo Crescent   Phone: 0304 201388
Dover CT16 1CA   Fax: 0304 241010

Dudley Chamber of Industry & Commerce
1st Floor
Falcon House   Phone: 0384 237653
The Minories   Fax: 0384 238068
Dudley DY2 8PG

Dundee & Tayside Chamber of Commerce & Industry
Chamber of Commerce
  Buildings   Phone: 0382 201122
Panmure St   Fax: 0382 29544
Dundee DD1 1ED

Dunfermline & West Fife Chamber of Commerce
10 Viewfield Terrace
Dunfermline KY12 7JH   Phone: 0383 721156

Ealing Chamber of Commerce & Industry
6 Ruislip Rd
Greenford UB6 9QN   Phone: 081-566 5270

East Kilbride Chamber of Commerce & Trade
113 Olympia House
East Kilbride   Phone: 03552 41740
Strathclyde G74 1LX   Fax: 03552 64643

East Lancashire Chamber of Commerce & Industry
16 Keirby Walk   Phone: 0254 664747
Burnley BB1 2DE   Fax: 0254 55465

Eastbourne & District Chamber of Commerce
6 Hyde Gardens   Phone: 0323 20515
Eastbourne BN21 4PN   Fax: 0323 30454

Eastleigh & District Chamber of Commerce
6 Julius Close
Chandler's Ford   Phone: 0703 269960
Eastleigh SO5 2AB

Edinburgh Chamber of Commerce & Manufacturers
3 Randolph Crescent   Phone: 031-225 5851
Edinburgh EH3 7UD   Telex: 72465

Exeter & District Chamber of Commerce & Trade
Concord House
South St   Phone: 0392 436641
Exeter EX4 2LJ   Fax: 0392 50402

Exmouth Chamber of Trade & Commerce
Information Bureau
Manor Gardens   Phone: 0395 263744
Exmouth EX8 1NZ

Falmouth Chamber of Commerce
61 Church St
Falmouth TR11 3DS   Phone: 0326 317429

Fareham Chamber of Commerce
75 High St
Fareham PO16 7BB   Phone: 0329 822250

Federation of Sussex Industries & Chambers of Commerce
c/o D Jackson
Seven Dials   Phone: 0273 26282
Brighton BN1 3JS   Fax: 0273 207965

Fife Chamber of Commerce & Industry
17 Toolbooth St   Phone: 0592 201932
Kirkcaldy KY1 1RW   Fax: 0592 641187

Finchley & Whetstone Chamber of Commerce
17 Finchley Lodge
Gainsborough Rd   Phone: 081-445 4175
London N12 8AL

Fleet & District Chamber of Trade & Commerce
57 Victoria Rd
Fleet   Phone: 0252 615949
Aldershot GU13 8OW

Glasgow Chamber of Commerce
30 George Square   Phone: 041-204 2121
Glasgow G2 1EQ   Fax: 041-221 2336

Glastonbury & District Chamber of Commerce
c/o J C Phillips
18 High St   Phone: 0458 32288
Glastonbury BA6 9DU

Gloucester & County Chamber of Commerce
20 Cheltenham Rd
Gloucester GL2 0LS   Phone: 0452 23383

Goole & District Chamber of Commerce & Shipping
48 Aire St
Goole DN14 5QE   Phone: 0405 69164

Gosport Chamber of Trade
The Sanderson Centre
Lees Lane   Phone: 0705 520543
Gosport PO12 3UL

Grantham Chamber of Commerce
39 Westgate   Phone: 0476 68626
Grantham NG31 6LY   Fax: 0476 590585

Greater Harrow Chamber of Commerce
1a High St
Wealdstone   Phone: 081-427 2648
Harrow HA3 5BY

Greenock Chamber of Commerce
14 Union St
Greenock PA16 8BH   Phone: 0475 83678

Greenwich Chamber of Commerce
83-85 Powis St
London SE18 6JB   Phone: 081-854 8649

Grimsby & Immingham Chamber of Commerce & Shipping
4 Victoria St   Phone: 0472 342981
Grimsby DN31 1DP   Fax: 0472 250579

Guildford & District Chamber of Commerce
28 Commercial Rd
Guildford GU1 4SU   Phone: 0483 37449

Hackney & Tower Hamlets Chamber of Commerce
1-5 Vyner St
London E2 9DG   Phone: 081-981 2349

Halton Chamber of Commerce
57-61 Church St
Runcorn WA7 1LG   Phone: 09285 60958

Hammersmith & Fulham Chamber of Commerce
Britannia House
Glenthorne Rd   Phone: 081-748 1893
London W6 0LF

Hartley Wintney & District Chamber of Trade & Commerce
5 Primrose Drive
Hartley Wintney   Phone: 025-126 3639
RG27 8TN

Hastings & St Leonards Chamber of Commerce
1st Floor
34 Robertson St   Phone: 0424 722130
Hastings TN34 1BP   Fax: 0424 722129

Hereford & District Chamber of Commerce
c/o J L Hart
Yeoman's Office
  Complex   Phone: 0432 268795
Commercial Rd   Fax: 0432 355139
Hereford HR1 2BL

Hertfordshire Chamber of Commerce & Industry
Andre House,
  Sailisbury Square   Phone: 07072 72771
Hatfield AL9 5BH   Fax: 07072 72442

Hinckley & District Chamber of Trade
c/o Arthur Edwards
1 Trinity Vicarage Rd   Phone: 0455 238865
Hinckley LE10 0BU

Hounslow Chamber of Commerce
2 Gerard Avenue
Hounslow TW4 0PU   Phone: 081-894 6095

Hull Incorporated Chamber of Commerce & Shipping
Samman House
Bowlalley Lane   Phone: 0482 24976
Hull HU1 1XT   Fax: 0482 213962

Inverness & District Chamber of Commerce
13a Island Bank Rd
Inverness IV2 4QN   Phone: 0463 233570

Ipswich & Suffolk Chamber of Commerce, Industry & Shipping
Agriculture House
Foundation St
Ipswich IP4 1BJ
Phone: 0473 210611
Fax: 0473 225488

Isle of Man Chamber of Commerce
17 Drinkwater St
Douglas
Isle of Man
Phone: 0624 674941
Fax: 0624 663367

Isle of Wight Chamber of Commerce
24 The Mall
Carisbrooke Rd
Newport PO30 1BW
Phone: 0983 524390
Fax: 0983 821811

Islington Chamber of Commerce & Trade
383 Holloway Rd
London N7 0RD
Phone: 071-607 9105

Kendal & District Chamber of Commerce & Manufacture
PO Box 27
Exchange Chambers
108 Highgate
Kendal LA9 4SX
Phone: 0539 720049
Fax: 0539 726177

Kensington & Chelsea Chamber of Commerce
1 Cromwell Place
London SW7 2JE
Phone: 071-589 2494
Fax: 071-225 0494

Kidderminster & District Chamber of Commerce
Slingfield Mill
Pitts Lane
Kidderminster
DY11 6YR
Phone: 0562 515515
Fax: 0562 747488

King's Lynn Chamber of Trade & Commerce
c/o J A Hannam
17a Tuesday Market
Place
King's Lynn PE30 1JN
Phone: 0553 768505
Fax: 0553 769322

Kingston upon Thames Chamber of Commerce
c/o R Knights
86-88 Richmond Rd
Kingston upon Thames
KT2 5EN
Phone: 081-546 7658
Fax: 081-541 5708

Kirkless & Wakefield Chamber of Commerce & Industry
Commerce House
New North Rd
Huddersfield HD1 5PJ
Phone: 0484 26591

Kirkwall Chamber of Commerce
5 Main St
Kirkwall KW15 1RW
Phone: 0856 2944

Lambeth Chamber of Commerce
90 Northwood High St
London SE27 2PJ
Phone: 081-670 2272

Lancaster District Chamber of Commerce, Trade & Industry
St Leonard's House
St Leonardgate
Lancaster LA1 1NN
Phone: 0524 39467
Fax: 0524 63280

Leeds & District Chamber of Trade
Commerce House
2 St Albans Place
Leeds LS2 8HZ
Phone: 0532 449655

Leeds Chamber of Commerce & Industry
Commerce House
2 St Alban's Place,
Leeds LS2 8HZ
Phone: 0532 430491
Telex: 55293
Fax: 0532 430504

Leicestershire Chamber of Commerce & Industry
4th Floor
York House
91 Granby St
Leicester LE1 6EA
Phone: 0533 551491
Fax: 0533 550548

Lewes Chamber of Commerce
The Elms
Newhaven Rd
Kingston
Lewes BN7 3NF
Phone: 0273 473412

Lewisham Chamber of Commerce
73 Lewisham High St
London SE13 0BX
Phone: 081-852 7517

Lincoln Incorporated Chamber of Commerce
Commerce House
Outer Circle Rd
Lincoln LN2 4HY
Phone: 0522 23713

London Chamber of Commerce & Industry
69 Cannon St
London EC4N 5AB
Phone: 071-248 4444
Fax: 071-489 0391

Londonderry Chamber of Commerce
15 Queen St
Londonderry
BT48 7EQ
Phone: 0504 262379
Fax: 0504 362826

Lowestoft Chamber of Commerce
Waveney Business
Centre
Gordon Rd
Lowestoft NR32 1NL
Phone: 0502 569383
Fax: 0502 501215

Luton, Bedford & District Chamber of Commerce & Industry
Commerce House
Stuart St
Luton LU1 5AU
Phone: 0582 23456
Fax: 0582 419422

Macclesfield Chamber of Commerce
Venture House
Cross St
Macclesfield
SK11 7PG
Phone: 0625 34680
Fax: 0625 616991

Maidstone & Mid-Kent Chamber of Commerce & Industry
Cornwallis House
Pudding Lane
Maidstone ME14 1NY
Phone: 0622 679744

Manchester Chamber of Commerce & Industry
56 Oxford St
Manchester M60 7HJ
Phone: 061-236 3210
Fax: 061-236 4160

Manchester Chamber of Trade
Arndale Centre
Manchester M4 3AA
Phone: 061-834 6436

Margate Chamber of Commerce
15 Hawley St
Margate CT9 1PU
Phone: 0843 223657

Medway & Gillingham Chamber of Commerce
149 New Rd
Chatham ME4 4PT
Phone: 0634 830001
Fax: 0634 830950

Merseyside Chamber of Commerce & Industry
1 Old Hall St
Liverpool L3 9HG
Phone: 051-227 1234
Fax: 051-236 0121

Milton Keynes Chamber of Commerce
Silbury Court
384 Silbury Boulevard
Milton Keynes
MK9 2HY
Phone: 0908 662123
Fax: 0908 662123

Neath, Briton Ferry & District Chamber of Commerce
c/o V Davies
17 Elm Rd
Briton Ferry SA11 2LY
Phone: 0639 820269

Newark Chamber of Commerce
67 London Rd
Newark NG24 1RZ
Phone: 0636 640555
Fax: 0636 605558

Newbury & West Berkshire Chamber of Commerce & Trade
24 Cheap St
Newbury RG14 4DB
Phone: 0635 36702

Newham Chamber of Commerce
27 Romford Rd
London E15 4LJ
Phone: 081-534 0363

Newport & Gwent Chamber of Commerce
Stelvio House
Bassaleg Rd
Newport NP9 3EB
Phone: 0633 256093
Fax: 0633 213188

North Derbyshire Chamber of Commerce & Industry
Commerce Centre
Canal Wharf
Chesterfield S41 7NA
Phone: 0246 211277
Fax: 0246 203173

North Staffs Chamber of Commerce & Industry
Commerce House,
Festival Park
Stoke-on-Trent
ST1 5BE
Phone: 0782 202222
Telex: 36250
Fax: 0782 202448

Northamptonshire Chamber of Commerce & Industry
65 The Avenue
Northampton
NN1 5BG
Phone: 0604 22422
Fax: 0604 29858

Northern Ireland Chamber of Commerce & Industry
22 Great Victoria St
Belfast BT2 7BJ
Phone: 0232 244113
Fax: 0232 247024

Northern Ireland Chamber of Trade
42-46 Fountain St
Belfast BT1 5EE
Phone: 0232 321980

Northwood & Pinner Chamber of Trade
38 Langton Grove
Northwood HA6 2PS
Phone: 09274 24749

Norwich & Norfolk Chamber of Commerce & Industry
112 Barrack St
Norwich NR3 1UB
Phone: 0603 625977
Fax: 0603 633032

Nottingham Chamber of Commerce & Industry
395 Mansfield Rd
Nottingham NG5 2DL
Phone: 0602 624624
Telex: 37605

Oldham & District Incorporated Chamber of Commerce
8 Clydesdale St
Oldham OL8 1BT
Phone: 061-624 2482

Orpington & District Chamber of Commerce
3 Chislehurst Rd
Orpington BR6 0DF
Phone: 0689 32703
Fax: 0959 34073

Oxford & District Chamber of Commerce
30 Cornmarket St
Oxford OX1 3EY   Phone: 0865 792020

Paignton Chamber of Trade & Commerce
248 Torquay Rd   Phone: 0803 521532
Paignton TQ3 2EZ   Fax: 0803 559930

Paisley Chamber of Commerce & Industry
6 Gilmour St   Phone: 041-889 9291
Paisley PA1 1BZ   Fax: 041-848 1565

Perthshire Chamber of Commerce
c/o M Watson
14-15 Tay St   Phone: 0738 37626
Perth PH1 5LQ   Fax: 0738 34998

**Peterborough Chamber of Commerce &
  Industry**
The Lawns
33 Thorpe Rd   Phone: 0733 342658
Peterborough   Fax: 0733 342747

**Plymouth Chamber of Commerce &
  Industry**
29 Looe St   Phone: 0752 21151
Plymouth PL4 0EA   Fax: 0752 222589

Pontefract & District Chamber of Trade
c/o Martin Richards
  Ltd
14 Wool Market   Phone: 0977 795200
Pontefract WF8 1AZ

**Reading & Central Berkshire Chamber of
  Commerce, Trade & Industry**
Commerce & Industry
  House   Phone: 0734 595049
2a Crambury Rd   Fax: 0734 500511
Reading RG3 2XD

Redbridge Chamber of Trade & Commerce
3rd Floor
38-40 Cranbrook Rd   Phone: 081-553 3703
Ilford IG1 4NF

**Rochdale Chamber of Commerce, Trade &
  Industry**
Lewis House
12 Smith St   Phone: 0706 343810
Rochdale OL16 1TX

**Romsey & District Chamber of Commerce
  & Industry**
Temple Court House
Church St   Phone: 0794 523633
Romsey SO51 8JH

**Ross-on-Wye & District Chamber of Trade
  & Industry**
Council Chambers
Broad St
Ross-on-Wye   Phone: 0989 62373
  HR9 7EB

**Rotherham & District Chamber of
  Commerce & Industry**
Carnson House
1 Moorgate Rd   Phone: 0709 828425
Rotherham S60 2ED   Fax: 0709 820448

Rugby & District Chamber of Commerce
9 Railway Terrace   Phone: 0788 544951
Rugby CV21 3EN   Fax: 0788 560901

**Salisbury & District Chamber of Commerce
  & Industry**
Farthing House
Pennyfarthing St   Phone: 0722 322708
Salisbury SP1 2PH

**Scunthorpe, Glanford & Gainsborough
  Chamber of Commerce**
58 Oswald Rd   Phone: 0724 842109
Scunthorpe DN15 7PQ   Fax: 0724 857659

Shaftesbury & District Chamber of Trade
c/o D L Beer
52 High St   Phone: 0747 53178
Shaftesbury SP7 8AA

**Sheffield Chamber of Commerce &
  Manufactures**
Commerce House
33 Earl St   Phone: 0742 766667
Sheffield S1 3FX   Fax: 0742 766644

Shepton Mallet Chamber of Commerce
c/o A Edwards
26-28 High St   Phone: 0749 342357
Shepton Mallet   Fax: 0749 342357
  BA4 5AN

Shetland Chamber of Commerce
122 Commercial St
Lerwick ZE1 0EX   Phone: 0595 4739

**Shropshire Chamber of Industry &
  Commerce**
Industry House
16 Halesfield   Phone: 0952 588766
Telford TF7 4TA   Fax: 0952 582503

**South Essex Chamber of Commerce, Trade
  & Industry**
845 London Rd
Westcliff-on-Sea   Phone: 0702 77090
  SS0 9SZ   Fax: 0702 77161

South of Scotland Chamber of Commerce
19 Buccleuch St
Hawick TD9 0HL
Phone: 0450 72267

South-East Hampshire Chamber of Commerce & Industry
27 Guildhall Walk
Portsmouth PO1 2RP
Phone: 0705 294111
Fax: 0705 296829

Southall Chamber of Commerce
Manor House
The Green
Southall UB2 3CJ
Phone: 081-374 0405

Southampton Chamber of Commerce
Bugle House
53 Bugle St
Southampton
SO9 4WP
Phone: 0703 223541
Fax: 0703 227426

Southend-on-Sea District Chamber of Commerce, Trade & Industry
845 London Rd
Westcliffe-on-Sea
SS0 9SZ
Phone: 0702 77090
Fax: 0702 77161

Southport & District Chamber of Trade, Commerce & Industry
72 King St
Southport PR8 1LG
Phone: 0704 531710
Fax: 0704 539255

Southwark Chamber of Commerce
Town Hall
Peckham Rd
London SE5 8UB
Phone: 071-703 6311
ext. 2376

St Albans, Harpenden & District Chamber of Commerce
10 Holywell Hill
St Albans AL1 8BZ
Phone: 0729 63054

Stafford Chamber of Trade
c/o T A Dunn, 1 Mill
St
Stafford ST16 2AJ
Phone: 0785 58648

Stockport Chamber of Commerce & Industry
27 Higher Hillgate
Stockport SK1 3ET
Phone: 061-480 0321
Fax: 061-476 0138

Swansea Chamber of Commerce & Shipping
Rooms F4/F5
Burrows Chambers
East Burrows Rd
Swansea SA1 1RF
Phone: 0792 653297
Fax: 0792 648345

Swindon Chamber of Industry & Commerce
1 Commercial Rd
Swindon SN1 5NE
Phone: 0793 616544
Fax: 619938

Teesside & District Chamber of Commerce & Industry
Commerce House
Exchange Square
Middlesbrough
TS1 1DW
Phone: 0642 230023
Fax: 0642 230105

Teignmouth Chamber of Commerce
5 Bligh Close
Teignmouth TQ14 9NQ
Phone: 0626 775889

Thames-Chiltern Chamber of Commerce & Industry
Commerce House
2-6 Bath Rd
Slough SL1 3SB
Phone: 0753 77877
Fax: 0753 24644

Torquay Chamber of Trade & Commerce
84 Union St
Torquay TQ2 5PY
Phone: 0803 24672

Twickenham & District Chamber of Commerce
Norman House
16 Bridgeway
Whitton
Twickenham TW2 7JJ
Phone: 081-894 6771

Tyne & Wear Chamber of Commerce & Industry
65 Quayside
Newcastle-upon-Tyne
NE1 3DS
Phone: 091-261 1142
Fax: 091-261 4035

Walsall Chamber of Commerce & Industry
Chamber of Commerce
House
Ward St
Walsall WS1 2AG
Phone: 0922 721777
Telex: 338212
Fax: 0922 647359

Waltham Forest Chamber of Commerce
306 Hoe St
London E17 9PX
Phone: 081-520 5494

Wandsworth Chamber of Commerce & Trade
25 East Hill
London SW18 2HZ
Phone: 071-732 9580
Fax: 081-877 3322

Warrington Chamber of Commerce & Industry
80 Sankey St
Warrington WA1 1SG
Phone: 0925 35054
Fax: 0925 444471

Watford Chamber of Commerce & Industry
c/o P Bailey
Barclays Bank
Chambers   Phone: 0923 34469
1a King St   Fax: 0923 223059
Watford WD1 8BT

Wellingborough & District Chamber of Trade & Commerce
Queen Anne House
29 High St   Phone: 0933 76565
Wellingborough   Fax: 0933 441213
NN8 4JZ

Westminster Chamber of Commerce
Mitre House
177 Regent St   Phone: 071-734 2851
London W1R 8DJ   Fax: 071-734 0670

Weymouth & Portland Chamber of Commerce
83 The Esplanade
Weymouth DT4 7AA   Phone: 0305 783971

Wigan & District Chamber of Commerce
107 Standishgate   Phone: 0942 496074
Wigan WN1 1XL   Fax: 0942 495469

Winchester Incorporated Chamber of Commerce
Staple House
Staple Gardens   Phone: 0962 66294
Winchester SO22 8SR

Windsor, Eton, Ascot & District Chamber of Trade & Commerce
c/o C T Carter
6 Rectory Close   Phone: 0753 860841
Windsor SL4 5ER

Wirral Chamber of Commerce
26 Hamilton Square   Phone: 051-647 8085
Birkenhead L41 6DF

Woking & District Chamber of Trade & Commerce
19a High St
Woking GU21 1BW   Phone: 0483 755017

Wolverhampton Chamber of Commerce & Industry
93 Tettenhall Rd
Wolverhampton   Phone: 0902 26726
WV3 9PE   Fax: 0902 26028

Worcester & Hereford Area Chamber of Commerce & Industry
Severn House   Phone: 0905 611611
10 The Moors   Telex: 335294
Worcester WR1 3EE   Fax: 0905 611093

Worthing Chamber of Trade & Commerce
2nd Floor
7 Chapel Rd   Phone: 0903 203252
Worthing BN11 1EG   Fax: 0903 820753

Yarmouth (Great) Chamber of Commerce
Norwich Union
Building
Hall Plain   Phone: 0493 842184
Great Yarmouth   Fax: 0493 857809
NR30 2QD

York Chamber of Commerce, Trade & Industry
c/o Joseph Terry &
Sons   Phone: 0904 629513
Bishopthorpe Rd   Fax: 0904 630985
York YO1 1YE

United Kingdom Offices
of Overseas Chambers of Commerce

American Chamber of Commerce (UK)
75 Brook St   Phone: 071-493 0381
London W1Y 2EB   Fax: 071-493 2394

Arab-British Chamber of Commerce
6 Belgrave Square   Phone: 071-235 4363
London SW1X 8PH   Fax: 071-245 6688

Australian British Chamber of Commerce
Suite 165
6th Floor
Linen Hall   Phone: 071-439 0086
162-168 Regent St   Fax: 071-734 0872
London W1R 5TB

**Belgo-Luxembourg Chamber of Commerce
in GB**
6 John St   Phone: 071-831 3508
London WC1 2ES   Fax: 071-831 9151

Brazilian Chamber of Commerce in GB
32 Green St   Phone: 071-499 0186
London W1Y 3FD   Fax: 071-493 5105

British-Israel Chamber of Commerce
14-15 Rodmarton St   Phone: 071-486 2371
London W1H 3FW   Fax: 071-224 1783

British-Soviet Chamber of Commerce
60a Pembroke Rd   Phone: 071-602 7692
London W8 6NX   Fax: 071-371 4788

**Canada-United Kingdom Chamber of
Commerce**
3 Regent St   Phone: 071-930 7711
London SW1Y 4NZ   Fax: 071-930 9703

Chinese Chamber of Commerce
19 Frith St   Phone: 071-734 5984
London W1V 2AL

Danish UK Chamber of Commerce
22 Sloane St   Phone: 071-259 6795
London SW17 2PE

Egyptian - British Chamber of Commerce
Kent House
Market Place   Phone: 071-323 2856
London W1N 2CL

French Chamber of Commerce in GB
197 Knightsbridge   Phone: 071-225 5250
London SW7 1RB   Fax: 071-225 5557

**German Chamber of Industry & Commerce
in the UK**
12-13 Suffolk St   Phone: 071-930 7251
London SW1Y 4HG   Fax: 071-930 2726

Indian Chamber of Commerce in GB
124 Middlesex St   Phone: 071-247 8078
London E1 7LP

**Italian Chamber of Commerce for GB in
London**
296 Regent St   Phone: 071-637 3153
London W1R 6AE   Fax: 071-436 6037

**Japanese Chamber of Commerce &
Industry in the UK**
2nd Floor
Salisbury House   Phone: 071-628 0069
29 Finsbury Circus   Fax: 071-628 0248
London EC2M 5QQ

Netherlands-British Chamber of Commerce
Dutch House   Phone: 071-405 1358
307-308 High Holborn   Fax: 071-405 1689
London WC1V 7LS

**New Zealand - United Kingdon Chamber of
  Commerce & Industry**
Suite 615
162-168 Regent St   Phone: 071-439 0086
London W1R 5TS   Fax: 071-734 0670

Norwegian-British Chamber of Commerce
Norway House
21-24 Cockspur St   Phone: 071-930 0181
London SW1Y 5BN   Fax: 071-930 7946

**Pakistan - UK Overseas Chamber of
  Industry & Commerce**
5 Bathurst St
London W2 3AJ   Phone: 071-262 7599

**Portuguese Chamber of Commerce &
  Industry in the UK**
1 New Bond St   Phone: 071-493 9973
London W1Y 0NP   Fax: 071-409 3307

Spanish Chamber of Commerce in GB
5 Cavendish Square   Phone: 071-637 9061
London W1M 0DP   Fax: 071-436 7188

Swedish Chamber of Commerce for the UK
72-73 Welbeck St   Phone: 071-486 4545
London W1M 7HA   Fax: 071-935 5487

**Turkish - British Chamber of Commerce &
  Industry**
360-366 Oxford St
London W1N 4AL   Phone: 071-499 4265

Subject Index

ABRASIVES

Abrasive Industries Association 1
British Abrasives Federation 506
Coated Abrasives Manufacturers'
Association 1198

Accident prevention see SPECIFIC
ASPECTS EG SAFETY

ACCOUNTANCY

Association of Accounting Technicians 112
Association of Authorised Public
Accountants 119
Association of Cost & Executive
Accountants 224
Association of International Accountants 301
Association of Practising Accountants 371
British Accounting Association 509
Chartered Association of Certified
Accountants 1156
Chartered Institute of Management
Accountants 1162
Chartered Institute of Public Finance &
Accountancy 1165
Institute of Chartered Accountants in
England & Wales 1849
Institute of Chartered Accountants of
Scotland 1848
Institute of Chartered Secretaries &
Administrators 1851
Institute of Company Accountants 1863
Institute of Internal Auditors 1910
International Accounting Standards
Committee 2048
International Association of Book-
keepers 2058
Society of Public Accountants 3235

ACOUSTICS

Association of Noise Consultants 354
Institute of Acoustics 1820
Noise Abatement Society 2698

Actuaries see FINANCIAL SERVICES

ACUPUNCTURE

British Acupuncture Association 511
British Medical Acupuncture Society 878
Council for Acupuncture 1286
Traditional Acupuncture Society 3361

ADHESIVE TAPE

Adhesive Tape Manufacturers
Association 2

Adhesives see BUILDING EQUIPMENT &
MATERIALS

Adoption see CHILD WELFARE

ADVERTISING & MARKETING

Advertising Association 5
Advertising Film & Videotape Producers
Association 6
Advertising Film Rights Society 7
Advertising Standards Authority 8
Association of Business Advertising
Agencies 182
Association of Distributors of
Advertising Material 243
Association of Free Newspapers 263
Association of Media Independents 337
Association of Point-of-Sale Advertising 367
Association of Print & Packaging Buyers 374

British Advertising Gift Distributors
Association 513
British Direct Marketing Association 700
British List Brokers Association 867
British Promotional Merchandise
Association 960
Bus Advertising Council 1108
Chartered Institute of Marketing 1163
Cinema Advertising Association 1183
Committee of Advertising Practice 1218
Committee of Marketing Organisations ...1221
Communication, Advertising &
Marketing Education Foundation 1231
Council of Outdoor Specialists 1311
Creative Services Association 1330
Dealer Advertising Information Service ...1344
Direct Mail Producers Association 1360
Direct Selling Association 1361
European Marketing & Promotion
Association 1481
European Marketing Association 1482
Incorporated Society of British
Advertisers 1769
Institute of Practitioners in Advertising ...1948
Institute of Sales Promotion 1969
International Advertising Association 2049
International Publishers' Advertising
Representatives Association 2159
Marketing Society 2307
Media Circle 2325
Media Society 2326
Outdoor Advertising Association of GB ...2734
Outdoor Advertising Council 2735
Overseas Press & Media Association 2738
Society of Arts Publicists 3143
Society of Incentive Travel Executives 3204
Society of Producers of Advertising
Music 3233
—see also MAIL ORDER TRADING

Aerobatics see SPORT & SPORTS
EQUIPMENT

Aeronautics see AVIATION &
AERONAUTICS

Aeroplanes see AVIATION & AERONAUTICS

Aerosols see PACKAGING MATERIALS &
EQUIPMENT

Aerospace see AVIATION & AERONAUTICS

After-dinner speakers see PUBLIC
SPEAKING

AGRICULTURAL EQUIPMENT

British Agricultural & Garden Machinery
Association 518
British Agricultural & Horticultural
Plastics Association 519
Garden Machinery Association 1642
Horticultural & Contractors' Tools
Association 1747
Milking Machine Manufacturers'
Association 2344
National Association of Agricultural
Contractors 2408

AGRICULTURE

Agricultural & Food Research Council 15
Agricultural Co-operative Training
Council 16
Agricultural Education Association 17
Agricultural Engineers' Association 18
Agricultural Law Association 19
Agricultural Manpower Society 21
Association of Agricultural Education
Staffs 113
Association of Agriculture 114
Association of Independant Crop
Consultants 283
British Agricultural Export Council 520
British Association of Feed Supplement
Manufacturers 568
British Association of Green Crop Driers 572
British Crop Protection Council 684
British Grassland Society 776
British Hay & Straw Merchants
Association 788
British Institute of Agricultural
Consultants 820
Centre for Agricultural Strategy 1144
Centre of Management in Agriculture 1150
Federation of Agricultural Co-operatives ...1516
Grain & Feed Trade Association 1675
Institution of Agricultural Engineers 2001
International Association of Agricultural
Economics 2057
International Farm Management
Association 2102
International General Produce
Association 2123
National Association of Principal
Agricultural Education Officers 2473
National Hedgelaying Society 2614
National Institute of Agricultural Botany ...2623
Northern Ireland Grain Trade
Association 2706
Processors' & Growers' Research
Organisation 2830
Royal Agricultural Society of England 2893
Royal Highland & Agricultural Society
of Scotland 2915

Scottish Agricultural Organisation
　　Society................................2993
Scottish Corn Trade Association 3011
Silsoe Research Institute 3091
Tropical Growers' Association 3369
United Kingdom Agricultural Supply
　　Trade Association.......................3379
–*see also* FARMING

Air conditioning *see* HEATING & VENTILATING

Air pollution control *see* POLLUTION CONTROL

Air transport *see* AVIATION & AERONAUTICS

Alchololic drinks *see* BEER & BREWING; WINES & SPIRITS

Alternative medicine *see* COMPLEMENTARY MEDICINE AND SPECIFIC ASPECTS EG ACUPUNCTURE

ALUMINIUM

Aluminium Extruders Association 36
Aluminium Federation........................ 37
Aluminium Finishing Association 38
Aluminium Powder & Paste Association 40
Aluminium Primary Producers
　　Association 41
Aluminium Rolled Products
　　Manufacturers Association 42
Aluminium Stockholders Association 43
British Aluminium Foil Rollers
　　Association............................. 524
International Primary Aluminium
　　Institute..............................2155
Organisation of European Aluminium
　　Smelters...............................2729

Ambulance services *see* HEALTHCARE, PUBLIC

Amusement parks *see* PARKS & GROUNDS ADMINISTRATION; ENTERTAINMENT & LEISURE ACTIVITIES

Amusements *see* ENTERTAINMENT & LEISURE ACTIVITIES

ANAESTHESIOLOGY

Anaesthetic Research Society 47
Association of Anaesthetists of GB &
　　Ireland 115
Association of Paediatric Anaesthetists
　　of GB and Ireland 359
International Federation of Dental
　　Anaesthesiology Societies 2108
Society for the Advancement of
　　Anaesthesia in Dentistry................3126

ANATOMY

Anatomical Society of GB & Ireland 48
International Anatomical Nomenclature
　　Committee 2051

Angling *see* FISHING & FISH INDUSTRY

Animal feedstuffs *see* AGRICULTURE

ANIMALS & ANIMAL WELFARE

Animal Diseases Research Association 52
Animal Health Distributors Association 53
Association of British Wild Animal
　　Keepers 175
British Hedgehog Preservation Society 793
Canine Studies Institute 1122
Drinking Fountain Association 1383
Institute for Animal Health 1810
Institute of Animal Health 1825
Institute of Animal Physiology 1827
Institute of Animal Physiology &
　　Genetics Research 1826
International Association Against Painful
　　Experiments on Animals 2052
Mammal Society.........................2294
National Federation of Zoological
　　Gardens of GB & Ireland 2606
Pet Health Council 2768
Pet Trade & Industry Association 2769
World Small Animal Veterinary
　　Association............................3477
World Society for the Protection of
　　Animals 3478
Zoological Society of London 3491
–*see also* VETERINARY PRACTICE; ZOOLOGY
　　and specific animals

ANTHROPOLOGY

International Union of Anthropological
　　& Ethnological Sciences................2186
Royal Anthropological Institute of GB &
　　Ireland 2894

ANTIQUE TRADES

British Antique Dealers' Association 529
London & Provincial Antique Dealers'
  Association 2264

ARBITRATION

Association of British Sailmakers 165
Chartered Institute of Arbitrators 1158
Scottish Agricultural Arbiters'
  Association 2992
Scottish Council for Arbitration 3012
Timber Arbitrators Associations of the
  UK 3344

ARCHAEOLOGY

Association for Industrial Archaeology 84
British Archaeological Association 532
British Classification Society 659
Council for British Archaeology 1287
Institute of Field Archaeologists 1886
Joint Association of Classical Teachers ... 2204
Prehistoric Society 2821
Royal Archaeological Institute 2895
Society for Post-Medieval Archaeology ... 3121
Society of Antiquaries 3136
Society of Antiquaries of Scotland 3137
Society of Museum Archaeologists 3225

ARCHERY

Grand National Archery Society 1676
National Association of Archery Coaches ... 2412

ARCHITECTURE

Architects & Surveyors Institute 59
Architects Registration Council of the
  UK 60
Architectural Association 62
Association of Chief Architects of
  Scottish Local Authorities 195
Association of Consultant Architects 217
British Institute of Architectural
  Technicians 821
Cathedral Architects Association 1132
Commonwealth Association of
  Architects 1225
Incorporated Association of Architects &
  Surveyors 1763
Royal Incorporation of Architects in
  Scotland 2918
Royal Institute of British Architects 2919
Society of Chief Architects of Local
  Authorities 3164

ARCHIVES

Association of County Archivists 227

British Records Association 973
Business Archives Council 1111
Society of Archivists 3141

AROMATHERAPY

Institute of Clinical Aromatherapy 1859
International Federation of
  Aromatherapists 2106

Arthritis *see* RHEUMATOLOGY

ARTS & ARTISTS

Art Workers Guild 66
Arts Development Association 69
Association of Art Historians 117
Association of British Picture Restorers 158
Association of Design & Arts Studies 235
Association of Illustrators 281
British Society of Painters in Oils 1024
British Society of Painters in Oils,
  Pastels & Acrylics 1025
British Watercolour Society 1086
Commercial Art Directors Association 1214
Ephemera Society 1448
Federation of British Artists 1520
Fine Art Trade Guild 1586
Guild of Aviation Artists 1685
Guild of Railway Artists 1704
International Institute for Conservation
  of Historic & Artistic Works 2129
National Artists Association 2383
National Association for Education in
  the Arts 2386
National Association of Decorative &
  Fine Arts Societies 2430
National Portraiture Association 2651
Oriental Ceramic Society 2732
Pastel Society 2752
Royal Institute of Oil Painters 2922
Royal Institute of Painters in Water
  Colours 2923
Royal Scottish Society of Painters in
  Water-Colours 2941
Royal Society of British Artists 2947
Royal Society of British Sculptors 2948
Royal Society of Marine Artists 2952
Royal Society of Miniature Painters,
  Sculptors & Gravers 2954
Royal Society of Painter-Etchers &
  Engravers 2956
Royal Society of Painters in Water-
  Colours 2957
Royal Society of Portrait Painters 2958
Society of Architectural & Industrial
  Illustrators 3140
Society of Artists in Architecture 3142
Society of Equestrian Artists 3191
Society of Graphic Fine Art 3199

Society of London Art Dealers 3217
Society of Miniaturists 3223
Society of Scottish Artists 3243
Society of Strip Illustration 3246
Society of Wildlife Artists 3255
United Society of Artists 3420

Arts & crafts *see* CRAFTS & CRAFTSMEN

ASBESTOS

Asbestos Removal Contractors
    Association 70
European Asbestos & Recycling
    Association 1453

ASTROLOGY

Faculty of Astrological Studies 1502

ASTRONOMY

Association for Astronomy Education 74
British Astronomical Association 608
Royal Astronomical Society 2899

Atomic energy *see* NUCLEAR ENERGY

AUCTIONEERING

Institute of Auctioneers & Appraisers in
    Scotland 1830
Society of Fine Art Auctioneers 3193

AUDIO/VISUAL INDUSTRIES

Advertising Film & Videotape Producers
    Association 6
Alliance of Video Retailers 32
Association of British Manufacturers of
    Photographic Cine & Audiovisual
    Equipment 149
Association of Independent Cinemas 285
Association of Independent Radio
    Contractors 291
Association of Professional Recording
    Studios 380
Association of Professional Video
    Distributors 381
Audio Engineering Society 447
Audio Visual Association 448
British Academy of Film & Television
    Arts 508
British Audio Dealers Association 609
British Federation of Film Societies 737
British Film Designers Guild 745
British Film Institute 746
British Interactive Video Association 841

British Kinematograph Sound &
    Television Society 856
British Phonographic Industry 939
British Radio & Electronic Equipment
    Manufacturers' Association 970
British Screen Advisory Council 991
British Society of Cinematographers 1017
British Tape Industry Association 1047
British Universities Film & Video Council . . . 1071
British Videogram Association 1080
British Vintage Wireless Society 1081
Cable Programme Providers Group 1115
Cable Television Association 1116
Car Radio Industry Specialists
    Association 1123
Cinema Theatre Association 1184
Cinematograph Exhibitors' Association
    of GB & Ireland 1185
Commercial Art Directors Association 1214
Community Radio Association 1232
Directors Guild of GB 1362
Educational Television Association 1400
European Institute for the Media 1476
Federation of British Audio 1521
Film & TV Press Guild 1582
Guild of British Animation 1686
Guild of British Film Editors 1687
Guild of Film Production Accountants &
    Financial Administrators 1693
Guild of Television Cameramen 1706
Incorporated Phonographic Society 1767
Independent Film Distributors'
    Association 1777
Independent Film, Video & Photography
    Association 1778
Independent Programme Producers
    Association 1782
Independent Television Association 1790
Institute of Sound & Communications
    Engineers 1975
International Consumer Electronics
    Association 2090
International Federation of the
    Phonographic Industry 2118
International Institute of
    Communications 2132
International Visual Communications
    Association 2192
Media Studies Association 2327
Music Film & Video Producers'
    Association 2373
National Association for Higher
    Education in Film & Video 2389
National Association of Sound &
    Lighting Companies 2490
National Audio Visual Aids Library 2511
Producers' Association 2833
Professional Lighting & Sound
    Association 2840
Radio Industry Council 2854
Radio Society of GB 2855

Radio, Electrical & Television Retailers'
 Association............................2856
Royal Television Society 2961
Scottish Film Council 3026
Society for Education in Film &
 Television 3113
Society of British Fight Directors...........3151
Society of Cable Television Engineers 3160
Society of Film Distributors...............3192
Society of Television Lighting Directors ...3250
Sound & Communications Contractors
 Association............................3267
Sound & Communications Industries
 Federation............................3268
Sound & Communications Suppliers
 Association............................3269
Video Trade Association..................3430
Videotex Industry Association 3431
–*see also* PHOTOGRAPHY

AUDIOLOGY

British Society of Audiology 1015
Society of Hearing Aid Audiologists........3201

Authors *see* WRITERS

Automatic vending *see* VENDING
 MACHINES

AUTOMATION

Article Number Association 68
Automatic Indentification Manufacturers 453
British Robot Association 983
Institute of Measurement & Control 1930
Numerical Engineering Society............2714
United Kingdom Automation Council 3383
–*see also* COMPUTER SCIENCE & DATA
 PROCESSING

Automotive industry *see* MOTOR
 INDUSTRY

AVIATION & AERONAUTICS

Aerodrome Owners Association 12
Air League 23
Aircraft Owners & Pilots Association 24
Aircraft Research Association 25
Airship Association 26
Association of British Aviation
 Consultants 128
Association of Licensed Aircraft
 Engineers 310
Baltic Air Charter Association...............464

Board of Airline Representatives in the
 UK..................................490
British Aviation Archaeological Council 611
British Helicopter Advisory Board 794
British Microlight Aircraft Association 887
Business Aircraft Users' Association........1110
European Regional Airlines Association ...1489
General Aviation Manufacturers &
 Traders Association....................1646
General Aviation Safety Committee........1647
Guild of Air Pilots & Air Navigators 1683
International Federation of Airworthiness ...2105
National Joint Council for Civil Air
 Transport............................2630
Professional Flight Instructors'
 Association...........................2836
Royal Aeronautical Society 2892
Society of British Aerospace Companies ...3149

BABY PRODUCTS

Baby Equipment Hirers Association 457
Baby Products Association 458
Disposable Nappy Association 1368

Bacteriology *see* BIOLOGY

Badminton *see* SPORT & SPORTS
 EQUIPMENT

BAKING INDUSTRY

British Confectioners Association 673
British Society of Baking 1016
Federation of Bakers 1519
Flour Advisory Bureau 1603
Flour Milling & Baking Research
 Association...........................1604
Institute of British Bakers..................1836
National Association of British & Irish
 Millers 2417
National Association of Master Bakers ...2463
National Council for Baking Education ...2537
Scottish Association of Master Bakers......3000
Scottish Flour Millers' Association 3028

BALL BEARINGS

Ball & Roller Bearing Manufacturers
 Association............................462

Ballet *see* DANCING

Ballroom dancing *see* DANCING

BANKING

Association for Payment Clearing
  Services 90
Association of British Consortium Banks 131
British Bankers' Association 615
British Merchant Banking & Securities
  Houses Association 882
British Overseas & Commonwealth
  Banks Association 928
Chartered Institute of Bankers 1159
Committee of London & Scottish
  Bankers 1220
Committee of Scottish Clearing Bankers . . . 1222
Foreign Banks & Securities Houses
  Association 1614
Foreign Exchange & Currency Deposit
  Brokers' Association 1615
Institute of Bankers in Scotland 1832
Northern Ireland Bankers' Association 2703
–see also FINANCIAL SERVICES

BANKRUPTCY

Association of Bankrupts 122

Barges *see* SHIPS & SHIPPING

Barristers *see* LAW & LEGAL SERVICES

Bartending *see* LICENSED TRADES

Batteries *see* ELECTRICAL TRADES

BEAUTY THERAPY

British Association of Beauty Therapy &
  Cosmetology 555
Institute of Practitioners in Beauty 1947
International Health & Beauty Council . . . 2127
–see also COSMETICS &
  TOILETRIES;ELECTROLYSIS;SUNTANNING

Beds & bedding *see* FURNITURE &
UPHOLSTERY

BEER & BREWING

Allied Brewery Traders' Association 33
Brewers Association of Scotland 500
Brewers' Society 501
Brewing Research Foundation 502
Home Brewing & Winemaking
  Manufacturers Association 1742
Home Brewing & Winemaking Trade
  Association 1743

Hop Merchants' Association 1746
Incorporated Brewers' Guild 1766
Institute of Brewing 1835
Small Independent Brewers' Association . . . 3100

BEER MATS

British Beer-Mat Collectors Society 620

BEES & BEE-KEEPING

Association of Bee-Keeping Appliance
  Manufacturers of GB 123
British Bee-Keepers' Association 619
British Isles Bee Breeders' Association 849
Central Association of Bee-Keepers 1137
International Bee Research Association . . . 2073

BELTING & STRAPPING

British Tensional Strapping Association . . . 1050

BETTING & GAMBLING

Betting Office Licensees Association 479
Bookmakers' Association 496
British Casino Association 643
National Association of Bookmakers 2414

Beverages *see* FOOD & BEVERAGES

Bicycles *see* CYCLES & CYCLING

BILLIARDS, POOL & SNOOKER

Billiards & Snooker Control Council 482
British Association of Pool Table
  Operators 591
World Professional Billiards & Snooker
  Association 3475

BIOCHEMISTRY

Association of Clinical Biochemists 205
Biochemical Society 483

BIOLOGY

Association of Applied Biologists 116
British Mycological Society 897
British Photobiology Society 940
British Social Biology Council 1002
British Society for Parasitology 1006
Institute of Biology 1834
International Society for Evolutionary
  Protistology 2169
International Union of Microbiological
  Societies 2190

National Institute for Biological
  Standards of Control 2620
Physiological Society 2781
Society for Applied Bacteriology 3109
Society for Experimental Biology 3116
Society for General Microbiology 3117
Society for Low Temperature Biology 3119
–see also MARINE BIOLOGY

BIOPHYSICS

British Biophysical Society 621

BIOTECHNOLOGY

Bioindustry Association 484
Biological Engineering Society 485

Bird preservation see ORNITHOLOGY

BISCUITS & CAKES

Biscuit Cake Chocolate & Confectionery
  Alliance 486

Blacksmiths see FARRIERS

Blankets see FURNITURE & UPHOLSTERY

Blindness see SIGHT IMPAIRED

Boats & boatbuilding see SHIPS & SHIPPING

Boilers see HEATING & VENTILATING

Bolts & nuts see FASTENING DEVICES

Book-keeping see ACCOUNTANCY

Book publishing see PUBLISHING

BOOKBINDING

Society of Bookbinders 3148

BOOKSELLING

Antiquarian Booksellers Association 54
Book Development Council 493
Book Packagers Assocation 494
Booksellers Association of GB & Ireland 497
British Esperanto Association 726
Provincial Booksellers' Fairs Association . . . 2846
School Bookshop Association 2979

BOTANY

British Lichen Society 866
Phytochemical Society of Europe 2782

BOWLS & BOWLING

British Tenpin Bowling Association 1049
English Bowling Association 1428
English Bowling Federation 1429
English Indoor Bowling Association 1432

Brass see METALLURGY

Brewing see BEER & BREWING

BRICKS, TILES & SANITARY POTTERY

Brick Development Association 503
British Bathroom Council 616
British Ceramic Tile Council 651
Calcium Silicate Brick Association 1118
Concrete Brick Manufacturers
  Association 1241
Magnesite & Chrome Brickmakers
  Association 2289
–see also CERAMICS

BRUSH INDUSTRY

British Brush Manufacturers' Association 629

BUILDING & CIVIL ENGINEERING

Architects & Surveyors Institute 59
Architectural Precast Cladding
  Association 63
Association of Environment Conscious
  Builders 254
Association of Facilities Managers 258
Association of London Borough
  Engineers & Surveyors 317
Association of Municipal Engineers 347
Association of Project Managers 383
Auger Boring Association 449
British Council of Maintenance
  Associations 680
British Public Works Association 964
British Tunnelling Society 1066
Building Conservation Trust 1097
Building Employers Confederation 1099
Building Research Establishment 1102

Building Services Research &
Information Association 1103
Channel Tunnel Association 1155
Chartered Institute of Building 1160
Confederation of Associations of
Specialist Engineering Contractors 1245
Construction Industry Computing
Association 1261
Construction Industry Research &
Information Association 1262
Export Group for the Constructional
Industries 1496
Faculty of Building 1503
Federation of Associations of Specialists
& Sub-Contractors 1517
Federation of Civil Engineering
Contractors 1530
Federation of Environmental Trade
Associations 1540
Federation of Master Builders 1551
Federation of Piling Specialists 1559
House Builders Federation 1754
Institute of Building Control 1842
Institute of Clerks of Works of GB 1858
Institute of Maintenance & Building
Management 1920
Institution of Civil Engineering
Surveyors 2006
Institution of Civil Engineers 2007
Institution of Highways &
Transportation 2020
Institution of Structural Engineers 2036
Institution of Works & Highways
Management 2039
International Commission on Irrigation &
Drainage 2084
International Federation of Prestressing ... 2112
International Society for Soil Mechanics
& Foundation Engineering 2171
Land Drainage Contractors Association ... 2218
National Federation of Master
Steeplejacks Lightning Conductor
Engineers 2586
National House-Building Council 2616
National Joint Consultative Committee
for Building 2629
National Joint Council for the Building
Industry 2632
National Register of Warranted Builders .. 2655
Royal Institution of Chartered Surveyors ... 2927
Scottish Building Employers Federation ... 3005
Scottish House Builders Association 3032
Scottish Master Wrights & Builders
Association 3042
–*see also* specific applications eg PLUMBING

BUILDING EQUIPMENT & MATERIALS

Aggregate Concrete Block Association 14
Aluminium Window Association 44
Amalgamated Chimney Engineers 45

Architectural Aluminium Association 61
Association of British Plywood & Veneer
Manufacturers 159
Association of Builders' Hardware
Manufacturers 178
Association of Building Component
Manufacturers 179
Association of Lightweight Aggregate
Manufacturers 313
Automatic Door Suppliers Association 452
Bathroom & Kitchen Distributors
Association 470
Brick Development Association 503
British Adhesives & Sealants Association 512
British Aggregate Construction Materials
Industries 517
British Blind & Shutter Association 622
British Cement Association 647
British Ceramic Confederation 648
British Ceramic Tile Council 651
British Constructional Steelwork
Association 674
British Flue & Chimney Manufacturers
Association 751
British Institute of Kitchen Architecture 828
British Kitchen Furniture Manufacturers 857
British Reinforcement Manufacturers
Association 975
British Structural Bearings
Manufacturers Association 1039
British Timber Merchants' Association 1057
British Wood Preserving & Damp-
Proofing Association 1090
British Woodworking Federation 1093
Builders Merchants Federation 1096
Building Contractors Federation 1098
Building Employers Confederation 1099
Building Equipment & Materials Metal
Trades Organisations 1100
Building Materials Export Group 1101
Calcium Silicate Brick Association 1118
Chartered Institution of Building
Services Engineers 1167
Clay Pipe Development Association 1191
Compressed Air Equipment Distributors
Association 1237
Concrete Block Paving Association 1240
Concrete Brick Manufacturers
Association 1241
Concrete Pipe Association 1242
Construction Fixings Association 1260
Construction Plant-Hire Association 1263
Draught Proofing Advisory Association ... 1380
Drilling & Sawing Association 1382
Dry Stone Walling Association of GB 1385
Dry-Lining & Partition Association 1386
External Wall Insulation Association 1497
Federation of Building Specialist
Contractors 1528
Federation of Manufacturers of
Construction Equipment & Cranes 1549

Fencing Contractors Association 1574
Fibre Building Board Organisation 1577
Fibre Cement Manufacturers'
   Association 1578
Flat Roofing Contractors Advisory Board . . . 1599
Glass & Glazing Federation 1667
Glassfibre Reinforced Cement
   Association 1669
Guild of Architectural Ironmongers 1684
Gypsum Products Development
   Association 1709
Institute of Architectural Ironmongers 1828
Institute of Asphalt Technology 1829
Institute of Builders' Merchants 1841
International Cement Bonded
   Particleboard Federation 2075
International Conference in Composite
   Structures 2089
International Truss Plate Association 2179
Kitchen Specialists Association 2215
Lead Contractors Association 2227
London Association of Master
   Stonemasons 2267
Mastic Asphalt Council & Employer's
   Federation 2320
Mortar Producers' Association 2359
National Association of Chimney Lining
   Engineers 2422
National Association of Loft Insulation
   Contractors 2462
National Association of Scaffolding
   Contractors 2481
National Cavity Insulation Association 2522
National Clayware Federation 2528
National Contractors Group 2535
National Council of Building Material
   Producers 2549
National Federation of Painting &
   Decorating Contractors 2590
National Federation of Plastering & Dry
   Lining Partition Contractors 2591
National Federation of Roofing
   Contractors 2594
National Fireplace Council
   Manufacturers' Association 2608
National Glass Reinforced Plastics
   Construction Federation 2611
National Panel Products Association 2643
National Prefabricated Building
   Association 2652
Natural Slate Quarries Association 2688
Northern Ireland Builders Merchants'
   Association 2704
Northern Ireland Wholesale Merchants'
   & Manufacturers' Association 2711
Partitioning Industry Association 2750
Patent Glazing Contractors Association . . . 2753
Pipe Jacking Association 2787
Plastic Tanks & Cisterns Manufacturers'
   Association 2794

Plastics Land Drainage Manufacturers'
   Association 2797
Plastics Window Federation 2800
Precast Flooring Federation 2819
Prefabricated Aluminium Scaffold
   Manufacturers Association 2820
Scottish Building Contractors
   Association 3004
Scottish Master Plasterers' Association . . . 3041
Single Ply Association 3094
Single Ply Roofing Association 3095
Sprayed Concrete Association 3278
Steel Construction Institute 3292
Steel Lintel Manufacturers Association . . . 3293
Steel Window Association 3294
Stone Federation 3300
Suspended Access Equipment
   Manufacturers' Association 3312
Suspended Ceilings Association 3313
Thermal Insulation Contractors
   Association 3340
Thermal Insulation Manufacturers &
   Suppliers Association 3341
Timber & Brick Homes Consortium 3343
Trussed Rafter Fabricators Association . . . 3370
United Kingdom & Ireland Particleboard
   Association 3378
United Kingdom Mineral Wool
   Association 3401
Wood Wool Slab Manufacturers
   Association 3465
—see also under specific materials eg CONCRETE

BUILDING SOCIETIES

Building Societies Association 1104
Chartered Building Societies Institute 1157

Burglar alarms *see* SECURITY

BURIAL & CREMATION

British Institute of Embalmers 823
Cremation Society of GB 1331
Federation of British Cremation
   Authorities 1522
Funeral Furnishing Manufacturers
   Association 1629
Institute of Burial & Cremation
   Administration 1843
National Association of Funeral
   Directors 2439
Proprietary Crematoria Association 2845

Business & business education *see*
   MANAGEMENT & MANAGEMENT TRAINING

Business equipment *see* OFFICE AUTOMATION & MANAGEMENT; STATIONERY & ALLIED PRODUCTS

Business records *see* ARCHIVES

Butchers *see* MEAT TRADES

Butter *see* DAIRY PRODUCTS

BUTTONS & BUTTONHOOKS

Association of Button Merchants 185
British Button Manufacturers Society 633
Buttonhook Society 1114

CABLES

British Cable Makers' Confederation 634
British Electrical Systems Association 716
Electrical & Electronic Insulation
    Association 1404
International Wire & Machinery
    Association 2195
Super Tension Cables Group 3308

CADMIUM

Cadmium Association 1117

Cakes *see* BISCUITS & CAKES

CALLIGRAPHY

Society for Italic Handwriting 3118
Society of Scribes & Illuminators 3244

Canals *see* WATERWAYS, INLAND

Canned food *see* FOOD & BEVERAGES

Cans *see* PACKAGING MATERIALS & EQUIPMENT

Car hire *see* VEHICLE HIRE

CARAVANS & CAMPING

British Holiday & Home Parks
    Association 798
Camping & Outdoor Leisure Association . . . 1120

European Caravan Federation 1456
National Caravan Council 2517

Career guidance *see* EMPLOYMENT & RECRUITMENT

Cargo handling *see* MATERIALS HANDLING

Carpentry *see* BUILDING EQUIPMENT & MATERIALS; WOOD & WOODWORKING

Carpets *see* FLOORING & FLOORCOVERING

Cartography *see* GEOGRAPHY

Catering *see* HOTEL & CATERING MANAGEMENT

Catering equipment *see* HOTEL & CATERING EQUIPMENT

CAVES

British Cave Research Association 646
National Caving Association 2521

CEMENT

British Cement Association 647
Cement Admixtures Association 1135
Fibre Cement Manufacturers'
    Association 1578
Scottish Cement Merchants Association . . . 3006

CERAMICS

British Ceramic Confederation 648
British Ceramic Plant & Machinery
    Manufacturers' Association 649
British Ceramic Research 650
Institute of Ceramics 1846
–*see also* BRICKS, TILES, etc.; CLAY
    TECHNOLOGY; POTTERY & CHINA

CHAINS

British Chain Manufacturers Association 652

CHAMBERS OF COMMERCE & TRADE

Association of British Chambers of
    Commerce 129

British Junior Chamber 855
International Chamber of Commerce 2077
National Chamber of Trade 2524
–*see also* part 3 for individual chambers

Champagne *see* WINES & SPIRITS

Charities *see* SOCIAL WELFARE

Cheese *see* DAIRY PRODUCTS

CHEMICAL ENGINEERING & CHEMICAL PLANT

British Chemical Engineering
  Contractors Association 654
Institution of Chemical Engineers 2005
Oil & Chemical Plant Constructors'
  Association 2718
Process Plant Association 2827

CHEMICAL INDUSTRY

British Agrochemicals Association 522
British Association for Chemical
  Specialities 538
British Calcium Carbonates Federation 635
British Chemical Distributors & Traders
  Association 653
British Colour Makers' Association 667
British Industrial Biological Research
  Association 815
Chemical Industries Association 1171
Food Additives Industry Association 1609
National Sulphuric Acid Association 2673
Royal Society of Chemistry 2949
Society of Chemical Industry 3163
Solvents Industry Association 3265
–*see also* specific aspects

Chess *see* SPORT & SPORTS EQUIPMENT

Chickens *see* POULTRY

CHILD WELFARE

Association for all Speech Impaired
  Children 73
Association for Child Psychology &
  Psychiatry 77
Association of British Paediatric Nurses 156
Association of Nursery Training Colleges 355
Association of Workers for Maladjusted
  Children 444

British Agencies for Adoption &
  Fostering 516
British Association for Early Childhood
  Education 542
British Paediatric Association 929
Federation of Resource Centres 1563
International Society of Paediatric
  Oncology 2174
London Adventure Playground
  Association 2265
National Association for Gifted Children . . . 2388
National Association for Maternal &
  Child Welfare 2390
National Association for Primary
  Education 2396
National Association for the Welfare of
  Children in Hospital 2404
National Children's Bureau 2525
National Council of Voluntary Child
  Care Organisations 2551
National Toy Libraries Association 2677
Pre-School Playgroups Association 2818
Scottish Pre-School Play Association 3056

Chimney sweeps *see* CLEANING TECHNOLOGY

Chimneys *see* BUILDING EQUIPMENT & MATERIALS

China *see* POTTERY & CHINA

CHIROPODY

Institute of Chiropodists 1853
Society of Chiropodists 3169

Chiropractice *see* COMPLEMENTARY MEDICINE

Chocolate *see* COCOA & CHOCOLATE PRODUCTS

CHROMATOGRAPHY

Chromatographic Society 1181

CHURCH FURNISHINGS

National Church Crafts Association 2527

Cigarettes *see* TOBACCO TRADES

Cinema advertising *see* ADVERTISING & MARKETING

Cinemas *see* AUDIO/VISUAL INDUSTRIES

Circuses *see* ENTERTAINMENT & LEISURE ACTIVITIES

CIVIL DEFENCE

Association of Civil Defence & Emergency Planning Officers 204
County Emergency Planning Officers' Society 1322
Institute of Civil Defence & Disaster Studies 1854
–see also DEFENCE & DEFENCE EQUIPMENT

CLASSICAL STUDIES

Association for the Reform of Latin Teaching 105
Classical Association 1189
Institute of Classical Studies 1855
Joint Association of Classical Teachers . . . 2204
Society for the Promotion of Hellenic Studies 3128
Society for the Promotion of Roman Studies 3130

CLAY TECHNOLOGY

British Ball Clay Producers' Federation 612
British Ceramic Confederation 648
China Clay Association 1179
Institute of Clay Technology 1856
National Clayware Federation 2528
Scottish Employers' Council for the Clay Industries 3020
–see also BRICKS, TILES, etc.; CERAMICS; POTTERY & CHINA

CLEANING TECHNOLOGY

British Institute of Cleaning Science 822
Cleaning & Hygiene Suppliers' Association 1193
Cleaning & Support Services Association 1194
Contract Cleaning & Maintenance Association 1269
Fabric Care Research Association 1498
Home Laundering Consultative Council . . . 1744
Industrial Cleaning Machine Manufacturers' Association 1795
National Association of Chimney Sweeps 2421

National Association of the Launderette Industry 2495
National Carpet Cleaners Association 2519
Society of Hospital Linen Service & Laundry Managers 3203
Society of Laundry Engineers & Allied Trades 3212
Textile Services Association 3335

Climatology *see* METEOROLOGY

CLOCKS & WATCHES

Antiquarian Horological Society 55
British Clock & Watch Manufacturers' Association 661
British Horological Institute 804
British Watch & Clock Makers' Guild 1083
National Association of Goldsmiths 2440
Watch & Clock Importers Association of GB 3441

Clothing *see* TEXTILE INDUSTRIES - CLOTHING

COAL & COKE

British Coal Exporters' Federation 663
Chamber of Coal Traders 1153
Coal Merchants' Federation 1196
Coal Preparation Plant Association 1197
Coke Oven Managers' Association 1202
Domestic Coal Consumers' Council 1374
Low Temperature Coal Distillers Association of GB 2283
National Association of Solid Fuel Wholesalers 2489
Solid Smokeless Fuels Federation 3263
Underfeed Stoker Makers' Association . . . 3374

COCOA & CHOCOLATE PRODUCTS

Cocoa Association of London 1199
International Cocoa Organization 2079

Coffee *see* FOOD & BEVERAGES

Coins *see* NUMISMATICS

Coke *see* COAL & COKE

Cold storage *see* REFRIGERATION

COMBUSTION ENGINEERING

British Combustion Equipment
  Manufacturers Association 668
British Internal Combustion Engine
  Research Institute 844
Combustion Engineering Association 1213
Institution of Diesel & Gas Turbine
  Engineers 2010

COMMERCE

British Society of Commerce 1018
–*see also* CHAMBERS OF COMMERCE and
  specific aspects

Commercial travellers *see* SALES
  MANAGEMENT

Commercial vehicles *see* MOTOR
  INDUSTRY

Commodity trading *see* FINANCIAL
  SERVICES AND SPECIFIC COMMODITIES

Community services *see* SOCIAL
  WELFARE

Company registration *see* FINANCIAL
  SERVICES

COMPLEMENTARY MEDICINE

British Chiropractic Association 657
British Holistic Medical Association 799
Council for Complementary &
  Alternative Medicine 1288
Council for Professions Supplementary
  to Medicine 1298
Institute for Complementary Medicine 1811
Institute of Holistic Therapies 1901
International Register of Oriental
  Medicine 2160
Metamorphic Association 2339
Radionics Association 2857
Register of Traditional Chinese Medicine ... 2872
School of Herbal Medicine Phytotherapy ... 2983
–*see also* under specific areas eg
  ACUPUNCTURE

COMPRESSED AIR

British Compressed Air Society 670
British Compressed Gases Association 671
Compressed Air Equipment Distributors
  Association 1237

COMPUTER SCIENCE & DATA PROCESSING

Association for Literary & Linguistic
  Computing 87
Association of Independent Computer
  Specialists 286
Association of Professional Computer
  Consultants 377
British Computer Society 672
British Management Data Foundation 870
Business Equipment & Information
  Technology Association 1112
Computer & Peripheral Equipment Trade
  Association 1238
Computing Services Association 1239
Construction Industry Computing
  Association 1261
Independent Contractors Association 1776
Independent National Computing
  Association 1781
Institute of Data Processing
  Management 1869
Institution of Analysts & Programmers 2002
Society for Computers & Law 3110
Society of Information Technology
  Managers 3208
United Kingdom Council for Computing
  Development 3385
–*see also* AUTOMATION

CONCRETE & CONCRETE PRODUCTS

Aggregate Concrete Block Association 14
British Aggregate Construction Materials
  Industries 517
British Precast Concrete Federation 956
British Ready Mixed Concrete
  Association 971
British Reinforcement Manufacturers
  Association 975
Concrete Brick Manufacturers
  Association 1241
Concrete Society 1243
Institute of Concrete Technology 1864
Mortar Producers' Association 2359
Sprayed Concrete Association 3278

CONFECTIONERY TRADES

Biscuit Cake Chocolate & Confectionery
  Alliance 486
Retail Confectioners & Tobacconists
  Association 2878
Wholesale Confectionery & Tobacco
  Alliance 3452

Conferences *see* EXHIBITIONS &
  CONFERENCES

Conservation see ENVIRONMENTAL PROTECTION AND UNDER SPECIFIC ASPECTS

Construction see BUILDING & CIVIL ENGINEERING; BUILDING EQUIPMENT & MATERIALS

Consumer credit see CREDIT TRADING

CONSUMER PROTECTION

Electricity Consumers' Council 1410
Gas Consumers Council 1643
Institute of Consumer Advisers 1865
National Association of Citizens Advice
    Bureaux 2425
National Federation of Consumer
    Groups 2576
Post Office Users National Council 2808

Contact lenses see OPHTHALMOLOGY

Containers see PACKAGING MATERIALS & EQUIPMENT

Control apparatus see SCIENTIFIC INSTRUMENTS

Conveyancing see LAW & LEGAL SERVICES

Cooperative societies see RETAIL TRADES

COPPER

British Non-Ferrous Metals Federation   907
Copper Development Association 1275
Copper Smelters & Refiners Association ... 1276
International Copper Association 2091

Copyright see INTELLECTUAL PROPERTY

CORDAGE, ROPE & TWINE

Coir Association 1201
London Sisal Association 2278
Manila Hemp Association 2296

CORK

Cork Industry Federation 1277

Coroners see LAW & LEGAL SERVICES

CORRESPONDENCE COLLEGES

Association of British Correspondence
    Colleges 133
Council for the Accreditation of
    Correspondence Colleges 1299

CORROSION TECHNOLOGY

European Federation of Corrosion 1464
Institution of Corrosion Science &
    Technology 2008

COSMETICS & TOILETRIES

British Essential Oils Association 728
British Fragrance Association 760
British Society of Perfumers 1026
Cosmetic, Toiletry & Perfumery
    Association 1284
International Federation of Essential Oils
    & Aroma Trades 2109
International Federation of Societies of
    Cosmetic Chemists 2115
Society of Cosmetic Scientists 3175

Cost accounting see ACCOUNTANCY

COTTON

British Cotton Growing Association 678

CRAFTS & CRAFTSMEN

Art Workers Guild 66
Association of British Pewter Craftsmen 157
Conference & Lecturers in Craft &
    Design Education 1250
Crafts Council 1327
Craftsmen Potters Association 1328
Federation of Crafts & Commerce 1534
Guild of Master Craftsmen................ 1699
Master Craftsmen's Association & Retail
    Export Group 2311
Rural Crafts Association 2967

Cranes see LIFTING & LOADING EQUIPMENT

CREDIT TRADING

Association of British Credit Unions 134
Association of Manufacturing Chemists   330
Consumer Credit Association of the UK ... 1267
Consumer Credit Trade Association 1268
Finance Houses Association 1584

Institute of Credit Management 1868
National Association of Trade Protection
     Societies 2500
National Consumer Credit Federation 2534
Scottish Consumer Credit Association 3010

Cremation see BURIAL & CREMATION

CRICKET

Cricket Council 1332
English Schools Cricket Association 1435
National Cricket Association 2554

Crop protection see AGRICULTURE

CRYOGENICS

British Cryogenics Council 685

CRYSTALLOGRAPHY

British Crystallographic Association 686
International Union of Crystallography . . . 2189

Curtains see FURNITURE & UPHOLSTERY

CUTLERY

British Cutlery & Silverware Association 687
Cutlery & Allied Trades Research
     Association 1341

CYCLES & CYCLING

Association of Cycle Traders 233
Bicycle Association of GB 481
British Cycling Federation 688
British Motorcyclists Federation 892
Institute of Motorcycling 1935
Lightweight Cycle Association of GB 2248
Lightweight Cycle Manufacturers'
     Association 2249
Motorcycle Industry Association 2365

DAIRY PRODUCTS

Association of British Preserved Milk
     Manufacturers 160
Association of Cheese Processors 194
Butter Information Council 1113
Creamery Proprietors' Association 1329
Dairy Trade Federation 1343
English Country Cheese Council 1430
European Federation of Dairy Retailers . . . 1465
National Dairy Council 2555
National Dairy Producers Association 2556

National Dairymen's Association 2557
Northern Ireland Dairy Trade Federation . . . 2705
Scottish Association of Milk Product
     Manufacturers 3001
Scottish Dairy Trade Federation 3017
Scottish Milk Records Association 3043
Society of Dairy Technology 3182
Stilton Cheese Makers Association 3299
United Kingdom Provision Trade
     Federation 3408

DANCING

Association for Dance Movement
     Therapy 79
Ballroom Dancers Federation 463
British Ballet Organization 613
British Council of Ballroom Dancing 679
British Entertainment & Dancing
     Association 721
Council for Dance Education & Training . . . 1289
Imperial Society of Teachers of Dancing . . . 1761
International Council of Ballroom
     Dancing 2094
International Dance Teachers'
     Association 2099
National Association of Teachers of
     Dancing 2493
Scottish Dance Teachers' Alliance 3018
United Kingdom Alliance of Professional
     Teachers of Dancing 3380

Data processing see COMPUTER SCIENCE
& DATA PROCESSING

Deafness see HEARING DISABILITIES

DECORATING

Association of Painting Craft Teachers 360
British Decorators Association 690
Interior Decorators & Designers
     Association 2047
London Association of Master
     Decorators 2266
National Federation of Painting &
     Decorating Contractors 2590
Northern Ireland Master Painters'
     Association 2708
Scottish Decorators Federation 3019
Wallpaper, Paint & Wallcovering
     Retailers Association 3439
–see also DESIGN; DISPLAY

DEER

British Deer Farmers' Association 691
British Deer Producers' Society 692
British Deer Society 693

DEFENCE & DEFENCE EQUIPMENT

Defence Manufacturers Association 1347
International Institute for Strategic
    Studies. 2131

DEMOLITION

Institute of Explosives Engineers 1882
National Federation of Demolition
    Contractors. 2577

DENTISTRY

Association for Denture Prosthesis 80
Association of British Dental Surgery
    Assistants 135
Association of Dental Hospitals of the
    UK. 234
British Association of Orthodontists 584
British Dental Association 694
British Dental Hygienists' Association 695
British Dental Trade Association 696
British Fluoridation Society 754
British Society for the Study of
    Prosthetic Dentistry .1013
British Society of Medical & Dental
    Hypnosis. 1023
British Society of Periodontology 1027
European Organisation of Caries
    Research 1484
Faculty of Dental Surgery 1507
General Dental Council. 1652
General Dental Practitioners Association . . .1653
International Dental Federation 2101
International Federation of Dental
    Anaesthesiology Societies 2108
Society for the Advancement of
    Anaesthesia in Dentistry. 3126

DESIGN

Art Workers Guild. 66
Association of Art Historians 117
Association of Design & Arts Studies 235
Association of Illustrators. 281
Association of Industrial Graphics &
    Nameplate Manufacturers 295
Association of Interior Design Degree
    Courses 300
Chartered Society of Designers 1169
Conference & Lecturers in Craft &
    Design Education 1250
Design & Industries Association 1350
Design & Technology Association 1351
Design Business Association 1352
Design Council 1353
Designers & Art Directors Association of
    London 1354
Ecological Design Association 1392
Faculty of Royal Designers for Industry . . .1509

International Council of Graphic Design
    Associations. 2095
International Society of Interior
    Designers 2173
National Association for Design
    Education 2385
National Society for Education in Art &
    Design 2668
Society of Designer-Craftsmen. 3183
–see also ARTS & ARTISTS

Detectives see SECURITY

Detergents see SOAP & DETERGENTS

DIABETES

British Diabetic Association 697
Diabetes Foundation .1357

Diecasting see METALLURGY

Diesel engines see INTERNAL
COMBUSTION ENGINEERING

Dietetics see NUTRITION

Direct mail see ADVERTISING &
MARKETING

Direct selling see ADVERTISING &
MARKETING

DISABILITY & REHABILITATION

Association for the Prevention of
    Disabilities 103
Association of Disabled Professionals 242
British Council of Organisations of
    Disabled People 681
British Society for Music Therapy 1004
British Sports Association for the
    Disabled 1036
Disability Alliance Education & Research
    Association. 1364
Disabled Drivers' Association 1365
National Association of Industries for
    the Blind & Disabled. 2453
National Association of Orientation &
    Mobility Instructors 2467
National Autistic Society 2512
National Council for Special Education . . .2543

National League for the Blind &
  Disabled 2635
Royal Association for Disability &
  Rehabilitation..........................2896

DISPLAY

British Display Society 701
British Sign Association 998
Shop & Display Equipment Association ...3088
–see also SHOPFITTING

Distributive trades see RETAIL TRADES

Docks see PORTS, DOCKS & HARBOURS

DOGS, DOG RACING & HUNTING

Masters of Basset Hounds Association ...2316
Masters of Deerhounds Association 2317
Masters of Draghounds Association 2318
Masters of Foxhounds Association 2319

Domestic appliances see ELECTRICAL
TRADES

DOORS & DOOR FURNITURE

Automatic Door Suppliers Association.......452
British Lock Manufacturers Association 868
Door & Shutter Manufacturers
  Association...........................1378

Dowsing see WATER & WATER TREATMENT

Drainage see WATER & WATER TREATMENT

Drama see THEATRE

Drawing see ARTS & ARTISTS

DRILLING

Auger Boring Association 449
British Drilling Association 705

DRIVING INSTRUCTION

Association of Motor Vehicle Teachers 346
Driving Instructors Association.............1384
Institute of Advanced Motorists............1823
Motor Schools Association of GB..........2363

National Association of Approved
  Driving Instructors 2410

DRUG ABUSE

Institute for the Study of Drug
  Dependence...........................1819

Drugs see PHARMACEUTICAL INDUSTRY &
PRACTICE

Dyeing & cleaning see CLEANING
TECHNOLOGY

DYES & PIGMENTS

Society of Dyers & Colourists..............3186

DYSLEXIA

British Dyslexia Association 706
Dyslexia Institute 1389

Earthenware see CLAY TECHNOLOGY;
POTTERY & CHINA

EARTHQUAKES

Society for Earthquake & Civil
  Engineering Dynamics 3112

Ecology see ENVIRONMENTAL PROTECTION

ECONOMICS

Economics Association....................1394
Institute of Economics & Statistics 1872
International Institute of Social
  Economics 2135
National Institute of Economic & Social
  Research 2625
Royal Economic Society...................2910
Society of Business Economists...........3159

EDUCATION

Adult Residential Colleges Association 3
Advisory Centre for Education 9
Association for Sandwich Education &
  Training 93
Association for Science Education 94
Association for Student Counselling 96
Association for Technological Education
  in Schools..............................99
Association for the Study of Primary
  Education (ASPE) 109

Association for the Teaching of the
Social Sciences 110
Association of Career Teachers 187
Association of College Registrars &
Administrators 207
Association of Colleges for Further &
Higher Education 208
Association of Commonwealth
Universities 210
Association of Directors of Education in
Scotland 237
Association of Educational Advisers in
Scotland 249
Association of Heads of Independent
Schools 274
Association of Heads of Outdoor
Education Centres 275
Association of Higher Academic Staff in
Colleges of Education in Scotland 278
Association of Polytechnic Teachers 370
Association of Principals of Colleges 372
Association of Principals of Sixth Form
Colleges 373
Association of Recognised English
Language Schools 392
Association of Religious in Education 397
Association of Tutors Incorporated 429
Association of University Teachers 432
Association of University Teachers
(Scotland) 433
Association of Vice-Principals of
Colleges 439
Boarding Schools Association 491
British Association for Early Childhood
Education 542
British Association of State Colleges in
English Language Teaching 599
British Educational Equipment
Association 709
British Educational Research Association 711
Business & Technician Education
Council 1109
Catholic Teachers' Federation.............1134
Centre for Urban Educational Studies 1149
College of Preceptors 1208
Committee of Directors of Polytechnics ...1219
Committee of Vice-Chancellors &
Principals 1223
Conference for Independent Further
Education 1251
Conference of Catholic Secondary
Schools & Colleges 1252
Conference of University Administrators ...1255
Council for Educational Advance 1290
Council for National Academic Awards ...1296
Council of Local Education Authorities ...1306
Council of Subject Teaching
Associations............................1315
Council on International Educational
Exchange 1317
County Education Officers' Society 1321

Curriculum Association....................1340
Educational Centres Association 1395
Educational Development Association 1396
Educational Institute of Scotland..........1398
Engineering Teaching Equipment
Manufacturers Association 1424
Environmental Education Advisors
Association..............................1447
European Association of Teachers..........1455
European Council of International
Schools 1461
Federation of English Language Course
Organisations..........................1539
General Studies Association 1657
General Teaching Council for Scotland ...1658
Girls' Schools Association 1665
Governing Bodies Association 1673
Governing Bodies of Girls Schools
Association..............................1674
Headmasters' Conference................1718
Headteachers' Association of Scotland ...1719
Home & School Council 1741
Incorporated Association of Preparatory
Schools 1765
Independent Schools Association 1784
Independent Schools Bursars'
Association..............................1785
Independent Schools Information
Service 1787
Independent Schools Joint Council 1788
Institute of Tape Learning 1982
International Association for Educational
& Vocational Guidance..................2055
International Association for Teachers of
English as a Foreign Language 2056
Joint University Council....................2211
National & International Society for
Education through Art 2380
National Adult School Organisation 2381
National Association for Curriculum
Enrichment & Extension 2384
National Association for Environmental
Education 2387
National Association for Gifted Children ...2388
National Association for Pastoral Care in
Education 2395
National Association for Remedial
Education 2397
National Association for Staff
Development in Further & Higher
Education 2398
National Association for Teaching
English & other Community
Languages to Adults 2399
National Association for the Support of
Small Schools 2401
National Association for the Teaching of
Drama 2403
National Association for the Teaching of
English................................2402

National Association of Advisers in Craft
  Design & Technology 2406
National Association of Advisory
  Officers for Special Education 2407
National Association of Counsellors in
  Education 2428
National Association of Development
  Education Centres 2431
National Association of Governors &
  Managers 2441
National Association of Head Teachers
  & Deputies 2442
National Association of Inspectors &
  Educational Advisers 2455
National Association of Schoolmaster &
  Union of Women Teachers 2483
National Association of Youth &
  Community Education Officers 2510
National Confederation of Parent-
  Teacher Associations 2532
National Council for Advisers for
  Educational Technology 2536
National Council for Educational
  Standards 2539
National Council for Educational
  Technology 2540
National Council for Mother Tongue
  Teaching 2541
National Council for Teacher-centred
  Professional Development 2544
National Council for Vocational
  Qualifications 2546
National Education Association 2563
National Federation of Voluntary
  Literacy Schemes 2602
National Foundation for Educational
  Research in England & Wales 2609
National Institute of Adult Continuing
  Education 2622
Primary History Association 2823
School Examination & Assessment
  Council 2980
School Journey Association 2981
Scottish Community Education Council ... 3009
Scottish Council for Educational
  Technology 3013
Scottish Council for Research in
  Education 3014
Scottish Institute of Adult & Continuing
  Education 3033
Scottish Secondary Teachers'
  Association 3061
Scottish Vocational Education Council ... 3069
Secondary Heads Association 3078
Simplified Spelling Society 3092
Society for Research into Higher
  Education 3123
Society of Education Officers 3187
Society of Headmasters of Independent
  Schools 3200
Society of Industrial Tutors 3207

Standing Conference of Heads of
  Modern Languages in Polytechnics &
  other Colleges 3285
Standing Conference of Principals 3286
Standing Conference of Regional
  Advisory Councils for Further
  Education 3287
Standing Conference on Principals of
  Sixth Form & Tertiary Colleges 3289
Tertiary College Association 3329
United Kingdom Reading Association 3409
Universities Council for Adult &
  Continuing Education 3421
Universities Council for the Education of
  Teachers 3422
—see also specific aspects

Effluents see WATER & WATER TREATMENT

EGGS

British Egg Association 713
British Egg Products Association 714
National Egg Marketing Association 2564
United Kingdom Egg Producers
  Association 3387

ELECTRICAL TRADES

Association of British Generating Set
  Manufacturers 141
Association of Control Manufacturers 222
Association of Electrical Machinery
  Trades 251
Association of Flow Survey Contractors ... 260
Association of Independent Electricity
  Producers 287
Association of Manufacturers Allied to
  the Electrical & Electronic Industries ... 328
Association of Manufacturers of
  Domestic Electrical Appliances 329
BEAMA 472
BEAMA Ancillery Metering Equipment
  Manufacturers' Association 473
BEAMA Capacitor Manufacturers'
  Association 474
BEAMA Interactive & Mains Systems
  Association 475
BEAMA Metering Association 476
BEAMA Transmission & Distribution
  Association 477
British Battery Manufacturers
  Association 618
British Cable Makers' Confederation 634
British Electro-Static Manufacturers
  Association 718
British Electrotechnical Approvals Board ... 720
Confederation of Aerial Industries 1244
Covered Conductors Association 1326
Domestic Appliance Service Association ... 1373

Electric Vehicle Association of GB 1403
Electrical & Electronic Insulation
  Association...........................1404
Electrical Contractors Association 1405
Electrical Contractors Association of
  Scotland 1406
Electrical Installation Equipment
  Manufacturers Association 1407
Electrical Wholesalers Federation..........1408
Electricity Association 1409
Engineering Industries Association 1423
European Committee of Manufacturers
  of Electrical Installation Equipment.......1459
European Committee of Manufacturers,
  Compressors, Vacuum Pumps &
  Pneumatic Tools.....................1458
Institution of Electrical Engineers 2011
Institution of Electronics & Electrical
  Incorporated Engineers.................2012
International Coil Winding Association ...2082
Joint Industry Board for the Electrical
  Contracting Industry 2210
Membrane Switch Manufacturers'
  Association............................2331
National Association of Range
  Manufacturers 2479
National Inspection Council for
  Electrical Installation Contracting 2619
Power Actuated Systems Association 2813
Power Generation Contractors
  Association...........................2815
Scottish Joint Industry Board for the
  Electrical Contracting Industry 3034
Small Electrical Appliance Marketing
  Association...........................3099
Society of Automotive-Electrical
  Technicians 3146
Society of Battery Manufacturers 3147
Society of British Battery Manufacturers ...3150
Society of Chief Electrical & Mechanical
  Engineers in Local Government 3166

ELECTROLYSIS

British Association of Electrolysists..........567

ELECTRONICS

Association of Franchised Distributors of
  Electronic Components...................261
BEAMA 472
Electronic Components Industry
  Federation............................1414
Electronic Engineering Association 1415
Institution of Electrical Engineers 2011
Institution of Electronics & Electrical
  Incorporated Engineers.................2012
International Consumer Electronics
  Association............................2090
National Electronics Council...............2565

Society of Automotive-Electrical
  Technicians 3146

EMBROIDERY & NEEDLEWORK

British Needlecrafts Council 906
Embroiderers' Guild 1416
Linen Sewing Thread Manufacturers'
  Association of GB & N Ireland...........2250
Quilters' Guild 2851

EMPLOYERS ORGANISATIONS

Alliance of Small Firms & Self-Employed
  People 31
Association of Independent Businesses 284
Confederation of British Industry...........1247
Institute of Directors 1870
National Federation of Self-Employed 2597
Union of Independent Companies..........3376
–see also specific trades and industries

EMPLOYMENT & RECRUITMENT

Association of Graduate Careers
  Advisory Services 269
Association of Graduate Recruiters 270
Association of Temporary & Interim
  Executive Services 425
Careers Research & Advisory Centre 1124
Federation of Recruitment &
  Employment Services 1562
Independent Schools Careers
  Organisation..........................1786
Institute of Careers Officers 1844
Institute of Employment Consultants 1874
National Association of Careers &
  Guidance Teachers.....................2419

EMPLOYMENT LAW & RIGHTS

Institute of Employment Rights 1875
Trades Union Congress 3360

ENDOCRINOLOGY

Society for Endocrinology 3114

ENERGY

Association for the Conservation of
  Energy 100
British Wind Energy Association 1089
Combined Heat & Power Association 1212
Energy Industries Council 1418
Energy Systems Trade Association 1419
Institute of Energy 1876
Institute of Petroleum 1942
National Energy Efficiency Association ...2566
Network for Alternative Technology &
  Technology Assessment 2693

Solar Energy Society 3260
Solar Trade Association 3261
—see also specific aspects eg NUCLEAR ENERGY

ENGINEERING

Association of Consulting Engineers 219
Association of Cost Engineers 225
British Council of Maintenance
    Associations........................... 680
Commonwealth Engineers Council 1227
Confederation of Associations of
    Specialist Engineering Contractors 1245
Conference of Heavy Engineering
    Industries Abnormal Loads Committee ...1254
Contractors Mechanical Plant Engineers ...1271
Council of Mechanical & Metal Trades
    Associations...........................1307
Engineering Council 1420
Engineering Employers' Federation 1421
Engineering Equipment & Materials
    Users Association......................1422
Engineering Industries Association 1423
Federation of Engineering Design
    Companies 1538
Fellowship of Engineering 1570
Institute of Engineers & Technicians 1877
Institution of British Engineers 2003
Institution of Engineering Designers.......2013
Institution of Incorporated Executive
    Engineers 2021
Institution of Mechanical Engineers 2024
Institution of Mechanical Incorporated
    Engineers 2025
Institution of Mining Electrical & Mining
    Mechanical Engineers 2027
International Association for Vehicle
    System Dynamics......................2054
International Society for Boundary
    Elements 2168
International Society for Soil Mechanics
    & Foundation Engineering..............2171
National Association of Industrial
    Distributors..........................2452
National Engineering Construction
    Employers' Association 2567
North East Coast Institution of
    Engineers & Shipbuilders..............2699
Scottish Engineering Employers'
    Association...........................3021
Society of Chief Electrical & Mechanical
    Engineers in Local Government 3166
Society of Engineers 3189
Society of Environmental Engineers 3190
Society of Professional Engineers 3234
United Kingdom Module Constructors
    Association...........................3402
Women's Engineering Society 3464
—see also specific aspects

ENTERTAINMENT & LEISURE ACTIVITIES

Alliance of British Clubs...................... 27
Association of Circus Proprietors of GB 203
Association of Directors of Recreation,
    Leisure & Tourism 239
Association of Entertainment & Arts
    Management 253
Association of London Clubs 319
Association of Recreation Managers 393
Association of Sun Tanning
    Organisations 415
British Arts Festivals Association 534
British Music Hall Society 894
Central Entertainment Agents Council 1143
Chief Leisure Officers Association..........1176
Council of Regional Arts Associations 1313
Entertainment Industry Suppliers
    Association...........................1443
Fairground Society........................1511
Institute of Entertainment & Arts
    Management 1878
Institute of Leisure & Amenity
    Management 1915
Leisure Studies Association.................2235
Personal Managers' Association.............2766
Ramblers Association.....................2860
Recreation Managers Association of GB ...2864
Showmen's Guild of GB 3089
Variety & Allied Entertainments Council
    of GB................................3425
—see also under individual activities eg THEATRE

ENTOMOLOGY

British Butterfly Conservation Society 632
British Dragonfly Society 704
Royal Entomological Society 2911
—see also BEES & BEE-KEEPING

ENVIRONMENTAL PROTECTION

Association of Environment Conscious
    Builders 254
British Association of Nature
    Conservationists 579
British Ecological Society 707
British Naturalists' Association 903
British Trust for Conservation Volunteers ...1063
Conservation Foundation 1257
Conservation Trust 1258
Council for Environmental Education 1292
Council for the Protection of Rural
    England 1301
Environment Council 1445
Industry & Environment Association........1803
Institute of Ecotechnics 1873
Institute of Environmental Assessment......1879
Institute of Freshwater Ecology 1893
Institution of Environmental Sciences 2016

International Centre for Conservation
   Education 2076
International Institute for Environment &
   Development 2130
Joint Committee of National Amenity
   Societies 2207
National Society for Clean Air &
   Environmental Protection, ... 2667
Natural Environment Research Council ... 2686
Open Spaces Society 2721
Professional Institutions Council for
   Conservation 2839
Royal Society for Nature Conservation ... 2944
United Kingdom Institute for
   Conservation 3396
–*see also* POLLUTION CONTROL

EPILEPSY

British Epilepsy Association 722
National Society for Epilepsy 2669

Ergonomics *see* MANAGEMENT &
   MANAGEMENT TRAINING

ESPERANTO

British Esperanto Association 726
Esperanto Teachers Association 1451

ESTATE AGENTS

Corporation of Estate Agents 1281
Estate Agents Services Association 1452
National Association of Estate Agents 2432
Property Consultants Society 2842

EXHIBITIONS & CONFERENCES

Agricultural Show Exhibitors'
   Association 22
Association of British Professional
   Conference Organisers 162
Association of Conference Executives 215
Association of Exhibition Organisers 257
Association of Show & Agricultural
   Organisations 407
British Association of Conference Towns 562
British Exhibition Contractors
   Association 729
British Exhibition Venues Association 730
European Federation of Conference
   Towns 1463
Exhibition Industry Federation 1494
National Exhibitors Association 2568
Simultaneous Interpretation Equipment
   Suppliers Association 3093

EXPLOSIVES

Association for Petroleum & Explosives
   Administration 91
Institute of Explosives Engineers 1882

EXPORT & IMPORT

British Exporters Association 731
British Importers Confederation 810
Export Buying Offices Association 1495
Institute of European Trade &
   Technology 1880
Institute of Export 1883

Fabric care *see* CLEANING TECHNOLOGY

Facsimile machines *see* OFFICE
   AUTOMATION & MANAGEMENT

Factoring *see* FINANCIAL SERVICES

Fairgrounds *see* ENTERTAINMENT &
   LEISURE ACTIVITIES

Family history *see* GENEALOGY &
   HERALDRY

FAMILY PLANNING

International Planned Parenthood
   Federation 2150

FARMING

Association of Agriculture 114
British Growers Association 778
British Organic Farmers Association 922
British Society of Animal Production 1014
Guild of Conservation Food Producers ...1691
International Farm Management
   Association 2102
International Sheepdog Society 2164
National Association of Breeders'
   Services 2416
National Cattle Breeders' Association 2520
National Farmers' Union 2569
National Farmers' Union of Scotland 2570
National Federation of City Farms 2573
National Federation of Young Farmers
   Clubs 2605
National Pig Breeders' Association 2647
National Sheep Association 2663
Permaculture Association 2761
Royal Association of British Dairy
   Farmers 2898

Snail Centre 3103
Society of Ploughmen 3231
Soil Association 3259
Tenant Farmers' Association 3328
Ulster Farmers' Union 3373
United Kingdom Irrigation Association ... 3397
World Jersey Cattle Bureau 3471
World Ploughing Organisation 3474
–see also AGRICULTURE and specific aspects

FARRIERS

Farriers Registration Council 1513
National Association of Farriers,
   Blacksmiths & Agricultural Engineers ... 2434

FASTENING DEVICES

Association of Stainless Fastener
   Distributors 411
Black Bolt & Nut Association of GB 488
British Industrial Fasteners Federation 817
British Turned-Parts Manufacturers
   Association 1069
National Association of Fastener
   Stockholders 2435
Power Fastenings Association 2814
Zip Fastener Manufacturers' Association ... 3490

FELT

Association of British Roofing Felt
   Manufacturers 164
Needleloom Felt Manufacturers'
   Association 2691
Pressed Felt Manufacturers Association ... 2822

FERTILISERS

Agricultural Lime Producers' Council 20
Fertiliser Manufacturers' Association 1576

Field sports *see* SPORT & SPORTS
   EQUIPMENT

FIELD STUDIES

Field Studies Council 1579
National Association of Field Studies
   Officers 2436
Scottish Field Studies Association 3025

Film industry *see* AUDIO/VISUAL
   INDUSTRIES

FILTRATION

Filtration Society 1583

FINANCIAL SERVICES

Association of British Factors &
   Discounters 139
Association of Company Registration
   Agents 214
Association of Consulting Actuaries 218
Association of Corporate Trustees 223
Association of International Bond
   Dealers 302
Association of Investment Trust
   Companies 303
Association of Invoice Factors 304
Association of Mortgage Lenders 344
Association of Property Unit Trusts 384
British Insurance & Investment Brokers'
   Association 839
British Merchant Banking & Securities
   Houses Association 882
British Venture Capital Association 1078
Corporation of Insurance & Financial
   Advisors 1282
Council of Mortgage Lenders 1310
Equipment Leasing Association 1449
European Food Brokers Association 1471
Faculty of Actuaries 1499
Federation of Commodity Associations 1532
Finance Houses Association 1584
Financial Intermediaries, Managers &
   Brokers Regulatory Authority 1585
Foreign Banks & Securities Houses
   Association 1614
Gilt Edged Market Makers Association
   Committee 1663
Insolvency Practitioners Association 1809
Institute of Actuaries 1821
Institute of Financial Planning 1889
Institute of Legal Cashiers 1913
Institutional Fund Managers'
   Association 2040
International Primary Market Association ... 2156
International Union of Credit &
   Investment Insurers 2188
Investment Managers Regulatory
   Organisation 2198
Investor Relations Society 2199
Life Assurance & Unit Trust Regulatory
   Authority 2241
London Discount Market Association 2269
London International Financial Futures
   Exchange 2275
Money Advice Association 2357
National Association of Investment
   Clubs 2456
National Conference of Friendly
   Societies 2533
National Pawnbrokers' Association 2644
Securities & Futures Authority 3079
Securities & Investments Board 3080
Society of Investment Analysts 3210
Soya Bean Meal Futures Association 3271
Sterling Brokers Association 3298

Unit Trust Association 3377
Wider Share Ownership Council 3457
–see also BANKING and other specific areas

Fingerprinting *see* FORENSIC SCIENCE

FIRE PROTECTION

Association of British Fire Trades 140
Association of Structural Fire Protection
    Contractors & Manufacturers 413
British Approvals for Fire Equipment 531
British Automatic Sprinkler Association 610
British Fire Protection Systems
    Association 747
British Fire Services Association 748
Chief & Assistant Chief Fire Officers
    Association 1174
Commonwealth & Overseas Fire
    Services Association 1224
Fire Extinguishing Trades Association 1588
Fire Industry Council .1590
Fire Protection Association 1591
Institution of Fire Engineers 2017
Intumescent Fire Seals Association 2197
National Association of Fire Officers 2437
Society of Fire Protection Engineers 3194

Fiscal studies *see* TAXATION

FISHING & FISH INDUSTRY

Angling Foundation 50
Angling Trade Association 51
Association of British Salted Fish Curers
    & Exporters 166
Association of Sea Fisheries Committees
    of England & Wales 403
British Trout Association 1062
European Fishing Tackle Trade
    Association 1468
Federation of British Kipperers, Herring
    Merchants & Herring Trade Quick
    Freezers Associations 1526
Federation of British Port Wholesale
    Fish Merchants Association 1527
Fisheries Society of the British Isles 1593
Fishing Boat Builders' Association 1594
Herring Buyers Association 1731
Institute of Fisheries Management 1890
International Association of Fish Meal
    Manufacturers 2060
London Fish Merchants Association 2272
National Anglers' Council 2382
National Federation of Anglers 2571
National Federation of Fishermen's
    Organisations 2579
National Federation of Inland Wholesale
    Fish Merchants 2585
National Federation of Sea Anglers 2596
Northern Ireland Retail Fish Trade
    Association 2709
Salmon & Trout Association 2972
Scottish Fishermen's Federation 3027
Scottish Pelagic Fishermens Association . . .3050
Scottish Salmon Smokers Association 3059
Shellfish Association of GB 3083
Shetland Salmon Farmers' Association . . .3085
Torry Research Station 3353

FLAGS

Flag Institute 1596

Flax *see* TEXTILE INDUSTRIES - GENERAL

FLOORING & FLOORCOVERING

Association of Oriental Carpet Traders of
    London 358
British Carpet Manufacturers'
    Association 639
British Carpets Export Council 640
British Floorcovering Manufacturers
    Association 750
British Home Furnishing Bureau 800
Contract Flooring Association 1270
National Federation of Terrazzo-Mosaic
    Specialists 2601
National Institute of Carpet Fitters 2624
Precast Flooring Federation 2819
Wholesale Floorcovering Distributors'
    Association 3455

Flour *see* BAKING INDUSTRY

FLOWERS & FLORISTRY

British Orchid Growers Association 921
British Retail Florists Association 978
Bulb Distributors Association 1105
Cottage Garden Society 1285
Flowers & Plants Association 1605
Garden History Society 1640
National Association of Flower
    Arrangement Societies of GB 2438
Rose Trade Association 2890
Royal National Rose Society 2934
Society of Floristry 3195

Flutes *see* MUSICAL INSTRUMENTS

Flying *see* AVIATION & AERONAUTICS

FOOD & BEVERAGES

British Association of Canned Food
  Importers & Distributors.................557
British Edible Pulse Association............708
British Food Export Council 756
British Frozen Food Federation 763
British Fruit Juice Importers Association 765
British Peanut Council 935
British Soft Drinks Association............1032
Campden Food & Drink Research
  Association.............................1119
Coffee Trade Federation 1200
Combined Edible Nut Trade Association ...1211
Delicatessen & Fine Food Association......1349
Federation of Oils, Seeds & Fats
  Associations...........................1555
Food & Drink Federation 1608
International Association of Seed
  Crushers 2066
International Coffee Organization 2081
International Tea Committee 2177
Lard Association 2222
National Association of Perry Makers 2470
Pizza & Pasta Association 2791
Salt Manufacturers Association 2973
Snack, Nut & Crisp Manufacturers
  Association.............................3102
Tea Brokers Association of London 3321
Tea Buyers' Association 3322
Tea Council 3323
Tea Producers Association.................3324
United Kingdom Association of Frozen
  Food Producers........................3382
United Kingdom Renderers' Association ...3411
United Kingdom Rice Standards
  Association.............................3412
United Kingdom Tea Association 3417
Vinegar Brewers' Federation 3432
—see also HEALTH FOODS and specific aspects

FOOD SCIENCE

Institute of Food Science & Technology
  of the UK 1891

FOOTBALL & FOOTBALL POOLS

English Schools Football Association.......1436
Football Association 1610
Pool Promoters Association 2806
Referees' Association 2865
Rugby Football Union 2966

FOOTWEAR

Boot & Shoe Manufacturers'
  Association.............................498
British Footwear Manufacturers
  Federation.............................757
Clothing & Footwear Institute 1195

Footwear Components Federation 1612
Footwear Distributors Federation..........1613
Independent Footwear Retailers'
  Association.............................1779
Instock Footwear Suppliers Association ...2041
London Footwear Manufacturers
  Association.............................2273
Multiple Shoe Retailers' Association 2368
Society of Master Shoe Repairers 3219

FORENSIC SCIENCE

Association of Police Surgeons 369
Fingerprint Society.......................1587
Forensic Science Society 1617

FORESTRY

Arboricultural Association 58
Association of Professional Foresters 378
British Christmas Tree Growers
  Association.............................658
Council of Forest Industries of British
  Columbia..............................1305
Forestry Industry Committee of GB 1618
Institute of Chartered Foresters 1850
National Small Woods Association.........2665
Royal Forestry Society of England,
  Wales & N Ireland 2913
Royal Scottish Forestry Society 2939
Tree Council.............................3368
—see also WOOD & WOODWORKING

Foundry trades *see* METALLURGY

FOUNTAINS

Fountain Society.........................1624

Foxhunting *see* DOGS, DOG RACING &
HUNTING

FRANCHISING

British Franchise Association 761

Freight *see* MATERIALS HANDLING

FRUIT & VEGETABLES

Fruit Importers Association 1628
Mushroom Growers' Association..........2371
National Association of Seed Potato
  Merchants.............................2484
National Dried Fruit Trade Association ...2560
National Federation of Fruit & Potato
  Trades................................2581

National Institute of Fresh Produce 2626
Nuclear Stock Association 2713
Processed Vegetable Growers
    Association............................2828
Processors' & Growers' Research
    Organisation..........................2830
Produce Packaging & Marketing
    Association............................2832
Retail Fruit Trade Federation..............2880
Wellesbourne Vegetable Research
    Association............................3449

Fruit juice see FOOD & BEVERAGES

FUEL

Chamber of Coal Traders 1153
Solid Smokeless Fuels Federation 3263
–see also specific fuels

FUND RAISING

Institute of Charity Fund Raising
    Managers 1847

Funerals see BURIAL & CREMATION

FUR

British Fur Trade Association 766
Fur Education Council 1630
International Fur Trade Federation 2122

FURNITURE & UPHOLSTERY

Association of Master Upholsterers.......... 335
Association of Suppliers to the Furniture
    Industry 417
Basketware Importers Association.......... 469
Blanket Manufacturers Association 489
British Contract Furnishing Association ... 676
British Furniture Manufacturers'
    Federation Associations 767
British Home Furnishing Bureau 800
Castor Manufacturers (UK) Association ...1127
Furniture Industry Research Association ...1632
Leisure & Outdoor Furniture Association ...2234
Master Carvers Association 2310
National Association of Retail Furnishers ...2480
National Bed Federation..................2514
National Fillings Trades Association 2607
Northern Furniture Manufacturers
    Association............................2700
Strip Curtain Suppliers Association........3304

FURNITURE REMOVAL & STORAGE

British Association of Removers 594

Institute of the Furniture Warehousing &
    Removing Industry 1984

Gambling see BETTING & GAMBLING

GAME & GAMEKEEPING

Game Conservancy Trust 1635
Game Farmers Association 1636
National Game Dealers Association 2610

GARAGE EQUIPMENT

Garage Equipment Association.............1638
Petrol Pump Manufacturers Association ...2770

Garden administration see PARKS &
    GROUNDS ADMINISTRATION

Gardening see HORTICULTURE; FLOWERS
    & FLORISTRY

GAS INDUSTRY

Council for the Registration of Gas
    Installers 1302
Gas Consumers Council 1643
Institution of Gas Engineers 2018
National Joint Industrial Council for the
    Gas Industry..........................2634
Society of British Gas Industries 3152

Gauges see SCIENTIFIC INSTRUMENTS

GENEALOGY & HERALDRY

Association of Genealogists & Record
    Agents 265
British Record Society 972
Federation of Family History Societies......1544
Heraldry Society 1729
Institute of Heraldic & Genealogical
    Studies...............................1899
Society of Antiquaries....................3136
Society of Antiquaries of Scotland 3137
Society of Genealogists 3197

Generating equipment see ELECTRICAL
    TRADES

GEOGRAPHY

Association of British Climatologists 130
British Cartographic Society 641
Geographical Association..................1659

GEOGRAPHY

Institute of British Geographers 1840
International Map Collectors Society 2140
Remote Sensing Society 2875
Royal Geographical Society 2914
Royal Scottish Geographical Society 2940
Scottish Association of Geography
    Teachers 2999

GEOLOGY

British Geological Survey 769
British Geotechnical Society 770
Earth Science Teachers Association 1390
Geological Society 1660
Geologists Association 1661
Institution of Geologists 2019
Institution of Mining & Metallurgy 2026
Palaeontographical Society 2744
Palaeontological Association 2745

GLACIOLOGY

International Glaciological Society 2124

GLASS

British Glass Confederation 772
China & Glass Retailers' Association 1178
European Glass Container
    Manufacturers' Committee 1474
Flat Glass Council 1597
Flat Glass Manufacturers Association 1598
Glass & Allied Trades Association 1666
Glass & Glazing Federation 1667
National Joint Council for the Flat Glass
    Industry 2631
Scottish Glass Association 3029
Society of Glass Technology 3198

GLIDING & HANG GLIDING

British Association of Paragliding Clubs 587
British Gliding Association 773
British Hang Gliding & Paragliding
    Association 783

Glucose see SUGAR & SUGAR PRODUCTS

GOATS

British Angora Goat Society 527
British Goat Society 774

GOLF & GOLF COURSES

Association of Golf Club Secretaries 267
British & International Golf
    Greenkeepers' Association 504

British Association of Golf Course
    Architects 570
British Association of Golf Course
    Constructors 571
Golf Ball Manufacturers Conference 1671
National Association of Public Golf
    Courses 2476
National Golf Clubs Advisory
    Association 2612
Professional Golfers' Association 2838

Graphic arts see PRINTING & PRINTING
EQUIPMENT

Graphic design see DESIGN

Greeting cards see STATIONERY & ALLIED
PRODUCTS

GROCERY TRADES

British Independent Grocers Association 812
Institute of Grocery Distribution 1894
Joint Industrial Council for the
    Wholesale Grocery & Provision Trade . . . 2209
Scottish Federation of Grocers' & Wine
    Merchants Associations 3022
Scottish Grocers Federation 3030
Scottish Provision Trade Association 3057
Voluntary Group Association 3436
Wholesale Grocers' Association of
    Scotland 3456

GUNS & SHOOTING

British Association for Shooting &
    Conservation 548
Clay Pigeon Shooting Association 1190
Great Britain Pistol Council 1678
Great Britain Target Shooting Federation . . . 1679
Gun Trade Association 1708
Historical Breechloading Smallarms
    Association 1736
Muzzle Loaders Association of GB 2378
National Pistol Association 2648
National Rifle Association 2659
National Small-Bore Rifle Association 2666
Scottish Shooting Council 3063
Vintage Arms Association 3433

GYNAECOLOGY & OBSTETRICS

Royal College of Obstetricians &
    Gynaecologists 2903

GYPSIES

Advisory Council for the Education of
 Romany & other Travellers 11
Association of Gypsy Organisations 273
Romani Institute 2888

HAIRDRESSING

British Association of Professional
 Hairdressing Employers.................. 592
Guild of Hairdressers 1695
Hairdressing Council 1710
Hairdressing Manufacturers' &
 Wholesalers' Association 1711
Institute of Trichologists................... 1994
National Hairdressers' Federation 2613

HALLMARKING

British Hallmarking Council................. 781

Handkerchieves *see* TEXTILE INDUSTRIES - GENERAL

Hang gliding *see* GLIDING & HANG GLIDING

Harbours *see* PORTS, DOCKS & HARBOURS

HARDWARE

British Hardware & Housewares
 Manufacturers' Association 785
British Hardware Federation 786
National Institute of Hardware 2627

Harps *see* MUSICAL INSTRUMENTS

HATS & HEADWEAR

British Hat Guild.......................... 787

Hay *see* AGRICULTURE

Health *see* HEALTHCARE AND SPECIFIC ASPECTS

HEALTH CLUBS

Fitness Industry Association 1595

HEALTH FOODS

British Health Food Trade Association 791
Health Food Manufacturers' Association ...1720
National Association of Health Stores 2446
Organic Food Manufacturers Federation ...2728

HEALTHCARE, PRIVATE

Association of British Health Care
 Industries 142
Association of Registered Care Homes 394
British Federation of Care Home
 Proprietors 736
British Health Care Association 789
Independent Healthcare Association........ 1780
Joint Care Committee 2206
National Care Homes Association 2518
Registered Nursing Home Association...... 2873
United Kingdom Home Care Association ...3393

HEALTHCARE, PUBLIC

Ambulance Service Institute 46
Association of Community Health
 Councils for England & Wales 211
Association of County Public Health
 Officers 230
Association of Directors of Public Health 238
Association of General Practitioner
 Community Hospitals 266
Association of Health Care Information
 & Medical Records Officers 276
Association of Public Analysts 385
Association of Public Analysts of
 Scotland 386
Association of Scottish Local Health
 Councils 402
British Association of Operating
 Department Assistants 582
English National Board for Nursing,
 Midwifery & Health Visiting 1433
Guild of Hospital Pharmacists 1696
Health Visitors' Association 1721
Healthcare Financial Management
 Association............................ 1722
Institute of Health Services Management ...1898
Institute of Physical Sciences in
 Medicine.............................. 1944
Institution of Environmental Health
 Officers 2015
National Association of Health
 Authorities 2445
National Association of Health Service
 Personnel Officers 2444
National Association of National Health
 Care Supplies Managers................. 2466
Royal Environmental Health Institute of
 Scotland 2912
Royal Institute of Public Health &
 Hygiene.............................. 2926

HEALTHCARE, PUBLIC

Society of Community Health Council
  Staff 3170
Society of Public Health 3236
—see also specific aspects eg HOSPITALS

HEARING AIDS

Hearing Aid Council 1723
Hearing Aid Industry Association 1724
Society of Hearing Aid Audiologists 3201

HEARING DISABILITIES

British Association of Teachers of the
  Deaf 602
British Association of the Hard of
  Hearing 603
British Deaf Association 689
British Tinnitus Association 1058
Council for the Advancement of
  Communication with Deaf People 1300
International Audiology Society to Help
  the Deaf 2071
National Association of Deafened
  People 2429
National Deaf Childrens' Society 2558
Royal Association in Aid of Deaf People . . . 2897
Royal National Institute for the Deaf 2933

HEATING & VENTILATING

Association of British Solid Fuel
  Appliance Manufacturers 169
Association of Installers & Unvented
  Hot Water Systems (Scotland &
  Ireland) 298
Association of Shell Boilermakers 405
Boiler & Radiator Manufacturers
  Association 492
British Industrial Furnace Constructors
  Association 818
British National Committee for
  Electroheat 900
Combined Heat & Power Association 1212
Decorative Gas Fire Manufacturers
  Association 1345
Domestic Heating Council 1375
Domestic Heating Society 1376
Heating & Ventilating Contractors'
  Association 1725
Heating, Ventilating & Air Conditioning
  Manufacturers' Association 1726
Institute of Domestic Heating &
  Environmental Engineers 1871
National Association of Plumbing,
  Heating & Mechanical Services
  Contractors 2471
—see also INSULATION

Helicopters see AVIATION & AERONAUTICS

Heraldry see GENEALOGY & HERALDRY

HERBS & HERBALISM

British Herbal Medicine Association 795
Herb Society 1730
National Institute of Medical Herbalists . . . 2628

HISTORIC BUILDINGS PRESERVATION

Ancient Monuments Society 49
Association for Studies in the
  Conservation of Historic Buildings 97
Association for the Study & Preservation
  of Roman Mosaics 107
Church Monuments Society 1182
Country Houses Association 1318
Folly Fellowship 1607
Fortress Study Group 1621
Historic Houses Association 1734
International Council on Monuments &
  Sites 2098
International Institute for Conservation
  of Historic & Artistic Works 2129
Joint Committee of National Amenity
  Societies 2207
Scottish Society for Conservation &
  Restoration 3064
Society for the Protection of Ancient
  Buildings 3131

HISTORY

Association of Contemporary Historians 221
British Agricultural History Society 521
British Association for Local History 546
British Society for the History of
  Medicine 1011
British Society for the History of Science . . . 1010
Ecclesiastical History Society 1391
Economic History Society 1393
Furniture History Society 1631
Historical Association 1735
Historical Metallurgy Society 1738
Institute of Contemporary History 1866
Joint Association of Classical Teachers 2204
Manorial Society of GB 2297
Police History Society 2804
Postal History Society 2809
Printing Historical Society 2824
Royal Historical Society 2916
Social History Society of the UK 3106
Society for the Social History of
  Medicine 3132
Society of Antiquaries 3136
Society of Antiquaries of Scotland 3137
Society of Archer-Antiquaries 3139
Society of Jewellery Historians 3211
Tool & Trades History Society 3352
—see also specific aspects eg ARCHIVES

Holidays see TRAVEL, TOURISM & HOLIDAYS

HOME ECONOMICS

Association of Higher Education
  Institutions Concerned with Home
  Economics 279
Institute of Home Economics 1902
National Association of Teachers of
  Home Economics 2494
United Kingdom Home Economics
  Federation.............................. 3394

HOMOEOPATHY

British Homoeopathic Association 801
Faculty of Homoeopathy 1508
Society of Homoeopaths 3202

Honey see SUGAR & SUGAR PRODUCTS

Hops see BEER & BREWING

Horns see MUSICAL INSTRUMENTS

Horology see CLOCKS & WATCHES

HORSES, HORSE RACING & RIDING

Arab Horse Society 57
Association of British Riding Schools 163
British Equestrian Federation 723
British Equestrian Trade Association........ 724
British Horse Society...................... 805
British Show Jumping Association......... 997
Jockeys' Association of GB 2203
National Pony Society 2650
National Trainers Federation 2678
Point-to-Point Secretaries Association ...2802
Racecourse Association 2852
Racehorse Owners Association 2853
Thoroughbred Breeders' Association 3342
World Arabian Horse Organisation 3468

HORTICULTURE

Bedding Plant Growers Association 478
British Association of Landscape
  Industries 576
British Association of Seed Analysts 595
British Seeds Council 994
British Society of Plant Breeders.......... 1028
British Sugar Beet Seed Producers
  Association............................1040
Commercial Horticulture Association 1215

Federation of Garden & Leisure
  Manufacturers 1546
Garden Centre Association 1639
Garden Industry Manufacturers
  Association............................1641
Garden Machinery Association........... 1642
Good Gardeners Association............. 1672
Guernsey Growers Association........... 1681
Horticultural Trades Association 1748
Institute of Horticulture 1904
National Association for Organic
  Gardening.............................2393
National Council for the Conservation of
  Plants & Gardens 2545
National Federation of City Farms......... 2573
National Society of Allotment & Leisure
  Gardeners 2670
Professional Gardeners Guild 2837
Professional Plant Users Group 2841
Royal Horticultural Society 2917
Scottish Seed & Nursery Trade
  Association............................3062
Society of Garden Designers.............. 3196
Soil Association 3259
Wellesbourne Vegetable Research
  Association............................3449
–see also specific aspects

Hosiery see TEXTILE INDUSTRIES -
  HOSIERY & KNITWEAR

HOSPITALS

Association of General Practitioner
  Community Hospitals 266
Council for Music in Hospitals............. 1294
Institute of Hospital Engineering 1905
International Hospital Federation........... 2128
National Association of Health Estate
  Managers 2443
National Association of Hospital
  Broadcasting Organisations............. 2450
National Association of Hospital Fire
  Officers 2451

HOTEL & CATERING EQUIPMENT

British Amusement Catering Trades
  Association............................ 525
Catering Equipment Distributors
  Association of GB 1128
Catering Equipment Manufacturers
  Association............................1129
European Catering Association............. 1457
Microwave Association................... 2341

HOTEL & CATERING MANAGEMENT

Association of Domestic Management....... 247

Association of Marine Catering
Superintendents 331
British Association of Hotel Accountants 573
British Association of Hotel Reservations
Representatives 574
British Federation of Hotel, Guest House
& Self-Catering Associations 738
British Hotels, Restaurants & Caterers
Association 806
Catering Managers Association of GB 1130
Catering Teachers' Association 1131
Civic Catering Association 1187
Corporate Hospitality Association 1280
European Motel Federation 1483
Hotel, Catering & Institutional
Management Association 1753
Mobile & Outside Caterers Association
of GB 2353
National Federation of Fish Friers 2578
Northern Ireland Hotels & Caterers
Association 2707
Restaurateurs Association of GB 2877
Society of Catering & Hotel
Management Consultants 3162
United Kingdom Standing Conference
on Hospitality Management Education . . . 3415

HOUSING

Institute of Housing 1906
Institute of Rent Officers 1962
National Federation of Housing
Associations 2584
National Federation of Housing Co-
operatives 2583
National Home Improvement Council 2615
National Housing & Town Planning
Council 2617
National Tenants Organization 2675
National Union of Residents'
Association 2681
Scottish National Housing & Town
Planning Council 3046

HUMANISM

British Humanist Association 807

Hunting see DOGS, DOGRACING &
HUNTING

HYDRAULICS & HYDROMECHANICS

British Fluid Power Association 752
British Fluid Power Distributors
Association 753
British National Committee on Large
Dams 902
International Powered Access Federation . . . 2152

HYDROLOGY

Hydrological Society 1756
Institute of Hydrology 1907

HYPNOSIS & HYPNOTHERAPY

British Hypnotherapy Association 808
British Society of Experimental &
Clinical Hypnosis 1020
British Society of Hypnotherapists 1022
British Society of Medical & Dental
Hypnosis 1023
Federation of Ethical Stage Hypnotists . . . 1542
National College of Hypnosis &
Psychotherapy 2530
National Council of Psychotherapists &
Hypnotherapy Register 2550
National Register of Hypnotherapists &
Psychotherapists 2654

ICE CREAM

Ice Cream Alliance 1757
Ice Cream Federation 1758

Ice hockey see SPORT & SPORTS
EQUIPMENT

Importing see EXPORT & IMPORT

Income tax see TAXATION

INDEXING

Society of Indexers 3205

INDUSTRIAL RELATIONS

Confederation of British Industry 1247
Industrial Participation Association 1798
Industrial Society 1800
Trades Union Congress 3360
–see also specific branches of industry

INFORMATION MANAGEMENT

Association for Education & Training
Technology 81
Association for Information Management 85
Association of British Library &
Information Studies Schools 148
Association of Information Officers in
the Pharmaceutical Industry 297
British Urban & Regional Information
Systems Association 1072
Centre for Information Media &
Technology 1145

Confederation of Information
   Communication Industries 1249
European Information Association 1475
Institute for Scientific Information 1816
Institute of Information Scientists 1908
Institute of Scientific & Technical
   Communicators 1971
International Council for Technical
   Communication 2093
–*see also* LIBRARY SCIENCE

Information technology *see* COMPUTER
SCIENCE & DATA PROCESSING

Inland waterways *see* WATERWAYS,
INLAND

Insects *see* ENTOMOLOGY

Instruments *see* SCIENTIFIC INSTRUMENTS

INSULATION

Asbestos Removal Contractors
   Association 70
Draught Proofing Advisory Association   . . . 1380
External Wall Insulation Association 1497
National Association of Loft Insulation
   Contractors 2462
National Cavity Insulation Association 2522
Phenolic Foam Manufacturers
   Association 2776
Thermal Insulation Contractors
   Association 3340
Thermal Insulation Manufacturers &
   Suppliers Association 3341
United Kingdom Mineral Wool
   Association 3401

INSURANCE

Associated Scottish Life Offices 72
Association of Average Adjusters 121
Association of British Insurers 144
Association of Brokers & Yacht Agents   176
Association of Burglary Insurance
   Surveyors 180
Association of Insurance & Risk
   Managers in Industry & Commerce 299
Aviation Insurance Offices' Association   . . . 456
British Insurance & Investment Brokers'
   Association 839
British Insurance Law Association 840
Chartered Institute of Loss Adjusters 1161
Chartered Insurance Institute 1168
Institute of Chartered Shipbrokers 1852
Institute of Insurance Brokers 1909

Institute of London Underwriters 1918
Institute of Public Loss Assessors 1953
Institute of Risk Management 1963
Insurance Adjusters Association 2042
Insurance Brokers Registration Council   . . . 2043
Insurance Institute of London 2044
International Union of Aviation Insurers   . . . 2187
International Union of Credit &
   Investment Insurers 2188
Life Insurance Association 2242
Lloyd's Aviation Underwriters'
   Association 2256
Lloyd's Motor Underwriters' Association   . . . 2257
Lloyd's Underwriters Association 2258
Lloyd's Underwriters' Non-Marine
   Association 2259
London Insurance & Reinsurance
   Market Association 2274
United Kingdom Credit Insurance
   Brokers' Committee 3386

INTELLECTUAL PROPERTY

Advertising Film Rights Society 7
Association of European Trade Mark
   Proprietors 256
British Copyright Council 677
British Videogram Association 1080
Chartered Institute of Patent Agents 1164
Federation against Copyright Theft 1515
Institute for Social Inventions 1817
Institute of International Licensing
   Practitioners 1911
Institute of Inventors 1912
Institute of Patentees & Inventors 1940
Institute of Trade Mark Agents 1986
International Association for the
   Protection of Industrial Property 2053
International Federation of the
   Phonographic Industry 2118
Licensing Executives Society 2240
Mechanical-Copyright Protection
   Society 2324
Performing Right Society 2759
Scottish Woollen Trade Mark
   Association 3074
Trade Mark Owners Association 3358
Trade Marks Patents & Designs
   Federation 3359

INTERFIRM COMPARISON

Centre for Interfirm Comparison 1147

INTERNATIONAL AFFAIRS

Institute for International Research 1815
International Institute for Strategic
   Studies 2131
Royal Institute of International Affairs 2920

Interpreters *see* LANGUAGES

INTRODUCTION AGENCIES
Association of British Introduction
    Agencies 145

Inventions *see* INTELLECTUAL PROPERTY

Investment *see* FINANCIAL SERVICES

Iron *see* METALLURGY

Irrigation *see* WATER & WATER
TREATMENT

Issuing houses *see* BANKING

Jazz *see* MUSIC

JEWELLERY
Art Metalware Manufacturers'
    Association 65
British Association of Cultured Pearl
    Importers 564
British Jewellers' Association 851
British Jewellery & Giftware Federation 852
Gemmological Association of GB 1645
Giftware Association 1662
Jewellery Distributors' Association of
    GB 2202
National Association of Goldsmiths 2440

Journalism *see* WRITERS

JUDO
British Judo Association 853
British Judo Council 854

JUTE
Association of Jute Spinners &
    Manufacturers 305
Jute Importers' Association 2213
Jute Spinners & Manufacturers
    Association 2214
London Jute Association 2276
United Kingdom Jute Goods
    Association 3398

Kitchens *see* BUILDING EQUIPMENT &
MATERIALS

Knitwear *see* TEXTILE INDUSTRIES -
HOSIERY & KNITWEAR

LABORATORY EQUIPMENT & TECHNOLOGY
Association of British Steriliser
    Manufacturers 171
British Laboratory Ware Association 858
British Society of Scientific
    Glassblowers 1030
Institute of Medical Laboratory Sciences . . . 1932
Institute of Science Technology 1970
–see also SCIENTIFIC INSTRUMENTS

Lace *see* TEXTILE INDUSTRIES - GENERAL

LADDERS
British Ladder Manufacturers
    Association 860

Land usage *see* ARGRICULTURE; FARMING

Landscape *see* TOWN & COUNTRY
PLANNING

LANGUAGES
Association for Language Learning 86
Association of Hispanists of GB &
    Ireland 280
Association of Police & Court
    Interpreters 368
Association of University Professors of
    French & Heads of French
    Departments 431
British Association for Soviet Slavonic &
    East European Studies 549
British Association of State Colleges in
    English Language Teaching 599
British Interlingua Society 842
Centre for Information on Language
    Teaching & Research 1146
Conference of University Teachers of
    German in GB & Ireland 1256
Institute of Linguists 1916
Institute of Translation & Interpreting 1990
International Association of University
    Professors of English 2069
International Federation for Modern
    Languages & Literatures 2103
International Phonetic Association 2149

Linguistics Association of GB.............2251
Modern Humanities Research
  Association............................2354
National Association of Language
  Advisers..............................2457
Philological Society.....................2778
Translators Association..................3363
—see also CLASSICAL STUDIES; ESPERANTO

Laundries & launderettes *see* CLEANING
  TECHNOLOGY

LAW & LEGAL SERVICES

Agricultural Law Association 19
Association of Law Costs Draftsmen 306
Association of Law Teachers 307
Association of Legal Personnel 309
Bar Association for Commerce, Finance
  & Industry............................. 465
Bar Association for Local Government...... 466
Barristers' Clerks' Association 468
British Academy of Experts 507
British Institute of International &
  Comparative Law 827
Commonwealth Lawyers Association 1229
Commonwealth Magistrates' & Judges'
  Association........................... 1230
Coroners' Society of England & Wales   ...1279
Council for Licensed Conveyancers 1293
Criminal Bar Association 1335
European Food Law Association 1472
Faculty of Advocates..................... 1500
General Council of the Bar 1651
Immigration Law Practitioners'
  Association........................... 1760
Institute of Legal Executives 1914
International Bar Association 2072
International Law Association 2138
International Property Lawyers
  Association........................... 2158
Justices' Clerks' Society 2212
Law Centres Federation 2223
Law Society 2224
Law Society of Scotland 2225
National Association of Sole
  Practitioners......................... 2488
Procurators Fiscal Society 2831
Scottish Law Agents Society 3037
Society of Construction Law 3173
Society of Public Notaries of London 3237
Society of Public Teachers of Law 3238
Society of Solicitors in the Supreme
  Courts of Scotland.................... 3245
Statute Law Society 3290
United Kingdom Environmental Law
  Association........................... 3388
—see also MAGISTRATES

LAWN TENNIS

Lawn Tennis Association 2226

LAWNMOWERS

British Lawnmower Manufacturers
  Federation.............................. 862

LEAD & LEAD PRODUCTS

European Lead Development Committee ...1478
International Lead & Zinc Study Group   ...2139
Lead Contractors Association 2227
Lead Development Association 2228
Lead Sheet Association 2229
Lead Smelters & Refiners Association 2230

LEATHER

British Leather Confederation 864
British Leathergoods Manufacturers
  Association.............................865
International Council of Hides & Skins
  Traders Association 2096
Leather Producers' Association 2232
Master Tanners Association................2315
National Federation of Hide & Skin
  Markets 2582
Skin Hide & Leather Traders Association ...3098
Society of Leather Technologists &
  Chemists...............................3213
United Kingdom Fellmongers
  Association.............................3391

Legal services *see* LAW & LEGAL SERVICES

Leisure activities *see* ENTERTAINMENT &
  LEISURE ACTIVITIES

LIBRARY SCIENCE

Association for Information Management 85
Association of Assistant Librarians 118
Association of British Library &
  Information Studies Schools.............. 148
Association of British Theological &
  Philosophical Libraries 173
Association of Independent Libraries 288
Association of London Chief Librarians   318
Association of UK Media Librarians 430
Bibliographical Society..................... 480
British & Irish Association of Law
  Librarians 505
International Association of Music
  Libraries................................2062
Librarians of Institutes & Schools of
  Education 2237
Library Association........................2238

Marine Librarians' Association 2302
School Library Association 2982
Scottish Library Association 3038
Society of County Children's &
    Education Librarians 3177
Society of County Librarians..............3178
–see also INFORMATION MANAGEMENT

LICENSED TRADES

British Institute of Innkeeping 825
Incorporated Society of Licensed Trade
    Stocktakers.............................1770
National Association of Licensed House
    Managers 2459
National Licensed Victuallers'
    Association.............................2636
Scottish Licensed Trade Association 3039
Society of Licensed Victuallers.............3214
United Kingdom Bartenders Guild..........3384

Licensing practice see INTELLECTUAL
PROPERTY

LIFTING & LOADING EQUIPMENT

Association of Loading & Elevating
    Equipment Manufacturers 315
Federation of Manufacturers of
    Construction Equipment & Cranes 1549
Lifting Equipment Engineers Association ...2243
National Association of Lift Makers 2460

LIGHTING

Association of Lighting Designers...........312
Association of Street Lighting
    Contractors.............................412
Decorative Lighting Association 1346
Film & Television Lighting Contractors
    Association.............................1581
Institution of Lighting Engineers 2023
Lighting Industry Federation...............2247
National Association of Sound &
    Lighting Companies.....................2490
National Illumination Committee of GB ...2618
Society of Television Lighting Directors ...3250

Linen see TEXTILE INDUSTRIES - GENERAL

Linguistics see LANGUAGES

LITERATURE & POETRY

Alliance of Literary Societies.................30
British Fantasy Society 734
British Science Fiction Association 989

English Association 1426
Folklore Society 1606
International Federation for Modern
    Languages & Literatures.................2103
Poetry Society 2801
Royal Society of Literature 2951
Schools Poetry Association 2985
Scottish Poetry Library Association 3054

Loading equipment see LIFTING &
LOADING EQUIPMENT

LOCAL GOVERNMENT

Association of Charter Trustees & Urban
    Parish Councils 193
Association of Chief Technical Officers 200
Association of Conservation Officers 216
Association of Councillors...................226
Association of County Chief Executives 228
Association of County Councils.............229
Association of County Supplies Officers 231
Association of Direct Labour
    Organisations 236
Association of District Council
    Treasurers 244
Association of District Councils 245
Association of District Secretaries 246
Association of London Authorities 316
Association of London Borough
    Engineers & Surveyors 317
Association of Metropolitan Authorities 342
Association of Registrars of Scotland........396
Borough Engineers' Society 499
Convention of Scottish Local Authorities ...1272
County Surveyors' Society.................1325
District Auditors' Society 1369
District Council Technical Association......1370
District Planning Officers' Society.........1371
Local Authority Caterers Association 2260
Local Government Management Board ...2262
London Boroughs Association 2268
National Association of Local Councils ...2461
Society of Chief Architects of Local
    Authorities 3164
Society of Chief Building Regulation
    Officers 3165
Society of Chief Electrical & Mechanical
    Engineers in Local Government 3166
Society of Chief Personnel Officers 3167
Society of Chief Quantity Surveyors in
    Local Government 3168
Society of County Secretaries.............3179
Society of County Treasurers 3181
Society of Information Technology
    Managers 3208
Society of Local Authority Chief
    Executives..............................3215
Society of Local Council Clerks...........3216
Society of Metropolitan Treasurers 3222

LOCKS

British Lock Manufacturers Association 868
Master Locksmiths Association 2312

LONG RANGE PLANNING

Strategic Planning Society.................3303

Lubricants *see* PETROLEUM & OIL TECHNOLOGY

Lutes *see* MUSICAL INSTRUMENTS

MACHINE TOOLS

Advanced Manufacturing Technology
 Research Institute..........................4
Association of European Machine Tool
 Merchants................................255
Machine Tool Technologies Association ...2285

Machinery *see* PLANT, INDUSTRIAL AND SPECIFIC MACHINE-USING TRADES

MAGISTRATES

Association of Magisterial Officers..........320
Association of Magistrates' Courts..........321
Magistrates' Association...................2288

MAIL ORDER TRADING

Association of Mail Order Publishers........322
Mail Order Traders' Association............2290
Mail Users' Association...................2291

Malt *see* WINES & SPIRITS

Man-made fibres *see* TEXTILE INDUSTRIES
 - GENERAL

MANAGEMENT & MANAGEMENT TRAINING

Association for Management Education
 & Development...........................88
Association of Business Administration
 Studies.................................181
Association of Business Executives..........184
Association of Facilities Managers..........258
Association of Incorporated Managers &
 Administrators..........................282
Association of Quality Management
 Consultants............................389
Association of Relocation Agents...........398

British Association for Commercial &
 Industrial Education.....................539
British Business Graduates Society..........631
British Educational Management &
 Administration Society...................710
British Institute of Management............829
British Junior Chamber....................855
Confederation of British Industry..........1247
Consultative Council of Professional
 Management Organisations..............1266
Ergonomics Society.......................1450
Faculty of Business Education.............1504
Foundation for Management Education ...1622
Industrial Participation Association.........1798
Industrial Society........................1800
Institute for Consumer Ergonomics........1812
Institute for International
 Communication........................1814
Institute of Commerce....................1860
Institute of Commercial Management......1861
Institute of Directors.....................1870
Institute of Facilities Management.........1884
Institute of Financial & Management
 Studies...............................1887
Institute of Management Consultants......1921
Institute of Management Services.........1922
Institute of Management Specialists.......1923
Institute of Manpower Studies............1924
Institute of Supervisory Management.......1979
Institute of Training & Development.......1988
Institution of Industrial Managers.........2022
International Federation of Business &
 Professional Women....................2107
International Federation of Training &
 Development Organisations..............2120
Management Consultancies Association ...2295
Manpower Society........................2298
Professional Business & Technical
 Management...........................2835
Society of Teachers in Business
 Education.............................3248
Strategic Planning Society.................3303
United Kingdom Federation of Business
 & Professional Women..................3389

Maps & mapping *see* GEOGRAPHY

MARINE BIOLOGY

Scottish Marine Biological Association ...3040

MARINE ENGINEERING

Association of Marine Engineering
 Schools................................332
British Nautical Instrument Trade
 Association.............................904
Institute of Marine Engineers.............1925
International Ship Electric Service
 Association............................2165

Marine Engine & Equipment
  Manufacturers' Association 2301
Marine Society 2303
Society of Consulting Marine Engineers
  & Ship Surveyors 3174
–see also SHIPS & SHIPPING

Marine science see OFFSHORE
TECHNOLOGY

MARKET RESEARCH

Association of British Market Research
  Companies 150
Association of Market Survey
  Organisations.......................... 333
Association of Qualitative Research
  Practitioners 388
Association of Social Research
  Organisations.......................... 409
Association of Users of Research
  Agencies 434
Federation of European Marketing
  Research Associations,................. 1543
Industrial Marketing Research
  Association............................ 1797
Market Research Society 2306
Social Research Association 3108

Marketing see ADVERTISING &
MARKETING

MARQUEES

Marquee Contractors Association 2308

MATCHES

Society of British Match Manufacturers ...3153

MATERIALS HANDLING

Association of Webbing Load Restraint
  Equipment Manufacturers 441
Automated Material Handling Systems
  Association............................ 451
British International Freight Association 845
British Materials Handling Federation 875
European Flexible Intermediate Bulk
  Container Association 1469
Flexible Intermediate Bulk Container
  Association............................ 1602
Freight Transport Association 1625
Institute of Logistics & Distribution
  Management 1917
Institute of Materials Management 1928
International Cargo Handling Co-
  ordination Association 2074

National Materials Handling Centre 2639
Shipowners Refrigerated Cargo
  Research Association 3086
Solids Handling & Processing
  Association............................ 3264
Storage & Handling Equipment
  Distributors' Association................ 3301
Timber Packaging & Pallet
  Confederation 3346

Materials recovery see RECLAMATION &
RECYCLING

MATERIALS TESTING

British Institute of Non-Destructive
  Testing................................ 831
British Measurement & Testing
  Association............................ 876

MATHEMATICS & STATISTICS

Association of Teachers of Mathematics 420
Institute of Economics & Statistics 1872
Institute of Mathematics & its
  Applications........................... 1929
Institute of Statisticians 1977
Mathematical Association 2321
National Association of Mathematics
  Advisors 2464
Organisation of Professional Users of
  Statistics 2730
Royal Statistical Society.................. 2960

MEAT TRADES

Association of British Meat Processors 151
Association of Meat Inspectors in GB 336
British Meat Manufacturers' Association 877
Federation of Fresh Meat Wholesalers 1545
Institute of Market Officers 1926
International Meat Trade Association 2144
Livestock Auctioneers' Market
  Committee for England & Wales 2254
Livestock Traders Association of GB 2255
National Association of British Market
  Authorities 2418
National Association of Catering
  Butchers 2420
National Association of Tripedressers....... 2501
National Federation of Meat Traders 2588
National Market Traders Federation 2637
Natural Sausage Casing Association 2687
Scotch Quality Beef & Lamb
  Association............................ 2989
Scottish Federation of Meat Traders'
  Associations........................... 3023
Ulster Curers' Association 3372
–see also POULTRY

Mechanical engineering see
ENGINEERING AND SPECIFIC ASPECTS

MECHANICAL HANDLING

Fork Truck Hire Association 1619
International Powered Access Federation ... 2152
Mechanical Handling Engineers
    Association 2323
–see also MATERIALS HANDLING

Medals see NUMISMATICS

Medical equipment see SURGICAL
EQUIPMENT & MATERIALS

MEDICAL PRACTICE

Association for Clinical Research 78
Association for the Study of Medical
    Education 108
Association of Medical Research
    Charities 338
Association of Medical Technologists 340
Association of Police Surgeons 369
Association of Teaching Hospital
    Pharmacists 423
British Association for Accident &
    Emergency Medicine 535
British Association for Dramatherapists 541
British Association for Immediate Care 543
British Association of Art Therapists 553
British Association of Dermatologists 565
British Association of Manipulative
    Medicine 578
British Association of Pharmaceutical
    Physicians 588
British Burn Association 630
British Medical Association 879
British Medical Ultrasound Society 880
British Migraine Association 888
British Society for the Study of Infection ... 1012
British Society of Gastroenterology 1021
Chest Heart & Stroke Association 1173
Cystic Fibrosis (Mucoviscidosis)
    Association 1342
Diving Medical Advisory Committee 1372
European Federation of Societies for
    Ultrasound in Medicine & Biology 1467
Faculty of Community Medicine 1506
General Medical Council 1654
Hospital Doctors' Association 1751
Institute of Medical Ethics 1931
Institute of Physical Sciences in
    Medicine 1944
Medical Officers of Schools Association ... 2329
Medical Women's Federation 2330

National Association of Family Planning
    Doctors 2433
National Association of Postgraduate
    Medical Education Centre
    Administrators 2472
National Osteoporosis Society 2642
Royal College of General Practitioners 2900
Royal Society of Medicine 2953
Royal Society of Tropical Medicine &
    Hygiene 2959
Society for Drug Research 3111
Society for Environmental Therapy 3115
Society for Research into Hydrocephalus
    & Spina Bifida 3124
Society of Apothecaries of London 3138
World Association of Sarcoidosis 3469
–see also SURGICAL PRACTICE;
    COMPLEMENTARY MEDICINE and specific
    branches of medicine

MEMORIALS & MONUMENTS

Monumental Brass Society 2358
National Association of Memorial
    Masons 2465

MENTAL HEALTH

Association for Residential Care 92
Association of Professions for the
    Mentally Handicapped People 382
British Institute of Mental Handicap 830
Mental After Care Association 2333
Mental Health Film Council 2334
National Association for Mental After-
    care in Registered Care Homes 2391
National Association for Mental Health ... 2392
Northern Ireland Association for Mental
    Health 2701
Royal Society for Mentally Handicapped
    Children & Adults 2943
Scottish Association for Mental Health ... 2995

METALLURGY

Art Metalware Manufacturers'
    Association 65
Association of British Pewter Craftsmen 157
Association of Bronze & Brass Founders 177
Association of Light Alloy Refiners 311
Association of Metal Sprayers 341
Association of Welding Distributors 442
BCIRA Cast Metals Technology 471
British Association for Brazing &
    Soldering 537
British Bronze & Brass Ingot
    Manufacturers Association 628
British Electroless Nickel Society 719
British Forging Industry Association 758
British Foundry Association 759
British Hardmetal Association 784

British Investment Casting Trade
  Association 847
British Metal Castings Council 883
British Powder Metal Federation 955
Cold Rolled Sections Association 1203
Cornish Mining Development
  Association 1278
Diecasting Society 1359
Ductile Iron Producers Asssociation 1388
European General Galvanizers
  Association 1473
European Investment Casters' Federation ... 1477
European Pressure Die Casting
  Committee 1488
Ferro Alloys & Metals Producers
  Association 1575
Foundry Equipment & Supplies
  Association 1623
Galvanizers Association 1633
Guild of Metal Perforators 1700
Historical Metallurgy Society 1738
Institute of British Foundrymen 1839
Institute of Metal Finishing 1933
Institute of Metals 1934
Institute of Sheet Metal Engineering 1972
Institution of Mining & Metallurgy 2026
International Deep Drawing Research
  Group 2100
International Lead & Zinc Study Group ... 2139
International Tungsten Industry
  Association 2182
Light Metal Founders Association 2244
Mechanical & Metal Trades
  Confederation 2322
Metal Finishing Association 2335
Midland General Galvanizers Association ... 2342
Minor Metals Trades Association 2352
National Association of Arc Welding
  Equipment Repairers 2411
National Metal Trades Federation 2640
National Society of Master Pattern
  Makers 2671
Nickel Development Institute 2697
Scottish Association for Metals 2996
Scottish Steel Founders' Association 3066
Solder Makers Association 3262
Steel Castings Research & Trade
  Association 3291
Welding Institute 3446
Welding Manufacturers' Association 3447
White Metal Casting Association 3450
World Bureau of Metal Statistics 3470
Zinc Alloy Die Casters Association 3487
Zinc Development Association 3488
Zinc Pigment Development Association ... 3489
–see also specific metals eg STEEL

Metaphysics *see* PARANORMAL
  PHENOMENA

METEOROLOGY

Association of British Climatologists 130
Royal Meteorological Society 2929

Microbiology *see* BIOLOGY

Midwifry *see* NURSING & MIDWIFRY

MILITARY HISTORY

Army Records Society 64
Military Historical Society 2343
Naval Historical Collectors & Research
  Association 2690
Orders & Medals Research Society 2727

Milk *see* DAIRY PRODUCTS

MINERALOGY

Mineral Industry Research Organisation ... 2346
Mineralogical Society of GB & Ireland ... 2347
Minerals Engineering Society 2348

MINING

Association of British Mining Equipment
  Companies 152
Association of Calendered UPV
  Suppliers 186
British Association of Colliery
  Management 560
Cornish Mining Development
  Association 1278
Council of Mining & Metallurgical
  Institutions 1309
Federation of Small Mines of GB 1565
Institution of Mining & Metallurgy 2026
Institution of Mining Electrical & Mining
  Mechanical Engineers 2027
Institution of Mining Engineers 2028
Miners' Lamp Manufacturers'
  Association 2349
Mining Association of the UK 2350
Mining Institute of Scotland 2351
National Association of Colliery
  Managers 2427

MODEL ENGINEERING

British Model Soldier Society 890

Motor cycles *see* CYCLES & CYCLING

MOTOR INDUSTRY

Automotive Distributors Federation 455
British Car Wash Association 637
British Friction Materials Council 762
British Gear Association 768
British Industrial Truck Association 819
Car Radio Industry Specialists
  Association 1123
Commercial Trailer Association 1217
Electric Vehicle Association of GB 1403
Federation of Automatic Transmission
  Engineers 1518
Federation of Engine Remanufacturers . . . 1537
Fire Fighting Vehicle Manufacturers'
  Association 1589
Historical Commercial Vehicle Society 1737
Institute of Automotive Engineer
  Assessors 1831
Institute of British Carriage &
  Automobile Manufacturers 1837
Institute of the Motor Industry 1985
Institute of Vehicle Recovery 1995
International Association for Vehicle
  System Dynamics 2054
Motor Industry Research Association 2362
National Association of Radiator
  Specialists 2478
National Joint Council for the Motor
  Vehicle Retail & Repair Industry 2633
Retail Motor Industry Federation 2881
Scottish Motor Trade Association 3044
Society of Motor Manufacturers &
  Traders 3224
Tachograph Analysis Association 3318
Vehicle Builders' & Repairers'
  Association 3429
–see also TYRES

MOTOR RACING

Association of Motor Racing Circuit
  Owners 345

Motor schools see DRIVING INSTRUCTION

MOUNTAINEERING

British Association of British Mountain
  Guides 556
British Mountaineering Council 893

Multiple sclerosis see NEUROLOGY

MUSEUMS

Association of Independent Museums 289
British Association of Friends of
  Museums 569
Interational Council of Museums 2045
Museum Training Institute 2369
Museums Association 2370
Scottish Museums Council 3045

MUSIC

Association for British Music 75
Association of British Orchestras 155
Association of Music Advisers in
  Scotland 348
Association of Professional Composers . . . 376
Association of Professional Music
  Therapists 379
Association of Teachers of Singing 422
British Arts Festivals Association 534
British Association for Jazz Education 544
British Association of Barbershop
  Singers 554
British Association of Concert Agents 561
British Federation of Music Festivals 739
British Federation of Young Choirs 741
British Jazz Society 850
British Music Information Centre 895
British Music Society 896
Cathedral Organists' Association 1133
Choir Schools Association 1180
Composers' Guild of GB 1235
Council for Music in Hospitals 1294
Council of Regional Arts Associations 1313
Country Music Association 1320
Faculty of Church Music 1505
Federation of Recorded Music Societies . . . 1561
Guild of Church Musicians 1690
Guild of International Songwriters &
  Composers 1697
Incorporated Society of Musicians 1772
International Society for Music
  Education 2170
Light Music Society 2245
Master Music Printers & Engravers
  Association 2313
Music Advisers' National Association 2372
Music Masters' & Mistresses'
  Association 2375
National Association of Youth
  Orchestras 2509
National Early Music Association 2561
National Federation of Music Societies . . . 2589
National Music Council of GB 2641
Royal Musical Association 2931
Royal Society of Musicians of GB 2955
Society for the Promotion of New Music . . . 3129
Sonic Arts Network 3266
United Kingdom Federation of Jazz
  Bands 3390

MUSICAL INSTRUMENTS

Association of Blind Piano Tuners 125

British Association of Symphonic Bands
& Wind Ensembles 601
British Flute Society 755
British Horn Society 803
British Institute of Organ Studies 832
Clarinet & Saxaphone Society of GB 1188
European Piano Teachers Association 1485
Federation of Master Organ Builders 1552
Federation of Music Industries 1554
Fellowship of Makers & Researchers of
Historical Instruments 1571
Incorporated Association of Organists 1764
Incorporated Society of Organ Builders   . . . 1773
Institute of Musical Instrument
Technology 1936
Lute Society 2284
Music Industries Association 2374
National School Band Association 2661
Piano Trade Suppliers Association 2783
Pianoforte Manufacturers & Distributors'
Association 2784
Pianoforte Tuners' Association 2785
Scottish Pipers' Association 3052
Society of Recorder Players 3240
United Kingdom Harp Association 3392

NAME STUDIES

Council for Name Studies in GB &
Ireland 1295
English Place-Name Society 1434
Names Society 2379

Naturopathy *see* OSTEOPATHY &
NATUROPATHY

Naval architecture *see* SHIPS & SHIPPING

Navigation *see* SHIPS & SHIPPING

NEEDLES

Needlemakers Association 2692

Needlework *see* EMBROIDERY &
NEEDLEWORK

NEUROLOGY

Association of British Neurologists 153
British Society for Clinical
Neurophysiology 1003
Electro-Physiological Technologists'
Association 1413
International Federation of Multiple
Sclerosis Societies 2110

Multiple Sclerosis Society of GB &
Ireland 2367
Society of British Neurological Surgeons . . . 3154

NEWSPAPERS & PERIODICALS

Association of British Editors 138
Association of Circulation Executives 202
Association of Free Magazines &
Periodicals 262
Association of Free Newspapers 263
Association of Newspaper & Magazine
Wholesalers 353
Association of Newspaper & Magazine
Wholesalers 352
Association of Subscription Agents 414
British Association of Industrial Editors   575
British Association of Picture Libraries &
Agencies 589
European Institute for the Media 1476
Guild of British Newspaper Editors 1688
Guild of Newspaper Editors 1702
International Federation of the Periodical
Press 2117
International Press Institute 2153
International Press Telecommunications
Council 2154
Media Studies Association 2327
Newspaper Conference 2694
Newspaper Publishers Association 2695
Newspaper Society 2696
Periodical Publishers Association 2760
Scottish Daily Newspaper Society 3016
Scottish Newspaper Proprietors'
Association 3048
Scottish Newspaper Publishers
Association 3049
Society of Picture Researchers & Editors . . . 3230
Talking Newpaper Association of the UK . . . 3319
United Kingdom Picture Editors Guild 3406
Web Offset Newspaper Association 3445

Noise *see* ACOUSTICS

Non-destructive testing *see* MATERIALS
TESTING

Non-ferrous metals *see* METALLURGY

NUCLEAR ENERGY

British Nuclear Energy Society 909
British Nuclear Forum 910
Institution of Nuclear Engineers 2029
Uranium Institute 3424

Numerical control *see* AUTOMATION

NUMISMATICS

British Art Medal Society 533
British Association of Numismatic
    Societies 580
British Numismatic Society 911
British Numismatic Trade Association 912
Royal Numismatic Society 2935

Nursery schools *see* CHILD WELFARE

NURSING & MIDWIFRY

Association of Radical Midwives 390
Association of Supervisors of Midwives   416
English National Board for Nursing,
    Midwifery & Health Visiting 1433
Infection Control Nurses' Association 1806
International Confederation of Midwives . . 2088
National Association of Theatre Nurses   . . 2496
National Board for Nursing, Midwifery &
    Health Visiting for Northern Ireland 2515
National Board for Nursing, Midwifery &
    Health Visiting for Scotland 2516
Royal College of Midwives 2901
Royal College of Nursing of the UK 2902

Nursing homes *see* HEALTHCARE

NUTRITION

British Dietetic Association 698
British Digestive Foundation 699
British Nutrition Foundation 913
British Society for Nutritional Medicine . . . 1005
International Food Information Service . . . 2121

Obstetrics *see* GYNAECOLOGY &
    OBSTETRICS

OCCUPATIONAL MEDICINE

British Association of Occupational
    Therapists 581
British Institute of Industrial Therapy 824
British Occupational Hygiene Society 915
Institution of Occupational Safety &
    Health 2030
International Institute of Risk & Safety
    Management 2133
Occupational Hygiene Products
    Distributors Association 2715
Society for the Prevention of Asbestosis
    & Industrial Diseases 3127
Society of Occupational Medicine 3226

OCEANOGRAPHY

Permanent Service for Mean Sea Level   . . . 2764
Society for Underwater Technology 3134
Underwater Association for Scientific
    Research 3375

OFFICE AUTOMATION & MANAGEMENT

British Facsimile Industry Consultative
    Committee 733
British Office Systems & Stationery
    Federation 916
British Office Technology Manufacturers
    Alliance 917
Business Equipment & Information
    Technology Association 1112
Institute of Administrative Management   . . . 1822
Institute of Word Processing 2000
–*see also* COMPUTER SCIENCE & DATA
    PROCESSING; SECRETARIAL PRACTICE

OFFSHORE TECHNOLOGY

Association of British Offshore
    Industries 154
British Offshore Support Vessels
    Association 918
British Rig Owners' Association 981
Institute of Marine Engineers 1925
International Underwater Engineering
    Contractors 2184
Offshore Contractors Council 2717
United Kingdom Offshore Operators
    Association 3403
United Kingdom Onshore Operators
    Group 3404

Oil fuel *see* PETROLEUM & OIL
    TECHNOLOGY

Oil pollution *see* POLLUTION CONTROL

Opera *see* MUSIC

OPERATIONAL RESEARCH

Operational Research Society 2722

OPHTHALMOLOGY

Association for Eye Research 82
Association of British Dispensing
    Opticians 137
Association of Optometrists 357
British College of Optometrists 665

British Ophthalmic Lens Manufacturers
& Distributors' Association 920
British Orthoptic Society 926
British Spectacle Frame Makers'
Association 1034
Case Makers' Association 1126
College of Ophthalmologists 1206
Comprehensive Prescription House
Association 1236
Federation of Manufacturing Opticians ... 1550
Federation of Ophthalmic & Dispensing
Opticians 1556
General Optical Council 1655
Institute of Ophthalmology 1937
International Glaucoma Association 2125
International Guild of Opticians 2126
International Optometric & Optical
League 2147
Ophthalmic Exhibitors' Association 2723
Ophthalmic Prescription Manufacturers'
Association 2724
Optical Frame Importers' Association 2725
Optical Information Council 2726
Scottish Committee of Optometrists 3008

Orchestras see MUSIC

Organs see MUSICAL INSTRUMENTS

ORNITHOLOGY

British Ornithologists' Union 924
British Trust for Ornithology 1064
British Waterfowl Association 1087
Fauna & Flora Preservation Society 1514
International Council for Bird
Preservation 2092
International Waterfowl & Wetlands
Research Bureau 2194
Parrot Society 2748
Wildfowl & Wetlands Trust 3458
World Pheasant Association 3473

Orthodontics see DENTISTRY

Orthopaedics see SURGICAL PRACTICE

OSTEOPATHY & NATUROPATHY

British College of Naturopathy &
Osteopathy 664
British Osteopathic Association 927
College of Osteopaths & Practitioners 1207
General Council & Register of
Naturopaths 1648
General Council & Register of
Osteopaths 1649
National Therapeutic & Osteopathic
Society 2676
Osteopathic Association Of GB 2733

PACKAGING MATERIALS & EQUIPMENT

Aluminium Foil Container Manufacturers
Association 39
Association of Carton Board Makers 188
Association of Greyboard Makers 271
British Aerosol Manufacturers'
Association 515
British Bottlers' Institute 625
British Box & Packaging Association 626
British Carton Association 642
British Disposable Products Association 702
British Fibreboard Packaging
Association 742
Can Makers Information Service 1121
Corrugated Case Materials Association ... 1283
European Flexographic Technical
Association 1470
European Glass Container
Manufacturers' Committee 1474
Industry Council for Packaging & the
Environment 1804
Institute of Packaging 1938
International Association of Packaging
Research Institutes 2064
Liquid Food Carton Manufacturers
Association 2253
Metal Packaging Manufacturers
Association 2336
Packaging & Industrial Films
Association 2739
Packaging Distributors Association 2740
PIRA 2790
Plastic Industrial Containers Association ... 2792
Plastics Crate Manufacturers'
Association 2796
Sterilization Packaging Materials
Association 3297
Timber Packaging & Pallet
Confederation 3346

Paediatrics see CHILD WELFARE

PAINT

British Colour Makers' Association 667
Oil & Colour Chemists' Association 2719
Paint Research Association 2742
Paintmakers Association of GB 2743
Wallpaper, Paint & Wallcovering
Retailers Association 3439

PALAEONTOGRAPHY & PALAEONTOLOGY

Palaeontographical Society 2744
Palaeontological Association 2745

PAPER & BOARD

Association of Board Makers 126
Association of Carton Board Makers 188
Association of Greyboard Makers 271
Association of Makers of Newsprint 323
Association of Makers of Packaging
   Papers 324
Association of Makers of Printings &
   Writings 325
Association of Makers of Soft Tissue
   Papers 326
British Association of Paper Exporters 586
British Paper & Board Industry
   Federation 930
British Paper Machinery Makers
   Association 931
British Wood Pulp Association 1091
Independent Waste Paper Processors
   Association 1792
Institute of Paper Conservation 1939
National Association of Paper
   Merchants 2468
Paper Agents' Association 2746
Paper Makers' Allied Trades Association ... 2747
PIRA 2790
Release Paper Manufacturers
   Association 2874
United Kingdom & Ireland Particleboard
   Association 3378

PARACHUTING

British Parachute Association 932

Paragliding see GLIDING & HANG GLIDING

PARANORMAL PHENOMENA

Association for the Scientific Study of
   Anomalous Phenomena 106
British Unidentified Flying Object
   Research Association 1070
Society of Metaphysicians 3220
—see also PSYCHICAL RESEARCH

PARKS & GROUNDS ADMINISTRATION

Association of National Park Officers 350
Association of Playing Field Officers &
   Landscape Managers 365
British Association of Leisure Parks,
   Piers & Attractions 577

Conservatory Association 1259
Council for National Parks 1297
Institute of Groundsmanship 1895
Institute of Leisure & Amenity
   Management 1915
International Federation of Park &
   Recreation Administration 2111
Metropolitan Public Gardens
   Association 2340
National Playing Fields Association 2649
National Turf Grass Council 2679
Sports Turf Research Institute 3276
—see also GOLF & GOLF COURSES

PARLIAMENTARY AGENTS

Society of Parliamentary Agents 3227

Passenger transport see TRANSPORT

Patents see INTELLECTUAL PROPERTY

PATHOLOGY

Association of Clinical Biochemists 205
Association of Clinical Pathologists 206
Pathological Society of GB & Ireland 2754
Royal College of Pathologists 2904

PENSIONS

Association of Pensioneer Trustees 361
National Association of Pension Funds ... 2469
Pensions Management Institute 2757
Society of Pension Consultants 3228

Performing rights see INTELLECTUCAL PROPERTY

Perfume see COSMETICS & TOILETRIES

Periodicals see NEWSPAPERS & PERIODICALS

Periodontology see DENTISTRY

PERSONNEL MANAGEMENT

Institute of Administrative Management ... 1822
Institute of Personnel Management 1941
Society of Chief Personnel Officers 3167

PEST CONTROL

British Pest Control Association............936
Collaborative International Pesticides
    Analytical Council 1205

PET FOODS

Pet Trade & Industry Association 2769

Petrol pumps *see* GARAGE EQUIPMENT

PETROLEUM & OIL TECHNOLOGY

Association for Petroleum & Explosives
    Administration...........................91
Association of British Independent Oil
    Exploration Companies...................143
British Lubricants Federation 869
Federation of Petroleum Suppliers 1558
Institute of Petroleum 1942
International Petroleum Industry
    Environmental Conservation
    Association...........................2148
Liquefied Petroleum Gas Industry
    Technical Association 2252
National Centre of Tribology..............2523
Petroleum Exploration Society of GB.......2772
United Kingdom Onshore Operators
    Group................................3404
United Kingdom Petroleum Industry
    Association...........................3405
World Petroleum Congresses 3472

PHARMACEUTICAL INDUSTRY & PRACTICE

Association of the British
    Pharmaceutical Industry..................426
European Confederation of Medical
    Suppliers Associations 1460
Institute of Pharmacy Management
    International...........................1943
National Pharmaceutical Association 2645
Pharmaceutical General Council
    (Scotland) 2773
Pharmaceutical Society of Northern
    Ireland 2775
Proprietary Articles Trade Association 2843
Proprietary Association of GB 2844
Royal Pharmaceutical Society of GB 2936
Scottish Pharmaceutical Federation 3051
Scottish Wholesale Druggists
    Association...........................3070
Society of Pharmaceutical Medicine.......3229

PHARMACOLOGY

British Pharmacological Society............937

PHILATELY

British Philatelic Federation.................938
British Thematic Association...............1055
International Federation of Stamp
    Dealers Associations 2116
National Philatelic Society.................2646
Philatelic Traders' Society 2777
Royal Philatelic Society 2937

PHILOSPHY

Royal Institute of Philosophy 2924

PHOTOGRAPHY

Affiliation of Honourable Photographers 13
Association of Model Agents 343
Association of Photographers..............363
Association of Photographic
    Laboratories 364
British Air Survey Association 523
British Institute of Professional
    Photography 834
British Photographers' Liaison
    Committee 941
British Photographic Association...........942
British Photographic Export Group 943
British Photographic Importers'
    Association...........................944
British Society of Cinematographers.......1017
Bureau of Freelance Photographers 1106
Council of Photographic News Agencies ...1312
Master Photographers Association 2314
Photographic Instrument Repairing
    Authority.............................2779
Remote Sensing Society 2875
Royal Photographic Society 2938
Stereoscopic Society 3295

PHYSICAL EDUCATION

British Association of Advisers &
    Lecturers in Physical Education 551
British Council of Physical Education 682
British Schools Gymnastics Association 987
Central Council of Physical Recreation ...1139
National Association for Outdoor
    Education 2394
National Association of Health &
    Exercise Teachers 2448
National Council for Schools Sports 2542
Physical Education Association of GB &
    N Ireland 2780
Scottish Association of Advisers in
    Physical Education.....................2997
Society for the Advancement of Games
    & Simulation in Education...............3125
Standing Conference on Physical
    Education in Teacher Education.........3288

PHYSICS

British Vacuum Council 1075
Institute of Physics.......................1945

PHYSIOTHERAPY

Association of Blind Chartered
    Physiotherapists 124
Chartered Society of Physiotherapy 1170
Fellowship of Sports Masseurs &
    Therapists 1573

Pianofortes *see* MUSICAL INSTRUMENTS

Picture restoring *see* ARTS & ARTISTS

PIGEONS

Scottish Homing Union 3031

PIPES, TUBES & TUNNELS

British Plumbing Fittings Manufacturers
    Association..............................947
Clay Pipe Development Association 1191
Concrete Pipe Association 1242
High Performance Pipe Association 1732
International Tube Association 2181
Pipe Jacking Association 2787
Pipeline Industries Guild 2788
Plastic Pipe Manufacturers Society 2793
Plastics Land Drainage Manufacturers'
    Association.............................2797

Place names *see* NAME STUDIES

PLANT, INDUSTRIAL

British Ceramic Plant & Machinery
    Manufacturers' Association 649
British Metallurgical Plant Constructors'
    Association..............................885
Contractors Mechanical Plant Engineers ...1271
Institution of Diagnostic Engineers 2009
Institution of Plant Engineers 2031
Metalforming Machinery Makers'
    Association.............................2338
Plastics Machinery Distributors
    Association.............................2798
Process Plant Association 2827
Rotating Electrical Machines Association ...2891
Scottish Plant Owners Association 3053

Plastic surgeons *see* SURGICAL PRACTICE

PLASTICS

British Independent Plastic Extruders'
    Association...............................813
British Laminated Plastic Fabricators
    Association...............................861
British Plastics Federation 945
British Plastics Stockholders'
    Association...............................946
British Urethane Foam Contractors
    Association.............................1074
European Plasticised PVC Film
    Manufacturers' Association 1486
European Plastics Distributors
    Association.............................1487
Plastics & Rubber Institute 2795

PLUMBING

British Plumbing Fittings Manufacturers
    Association...............................947
Institute of Plumbing.....................1946
National Association of Plumbing,
    Heating & Mechanical Services
    Contractors...........................2471
Scottish & N Ireland Plumbing
    Employers' Federation 2991

Poetry *see* LITERATURE & POETRY

POLAROGRAPHY

British Polarological Research Society 948

POLICE

Association of Chief Police Officers
    (Scotland) 199
Association of Chief Police Officers of
    England, Wales & Northern Ireland........198
Association of Police & Court
    Interpreters 368
International Police Association 2151
Police Federation (England & Wales) 2803
Police Superintendents' Association of
    England & Wales 2805
Scottish Police Federation 3055

POLLUTION CONTROL

Advisory Committee on Pollution of the
    Sea 10
British Oil Spill Control Association 919
International Association on Water
    Pollution Research & Control...........2070
International Petroleum Industry
    Environmental Conservation
    Association.............................2148
International Society for the Prevention
    of Water Pollution 2172

International Tanker Owners Pollution
  Federation 2176
National Pure Water Association 2653
National Society for Clean Air &
  Environmental Protection, ... 2667

POPULATION REGISTRATION

Institution of Population Registration 2032
Society of Registration Officers 3241

PORTS, DOCKS & HARBOURS

Association of Master Lightermen &
  Barge Owners 334
British Ports Federation 950
London Wharfingers Association 2281
National Association of Warehouse
  Keepers 2504
Society of International Gas Tankers &
  Terminal Operators 3209
Yacht Harbour Association 3485
—see also SHIPS & SHIPPING

Postal services *see*
  TELECOMMUNICATIONS

Poster advertising *see* ADVERTISING &
MARKETING

Potatoes *see* FRUIT & VEGETABLES

POTTERY & CHINA

British Pottery Managers' Association 952
China & Glass Retailers' Association 1178
Tableware Distributors Association 3317
—see also CERAMICS

POULTRY

British Chicken Association 656
British Goose Producers Association 775
British Poultry Breeders & Hatcheries
  Association 953
British Poultry Federation 954
British Turkey Federation 1068
Duck Producers Association 1387
Hen Packers Association 1728
National Federation of Wholesale
  Poultry Merchants 2603
Poultry Industry Conference 2812
World's Poultry Science Association 3479

PRINTING & PRINTING EQUIPMENT

Association of Industrial Graphics &
  Nameplate Manufacturers 295
Association of Printing Machinery
  Importers 375
Association of Teachers of Printing &
  Allied Subjects 421
British Federation of Printing Machinery
  & Supplies 740
British Printing Industries Federation 958
Graphic Reproduction Federation 1677
Institute of Printing 1949
International Association of Research
  Institutes for the Graphic Arts Industry ... 2065
Master Music Printers & Engravers
  Association 2313
Oil & Colour Chemists' Association 2719
PIRA 2790
Screen Printing Association 3075
Society of British Printing Ink
  Manufacturers 3155
Society of Master Printers of Scotland ... 3218
Society of Typographical Designers 3253

PRISON & PROBATION SERVICES

Association of Chief Officers of
  Probation 197
Central Council of Probation
  Committees 1140
National Association for the Care &
  Resettlement of Offenders 2400
National Association of Prison Visitors ... 2474
National Association of Probation
  Officers 2475
Prison Officers' Association 2825

Process plant *see* PLANT, INDUSTRIAL

Product quality *see* QUALITY CONTROL

PRODUCTION ENGINEERING

Institution of Production Engineers 2033
Production Engineering Research
  Association of GB 2834

PRODUCTIVITY

British Production & Inventory Control
  Society 959

PROPERTY - LAND & BUILDINGS

Association of Residential Letting
  Agents 399
British Property Federation 961

Central Association of Agricultural
 Valuers 1136
Certificated Bailiffs' Association of
 England & Wales 1151
Chief Building Surveyors' Society 1175
Country Landowners' Association 1319
Farm & Rural Buildings Centre 1512
Federation of Overseas Property
 Developers Agents & Consultants 1557
Federation of Private Residents'
 Associations 1560
Incorporated Society of Valuers &
 Auctioneers 1774
Industrial Agents Society 1793
International Commercial Property
 Association 2083
International Property Lawyers
 Association 2158
Local Authority Valuers Association 2261
Property Consultants Society 2842
Rating & Valuation Association 2861
Rating Surveyors Association 2862
Scottish Assessors' Association 2994
Scottish Landowners' Federation.......... 3036
Small Landlords Association 3101
Timeshare Council 3350

PSYCHIATRY

Institute of Social Psychiatry.............. 1974
Royal College of Psychiatrists 2906

PSYCHICAL RESEARCH

Incorporated Society for Psychical
 Research 1768
National Federation of Spiritual Healers ... 2599
Spiritualist Association of GB.............. 3273

PSYCHOLOGY

Association for Teaching Psychology 98
Association of Educational
 Psychologists........................... 250
British Institute of Practical Psychology 833
British Psycho-Analytical Society 962
British Psychological Society 963
Society of Analytical Psychology.......... 3135

PSYCHOTHERAPY

Association of Child Psychotherapists 201
Association of Sexual & Marital
 Therapists 404
British Association for Behavioural
 Psychotherapy 536
British Association of Psychotherapists 593
Institute of Group Analysis 1896
Institute of Psycho-Analysis 1951
Institute of Psychosexual Medicine........ 1952
Institute of Transactional Analysis.......... 1989

International Association of Group
 Psychotherapy 2061
National College of Hypnosis &
 Psychotherapy 2530
National Council of Psychotherapists &
 Hypnotherapy Register 2550
National Register of Hypnotherapists &
 Psychotherapists........................ 2654
United Kingdom Standing Conference
 for Psychotherapy...................... 3414

Public address systems *see*
 AUDIO/VISUAL INDUSTRIES

PUBLIC ADMINISTRATION

Chartered Institute of Public Finance &
 Accountancy 1165
Royal Institute of Public Administration ...2925
–*see also* LOCAL GOVERNMENT

PUBLIC RELATIONS

Communication, Advertising &
 Marketing Education Foundation 1231
Institute of Public Relations 1954
Public Relations Consultants
 Association.............................. 2848
Society of County & Regional Public
 Relations Officers 3176
Society of District Councils Public
 Relations Officers 3185

PUBLIC SPEAKING

Association of Speakers Clubs 410
Guild of Professional After Dinner
 Speakers 1703

PUBLISHING

Association of British Directory
 Publishers.............................. 136
Association of Learned & Professional
 Society Publishers 308
Association of Little Presses 314
Association of Publishers' Educational
 Representatives 387
Book Publishers' Representatives'
 Association.............................. 495
Directory Publishers Association 1363
Educational Publishers Council 1399
Federation of Children's Book Groups...... 1529
Independent Publishers Guild............. 1783
Music Publishers' Association 2376
Private Libraries Association 2826
Publishers Association 2849
Scottish Publishers Association 3058
Society of Private Printers 3232
Society of Young Publishers.............. 3258

University, College & Professional
  Publishers Council 3423

PUMPS

British Pump Manufacturers Association 965
European Committee of Manufacturers,
  Compressors, Vacuum Pumps &
  Pneumatic Tools 1458
Pump Distributors Association of GB 2850

PURCHASING MANAGEMENT

Institute of Purchasing & Supply 1955
Institute of Purchasing Management 1956

PYROTECHNICS

British Pyrotechnists Association 966

QUALITY CONTROL

British Quality Association 967
Institute of Quality Assurance 1958

QUARRYING

Institute of Quarrying 1959

RABBITS

British Commercial Rabbit Association 669
British Rabbit Council 968

Racing & racecourses see DOGS, DOG
  RACING & HUNTING; HORSES & HORSE
  RACING

Radio industry see AUDIO/VISUAL
  INDUSTRIES

RADIOGRAPHY & RADIOLOGY

Association of X-ray Equipment
  Manufacturers 445
British Institute of Radiology 835
College of Radiographers 1209
International Commission on
  Radiological Protection 2085
Royal College of Radiologists 2907
Society for Radiological Protection 3122
Society of Radiographers 3239

RAIL TRANSPORT

Association of Independent Railways 292
Association of Railway Preservation
  Societies 391

Association of Wagon Builders &
  Repairers 440
Institution of Railway Signal Engineers . . . 2035
Light Rail Transit Association 2246
Locomotive & Carriage Institution 2263
Permanent Way Institution 2765
Railway Development Society 2858
Railway Industry Association 2859
Tramway & Light Railway Society 3362

RATING & VALUATION

Association of Valuers of Licensed
  Property 435
Local Authority Valuers Association 2261
Machinery Users' Association 2286
Rating & Valuation Association 2861
Rating Surveyors Association 2862
−see also PROPERTY - LAND & BUILDINGS

RECLAMATION & RECYCLING

Aluminium Can Recycling Association 35
British Scrap Federation 990
British Secondary Metals Association 992
British Textile By-Products Association . . . 1051
British Waste Paper Association 1082
Chemical Recovery Association 1172
European Asbestos & Recycling
  Association 1453
Federation of Drum Reconditioners 1536
Independent Waste Paper Processors
  Association 1792
Institute of Wastes Management 1997
International Salvage Union 2163
International Tyre, Rubber & Plastics
  Federation 2183
Motor Vehicle Dismantlers' Association
  of GB 2364
National Association of Waste Disposal
  Contractors 2505
National Renderers Association 2656
Reclamation Association 2863
Salvage Association 2974
Scottish Scrap Association 3060
United Kingdom Reclamation Council 3410
Waste Disposal Engineers Association 3440
Wiping Cloth Manufacturers'
  Association 3460

Recreation see ENTERTAINMENT &
  LEISURE ACTIVITIES

Recruitment see EMPLOYMENT &
  RECRUITMENT

Recycling see RECLAMATION &
  RECYCLING

REFRACTORY MATERIALS

Institute of Refractories Engineers..........1960
Refractory Contractors Association.........2868
Refractory Users Federation 2869

REFRIGERATION

British Refrigeration Association 974
Cold Storage & Distribution Federation ...1204
Institute of Refrigeration...................1961

Rehabilitation *see* DISABILITY &
REHABILITATION

Reindeer *see* DEER

REPTILES & AMPHIBIANS

British Herpetological Society 796

RESEARCH & DEVELOPMENT

British Association for the Advancement
    of Science................................550
Research & Development Society 2876

Resins *see* SURFACE COATINGS

Restaurants *see* HOTEL & CATERING
MANAGEMENT

RETAIL TRADES

Alliance of Independent Retailers 28
Article Number Association 68
British Council of Shopping Centres 683
British Shops & Stores Association 996
Company Chemists Association 1234
Cooperative Employers Association 1273
Cooperative Union....................1274
Institute of Cooperative Directors 1867
London Fish & Poultry Retailers'
    Association............................2271
Music Retailers Association...............2377
National Association of Colleges in
    Distributive Education & Training 2426
National Association of Shopkeepers.......2486
National Federation of Fishmongers 2580
National Federation of Retail
    Newsagents 2593
National Pharmaceutical Association 2645
National Retail Training Council 2657
Radio, Electrical & Television Retailers'
    Association............................2856

Retail Confectioners & Tobacconists
    Association..............................2878
Retail Consortium.......................2879
—see also specific aspects eg GROCERY TRADES

RETIREMENT PLANNING

Association of Retired Persons.............400

RHEOLOGY

British Society of Rheology...............1029

RHEUMATOLOGY

Arthritis & Rheumatism Council..............67
British Society for Rheumatology 1007

Rifles *see* GUNS & SHOOTING

ROAD TRANSPORT

British Road Federation 982
Bus & Coach Council 1107
Heavy Transport Association...............1727
Institute of Road Transport Engineers 1965
Institute of Transport Administration 1991
National Federation of Bus Users 2572
Omnibus Society 2720
Road Haulage Association.................2884

ROADS & ROAD SAFETY

Association of Industrial Road Safety
    Officers 296
Association of Road Traffic Sign Makers 401
British Institute of Traffic Education
    Research 838
British Parking Association 933
County Road Safety Offices' Association ...1324
Guild of Experienced Motorists 1692
Institute of Highway Incorporated
    Engineers 1900
Institute of Road Safety Officers 1964
Institution of Highways &
    Transportation 2020
National Automobile Safety Belt
    Association...............................2513
Pedestrians Association for Road Safety ...2756
Permanent International Association of
    Road Congresses 2763
Road Operators' Safety Council...........2885
Road Surface Dressing Association 2886
Transport & Road Research Laboratory ...3364

Robotics *see* AUTOMATION

ROOFING

Association of British Roofing Felt
    Manufacturers 164
British Flat Roofing Council 749
European Liquid Roofing Association 1479
Flat Roofing Contractors Advisory Board ... 1599
Institute of Roofing 1966
Metal Roofing Contractors Association ... 2337
National Federation of Roofing
    Contractors 2594
National Master Tile Fixers Association ... 2638
National Society of Master Thatchers 2672
Single Ply Roofing Association 3095

Ropes see CORDAGE, ROPE & TWINE

RUBBER & RUBBER PRODUCTS

British Rubber Industry Training
    Organisation 984
British Rubber Manufacturers
    Association 985
International Institute of Synthetic
    Rubber Producers 2137
International Rubber Research &
    Development Board 2161
International Rubber Study Group 2162
Malaysian Rubber Producers' Research
    Association 2292
Plastics & Rubber Institute 2795
Rubber Trade Association of London 2965

Rural conservation see ENVIRONMENTAL
PROTECTION

SAFETY

British Safety Council 986
Industrial Safety (Protective Equipment)
    Manufacturers Association 1799
Institute of Home Safety 1903
Institute of Safety & Public Protection ... 1967
Institution of Occupational Safety &
    Health 2030
International Institute of Risk & Safety
    Management 2133
Royal Society for the Prevention of
    Accidents 2946
Society of Industrial Emergency Services
    Officers 3206
–see also specific aspects eg ROADS & ROAD
SAFETY

SALES MANAGEMENT

Institute of Sales & Marketing
    Management 1968

Manufacturers' Agents' Association of
    GB & Ireland 2299
Scottish Commercial Travellers
    Association 3007
Society of Sales Management
    Administrators 3242
–see also ADVERTISING & MARKETING

Sales promotion see ADVERTISING &
MARKETING

Salmon see FISHING & FISH INDUSTRY

Salvage see RECLAMATION & RECYCLING

SAND, GRAVEL & GRIT

British Grit Association 777
Sand & Ballast Hauliers & Allied Trades
    Alliance 2975
Sand & Gravel Association 2976

Sanitary pottery see BRICKS, TILES &
SANITARY POTTERY

Saws see TOOLS

Saxaphones see MUSICAL INSTRUMENTS

Scaffolding see BUILDING EQUIPMENT &
MATERIALS

Schools see EDUCATION

SCIENCE & TECHNOLOGY

Association of Consulting Scientists 220
British Association for the Advancement
    of Science 550
British Consultants Bureau 675
Council of Science & Technology
    Institutes 1314
Royal Society 2942
Royal Society for the Encouragement of
    Arts, Manufactures & Commerce 2945
United Kingdom Technology
    Organisation 3418
–see also under specific branches

SCIENTIFIC INSTRUMENTS

Association for the Instrumentation,
Control & Automation Industry in the
UK..102
Association of British Spectroscopists.......170
British Pressure Gauge Manufacturers
Association.....................................957
Diamond Industrial Products Association ...1358
Institute of Measurement & Control.......1930
Milling Cutter & Toolbit Association.......2345
Royal Microscopical Society.............2930
Sira..3096

Screen advertising *see* ADVERTISING &
MARKETING

Sculptors *see* ARTS & ARTISTS

SECRETARIAL PRACTICE

Association of Business Centres............183
Association of Medical Secretaries,
Practice Administrators &
Receptionists.................................339
Association of Official Shorthandwriters 356
Association of Personal Assistants &
Secretaries...................................362
Faculty of Secretaries & Administrators ...1510
Fellowship of Skilled Secretaries..........1572
Independent Secretarial Training
Association..................................1789
Institute of Agricultural Secretaries........1824
Institute of Qualified Private Secretaries ...1957
Institute of Shorthand Writers..............1973
School Secretaries' Association...........2984

SECURITY

Association for the Prevention of Theft
in Shops.....................................104
Association of British Investigators..........146
Association of British Private Detectives 161
Association of British Security Officers 168
British Security Industry Association........993
Institute of British Detective
Investigative Security & Forensic
Specialists...................................1838
Institute of Professional Investigators.......1950
International Institute of Security..........2134
International Professional Security
Association..................................2157
Loss Prevention Council....................2282
National Association of Health Service
Security Officers............................2447
Safety Equipment Distributors
Association..................................2969

Self-employed *see* EMPLOYERS
ORGANISATIONS

SEWING MACHINES

Sewing Machine Trade Association........3082

SHEEP

British Milksheep Association..............889
National Sheep Association 2663

SHIPS & SHIPPING

Association of British Container Lessors 132
Association of Brokers & Yacht Agents 176
Association of Master Lightermen &
Barge Owners..............................334
British Boatbuilders Association............623
British Hire Cruiser Federation..............797
British Marine Equipment Association......871
British Marine Equipment Council.........872
British Marine Industries Federation........873
British Motor Ship Owners Association 891
British Naval Equipment Association.......905
British Offshore Support Vessels
Association..................................918
British Shippers' Council...................995
British Tugowners' Association...........1065
Council of European & Japanese
National Shipowners' Associations.......1304
Cruising Association.......................1339
European Tugowners Association..........1492
General Council of British Shipping.......1650
Institution of Engineers & Shipbuilders
in Scotland.................................2014
International Association of Dry Cargo
Shipowners................................2059
International Association of Navigation
Schools....................................2063
International Chamber of Shipping........2078
International Federation of Shipmasters
Associations...............................2114
International Maritime Industries Forum ...2141
International Maritime Pilots Association ...2142
International Ship Suppliers Association ...2166
International Shipping Federation..........2167
International Tanker Owners Pollution
Federation.................................2176
London Tugowners Association...........2280
Marine Training Association...............2305
Nautical Institute.........................2689
Passenger Shipping Association..........2751
Permanent International Association of
Navigation Congresses..................2762
Royal Institute of Navigation.............2921
Royal Institution of Naval Architects.......2928
Sailing Barge Association.................2971
Scottish Boat Builders Association........3003

Shiprepairers & Shipbuilders
  Independent Association 3087
Society for Nautical Research.............3120
Society of International Gas Tankers &
  Terminal Operators......................3209
Standby Ship Operators Association 3284
World Ship Society 3476
Yacht Brokers Designers & Surveyors
  Association.............................3483
Yacht Charter Association 3484

Shoes *see* FOOTWEAR

Shooting *see* GUNS & SHOOTING

SHOPFITTING

Association of Shopfront Section
  Manufacturers 406
National Association of Shopfitters.........2485
Shop & Display Equipment Association   ...3088
–*see also* DISPLAY

Shops *see* RETAIL TRADES

Show jumping *see* HORSES, HORSE
  RACING & RIDING

SIGHT IMPAIRED

Association for the Education & Welfare
  of the Visually Handicapped 101
Association of Blind Piano Tuners 125
British Retinitis Pigmentosa Society 980
National Association of Industries for
  the Blind & Disabled....................2453
National League for the Blind &
  Disabled 2635
Partially Sighted Society 2749
Royal National Institute for the Blind.......2932
Talking Newspaper Association of the UK ...3319

Silk *see* TEXTILE INDUSTRIES - GENERAL

Silver *see* JEWELLERY

Silverware *see* CUTLERY

Singing *see* MUSIC

SKATING & SKATEBOARDING

English Curling Association................1431
National Skating Association of GB 2664

SKIING

Association of Ski Schools in GB 408
British Association of Ski Instructors 597
British Ski Federation 999
British Water Ski Federation 1085
English Ski Council 1439
Skibob Association of GB 3097

Smoke abatement *see* POLLUTION
  CONTROL

Smokeless fuel *see* FUEL

Snooker *see* BILLIARDS, POOL & SNOOKER

SNUFF

Society of British Snuff Blenders...........3156

SOAP & DETERGENTS

Soap & Detergent Industry Association   ...3104

SOCIAL WELFARE

Almshouse Association 34
Association for Family Therapy 83
Association for Neighbourhood Councils 89
Association of Accommodation &
  Welfare Officers.........................111
Association of Charity Officers 192
Association of Chief Education Social
  Workers.................................196
Association of Community Technical Aid
  Centres 212
Association of Community Workers in
  the UK 213
Association of Directors of Social
  Services..................................241
Association of Directors of Social Work 240
British Association for Counselling 540
British Association for Service to the
  Elderly 547
British Association of Domiciliary Care
  Officers 566
British Association of Settlements &
  Social Action Centres 596
British Association of Social Workers........598
British Geriatrics Society 771
British Sociological Association 1031
Carers National Association...............1125

Central Council for Education &
  Training in Social Work 1138
Centre for Policy on Ageing 1148
Council of Voluntary Welfare Work........1316
Federation of Independent Advice
  Centres 1547
Health Visitors' Association 1721
Incorporated Society of Managers &
  Administrators.........................1771
Institute for Social Studies in Medical
  Care 1818
Institute of Community Development.......1862
Institute of Family Therapy 1885
Institute of Health Education 1897
Institute of Welfare Officers...............1998
International Federation of Settlements   ...2113
Joint Council for Welfare of Immigrants   ...2208
National Association for Voluntary
  Hostels................................2405
National Association of Bereavement
  Services 2413
National Association of Citizens Advice
  Bureaux................................2425
National Association of Leagues of
  Hospital Friends 2458
National Association of Racial Equality   ...2477
National Association of Social Workers
  in Education...........................2487
National Association of Victims Support
  Schemes 2502
National Association of Voluntary Help
  Organisers.............................2503
National Council for Voluntary
  Organisations..........................2547
National Federation of Community
  Organisations..........................2575
National Federation of Self-Help
  Organisations..........................2598
National Institute for Social Work 2621
Office of Health Economics................2716
Patients Association 2755
Pre-Retirement Association of GB &
  Northern Ireland 2817
Refugee Council 2870
Royal Society of Health 2950
Scottish Council for Voluntary
  Organisations..........................3015
Social Care Association 3105
Social Policy Association 3107
Tavistock Institute of Human Relations   ...3320
—*see also* CHILD WELFARE

Soft drinks *see* FOOD & BEVERAGES

Solicitors *see* LAW & LEGAL SERVICES

Sound engineering *see* AUDIO/VISUAL
  INDUSTRIES

Sound recording *see* AUDIO/VISUAL
  INDUSTRIES

SPACE RESEARCH

British Interplanetary Society 846
Interdisciplinary Scientific Committee on
  Space Research.........................2046
United Kingdom Industrial Space
  Committee 3395

SPEECH & SPEECH THERAPY

Association for Stammerers.................. 95
College of Speech & Language
  Therapists 1210

Spiritualism *see* PSYCHICAL RESEARCH

SPONSORSHIP

Association for Business Sponsorship of
  the Arts 76
European Sponsorship Consultants
  Association.............................1491
Institute of Sports Sponsorship 1976
—*see also* ADVERTISING & MARKETING

SPORT & SPORTS EQUIPMENT

Badminton Association of England.......... 460
British Aerobatic Association 514
British Association of Canoe Trades......... 558
British Balloon & Airship Club 614
British Bobsleigh Association 624
British Canoe Union 636
British Chess Federation................... 655
British Field Sports Society 743
British Ice Hockey Association............. 809
British Institute of Sports Coaches 836
British Orienteering Federation............. 923
British Racketball Association.............. 969
British Schools' Canoeing Association....... 988
British Slot Car Racing Association 1000
British Sports & Allied Industries
  Federation.............................1035
British Trampoline Federation.............1061
Croquet Association 1338
English Basketball Association 1427
Federation of Sailing & Motor Cruising
  Schools 1564
Federation of Sports Goods Distributors   ...1566
Formula Air Racing Association............1620
Hockey Association 1739
International Council of Marine Industry
  Associations...........................2097
International Institute of Sports Therapy   ...2136
Martial Arts Commission 2309
Modern Pentathlon Association of GB   ...2356

National School Sailing Association........2662
Royal Yachting Association.................2963
Sail Training Association 2970
Sports Council...........................3274
Sports Council for Northern Ireland.......3275
Squash Rackets Association 3280
–see also individual sports

SPRINGS

Spring Research & Manufacturers'
     Association.........................3279

Stamps *see* PHILATELY

STATIONERY & ALLIED PRODUCTS

British Association of Trade Computer
     Label Manufacturers 606
Domestic Manufacturing Stationers'
     Association.........................1377
Drawing Office Material Manufacturers
     & Dealers Association...............1381
Envelope Makers' & Manufacturing
     Stationers' Association 1444
Greeting Card & Calendar Association......1680
Letter File Manufacturers Association 2236
Postcard Association 2810
Rubber Stamp Manufacturers' Guild 2964
Writing Equipment Society 3481
Writing Instruments Association 3482

Statistics *see* MATHEMATICS & STATISTICS

STEEL

British Independent Steel Producers
     Association.........................814
British Iron & Steel Consumers' Council 848
Electric Steel Makers' Guild 1402
National Association of Steel
     Stockholders 2492
Stainless Steel Fabricators' Association ...3282

Stockbroking *see* FINANCIAL SERVICES

STONE INDUSTRY

Dry Stone Walling Association of GB 1385
London Association of Master
     Stonemasons 2267
Stone Federation 3300

STORAGE EQUIPMENT

Storage & Handling Equipment
     Distributors' Association............3301

Storage Equipment Manufacturers
     Association.........................3302

STRAIN MEASUREMENT

British Society for Strain Measurement ...1008
Joint British Committee for Stress
     Analysis............................2205

Structural engineering *see* BUILDING &
CIVIL ENGINEERING

SUGAR & SUGAR PRODUCTS

British Honey Importers & Packers
     Association.........................802
British Sugarcraft Guild 1041
European Federation of Honey Packers
     & Distributors 1466
Honey Importers & Packers Association ...1745
International Sugar Organization 2175
London Sugar Brokers' Association 2279
Refined Sugar Association...............2866
Sugar Association of London 3305
Sugar Bureau 3306
Sugar Traders Association of the UK 3307
United Kingdom Sugar Industry
     Association.........................3416

SUN TANNING

Association of Sun Tanning
     Organisations.......................415
British Sunbed Hire Federation 1042

Supermarkets *see* RETAIL TRADES;
GROCERY TRADES

SURFACE COATINGS

British Aggregate Construction Materials
     Industries 517
British Resin Manufacturers' Association 976
British Surface Treatment Suppliers
     Association.........................1043
Federation of Epoxy Resin Formulators
     & Applicators.......................1541
Institute of Vitreous Enamellers 1996
International Union for Surface Finishing ...2185
Vitreous Enamel Development Council ...3434

Surfing *see* SWIMMING & SURFING

SURGICAL EQUIPMENT & MATERIALS

British Anaesthetic & Respiratory
     Equipment Manufacturers Association; 526

British Surgical Export Group 1045
British Surgical Trades Association 1046
Disposable Hypodermic & Allied
   Equipment Manufacturers' Association
   of Europe 1367
Electro-Medical Trade Association 1412
European Confederation of Medical
   Suppliers Associations 1460
Hospital Disposable Fabric Convertors'
   Association 1750
Institute of Sterile Services Management . . . 1978
Sterilised Suture Manufacturers'
   Association 3296
Surgical Dressing Manufacturers'
   Association 3310
Surgical Textiles Conference 3311
United Kingdom Medical Equipment
   Industries Group 3400

SURGICAL PRACTICE

Association of Coloprociology of GB &
   Ireland 209
Association of Surgeons of GB &
   Ireland 418
British Association of Aesthetic Plastic
   Surgeons 552
British Association of Cosmetic
   Surgeons 563
British Association of Oral &
   Maxillofacial Surgeons 583
British Association of Otolaryngologists 585
British Association of Plastic Surgeons 590
British Association of Surgical Oncology 600
British Association of Urological
   Surgeons 607
British Colostomy Association 666
British Institute of Surgical
   Technologists 837
British Orthopaedic Association 925
British Society for Surgery of the Hand . . . 1009
British Thoracic Society 1056
European Society of Ophthalmic Plastic
   & Reconstructive Surgery 1490
Ileostomy Association of GB & Ireland . . . 1759
International Medical Society of
   Paraplegia 2145
Royal College of Physicians 2905
Royal College of Surgeons of England . . . 2908
Society of Cardiological Technicians 3161

SURVEYING

Architects & Surveyors Institute 59
Association of CCTV Surveyors 189
Association of London Borough
   Engineers & Surveyors 317
Commonwealth Association of
   Surveying & Land Economy 1226
Consultant Quantity Surveyors
   Association 1265

Hydrographic Society 1755
Incorporated Association of Architects &
   Surveyors 1763
London District Surveyors Association . . . 2270
Rating & Valuation Association 2861
Royal Institution of Chartered Surveyors . . . 2927
Society of Chief Quantity Surveyors in
   Local Government 3168
Society of Surveying Technicians 3247
United Kingdom Land & Hydrographic
   Survey Association 3399

SWIMMING & SURFING

British Surfing Association 1044
English Schools Swimming Association . . . 1437
Institute of Swimming Teachers &
   Coaches 1981
Surf Life Saving Association of GB 3309
Swimming Teachers' Association 3315

SWIMMING POOLS

Institute of Baths & Recreation
   Management 1833
Institute of Swimming Pool Engineers 1980
Swimming Pool & Allied Trades
   Association 3314

TABLE TENNIS

English Schools Table Tennis
   Association 1438
English Table Tennis Association 1440

TANKS

Plastic Tanks & Cisterns Manufacturers'
   Association 2794

TAR

Low Temperature Coal Distillers
   Association of GB 2283

TATTOOISTS

British Tattoo Artists Federation 1048

TAXATION

Institute for Fiscal Studies 1813
Institute of Taxation 1983

Taxi cabs *see* VEHICLE HIRE

TAXIDERMY

Guild of Taxidermists 1705

Tea *see* FOOD & BEVERAGES

Teaching *see* EDUCATION

TELECOMMUNICATIONS

Association of Telephone Information &
   Entertainment Providers 424
British Approvals Board for
   Telecommunications 530
Federation of Communication Services ...1533
Independent Cellular Retailers
   Federation................................1775
Institution of British
   Telecommunications Engineers 2004
International Maritime Satellite
   Organisation............................2143
Overhead Transmission Line Contractors ...2737
Society of Cable Television Engineers 3160
Super Tension Cables Group 3308
Telecommunication Engineering &
   Manufacturing Association 3325
Telecommunications Industry
   Association..............................3326
Telecommunications Users' Association ...3327

Television & video *see* AUDIO/VISUAL
INDUSTRIES

Tennis *see* LAWN TENNIS; TABLE TENNIS

TEXTILE INDUSTRIES - CLOTHING

Apparel Knitting & Textiles Alliance 56
Athletic Clothing Manufacturers
   Association............................. 446
British Clothing Industry Association 662
British Fashion Council 735
British Menswear Guild 881
Clothing & Footwear Institute 1195
Federation of Clothing Designers &
   Executives...............................1531
Federation of Merchant Tailors 1553
Menswear Association of Britain 2332
National Childrens' Wear Association of
   GB & NI 2526
Scottish Federation of Merchant Tailors ...3024
–see also HATS & HEADWEAR

TEXTILE INDUSTRIES - GENERAL

British Fabric Association 732
British Interlining Manufacturers
   Association............................. 843
British Lace Federation.................... 859
British Narrow Fabrics Association 898

British Nonwovens Manufacturers'
   Association............................. 908
British Polyolefin Textiles Association 949
British Textile Confederation 1052
British Textile Employers' Association 1053
Central Council of the Irish Linen
   Industry 1141
Coir Association 1201
Employers' Association of the Linen &
   Cotton Handkerchief & Household
   Goods Wages Council 1417
Fabric Care Research Association 1498
Flax & Linen Association 1600
Flax Merchants Association................1601
Handkerchief & Household Linens
   Association..............................1713
Home & Contract Furnishing Textiles
   Association..............................1740
International Association of Textile
   Dyers & Printers 2067
Irish Linen Guild.........................2200
Lambeg Industrial Research Association ...2217
Made-up Textile Association 2287
Scottish Lace & Window Furnishing
   Association..............................3035
Scottish Net Manufacturers Association ...3047
Silk Association of GB 3090
Textile Converters Association 3330
Textile Distributors Association 3331
Textile Finishers' Association 3332
Textile Institute 3333
Textile Research Council 3334

TEXTILE INDUSTRIES - HOSIERY & KNITWEAR

Apparel Knitting & Textiles Alliance 56
British Branded Hosiery Group 627
British Hand Knitting Confederation......... 782
Hand Knitting Association 1712
Hawick Knitwear Manufacturers
   Association..............................1717
Hosiery & Allied Trades Research
   Association..............................1749
Knitting Industries' Federation 2216
Leicester & District Knitting Industry
   Association..............................2233
National Wool Textile Export
   Corporation 2685

TEXTILE MACHINERY & EQUIPMENT

British Association of Clothing
   Machinery Manufacturers 559
British Textile Machinery Association.......1054

THEATRE

Association of British Theatre
   Technicians 172
British Music Hall Society 894

Conference of Drama Schools 1253
Directors Guild of GB 1362
Entertainment Agents Association 1442
Federation of Ethical Stage Hypnotists ...1542
Independent Theatre Council 1791
Institute of Entertainment & Arts
     Management 1878
International Federation for Theatre
     Research 2104
National Council for Drama Training 2538
National Federation of Playgoers'
     Societies 2592
Provincial Theatre Council................2847
Society for Theatre Research 3133
Society of British Theatre Designers.......3157
Society of Teachers of Speech & Drama ...3249
Society of Theatre Consultants............3251
Society of West End Theatre..............3254
Stage Management Association...........3281
Theatres Advisory Council 3337
Theatres National Committee 3338
Theatrical Management Association 3339
Variety & Allied Entertainments Council
     of GB 3425

Tiles see BRICKS, TILES & SANITARY POTTERY

Timber see WOOD & WOODWORKING

Timesharing see PROPERTY - LAND & BUILDINGS

TIN

International Tin Research Institute 2178

TOASTMASTERS

National Association of Toastmasters.......2497

TOBACCO TRADES

Association of Independent Tobacco
     Specialists..........................293
National Association of Cigarette
     Machine Operators....................2424
Pipesmokers' Council 2789
Retail Confectioners & Tobacconists
     Association..........................2878
Tobacco Advisory Council.................3351
Wholesale Confectionery & Tobacco
     Alliance 3452

Toilet preparations see COSMETICS & TOILETRIES

TOOLS

Association of Engineering Distributors 252
British Hacksaw & Bandsaw Makers'
     Association...........................780
British Masonry Drill Bit Association 874
Diamond Industrial Products Association ...1358
Drilling & Sawing Association 1382
Engineers' Hand Tools Association........1425
European Committee of Manufacturers,
     Compressors, Vacuum Pumps &
     Pneumatic Tools.....................1458
Federation of British Engineers' Tool
     Manufacturers 1523
Federation of British Hand Tool
     Manufacturers 1525
File Association...........................1580
Gauge & Tool Makers' Association.......1644
Handsaw Association 1714
Milling Cutter & Toolbit Association 2345
Portable Electric Tool Manufacturers'
     Association...........................2807
Saw Association 2977
Screw Thread Tool Manufacturers'
     Association...........................3076
Twist Drill & Reamer Association 3371
Woodworkers', Builder's &
     Miscellaneous Tools Association 3466
–see also MACHINE TOOLS

Tourism see TRAVEL, TOURISM & HOLIDAYS

TOWN & COUNTRY PLANNING

British Association of Landscape
     Industries 576
British Urban Regeneration Association ...1073
County Planning Officers' Society.........1323
Land Institute 2219
Landscape Institute 2220
Landscape Research Group...............2221
National Housing & Town Planning
     Council 2617
Regional Studies Association 2871
Royal Town Planning Institute 2962
Scottish National Housing & Town
     Planning Council 3046
Society of Town Planning Technicians ...3252
Town & Country Planning Association ...3356

TOYS

British Association of Toy Retailers 605
British Doll Artists Association 703
British Toy & Hobby Manufacurers
     Association...........................1059
British Toymakers Guild 1060
International Committee of Toy
     Industries 2087

National Association of Toy Distributors ...2498
National Association of Toy Retailers.......2499
National Toy Libraries Association 2677
Toy & Giftware Importers Association 3357

TRADE ASSOCIATIONS

Confederation of British Associations 1246
Society of Association Executives 3144

Trademarks *see* INTELLECTUAL PROPERTY

Trades unions *see* EMPLOYMENT LAW & RIGHTS

TRADING STANDARDS

Association of Certification Bodies 191
Association of Trading Standards
    Officers 428
Institute of Trading Standards
    Administration..........................1987
Society of County Trading Standards
    Officers 3180
Society of Directors of Trading
    Standards in Scotland 3184
Society of Metropolitan Chief Trading
    Standards Officers 3221

Traffic *see* ROADS & ROAD SAFETY

Training *see* MANAGEMENT & MANAGEMENT TRAINING; EDUCATION; AND SPECIFIC ASPECTS

Translation *see* LANGUAGES

TRANSPORT

Chartered Institute of Transport 1166
Community Transport Association..........1233
Despatch Association 1355
London Regional Passengers Committee ...2277
National Council on Inland Transport 2553
Organisation of Teachers of Transport
    Studies.................................2731
Thames Passenger Services Federation   ...3336
Transport Association 3365
Transport Ticket Society...................3366
Transport Users Consultative Committee ...3367
–see also specfic areas eg ROAD TRANSPORT

TRAVEL, TOURISM & HOLIDAYS

Alliance of Independent Travel Agents   29
Association of British Travel Agents 174
Association of Couriers in Tourism 232
Association of Directors of Recreation,
    Leisure & Tourism 239
Association of Guide-Booking Agency
    Services 272
Association of Independent Tour
    Operators 294
Association of National Tourist Office
    Representatives in the UK 351
Association of Pleasurecraft Operators
    on Inland Waterways.....................366
British Activity Holiday Association 510
British Association of Hotel Reservations
    Representatives.........................574
British Association of Tourist Officers 604
British Holiday & Home Parks
    Association.............................798
British Incoming Tour Operators'
    Association.............................811
British Resorts Association 977
Guild of Business Travel Agents 1689
Guild of Guide Lecturers 1694
Institute of Travel & Tourism 1992
Institute of Travel Management 1993
International Airline Passengers
    Assocation 2050
International Association of Tour
    Managers 2068
International Federation of Tour
    Operators 2119
National Association of Holiday Centres ...2449
National Committee of Skal Clubs of the
    UK.....................................2531
National Retreat Centre 2658
School & Group Travel Association 2978
Scottish Tourist Guides Association 3068
Tour Operators Study Group..............3354
Tourism Society 3355
–see also HOTEL & CATERING MANAGEMENT

Trees *see* FORESTRY

Tropical medicine *see* MEDICAL PRACTICE

Tubing *see* PIPES, TUBES & TUNNELS

Turkeys *see* POULTRY

Typography *see* PRINTING & PRINTING EQUIPMENT

TYRES

Industrial Tyre Association.................1801
National Tyre Distributors' Association   ...2680

Retread Manufacturers' Association 2882

Underwater technology *see*
OCEANOGRAPHY; OFFSHORE
TECHNOLOGY

Unit trusts *see* FINANCIAL SERVICES

Universities *see* EDUCATION

Upholstery *see* FURNITURE & UPHOLSTERY

Valuation *see* RATING & VALUATION

VALVES

British Valve & Actuator Manufacturers
Association 1076

Vegetables *see* FRUIT & VEGETABLES

VEGETARIANISM

International Vegetarian Union 2191
Vegan Society 3426
Vegetarian Society 3428

Vehicle components *see* MOTOR
INDUSTRY

VEHICLE HIRE

Association of Registered Chauffeurs 395
British Vehicle Rental & Leasing
Association 1077
Licensed Taxi Drivers Association 2239
National Federation of Taxicab
Associations 2600

VENDING MACHINES

Automatic Vending Association of
Britain 454
National Association of Cigarette
Machine Operators 2424

Ventilation *see* HEATING & VENTILATING

VETERINARY PRACTICE

Association of Veterinary Anaesthetists
of GB & Ireland 437

Association of Veterinary Teachers &
Research Workers 438
British Cattle Veterinary Association 645
British Equine Veterinary Association 725
British Small Animal Veterinary
Association 1001
British Veterinary Association 1079
Royal College of Veterinary Surgeons 2909
—*see also* ANIMALS & ANIMAL WELFARE

Video *see* AUDIO/VISUAL INDUSTRIES

Visual aids *see* AUDIO/VISUAL INDUSTRIES

Visually handicapped *see* SIGHT
IMPAIRED

Vodka *see* WINES & SPIRITS

WALLCOVERINGS

Wall Covering Distributors Association . . . 3437
Wallcovering Manufacturers Association
of GB 3438
Wallpaper, Paint & Wallcovering
Retailers Association 3439

Waste disposal *see* RECLAMATION &
RECYCLING

Watchmaking *see* CLOCKS & WATCHES

WATER & WATER TREATMENT

Association of CCTV Surveyors 189
Association of Drainage Authorities 248
Association of High Pressure Water
Jetting Contractors 277
British Effluent & Water Association 712
British Society of Dowsers 1019
British Turf & Landscape Irrigation
Association 1067
British Water Industries Group 1084
European Desalination Association 1462
Federation of Dredging Contractors 1535
Freshwater Biological Association 1626
Industrial Water Society 1802
Institution of Water & Environmental
Management 2037
Institution of Water Officers 2038
International Association on Water
Pollution Research & Control 2070
International Commission on Irrigation &
Drainage 2084

International Water Supply Association ...2193
National Association of Water Power
    Users 2506
National Pure Water Association 2653
Scottish Association of Directors of
    Water & Sewerage Services 2998
Society of British Water Industries 3158
Water Companies' Association 3442
Water Research Centre 3443
Water Services Association of England
    & Wales.................................3444
Well Drillers Association..................3448

Water pipes *see* PIPES, TUBES & TUNNELS

Water pollution *see* POLLUTION CONTROL

WATERWAYS, INLAND

Association of Pleasurecraft Operators
    on Inland Waterways......................366
Barge & Canal Development Association 467
Inland Waterways Amenity Advisory
    Council 1807
Inland Waterways Association 1808
National Association of Inland
    Waterway Carriers 2454
National Waterways Transport
    Association.............................2684
Paddle Steamer Preservation Society 2741

WEIGHING MACHINES

National Federation of Scale &
    Weighing Machine Manufacturers 2595

Welding *see* METALLURGY

Welfare *see* CHILD WELFARE; SOCIAL
WELFARE

Whisky *see* WINES & SPIRITS

WHOLESALE TRADES

British Wholesale Traders Association 1088
Federation of Wholesale & Industrial
    Distributors Co-ordinating Committee ...1567
Federation of Wholesale Distributors 1568
Wholesale Cash & Carry Association 3451
Wholesale Delivered Group Trade
    Association.............................3454

WINDOW CLEANERS

National Federation of Master Window
    Cleaners...............................2587

Windows *see* BUILDING EQUIPMENT &
MATERIALS

WINES & SPIRITS

Association of Malt Products
    Manufacturers 327
Champagne Agents Association............1154
English Vineyard Association 1441
European Malt Extract Manufacturers
    Association.............................1480
Gin & Vodka Assocation of GB 1664
Home Brewing & Winemaking
    Manufacturers Association 1742
Home Brewing & Winemaking Trade
    Association.............................1743
Importers of Madeira Wine 1762
Institute of Masters of Wine 1927
Malt Distillers Association of Scotland ...2293
Scotch Whisky Association 2990
Sherry Producers Committee.............3084
Wine & Spirit Association of GB & N
    Ireland 3459

WIRE & WIRE PRODUCTS

British Woven Wire Export Association ...1094
European Wire Rope Information Service ...1493
Federation of Wire Rope Manufacturers
    of GB 1569
International Wire & Machinery
    Association.............................2195
Scottish Wirework Manufacturers'
    Association.............................3071
Stainless Steel Industry Association 3283
Wire & Wire Rope Employers'
    Association.............................3461
Wire Products Association................3462
Wire Rope Export Conference 3463
Woven Wire Association 3480

WOMEN'S ORGANISATIONS

International Federation of Business &
    Professional Women 2107
National Association of Women's Clubs ...2507
National Council of Women of GB 2552
National Federation of Women's
    Institutes 2604
National Union of Townswomen's
    Guilds 2682
United Kingdom Federation of Business
    & Professional Women 3389

WOOD & WOODWORKING

Association of British Plywood & Veneer
    Manufacturers 159
Association of Timber Agents & Brokers 427
British Timber Merchants' Association 1057
British Wood Turners Association 1092
British Woodworking Federation 1093
Institute of Carpenters 1845
Institute of Machine Woodworking
    Technology 1919
Institute of Wood Science 1999
Master Carvers Association 2310
National Sawmilling Association 2660
Northern Ireland Timber Importers
    Association 2710
Processed Woodchip, Sawdust &
    Woodflour Association 2829
Scottish Timber Trade Association 3067
Society of Wood Engravers 3257
Timber Drying Association 3345
Timber Research & Development
    Association 3347
Timber Trade Federation 3348
Timber Trade Training Association 3349
United Kingdom Softwood Sawmillers'
    Association 3413
Woodworking Machinery Suppliers
    Association 3467
–see also FORESTRY

WOOL

Association of Wholesale Woollen
    Merchants 443
Confederation of British Wool Textiles ... 1248
Harris Tweed Association 1715
Hawick Knitwear Manufacturers
    Association 1717
International Mohair Association 2146
International Wool Secretariat 2196
National Wool Textile Export
    Corporation 2685
Northern Ireland Wool Users'
    Association 2712
Scottish Woollen Industry Association 3072
Scottish Woollen Publicity Council 3073
United Kingdom Wool Growers
    Federation 3419

WRITERS

Association of Authors' Agents 120
Association of British Science Writers 167
Association of Golf Writers 268
Authors' Licensing & Collecting Society 450
British Guild of Travel Writers 779
Broadcasting Press Guild 1095
Central Criminal Court Journalists'
    Association 1142
Circle of Wine Writers 1186
Commonwealth Journalists Association ... 1228
Crime Reporters' Association 1333
Crime Writer's Association 1334
Critics' Circle 1336
Critics' Guild 1337
Environmental Communicators
    Organisation 1446
European Association of Science Editors ... 1454
Football Writers' Association 1611
Foreign Press Association in London 1616
Guild of Agricultural Journalists 1682
Guild of Jewish Journalists 1698
Guild of Motoring Writers 1701
Guild Of Travel Writers 1707
Medical Journalists' Association 2328
Outdoor Writer's Guild 2736
Romantic Novelists' Association 2889
Science Fiction Foundation 2986
Society of Authors 3145
Society of Women Writers & Journalists ... 3256
Sports Writers' Association of GB 3277
Yachting Journalists Association 3486

X-ray equipment *see* RADIOGRAPHY &
RADIOLOGY

Yachts & yachting *see* SPORT & SPORTS
EQUIPMENT

YOUTH SERVICES

Association of Boys' Clubs Organisers 127
National Association of Boys' Clubs 2415
National Association of Youth Hostel
    Wardens 2508
National Council for Voluntary Youth
    Services 2548
Northern Ireland Association of Youth
    Clubs 2702
Scottish Association of Youth Clubs 3002
Scottish Standing Conference of
    Voluntary Youth Organisations 3065

Zinc *see* METALLURGY

ZOOLOGY

International Commission on Zoological
    Nomenclature 2086
International Trust for Zoological
    Nomenclature 2180

Geographic Index
by City

Aberdare

Combustion Engineering Association 1213

Aberdeen

Association of Directors of Social Work 240
British Boatbuilders Association 623
Federation of British Kipperers, Herring
  Merchants & Herring Trade Quick
  Freezers Associations 1526
Fishing Boat Builders' Association 1594
Scottish Association of Directors of
  Water & Sewerage Services 2998
Scottish Fishermen's Federation 3027
Scottish Pelagic Fishermens Association . . . 3050
Torry Research Station 3353

Airdrie

Scottish Commercial Travellers
  Association 3007

Alderley Edge

Association of Shell Boilermakers 405

Aldershot

Architectural Precast Cladding
  Association 63
Association of Structural Fire Protection
  Contractors & Manufacturers 413
British Waste Paper Association 1082
Federation of Epoxy Resin Formulators
  & Applicators 1541
Institute of Carpenters 1845
National Caravan Council 2517
Phenolic Foam Manufacturers
  Association 2776
Sprayed Concrete Association 3278
Thermal Insulation Manufacturers &
  Suppliers Association 3341

Alton

Association of Brokers & Yacht Agents 176
British Bottlers' Institute 625
International Society for the Prevention
  of Water Pollution 2172
National Pony Society 2650
United Kingdom Technology
  Organisation 3418
Yacht Brokers Designers & Surveyors
  Association 3483

Altrincham

Institute of Health Education 1897
Institution of Civil Engineering
  Surveyors 2006
National Association of Approved
  Driving Instructors 2410
Salt Manufacturers Association 2973

Ambleside

Freshwater Biological Association 1626
Institute of Freshwater Ecology 1893

Amersham

British Button Manufacturers Society 633
British Dental Trade Association 696
Institute of Public Loss Assessors 1953
Master Music Printers & Engravers
  Association 2313
National Federation of Hide & Skin
  Markets 2582
Society of Chief Quantity Surveyors in
  Local Government 3168

Ampthill

International Federation of Dental
  Anaesthesiology Societies 2108
United Kingdom Irrigation Association . . . 3397

Andover

Association of British Steriliser
   Manufacturers 171
Association of General Practitioner
   Community Hospitals 266
Gin & Vodka Assocation of GB 1664
Swimming Pool & Allied Trades
   Association 3314

Arundel

Property Consultants Society 2842

Ascot

Association of Licensed Aircraft
   Engineers 310
Automated Material Handling Systems
   Association 451
British Industrial Truck Association 819
Chartered Institute of Building 1160
Hospital Doctors' Association 1751
Racecourse Association 2852
Society of Licensed Victuallers 3214
Steel Construction Institute 3292

Ashford

Architectural Aluminium Association 61
British Association of Barbershop
   Singers 554
British Society of Dowsers 1019
Yacht Harbour Association 3485

Ashtead

Omnibus Society 2720

Aviemore

Association of Ski Schools in GB 408
British Association of Ski Instructors 597

Aylesbury

Association of County Supplies Officers 231
County Education Officers' Society 1321
General Aviation Manufacturers &
   Traders Association .1646
International Medical Society of
   Paraplegia 2145
Marine Training Association 2305
National Association of Memorial
   Masons 2465
National Tyre Distributors' Association . . .2680

Aylesford

Association of Building Component
   Manufacturers 179

Ayr

Scottish Association of Advisers in
   Physical Education 2997

Bakewell

National Golf Clubs Advisory
   Association 2612

Banbury

British Shops & Stores Association 996
European Food Brokers Association 1471
Radionics Association .2857

Bangor

Association for Literary & Linguistic
   Computing 87
International Union of Anthropological
   & Ethnological Sciences 2186
National Audio Visual Aids Library 2511
Natural Slate Quarries Association 2688

Bangor, Co Down

Northern Ireland Builders Merchants'
   Association 2704
Northern Ireland Timber Importers
   Association 2710

Banstead

Automatic Vending Association of
   Britain 454
National Federation of Terrazzo-Mosaic
   Specialists 2601

Barking

Association of London Chief Librarians 318
National Association of Language
   Advisers 2457
Rubber Trade Association of London 2965

Barnet

British Society for Music Therapy 1004
Society of Women Writers & Journalists . . .3256

Barnsley

Federation of Ethical Stage Hypnotists . . .1542
Institute of Market Officers 1926
National Market Traders Federation 2637
Permanent Way Institution 2765

Basingstoke

Association for the Reform of Latin
    Teaching 105
Association of Business Advertising
    Agencies 182
Association of Industrial Road Safety
    Officers 296

Bath

British Toymakers Guild 1060
National Osteoporosis Society 2642
Royal Photographic Society 2938
Sterilization Packaging Materials
    Association 3297

Bathgate

Association of Chief Architects of
    Scottish Local Authorities 195

Beckenham

Association of Learned & Professional
    Society Publishers 308

Bedford

Aircraft Research Association 25
Association of Conservation Officers 216
British Association of Orthodontists 584
Institute of Legal Executives 1914
Institution of Agricultural Engineers 2001
Institution of Diesel & Gas Turbine
    Engineers 2010
International Sheepdog Society 2164
Music Masters' & Mistresses'
    Association 2375
National Association of Prison Visitors . . . 2474
National Hairdressers' Federation 2613
Parrot Society 2748
Pet Trade & Industry Association 2769
Radio, Electrical & Television Retailers'
    Association 2856
Silsoe Research Institute 3091

Belfast

International Association for Educational
    & Vocational Guidance 2055
National Board for Nursing, Midwifery &
    Health Visiting for Northern Ireland 2515
Northern Ireland Association for Mental
    Health 2701
Northern Ireland Association of Youth
    Clubs 2702
Northern Ireland Bankers' Association 2703
Northern Ireland Dairy Trade Federation . . . 2705
Northern Ireland Grain Trade
    Association 2706

Northern Ireland Hotels & Caterers
    Association 2707
Northern Ireland Retail Fish Trade
    Association 2709
Northern Ireland Wholesale Merchants'
    & Manufacturers' Association 2711
Pharmaceutical Society of Northern
    Ireland 2775
Sports Council for Northern Ireland 3275
Ulster Curers' Association 3372
Ulster Farmers' Union 3373

Benfleet

Institute of Domestic Heating &
    Environmental Engineers 1871

Berkhamsted

Association of European Machine Tool
    Merchants 255

Bexley

Drinking Fountain Association 1383

Bexleyheath

Association of Trading Standards
    Officers 428
Mastic Asphalt Council & Employer's
    Federation 2320

Bidford-on-Avon

Aluminium Foil Container Manufacturers
    Association 39

Biggleswade

National Exhibitors Association 2568

Billingshurst

International Powered Access Federation . . . 2152

Bingley

British Turf & Landscape Irrigation
    Association 1067
National Turf Grass Council 2679
Sports Turf Research Institute 3276

Birmingham

Alliance of Literary Societies 30
Aluminium Can Recycling Association 35
Aluminium Extruders Association 36
Aluminium Federation 37
Aluminium Finishing Association 38

Aluminium Powder & Paste Association 40
Aluminium Primary Producers
  Association 41
Aluminium Rolled Products
  Manufacturers Association 42
Art Metalware Manufacturers'
  Association........................ 65
Association for Neighbourhood Councils 89
Association for the Education & Welfare
  of the Visually Handicapped 101
Association of Blind Chartered
  Physiotherapists 124
Association of British Pewter Craftsmen 157
Association of British Private Detectives 161
Association of British Security Officers 168
Association of Bronze & Brass Founders 177
Association of Dental Hospitals of the
  UK............................... 234
Association of Engineering Distributors 252
Association of Hispanists of GB &
  Ireland 280
Association of Light Alloy Refiners.......... 311
Association of Paediatric Anaesthetists
  of GB and Ireland 359
Association of Stainless Fastener
  Distributors....................... 411
Association of University Professors of
  French & Heads of French
  Departments...................... 431
Automotive Distributors Federation.......... 455
Ball & Roller Bearing Manufacturers
  Association........................ 462
BCIRA Cast Metals Technology 471
Bookmakers' Association 496
British & Irish Association of Law
  Librarians 505
British Association of Cultured Pearl
  Importers......................... 564
British Association of Social Workers........ 598
British Balloon & Airship Club............ 614
British Bronze & Brass Ingot
  Manufacturers Association 628
British Chain Manufacturers Association 652
British Constructional Steelwork
  Association........................ 674
British Dietetic Association 698
British Forging Industry Association......... 758
British Foundry Association 759
British Gear Association 768
British Hallmarking Council............... 781
British Hardware Federation 786
British Independent Plastic Extruders'
  Association........................ 813
British Industrial Furnace Constructors
  Association........................ 818
British Institute of Traffic Education
  Research 838
British Investment Casting Trade
  Association........................ 847
British Jewellers' Association 851
British Jewellery & Giftware Federation 852

British Leathergoods Manufacturers
  Association........................ 865
British Materials Handling Federation 875
British Metal Castings Council............ 883
British Non-Ferrous Metals Federation ... 907
British Plumbing Fittings Manufacturers
  Association........................ 947
British Powder Metal Federation........... 955
British Pressure Gauge Manufacturers
  Association........................ 957
British Racketball Association............. 969
British Robot Association 983
British Rubber Industry Training
  Organisation....................... 984
British Surface Treatment Suppliers
  Association........................ 1043
British Turned-Parts Manufacturers
  Association........................ 1069
British Valve & Actuator Manufacturers
  Association........................ 1076
Castor Manufacturers (UK) Association ...1127
Cold Rolled Sections Association 1203
Compressed Air Equipment Distributors
  Association........................ 1237
Copper Smelters & Refiners Association ...1276
Drilling & Sawing Association 1382
Ductile Iron Producers Asssociation 1388
Electro-Physiological Technologists'
  Association........................ 1413
English Ski Council 1439
European Investment Casters' Federation ...1477
Federation of Family History Societies...... 1544
Funeral Furnishing Manufacturers
  Association........................ 1629
Galvanizers Association 1633
Garden Industry Manufacturers
  Association........................ 1641
Giftware Association 1662
Institute of British Carriage &
  Automobile Manufacturers 1837
Institute of British Detective
  Investigative Security & Forensic
  Specialists........................ 1838
Institute of British Foundrymen 1839
Institute of Field Archaeologists........... 1886
Institute of Metal Finishing 1933
Institute of Sheet Metal Engineering 1972
International Federation of Settlements 2113
Jewellery Distributors' Association of
  GB 2202
Light Metal Founders Association.......... 2244
Mechanical Handling Engineers
  Association........................ 2323
Metal Finishing Association 2335
Motor Vehicle Dismantlers' Association
  of GB 2364
National Adult School Organisation 2381
National Association for Teaching
  English & other Community
  Languages to Adults 2399

National Association of Arc Welding
    Equipment Repairers 2411
National Association of Archery Coaches . . . 2412
National Association of Fastener
    Stockholders 2435
National Association of Health
    Authorities 2445
National Association of Industrial
    Distributors 2452
National Association of Schoolmaster &
    Union of Women Teachers 2483
National Association of Steel
    Stockholders 2492
National Small Woods Association 2665
National Union of Townswomen's
    Guilds 2682
Nickel Development Institute 2697
Occupational Hygiene Products
    Distributors Association 2715
Operational Research Society 2722
Organisation of European Aluminium
    Smelters 2729
Plastic Pipe Manufacturers Society 2793
Plastics Land Drainage Manufacturers'
    Association 2797
Professional Golfers' Association 2838
Registered Nursing Home Association 2873
Royal Society for the Prevention of
    Accidents 2946
Safety Equipment Distributors
    Association 2969
School Secretaries' Association 2984
Storage & Handling Equipment
    Distributors' Association 3301
Storage Equipment Manufacturers
    Association 3302
Transport Association 3365
United Kingdom Bartenders Guild 3384
Zip Fastener Manufacturers' Association . . . 3490

Bishop's Castle

Decorative Lighting Association 1346

Bishop's Stortford

Lifting Equipment Engineers Association . . . 2243

Blackburn

Association of Circus Proprietors of GB 203
Borough Engineers' Society 499
Institute of Professional Investigators 1950

Blackpool

Baby Equipment Hirers Association 457
British Federation of Hotel, Guest House
    & Self-Catering Associations 738
United Kingdom Alliance of Professional
    Teachers of Dancing 3380

Blairgowrie

Scottish Field Studies Association 3025

Bo'ness

Incorporated Society of Licensed Trade
    Stocktakers 1770

Bognor Regis

British Doll Artists Association 703

Boston

Association for British Music 75
English Bowling Federation 1429
National Association of Health Stores 2446
Plastics Crate Manufacturers'
    Association 2796

Bournemouth

British Ceramic Plant & Machinery
    Manufacturers' Association 649
British Ice Hockey Association 809
British Slot Car Racing Association 1000
Institute of Commercial Management 1861
National Committee of Skal Clubs of the
    UK 2531
Society of Chief Building Regulation
    Officers 3165

Bracknell

Building Services Research &
    Information Association 1103
Canine Studies Institute 1122

Bradford

Blanket Manufacturers Association 489
Confederation of British Wool Textiles . . . 1248
Museum Training Institute 2369
National Wool Textile Export
    Corporation 2685
Society of Dyers & Colourists 3186

Brentford

British Nonwovens Manufacturers'
    Association 908

Brentwood

British Drilling Association 705

Bridgend

Plastic Tanks & Cisterns Manufacturers'
    Association 2794

Bridgwater

National Clayware Federation 2528
National Council for Teacher-centred
  Professional Development 2544
Society of County Children's &
  Education Librarians 3177

Bridlington

Society of Archer-Antiquaries 3139

Brightlingsea

Tramway & Light Railway Society 3362

Brighton

Affiliation of Honourable Photographers 13
Association of Corporate Trustees 223
British Association of Art Therapists 553
British Floorcovering Manufacturers
  Association 750
Fauna & Flora Preservation Society 1514
Federation of Overseas Property
  Developers Agents & Consultants 1557
Institute of Manpower Studies 1924
Institution of British Engineers 2003
International Dance Teachers'
  Association 2099
Microwave Association 2341
National Association of Orientation &
  Mobility Instructors 2467
National Society for Clean Air &
  Environmental Protection, ... 2667
Proprietary Crematoria Association 2845
Single Ply Association 3094

Bristol

Aerodrome Owners Association 12
Association of British Wild Animal
  Keepers 175
Association of Consultant Architects 217
Association of District Secretaries 246
British Dental Hygienists' Association 695
British Growers Association 778
British Herbal Medicine Association 795
British Organic Farmers Association 922
British Society for Clinical
  Neurophysiology 1003
European Flexographic Technical
  Association 1470
Institute of Company Accountants 1863
National Federation of City Farms 2573
Naval Historical Collectors & Research
  Association 2690
Society for Computers & Law 3110
Society for Endocrinology 3114
Society of County & Regional Public
  Relations Officers 3176

Soil Association 3259
United Kingdom Egg Producers
  Association 3387
World Professional Billiards & Snooker
  Association 3475

Brixham

European Marketing Association 1482

Bromley

British Association of Manipulative
  Medicine 578
British Friction Materials Council 762
British Lawnmower Manufacturers
  Federation 862
Military Historical Society 2343
Noise Abatement Society 2698
Society of Artists in Architecture 3142
Society of Investment Analysts 3210

Buckfastleigh

Permaculture Association 2761

Buckhurst Hill

Clay Pigeon Shooting Association 1190

Buckingham

Society of Public Teachers of Law 3238

Burnham-on-Crouch

British Watch & Clock Makers' Guild 1083

Burton upon Trent

National Association of Postgraduate
  Medical Education Centre
  Administrators 2472

Bury

Needleloom Felt Manufacturers'
  Association 2691
Pressed Felt Manufacturers Association . . . 2822

Bury St Edmunds

Fibre Cement Manufacturers'
  Association 1578

Buxton

Stilton Cheese Makers Association 3299

Caernarfon

Association of Heads of Outdoor
  Education Centres 275

Calne

Alliance of Small Firms & Self-Employed
  People 31

Camberley

Army Records Society 64
British Institute of Innkeeping 825
Independent Schools Careers
  Organisation 1786

Cambridge

Association of British Neurologists 153
Association of British Theological &
  Philosophical Libraries 173
Association of Graduate Recruiters 270
Association of Professional Music
  Therapists 379
Bathroom & Kitchen Distributors
  Association 470
British Association for Brazing &
  Soldering 537
Careers Research & Advisory Centre 1124
Construction Industry Computing
  Association 1261
County Road Safety Offices' Association . . . 1324
Economic History Society 1393
Institute of Animal Physiology 1827
International Council for Bird
  Preservation 2092
International Glaciological Society 2124
International Society for Soil Mechanics
  & Foundation Engineering 2171
National Early Music Association 2561
National Institute of Agricultural Botany . . 2623
Nuclear Stock Association 2713
Palaeontological Association 2745
Provincial Booksellers' Fairs Association . . 2846
Shipowners Refrigerated Cargo
  Research Association 3086
Welding Institute 3446

Canterbury

Institute of Heraldic & Genealogical
  Studies 1899
International Federation for Theatre
  Research 2104

Cardiff

Association for Family Therapy 83
European Information Association 1475

Carlisle

International Bee Research Association . . . 2073
United Kingdom Federation of Jazz
  Bands 3390

Carlisle

British Deaf Association 689
Society of County Secretaries 3179
World Ploughing Organisation 3474

Carnforth

Association for the Teaching of the
  Social Sciences 110

Carshalton

British Industrial Biological Research
  Association 815
Federation of British Cremation
  Authorities 1522
Institute of Refrigeration 1961
National Union of Residents'
  Association 2681

Caterham

Shop & Display Equipment Association . . . 3088

Cheadle

British Association of Pool Table
  Operators 591

Cheam

British Confectioners Association 673
Natural Sausage Casing Association 2687

Chelmsford

Asbestos Removal Contractors
  Association 70
British Lubricants Federation 869
British Schools' Canoeing Association 988
European Asbestos & Recycling
  Association 1453

Cheltenham

British Association of Beauty Therapy &
  Cosmetology 555
British Small Animal Veterinary
  Association 1001
Federation of Resource Centres 1563
International Centre for Conservation
  Education 2076
Masters of Basset Hounds Association . . . 2316
Standing Conference of Principals 3286

Chepstow

Industrial Tyre Association..................1801
National Association of Youth Hostel
   Wardens 2508

Chessington

Stereoscopic Society 3295

Chester

Association of Civil Defence &
   Emergency Planning Officers 204
Consumer Credit Association of the UK ...1267
Flag Institute 1596
Guild of Hairdressers 1695
Heavy Transport Association...............1727
International Union of Crystallography ...2189

Chesterfield

Association for Residential Care 92
Low Temperature Coal Distillers
   Association of GB 2283

Chichester

Association of Principals of Colleges 372
British Association for Jazz Education 544
British Association for Local History 546
British Vehicle Rental & Leasing
   Association................................1077
Society of Automotive-Electrical
   Technicians 3146

Chippenham

Architects & Surveyors Institute.............. 59
Association of Motor Racing Circuit
   Owners 345
National Association for Curriculum
   Enrichment & Extension 2384

Chipping Campden

Campden Food & Drink Research
   Association...........................1119

Cirencester

International Federation of Training &
   Development Organisations..............2120
Masters of Foxhounds Association 2319

Clacton-on-Sea

General Dental Practitioners Association ...1653

Colchester

Association of Teachers of Singing......... 422
British Flute Society 755
British Ladder Manufacturers
   Association............................... 860
National Association for Staff
   Development in Further & Higher
   Education 2398
National Association of Health Estate
   Managers 2443
National Association of Leagues of
   Hospital Friends 2458

Coleraine

British Air Survey Association 523

Colwyn Bay

Snail Centre 3103

Corby

British Institute of Management............ 829
Institute of Logistics & Distribution
   Management 1917
National Society of Allotment & Leisure
   Gardeners 2670

Corsham

British Equine Veterinary Association........ 725
National & International Society for
   Education through Art 2380
National Society for Education in Art &
   Design 2668

Coulsdon

British Bobsleigh Association 624

Coventry

Association of Independent Cinemas 285
Association of Industrial Graphics &
   Nameplate Manufacturers 295
Bicycle Association of GB 481
Black Bolt & Nut Association of GB 488
British Deer Farmers' Association 691
British Industrial Fasteners Federation 817
British Numismatic Trade Association 912
British Production & Inventory Control
   Society.................................. 959
British Urethane Foam Contractors
   Association............................1074
Institute of Housing.......................1906
Livestock Auctioneers' Market
   Committee for England & Wales 2254
Motorcycle Industry Association 2365

National Association for Organic
  Gardening............................2393
National Association for Pastoral Care in
  Education 2395
National Association of Plumbing,
  Heating & Mechanical Services
  Contractors..........................2471
National Association of Seed Potato
  Merchants............................2484
National Council for Special Education ...2543
Referees' Association 2865
Universities Council for Adult &
  Continuing Education 3421

Cranbrook

British Association of Feed Supplement
  Manufacturers 568

Cranfield

British Hang Gliding & Paragliding
  Association............................ 783
Institute of Materials Management 1928
International Association for Vehicle
  System Dynamics.......................2054
International Deep Drawing Research
  Group.................................2100
National Materials Handling Centre 2639

Crawley

Association of Magisterial Officers 320
British Compressed Gases Association 671
Guild of Motoring Writers 1701
Hearing Aid Industry Association 1724
Locomotive & Carriage Institution..........2263

Crewe

British Waterfowl Association..............1087
International Association of University
  Professors of English 2069

Crowborough

British Institute of Kitchen Architecture 828

Crowthorne

Society of Teachers in Business
  Education 3248
Transport & Road Research Laboratory ...3364

Croydon

Angling Foundation........................ 50
Angling Trade Association.................. 51
Association of Loading & Elevating
  Equipment Manufacturers 315

British Chemical Distributors & Traders
  Association............................ 653
British Dragonfly Society 704
British Egg Products Association........... 714
British Photographic Association........... 942
British Photographic Importers'
  Association............................ 944
British Society of Baking 1016
British Sports & Allied Industries
  Federation............................1035
British Tape Industry Association 1047
Cathedral Organists' Association 1133
Driving Instructors Association............1384
Federation of Manufacturers of
  Construction Equipment & Cranes 1549
Fellowship of Skilled Secretaries 1572
Golf Ball Manufacturers Conference.......1671
Guild of Metal Perforators 1700
Institute of Trade Mark Agents............1986
Institute of Word Processing..............2000
International Airline Passengers
  Assocation 2050
Marquee Contractors Association 2308
Metropolitan Public Gardens
  Association............................2340
National Association of Fire Officers 2437
National Association of Mathematics
  Advisors 2464
National Association of Retail Furnishers ...2480
National Council for Schools Sports 2542
Orders & Medals Research Society........2727
Small Electrical Appliance Marketing
  Association............................3099

Dagenham

Hydrographic Society 1755
Science Fiction Foundation................2986

Darlington

Arts Development Association 69
Society of Local Council Clerks............3216

Dartford

British Display Society 701
Institute of Home Safety 1903
Tool & Trades History Society 3352

Daventry

Independent Waste Paper Processors
  Association............................1792
Master Locksmiths Association 2312
Wiping Cloth Manufacturers'
  Association............................3460

Dawlish

Institution of Railway Signal Engineers   ...2035

Denbigh

British Electroless Nickel Society 719

Derby

Association of Teachers of Mathematics 420
British Association of Canoe Trades 558
British Educational Research Association 711
British Isles Bee Breeders' Association 849
British Pest Control Association 936
English Schools Table Tennis
    Association 1438
Media Studies Association 2327
Minerals Engineering Society 2348
National Federation of Anglers 2571

Dewsbury

Cottage Garden Society 1285

Didcot

International Commission on
    Radiological Protection 2085
Society for Radiological Protection 3122

Doncaster

Association for Technological Education
    in Schools 99
British Sunbed Hire Federation 1042
Institution of Mining Electrical & Mining
    Mechanical Engineers 2027
Institution of Mining Engineers 2028
Partially Sighted Society 2749
Society of Ploughmen 3231

Dorchester

British Association for Dramatherapists 541

Droitwich

Association of Independent Tobacco
    Specialists 293
British Milksheep Association 889

Dundee

Association for the Study of Medical
    Education 108
Association of Independent Museums 289
Association of Jute Spinners &
    Manufacturers 305
British Polyolefin Textiles Association 949
European Flexible Intermediate Bulk
    Container Association 1469
Flax & Linen Association 1600
Flexible Intermediate Bulk Container
    Association 1602

Jute Importers' Association 2213
Jute Spinners & Manufacturers
    Association 2214
Made-up Textile Association 2287

Dunstable

Association of Tutors Incorporated 429
National Association of Industries for
    the Blind & Disabled 2453

Dunster

Society of British Battery Manufacturers . . . 3150

Durham

Association of Educational
    Psychologists 250
Council for the Advancement of
    Communication with Deaf People 1300

East Dereham

Organic Food Manufacturers Federation . . . 2728

East Grinstead

Guild of Experienced Motorists 1692
International Register of Oriental
    Medicine 2160

East Molesey

British Cable Makers' Confederation 634
Covered Conductors Association 1326
Embroiderers' Guild 1416
Personal Managers' Association 2766
Society for the Advancement of Games
    & Simulation in Education 3125
Super Tension Cables Group 3308

East Moseley

Independent Publishers Guild 1783

Eastbourne

Association of Authorised Public
    Accountants 119
British Council of Physical Education 682
Central Entertainment Agents Council 1143
Federation of Wholesale Distributors 1568
Leisure Studies Association 2235
National Association for Mental After-
    care in Registered Care Homes 2391
Professional Lighting & Sound
    Association 2840
Wholesale Cash & Carry Association 3451

Wholesale Delivered Group Trade
  Association 3454

Edgware

British Association of Hotel Accountants 573
British Numismatic Society 911
Infection Control Nurses' Association 1806

Edinburgh

Animal Diseases Research Association 52
Associated Scottish Life Offices 72
Association of Chief Police Officers
  (Scotland) 199
Association of Directors of Education in
  Scotland 237
Association of Educational Advisers in
  Scotland 249
Association of Higher Academic Staff in
  Colleges of Education in Scotland 278
Association of Installers & Unvented
  Hot Water Systems (Scotland &
  Ireland) 298
Association of Relocation Agents 398
Association of Scottish Local Health
  Councils 402
Association of University Teachers
  (Scotland) 433
Brewers Association of Scotland 500
British Ski Federation 999
British Society of Animal Production 1014
Committee of Scottish Clearing Bankers . . . 1222
Convention of Scottish Local Authorities . . . 1272
Council for Name Studies in GB &
  Ireland 1295
Domestic Heating Council 1375
Educational Institute of Scotland 1398
Electrical Contractors Association of
  Scotland 1406
Faculty of Actuaries 1499
Faculty of Advocates 1500
General Teaching Council for Scotland . . . 1658
Guild of Newspaper Editors 1702
Herring Buyers Association 1731
Institute of Animal Physiology &
  Genetics Research 1826
Institute of Auctioneers & Appraisers in
  Scotland 1830
Institute of Bankers in Scotland 1832
Institute of Chartered Accountants of
  Scotland 1848
Institute of Chartered Foresters 1850
Law Society of Scotland 2225
Mining Institute of Scotland 2351
National Association of Youth
  Orchestras 2509
National Board for Nursing, Midwifery &
  Health Visiting for Scotland 2516
National Farmers' Union of Scotland 2570

Pharmaceutical General Council
  (Scotland) 2773
Procurators Fiscal Society 2831
Royal Highland & Agricultural Society
  of Scotland 2915
Royal Incorporation of Architects in
  Scotland 2918
Royal Scottish Forestry Society 2939
Royal Scottish Geographical Society 2940
Scotch Quality Beef & Lamb
  Association 2989
Scottish & N Ireland Plumbing
  Employers' Federation 2991
Scottish Agricultural Arbiters'
  Association 2992
Scottish Agricultural Organisation
  Society 2993
Scottish Assessors' Association 2994
Scottish Association for Mental Health . . . 2995
Scottish Association of Master Bakers 3000
Scottish Association of Youth Clubs 3002
Scottish Community Education Council . . . 3009
Scottish Corn Trade Association 3011
Scottish Council for Arbitration 3012
Scottish Council for Research in
  Education 3014
Scottish Council for Voluntary
  Organisations 3015
Scottish Federation of Grocers' & Wine
  Merchants Associations 3022
Scottish Federation of Merchant Tailors . . . 3024
Scottish Grocers Federation 3030
Scottish Institute of Adult & Continuing
  Education 3033
Scottish Joint Industry Board for the
  Electrical Contracting Industry 3034
Scottish Landowners' Federation 3036
Scottish Law Agents Society 3037
Scottish Licensed Trade Association 3039
Scottish Master Plasterers' Association . . . 3041
Scottish Motor Trade Association 3044
Scottish Museums Council 3045
Scottish Newspaper Proprietors'
  Association 3048
Scottish Newspaper Publishers
  Association 3049
Scottish Poetry Library Association 3054
Scottish Publishers Association 3058
Scottish Salmon Smokers Association 3059
Scottish Secondary Teachers'
  Association 3061
Scottish Seed & Nursery Trade
  Association 3062
Scottish Standing Conference of
  Voluntary Youth Organisations 3065
Scottish Tourist Guides Association 3068
Scottish Wholesale Druggists
  Association 3070
Scottish Woollen Industry Association 3072
Scottish Woollen Publicity Council 3073

Scottish Woollen Trade Mark
　Association 3074
Society of Antiquaries of Scotland 3137
Society of Master Printers of Scotland ... 3218
Society of Scottish Artists 3243
Society of Solicitors in the Supreme
　Courts of Scotland 3245
United Kingdom Module Constructors
　Association 3402
Wholesale Grocers' Association of
　Scotland 3456

Elgin

Malt Distillers Association of Scotland ... 2293

Elstree

Faculty of Building 1503

Ely

British Society of Plant Breeders 1028

Enfield

British Retail Florists Association 978
Institute of Management Services 1922
Society for the Prevention of Asbestosis
　& Industrial Diseases 3127
Society of Industrial Tutors 3207

Epping

Association of Suppliers to the Furniture
　Industry 417
College of Preceptors 1208
Woodworking Machinery Suppliers
　Association 3467

Epsom

Domestic Heating Society 1376
Institute of Building Control 1842
Master Photographers Association 2314
Patent Glazing Contractors Association ... 2753
Society of Hearing Aid Audiologists 3201

Esher

Catering Equipment Distributors
　Association of GB 1128
National Association of Toastmasters 2497
National Council for Educational
　Standards 2539
National Education Association 2563
Organisation of Professional Users of
　Statistics 2730

Exeter

Association of Mortgage Lenders 344
Association of Wholesale Woollen
　Merchants 443
Conference for Independent Further
　Education 1251
Federation of Wholesale & Industrial
　Distributors Co-ordinating Committee ... 1567
Institute of Rent Officers 1962
National Institute of Medical Herbalists ... 2628
Surf Life Saving Association of GB 3309
Textile Distributors Association 3331
Wholesale Floorcovering Distributors'
　Association 3455

Exmouth

British Association of Advisers &
　Lecturers in Physical Education 551

Fakenham

Media Society 2326

Falkirk

Society of Hospital Linen Service &
　Laundry Managers 3203

Fareham

Association of Genealogists & Record
　Agents 265

Farnborough

British Independent Grocers Association 812

Farnham

Association of Wagon Builders &
　Repairers 440
British Crop Protection Council 684
British Vintage Wireless Society 1081
Institute of Maintenance & Building
　Management 1920
National Association for Higher
　Education in Film & Video 2389
National Licensed Victuallers'
　Association 2636

Felpham

International Health & Beauty Council ... 2127
International Institute of Sports Therapy ... 2136

Feltham

British International Freight Association 845
Fibre Building Board Organisation 1577

National Tenants Organization 2675

Fleetwood

Association of British Dental Surgery
   Assistants 135

Folkestone

National Church Crafts Association 2527
National School Sailing Association 2662

Fordingbridge

Game Conservancy Trust 1635

Forfar

Association of Directors of Recreation,
   Leisure & Tourism 239

Frome

Association for the Scientific Study of
   Anomalous Phenomena 106

Gerrards Cross

British Music Society 896
British Society of Cinematographers 1017
National Society for Epilepsy 2669

Gillingham, Kent

Association of Independent Railways 292

Glasgow

Association of Public Analysts of
   Scotland 386
Association of Veterinary Anaesthetists
   of GB & Ireland 437
Association of Veterinary Teachers &
   Research Workers 438
Boiler & Radiator Manufacturers
   Association 492
British Nautical Instrument Trade
   Association 904
British Society for the Study of Infection ... 1012
British Wholesale Traders Association 1088
Building Equipment & Materials Metal
   Trades Organisations 1100
European Desalination Association 1462
Guild of Taxidermists 1705
Headteachers' Association of Scotland   ... 1719
Institution of Engineers & Shipbuilders
   in Scotland 2014
International Association of Navigation
   Schools 2063
Linguistics Association of GB 2251

National Metal Trades Federation 2640
Royal Environmental Health Institute of
   Scotland 2912
Royal Scottish Society of Painters in
   Water-Colours 2941
Scottish Association for Metals 2996
Scottish Association of Milk Product
   Manufacturers 3001
Scottish Boat Builders Association 3003
Scottish Building Contractors
   Association 3004
Scottish Building Employers Federation   ... 3005
Scottish Cement Merchants Association   ... 3006
Scottish Committee of Optometrists 3008
Scottish Consumer Credit Association 3010
Scottish Council for Educational
   Technology 3013
Scottish Daily Newspaper Society 3016
Scottish Dairy Trade Federation 3017
Scottish Dance Teachers' Alliance 3018
Scottish Decorators Federation 3019
Scottish Engineering Employers'
   Association 3021
Scottish Film Council 3026
Scottish Flour Millers' Association 3028
Scottish Glass Association 3029
Scottish Homing Union 3031
Scottish House Builders Association 3032
Scottish Master Wrights & Builders
   Association 3042
Scottish Pharmaceutical Federation 3051
Scottish Pipers' Association 3052
Scottish Plant Owners Association 3053
Scottish Police Federation 3055
Scottish Pre-School Play Association 3056
Scottish Provision Trade Association 3057
Scottish Scrap Association 3060
Scottish Society for Conservation &
   Restoration 3064
Scottish Vocational Education Council   ... 3069
Scottish Wirework Manufacturers'
   Association 3071
Social Policy Association 3107
Society of British Neurological Surgeons ... 3154
Stainless Steel Fabricators' Association   ... 3282
United Kingdom Softwood Sawmillers'
   Association 3413

Gloucester

Association of Distributors of
   Advertising Material 243
Association of Environment Conscious
   Builders 254
Association of Free Magazines &
   Periodicals 262
Association of Free Newspapers 263
Association of Playing Field Officers &
   Landscape Managers 365
British Cattle Veterinary Association 645

British Holiday & Home Parks
  Association 798
County Planning Officers' Society 1323
Dealer Advertising Information Service . . . 1344
Good Gardeners Association 1672
International Waterfowl & Wetlands
  Research Bureau 2194
Music Advisers' National Association 2372
Society of Floristry 3195
Wildfowl & Wetlands Trust 3458

Godalming

Association of Professional Video
  Distributors 381
British Health Food Trade Association 791
Faculty of Secretaries & Administrators . . 1510
Health Food Manufacturers' Association . . . 1720
Institution of Incorporated Executive
  Engineers 2021
Rural Crafts Association 2967
Society of Bookbinders 3148
Society of Equestrian Artists 3191

Grantham

Association of Independant Crop
  Consultants . . . . : 283
British Edible Pulse Association 708
British Frozen Food Federation 763
Institute of Environmental Assessment 1879
Institute of Sterile Services Management . . . 1978

Gravesend

London Tugowners Association 2280
National Confederation of Parent-
  Teacher Associations 2532
Society of District Councils Public
  Relations Officers 3185

Great Yarmouth

Association of Supervisors of Midwives 416
Vintage Arms Association 3433

Greenford

Association of Information Officers in
  the Pharmaceutical Industry 297

Grimsby

Federation of British Port Wholesale
  Fish Merchants Association 1527
National Federation of Fishermen's
  Organisations 2579

Guildford

British Electro-Static Manufacturers
  Association 718
British List Brokers Association 867
Corporation of Insurance & Financial
  Advisors 1282
Defence Manufacturers Association 1347
Earth Science Teachers Association 1390
Folly Fellowship 1607
International Association of Packaging
  Research Institutes 2064
Local Authority Caterers Association 2260
Pre-Retirement Association of GB &
  Northern Ireland 2817
Society for Italic Handwriting 3118
Society for Research into Higher
  Education 3123
Society of Producers of Advertising
  Music 3233

Hadleigh

Institute of Trading Standards
  Administration 1987

Hailsham

School of Herbal Medicine Phytotherapy . . . 2983

Halifax

Automatic Indentification Manufacturers 453
British Interlining Manufacturers
  Association 843
British Needlecrafts Council 906
Quilters' Guild 2851
United Kingdom Home Care Association . . . 3393

Halstead

Corporation of Estate Agents 1281

Harlow

Advisory Council for the Education of
  Romany & other Travellers 11
British Car Wash Association 637
Institute of Builders' Merchants 1841
Institute of Swimming Pool Engineers 1980

Harpenden

Collaborative International Pesticides
  Analytical Council 1205

Harrogate

British Decorators Association 690
Fabric Care Research Association 1498
Forensic Science Society 1617

National Association of Theatre Nurses ...2496
Textile Research Council 3334

Harrow

Association of Professional Computer
    Consultants 377
British Association of Removers 594
British Trampoline Federation 1061
Institute of the Furniture Warehousing &
    Removing Industry......................1984
Textile Services Association 3335
Voluntary Group Association 3436

Hartlepool

British Science Fiction Association 989

Haslemere

Draught Proofing Advisory Association ...1380
External Wall Insulation Association.......1497
National Association of Loft Insulation
    Contractors...........................2462
National Cavity Insulation Association......2522

Hastings

Association of Painting Craft Teachers 360
British Chess Federation.................... 655
English Table Tennis Association 1440
National Federation of Bus Users 2572
Society of Metaphysicians.................3220
Vegan Society 3426

Hatfield

Association for Science Education 94
British Hay & Straw Merchants
    Association............................. 788
Centre for Information Media &
    Technology............................1145
Solvents Industry Association.............3265
World Small Animal Veterinary
    Association............................3477

Haverfordwest

National Dairy Producers Association 2556

Hawick

Hawick Knitwear Manufacturers
    Association............................1717

Hay-on-Wye

Mail Users' Association 2291

Hayes

Soap & Detergent Industry Association ...3104

Haywards Heath

British Unidentified Flying Object
    Research Association 1070
Economics Association.....................1394
European Liquid Roofing Association 1479
Federation of Sports Goods Distributors ...1566
Flat Roofing Contractors Advisory Board ...1599
Hairdressing Manufacturers' &
    Wholesalers' Association 1711
National Association of Head Teachers
    & Deputies..........................2442
National Association of Inspectors &
    Educational Advisers 2455
World Ship Society 3476

Heathfield

Talking Newspaper Association of the UK ...3319

Helmsley

Association of National Park Officers 350

Hemel Hempstead

Institute of Tape Learning 1982
Solder Makers Association 3262
Suspended Ceilings Association 3313

Henley-on-Thames

British Franchise Association 761
General Aviation Safety Committee 1647
Open Spaces Society 2721

Hereford

Association of Art Historians 117
Chief Building Surveyors' Society 1175
Garden History Society...................1640
Institute of Financial Planning 1889
Institute of Fisheries Management 1890

Herne Bay

Pianoforte Tuners' Association.............2785
Society of Indexers 3205

Hertford

Environmental Communicators
    Organisation..........................1446
Institute of the Motor Industry............1985
International Rubber Research &
    Development Board.....................2161

Malaysian Rubber Producers' Research
    Association 2292
Society of Chief Electrical & Mechanical
    Engineers in Local Government 3166
Society of County Trading Standards
    Officers 3180

High Wycombe

Association of Project Managers 383
British Effluent & Water Association 712
British Timber Merchants' Association 1057
Guild of British Film Editors 1687
Institute of Concrete Technology 1864
Institute of Wood Science 1999
Intumescent Fire Seals Association 2197
National Federation of Scale &
    Weighing Machine Manufacturers 2595
Paddle Steamer Preservation Society 2741
Society of British Match Manufacturers 3153
Timber Drying Association 3345
Timber Research & Development
    Association 3347
Timber Trade Training Association 3349
Videotex Industry Association 3431

Hindhead

National Association of Agricultural
    Contractors 2408

Hornchurch

Institute of Plumbing 1946

Horsham

Association of Chief Technical Officers 200

Hounslow

International Press Telecommunications
    Council 2154

Huddersfield

Association of Councillors 226
Society of Community Health Council
    Staff 3170

Hull

Association of British Salted Fish Curers
    & Exporters 166
British Accounting Association 509
British Association of State Colleges in
    English Language Teaching 599
International Institute of Social
    Economics 2135

National Association of Inland
    Waterway Carriers 2454

Hungerford

Association for the Study & Preservation
    of Roman Mosaics 107

Huntingdon

Association for Petroleum & Explosives
    Administration 91
Association of Conference Executives 215
Association of Drainage Authorities 248
British Scrap Federation 990
Conservatory Association 1259
National Federation of Taxicab
    Associations 2600
Reclamation Association 2863
Society of Dairy Technology 3182
United Kingdom Reclamation Council 3410

Ilford

British Tenpin Bowling Association 1049
London Fish & Poultry Retailers'
    Association 2271
Thermal Insulation Contractors
    Association 3340

Ilkley

Association of Higher Education
    Institutions Concerned with Home
    Economics 279
British Society of Painters in Oils 1024
British Society of Paints in Oils, Pastels
    & Acrylics 1025
British Watercolour Society 1086
International Mohair Association 2146
Society of Miniaturists 3223

Inverness

Harris Tweed Association 1715

Ipswich

Adult Residential Colleges Association 3
Animal Health Distributors Association 53
British Association for Immediate Care 543
County Surveyors' Society 1325
Society for Environmental Therapy 3115

Isleworth

Association of Independent Tour
    Operators 294
Federation against Copyright Theft 1515

Keele

British Society for Parasitology 1006
Classical Association 1189

Keighley

British Association of Landscape
   Industries 576
British Hand Knitting Confederation 782
Hand Knitting Association 1712

Kenilworth

British Angora Goat Society 527
British Bee-Keepers' Association 619
British Equestrian Federation 723
British Horse Society......................805
British Show Jumping Association 997
Dry Stone Walling Association of GB 1385
Farm & Rural Buildings Centre 1512
Grand National Archery Society...........1676
Institute of Agricultural Secretaries 1824
Land Drainage Contractors Association ...2218
National Association of Farriers,
   Blacksmiths & Agricultural Engineers ...2434
National Federation of Young Farmers
   Clubs 2605
National Hedgelaying Society.............2614
National Prefabricated Building
   Association...............................2652
Royal Agricultural Society of England 2893

Kettering

British Cycling Federation 688
Institution of Works & Highways
   Management 2039
Society of Master Shoe Repairers 3219

Kew

Association of British Picture Restorers 158
Design & Industries Association 1350

Kidderminster

Association of Charter Trustees & Urban
   Parish Councils...........................193
British Institute of Mental Handicap........830

Kingsbridge

Church Monuments Society 1182
National Association of Youth &
   Community Education Officers..........2510

Kingston upon Thames

Association of British Fire Trades 140
Association of British Investigators..........146

Association of College Registrars &
   Administrators 207
British Approvals for Fire Equipment 531
British Fire Protection Systems
   Association...............................747
Building Conservation Trust 1097
Fire Extinguishing Trades Association 1588
Fire Industry Council 1590
International Advertising Association 2049

Kirkcaldy

Association of Registrars of Scotland........396
Scottish Employers' Council for the Clay
   Industries 3020

Knaresborough

British Health Care Association 789

Knutsford

Primary History Association................2823

Lancaster

Association of Bankrupts 122
Phytochemical Society of Europe 2782
Social History Society of the UK 3106

Leamington Spa

Association of Personal Assistants &
   Secretaries 362
Design & Technology Association 1351
Federation of Agricultural Co-operatives ...1516
Institute of Management Specialists........1923
International Tube Association 2181
International Wire & Machinery
   Association...............................2195
Mortar Producers' Association 2359
National Institute of Hardware 2627
Professional Business & Technical
   Management 2835
Society of British Gas Industries 3152
Society of British Water Industries 3158
United Kingdom Wool Growers
   Federation................................3419

Leatherhead

Council for Music in Hospitals............1294
Institute of Purchasing Management 1956
International Association of Research
   Institutes for the Graphic Arts Industry ...2065
PIRA...2790
Railway Development Society 2858
Society of British Printing Ink
   Manufacturers 3155
Wholesale Confectionery & Tobacco
   Alliance 3452

Leeds

Association of Publishers' Educational
  Representatives 387
Billiards & Snooker Control Council 482
British Epilepsy Association 722
British Institute of Sports Coaches 836
British Society of Medical & Dental
  Hypnosis 1023
English Basketball Association 1427
European Organisation of Caries
  Research 1484
Federation of Engine Remanufacturers . . . 1537
International Phonetic Association 2149
International Society of Paediatric
  Oncology 2174
National Federation of Fish Friers 2578
National Institute of Carpet Fitters 2624
Northern Furniture Manufacturers
  Association 2700
Physiological Society 2781
Road Surface Dressing Association 2886
Standing Conference on Physical
  Education in Teacher Education 3288
Vehicle Builders' & Repairers'
  Association 3429

Leek

Association of Webbing Load Restraint
  Equipment Manufacturers 441

Leicester

Aggregate Concrete Block Association 14
Association for Teaching Psychology 98
Association of European Trade Mark
  Proprietors 256
Association of Registered Care Homes 394
Association of Teachers of Printing &
  Allied Subjects 421
British Association of Paragliding Clubs 587
British Automatic Sprinkler Association 610
British Branded Hosiery Group 627
British Federation of Care Home
  Proprietors 736
British Fire Services Association 748
British Gliding Association 773
British Narrow Fabrics Association 898
British Parachute Association 932
British Precast Concrete Federation 956
British Psychological Society 963
British Pyrotechnists Association 966
Concrete Block Paving Association 1240
Concrete Brick Manufacturers
  Association 1241
Concrete Pipe Association 1242
Confederation of British Associations 1246
Filtration Society 1583
Girls' Schools Association 1665
Headmasters' Conference 1718

Independent Contractors Association 1776
Independent National Computing
  Association 1781
Institute of Explosives Engineers 1882
Institution of Diagnostic Engineers 2009
Institution of Fire Engineers 2017
Institution of Occupational Safety &
  Health 2030
International Coil Winding Association . . . 2082
Leicester & District Knitting Industry
  Association 2233
Librarians of Institutes & Schools of
  Education 2237
Manpower Society 2298
Mathematical Association 2321
National Association of Trade Protection
  Societies 2500
National Council for Advisers for
  Educational Technology 2536
National Council for Voluntary Youth
  Services 2548
National Federation of Master
  Steeplejacks Lightning Conductor
  Engineers 2586
National Institute of Adult Continuing
  Education 2622
Photographic Instrument Repairing
  Authority 2779
Precast Flooring Federation 2819
Secondary Heads Association 3078
Society of Local Authority Chief
  Executives 3215

Leighton Buzzard

Association for Denture Prosthesis 80
British Wood Pulp Association 1091
Institution of Corrosion Science &
  Technology 2008
Process Plant Association 2827

Lerwick

Shetland Salmon Farmers' Association . . . 3085

Letchworth

International Council for Technical
  Communication 2093
National Pistol Association 2648

Leven

Scottish Steel Founders' Association 3066

Lewes

Guild of Master Craftsmen 1699
International Federation of Tour
  Operators 2119
Tour Operators Study Group 3354

Lichfield

Industrial Marketing Research
   Association.............................1797
Institute of Science Technology............1970
Institute of Supervisory Management.......1979
Paper Agents' Association.................2746

Lincoln

Association of Bee-Keeping Appliance
   Manufacturers of GB.....................123
International Association of Music
   Libraries................................2062
Royal Society for Nature Conservation ...2944

Lingfield

National Association of Colliery
   Managers 2427

Lisburn

Central Council of the Irish Linen
   Industry 1141
Irish Linen Guild..........................2200
Lambeg Industrial Research Association ...2217
Linen Sewing Thread Manufacturers'
   Association of GB & N Ireland...........2250

Liskeard

Association of Independent Electricity
   Producers 287

Liverpool

Association of Community Technical Aid
   Centres 212
Association of Marine Engineering
   Schools 332
Conference of Catholic Secondary
   Schools & Colleges 1252
English Schools Swimming Association ...1437
Institute of Pharmacy Management
   International............................1943
Mail Order Traders' Association 2290
Master Tanners Association.................2315
Metal Roofing Contractors Association ...2337
National Association of Health Service
   Personnel Officers 2444
National Association of Investment
   Clubs 2456
Permanent Service for Mean Sea Level ...2764
Pool Promoters Association 2806
Tachograph Analysis Association 3318
Wall Covering Distributors Association ...3437

Livingston

Hospital Disposable Fabric Convertors'
   Association............................1750

Llandrindod Wells

British Activity Holiday Association 510

Loughborough

Association of Career Teachers 187
Association of Health Care Information
   & Medical Records Officers 276
British Butterfly Conservation Society 632
British Federation of Young Choirs..........741
Ergonomics Society........................1450
Institute for Consumer Ergonomics.........1812
Institute of Swimming Teachers &
   Coaches................................1981
Society of Chief Personnel Officers 3167

Louth

Processed Vegetable Growers
   Association............................2828

Lowestoft

British Aviation Archaeological Council 611
Fisheries Society of the British Isles........1593
Pianoforte Manufacturers & Distributors'
   Association............................2784
Trussed Rafter Fabricators Association ...3370

Ludlow

British Hedgehog Preservation Society 793

Luton

British Association of Teachers of the
   Deaf 602
British Hat Guild..........................787
Institute of Sales & Marketing
   Management 1968
Institute of Scientific & Technical
   Communicators........................1971
International Federation of Societies of
   Cosmetic Chemists.....................2115
Plastic Industrial Containers Association ...2792
Plastics Window Federation 2800
Society of Cosmetic Scientists 3175

Lutterworth

Landscape Research Group................2221

Lymington

British Cartographic Society 641

Engineering Teaching Equipment
　　Manufacturers Association 1424

Lytham St Annes

Association of Sea Fisheries Committees
　　of England & Wales.....................403

Macclesfield

Advanced Manufacturing Technology
　　Research Institute........................4
British Federation of Music Festivals 739

Maidenhead

British Flue & Chimney Manufacturers
　　Association................................751
British Grassland Society 776
British Refrigeration Association 974
Chartered Institute of Marketing 1163
Computer & Peripheral Equipment Trade
　　Association..............................1238
District Planning Officers' Society 1371
Federation of Environmental Trade
　　Associations............................1540
Heating, Ventilating & Air Conditioning
　　Manufacturers' Association 1726

Maidstone

Association of Workers for Maladjusted
　　Children..................................444
British Promotional Merchandise
　　Association................................960
Buttonhook Society........................1114
Cremation Society of GB 1331
High Performance Pipe Association 1732
Society of Construction Law 3173

Malvern

National Sheep Association 2663

Manchester

Association of British Climatologists 130
Association of British Library &
　　Information Studies Schools..............148
Association of Direct Labour
　　Organisations............................236
Association of Graduate Careers
　　Advisory Services 269
Association of Incorporated Managers &
　　Administrators 282
Association of Independent Libraries 288
Association of Law Teachers 307
Association of Nursery Training Colleges 355
British Association of British Mountain
　　Guides 556

British Association of Domiciliary Care
　　Officers 566
British Association of Friends of
　　Museums 569
British Association of Numismatic
　　Societies 580
British Mountaineering Council 893
British Textile By-Products Association ...1051
British Textile Employers' Association 1053
British Textile Machinery Association.......1054
Community Transport Association.........1233
Conference of University Administrators ...1255
Cooperative Employers Association 1273
Cooperative Union........................1274
Employers' Association of the Linen &
　　Cotton Handkerchief & Household
　　Goods Wages Council 1417
European Institute for the Media 1476
Federation of Petroleum Suppliers 1558
Home & Contract Furnishing Textiles
　　Association...............................1740
Incorporated Society of Managers &
　　Administators...........................1771
Independent Cellular Retailers
　　Federation..............................1775
Institute of Community Development.......1862
Institute of Cooperative Directors 1867
Institute of Welfare Officers...............1998
International Association of Textile
　　Dyers & Printers 2067
Lard Association...........................2222
Local Authority Valuers Association 2261
Lute Society...............................2284
National Association of Field Studies
　　Officers 2436
National Fillings Trades Association 2607
Paper Makers' Allied Trades Association ...2747
Professional Institutions Council for
　　Conservation 2839
Society for the Social History of
　　Medicine................................3132
Textile Converters Association 3330
Textile Finishers' Association 3332
Textile Institute 3333
United Kingdom Fellmongers
　　Association...............................3391
United Kingdom Standing Conference
　　on Hospitality Management Education ...3415
Wire & Wire Rope Employers'
　　Association..............................3461
World Arabian Horse Organisation 3468

Mansfield

Ileostomy Association of GB & Ireland ...1759
National Association for Design
　　Education 2385
Society of Teachers of Speech & Drama ...3249
Solid Smokeless Fuels Federation 3263

Market Harborough

Association of CCTV Surveyors 189
British Association of Golf Course
    Constructors 571
Well Drillers Association 3448

Marlborough

Commercial Horticulture Association 1215
Federation of Children's Book Groups 1529
Federation of Garden & Leisure
    Manufacturers 1546
Pump Distributors Association of GB 2850

Marlow

Institute of Training & Development 1988
Water Research Centre 3443

Matlock

Association of Lightweight Aggregate
    Manufacturers 313
Association of Speakers Clubs 410
British Orienteering Federation 923
Institute of Clay Technology 1856

Maybole

World's Poultry Science Association 3479

Melksham

Federation of Recorded Music Societies . . . 1561

Melton Mowbray

Institute of Baths & Recreation
    Management 1833
Institute of Packaging 1938
Production Engineering Research
    Association of GB 2834

Mexborough

Coke Oven Managers' Association 1202

Middlesbrough

Association of Flow Survey Contractors 260
Society of Chief Architects of Local
    Authorities 3164

Midhurst

British Combustion Equipment
    Manufacturers Association 668

Milton Keynes

Badminton Association of England 460
Bar Association for Local Government 466
Curriculum Association 1340
Guild of Conservation Food Producers . . . 1691
Hearing Aid Council 1723
Institute of Groundsmanship 1895
Light Rail Transit Association 2246
Network for Alternative Technology &
    Technology Assessment 2693

Minehead

Society of Battery Manufacturers 3147

Morden

Association of London Borough
    Engineers & Surveyors 317
British Fantasy Society 734
Medical Officers of Schools Association . . . 2329

Moreton-in-Marsh

Game Farmers Association 1636

Motherwell

Scottish Library Association 3038

Musselburgh

Scottish Net Manufacturers Association . . . 3047

Nantwich

British Commercial Rabbit Association 669

Nelson

National College of Hypnosis &
    Psychotherapy 2530
National Register of Hypnotherapists &
    Psychotherapists 2654

New Malden

British Motorcyclists Federation 892
Licensing Executives Society 2240

New Milton

Yacht Charter Association 3484

Newark

Association of Show & Agricultural
    Organisations 407
British Clock & Watch Manufacturers'
    Association 661

Newark

British Horological Institute................804
British Rabbit Council.....................968

Newbury

British Facsimile Industry Consultative
   Committee 733
Delicatessen & Fine Food Association......1349
Institute for Animal Health 1810
Jockeys' Association of GB 2203
National Association of Teachers of
   Dancing.................................2493
Society of Garden Designers..............3196
Solar Trade Association 3261

Newcastle under Lyme

British Association for Service to the
   Elderly 547
European Motel Federation................1483
Federation of Small Mines of GB 1565
Retread Manufacturers' Association 2882

Newcastle upon Tyne

Association of Community Workers in
   the UK..................................213
Association of International Accountants 301
Association of Medical Technologists 340
British Mycological Society................897
British Society for Strain Measurement ...1008
Cathedral Architects Association 1132
Institution of Water Officers 2038
International Union of Microbiological
   Societies 2190
National Federation of Consumer
   Groups..................................2576
North East Coast Institution of
   Engineers & Shipbuilders...............2699
Outdoor Writer's Guild 2736
Society of Metropolitan Treasurers 3222
Society of Museum Archaeologists.........3225

Newmarket

Thoroughbred Breeders' Association 3342

Newmilns

Scottish Lace & Window Furnishing
   Association.............................3035

Newport

Association of Heads of Independent
   Schools 274
Steel Lintel Manufacturers Association ...3293

Newport, Isle of Wight

Fortress Study Group 1621

Newton Abbot

British Ball Clay Producers' Federation 612
British Goat Society......................774
British Orchid Growers Association 921
National Federation of Sea Anglers 2596
Society for Applied Bacteriology 3109

Newtownards

Northern Ireland Master Painters'
   Association.............................2708

Northampton

Association of Police Surgeons 369
British Brush Manufacturers' Association 629
British Fibreboard Packaging
   Association.............................742
British Hardware & Housewares
   Manufacturers' Association 785
British Institute of Cleaning Science 822
British Institute of Non-Destructive
   Testing 831
British Leather Confederation 864
Footwear Components Federation 1612
Incorporated Association of Architects &
   Surveyors 1763
Institute of Insurance Brokers.............1909
Institute of Wastes Management 1997
Leather Producers' Association 2232
National Association for Gifted Children ...2388
National Association for Primary
   Education 2396
National Society of Master Thatchers 2672
Society of Homoeopaths 3202
Society of Information Technology
   Managers 3208
Society of Leather Technologists &
   Chemists 3213

Northwood

Society of Television Lighting Directors ...3250
Video Trade Association..................3430

Norwich

Association of District Council
   Treasurers 244
Disabled Drivers' Association 1365
National Association for the Support of
   Small Schools 2401
Single Ply Roofing Association 3095

Nottingham

Association of Interior Design Degree
  Courses 300
British Association of Colliery
  Management 560
British Canoe Union 636
British Flat Roofing Council 749
British Geological Survey 769
British Lace Federation 859
Chromatographic Society 1181
Company Chemists Association 1234
Contract Flooring Association 1270
English Place-Name Society 1434
Hosiery & Allied Trades Research
  Association 1749
Institute of Consumer Advisers 1865
Institute of Quarrying 1959
International Police Association 2151
Knitting Industries' Federation 2216
Livestock Traders Association of GB 2255
National Association of Shopkeepers 2486
Palaeontographical Society 2744
Remote Sensing Society 2875

Nuneaton

Motor Industry Research Association 2362

Oakham

National Association for Education in
  the Arts 2386

Oban

Scottish Marine Biological Association ... 3040

Ormskirk

Association of Radical Midwives 390
United Kingdom Reading Association 3409

Orpington

Institute of Administrative Management ... 1822
Institute of Facilities Management 1884
Sira 3096

Oswestry

Faculty of Business Education 1504
National Pure Water Association 2653
Tertiary College Association 3329

Oxford

Agricultural Co-operative Training
  Council 16
Anaesthetic Research Society 47

Association of British Container Lessors 132
Association of Subscription Agents 414
British Anaesthetic & Respiratory
  Equipment Manufacturers Association; 526
British Association of Golf Course
  Architects 570
British Cryogenics Council 685
British Hire Cruiser Federation 797
British Microlight Aircraft Association 887
British Tattoo Artists Federation........... 1048
Central Association of Agricultural
  Valuers 1136
Fellowship of Makers & Researchers of
  Historical Instruments 1571
Foundation for Management Education ... 1622
Institute of Economics & Statistics 1872
Institute of Financial & Management
  Studies 1887
International Association of Agricultural
  Economics 2057
National Association of Sole
  Practitioners 2488
Professional Flight Instructors'
  Association 2836
Royal Microscopical Society 2930

Paignton

International Institute of Security 2134
International Professional Security
  Association 2157

Paisley

International Conference in Composite
  Structures 2089
Scottish Milk Records Association 3043
Scottish National Housing & Town
  Planning Council 3046

Penrith

Association of Agricultural Education
  Staffs 113

Penzance

Association of British Riding Schools 163
British Surfing Association 1044
Cornish Mining Development
  Association 1278
Guild of International Songwriters &
  Composers 1697

Perth

Agricultural Education Association 17
Scottish Federation of Meat Traders'
  Associations 3023

Peterborough

Agricultural Engineers' Association 18
Alliance of Independent Travel Agents 29
Association for the Study of Primary
   Education (ASPE) 109
British Agrochemicals Association 522
Farriers Registration Council 1513
Fertiliser Manufacturers' Association 1576
National Anglers' Council 2382
Police History Society 2804
Processors' & Growers' Research
   Organisation 2830

Petersfield

European Council of International
   Schools 1461
Federation of Master Organ Builders 1552
Incorporated Society of Organ Builders ...1773

Pinner

British Fabric Association 732
Lead Contractors Association 2227
Private Libraries Association 2826
Society of Private Printers 3232

Plymouth

British Association of Tourist Officers 604
National Caving Association 2521
Society of Cardiological Technicians 3161

Pontypridd

Waste Disposal Engineers Association 3440

Portadown

Handkerchief & Household Linens
   Association 1713
Northern Ireland Wool Users'
   Association 2712

Portsmouth

Association of Polytechnic Teachers 370
Federation of Crafts & Commerce 1534
Independent Schools Bursars'
   Association 1785
Institute of Hospital Engineering 1905
International Society for Evolutionary
   Protistology 2169
Rating Surveyors Association 2862
Sail Training Association 2970
Standing Conference of Heads of
   Modern Languages in Polytechnics &
   other Colleges 3285
Sterilised Suture Manufacturers'
   Association 3296

Potters Bar

Copper Development Association 1275
International Association of Fish Meal
   Manufacturers 2060
International Copper Association 2091
National Institute for Biological
   Standards of Control 2620
Radio Society of GB 2855
United Society of Artists 3420

Preston

Catering Teachers' Association 1131
English Curling Association 1431
Institute of Statisticians 1977
Light Music Society 2245
National Association of Careers &
   Guidance Teachers 2419
Surgical Textiles Conference 3311

Princes Risborough

Gauge & Tool Makers' Association 1644

Rayleigh

Certificated Bailiffs' Association of
   England & Wales 1151

Reading

Agricultural Manpower Society 21
Almshouse Association 34
Association of Professional Recording
   Studios 380
Association of Recreation Managers 393
Association of Vice-Principals of
   Colleges 439
British Agricultural History Society 521
British Colostomy Association 666
British Council of Shopping Centres 683
British Deer Producers' Society 692
British Deer Society 693
British Dyslexia Association 706
British Institute of Organ Studies 832
British Schools Gymnastics Association 987
British Society of Audiology 1015
Centre for Agricultural Strategy 1144
Centre of Management in Agriculture 1150
Conservation Trust 1258
Council for Environmental Education 1292
Garden Centre Association 1639
General Council & Register of
   Osteopaths 1649
Governing Bodies Association 1673
Horticultural Trades Association 1748
Institute of Leisure & Amenity
   Management 1915
International Farm Management
   Association 2102

International Federation of Park &
    Recreation Administration 2111
International Food Information Service   ...2121
International Society for Music
    Education 2170
International Tyre, Rubber & Plastics
    Federation...........................2183
Modern Pentathlon Association of GB   ...2356
National Association of Advisers in Craft
    Design & Technology 2406
National Chamber of Trade 2524
Police Superintendents' Association of
    England & Wales 2805
Royal Meteorological Society 2929
Sand & Ballast Hauliers & Allied Trades
    Alliance 2975
School & Group Travel Association 2978
Society for General Microbiology 3117
Tenant Farmers' Association 3328
World Pheasant Association 3473

Redbourn

United Kingdom Mineral Wool
    Association..........................3401

Redditch

Incorporated Association of Organists 1764
Needlemakers Association 2692

Redhill

Brewing Research Foundation 502
British Resin Manufacturers' Association 976
Commonwealth & Overseas Fire
    Services Association 1224
Diecasting Society 1359
Formula Air Racing Association 1620
Foundry Equipment & Supplies
    Association..........................1623
Metalforming Machinery Makers'
    Association..........................2338
Miners' Lamp Manufacturers'
    Association..........................2349
National Society of Master Pattern
    Makers..............................2671

Reigate

Association of Consulting Actuaries 218
British Fruit Juice Importers Association 765
Guild of Church Musicians 1690
International Association of Group
    Psychotherapy.......................2061
Liquefied Petroleum Gas Industry
    Technical Association 2252
Manufacturers' Agents' Association of
    GB & Ireland 2299
Screen Printing Association 3075

Rhyl

Muzzle Loaders Association of GB 2378

Richmond-on-Thames

British Iron & Steel Consumers' Council 848
Coroners' Society of England & Wales   ...1279
European Catering Association.............1457
European Federation of Conference
    Towns 1463
Institute of Burial & Cremation
    Administration 1843
Society of Wood Engravers 3257

Rickmansworth

British Agricultural & Garden Machinery
    Association.......................... 518
Flour Milling & Baking Research
    Association..........................1604
Garden Machinery Association.............1642
Life Insurance Association 2242
Timber & Brick Homes Consortium 3343

Ripley

Institute of Vitreous Enamellers 1996

Ripon

National Association of Breeders'
    Services 2416

Rochdale

Association of Newspaper & Magazine
    Wholesalers 352
Educational Development Association 1396
National Association of British Market
    Authorities 2418

Rochester

Council of Subject Teaching
    Associations 1315

Romford

Association of Principals of Sixth Form
    Colleges 373
Institute of Social Psychiatry..............1974
National Association for Outdoor
    Education 2394

Romsey

Arboricultural Association 58
Gun Trade Association 1708

Ross-on-Wye

Association of Professions for the
   Mentally Handicapped People 382
Milking Machine Manufacturers'
   Association 2344

Rotherfield

Guild of Agricultural Journalists 1682

Rotherham

Institute of Safety & Public Protection   ...1967

Roxburgh

Association of Music Advisers in
   Scotland 348

Royston

Association of Franchised Distributors of
   Electronic Components 261
British Office Technology Manufacturers
   Alliance 917
British Society of Rheology 1029
Society of Environmental Engineers 3190

Rugby

Association for Language Learning 86
British Association for Counselling 540
British Junior Chamber 855
Institution of Chemical Engineers 2005
Institution of Lighting Engineers 2023
National Cattle Breeders' Association 2520

Ruislip

Association of British Manufacturers of
   Photographic Cine & Audiovisual
   Equipment 149
British Advertising Gift Distributors
   Association 513
British Photographic Export Group 943
Camping & Outdoor Leisure Association ...1120
Envelope Makers' & Manufacturing
   Stationers' Association 1444
International Federation of Airworthiness ...2105
National Association of Range
   Manufacturers 2479
National Federation of Fishmongers 2580

Runcorn

British Secondary Metals Association 992

Ryde

Association of Printing Machinery
   Importers 375

Saffron Walden

Independent Schools Association 1784
National Association of Advisory
   Officers for Special Education 2407

Salisbury

Agricultural Law Association 19
Arab Horse Society 57
Association of British Professional
   Conference Organisers 162
Association of Pensioneer Trustees 361
British Archaeological Association 532
British Wood Turners Association 1092

Sandbach

Association of Cost Engineers 225

Sandwich

Association of British Spectroscopists 170

Scarborough

Institute of Entertainment & Arts
   Management 1878
Institute of Holistic Therapies 1901

Sevenoaks

British Association of Industrial Editors   575
British Institute of Surgical
   Technologists 837
British Surgical Export Group 1045
British Surgical Trades Association 1046
Butter Information Council 1113
Contractors Mechanical Plant Engineers ...1271
International Association of Book-
   keepers 2058

Sheffield

Association for Sandwich Education &
   Training 93
Association of British Mining Equipment
   Companies 152
Association of Calendered UPV
   Suppliers 186
Association of Sexual & Marital
   Therapists 404
British Council of Maintenance
   Associations 680
British Crystallographic Association 686
British Cutlery & Silverware Association   687

British Glass Confederation 772
British Hacksaw & Bandsaw Makers'
    Association 780
British Hardmetal Association 784
British Interlingua Society 842
British Masonry Drill Bit Association 874
British Society of Experimental &
    Clinical Hypnosis 1020
British Society of Periodontology 1027
Coal Preparation Plant Association 1197
Construction Fixings Association 1260
Cutlery & Allied Trades Research
    Association 1341
Electric Steel Makers' Guild 1402
Engineers' Hand Tools Association 1425
European Glass Container
    Manufacturers' Committee 1474
European Plasticised PVC Film
    Manufacturers' Association 1486
European Wire Rope Information Service . . . 1493
Federation of British Engineers' Tool
    Manufacturers 1523
Federation of British Hand Tool
    Manufacturers 1525
Ferro Alloys & Metals Producers
    Association 1575
File Association 1580
Geographical Association 1659
Handsaw Association 1714
Home & School Council 1741
Horticultural & Contractors' Tools
    Association 1747
Institute of British Bakers 1836
Magnesite & Chrome Brickmakers
    Association 2289
Milling Cutter & Toolbit Association 2345
Money Advice Association 2357
National Association for the Teaching of
    English 2402
National Association of Governors &
    Managers 2441
National Consumer Credit Federation 2534
Packaging & Industrial Films
    Association 2739
Power Actuated Systems Association 2813
Saw Association 2977
Screw Thread Tool Manufacturers'
    Association 3076
Society of Glass Technology 3198
Spring Research & Manufacturers'
    Association 3279
Stainless Steel Industry Association 3283
Steel Castings Research & Trade
    Association 3291
Twist Drill & Reamer Association 3371
United Kingdom Home Economics
    Federation 3394
Woodworkers', Builder's &
    Miscellaneous Tools Association 3466
Writing Equipment Society 3481

Shepperton

Commercial Art Directors Association 1214

Shepton Mallet

National Association of Perry Makers 2470

Shrewsbury

Field Studies Council 1579
Institute of Machine Woodworking
    Technology 1919
National Association of Cigarette
    Machine Operators 2424

Sidcup

Association of Manufacturing Chemists 330
Institute of Commerce 1860
Institute of Data Processing
    Management 1869
Joint Industry Board for the Electrical
    Contracting Industry 2210

Sissinghurst

Medical Journalists' Association 2328

Slough

Audio Engineering Society 447
British Cement Association 647
British Internal Combustion Engine
    Research Institute 844
Institute of Qualified Private Secretaries . . . 1957
Institute of Sound & Communications
    Engineers 1975
Metal Packaging Manufacturers
    Association 2336
Music Industries Association 2374
National Foundation for Educational
    Research in England & Wales 2609
Sound & Communications Contractors
    Association 3267
Sound & Communications Industries
    Federation 3268
Sound & Communications Suppliers
    Association 3269

Solihull

Association of Metal Sprayers 341
British Association of Symphonic Bands
    & Wind Ensembles 601
British Institute of Embalmers 823
British Plastics Stockholders'
    Association 946
Catholic Teachers' Federation 1134
European Plastics Distributors
    Association 1487

Solihull

Justices' Clerks' Society 2212
National Association of Funeral
   Directors 2439
Partitioning Industry Association 2750
Society of Cable Television Engineers 3160

Southall

Retail Fruit Trade Federation 2880

Southampton

Association of British Sailmakers 165
British Biophysical Society 621
British Institute of Industrial Therapy 824
Decorative Gas Fire Manufacturers
   Association 1345
Federation of Sailing & Motor Cruising
   Schools 1564
Institute of Transport Administration 1991
International Society for Boundary
   Elements 2168
National Association of the Launderette
   Industry 2495
Royal Yachting Association 2963
Society of Registration Officers 3241
Yachting Journalists Association 3486

Southend-on-Sea

British Resorts Association 977
Institute of Mathematics & its
   Applications 1929
National Federation of Playgoers'
   Societies 2592
Produce Packaging & Marketing
   Association 2832

Southport

Institute of Chiropodists 1853
Romantic Novelists' Association 2889

Spalding

British Sugar Beet Seed Producers
   Association 1040
Bulb Distributors Association 1105
Fairground Society 1511

St Albans

British Parking Association 933
Institute of Acoustics 1820
Institute of Travel & Tourism 1992
International Association Against Painful
   Experiments on Animals 2052
National Carpet Cleaners Association 2519
National Pharmaceutical Association 2645
Rose Trade Association 2890

Royal National Rose Society 2934
Society of Recorder Players 3240

St Andrews

Anatomical Society of GB & Ireland 48

St Austell

China Clay Association 1179
Society of British Snuff Blenders 3156

St Helens

Aluminium Stockholders Association 43
British Society of Scientific
   Glassblowers 1030
Flat Glass Manufacturers Association 1598

St Lawrence, Jersey

World Jersey Cattle Bureau 3471

St Peter Port, Channel Island

Guernsey Growers Association 1681

Stafford

Association of British Generating Set
   Manufacturers 141
English Schools Football Association 1436
Instock Footwear Suppliers Association . . . 2041
National Association for Remedial
   Education 2397
National Association of Principal
   Agricultural Education Officers 2473
National Association of Radiator
   Specialists 2478
Society of County Treasurers 3181
White Metal Casting Association 3450

Staines

British Public Works Association 964
Conference & Lecturers in Craft &
   Design Education 1250
Dyslexia Institute 1389
Institute of Asphalt Technology 1829
National Joint Council for Civil Air
   Transport 2630
Showmen's Guild of GB 3089

Stamford

Institute of Credit Management 1868
Institute of Purchasing & Supply 1955
Mushroom Growers' Association 2371

Staplehurst

Historical Commercial Vehicle Society 1737

Stevenage

Abrasive Industries Association 1
Association of Street Lighting
  Contractors............................... 412
British Abrasives Federation 506
British Adhesives & Sealants Association 512
British Institute of Agricultural
  Consultants 820
Chief Leisure Officers Association 1176
Coated Abrasives Manufacturers'
  Association.............................1198
Diamond Industrial Products Association ...1358
District Auditors' Society 1369
Federation of Associations of Specialists
  & Sub-Contractors.......................1517
Fingerprint Society.......................1587
Furniture Industry Research Association ...1632
International Cement Bonded
  Particleboard Federation..................2075
Professional Gardeners Guild 2837
Skibob Association of GB 3097
Society of Catering & Hotel
  Management Consultants 3162
United Kingdom & Ireland Particleboard
  Association............................3378

Stirling

Scottish Association of Geography
  Teachers 2999
Scottish Shooting Council.................3063
Scottish Timber Trade Association 3067

Stockport

Alliance of British Clubs..................... 27
Association of Directors of Social
  Services................................. 241
British Paper Machinery Makers
  Association.............................. 931
Federation of Automatic Transmission
  Engineers 1518
International Vegetarian Union.............2191
Motor Schools Association of GB.........2363
National Federation of Master Window
  Cleaners...............................2587
National School Band Association 2661
Standing Conference on Principals of
  Sixth Form & Tertiary Colleges 3289
Surgical Dressing Manufacturers'
  Association.............................3310

Stoke-on-Trent

Amalgamated Chimney Engineers 45

[Stoke-on-Trent continued]

Association of Accommodation &
  Welfare Officers..........................111
British Bathroom Council...................616
British Ceramic Confederation 648
British Ceramic Research 650
British Ceramic Tile Council 651
British Pottery Managers' Association 952
Institute of Ceramics 1846
National Association of Chimney Lining
  Engineers 2422
National Association of Chimney
  Sweeps 2421
National Fireplace Council
  Manufacturers' Association 2608
Tableware Distributors Association 3317

Stone

British Electrical Systems Association 716

Stornoway

Society of Directors of Trading
  Standards in Scotland...................3184

Stourbridge

Institute of Careers Officers...............1844

Stratford upon Avon

Association of Applied Biologists 116
Traditional Acupuncture Society 3361

Stroud

British Management Data Foundation 870
Ecological Design Association 1392
Energy Systems Trade Association 1419
Society of Architectural & Industrial
  Illustrators.............................3140

Sunbury-on-Thames

National Federation of Spiritual Healers ...2599

Surbiton

Association of Malt Products
  Manufacturers 327
Association of Valuers of Licensed
  Property................................ 435
Baby Products Association 458
Clarinet & Saxophone Society of GB 1188
European Malt Extract Manufacturers
  Association.............................1480
Independent Film Distributors'
  Association.............................1777
Leisure & Outdoor Furniture Association ...2234
National Association of Bookmakers 2414

Surbiton

National Association of Tripedressers 2501
National Automobile Safety Belt
　　Association 2513
Police Federation (England & Wales) 2803
Social Care Association 3105
Solids Handling & Processing
　　Association 3264
United Kingdom Renderers' Association ... 3411

Sutton, Surrey

British Association for Chemical
　　Specialities 538
British Urban Regeneration Association ... 1073
Cleaning & Hygiene Suppliers'
　　Association 1193
Federation of Clothing Designers &
　　Executives 1531

Swansea

Association of Motor Vehicle Teachers 346
National Association of Health Service
　　Security Officers 2447

Swindon

Agricultural & Food Research Council 15
Association of Board Makers 126
Association of Carton Board Makers 188
Association of Colleges for Further &
　　Higher Education 208
Association of Greyboard Makers 271
Association of Makers of Newsprint 323
Association of Makers of Packaging
　　Papers 324
Association of Makers of Printings &
　　Writings 325
Association of Makers of Soft Tissue
　　Papers 326
British Association of Trade Computer
　Label Manufacturers 606
British Box & Packaging Association 626
British Disposable Products Association 702
British Paper & Board Industry
　　Federation 930
British Society for the History of Science ... 1010
Car Radio Industry Specialists
　　Association 1123
Corrugated Case Materials Association ... 1283
Faculty of Church Music 1505
National Association of Counsellors in
　　Education 2428
National Association of Paper
　　Merchants 2468
Natural Environment Research Council ... 2686
Packaging Distributors Association 2740
School Library Association 2982
Underwater Association for Scientific
　　Research 3375

Tadworth

British Colour Makers' Association 667
Corporate Hospitality Association 1280

Tamworth

Association of Builders' Hardware
　　Manufacturers 178
British Blind & Shutter Association 622
British Lock Manufacturers Association 868
Chief & Assistant Chief Fire Officers
　　Association 1174
Door & Shutter Manufacturers
　　Association 1378
Industrial Water Society 1802
Power Fastenings Association 2814
Timber Packaging & Pallet
　　Confederation 3346

Taunton

Association of Meat Inspectors in GB 336
European Caravan Federation 1456
Institute of Road Safety Officers 1964

Tavistock

Guild of Television Cameramen 1706

Teddington

British Measurement & Testing
　　Association 876
Central Association of Bee-Keepers 1137
Interior Decorators & Designers
　　Association 2047
Paint Research Association 2742

Telford

Association for Industrial Archaeology 84
Association of Pleasurecraft Operators
　　on Inland Waterways 366
Glassfibre Reinforced Cement
　　Association 1669

Thame

British Association of Electrolysists 567
British Beer-Mat Collectors Society 620

Thames Ditton

College of Osteopaths & Practitioners 1207
Names Society 2379

Thetford

British Trust for Ornithology 1064

Tiptree

Book Publishers' Representatives'
Association 495

Tiverton

Masters of Deerhounds Association 2317

Tonbridge

British Society for the History of
Medicine 1011
Chemical Recovery Association 1172
Coffee Trade Federation 1200
Hop Merchants' Association 1746
London Jute Association 2276
London Sisal Association 2278
Postal History Society 2809
Silk Association of GB 3090
Toy & Giftware Importers Association 3357

Torquay

National Association of Water Power
Users 2506

Towcester

British Retinitis Pigmentosa Society 980
Transport Ticket Society 3366

Tring

British Ornithologists' Union 924
Crime Writer's Association 1334
Royal Forestry Society of England,
Wales & N Ireland 2913
Steel Window Association 3294

Trowbridge

Association of County Public Health
Officers 230
Association of Road Traffic Sign Makers 401
County Emergency Planning Officers'
Society 1322

Truro

Association of County Archivists 227
Environmental Education Advisors
Association 1447
International Truss Plate Association 2179

Tunbridge Wells

Antiquarian Horological Society 55
Association of Cycle Traders 233
British Association of Conference Towns 562

British Association of Green Crop Driers 572
British Exhibition Venues Association 730
British Shippers' Council 995
Circle of Wine Writers 1186
Freight Transport Association 1625
Governing Bodies of Girls Schools
Association 1674
Institute of Printing 1949
International Property Lawyers
Association 2158
National Federation of Meat Traders 2588
National Federation of Wholesale
Poultry Merchants 2603
National Game Dealers Association 2610
Vitreous Enamel Development Council ... 3434

Twickenham

Association of Electrical Machinery
Trades 251
British Jazz Society 850
Guild of Film Production Accountants &
Financial Administrators 1693
Home Brewing & Winemaking Trade
Association 1743
Rugby Football Union 2966
Society of Incentive Travel Executives 3204

Uckfield

Masters of Draghounds Association 2318

Uxbridge

Institute for Scientific Information 1816
International Tin Research Institute 2178
National Association of National Health
Care Supplies Managers 2466

Ventnor

British Polarological Research Society 948

Wakefield

Association of Chief Officers of
Probation 197
Association of Disabled Professionals 242
Athletic Clothing Manufacturers
Association 446
Barge & Canal Development Association 467
British Burn Association 630
Great Britain Pistol Council 1678

Wallingford

British Trust for Conservation Volunteers ... 1063
Business Aircraft Users' Association 1110
Institute of Hydrology 1907

Wallington

Mobile & Outside Caterers Association
of GB 2353

Walsall

British Tensional Strapping Association ...1050
National Association for Environmental
    Education 2387
Swimming Teachers' Association 3315
Wallpaper, Paint & Wallcovering
    Retailers Association 3439

Walton-on-Thames

British Approvals Board for
    Telecommunications 530
British Electrotechnical Approvals Board 720
Marine Engine & Equipment
    Manufacturers' Association 2301

Wantage

Pizza & Pasta Association 2791

Ware

British Institute of Professional
    Photography 834
Chartered Building Societies Institute 1157
Coal Merchants' Federation 1196
Domestic Appliance Service Association . . . 1373
National Association of Master Bakers . . . 2463
World Bureau of Metal Statistics 3470

Warlingham

Association of Shopfront Section
    Manufacturers 406
Automatic Door Suppliers Association 452
Boarding Schools Association 491
National Association of Shopfitters 2485

Warrington

British Medical Acupuncture Society 878
British Woven Wire Export Association ...1094
National Association of Voluntary Help
    Organisers 2503
National Centre of Tribology 2523
Woven Wire Association 3480

Warwick

Association of County Chief Executives 228
Association of Market Survey
    Organisations 333
Guild of Railway Artists 1704
National Association of Estate Agents 2432

Wellesbourne Vegetable Research
    Association 3449

Washington

Association of Chief Education Social
    Workers 196

Watford

Association of Print & Packaging Buyers 374
Association of Railway Preservation
    Societies 391
Building Research Establishment 1102
Cement Admixtures Association 1135
Fencing Contractors Association 1574
Institute of Grocery Distribution 1894
National Pig Breeders' Association 2647
Proprietary Articles Trade Association 2843
Society of Business Economists 3159

Wellingborough

British Naturalists' Association 903
British Society of Perfumers 1026

Welwyn Garden City

British Calcium Carbonates Federation 635
Calcium Silicate Brick Association 1118

Wembley

Despatch Association 1355
International Rubber Study Group 2162
Oil & Colour Chemists' Association 2719

Westbury

Association of Professional Foresters 378
Institution of Engineering Designers 2013
Society of Association Executives 3144

Weston-super-Mare

Association of Golf Club Secretaries 267
District Council Technical Association 1370
International Audiology Society to Help
    the Deaf 2071

Wetherby

British Equestrian Trade Association 724

Weybridge

British Marine Industries Federation 873
British Migraine Association 888
Cork Industry Federation 1277

Home Brewing & Winemaking Manufacturers Association 1742

International Council of Marine Industry Associations 2097

Recreation Managers Association of GB ... 2864

Road Haulage Association 2884

Wheathampstead

National Therapeutic & Osteopathic Society 2676

Whitby

Catering Managers Association of GB 1130

Whitstable

International Association for Teachers of English as a Foreign Language 2056

Wigan

British Society of Commerce 1018

Civic Catering Association 1187

Society of Public Accountants 3235

Winchester

Ambulance Service Institute 46

Association of Quality Management Consultants 389

British Urban & Regional Information Systems Association 1072

Centre for Interfirm Comparison 1147

Council of Regional Arts Associations 1313

English Schools Cricket Association 1435

National Association of Social Workers in Education 2487

Schools Poetry Association 2985

Windermere

Association of Entertainment & Arts Management 253

Windsor

Brick Development Association 503

Channel Tunnel Association 1155

Woking

British Aerobatic Association 514

British Helicopter Advisory Board 794

European Regional Airlines Association ... 1489

Great Britain Target Shooting Federation ... 1679

Institute of Animal Health 1825

Institute of Employment Consultants 1874

National Council for the Conservation of Plants & Gardens 2545

National Rifle Association 2659

National Small-Bore Rifle Association 2666

Optical Information Council 2726

Society of Headmasters of Independent Schools 3200

Underfeed Stoker Makers' Association ... 3374

Wolverhampton

Allied Brewery Traders' Association 33

British Grit Association 777

Institute of Refractories Engineers 1960

Midland General Galvanizers Association ... 2342

Woodbridge

Agricultural Show Exhibitors' Association 22

London Association of Master Decorators 2266

Worcester

Alliance of Independent Retailers 28

British Security Industry Association 993

Choir Schools Association 1180

Institute of Paper Conservation 1939

Kitchen Specialists Association 2215

Society of County Librarians 3178

Worksop

Federation of Wire Rope Manufacturers of GB 1569

Wire Rope Export Conference 3463

Worthing

English Bowling Association 1428

Land Institute 2219

Wrexham

British Association for Shooting & Conservation 548

Wylam

Association of Domestic Management 247

York

Association of Welding Distributors 442

British & International Golf Greenkeepers' Association 504

Educational Television Association 1400

General Studies Association 1657

Institute of Physical Sciences in
  Medicine 1944

Master Carvers Association 2310